THE CAMBRI

NEWTC The Cambridge companion to
Newton

Sir Isaac Newton (1642–1727) was one of the greatest scientists of all time, a thinker of extraordinary range and creativity who has left enduring legacies in mathematics and the natural sciences. In this volume a team of distinguished contributors examines all the main aspects of Newton's thought, including not only his approach to space, time, and universal gravity in his *Principia*, his research in optics, and his contributions to mathematics, but also his more clandestine investigations into alchemy, theology, and prophecy, which have sometimes been overshadowed by his mathematical and scientific interests. New readers and non-specialists will find this the most convenient and accessible guide to Newton currently available. Advanced students and specialists will find a conspectus of recent developments in the interpretation of Newton.

OTHER VOLUMES IN THE SERIES OF CAMBRIDGE COMPANIONS:

AQUINAS *Edited by* NORMAN KRETZMANN *and*
ELEONORE STUMP

HANNAH ARENDT *Edited by* DANA VILLA

AUGUSTINE *Edited by* ELEONORE STUMP *and*
NORMAN KRETZMANN

BACON *Edited by* MARKKU PELTONEN

DESCARTES *Edited by* JOHN COTTINGHAM

EARLY GREEK PHILOSOPHY *Edited by* A. A. LONG

FEMINISM IN PHILOSOPHY *Edited by* MIRANDA
FRICKER *and* JENNIFER HORNSBY

FOUCAULT *Edited by* GARY GUTTING

FREUD *Edited by* JEROME NEU

GALILEO *Edited by* PETER MACHAMER

GERMAN IDEALISM *Edited by* KARL AMERIKS

HABERMAS *Edited by* STEPHEN K. WHITE

HEGEL *Edited by* FREDERICK BEISER

HEIDEGGER *Edited by* CHARLES GUIGNON

HOBBES *Edited by* TOM SORELL

HUME *Edited by* DAVID FATE NORTON

HUSSERL *Edited by* BARRY SMITH *and*
DAVID WOODRUFF SMITH

WILLIAM JAMES *Edited by* RUTH ANNA PUTNAM

KANT *Edited by* PAUL GUYER

KIERKEGAARD *Edited by* ALASTAIR HANNAY *and*
GORDON MARINO

LEIBNIZ *Edited by* NICHOLAS JOLLEY

LOCKE *Edited by* VERE CHAPPELL

MARX *Edited by* TERRELL CARVER

NIETZSCHE *Edited by* BERND MAGNUS *and*
KATHLEEN HIGGINS

NEWTON *Edited by* I. BERNARD COHEN *and*
GEORGE E. SMITH

OCKHAM *Edited by* PAUL VINCENT SPADE

PLATO *Edited by* RICHARD KRAUT

PLOTINUS *Edited by* LLOYD P. GERSON

SARTRE *Edited by* CHRISTINA HOWELLS

SCHOPENHAUER *Edited by* CHRISTOPHER
JANAWAY

SPINOZA *Edited by* DON GARRETT

WITTGENSTEIN *Edited by* HANS SLUGA *and*
DAVID STERN

The Cambridge Companion to
NEWTON

Edited by

I. Bernard Cohen
Harvard University

and

George E. Smith
Tufts University

CAMBRIDGE
UNIVERSITY PRESS

PUBLISHED BY THE PRESS SYNDICATE OF THE UNIVERSITY OF CAMBRIDGE
The Pitt Building, Trumpington Street, Cambridge, United Kingdom

CAMBRIDGE UNIVERSITY PRESS
The Edinburgh Building, Cambridge CB2 2RU, UK
40 West 20th Street, New York, NY 10011-4211, USA
477 Williamstown Road, Port Melbourne, VIC 3207, Australia
Ruiz de Alarcón 13, 28014 Madrid, Spain
Dock House, The Waterfront, Cape Town 8001, South Africa

http://www.cambridge.org

First published 2002

Printed in the United Kingdom at the University Press, Cambridge

Typeface Trump Medieval 10/13 pt.   *System* LATEX 2ε [TB]

A catalogue record for this book is available from the British Library

Library of Congress Cataloguing in Publication data

The Cambridge companion to Newton / edited by I. Bernard Cohen and
George E. Smith.
    p. cm.
Includes bibliographical references and index.
ISBN 0 521 65177 8 (hardback) – ISBN 0 521 65696 6 (paperback)
1. Newton, Isaac, Sir, 1642–1727. 2. Physics–Europe–History–17th century.
3. Physics–Europe–History–18th century. 4. Science–Europe–
History–17th century. 5. Science–Europe–History–18th century.
I. Cohen, I. Bernard, 1914– II. Smith, George E. (George Edwin), 1938–
QC16.N7 C35 2002
530′.092–dc21   2001037836

ISBN 0 521 65177 8 hardback
ISBN 0 521 65696 6 paperback

CONTENTS

List of figures   *page* vii
List of contributors   ix
Preface   xiii

Introduction
I. BERNARD COHEN AND GEORGE E. SMITH   I

1   Newton's philosophical analysis of space and time
    ROBERT DISALLE   33

2   Newton's concepts of force and mass, with notes on the
    Laws of Motion
    I. BERNARD COHEN   57

3   Curvature in Newton's dynamics
    J. BRUCE BRACKENRIDGE AND
    MICHAEL NAUENBERG   85

4   The methodology of the *Principia*
    GEORGE E. SMITH   138

5   Newton's argument for universal gravitation
    WILLIAM HARPER   174

6   Newton and celestial mechanics
    CURTIS WILSON   202

7   Newton's optics and atomism
    ALAN E. SHAPIRO   227

8   Newton's metaphysics
    HOWARD STEIN   256

v

9   Analysis and synthesis in Newton's mathematical
    work
    NICCOLÒ GUICCIARDINI   308

10 Newton, active powers, and the mechanical philosophy
    ALAN GABBEY   329

11 The background to Newton's chymistry
    WILLIAM NEWMAN   358

12 Newton's alchemy
    KARIN FIGALA   370

13 Newton on prophecy and the Apocalypse
    MAURIZIO MAMIANI   387

14 Newton and eighteenth-century Christianity
    SCOTT MANDELBROTE   409

15 Newton versus Leibniz: from geometry to metaphysics
    A. RUPERT HALL   431

16 Newton and the Leibniz–Clarke correspondence
    DOMENICO BERTOLONI MELI   455

    Bibliography   465
    Index   481

FIGURES

2.1 Newton's parallelogram rule for motions
produced by impulsive forces. *page* 66

2.2 The area law for uniform rectilinear motion. 71

2.3 Newton's polygonal path (from the first edition
of the *Principia*, 1687). 71

2.4 The trajectory of a moving body that has received
a blow or has been struck by an impulsive force. 77

3.1 A particle at *A* rotates uniformly in a circle *AD*
constrained by a string attached to the center *C*,
the center of the circle. 89

3.2 A polygon *AB*, *BC*, etc. is inscribed in a circle
of radius *R*. 90

3.3 A particle moves along a circular arc from *P* to
Q under the influence of a force directed toward
the center of the circle *S*. 92

3.4 Newton's drawing of the orbit for a constant radial
force which appears on the upper right-hand
corner of his letter to Hooke written on
13 December 1679. 98

3.5 Illustrating how a segment *P P'* of an orbit is
obtained by rotating the radius of curvature vector
P Q into *P'Q* about its fixed center of curvature *Q*
through an angle ϕ, while the center of force is
located at *C*. 101

3.6 The upper segment *AO* of the orbit for constant
radial force as obtained by the iterations of the
curvature method. 104

vii

3.7   A simulation which accounts for the angular error
      in Newton's drawing.   105
3.8   Taken from Proposition 1, Book 1, 1687 *Principia*.   108
3.9   The triangles SAB and SBc have equal bases $AB =$
      Bc and a common slant height. The triangles SBC
      and SBc have a common base SB and equal slant
      heights.   109
3.10 Taken from Proposition 6, Book 1, 1687 *Principia*.   111
3.11 Taken from Lemma 11, Book 1, 1687 *Principia*.   113
3.12 Taken from Lemma 11, Book 1, 1687 *Principia*.   114
3.13 Taken from Proposition 6, Book 1, 1713 *Principia*.   115
3.14 An enhanced version of Newton's diagram shown
      in Fig. 3.13.   116
3.15 Figure in Proposition 15, Book 2, describing an
      equiangular spiral curve $PQRr$ for an orbit under
      the action of a gravitational force centered at S
      and a resistance force.   119
3.16 Figure in Proposition 28, Book 3, for an ellipse
      $CPADB$ representing a hypothetical orbit of the
      Moon around the Earth.   123
5.1   Log mean distances versus log periodic times for
      the planets.   179
7.1   Refraction at the surface EG decomposes a ray
      of sunlight OF into rays of different degrees of
      refrangibility and color.   231
7.2   Newton's dispersion model from his *Optical
      Lectures*.   234
7.3   Newton's derivation of Snell's law of refraction in
      the *Principia*, Book 1, Proposition 94.   236
7.4   Newton's method for determining the thickness
      d of a thin film of air formed between a spherical
      lens and a plane.   239
7.5   One quadrant of Newton's rings produced with light
      of a single color.   244
7.6   A compound corpuscle of matter illustrating
      Newton's hierarchical conception of the structure
      of matter.   248

CONTRIBUTORS

DOMENICO BERTOLONI MELI is a professor in the Department of History and Philosophy of Science at Indiana University. He specializes in seventeenth- and eighteenth-century science and medicine and is the author of *Equivalence and Priority: Newton versus Leibniz*.

J. BRUCE BRACKENRIDGE is Alice G. Chapman Professor of Physics Emeritus at Lawrence University. He is the author of *The Key to Newton's Dynamics: The Kepler Problem and the Principia*, as well as several papers on the role of curvature in Newton's dynamics.

I. BERNARD COHEN is Victor S. Thomas Professor of the History of Science Emeritus at Harvard University. He is the author of numerous books in the history of science generally and on Newton in particular, including *The Newtonian Revolution*, and is co-editor of the Variorum Latin edition of Newton's *Principia* and co-author of the new English translation.

ROBERT DISALLE is a professor in the Department of Philosophy at the University of Western Ontario. He has published several papers on Newton, Einstein, and Mach, especially on their respective treatments of space, time, and motion.

KARIN FIGALA is University Professor for the History of the Sciences at Deutsches Museum in Munich. She is author of many papers on alchemy and co-editor of the recent *Alchemie, Lexicon einer hermetischen Wissenschaft*.

ALAN GABBEY is Professor of Philosophy at Barnard College. He has published numerous papers on seventeenth-century mechanics and philosophy, including a prominent paper on the principle of inertia.

NICCOLÒ GUICCIARDINI teaches history of science at the University of Bologna. He is author of *The Development of Newtonian Calculus in Britain, 1700–1800* and *Reading the Principia: The Debate on Newton's Mathematical Methods for Natural Philosophy from 1687 to 1736.*

RUPERT HALL is Professor Emeritus of History of Science and Technology at Imperial College, University of London. His many works in the history of science include *Philosophers at War: The Quarrel between Newton and Leibniz, Isaac Newton, Adventurer in Thought*, and, as co-editor (with Marie Boas Hall), *Unpublished Scientific Papers of Isaac Newton.*

WILLIAM HARPER is Professor of Philosophy at Western Ontario University. He has written extensively on Newton's methodology and the relationship between Newton's and Einstein's theories of gravity, as well as on Kant and on causal decision theory.

MAURIZIO MAMIANI is Professor of History of Science and Technology at the University of Udine, Italy. Among his books and papers on Newton are *I. Newton filosofo della natura, Il prisma di Newton*, and *Introduzione a Newton.*

SCOTT MANDELBROTE is Official Fellow and Director of Studies in History at Peterhouse, Cambridge, and a Fellow of All Souls College, Oxford. He is one of the editorial directors of a project to transcribe and edit the alchemical, administrative, and theological manuscripts of Isaac Newton.

MICHAEL NAUENBERG is Professor of Physics Emeritus at the University of California, Santa Cruz. In addition to the many papers from his distinguished career in physics, he has published several articles on the technical development of Newton's physics.

WILLIAM R. NEWMAN is a professor in the Department of History and Philosophy of Science at Indiana University. His work on early chemistry and alchemy includes *The "Summa Perfectionis" of Pseudo-Geber: A Critical Edition, Translation, and Study,* and *Gehennical Fire: The Lives of George Starkey, An American Alchemist in the Scientific Revolution.*

ALAN E. SHAPIRO is Professor of the History of Science and Technology at the University of Minnesota. He is author of *Fits, Passions, and Paroxysms: Physics, Method, and Chemistry* and *Newton's Theories of Colored Bodies and Fits of Easy Reflection,* and is the editor of Newton's optical papers.

GEORGE E. SMITH is Professor of Philosophy at Tufts University and Acting Director of the Dibner Institute for the History of Science and Technology at MIT. He specializes in the development of evidence in the advanced sciences and engineering and is the author of several papers on Newton.

HOWARD STEIN is a professor emeritus in the Department of Philosophy of the University of Chicago. His research has focused on the philosophical foundations of physics and mathematics, and he has published several highly influential papers on Newton, as well as on Huygens, Maxwell, and Einstein.

CURTIS WILSON is a tutor at St. John's College, Annapolis. His writings on the history of science reach from the Middle Ages through the nineteenth century, most extensively on astronomy; he is co-editor of the two parts of *Planetary Astronomy from the Renaissance to the Rise of Astrophysics,* the second volume of *The General History of Astronomy.*

PREFACE

At the time of his death in 1996, our colleague Sam Westfall had begun to plan a Newton volume for the Cambridge Companions series. He had made contact with potential contributors, but had not reached the final stages of planning. When Cambridge University Press invited us to succeed Sam as editors of this volume, we received generous help from his wife, Gloria. For this we are profoundly grateful. Studying Sam's preliminary table of contents revealed to us that his orientation to a book for this series, though reflecting his deep scholarship, was nevertheless entirely different from ours. For practical purposes, therefore, we started afresh. Still, it was a source of constant regret that we could not draw on Sam's wisdom and knowledge of Newton, a loss aggrandized by the tragic early death of Betty Jo Teeter Dobbs.

Our original plan for this book included a chapter on the reception and assimilation of Newton's science among late-seventeenth- and eighteenth-century philosophers. Two considerations led us to abandon this plan and restrict attention to philosophers with whom Newton actually interacted, most notably Leibniz. First, the number of philosophers such a chapter ought to examine is too large, and their individual responses to Newton are too diverse, to be manageable within the scope of one or two chapters of reasonable length. Second, many of these responses shed more light on the philosopher in question than on Newton, often because they are responses to a caricature of Newton's science. There is a book to be written that examines philosophers' reactions to Newton's science from Locke through Kant (if not through Mill and Whewell, or even Mach), carefully comparing their construals of that science both with what

Newton actually did and with the contemporaneous responses to it by "scientists" from Huygens through Laplace. Such a book, however, would not be a Companion to Newton in the sense of this series.

Hilary Gaskin, our editor at Cambridge University Press, was extremely helpful to us in many ways in preparing this volume. It is a far better volume than it would have been without her. We also acknowledge Frances Brown's effort in copy-editing, Andrew Janiak's help in reading the page-proofs, and Tobiah Waldron's preparation of the index.

The editors dedicate this volume to their wives, India and Susan.

Introduction

Isaac Newton deserves to be included in a series of companions to major philosophers even though he was not a philosopher in the sense in which Descartes, Locke, and Kant were philosophers. That is, Newton made no direct contributions to epistemology or metaphysics that would warrant his inclusion in the standard list of major philosophers of the seventeenth and eighteenth centuries – Descartes, Spinoza, Locke, Leibniz, Berkeley, Hume, and Kant – or even in a list of other significant philosophers of the era – Bacon, Hobbes, Arnauld, Malebranche, Wolff, and Reid. The contributions to knowledge that made Newton a dominant figure of the last millennium were to science, not to philosophy. By contrast, Galileo, the other legendary scientific figure of the era, not only published the most compelling critique of Aristotelian scholasticism in his *Dialogues on the Two Chief World Systems*, but in the process turned the issue of the epistemic authority of theology versus the epistemic authority of empirical science into a hallmark of modern times. Although Newton clearly sympathized with Galileo, he wrote virtually nothing critical of the Aristotelian tradition in philosophy, and the immense effort he devoted to theology was aimed not at challenging its epistemic authority, but largely at putting it on a firmer footing. Newton made no direct contributions to philosophy of a similar magnitude. Indeed, from his extant writings alone Newton has more claim to being a major theologian than a major philosopher.[1]

Without dispute Newton was *the* giant of science in the seventeenth and eighteenth centuries, just as James Clerk Maxwell was *the* giant of science during the latter nineteenth century. But the very thought of a companion to Maxwell for non-specialist students in philosophy would seem to be beyond serious consideration. Why then a companion to Newton?

A superficial answer is that what we now call science was then still part of philosophy, so-called "natural philosophy" as in the full title of the work that turned Newton into a legend, *Philosophiae Naturalis Principia Mathematica*, or *Mathematical Principles of Natural Philosophy*. While historically correct, this answer is seriously misleading. Newton's *Principia* is the single work that most effected the divorce of physics, and hence of science generally, from philosophy. Newton chose his title to parallel Descartes's *Principia Philosophiae* (1644), a work that he viewed as filled with "figmenta" – imaginings – and that he intended his own *Principia* (1687) to supplant, once and for all. Descartes thought of his *Principia* as a culmination of his philosophy, laying out not merely a full natural philosophy to replace Aristotle's, but also point by point the epistemological principles that he had developed in his *Meditations*. It is a comment on the radical split between science and philosophy that because of Newton's *Principia* we no longer read Descartes's *Principia* as central to his philosophy, viewing it instead as Descartes's science. Correspondingly, to say that Newton's *Principia* is a work in philosophy is to use this term in a way that it rendered obsolete.

A better answer to why a companion to Newton for philosophers is that his *Principia* gave us a new world-view in which a taxonomy of interactive forces among particles of matter is fundamental. This supplanted not only the Aristotelian world-view, but also that of the so-called "mechanical philosophy" espoused by Descartes and others in the seventeenth century to replace the Aristotelian, a view in which physical change takes place strictly through contact of matter with matter. The trouble with this new-world-view answer is that the new "experimental philosophy" which Newton put forward as his alternative to the "mechanical philosophy" did not as such include any ontological claims at all. Rather, its point was that questions about what there is physically should be settled purely through experimental inquiry; classical philosophical arguments on issues like whether atoms or vacuums exist should cease carrying any weight. So, the revolution in physical ontology wrought by Newton was just an ancillary product of his science, and hence it too was part of the split between science and philosophy. With this split, most questions about what physically exists would no longer fall within the scope of traditional metaphysics.

The best answer to why a companion to Newton for philosophers is that Newtonian science created a new problem for philosophy, a problem that remained at the forefront of philosophy for the next two hundred years and is still central today. Questions about the nature and scope of the knowledge we can achieve of the empirical world have been part of philosophy since Plato and Aristotle. In part because of the challenge of Pyrrhonic skepticism, they became especially important in the rise of modern philosophy during the seventeenth and eighteenth centuries, that is, among philosophers from Bacon and Descartes through Hume, if not Kant. Philosophical considerations led virtually all of these philosophers to the same largely negative conclusion: given the limited character of the information we receive through our senses, empirical inquiry in itself cannot establish much in the way of general theoretical knowledge. For Descartes and Leibniz this meant that empirical inquiry has to be amply supplemented by philosophical reasoning, an alternative dismissed by Locke and Hume. On the face of it, the science coming out of Newton's *Principia* defied such skeptical conclusions. The initial problem this science posed for philosophers was to make clear just what sort of knowledge it was achieving. As the spectacular success of this science became increasingly evident during the course of the eighteenth century, the problem took on the added dimension of explaining how such knowledge is possible. Both aspects of this problem have been with us ever since.

The success of the science coming out of Newton's *Principia* created a second, more indirect problem for philosophy. This science portrays the natural world as governed by laws. But we are part of nature and hence to a considerable extent must also be governed by such laws. The upshot is a tension between our conception of ourselves as moral, reason-giving beings, on the one hand, and modern science, on the other, that took root during the eighteenth century and has again been with us ever since.

The compelling reason for a companion to Newton for philosophers, then, is that Newtonian science has been a backdrop to modern philosophy in much the way Euclidean geometry was to philosophy before Newton. One has trouble understanding many of the writings of philosophers after Newton without taking into account what they thought, rightly or wrongly, he had done. Newton was not a philosopher in our present sense of the term. Nevertheless, he gave careful consideration to how to go about establishing scientific knowledge, reaching conclusions that prima facie conflict with much of what philosophers have said about modern science. Even though he did not engage much in metaphysics in the grand sense of the term, he was more sensitive to issues of metaphysics than most subsequent scientists have been and also more aware of the metaphysical foundations implicit in science. Because of the attention he did give to philosophical concerns, the issues his work initiated in subsequent philosophy are better understood by putting them in the context of an accurate picture of what he did.

The goal of this volume is to provide an introduction to Newton's work, enabling readers to gain more rapid access to it and to become better judges of how well subsequent philosophers have dealt with it. The primary emphasis is on Newton's science, especially on making it accessible to a philosophical audience. The science for which he is known, however, occupied a much smaller fraction of his total intellectual life than one might think. Recent scholarship has made clear that an appreciation of his efforts in such other areas as theology, prophecy, and alchemy gives added perspective to the work for which he is best known. Moreover, he lived in a time when philosophic controversy was at the center of intellectual life. Even though he wrote little in pure philosophy, he was thoroughly familiar with the philosophic writings of others, especially Descartes, and consequently his work is highly responsive, often in subtle ways, to the philosophy of his times.

Because our goal is to acquaint philosophers with the main aspects of Newtonian science that actually influenced the development of philosophy, the chapters that follow deal primarily with those writings of Newton that were published in his life-time or soon thereafter. Nevertheless, almost every chapter draws heavily on the enormous stock of Newton's manuscripts and on the scholarship of recent decades that has used these manuscripts to produce a fuller perspective on the many facets of Newton's intellectual activity.

THE GENUINE NEWTON VERSUS
THE FIGURE OF LEGEND

The philosophic and popular literature on Newton abounds with misinformation and myths that have saddled the educated public with continuing misconceptions about him. As the close scrutiny given to his unpublished papers over the last fifty years has shown, Newton is a figure of truly legendary proportions even without the myths. Nevertheless, the myths and misconceptions seem to have a life of their own, persisting in spite of the high quality of Newton scholarship. As Rupert Hall shows in his chapter, some of the myths arose, at times with assistance from Newton himself, during the heated priority dispute with Leibniz over the calculus. Many of them, however, derive either from the philosophic literature or from works of intellectual history and careless remarks by authors of science textbooks, and they continue to gain new life from these sources. One of the goals of the volume is to dispel myths about Newton that hamper current philosophic research and understanding.

Myths about Newton are too numerous to list here. A few of them, however, have had such distortive effects on philosophic discussion as to warrant their being singled out. The most prominent myth of twentieth-century origin is that Einstein has shown that Leibniz was correct all along about the relativity of motion. Robert DiSalle's chapter shows that the relationship between Einstein's theories of special and general relativity and Newton's theories of motion and gravity is intricate. Still, one point that is certain is that Einstein did not show that Leibniz had been correct in his claims about the relativity of space. For Leibniz denied that there can be any fact of the matter about whether the Earth is orbiting the Sun, or the Sun the Earth, and Einstein's theories do not show this. Newtonian gravity holds in the weak-field limit of Einsteinian gravity, so that the former bears the same sort of relationship to the latter that Galilean uniform gravity bears to Newtonian gravity, allowing the evidence for the earlier theory in each case to carry over, with suitable qualifications about levels of accuracy, to the later theory. Moreover, as Euler showed in the late 1740s, and as Kant learned from Euler,[2] Newton's approach to space and time is inextricably tied to his laws of motion, in particular to the law of inertia. Abandoning Newtonian space and time in the manner Leibniz called for would entail abandoning the law of inertia as formulated in the seventeenth century, a law at the heart of Leibniz's dynamics. In gaining ascendancy over Leibniz's objections, Newton did not set physics down a dead-end path from which it was finally rescued by Einstein; rather, Einstein's theories of relativity represent a further major step along the path initiated by Newton.

Nothing about Newton is better known than the story that he came upon his theory of gravity while contemplating the fall of an apple in his mother's garden when away from Cambridge during the plague. To quote R. S. Westfall, this story

has contributed to the notion that universal gravitation appeared to Newton in a flash of insight in 1666 and that he carried the *Principia* about with him essentially complete for twenty years until Halley pried it loose and gave it to the world. Put in this form, the story does not survive comparison with the record of his early work in mechanics. The story vulgarizes universal gravitation by treating it as a bright idea.[3]

Newton definitely did give careful thought at some point during the late 1660s to the possibility that terrestrial gravity extends, in an inverse-square proportion, to the Moon. From his papers and correspondence, however, we can clearly see that the earliest date that can be assigned to his theory of universal gravity is late 1684 or early 1685, during the course of his revision of the tract "De motu." In their chapter Bruce Brackenridge and Michael Nauenberg show that Newton had employed novel mathematics to explore orbital trajectories from an early time. But because Newton did not make use of Kepler's area rule in these efforts, they fell significantly short of the orbital mechanics he developed in the 1680s and that ultimately led him in a sequence of steps to universal gravity. As I. B. Cohen shows in his chapter, an important part of this sequence was Newton's arriving at new concepts of *mass* and *force* that were required for both his laws of motion and the law of gravity. The theory of gravity was thus a product of twenty years of maturing thought about orbital motion.

In addition to being historically inaccurate, the bright-idea picture is an impediment to an appreciation of how complicated and how revolutionary the Newtonian theory of gravity actually was. From the point of view of his contemporaries, Newton's theory consists of a sequence of progressively more controversial claims: from the inverse-square centripetal acceleration of orbiting bodies to interactive forces not merely between orbiting and central bodies, but among the different orbiting bodies as well; to the law of gravity according to which the forces on orbiting bodies are proportional to the masses of the distant bodies toward which these forces are directed; and finally to the sweeping claim that there are gravitational forces between every two particles of matter in the universe.

William Harper's chapter on Newton's "deduction" of his theory of gravity examines how Newton put this sequence forward, invoking specific evidence for each claim in turn. Even the most outspoken critics of universal gravity thought Newton had established some of the claims in the sequence. Though they balked at different points, the common feature was where they thought concession of a claim was tantamount to conceding action at a distance. Newton himself was troubled by action at a distance – so much so that it seems to have driven him into thinking through and then laying out a new, elaborate approach to how empirical science ought to be done, an approach that the *Principia* was expressly intended to illustrate.

A further myth, complementing the bright-idea picture, is that everything in orbital mechanics immediately fell into place under Newton's theory of gravity. A corollary to this myth is that the continuing opposition to Newton's theory represented philosophic obstinacy in the face of overwhelming empirical evidence. Curtis Wilson's chapter dispels myths about Newton's achievements in celestial mechanics. Newton's most important achievement involved two superficially opposing points. On the one hand, the *Principia* raised Kepler's rules, especially the area rule, from the status of one among several competing approaches to calculating orbits, to the status where they came to be thought of as laws, *the* laws of planetary motion. On the other hand, the *Principia* concludes that none of Kepler's "laws" is in fact true of the actual system of planets or their satellites, and this in turn shifted the focus of orbital mechanics to deviations from Keplerian motion. With the exception of a few results on the lunar orbit, the *Principia* made no attempt to derive these deviations, and even in the case of the lunar orbit it left one major loose end that became a celebrated issue during the 1740s. The difficult task of reconciling Newtonian theory with observation occupied the remainder of the eighteenth century following Newton's death. This effort culminated with Laplace's *Celestial Mechanics*, the first volumes of which appeared in the last years of the century. It was in these volumes that what physicists now speak of as Newtonian physics first appeared comprehensively in print, more than a hundred years after the first edition of the *Principia*.

A statement often made about less successful sciences, "they have not had their Newton yet," rightly evokes Newton's singular place in the history of physics and astronomy. The combination of the bright-idea and the everything-fell-into-place myths, however, fosters an unfortunate misconception of just what was involved in the breakthrough he achieved and other such major breakthroughs. On this misconception, the key to successful science is for someone to come along who almost magically devises a new way of thinking about the relevant aspect of the world and who is then somehow able to see almost immediately how effective this new way of thinking is going to prove to be over the long run. Such an idea is plausible only with the help of a still further myth about Newton: that he was in some extraordinary way in tune with the world. One need look no further than his unsuccessful efforts to develop a theory of fluid resistance forces in Book 2 of the *Principia* in order to see that he was no more in tune with the world than other scientists of his time.[4] Newton was exceptional not because he had a capacity to leap to correct answers, but because of the speed and tenacity with which he would proceed step-by-step through a train of inquiry, putting questions to himself, working out answers to these questions, and then raising further questions through reflecting on these answers.

In the *Principia* (and to some degree in the *Opticks*) Newton telescoped the results of an enormous amount of detailed scientific research into an amazingly short duration of time. The research itself, however, is not other-worldly at all. It is disciplined empirical inquiry at its best. A good reason to study Newton's scientific efforts is that they provide insight into the ways in which science truly works.

An important feature of Newton's mature science is the union of mathematical analysis and the data of experience as manifested in experiment and critical observation. For example, Newton's analysis of resistance forces depended on the results of experiments he undertook in order to determine the parameters in laws for these forces. Another feature of Newton's science, as set forth in the *Principia*, was that the development of the subject matter should proceed without any appeal to religious principles or arguments in favor of one or another school of philosophy. That is, Newton consciously and purposely excluded from the scientific text any overt considerations of theology or fundamental philosophy. In later editions of the *Principia* (1713, 1726), he added a supplementary General Scholium, in which he introduced topics of theology and scientific method and the foundations of scientific knowledge. But the system of rational mechanics and the Newtonian gravitational system of the world were free of any overt reference to questions of theology and philosophy. In this sense, the *Principia* established a mode of scientific presentation that was free of what we today would call extra-scientific considerations.

A BRIEF BIOGRAPHICAL SKETCH

Newton lived into his eighty-fifth year, from 1642 to 1727, the year after the third edition of the *Principia* appeared. His life may be divided into four segments, the first ending in 1661 when he entered Trinity College, Cambridge, as an undergraduate, and the second extending to the publication of the *Principia* in 1687. The third period is marked by the renown that the *Principia* brought him; it concludes with his becoming disenchanted with Cambridge in the early 1690s and his permanent move to London and the Mint in 1696. In the final period, Newton remained intellectually active in London, though his achievements of legend occurred mostly during his Cambridge years, stretching from his early twenties to his early fifties.

Newton's pre-Cambridge youth spans the period from the start of the Civil War to the restoration of Charles II. He was born into a Puritan family in Woolsthorpe, a tiny village near Grantham, on Christmas Day 1642 (in the Julian calendar, old style), a little short of twelve months after Galileo had died. Newton's father, who had died the previous October, was a farmer. Three years after Newton's birth, his mother Hannah married a well-to-do preacher, 63-year-old Barnabas Smith, rector of North Witham. She moved to her new husband's residence, leaving young Isaac behind, to be raised by his aged maternal grandparents. Hannah returned to Woolsthorpe and the family farm in 1653, after Smith died, with three new children in tow. Two years later Isaac was sent to boarding school in Grantham, returning to Woolsthorpe in 1659. The family expected that he would manage his father's farm. It soon became evident, however, that he was not cut out to be a farmer. The headmaster of the Grantham school and Hannah's brother, who had received an M.A. from Cambridge, then persuaded her that Isaac should prepare for the university; and in 1661 he entered Trinity College as an undergraduate.

Newton's years at Trinity College, as a student and Fellow and then as a professor, appear to have been spent predominantly in solitary intellectual pursuits. As an undergraduate he read the works of

Aristotle and later commentators and some scientific works such as Kepler on optics. At some point within his first two years as a student, he began reading widely on his own, supplementing the classical education Cambridge was providing with more contemporary writings of such figures as Descartes.

Cambridge then had on its faculty one of the leading British mathematicians, Isaac Barrow, whose lectures he attended. Newton, however, largely taught himself mathematics through extensive reading of recent publications, most notably the second edition of van Schooten's Latin translation, with added commentary, of Descartes's *Géométrie*. Within an incredibly short period, less than two years, Newton mastered the subject of mathematics, progressing from a beginning student of university mathematics to being, *de facto*, the leading mathematician in the world. He reached this status during 1665–6, a time when the university was closed because of the great plague and he had returned to the family farm in Woolsthrope. It was during this period that Newton developed the basic results of the differential and integral calculus, including the fundamental theorem relating the two. No later than this time, he also made his experiments on refraction and color that similarly put him at the forefront in optics. His notebooks from the mid-1660s show him also working out answers to questions about motion, most notably uniform circular motion, questions that were undoubtedly provoked by his encountering the ideas of Galileo and especially Descartes (from whom, among much else, he learned the law of inertia). It was during this early period that Newton independently discovered the v^2/r rule for uniform circular motion, a few years before Christiaan Huygens published it in his renowned *Horologium Oscillatorium*.

On his return to Cambridge following the plague year, Newton was elected a Fellow of Trinity College, receiving his M.A. in 1668. The requirement of a fellowship in those days included a formal statement of allegiance to the principles of the Church of England. Before fulfilling this requirement, Newton initiated an intense study of theology, especially the implications of the doctrine of the Trinity. He ended up by rejecting this doctrine as a distortion of Christianity. At this time, Newton was appointed to the Lucasian Professorship of Mathematics, which was financed by private rather than state funds – the basis for Newton not being examined on his beliefs concerning the Trinity and the religious principles of the Church of England.

During these years, Newton continued his work in mathematics and optics, and he became immersed in chemical and alchemical research and experiments. He wrote a tract, "De analysi," or "On Analysis by Infinite Series," in which he presented his key discoveries in the calculus. This work was circulated among British mathematicians and, notably, a copy was sent to the publisher John Collins in London. It was undoubtedly because of this tract that Barrow recommended the youthful Newton to succeed him as Lucasian Professor of Mathematics. Newton occupied this chair from 1669 until he formally resigned in 1701, five years after moving to London.

Newton's sole formal publication before the *Principia* was a series of letters on the theory of light and colors, including the invention of a reflecting telescope, published in the *Philosophical Transactions of the Royal Society* from 1672 to 1676. He was so embittered by the controversies that were engendered by these publications that he vowed to publish no further discoveries from his research in natural philosophy. The publication of these optical letters and his circulating of tracts in mathematics gave Newton a reputation as a major scientist in Britain and abroad. His formal publications, however, were merely the tip of an iceberg. Newton's professorship required him to deposit in the University Library a copy of his lectures. Among these are his Optical Lectures of 1670–2, which, as Alan Shapiro has shown, present an enormous range of experiments bolstering and complementing those described in his publications. There are also Lectures on Algebra from 1673 to 1683. These registered lectures are ambitious to a point that one has trouble seeing how the students could have handled the material. These lectures too, however, represent but a fraction of Newton's intellectual efforts during the 1670s. For example, his private papers show much more extensive successful research in mathematics during this decade than the lectures reflect, and he continued his research in chemistry, alchemy, biblical chronology, prophecy, and theology, as well as occasional physics.

In late 1679, in an effort to reinvigorate the activities of the Royal Society, Robert Hooke wrote to Newton posing various research issues, with the goal of stimulating Newton to renew his active association with the Society. During the ensuing exchange of letters, Hooke told Newton of his "hypothesis" that curved or orbital motion could be analyzed by supposing two components: an inertial tangential motion and an accelerated motion directed toward a center of force. He also raised the question of the precise trajectory described by a body under an inverse-square force directed toward a central point in space. During the course of this brief correspondence, Newton discovered the relation between inverse-square centripetal forces and Keplerian motion that comprises the initial stepping stone of the *Principia*. Yet he communicated this to no one. Moreover, whatever further conclusions he reached at the time, universal gravity was not one of them, for in 1681 he concluded that comets do not generally button-hook around the Sun.

In the summer of 1684 Edmond Halley visited Newton in Cambridge in order to ask him a question that the London savants could not answer: what curved path results from an inverse-square force? Newton is reported to have replied without any hesitation: the curve produced by an inverse-square force is an ellipse. He promised Halley to send the proof on to London. Halley received a tract, Newton's "De motu corporum in gyrum," in November. He was so impressed by the magnitude of Newton's achievement that he hastened to Cambridge for a second visit. On arrival, he learned that Newton, evidently stimulated by Halley's first visit, was continuing research on orbital motion. Newton gave Halley permission to register his tract with the Royal Society while awaiting further results. Such were the beginnings of the *Principia*.

It was agreed that Newton's book would be published by the Royal Society. Halley was to supervise the actual publication. The manuscript of Book 1 of the *Principia* arrived in London in spring of 1686, prompting a controversy with Hooke, who claimed priority for the concept of an inverse-square solar force. Halley managed to keep Newton working in spite of the controversy, finally receiving Book 2 in March 1687 and Book 3 in April.

Publication of the *Principia* in 1687, which ended Newton's life of comparative isolation, led to adulation in Britain and intense opposition to his theory of gravity elsewhere. He was elected to represent Cambridge University in Parliament in 1689 (and again in 1701). He continued experimental research in chemistry, writing his principal alchemical essays in the early 1690s, and in optics, exploring diffraction phenomena and laying out but not finishing a book on optics. He also initiated work on a radically restructured second edition of the *Principia*, an effort he abandoned when he suffered some sort of mental breakdown in 1693. He had been pursuing positions in London before the breakdown, and his efforts were finally rewarded when he was appointed Warden of the Mint in 1696, and Master of it in 1699. This nine-year period between when Newton was thrust into prominence and when he departed from Cambridge, while intense in more ways than one, yielded only manuscripts, and no new publications. Clearly these years were marked by turmoil.

Newton's subsequent thirty years in London contrast sharply with his thirty-plus years of comparatively solitary research in Cambridge. He was elected President of the Royal Society in 1703, a post he held until his death, and he was knighted in 1705. Catherine Barton, the extraordinarily vivacious teenage daughter of his half-sister, moved in with him, gaining great prominence in London social circles; she continued to reside with him until he died, even after she married John Conduitt (who succeeded Newton as Master of the Mint) in 1717.

The first decade of the new century saw him publishing the first edition of his *Opticks*, a work written in English rather than in Latin. An appendix to the *Opticks* contained two earlier tracts in mathematics, one of which exhibited Newton's dot-notation for differentials. There was also an edition of Newton's lectures in algebra and a Latin edition of the *Opticks* (1706). During the last years of the decade he began work in earnest on a second edition of the *Principia*, which was finally published in 1713. Although this edition was not radically restructured, 397 of its 494 pages involved changes from the first edition – sometimes mere changes in wording, but in places a complete rewriting or the addition of new material. One important feature of the second edition was the concluding Scholium Generale with its slogan, "Hypotheses non fingo." As Alexandre Koyré determined, Newton meant "I do not feign hypotheses." He did not invent fictions in order to provide scientific explanation.

Continental natural philosophers found it difficult to accept Newton's concept of a force of universal gravity. Thus Leibniz, like Huygens and others, was strongly opposed to Newton's theory of gravity from the time it first appeared. Leibniz's response was to publish an alternative account of Keplerian motion in 1689, followed by his more important papers in dynamics. The relationship between the two did not turn nasty, however, until one of Newton's followers, John Keill, declared in 1709 that Leibniz had stolen the calculus from Newton. The ensuing priority dispute, which lasted beyond Leibniz's death in 1716, is described in Rupert Hall's chapter. It was complicated by the fact that Leibniz had been in England and had visited John Collins in the early 1680s, before publishing his own fundamental results in calculus. Furthermore, Newton had not then published his work on the calculus, instead only circulating his ideas in manuscript form. The priority dispute also spilled over into open disputes about the theory of gravity and its philosophical and theological implications, leading to the Leibniz–Clarke correspondence of 1715–16, analyzed in the chapter by Domenico Bertoloni Meli. Of course, Newton's calculus differed in key respects from Leibniz's, and we are now aware that the two men made their breakthroughs independently. Today we know that Newton was first in inventing the calculus, but that Leibniz was first in publishing it and then forming a group working on its further development and dissemination.

Newton remained intellectually engaged during the last ten years of his life, though less in science and mathematics than in theology, chronology, and prophecy. Further editions of his *Opticks* appeared in 1717/18 (and posthumously in 1730). Newton also produced a third edition of the *Principia*, appearing in 1726, when he was 83 years old. It does not differ in essentials from the second edition; the main change was some new text based on recent data. Though his theory of gravity remained still largely unaccepted on the Continent, there can be no question but that Newton had himself achieved the status of legend throughout the educated world. He died on 20 March 1727.

NEWTON THE SCIENTIST

Even after the myths and exaggerations have been discarded, Newton still occupies a singular place in the history of science, having contributed far more than any other single individual to the transformation of natural philosophy into modern science. An obvious question is, why him rather than someone else? What was it about Newton that enabled him to have such an extraordinary impact on empirical inquiry? The answer involves at least three factors: the historical situation in which he found himself, the attitude with which he approached empirical research, and the breadth as well as the depth of his genius.

Newton is well known for having remarked, "If I have seen further, it is by standing on the sholders of Giants."[5] This was not mere modesty. Newton knew better than anyone the extent to which he proceeded from the work of others before him. The two giants who are invariably cited are Kepler and Galileo, but this grossly oversimplifies the historical situation. In the case of astronomy, it makes little sense to cite Kepler without citing Tycho Brahe for providing the data that Kepler and all the other astronomers of the seventeenth century relied on. Newton, moreover, learned his orbital astronomy from reading not Kepler, but the generation that followed him, in particular Jeremiah Horrocks, Ishmaël Bouillau, Edward Streete, Vincent Wing, Nicholas Mercator, and G. A. Borelli. Most of these figures departed from Kepler in one respect or another, but in doing so they gave rise to questions that would have had far less force than without these departures. In his own generation, as well, Newton relied on John Flamsteed and, less directly, members of the French Academy for astronomical observations of increasingly high quality. Without this body of research in astronomy over the century before the *Principia*, Newton could never have made the enormous advances that he presented to the world in that book.

The situation is similar in physics. Christiaan Huygens extended Galileo's work on motion in important ways, including pendulum motion and an extraordinarily precise measurement of the strength of surface gravity. This research is presented in his *Horologium Oscillatorium* of 1673, a work Newton greatly admired – and appropriately so, for it would have been the most important work in the science of motion in the seventeenth century had it not been eclipsed by the *Principia*. Huygens himself was the culmination of a tradition represented not just by Galileo, but also by Marin Mersenne and Descartes as well. Huygens, not Newton, was the first in print with a mathematical account of the force required for a body to move uniformly in a circle, a force first called attention to by Descartes. Huygens, along with John Wallis and Christopher Wren, were the first in print with modern laws of impact, and the Royal Society, for which Robert Hooke was curator of experiments, had evaluated these laws experimentally. Much the same can be said of advances made in theoretical and practical optics by figures preceding Newton, starting with Kepler and Snell and including Descartes, Huygens, and others.

Newton learned the principles of making experiments from such masters as Robert Boyle and Robert Hooke. He became acquainted with the corpuscular philosophy, or the doctrines of atomism, by reading works of Boyle and from the writings of Pierre Gassendi and Walter Charleton. Thus, Newton was informed of current thinking in science by learning from great masters, the leading figures of an age well described as "the century of genius."

In short, although Newton worked largely as a solitary figure during his decades at Cambridge, he was anything but insulated from those who were forming an international scientific community during the century. Newton read widely, critically assimilating advances made by others and openly building from them. His singular place in the history of science is in no small part an accident of historical timing, his coming of age at a time when the labors of many others had created a singular opportunity.

A second factor enabling Newton to produce his extraordinary impact was the depth of his commitment to the principle that in matters of natural philosophy the empirical world should always be the sole arbiter. The view that the empirical world should be the ultimate arbiter was a hallmark of the era, whether as voiced by Tycho and Kepler, by Galileo, by Bacon and Boyle, or by Mersenne and Gassendi. Those engaged in empirical research were quick to realize, however, that it was one thing to express a commitment to this tenet and quite another to find ways in which the world would provide conclusive answers to theoretical questions. This realization led to a widespread guardedness, if not skepticism, toward theoretical claims. Perhaps all that could be hoped for was to describe the world accurately in the manner of a natural history, with purely theoretical claims never rising above the status of conjectural hypotheses not incompatible with the so-far observed world.

Newton, by contrast, took the commitment of the empirical world's being the ultimate arbiter as an obligation to insist on and hence to pursue ways in which the empirical world could be made to yield definite answers to theoretical questions. Throughout his career he maintained a sharp distinction between conjectural hypotheses and experimentally established results. He was never willing to rest content with any hypothesis. Whether in alchemy and chemistry, in optics, or in orbital mechanics, the challenge was to design sequences of experiments or to marshal complexes of observations that would warrant taking theoretical claims to be established. He saw himself as having met this challenge in the case of orbital mechanics, to a lesser extent in the case of optics in so far as he never thought he had established the corpuscular character of light, and to almost no extent at all in the case of alchemy and chemistry, despite years of effort and hundreds of experiments. The important point, however, is that the depth of his commitment to having the empirical world settle questions kept him going along lines of research, asking further questions and looking for further evidence, far beyond where anyone else would have stopped. One can easily fail to appreciate how strongly Newton felt about this, for he often voiced it in innocuous ways. For example, in a portion of the Preface to the first edition of the *Principia* that he decided to withhold from publication, he puts forward the idea that further progress in science will come from inquiring into the forces among particles of matter, beyond gravity, by which "bodies agitate one another and coalesce into various structures"; he then adds: "It remains therefore that we inquire by means of fitting experiments whether there are forces of this kind in nature, then what are their properties, quantities, and effects."[6] It is easy to underestimate how much is packed into the word "fitting."

Being unusually demanding and dogged in empirical research, even during exceptionally propitious times, means little by itself. The third, and most important, factor enabling Newton to have his extraordinary impact was the breadth of his genius. It goes without saying that he ranks among the two or three greatest theoretical scientists ever – one thinks of Maxwell and Einstein as well – where the skill involved is taking an initial line of thought and elaborating it into a full, detailed theory with a wide range of ramifications. Newton is commonly listed with Gauss as the greatest mathematicians in history, if not for his success in developing theoretical edifices, then for his ability to solve individual problems, first identifying the core difficulty of the problem, then devising apparatus to surmount this difficulty, and finally seeing the further potential of this apparatus.

Less widely recognized is the fact that Newton was among the most skillful experimental scientists in history. This is less widely recognized not merely because we tend to celebrate theoreticians, and not experimenters, but also because such a large fraction of Newton's experimental effort is not well known. His experiments in alchemy and chemistry have yet to be published, the experiments in the *Principia* are in the rarely read Book 2, and even the experiments that occupy much of the *Opticks*, which have indeed been widely heralded as examples of experimental science at its best, are rarely seen as the culminations of a much wider range of experiments that complement and support them. With the exception of Alan Shapiro's chapter, this book too may be guilty of not putting due emphasis on Newton the experimentalist, especially since the total fraction of his time put into designing and carrying out experiments has to have been far greater than the fraction put into devising theories. In-born talent is less of a factor in genius in experiment than it is in genius in mathematics and genius in theorizing. Great skill in experimental research is something that gets developed through extended practice over time. It involves more than just painstaking care, perseverance in the face of practical difficulties, and ingenuity in the schematic design of experiments. Telling experiments almost always have to be *developed*, and this usually entails designing and carrying out a large number of preliminary and complementary experiments in order to obtain well-behaved results and to foreclose alternative interpretations of these results. Newton belongs in the first rank of experimentalists because his experimental research displays mastery of all of these aspects.

To be among the first rank of experimentalists, mathematicians, and theoreticians is more than enough to put Newton in a class by himself among empirical scientists, for one has trouble thinking of any other candidate who was in the first rank of even two of these categories. Moreover, we have not emphasized enough the extent to which each of these dimensions of Newton's genius fed off and informed the other two in the way he approached empirical inquiry. Even granting all of this, however, we have yet to capture the full breadth of Newton's genius. At least in comparison to subsequent scientists, Newton was also exceptional in his ability to put his scientific effort in much wider perspective.[7] As one should expect, the substance of his science concerns recondite details, and as already noted he always maintained a sharp distinction between substantive science and conjecture. Nevertheless, as a child of his time, he was a *natural philosopher*, no less preoccupied with forming a comprehensive conception of the natural world than Descartes was. This dimension of Newton's science stands out most clearly in the Queries at the end of the *Opticks*, but once identified and appreciated, it is easy to find everywhere else. Newton's approach to natural philosophy differed from Descartes's first in his insistence that any conjectured broad conception of the natural world be grounded in experimental fact, and second in his view that the primary value of such conjecture lay in framing questions and suggesting further experiments. As a consequence, Newton's pursuit of a philosophy of nature was at all times part of his science, putting the science into a perspective that invested its recondite details with added significance.

This "philosophical" dimension of Newton's science shows up in the present volume in three ways. First, he did frame a conception of the natural world that, in addition to forming the core of our own current conception, contrasted in interesting ways with those put forward by other seventeenth- and eighteenth-century philosophers. This is the main topic of Alan Gabbey's chapter. Second, his pursuit of this conception forced him to be much more attentive to and careful about "metaphysical" aspects of his science than is at first apparent from reading this science. Howard Stein's chapter makes the metaphysics of Newtonian science explicit, a metaphysics that has been crucial to subsequent science; in the process Stein reveals how skillful a philosopher, in the grand sense of the word, Newton was. Third, the importance Newton attached to conjecture about nature as a whole, coupled with his insistence on a sharp epistemological distinction between such conjecture and established science, led him into meticulous critical reflection on what is required to establish scientific results. Few, if any, successful scientists have given so much thought to questions of scientific methodology. From both the point of view of understanding his science as he saw it and the point of view of philosophy of science generally, Newton's views about how science should be done are important. While this topic surfaces in many of the chapters in this volume, for example those by DiSalle, Cohen, Shapiro, and Stein, it is the central topic in the chapters by William Harper and George Smith.

NEWTON THE MATHEMATICIAN

This book emphasizes Newton the scientist because his importance both to the millennium and to modern philosophy derives mostly from the impact he had on science. This emphasis, however, gives a distorted picture of Newton the individual. For the time and effort he put into science, even including the huge number of hours he put into chemical experiments, represent a modest fraction of the total time and effort he put into intellectual pursuits. Furthermore, notwithstanding his strong insistence on strictly empirical criteria within science, his other intellectual preoccupations could not help but have some effect on how he did science. A full understanding of Newton's science, therefore, at the very least requires it to be seen as fitting harmoniously within his other pursuits. And an understanding of Newton the individual must put no less weight on his work in pure mathematics, and his efforts in alchemy and theology, than on the work that made him legendary.

Newton's achievements in mathematics were extraordinary, yet his impact on the history of theoretical mathematics, and consequently on aspects of mathematics of greatest interest to philosophers, is not in proportion to these achievements. Some reasons for this are less interesting than others. Although he circulated some manuscripts, he did not publish any of his work on the calculus until the first decade of the eighteenth century, and by then the Leibniz school had been going strong, with frequent publications, for over ten years. Moreover, many of his mathematical results were never published in his lifetime. A compelling case can be made that the full range and depth of his achievements in mathematics became evident only in the twentieth century with the publication of the eight magisterial volumes of his mathematical papers under the editorship of D. T. Whiteside. Whatever inkling Newton's contemporaries may have gained of the scope of his mathematics from his publication of individual solved problems in the *Principia*, their lack of access to the systematic development of the methods he had used in these solutions limited their ability to build a growing body of Newtonian mathematics. Instead, time and again, areas in which Newton made breakthroughs, such as differential geometry and the calculus of variations, had to be independently developed by later mathematicians – most often Euler – who then had the impact on the history of the subject.

Newton's style as a mathematician also helps account for his disproportionately limited impact on the history of the field. His approach to mathematics – especially during the early periods – tended to be primarily that of a problem solver, taking on the challenge of specific unsolved problems. As remarked above, he had an uncanny knack for identifying the core difficulty of a problem and then devising means for overcoming it, often adapting ideas and methods of others, but putting them to novel use. Thus, for example, his initial algorithms for derivatives combined techniques from Cartesian geometry with the idea of an indefinitely small, vanishing increment. Similarly, his initial algorithms for integrals adapted a method Wallis had devised for algebraic curves, first reconceptualizing it to represent an integral that grows as the curve extends incrementally and then combining this with the binomial series to obtain solutions for integrals of a much wider range of curves. Once he had these results and found, from geometric representations of them, the relationship between differentiation and integration, he adapted Barrow's way of treating curves as arising from the motion of a point to recast his results on derivatives in terms of quantities that change with time and their increments of change, "fluents" and "fluxions."[8] (His first full tract on fluxions, dated 1666, was called "To Resolve Problems by Motion."[9]) He continued to extend his methods over the next thirty years, applying them to a growing range of problems. For Newton, however, the calculus was always a collection of interrelated methods for solving problems, not a radically new, superior approach to mathematics.

This view of the calculus is symptomatic of the factor that was probably most responsible for limiting Newton's impact on the history of mathematics, his mathematical conservatism. Rupert Hall's chapter calls attention to ways in which this conservatism intensified the priority dispute with Leibniz. Leibniz and his school saw the calculus as opening the way to doing all mathematics purely through the manipulation of symbols. To this end they put great effort into devising a suitable notation for the calculus, resulting in the form familiar to us. With the exception of the dot-notation (representing derivatives with respect to time), which dates from the mid-1690s, after the *Principia*, the notations Newton devised were not at all perspicuous. Given the range of Newton's talents, this almost certainly reflects not so much an inability on his part to come up with good notations as a lack of interest in, if not opposition to, a revolutionary new mathematics dominated by symbol manipulation. Niccolò Guicciardini's chapter examines Newton's changing views on the relationship between geometry and symbol-dominated mathematics and the impact these views had on his work. Following an intense reexamination of classical mathematics during the early 1680s, Newton appears to have concluded that the true roots of all mathematics lie in classical geometry.

This conservatism is apparent in the mathematics of the *Principia*. Contrary to a myth endorsed by Newton himself, there is no evidence whatever that Newton first derived his results on celestial orbits by using the symbolic calculus and then recast them in geometric form. The differential calculus does appear in Book 2, where Newton is unable to find a geometric solution to problems of motion with resistance forces varying as velocity squared; and in a handful of places solutions for integrals are given, without derivations, that he surely obtained symbolically. Everywhere else, however, the mathematics of the *Principia* is his "method of first and last ratios," a quite elegant extension of synthetic geometry that incorporates limits in a way that avoids the extensive use of *reductio ad absurdum* proofs that others were resorting to when working with infinitesimals. It was left to individuals within the Leibnizian tradition to recast the *Principia* into the symbolic calculus. What became clear in this process was the superiority of purely symbolic methods in attacking perturbation problems in celestial mechanics. With this realization the fundamental step in problems of physics ceased being one of finding an adequate geometric representation of the quantities involved, and instead became one of formulating appropriate differential equations in purely symbolic form. In a real sense, then, it was Newton's physics that gave the greatest impetus to the Leibnizian approach to mathematics, disproportionately limiting the impact Newton's work in mathematics had on the history of the field.

For the philosopher, however, Newton's mathematics has some special interest because of its arousing a controversy in which a philosopher, Bishop Berkeley, was a major figure. Berkeley's anti-Newtonian polemic was called *The Analyst* and was addressed to an "infidel mathematician." It was long believed that the "infidel mathematician" was Edmond Halley, but the target of Berkeley's attack was later identified as the physician Samuel Garth. Berkeley was troubled by the use of infinitesimals in the Newtonian form of the calculus, holding that this method of limits provided an unsound foundation, one that was based on "ghosts of departed quantities."[10] Since the new mathematics was based on such insecure foundations, he argued, mathematicians should not presume to criticize the foundations of religion. Berkeley further insisted that Newton's gravitational mechanics provided only a description of the phenomena of the external world and not an explantion, the "how" but not the "why" of the physics of the world.[11] Philosophers should also be aware that other aspects of Newton's mathematics are of philosophic interest. For example, as Rupert Hall shows in his chapter, the controversy between Newton and the Leibnizians went beyond mere questions of chronology and priority and in fact had important philosophic implications.

THE "OTHER" NEWTON: ALCHEMY AND THEOLOGY

Although Newton's fame and reputation are built on his scientific work in rational mechanics, cosmology, optics, and mathematics, the creative force of his intellect was not limited to these subjects. Newton was also deeply committed to his research into what seem to us esoteric domains, including historical and biblical chronology, theology, prophecy, a tradition of ancient wisdom, and alchemy. (He disdained the study of astrology, however, having concluded early on that there was no validity to predictions based on horoscopes.) Some of the esoteric subjects Newton studied bear no apparent or direct relation to what we consider to have been his scientific work. But others were not so completely distinct. For example, with regard to the wisdom of the ancients, Newton alleged that certain aspects of the law of universal gravity were known to ancient sages. At one time he even thought to include in a new edition of the *Principia* some extracts from Lucretius and other ancient writers. His studies of biblical chronology, prophecy, or pure theology (exploring such questions as the existence of the Trinity and the heresies of Arius) do not have this close relationship with his science.

The situation is more complicated with his alchemical concerns. Newton appears not to have conceived his studies of alchemy and his explorations concerning certain kinds of active and passive forces, or of aetherial and vegetative "spirits," to be wholly separate from what we today would call his "hard science." These domains of thought were, for him, closely associated not just with the nature of matter itself, but with the construction of matter and the action of forces between the particles of which matter is composed.

One feature of alchemical writings that evidently had a special appeal to Newton was the belief that these texts, if properly interpreted, would reveal the wisdom handed down by God in the distant past. In this regard, Newton's studies of alchemical texts had a close kinship with his studies of prophecy in the Book of Daniel and the Book of Revelation. Newton was not singular in believing that there was a close connection between spiritual and experimental domains. Count Michael Maier, one of the most important of the "authores optimi" for Newton, had a plate in his book *Atalanta Fugiens* that symbolized the dual aspect of alchemy in a way that fits Newton's concerns. This plate shows an alchemical laboratory: on one side is an oratory where the student of alchemy kneels in prayer, while on the other is a furnace, well equipped for the "chymical" part of the study.

In the present volume several chapters are devoted to aspects of Newton's research that are not obviously part of his scientific work. William Newman clarifies the scope of seventeenth-century "chymistry" and explains the basic principles of Newton's alchemy and its relation to ideas of van Helmont. Karin Figala shows the importance for Newton's alchemical studies of Count Michael Maier and Michael Sendivogius, in the process calling attention to ways in which Newton's alchemy had a potential for more far-reaching ramifications. Maurizio Mamiami explores the extent to which Newton's discussions of methods of research in natural philosophy were tied to his early acquaintance with rules for studies of theology. Scott Mandelbrote examines Newton's distinctive version of Christianity and the reception of his posthumously published theological writings, which are strongly anti-Trinitarian, during the eighteenth century.

Newton's studies of alchemy are notoriously difficult to evaluate because Newton did not produce treatises or tracts setting forth his goals and interpretations. Almost all of the alchemical manuscripts consist of notes on his reading, summaries or extracts from various authors, or records of experiments. Newton had read widely in alchemy and knew the alchemical literature better than most of his contemporaries. Because much of this literature is still being discovered, it is often difficult for us to be certain whether any given document may be an original composition by Newton or a summary of someone else's ideas. A case in point is a document called "Clavis" or "Key," which was believed to be an essay by Newton until William

Newman showed it to be a Latin version of an English essay sent by George Starkey (a Harvard graduate who had moved to London) to Robert Boyle.

On the basis of her studies, Karin Figala has concluded that Newton found in alchemy a hierarchical scheme of matter in which particles of different substances could be set out in a table according to their size. She notes that this same hierarchy occurs in the planets, which in alchemy were associated with the different metals. Such schematization is related to Newton's science (as science is commonly understood today) because in the later Queries of the *Opticks* (and as recorded by David Gregory, in a memorandum of discussions with Newton), Newton set forth a view of the structure of matter based on a hierarchy of particles that is related to Maier's hierarchy of matter and of the planets with which he believed the different types of particles were associated.

In considering the life and thought of Newton, the words alchemy and alchemist must be used with caution. In Newton's day, and during earlier times, an alchemist was traditionally a charlatan, someone who claimed the ability to transmute base metals such as lead into the noble metal gold. In the words of John Harris, in his Newtonian *Lexicon Technicum*, published in 1704, the same year as Newton's *Opticks*, such alchemists are said to "amuse the Ignorant and Unthinking with hard Words and Nonsense." It is a subject, he wrote, that "begins with Lying, is continued with Toil and Labour, and at last ends in Beggary." As long ago as the fourteenth century, the poet Chaucer (in "The Canon's Yeoman's Tale") poked fun at the alchemist, an obvious fraud, whose motto was the traditional "Ignotum per ignotius," or explaining what is "unknown" by what is "more unknown." Just before Newton was born, Ben Jonson wrote a whole play (*The Alchemist*) poking fun at the charlatans who practiced this profession. Indeed, as late as the middle of the nineteenth century, David Brewster (in his biography of Newton) was appalled to find that Newton had been spending creative energy in such a subject as alchemy. He simply could not "understand how a mind of such power, and so nobly occupied with the abstractions of geometry, and the study of the material world, could stoop to be even the copyist of the most contemptible alchemical poetry."

And yet, even though in Newton's day an alchemist tended to be a charlatan, a purveyor of "get rich quick" schemes, there was also in Newton's day a serious tradition of the study of alchemy.

Thus John Harris, in another entry in his *Lexicon*, gave a lengthy discussion of "Transmutation," quoting many authorities, including Robert Boyle.

In a certain sense, Newton's and Boyle's concern were with the experimental side of alchemy. This is sometimes called "chymistry," not quite the subject of chemistry as it developed in a later period, but a kind of study based on laboratory experiments and not just speculation. According to Harris, the goal of "chymistry" was "to separate usefully the Purer Parts of any mix'd Body from the more gross and Impure." This could in some measure be an account of Newton's research program in alchemy.

Because Newton's thoughts on chymistry are closely related to his theory of matter, they appear in some of the later Queries of the *Opticks*, where the structure and properties of matter are under discussion. We should note, however, that these discussions of the structure of matter do not appear in the text of the *Opticks*, but are part of the speculative Queries that are an appendix.

Still, Newton's concern for alchemy was not limited to the strictly chemical or metallurgical aspects of the subject. He made copious notes or annotations on almost all aspects of alchemy, including the spiritual or allegorical matrix in which alchemical writings have traditionally been embedded. He was even deeply concerned to understand the symbolic illustrations that grace many alchemical texts and that at first glance seem only distantly related to the transmutation of metals. The seriousness of his concern is made evident by the bare fact that his manuscript writings and notes on this subject are so voluminous, coming to more than a million words, dating from the late 1660s, when he first became interested, to at least the 1690s, when he moved from Cambridge to London to become Warden and then Master of the Mint.

Two scholars in particular have made massive studies of Newton's alchemical writings: the late Betty Jo Dobbs and Karin Figala. Dobbs wrote two books on the subject, summarizing her findings and conjectures.[12] Her conclusions are of real significance for any philosopher wishing to understand the mind of Newton. Figala has rather concentrated on what she conceives to be Newton's hierarchy of matter. Her most complete presentation is available in a major monograph in German, published in 1984.[13] She has also summarized her findings in a lengthy essay-review of Dobbs's first book on

Newton and alchemy.[14] Yet a third presentation is available as an appendix to Rupert Hall's *Isaac Newton: Adventurer in Thought.*[15]

It is difficult to describe briefly all the findings and conjectures of Betty Jo Dobbs concerning Newton's actual goal in his alchemical studies and the relation of this goal to his more orthodox scientific work. Dobbs made much of a work she identified as a composition by Newton, "Of Nature's Obvious Laws and Processes in Vegetation." In her analysis of this document she finds evidence for an early belief by Newton in the existence of forces with which particles of matter are endowed.

In evaluating this area of Newton's creative activity, we must take note that it differs from his research in mathematics, rational mechanics, cosmology, and optics in one very important feature: his studies of alchemy were part of what Jan Golinski has called Newton's "private science." His explorations of alchemy differ from his work in physics and mathematics to the extent that these were public. However reluctant Newton was to publish or even to circulate his work in science and mathematics, the fact remains that he did publish and make known a tremendous body of new science and mathematics. But the results of his alchemical studies were virtually never communicated, save to a select few intimate fellow "adepts." Indeed, Newton himself set forth this distinction in the essay "On Nature's Obvious Laws and Processes in Vegetation." Here he made a clear separation between what he called "vulgar chymistry" and a process of growth and life ("vegetation"), considered to be a feature of "Nature's actions [which] are either vegetable or purely mechanical" and thus in a manner shared by plants and animals and also metals.[16]

Thus far we have not faced up to what may be the most important question concerning Newton's alchemical studies: how were they related to his work in rational mechanics or optics. There seems to be little doubt that Newton's explorations in alchemy and the associated esoteric philosophy were related to his thinking about various types of "aether" and the ways in which the forces of nature (such as gravitational attractions) could actually perform their functions. It also does seem to be the case that Newton's theory of matter was strongly related to his explorations of alchemy. And this could extend to that part of optics in which Newton explored the interactions of light particles and matter.

But the situation is quite different when it comes to evidence that Newton's explorations of alchemy were in any significant way related to either the creation of his rational mechanics or his cosmology based on universal gravitational interaction. In her last book, Betty Jo Dobbs took the opposite point of view, arguing that Newton's alchemy revealed the existence of forces between particles of matter and that this gave Newton the justification to produce the physics of attractive forces in the *Principia*. There is, however, not a single document that would indicate that while composing the *Principia* Newton was encouraged by his alchemical findings to deal with gross forces acting at a distance.

We should take note here that, in any event, the transition from short-range forces to long-range forces is far from simple. It is the inverse of the problem of a transition from long-range to short-range forces. In fact, Newton did at one time speculate on such transitions and even wrote up some discussions of them to be included in a preface (from which we quoted earlier) and in a conclusion to the original *Principia*. In the end, however, he rejected the idea of including such speculations in the book, no doubt because they had a degree of uncertainty and pure speculation that was out of place in the mathematical elaboration of his theory of forces. As the documents make plain, Newton was convinced that short-range forces of attraction and of repulsion do exist and do produce many of the observed properties of matter. Yet he was also aware (and gave expression to his dubiety) that the very existence of these forces was no more than an unsubstantiated hunch. In choosing not to include both this preface and the conclusion in the *Principia*, he evidently did not want the certainties of the *Principia* to be contaminated by speculations.

Newton seems to have believed that there was a unity in all the areas that he explored: the interpretation of the Bible, the tradition of ancient wisdom, Church history, alchemy, prophecy, optics and color theory, theory of matter, rational mechanics, and celestial dynamics. But it is a fact of record that in his writings on mathematics, in the *Principia*, and in his writing about optics proper, there was no trace of his concern for these esoteric subjects. Only in the later Queries to the *Opticks* do we find a hint of his concern for alchemy, in that part of the queries where he speculates about the structure of matter. In short, these esoteric subjects were not features of the known thought of the public Newton or the Newton of history, the Newton who has been so important a figure in modern thought. For the philosopher, therefore, it is important to be aware of the range of Newton's thought and concerns; yet the Newton who has had so important an influence in the historical development of thought is rather the Newton of experiments and scientific theory, the mathematician who was a creator of the calculus, and the Newton who established the science of rational mechanics and set forth the Newtonian system of the world.

VARIETIES OF NEWTONIAN NATURAL PHILOSOPHY

Although Newton's influence on science and on philosophy was primarily produced by the *Principia*, the men and women of the eighteenth century were aware that the Newtonian philosophy embraced more than the combination of mathematics and empirical evidence which characterized that great work. We may gain some insight into the ways in which Newton influenced science and philosophy by reference once again to the *Lexicon Technicum* of John Harris, of which the last edition was published in 1731. The varieties of Newtonian philosophy set forth in this dictionary were adopted as still valid and set forth once again in Ephraim Chambers's *Cyclopaedia* (of which the first edition was published in 1728), and still served as the basis of the entry "Newtonianisme" in the *Encyclopédie* of Diderot and d'Alembert. At the century's end, in 1796, this delineation of the varieties of Newtonian philosophy was still considered valid, appearing once again in Charles Hutton's *Mathematical and Philosophical Dictionary*.

Not surprisingly, the primary entry in the *Lexicon Technicum* under the heading "NEWTONIAN Philosophy" is "the doctrine of the universe, and particularly of the heavenly bodies; their laws, affections, etc., as delivered by Isaac Newton." The dictionary, however, goes on to record some other senses in which at that time the term "Newtonian philosophy" was used. One further sense was "the corpuscular philosophy, as it now stands corrected and reformed by the discoveries and improvements made in several parts thereof by Sir I. Newton." As the lexicon explains, this aspect of "Newtonian philosophy" was primarily founded on the third book of Newton's *Opticks* (the part containing the Queries) and sundry papers such

as the "De natura acidorum," first published in 1710 in the second
volume of Harris's *Lexicon*.

A third meaning of the term "Newtonian Philosophy," according to the *Lexicon*, was "the method or order which Sir I. Newton
observes in philosophizing." This "method" of doing science was
said to consist of the "drawing of conclusions directly from phaenomena, exclusive of all previous hypotheses; the beginning from simple
principles; deducing the first powers and laws of nature from a few
select phaenomena, and then applying those laws, etc., to account
for other things."

The fourth and fifth meanings of "Newtonian Philosophy," as
given in the *Lexicon*, refer rather particularly to the *Principia*. The
third equates the "Newtonian Philosophy" with the "Mechanical
and Mathematical Philosophy." In this philosophy, "Physical bodies are considered mathematically; and . . . geometry and mechanics
are applied to the solution of phaenomena." The fourth meaning is
"that part of physical knowledge, which Sir I. Newton has handled,
improved, and demonstrated in his *Principia*." Finally, there is the
sixth sense of this term: "the new principles which Sir I. Newton has
brought into philosophy; the new system founded thereon; and the
new solution of phaenomena thence deduced; or that which characterizes, and distinguishes his philosophy from all others."[17]

This record of the ways in which the Newtonian philosophy was
conceived during the eighteenth century is especially valuable for
a number of reasons. First of all, as we have seen, it reports a variety of beliefs concerning the Newtonian philosophy which lasted for
at least another three-quarters of a century. It indicates the significance of an aspect of Newton's thought that is not generally given
a just place of importance: the creation of new science based on
experiment, on the direct questioning of nature, and not produced
in the manner of the *Principia* by a combination of mathematics
(geometry, algebra, trigonometry, infinite series, and the calculus)
together with critical observations plus experiments. This other
form of Newtonian natural philosophy was found primarily in Book 1
of the *Opticks*, where the statement of each proposition one by one
is followed by "The Proof by Experiments," and in the Queries with
which the *Opticks* concludes.

In defining the nature of the influence of Newton's science, therefore, we must take account of the existence of two rather different

varieties of Newtonian natural philosophy. They were, in a sense, as different as the manner of presentation was different in the *Principia* and the *Opticks*. The *Principia* was written in austere and formal Latin, giving the appearance of a text on geometry, whereas the *Opticks* was written in a gentle manner in flowing English prose, a kind of record of experiments and conclusions in the form of an extended laboratory journal. This difference in form determined two classes of readers. John Locke, for example, could not follow the mathematical proofs of the *Principia*, and relied on the judgment of Christiaan Huygens concerning the validity of the proofs; by contrast, he read the *Opticks* again and again with great pleasure.

This separation between the two strands of Newtonian Philosophy became even more marked with the publication of the later Queries in the *Opticks*, which contain Newton's speculations on all sorts of scientific and philosophic questions. Scientists such as Stephen Hales (the founder of plant physiology), the chemists Joseph Black and Antoine-Laurent Lavoiser, and Benjamin Franklin could thus be Newtonian scientists without the necessity of having any competence in the science of the *Principia*. There is, perhaps, no greater tribute to the genius of Isaac Newton than that he could thus engender two related but rather different traditions of doing science.

NOTES

1 Newton did, however, produce an extensive critique of Descartes's philosophy (in an essay known by its beginning, "De gravitatione," discussed in the chapters by Gabbey and Stein in this volume), but this was not published until 1962.

2 See DiSalle's chapter in this book, note 31.

3 Richard S. Westfall, *Never at Rest: A Biography of Isaac Newton* (Cambridge: Cambridge University Press, 1983), p. 155.

4 See George E. Smith, "The Newtonian Style in Book II of the *Principia*," in Jed Z. Buchwald and I. Bernard Cohen (eds.), *Isaac Newton's Natural Philosophy* (Cambridge, MA: MIT Press, 2001), pp. 249–313.

5 This remark was made years before the *Principia*, in a letter to Hooke (of 5 February 1676); Hooke had offered a gesture of goodwill (in a letter of 20 January 1676) following criticism of him by Newton in one of his public letters on light. See *The Correspondence of Isaac Newton*, vol. 1, ed. H. W. Turnbull (Cambridge: Cambridge University Press, 1959), p. 416.

6   A. Rupert Hall and Marie Boas Hall (eds.), *The Unpublished Scientific Papers of Isaac Newton* (Cambridge: Cambridge University Press, 1962), p. 307.

7   We owe this point to Alan Shapiro.

8   For details on Newton's invention of the calculus, see D. T. Whiteside (ed.), *The Mathematical Papers of Isaac Newton*, vol. 1 (Cambridge: Cambridge University Press, 1967), part 2, esp. pp. 145–54.

9   In fact, the treatises on fluxions by Newton and his disciples read as if they were tracts on the motion of a particle. On this point see I. B. Cohen, *The Newtonian Revolution* (Cambridge: Cambridge University Press, 1980), ch. 3.

10   In his chapter Rupert Hall points out that Newton expressed similar objections to infinitesimals during the priority dispute with Leibniz.

11   See A. A. Luce (ed.), *The Works of George Berkeley, Bishop of Cloyne*, vol. 4 (London: Nelson, 1952); Sir Alan Cook, *Edmond Halley: Charting the Heavens and the Seas* (Oxford: Clarendon Press, 1998), pp. 408–11.

12   B. J. T. Dobbs, *The Foundations of Newton's Alchemy, or "The Hunting of the Green Lyon"* (Cambridge: Cambridge University Press, 1975); and *The Janus Faces of Genius: The Role of Alchemy in Newton's Thought* (Cambridge: Cambridge University Press, 1991).

13   K. Figala, "Die exakte Alchemie von Isaac Newton," *Verhandlungen der Naturforschenden Gesellschaft Basel* 94 (1984), pp. 155–228.

14   K. Figala, "Newton as Alchemist," *History of Science* 15 (1977), pp. 102–37.

15   See pp. 381–6 in A. Rupert Hall, *Isaac Newton: Adventurer in Thought* (Oxford: Blackwell, 1992).

16   An excellent summary of this work is given by Jan Golinski in "The Secret Life of an Alchemist," in J. Fauvel *et al.* (eds.), *Let Newton Be! A New Perspective on His Life and Works* (Oxford: Oxford University Press, 1988), pp. 147–67. For a more complete presentation, together with a transcript of the whole text, see Dobbs, *Janus Faces*.

17   See, further, I. B. Cohen, *Franklin and Newton* (Philadelphia: American Philosophical Society, 1956; Cambridge, MA: Harvard University Press, 1966), ch. 3, esp. pp. 179–82, "Varieties of Newtonian Philosophy."

1 Newton's philosophical analysis of space and time

INTRODUCTION: PHILOSOPHICAL CONTROVERSY OVER NEWTON'S IDEAS OF SPACE, TIME, AND MOTION

Newton's concepts of "absolute space," "absolute time," and "absolute motion" met with serious objections from such philosophical contemporaries as Huygens, Leibniz, and Berkeley. Among philosophers of the early twentieth century, after the advent of Special and General Relativity, the objections bordered on scorn: Newton's concepts were not only lately outmoded, but they were also epistemologically inherently defective, empirically unfounded – concepts not scientific at all, but "metaphysical," in so far as science is concerned precisely with "sensible measures" rather than obscure notions of what is "absolute." The prevailing idea was that Einstein had established not only a new theory of space and time, but a deeper philosophical viewpoint on space and time in general. From this viewpoint, space, time, and motion are essentially relative, and to call them absolute was an elementary philosophical error. As Einstein put it, General Relativity had taken from space and time "the last remnant of physical objectivity."[1]

The philosophical motivation for this viewpoint seems obvious. Space cannot be observed; all that we can observe is the relative displacement of observable things. Therefore, if we observe two bodies in relative motion, to say that one of them is "really" moving, or that it is moving "relative to absolute space," is to pass beyond the bounds of empirical science. If we wish to decide which bodies are moving, we have to construct a frame of reference – that is, we must designate some reference-points to be fixed, and compare the motions of other bodies to these. Einstein held that any such choice of a reference-frame is inherently arbitrary, and that a philosophically sound physics would be independent of such arbitrary choices; the "General Theory of Relativity" was supposed to be a theory in which all reference-frames are equivalent. To his philosophical followers, especially Hans Reichenbach and Moritz Schlick, Einstein was only saying what philosophers ought to have known, and a few had already suspected, on purely philosophical grounds. Contemporaries who had rejected Newton's views now seemed to have anticipated the eventual emergence of physics from its naive state.

In the 1960s and 1970s, however, many scientists and philosophers began to recognize what a few had known all along: that general relativity does not make space, time, and motion "generally relative," as Einstein had thought.[2] Instead, the theory postulates a spatio-temporal structure that is, in an obvious sense, just as "absolute" as the structures postulated by Newton. On the one hand, Einstein's field equation relates the geometry of space-time to the distribution of matter and energy. Thus, if "absolute" means "fixed and uniform," or "unaffected by material circumstances," then we can say that spacetime in general relativity is not "absolute," but "dynamical." On the other hand, spacetime in general relativity remains "absolute" in at least one philosophically decisive sense: it is not an abstraction from relations among material things, but a "physically objective" structure open to objective empirical investigation. Moreover, the theory does indeed make "absolute" distinctions among states of motion; it draws these distinctions in a way that departs dramatically from Newton's theory, but they remain physically objective distinctions that do not depend on the arbitrary choice of a reference-frame.

It became clear, then, that Newton's theory and Einstein's special and general theories all make essentially similar claims about the world: each specifies a certain "absolute" spatio-temporal structure, along with physical assumptions – primarily about the nature of force and inertia – that enable us to connect that structure with experience. In other words, conceptions of space and time are not arbitrary metaphysical hypotheses appended to otherwise empirical physics; they are assumptions implicit in the laws of physics. Defenders of Newton began to argue that "absolute" space-time structures are not so very different from other unobservable "theoretical entities" introduced into physics, such as fundamental particles and fields. Accordingly, they ought to be judged by how well they function in explanations of observed phenomena. Any reasonable metaphysical question about space, time, and motion could thus be translated into a straightforward question about physics. For example, "is rotation absolute?" becomes, "does our best-established physical theory distinguish between absolute rotation and relative rotation?" and "is there an equally good or a better physical theory that dispenses with absolute rotation, or that refers only to relative motions?"[3]

From this point of view, we can ask of Newton's conceptions of absolute time, absolute space, absolute rotation, and absolute motion, "are they required by Newtonian physics?" And the answer is straightforward: Newton's laws presuppose absolute time, but not absolute space; they enable us to distinguish a truly rotating or accelerating body from one that is merely relatively rotating or accelerating; but they do not enable us to distinguish which bodies are "at rest in absolute space," or to determine the "absolute velocity" of any thing. Therefore Newton's laws require not absolute space, but a four-dimensional structure known as "Newtonian space-time." A straight line of this structure represents uniform motion in a straight line, and therefore its physical counterpart is the motion of a body not subject to forces.[4] Einstein's theories postulate different spacetime structures, based on different physical assumptions. Thus the theories should not be judged on purely philosophical grounds; it is, rather, a simple question of which theory is best supported by the empirical evidence. Had Newton said, "Spacetime is a four-dimensional affine space," instead of "Absolute space remains similar and immovable," there would have been no philosophical grounds for objection, but only (eventually) new developments in physics demanding new spacetime structures. Generally, on this point of view, our philosophical views about space and time should depend on our beliefs about physics.

Yet this seemingly simple approach to space and time has always been under philosophical suspicion. Einstein's chief objection had been anticipated by Leibniz: only the relative motions of bodies are observable, while space and time are not. How, then, could space, time, and motion be absolute? If we could construct a theory that made no reference to absolute space, time, and motion, ought we not to prefer it just for that reason? And even if "our best" physical

oes make claims about space, time, and motion, do we not
eless have independent philosophical grounds to doubt their
lute" status? For it seems absurd that any argument about ob-
ed spatial relations could prove that space itself is "absolute."
Even to Newton's sympathizers, objections like these have always
seemed challenging; to his opponents, they have seemed decisive.
Hence whether motion is absolute or relative has appeared to be one
of the perennial questions of philosophy.

As we will see, however, this approach to the philosophical questions of space and time is based on a fundamental misunderstanding
of what Newton accomplished – indeed, a misunderstanding of the
role that space and time play in physics. What it assumes is that
what we *mean* by space, time, and motion, and what we mean by
claiming that they are "absolute," is already established on purely
philosophical grounds, so that we can then ask what physics has to
say about these philosophical concepts. What it overlooks is that
Newton was *not* taking any such meanings for granted, but *defining*
new theoretical concepts within a framework of physical laws. Independently of such a framework, it is premature to ask, "did Newton
successfully prove that space, time, and motion are absolute?" The
proper questions are, what were Newton's *definitions* of "absolute
space," "absolute time," and "absolute motion"? And, how do those
definitions function in his physical theory?

NEWTON'S PHILOSOPHICAL CONTEXT

It was natural for Newton's contemporaries to misunderstand his
purpose. Leibniz, for example, had an understanding of space, time,
and motion, and of what it means to be a "substance" or to be
"absolute," that arose from his own peculiar metaphysics. And to
say that "space," "time," and "motion," as he understood them, are
"absolute," rather than essentially relative, seemed to be an obvious
mistake. But Newton explicitly proposed to ignore the prevailing
philosophical uses of these terms, and to introduce theoretical notions of his own.

Although time, space, place, and motion are very familiar to everyone, it
must be noted that these quantities are popularly conceived solely with
reference to the objects of sense perception. And this is the source of certain

preconceptions; to eliminate them it is useful to distinguish these quantities into absolute and relative, true and apparent, mathematical and common.[5]

As Howard Stein first emphasized,[6] the preconceptions that Newton had in mind were those of Descartes and his followers. Descartes had purported to prove that space is identical with extended substance. It followed that a vacuum is impossible, for wherever there is extension, there is, by definition, substance as well; it also followed that what we call motion "in space" is really motion relative to a fluid material plenum. From these foundations, Descartes developed a vortex theory of planetary motion: the rotation of the Sun creates a vortex in the interplanetary fluid, and the planets are thereby carried around in their orbits; similarly, the planets with satellites create smaller vortices of their own. Descartes would thus seem to have advanced a version of the Copernican theory, and attributed real motion to the Earth. But he equivocated on this point by his definition of "motion in the philosophical sense": while motion "in the vulgar sense" is "the action by which a body passes from one place to another," its motion "in the philosophical sense" is the body's "transference from the vicinity of those bodies contiguous to it to the vicinity of others."[7] On this definition, Descartes could claim to hold both the heliostatic and geostatic views of the planetary system: the Earth is indeed revolving around the Sun in the vortex, but "in the philosophical sense" it is at rest, since it remains contiguous to the same particles of the fluid. Hence Descartes's assertion: "I deny the movement of the earth more carefully than Copernicus, and more truthfully than Tycho."[8]

Newton saw that such a definition is completely unsuitable for any *dynamical* analysis of motion, and in particular the dynamical understanding of the solar system. It implies that the choice between Copernicus or Kepler, on the one hand, and Ptolemy or Tycho, on the other, has nothing to do with the dynamical causes and effects of motion, but can only be made on the grounds of simplicity or convenience. From a certain philosophical point of view, of course, this is the desired conclusion. But the vortex theory itself – as advanced not only by Descartes, but by Leibniz and other "relativists" as well – assumed that the planetary system really is a dynamical system: that is, a system that is subject to the laws of motion, and whose parts are related by *causal interactions*. On that assumption, the fact that planets orbit the sun, instead of moving uniformly in a straight line, requires some kind of causal explanation. Thus, Descartes's theory, *as a causal explanation* of the planetary motions, required a distinction between inertial motion and motion under the causal influence of a force. But this requirement is completely neglected by his definition of "motion in the philosophical sense." We begin to understand Newton's Scholium by properly understanding the question it addresses: what concepts of time, space, and motion are required by a dynamical theory of motion?

Asking this question about Newton's theory does not deny its connection with his profound metaphysical convictions – not only about space and time, but about God and his relationship to the natural world. On the contrary, it illuminates the nature of those convictions and their relationship to Newton's physics. For Newton, God and physical things alike were located in space and time. But space and time also formed a framework within which things act on one another, and their causal relations became intelligible through their spatio-temporal relations – above all, through their effects on each other's state of motion. The latter principle, which was implicit in seventeenth-century physics, was for Newton the link between physics and metaphysics: if physics is to understand the real causal connections in the world, then physics must define space, time, and motion so as to make those connections intelligible.

NEWTON'S DEFINITIONS

Newton begins by defining "absolute time" as time that, "without reference to anything external, flows uniformly."[9] This means that, regardless of whether any particular mechanical or natural process flows equably – for example, regardless of whether the motion of any real clock or rotating planet really sweeps out equal angles in equal times – there is an objective fact, in "absolute time," about whether two intervals of time are truly equal. Absolute time also implies absolute simultaneity, so that each moment of time is defined everywhere, and it is an objective fact whether any two events happened at the same moment. These two principles define precisely what is presupposed about time in the subsequent arguments of the *Principia*. Newton's critics, however, have traditionally taken him to be asserting that "time is absolute," and that the meaning of such a claim is established independently of physics. Leibniz, for example, assumed that if time is absolute, it must be (what he would call) a "substance," and so each moment must be a distinguished individual. This would mean that if the beginning of the universe were shifted from one to another moment of absolute time, some real difference would be made. But no such difference could be discernible; absolute time therefore violates the "Principle of the Identity of Indiscernibles," by which there cannot be two distinct things that do not differ discernibly. Therefore, to Leibniz, time cannot be "absolute," but can only be an "order of succession."

Yet in the notion of absolute time *as defined by Newton*, no such difference is implied. In fact, Newton explicitly rejects the idea that the moments of time (or space) have any identity above and beyond their mutual order and position, asserting (in strikingly "Leibnizian" terms) that "all things are placed in time with reference to order of succession; and in space with reference to order of position."[10] The defining characteristic of absolute time is not the distinct individuality of its moments, but the *structure* of time, i.e., the fact that it flows equably and that equal intervals of time are objectively defined. The critical question is not whether Newton successfully proves that "time is absolute" – for this was never his purpose – but whether his definition of absolute time is a good one. And in the context of the *Principia*, this amounts to asking, does this definition have objective physical content? That is, can we define equal intervals of elapsed time without recourse to some arbitrary standard? Is there a good physical definition of what it means for time intervals to be equal, even if no actual clock measures such intervals exactly? The answer is "yes": this is precisely the definition of time implied by Newton's laws of motion, which postulate an objective distinction between inertial motions, which cross equal distances in equal times, and motions that are accelerated by an impressed force. In short, an ideal clock that keeps absolute time is simply an inertial clock: impossible to achieve in practice, but approachable to an arbitrary degree of approximation. Thus Newton's definition of absolute time is as well founded as his laws of motion. And this is why, in spite of all the traditional philosophical objections to it, it could only be overthrown by Einstein's introduction of new fundamental physical laws.

A similar analysis can be given of Newton's definitions of absolute space and motion. For Leibniz and others, to say that "space

is absolute" is to say that space is a substance, and thereby to attribute a distinct identity to each point of space. But if the locations
of all things in space were shifted any distance in any direction, no
real difference would be made; therefore (again by the Principle of
the Identity of Indiscernibles), space cannot be absolute. Here again,
however, in the definition of absolute space *given by Newton*, no
such difference is implied. The defining characteristics of absolute
space are that it remains "homogeneous and immovable," so that
the parts of absolute space (the "absolute places") are truly at rest,
and that translation from one to another absolute place is "absolute
motion."[11] This means that there is a real difference between motion
and rest in *the same* absolute place over time; but it does not imply any real difference between one universe, and another in which
everything is shifted to a *different* absolute place; a body's state of
motion depends on whether it remains in *the same* absolute place,
but not on *which* absolute place it occupies. (Similarly, in Newtonian
spacetime we can determine whether two velocities are the same,
independently of their actual magnitude.) So Leibniz's classic arguments from the Principle of the Identity of Indiscernibles, cogent
though they may be against a certain conception of space and time
as "substances," are *not* arguments against the concepts Newton
designated by "absolute time" and "absolute space."

Now, however, if we ask of absolute space what we asked of absolute time (is this a legitimate definition on physical grounds?) we
encounter a problem. Unlike absolute time, absolute space entails a
distinction that is not well defined according to Newton's laws: the
distinction between rest and motion in absolute space. According to
the laws of motion, a body moves uniformly in a straight line until
an applied force causes it to accelerate, and the effect of the force is
independent of the velocity of the body it acts upon. In other words,
Newton's laws embody the principle of Galilean relativity, which
Newton himself derived as Corollary 5 to the laws: "When bodies are
enclosed in a given space, their motions in relation to one another
are the same whether the space is at rest or whether it is moving
uniformly straight forward without circular motion."[12] This means
that nothing in the behavior of the solar system, for example, would
enable us to determine whether it is at rest or moving inertially.
Corollary 6 undermines absolute motion even further: "If bodies are
moving in any way whatsoever with respect to one another and are

urged by equal accelerative forces along parallel lines, they will all continue to move with respect to one another in the same way as they would if they were not acted on by those forces."[13] That is, nothing in the behavior of the solar system can even tell us whether the system is moving inertially, or being accelerated equally by some force from outside the system. Thus, though absolute space is invulnerable to the familiar criticisms from Leibniz, it is devastated by Newton's own concepts of force and inertia. Evidently this might have been otherwise: if the laws of physics measured force by velocity rather than acceleration, then dynamics could identify which bodies are truly at rest. Then we would have the physical definition of absolute space that Newtonian physics lacks. But in a Newtonian world, Newton's distinction between absolute motion and absolute rest cannot be realized.

That Newton was aware of this problem is clear from his discussion of absolute motion. He proposes to distinguish absolute from relative motion by its "properties, causes, and effects." And in the discussion of absolute translation, the properties can be simply defined: that bodies at rest are at rest relative to one another; that parts of a body partake of the motion of the whole; that whatever is contained in a given space shares the motion of that space. These properties together imply that we cannot determine the true state of rest or motion unless we refer motion to immovable space, rather than to some object or relative space that may be in motion. The latter properties, moreover, are directed against Descartes (without naming him, however). For they are not necessarily true of motion in Descartes's sense: if an apple moves, for example, the core remains at rest, as it is not moving relative to the skin that is contiguous to it. So Newton has given a more sensible analysis than Descartes of what we might mean by motion, assuming that we know which bodies are moving or resting in space. But that is precisely what we do *not* know: none of these properties enables us actually to determine empirically what a body's absolute motion is. An empirical distinction between absolute and relative motion first appears when we move from the properties of true motion to the causes and effects – causes and effects that have to do with inertia and force. And forces, as we have seen, can distinguish between acceleration and uniform motion, but not between "absolute motion" and "absolute rest."

The causes that distinguish absolute from relative motion are "the forces impressed upon bodies to generate motion."[14] Obviously, relative motion can be generated or changed without the action of any force, but true motion is only generated or changed by a force. By the same token, a body's true motion necessarily "suffers some change" from the application of a force, whereas its relative motion need not: for example, if the reference-point by which we measure its relative motion is subject to the same force. Here a "relativist" might be tempted to ask, how does Newton know all of this about true motion? To ask this is to forget that Newton is elaborating the *definition* of true motion that is implicit in the principle of inertia. The critical question is, instead, does the definition define exactly what Newton wanted to define? Corollary 5 (or Corollary 6, for that matter) shows explicitly that it does not: the effects of impressed forces on the "true motions" of bodies are completely independent of the initial velocities of those bodies; therefore the causes of "true motion" provide a definition, not of motion with respect to absolute space, but of acceleration.

The same is true of the effects that distinguish absolute from relative motion: "the forces of receding from the axis of circular motion," or centrifugal forces.[15] "For in purely relative circular motion these forces are null, while in true and absolute circular motion, they are larger or smaller in proportion to the quantity of motion."[16] Such effects, even if we assume that they distinguish a true rotation from a relative motion, certainly cannot reveal whether a rotating body is at rest in absolute space. But what do they reveal? Newton discusses this in the most controversial part of the Scholium, the "water-bucket experiment." The experiment is extremely simple: suspend a bucket of water by a rope, and turn the bucket in one direction until it is "strongly twisted"; then, turn the bucket in the contrary direction and let the rope untwist. As the bucket now rotates, the surface of the water will initially be flat, but relative to the bucket, it is rotating. By the friction of the rotating bucket, the water will gradually begin to rotate as well, eventually equaling the speed of the bucket, so that its motion relative to the bucket gradually ceases. Yet as the relative rotation of the water decreases, its "endeavor to recede from the axis of motion" – exhibited by the water's climbing the sides of the bucket – increases correspondingly. The significance of this is plain. Newton is identifying the water's rotation by its dynamical effect, which is least when the motion in Descartes's sense is greatest, and greatest when the Cartesian motion is least.

Therefore, that endeavor does not depend on the change of position of the water with respect to surrounding bodies, and thus true circular motion cannot be determined by such changes of position. The truly circular motion of each revolving body is unique, corresponding to a unique endeavor as its proper and sufficient effect.[17]

Thus the Cartesian definition of motion ignores the very dynamical effects with which physics ought to be concerned. Newton explicitly points out, however, that his dynamical concept of motion is implicit in Descartes's own vortex theory. For in that theory,

the individual parts of the heavens [i.e. of the fluid vortex], and the planets that are relatively at rest in the heavens to which they belong, are truly in motion. For they change their positions relative to one another (which is not the case with things that are truly at rest), and as they are carried around together with the heavens, they participate in the motions of the heavens and, being parts of revolving wholes, endeavour to recede from the axes of those wholes.[18]

The true rotation of a body, then, cannot be judged from its motion relative to contiguous bodies, but only from the magnitude of the centrifugal effects it causes.

Critics of this argument have generally not defended the Cartesian view of motion against Newton's objections. But Newton was evidently trying to do more than distinguish true rotation from rotation in Descartes's "philosophical sense." This is clear from another thought-experiment: suppose that two globes, joined by a cord, revolve around their common center of gravity; suppose, further, that there are no other bodies, contiguous or otherwise, to which we can refer their motions. Even then, "the endeavor of the balls to recede from the axis of motion could be known from the tension of the cord, and thus the quantity of circular motion could be computed."[19] In other words, the true rotation of a body is not only independent of its rotation relative to contiguous bodies; it is independent of *any* relative rotation. If Newton is correct, one could say of one body, in an otherwise empty universe, whether it is rotating or not.

This is the step that has always raised philosophical doubts: do the experiments prove that the water, or the pair of globes, is really rotating? Could such an experiment possibly demonstrate the existence of absolute space? Is rotation relative to absolute space really the cause of the observed centrifugal forces? Perhaps the centrifugal forces on the water are not caused by motion relative to the bucket, but does this mean that they are independent of *any* relative motion, as the experiment of the globes purports to show? According to Ernst Mach, writing two hundred years after Newton, if Newton saw no need to refer motion to contiguous bodies, this is because he was tacitly referring all motion to the "fixed stars". And even if we can deduce from Newton's laws how bodies would behave in the absence of the fixed stars, we cannot deduce whether, in those circumstances, Newton's laws would still hold anyway.[20]

To Einstein, under Mach's influence, Newton's argument illustrated the inherent "epistemological defect" of Newtonian physics. Consider two spheres S_1 and S_2, rotating relative to one another, and suppose that S_2 bulges at its equator; how do we explain this difference? Einstein says,

No answer can be admitted as epistemologically satisfactory, unless the reason given is an observable fact of experience...Newtonian mechanics does not give a satisfactory answer to this question. It pronounces as follows: The laws of mechanics apply to the space R_1, in respect to which the body S_1 is at rest, but not to the space R_2, in respect to which the body S_2 is at rest. But the privileged space R_1...is a merely factitious cause, and not a thing that can be observed.[21]

Einstein's view became the "received view" of absolute rotation among philosophers of science. And even philosophers who have defended absolute rotation have accepted this challenge to show that absolute motion does provide a legitimate explanation.[22] As our reading of Newton suggests, however, this critical view simply asks the wrong questions. Newton never claims to *prove* that the centrifugal forces on the water or the globes are caused by rotation relative to absolute space, or claims that any such experiment could demonstrate the existence of absolute space. What he says, instead, is that the centrifugal forces *define* absolute rotation. It makes no sense to ask, how does Newton know that S_2 is really rotating? S_2 is rotating *by definition* – more precisely, S_2 is rotating just because it satisfies the definition of absolute rotation. Thus Newton has not tried to *justify* the causal link between rotation and centrifugal effects, but simply to identify it as definitive of true rotation. Thus he has defined a theoretical quantity, absolute rotation, by exhibiting how it is detected and measured by centrifugal effects. His discussion of the water-bucket makes this explicit: from the endeavor to recede from the axis, "one can find out *and measure* the true and absolute circular motion of the water, which here is the direct opposite of its relative motion" [emphasis added].[23] And concerning the globes, he states not only that from the tension on the cord "we might compute the quantity of their circular motions," but also that changes in the tension would provide a measure of the increase or decrease in rotation. "In this way both the quantity and the direction of this circular motion could be found in any immense vacuum, where nothing external or sensible existed with which the balls could be compared."[24] Again, we might think to ask how we really know that these effects provide a measure of absolute rotation, or by what right we can infer from such effects the quantity of absolute rotation. But this is as pointless as asking, by what right do we infer the magnitude and direction of an impressed force from the magnitude and direction of an acceleration? For this is just how Newton's laws define impressed force. In both cases, we are not inferring a theoretical entity from a phenomenon, but defining a phenomenon as the measure of a theoretical quantity.[25]

Newton's argument, in sum, was never an argument from physical phenomena to metaphysical conclusions about the "absoluteness" of rotation. Instead, it was an argument of a sort that is fundamental to every empirical science: an argument that a novel theoretical concept has a well-defined empirical content. Like the definition of absolute time, and unlike the definition of absolute translation, the definition of absolute rotation does indeed have a basis in Newton's laws. And this means, again, that it is no less well founded than Newton's laws; if the universe in fact obeys those laws, we can always measure the true rotation of any body.

This interpretation of Newton's Scholium defies a long and continuing tradition, though its main point was already made by Stein in 1967.[26] But it is explicitly corroborated by Newton's other extended discussion of space, the manuscript "De gravitatione et aequipondio fluidorum."[27] For example, here Newton explicitly denies the conception of space and time as "substances" that provoked Leibniz's "indiscernibility" objection: "The parts of duration and space are only understood to be the same as they really are because of their mutual order and position; nor do they have any hint of individuality apart from that order and position which consequently cannot be altered."[28] Newton concludes that space "has its own way of being, which fits neither substances nor accidents." He even suggests, for reasons not unlike those later given by George Berkeley, that the philosophical notion of "substance" is itself "unintelligible."[29]

More important, "De gravitatione," much more explicitly than the Scholium, emphasizes that Newton's dynamical arguments concern the *definition* of true motion. His entire discussion of space and motion is contained in a "Note" to Definition 4: "Motion is change of place."[30] As Stein pointed out (1967), Newton begins immediately to justify this definition against "the Cartesians," by showing that Descartes's definition of motion is incompatible with the basic principles of mechanics. In particular, it is incompatible with the principle of inertia: if a body's true motion is defined relative to contiguous bodies, and the latter are the constantly flowing particles of the vortex, it will be impossible to define a definite path for the body. And in that case, it will be impossible to say whether that path is rectilinear or uniform. "On the contrary, there cannot be motion since there can be no motion without a certain velocity and determination."[31]

Newton also points out, however, that, alongside the "philosophical" conception of motion, Descartes makes casual or implicit use of a *physical* and *causal* conception of motion. For example, Descartes acknowledges that the revolution of a planet or comet around the sun creates centrifugal forces in the planet, a centrifugal tendency that must be balanced by the resistance of the fluid in the vortex. And this physical motion of the vortex itself is referred, not to "the ambient bodies," but to "generic" extension. Of course Descartes says that the latter is an abstraction from extended matter that exists only in thought; the vortical motion that produces the centrifugal forces is thus mere "motion in the vulgar sense," not true motion. But Newton observes that of these two parallel concepts of motion, it is the "vulgar" one, rather than the "philosophical" one, that Descartes appeals to in giving a *physical* and *causal* account of celestial motion. Therefore he argues that, of the possible ways of defining motion, we ought to choose that one that successfully defines a physical quantity, and that can therefore play a role in causal explanation: "And since the whirling of the comet around the Sun in his philosophical sense does not cause a tendency to recede from the center, which a gyration in the vulgar sense can do, surely motion in the vulgar sense should be acknowledged, rather than the philosophical."[32]

It might seem that Descartes's theory of motion is too easy a target, especially compared to a sophisticated account of the relativity of motion like that of Leibniz.[33] But Newton's objection to Descartes's definition is not merely its inadequacy or even incoherence, but also its inconsistency with dynamical principles that Descartes himself accepted. And this same objection applies to Leibniz: he appeals to a causal account of motion that is incompatible with his professed philosophical account. On philosophical grounds, as we have seen, Leibniz denies that there is a real distinction between one state of motion and another, and asserts the general "equivalence of hypotheses" about which bodies are at rest or in motion; consequently, he asserts that the Copernican and Ptolemaic systems are equivalent. Yet he very clearly does attach a *physical* meaning to the distinction between one state of motion and another. On the one hand, Leibniz presents a strange argument for the relativity of all motion. He claims to agree with Newton on "the equivalence of hypotheses in the case of rectilinear motions." But a curved motion is really made up of infinitesimal rectilinear motions, and so he concludes that a curved path is equivalent to a straight one, because they are equivalent in the mathematical sense that both are "locally straight." So all motions, rectilinear or curved, are equivalent.[34] On the other hand, according to Leibniz's own dynamical theory, the curved path is not *physically* – therefore not *causally* – equivalent to the straight path. This is because, on that theory, a body by its own inherent force can maintain its motion in a straight path, whereas a body cannot maintain a curved motion without the constant intervention of some other body. Indeed, the crux of his objection to Newtonian action at a distance is that it violates this principle:

If God wanted to cause a body to move free in the aether round about a certain fixed center, without any other creature acting upon it, I say it could not be done without a miracle, since it cannot be explained by the nature of bodies. For a free body naturally recedes from a curve in the tangent.[35]

This passage establishes that Leibniz's understanding of rotation and centrifugal force was, at least in the context of physical explanation, the same as Newton's. And this is a natural consequence of Leibniz's commitment to the vortex theory, in which the harmonic circulation of the planets results from a balance between their own "centrifugal tendencies" and the pressure of the ambient fluid.[36] More generally, such remarks reveal that, despite his "general law of equivalence," Leibniz's convictions about the fundamental nature of bodies, and their causal interactions with one another, depended on the concept of a privileged state of motion.

Leibniz's view exhibits the conflict, characteristic of seventeenth-century "relativist" views of space, time, and motion, between two opposing motives. On the one hand was the desire for a "relativistic" account of motion, in reaction against traditional Aristotelian objections to the motion of the earth. The classical argument was simply that terrestrial phenomena seem to reveal none of the expected effects of a rapid rotation or revolution; to accept the Copernican theory, one had to grasp the idea of "indistinguishable" states of motion, and to accept an "equivalence of hypotheses" about whether the earth is at rest. Only thus could Galileo argue that the terrestrial evidence is necessarily inconclusive, and appeal to the advantages of Copernicanism as an elegant account of celestial phenomena. On the other hand, the demise of Aristotle's theory of celestial motion – the "crystalline spheres" – produced the need for a causal account of motion, which would reveal the physical connections among the Sun and the planets. And the founding principle of that account, at least for Newton and Leibniz and their contemporaries, was Descartes's principle that the planets tend to travel in straight lines, but are forced by some physical cause into circulations around the sun. Leibniz maintained the mechanistic view that any such cause must act by immediate contact, while Newton accepted the possibility of "action at a distance," but, in any case, they shared the principle that a certain state of motion is "natural," and that any deviation from that state requires a causal explanation. Therefore, a "general law of equivalence" of states of motion would vitiate the very celestial mechanics that Leibniz and other Cartesians hoped to construct. If it made no *physical* difference whether the Sun orbited the Earth, or the Earth the Sun; if it made no physical difference whether the interplanetary medium were at rest, or rotating in a vortex; then there would be little hope of explaining the celestial motions by the physical interactions among the celestial bodies.

All of this shows that Newton's definition of absolute motion, in so far as it identifies the latter by its "causes and effects," is by no means an arbitrary definition, or an idiosyncratic one derived solely from his metaphysical views. Rather, Newton's definition identifies the very conception of motion that was implicit in seventeenth-century thinking about physical causes and physical explanations. His Scholium attempts (not entirely successfully, as we have seen) to characterize this conception precisely, and especially to separate it from philosophical "preconceptions" about relativity that are irrelevant to the task of physical explanation. In other words, instead of a metaphysical hypothesis to account for dynamical effects, Newton has offered a conceptual analysis of what is presupposed about motion – by Descartes, Leibniz, and every other seventeenth-century mechanist – in ordinary reasoning from motion to its physical cause.

THE SYSTEM OF THE WORLD

The Newtonian conception of motion has an obvious yet remarkable consequence: whether the planetary system is geocentric or heliocentric can no longer be settled by adopting the simplest hypothesis, but is now a straightforward empirical question. For, assuming the laws of motion, Book 3 of Newton's *Principia* argues from the celestial motions to the physical forces that cause them. Again, any post-Cartesian physicist would infer, from the fact that a planet travels in a closed orbit rather than a straight line, that *some* force keeps it from following the tangent; Newton, drawing on the work of Galileo, Huygens, and others, reasoned mathematically from the precise characteristics of the orbit to the precise characteristics of the force. And this reasoning leads eventually from Kepler's laws of planetary motion to universal gravitation.[37]

Throughout this reasoning from motions to forces, Newton remains neutral between the geocentric and heliocentric theories. Once the forces are known, however, we can compare the masses of the celestial bodies by comparing the forces they exert on their satellites. From there, a very simple argument determines the physical center of the system. First, suppose (Hypothesis 1) that the center of the system (whatever it is) is at rest.[38] "No one doubts this, although some argue that the earth, others that the sun, is at rest in the center of the system." Then (Proposition II) the common center of gravity of the system must be at rest. For by Corollary 4 to the laws of motion, "that center either will be at rest or move uniformly straight forward. But if that center always moves forward, the center of the universe will also move, contrary to the hypothesis." The conclusion is immediate: "Proposition 12: That the sun is engaged in continual motion but never recedes far from the common center of gravity of all the planets."[39] In other words, if the planetary system is a dynamical system, whose members interact according to the accepted dynamical laws, then no body is at rest, for, by the third law of motion, to every action of every body there is an equal and opposite reaction, and only the center of gravity of the system can remain at rest. However, the comparison of masses reveals that most of the mass of the system is contained in the sun. Therefore, "if that body toward which other bodies gravitate most had to be placed in the center... that privilege would have to be conceded to the sun."[40]

Newton's argument is that, given the laws of motion and the observed behavior of the planets and the sun, we can infer their causal influences on one another and their relative masses; when all of this is known, the structure and motion of the system – "the frame of the system of the world" – is determined. But, as Newton well knew, the system is determined only up to a point. By Corollary 5, no dynamical analysis of the solar system can reveal whether the system as a whole is at rest or in uniform motion. And Corollary 6 renders the analysis still less determinate. But none of this affects Newton's dynamical analysis:

It may be alleged that the sun and planets are impelled by some other force equally and in the direction of parallel lines; but by such a force (by Cor. VI of the Laws of Motion) no change would happen in the situation of the planets to one another, nor any sensible effect follow; but our business is with the causes of sensible effects. Let us, therefore, neglect every such force as imaginary and precarious, and of no use in the phenomena of the heavens.[41]

The causal analysis of the motions within the solar system establishes a close approximation to Kepler's heliocentric system, whatever the motion of the system as a whole. And the geocentric theory is revealed to be physically impossible, precisely as it would be physically impossible for a baby to whirl a large adult around its head on a string: in both cases the smaller body must revolve further from the center of gravity.

Philosophically this argument is not very different from the Leibnizian argument for a heliocentric vortex. The latter, too, reasons from accelerated motions to their physical causes, and it infers from the nature and magnitude of the Sun that it, rather than the Earth, has the required causal efficacy to serve as the physical center of the system. Therefore, on Leibniz's physical theory as well as on Newton's, whether Ptolemy or Copernicus was more nearly right is a physically meaningful question. It should be emphasized, moreover, that the same comparison can be made between Newton's theory and general relativity. Philosophers used to say that general relativity had finally established the equivalence of the Copernican and Ptolemaic systems, except to the extent that one might be "simpler" than the other.[42] Precisely as in Newton's theory, however, in general relativity the planetary orbits are determined by the mass of the Sun. The mass causes spacetime curvature, instead of a gravitational field in Newton's sense, but there remains an essential similarity: the mass required to account for the precise curvature of the planetary orbits is the same in both theories, and on either theory the Earth's mass is too small. So the two systems are, on physical grounds, as *in*equivalent in Einstein's theory as they are in Newton's. The decision between them is not an arbitrary choice of reference-frame, but the outcome of a dynamical analysis, based on the principle that states of motion can have genuine dynamical differences.

CONCLUSION: AN EMPIRICIST VIEW OF SPACE, TIME, AND MOTION

Newton's conceptions of space, time, and motion were long regarded as metaphysical ideas whose place in empirical science was open to dispute. Now we can finally see that they were, instead, exemplary of the way in which science gives empirical meaning to theoretical notions. A spatio-temporal concept belongs in physics just in case it is defined by physical laws that explain how it is to be applied, and how the associated quantity is to be measured; Newton called "absolute" precisely those quantities that could be so defined. By this standard, absolute space does not belong in Newtonian physics, since absolute translation in space is not a physically measurable quantity. But absolute time, absolute acceleration, and absolute rotation are well-defined concepts that are, as we saw, implicit in classical thinking about physical causes. Thus philosophical questions about these concepts could become empirical questions. In particular, the question of what is really moving in the solar system was reduced to simple empirical questions. Which bodies exhibit the dynamical effects that are definitive of true rotation? Where is the center of gravity of the system, and what body is closest to that center?

The controversy over this theory of motion can be compared to the controversy over Newton's theory of gravitation as an action at a distance. To his scientific and philosophical contemporaries, action at a distance contradicted the very concept of physical action, which was supposed to be possible only by direct contact. But for Newton, action is defined by the laws of motion, which provide empirical criteria for measuring the action of one thing on another; if the planets and the sun satisfy these criteria in their direct mutual relations, then they are acting on one another. Thus the question of action at a distance became an empirical question. We can also compare this to the controversy over non-Euclidean geometry in the nineteenth century. Many philosophers found it inconceivable that space could possibly be curved; this seemed contrary to the very concept of space.[43] According to Gauss, Riemann, and Helmholtz, however, when we make precise the empirical meaning of the claim that space is curved, we see that it is no more contradictory than the claim that space is not curved. Both claims derive their meaning from physical assumptions about the behavior of bodies and light – for example, that "light rays travel in straight lines"; just this understanding of the meaning of curvature makes it an empirically measurable quantity, and makes the question whether space is curved an empirical question. Similarly, Newton showed that the familiar assumptions about inertia and force – specifically, that "bodies not subject to forces travel uniformly in straight lines" – suffice to define acceleration and rotation as empirically measurable quantities. His critics insisted that, to be an empiricist about space and time, one had to define motion as change of relative position; Newton's philosophical insight was that empirical definitions of motion, space, and time come from the laws of empirical science.

NOTES

I would like to thank John Earman and William Demopoulos for their advice and comments. I also thank the Social Sciences and Humanities Research Council of Canada for financial support. This chapter is dedicated to my son Christopher.

1   Albert Einstein, "The Foundation of the General Theory of Relativity," in Einstein et al., The Principle of Relativity, trans. W. Perrett and G. B. Jeffery (New York: Dover Publications, 1952), p. 117. This is a translation of Einstein's "Die Grundlagen der allgemeinen Relativitätstheorie," Annalen der Physik (4) 49 (1916), 769–822.

2   Among the earliest expressions of this view was Hermann Weyl, Raum–Zeit–Materie (Berlin: Springer-Verlag, 1918); Weyl was followed by (for example) A. d'Abro, The Evolution of Scientific Thought (1927; Dover Publications reprint, 1950), and Karl Popper, "Three Views Concerning Human Knowledge" (1953, reprinted in Popper's Conjectures and Refutations, New York: Harper, 1963). This view was later brought to philosophical prominence by Howard Stein, "Newtonian Space-Time," Texas Quarterly 10 (1967), 174–200; this was followed by John Earman and Michael Friedman, "The Meaning and Status of Newton's Law of Inertia and the Nature of Gravitational Forces," Philosophy of Science 40 (1973), 329–59; Howard Stein, "Some Philosophical Prehistory of General Relativity," in J. Earman, C. Glymour, and J. Stachel (eds.), Foundations of Space-Time Theories, Minnesota Studies in Philosophy of Science 8 (Minneapolis: University of Minnesota Press, 1977), pp. 3–49.

3   See, for example, Roberto Torretti, Relativity and Geometry (Oxford: Pergamon Press, 1983); Michael Friedman, Foundations of Space-Time Theories (Princeton: Princeton University Press, 1983); and John Earman, World Enough and Spacetime: Absolute versus Relational Theories of Space and Time (Cambridge, MA: MIT Press, 1989).

4   For further explanation see Stein, "Newtonian Space-Time" and "Some Philosophical Prehistory," or Friedman, Foundations, ch. 1.

5   Isaac Newton, The Principia, Mathematical Principles of Natural Philosophy: A New Translation, trans. I. Bernard Cohen and Anne Whitman (Berkeley: University of California Press, 1999), p. 408.

6   Stein, "Newtonian Space-Time."

7   René Descartes, The Principles of Philosophy, trans. Valentine Rodger Miller and R. P. Miller (Dordrecht: Reidel, 1983), Part 2, article 28, p. 52.

8   *Ibid.*, part 3, article 19.
9   Newton, *The Principia*, p. 408.
10 *Ibid.*, p. 410.
11 *Ibid.*, pp. 408–9.
12 *Ibid.*, p. 423.
13 *Ibid.*, p. 423.
14 *Ibid.*, p. 412.
15 *Ibid.*, p. 412.
16 *Ibid.*, p. 412.
17 *Ibid.*, p. 413.
18 *Ibid.*, p. 413.
19 *Ibid.*, p. 414.
20 Ernst Mach, *Die Mechanik in ihrer Entwickelung, historisch-kritisch dargestellt.* (Leipzig: F. A. Brockhaus, 1883).
21 Einstein, "The Foundation of the General Theory of Relativity," p. 113.
22 For example, Friedman, *Foundations*.
23 Newton, *The Principia*, p. 414.
24 *Ibid.*, p. 414.
25 For further discussion, including a comparision of Newton's arguments with Einstein's arguments for special and general relativity, see Robert DiSalle, "Spacetime Theory as Physical Geometry," *Erkenntnis* 42 (1995), 317–37.
26 Stein, "Newtonian Space-Time." This paper has been frequently cited in literature on the "absolute versus relational" debate, but, I would argue, generally misinterpreted. To the extent that that debate takes the question, "are space, time and motion absolute?" to be well defined in purely philosophical terms, Stein is taken to have shown that Newton had good arguments, or better arguments than "relativists" or "relationalists" had ever acknowledged, for the "absolutist" side. (See, e.g., Friedman, *Foundations*, and Earman, *World Enough*.) Thus the essential point, that Newton's Scholium introduces *definitions* of absolute space, time, and motion – and to that extent transcends the traditional debate – has not been generally appreciated.
27 "On the gravity and equilibrium of fluids" (hereafter "De gravitatione"). In A. R. Hall and M. B. Hall (eds.), *Unpublished Scientific Papers of Isaac Newton* (Cambridge: Cambridge University Press, 1962), pp. 89–156. The most important philosophical commentary on this paper is found in Stein, "Newtonian Space-Time"; see also Stein, this volume.
28 Hall and Hall, *Unpublished Scientific Papers*, p. 136.
29 *Ibid.*, pp. 139–49. See also DiSalle, "On Dynamics, Indiscernibility, and Spacetime Ontology," *British Journal for the Philosophy of Science* 45 (1994), 265–87, and Stein, this volume.

30 Hall and Hall, *Unpublished Scientific Papers*, p. 122.

31 *Ibid.*, pp. 129–31. Stein suggests that "if Huygens and Leibniz...had been confronted with the argument of this passage, a clarification would have been forced that could have promoted appreciably the philosophical discussion of space-time" ("Newtonian Space-Time," p. 186). It is interesting to note that essentially the same argument was advanced by Leonhard Euler in 1748, and had a very serious impact on the philosophy of space and time. Euler's general theme was the relation between science and metaphysics; he claimed that the truths of physics – in particular the laws of mechanics – are so well founded that they must serve as a guide for metaphysical researches into the nature of bodies. "For one has the right to reject in this science [metaphysics] all reasoning and all ideas, however well founded they might otherwise appear, that lead to conclusions contrary to those truths [of mechanics]" ("Reflexions sur l'espace et le temps," in Euler's *Opera Omnia*, series 3, volume 2, pp. 377–83; p. 377). In particular, the principle that bodies continue to move in the same direction until a force is applied cannot be reconciled with the relativistic account of space: "For if space and place were nothing but the relation among co-existing bodies, what would be the same direction? ... However bodies may move or change their mutual situation, that doesn't prevent us from maintaining a sufficiently clear idea of a fixed direction that bodies endeavour to follow in their motion, in spite of the changes that other bodies undergo. From which it is evident that identity of direction, which is an essential circumstance in the general principles of motion, is absolutely not to be explicated by the relation or the order of co-existing bodies" (*ibid.*, p. 381). Euler's essay, in turn, profoundly influenced the development of Immanuel Kant's thought away from Leibnizian relationalism, toward a deeper understanding of the Newtonian theory of space, time, and motion, and eventually toward a complete reexamination of the roles of space and time in our understanding of the external world. See Michael Friedman, "Introduction" to *Kant and the Exact Sciences* (Cambridge, MA: Harvard University Press, 1993).

32 Hall and Hall, *Unpublished Scientific Papers*, p. 125.

33 See, especially, Julian Barbour, *Absolute or Relative Motion?* (Cambridge: Cambridge University Press, 1991).

34 Cf. "A Specimen of Dynamics," in Leibniz's *Philosophical Essays*, ed. and trans. R. Ariew and D. Garber (Indianapolis: Hackett Publishing Co., 1989), pp. 136–7. This argument is evidently based on a misunderstanding of Galilean relativity, which, again, asserts the equivalence of motions that are rectilinear *and uniform*. Even though curved lines may be considered "infinitesimally straight," their distinguishing

characteristic is that one "infinitesimal straight segment" has a different *direction* from the next; the tangent to a circle at one point, for example, is not parallel to the tangent at a nearby point. Of course Leibniz was well aware of this. But this is just the distinguishing characteristic of curvilinear motion that, on Leibniz's own theory, requires a causal explanation!

35 From Leibniz's Third Letter to Samuel Clarke, in *Philosophical Essays*, p. 327.

36 Cf. Leibniz's letter to Christiaan Huygens (1690), in *Philosophical Essays*, pp. 309–12.

37 See chapter by W. Harper, this volume.

38 This "Hypothesis" is sometimes misinterpreted as indicating Newton's belief that the center of the solar system is at absolute rest in the center of the universe. But Newton knew (cf. below and note 40) that the dynamical analysis of the solar system cannot determine whether the entire system is at rest, in uniform motion, or even uniformly accelerated. The function of Hypothesis 1 is, rather, purely *dialectical*. That is, it is taken as the common assumption of the Keplerian and Tychonic accounts of the structure of the planetary system, in order to show that *both sides are mistaken*: neither the earth nor the sun is in the center.

39 Newton, *The Principia*, p. 816.

40 *Ibid.*, p. 817.

41 Newton, *The System of the World*, in *Sir Isaac Newton's Mathematical Principles of Natural Philosophy and his System of the World*, ed. Florian Cajori, trans. Andrew Motte, 2 vols. (Berkeley: University of California Press, 1962), vol. 2, p. 558.

42 For example, Hans Reichenbach, *The Philosophy of Space and Time*, trans. Maria Reichenbach (New York: Dover Publications, 1957); Moritz Schlick, *Space and Time in Contemporary Physics*, trans. H. Brose (New York: Oxford University Press, 1920).

43 For the history of this controversy, see Roberto Torretti, *Philosophy of Geometry from Riemann to Poincaré* (Dordrecht: Reidel, 1977).

2 Newton's concepts of force and mass, with notes on the Laws of Motion

VARIETIES OF FORCE IN THE *PRINCIPIA* [1]

Newton's physics is based on two fundamental concepts: mass and force.[2] In the *Principia* Newton explores the properties of several types of force. The most important of these are the forces that produce accelerations or changes in the state of motion or of rest in bodies. In Definition 4 of the *Principia*, Newton separates these into three principal categories: impact or percussion, pressure, and centripetal force. In the *Principia*, Newton mentions other types of forces, including (in Book 2) the forces with which fluids resist motions through them.[3] Of a different sort is Newton's "force of inertia," which is neither an accelerative force nor a static force and is not, properly speaking in the context of dynamics, a force at all.[4]

The structure of Newton's *Principia* follows a classical pattern: definitions and axioms, followed by the statement of propositions and their demonstrations. Newton's treatise differs, however, from classical (or Greek) geometry in two respects. First, there is a constant appeal to the method of limits – Newton's "first and ultimate ratios," as set forth in Book 1, Section 1. Second, the validity of propositions is tied to evidence of experiment and critical observation.

In the demonstrations in the *Principia*, Newton generally proceeds by establishing a series of proportions from a geometric configuration. He then allows one or more of the parameters to be diminished without limit, thereby obtaining a limiting ("ultimate") value of the geometric ratio. It is in the limit that Newton's proofs are valid.

THE STRUCTURE OF THE *PRINCIPIA*

The propositions in the *Principia* are set forth in three "books." Book 1 analyzes motion in free spaces, that is, spaces devoid of fluid resistance. Book 2 then considers various conditions of fluid resistance and a variety of related topics. Finally, in Book 3, Newton applies the results of Book 1 to the physics of the heavens, to the "System of the World." Here he shows that gravity extends to the Moon and that the Earth is an oblate spheroid. He investigates the motions of the Moon, calculates planetary densities and relative masses, explains the motions of the tides, and shows that comets are like planets and thus move in conic sections, some of which are ellipses. Book 3, as Edmond Halley reported to the Royal Society, displays a demonstration of the Copernican system as amended by Kepler.[5]

As is well known, Book 3 centers on the concept of a universal gravitating force, one which is shown by Newton to act between any two particles in the universe. This force is directly proportional to the product of the masses and inversely proportional to the square of the distance between them.

In the final (second and third) editions, Newton has a concluding General Scholium which sets forth a philosophical point of view that has dominated most of physical science ever since. According to this philosophy, the goal of science is not to explore ultimate causes, as for example the cause of gravity, nor to "feign" hypotheses.[6] Rather, Newton writes, it "is enough" that "gravity really exists and acts according to the laws that we have set forth and is sufficient to explain the motions of the heavenly bodies and of our sea."

THE DEFINITIONS — NEWTON'S CONCEPT OF MASS

The *Principia* opens with a set of "Definitions," of which the first is "mass," a new concept formally introduced into physics by Newton and a fundamental concept of all physical science ever since. In the actual statement of the definition, Newton does not use the word "mass." Rather, he states what he means by the then-current expression, "quantity of matter" ("quantitas materiae"). He writes that *his* measure of quantity of matter is one that "arises from" (the Latin is "orta est") two factors jointly: density and volume. He indicates that this particular measure is what he means whenever he writes of "body" or "mass."

Newton introduced the concept of mass because his physics demanded a measure of matter that is not the result of a body happening to be at one place rather than another or being subject to some particular physical circumstance such as an external pressure. In other words, Newton's measure – to use the language of Aristotelian physics – is not an "accidental" property.

In Definition 1, Newton effectively rejects then-current measures of matter such as extension (favored by Descartes) or weight (Galileo's measure). He abandoned weight as the measure of matter because the reported experiences of Richer and Halley had shown that the weight of a body varies with its terrestrial latitude. Newton points out that, at any given place, the mass of a body "can always be known from a body's weight"; he has found "by making very accurate experiments with pendulums" that at any given place mass is proportional to weight. The report on these experiments is given in Book 3, Proposition 6.

Newton's views concerning density were strongly influenced by the pneumatic experiments of Boyle and others and by his own concept of the theory of matter. He was aware that a given quantity of air could be expanded or contracted. Under such varying conditions, the density would change, but the quantity of matter would remain fixed, depending on the volume and density jointly.

The quantity of matter in a given sample would, according to Newton, remain unaltered if it were transported from one place on Earth to another. According to Newton's concept, the quantity of matter would remain fixed even if the sample of matter were transported to the Moon or to Jupiter.

Newton's concept of mass has been criticized, notably by Ernst Mach,[7] on the grounds of circularity. If density is mass per unit volume, how can mass be defined as jointly proportional to density and volume?[8] In the *Principia*, however, Newton does not define density, nor did he ever write a gloss on his Definition 1. Apparently, however, he was thinking of density as a measure of the degree of concentration of the number of fundamental particles of which all matter is composed.[9] As such, density would not depend on mass and volume.

Newton came to his concept of mass only as the *Principia* was taking form. Mass does not occur in the several versions of "De motu", the tract that Newton wrote just before composing the *Principia*, a tract which he expanded into the *Principia*. In a list of definitions drawn up just before writing the *Principia*,[10] Newton used the noun "pondus" or "weight" as the measure of matter, but he was careful to note that he did not mean weight as commonly understood. He thus wrote that because of the "want of a suitable word," he will "represent and designate quantity of matter by weight," even though he is aware that this usage is not appropriate in all circumstances. Indeed, in an earlier statement in this same set of definitions, he wrote that by "weight" ("pondus"), "I mean the quantity or amount of matter being moved, apart from considerations of gravity, so long as there is no question of gravitating bodies."

NEWTON'S "QUANTITY OF MOTION"

The subject of Definition 2 is "quantity of motion," our momentum. Newton says that it "arises from the velocity and quantity of matter jointly." Here he uses the same verb ("oriri") as in the definition of quantity of matter.

NEWTON'S CONCEPT OF "INERTIA" – *VIS INSITA* AND "FORCE OF INERTIA"

In Definition 3, Newton declares the sense in which he will use a term then current in discussions of motion, *vis insita*.[11] This term was not an invention of Newton's; it occurs in many books with which Newton was familiar, even appearing as an entry in Rudolph Goclenius's widely read dictionary, *Lexicon Philosophicum* (1613). According to Goclenius, *vis insita* is a "natural power," a force (*vis*) that can be either *insita* (inherent or natural) or *violenta* (violent). In Aristotelian physics this means that force is either according to a body's nature or contrary to it. The term *vis insita* also appears in Johann Magirus's *Physiologiae Peripateticae Libri Sex* (1642), which Newton studied while a Cambridge undergraduate, entering many extracts in his college notebook. *Vis insita* occurs in both Magirus's text and his accompanying Latin version of Aristotle's *Nichomachean Ethics*. Newton would also have encountered this term in the writings of Henry More, an influential figure in Newton's intellectual development.[12]

In Definition 3, Newton declares that because he is giving a new sense to this term, he will give it another name: *vis inertiae* or "force of inertia."

The traditional or older physics held that if the motive force applied to a body were to cease acting, the body would then seek its natural place and there come to rest. Kepler, however, in his radical restructuring of the science of motion, held that a primary quality of matter is its "inertness," its inability to move by itself, by its own internal power. Accordingly, if an externally applied force producing motion were to cease, then – according to Kepler – the body would come to rest and do so wherever it happened to be.

Newton encountered this Keplerian concept of motion in a Latin edition of Descartes's correspondence, in an exchange of letters between Descartes and Mersenne concerning "natural inertia"; neither correspondent referred to Kepler by name in this context.[13] Newton made a radical transformation of this Keplerian concept. No longer would the inertia of matter merely bring a body to rest when an external force ceased to act; rather, this inertness would tend to maintain a body in whatever "state" it happened to be, whether a state of resting or of moving "uniformly straight forward."[14] The concept of a body being in a "state" of motion was taken by Newton from Descartes's *Principia*.

Two further aspects of Newton's concept of inertia should be noted. One is that generally Newton does not refer, as we do today, to "inertia" as such; rather he tends to write of a "force of inertia," a *vis inertiae*. The second is that he identified mass and inertia. The *vis insita* of a body, he writes in Definition 3, "is always proportional to the body," that is, proportional to the mass. Furthermore, it "does not differ from the inertia of the mass" save for "the manner in which it is conceived." Hence, he writes, we may give *vis insita* a new and "very significant name," force of inertia (*vis inertiae*). And, indeed, throughout the *Principia*, Newton generally uses *vis inertiae* rather than *vis insita*.

Newton explains that, because of "a body's inertia," a body is only "with difficulty" made to change its "state" of resting or moving uniformly. It is for this reason, he declares, that *vis inertiae* is a better name than *vis insita*. Although the use of *vis* or "force" in the context of inertia seems outlandish to a twenty-first-century reader, this was not the case for Newton's successors in developing the science of dynamics. For example, Jean d'Alembert, in his *Traité de dynamique* (1743), wrote: "I follow Newton in using the name 'force of inertia' for the properties which bodies have of remaining in the state in which they are."

Newton's concept of *vis inertiae* has one puzzling feature. As he makes clear, especially in Definition 4, this is not an "impressed" force, one that can produce a change in state or an acceleration. Therefore, this "force" cannot be combined by means of a force triangle with continuous or instantaneous external forces.

Newton never explained why he wrote of a *vis inertiae*, a "force of inertia," rather than a property of inertia and we have no basis for guessing what was his state of mind. Perhaps he was merely transforming *vis insita* into a *vis* of a new and different sort.

THREE VARIETIES OF IMPRESSED FORCE

In Definition 4, Newton deals with "impressed force," a term that has a long history of usage before the *Principia*. Newton is concerned with the "action" of forces to alter the "state" of a body, to alter a body's condition of resting or moving uniformly straight forward. According to Newton, this action occurs only while the force is being impressed, while the force is actually producing a change of state. It does not remain in the body after the action is over. Newton says explicitly that "a body perseveres in any new state solely by the force of inertia."

It is in the conclusion of Newton's discussion of Definition 4 that he declares that there are "various sources of impressed force, such as percussion, pressure, or centripetal force."

CENTRIPETAL FORCE

Newton has no need of comment on the first two of his three types of impressed force: percussion and pressure. The case is different, however, for centripetal force. The concept of centripetal force was introduced into rational mechanics and celestial dynamics in the *Principia*. In a memorandum, Newton said that he had invented the name in honor of Christiaan Huygens, who had used the oppositely directed *vis centrifuga*.

Centripetal force differs from percussion and pressure in one notable aspect. Percussion and pressure are the result of some kind of observable physical action. In both, there is a contact of one body with another, typically providing visual evidence of a force acting, for example, a billiard ball striking another billiard ball. These are the kinds of force on which the so-called "mechanical philosophy" was built, in particular the philosophy of nature of Descartes. These forces display the principle of matter in contact with other matter to produce or alter a motion.

Centripetal force, however, is very different. In important cases, such as orbital motion, we do not know that there is a centripetal force by seeing an action, as is the case for a pressure or a percussion; the only evidence that a centripetal force is acting is that there is a continuous change in a body's state, a continuing departure from a uniform rectilinear motion. Accordingly, in introducing centripetal force in Definition 5, Newton is in effect declaring his independence from the strait-jacket rigidity of the mechanical philosophy. It is a fact of record that Continental natural philosophers – notably Huygens and Leibniz – rejected the Newtonian science of motion because it departed from the strict condition that forces must occur only by the action of matter in contact with matter; they rejected the notion of centripetal force, as posited by Newton, because this "force" acts at a distance and is not produced by matter in contact with matter.

In Definition 5, Newton refers to three examples of centripetal force. One is gravity, by which he means terrestrial gravity, the force that causes bodies to descend downward, "toward the center of the Earth." Another is magnetic force, in which a piece of iron "seeks a lodestone." And, finally, there is the "force, whatever it may be, by which the planets are continually drawn back from rectilinear motions and compelled to revolve in curved lines." Note that it is the departure from uniform linear motion that provides evidence that there is a centripetal force acting.

Newton then turns to an important example of centripetal force taken from Descartes, a stone being whirled in a sling. The stone naturally tends to fly off on a tangent, but is restrained by the force of the hand, constantly pulling the body inward toward the center via the string. Newton calls such a force "centripetal" because "it is directed toward the hand as toward the center of an orbit." And then he boldly asserts that the case is the same for "all bodies that are made to move in orbits." They all tend to fly off "in straight lines with uniform motion" unless there is a force. We may note an anticipation of the first law in the statement that if there were no gravity, a projectile or an orbiting body would move off in a straight line "with uniform motion." It follows from this discussion that planets moving in orbits must similarly be subject to some kind of centrally directed force.

THREE MEASURES OF FORCE

The remaining definitions (Definitions 6–8) are concerned with the three measures of centripetal force. These are the absolute quantity (Definition 6), the accelerative quantity (Definition 7), and the motive quantity (Definition 8). The most important of these is the "accelerative" quantity, defined as the velocity which is generated "in a given time." This measure is the rate at which velocity changes, our acceleration. It is this measure that Newton has in mind during the first ten sections of Book 1.

In Definition 8, Newton introduces a measure that is "proportional to the motion" (i.e., momentum) which a force "generates in a given time." This measure is, in other words, the rate at which "motion" (i.e., momentum) changes.

THE LAWS OF MOTION: NEWTON'S FIRST LAW

In the *Principia*, the definitions are followed by Newton's "Axioms or Laws of Motion." Newton's "Axiomata sive leges motus" was an obvious transformation of Descartes's "Regulae ... sive leges naturae," which appear in the latter's *Principia*. This source of Newton's name for the "axioms" would have been obvious to most of Newton's readers, who would also have appreciated that the title of Newton's treatise, *Philosophiae Naturalis Principia Mathematica*, was a rather obvious recasting of the title of Descartes's *Philosophiae Principia*.[15]

The first law of motion, sometimes known as the law of inertia, states: "Every body perseveres in its state of being at rest or of moving uniformly straight forward [i.e., moving uniformly forward in a straight line] except insofar as it is compelled to change its state by forces impressed." In the brief paragraph which follows (consisting of three short sentences), Newton mentions three examples of inertial motion, each of which is based on an analysis of curved motion produced by the action of a form of centripetal force. In each case, the curved motion is, by Newton's analysis, compounded of a linear or tangential component of inertial motion and an inward accelerated motion produced by a centripetal force.

Thus a major purpose of the first law is to make explicit the condition under which we can infer the action of a continuously acting, centrally directed force. Newton's three examples, accordingly, invoke centripetal forces and not pressure or percussion.

The first example is the motion of projectiles. These "persevere in their [linear forward] motions" except in so far as they are retarded by air resistance and are "impelled downward by the force of gravity." Newton's second example is the circular notion of a spinner or a top. Here Newton explains that the particles that compose the spinning object tend to fly off in straight lines along tangents to their curves of motion. They do not fly off, however, but are kept in circular orbits by the cohesive forces that hold the top together. When a top is subjected to a degree of rotation beyond some structural limit, the cohesive force is no longer great enough and the particles fly off in all directions tangent to their original paths of rotation.[16] Newton's third example is the long-term orbital motion of the planets and of comets.

The "forces impressed" which Newton mentions in the statement of the law can be any of the three varieties of impressed force: pressure, percussion, or centripetal force. In other words, the law is equally valid for impulsive or instantaneous forces and continuous forces.

THE SECOND LAW OF MOTION

The second law states that a "change in motion" is proportional to "the motive force impressed" and adds that this change in motion is directed along "the straight line in which this force is impressed." Some commentators have added a word or phrase to Newton's law so as to have it read that the *rate* of "change in motion" (or the change in motion per unit time) is proportional to the force.[17] This alteration would make Newton's second law read like the one found in today's physics textbooks.

Newton, however, did not make an error here. He chose his words very carefully. In his formulation of the second law, Newton was explicitly stating a law for impulsive forces, not for continuous forces. Thus Newton's second law states quite correctly that an impulsive

force – that is, a force acting instantaneously or nearly instantaneously, or acting in an infinitesimally small "particle" of time –
produces a change in the "quantity of motion" or momentum.

Newton's discussion of this law, following its formal statement,
leaves no doubt that this is the correct reading of Newton's intention.
He says that the "effect" of the action of a force is the same "whether
the force is applied at once or successively by degrees."

Consider the following example. Let an impulsive force F produce a certain change in momentum $\Delta(mV)$ and let that force be
divided into three equal parts, each of which will produce a change
in momentum $1/3\ mV$. Then, the successive application of these
three forces will produce a corresponding total change in momentum of $3 \times 1/3 \times mV = mV$. The net change in momentum is the
same whether the impacts are delivered seriatim or all at once. This
makes perfect sense for impulsive forces, but has no meaning for
continuous forces since the latter produce a net change of momentum that depends on both the magnitude of the force and the time
during which the force acts.

This interpretation is further confirmed in Corollary 1 to the
Laws. Here (see Figure 2.1), Newton considers a body struck by a
blow. "Let a body in a given time," he writes, "by a force M impressed in A, be carried with uniform motion from A to B." Here is a
plain case of an impulsive force generating a motion. After receiving
the blow, the body then, according to Definition 4, "perseveres" in
the "new state" by its "force of inertia."

In such statements as these, we can see the influence of
Descartes. In explaining how refraction takes place, Descartes – in his
Dioptrique (1637) – invokes an analogy with the motion of a tennis

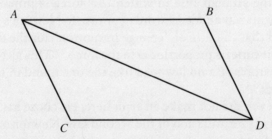

Fig. 2.1 Newton's parallelogram rule for motions produced by impulsive forces.

ball striking a body of water. At the moment of impact, at the interface between the air and the water, Descartes supposes, the ball is
given a blow or is struck by an impulsive force. The ensuing motion,
originating from the instantaneous action at the interface, is uniform
and rectilinear, with a new magnitude and direction, as is the case
in a refracted light beam.[18]

Of course, Newton knew the second law as a law for continuously
acting forces. This form of the second law is implied in Definitions
7 and 8. In Book 2, Proposition 24, Newton writes that "the velocity
that a given force can generate in a given time in a given quantity of
matter is as the force and the time directly and the matter inversely."
The factor of time shows that this is a case of the second law for
continuous forces.[19]

A reason why Newton may have given priority to the impulsive
form of the law rather than the continuous version is that in this case
one can witness an act of impact or pressure. As we have noted, the
most important class of continuous forces is in the orbital motion of
planets, planetary satellites, and eventually comets. In each of these
cases, the effect of the force is not associated with an observable
physical act.

Another factor of importance is that Newton formed his dynamics
in the context of the great advances in the science of motion made,
during the decades before the *Principia*, by studies of impact – the
work of such giants as Wallis, Wren, and Huygens. Descartes had set
the scene in his *Principia*, which contained a series of statements
about impacts which are wrong.

In the *Principia*, Newton described at length the experiments he
himself had made on impact, including the distinction between elastic and non-elastic collisions. In short, the primacy given by Newton
to impulsive forces would have been in keeping with the cutting edge
of the science of motion in those days.

Yet it is a fact that the propositions of Book 1, beginning with the
first group of propositions (Propositions 1–14), deal with varieties of
centripetal force and orbital motions and not with impulsive forces.
As we shall see shortly, in these opening propositions, Newton begins with a series of impulsive forces and effects a transition from
a sequence of impulsive forces to a continuous force. Indeed, from
Newton's point of view, the impact form of the second law led so
readily into the continuous form that he did not even bother to state

the continuous form as a separate entity. In other words, the distinction between the two forms of the law is more significant for us than it would have been for Newton.

THE THIRD LAW

Newton's third law has been characterized by Ernst Mach as the most original of the three Laws of Motion. It is the only one of the Laws of Motion that Newton did not allege had been known to Galileo. In fact, Newton had found the law some years before he composed the *Principia*.[20] As commonly stated, the third law declares that action is always equal and opposite to reaction. In Newton's own words, "To any action there is always an opposite and equal reaction."

This law, however, simple as it is, is easily subject to misinterpretation. For example, it is often mistakenly believed that this law provides for an equilibrium of two forces, the equal and oppositely directed action and reaction. But the law actually says that if a body A exerts a force F_a on body B, then body B will exert an equal and opposite force F_b on body A. There is no equilibrium because the forces F_a and F_b are exerted on different bodies, one on body A and the other on body B.

Newton himself apparently saw that this law might be subject to misinterpretation and so he included a second version in the statement of the third law. In "other words," he wrote, "the actions of two bodies upon each other are always equal and always opposite in direction."

In the discussion of the law, Newton says that it applies specifically to collisions. He shows the way in which this law is related to the law of conservation of momentum, previously announced by the mathematician John Wallis, and known to Huygens. He concludes with the important statement that this "law is valid also for attractions, as will be proved in the next scholium."

WHY A SEPARATE LAW 1 AND LAW 2

A number of critics and authors of textbooks on mechanics have criticized Newton for having a separate Law 1 and Law 2. After all, they argue, if there is no net external force F, the second law (for continuous forces) implies that the acceleration A is zero and so there is no change in a body's state. In the case of the impact form of the second law, there is similarly no change in state.

There are two sets of reasons, however, why Newton had a separate Law 1. First, in Newton's day – as during many preceding centuries – the common belief was that all motion requires a mover, a moving force. The very statement of this law as an axiom was a radical step, a declaration of an important new principle of motion, too important to be a special case of another law. Indeed, such a statement was possible only after Descartes's bold assertion that uniform rectilinear motion can be considered a "state," thus existing without a driving or motive external force.

Second, Newton's first two laws of motion depended heavily on the prior statements of Descartes, Galileo, and Huygens. The form in which Newton expressed the first law, including the choice of language and the separate statement of Law 1 and Law 2, shows the influence of Descartes's *Principia*, where these are part of the "regulae quaedam sive leges naturae."

In the 1660s, some two decades before developing the mature ideas expounded in the *Principia*, Newton had already seen how basic was Descartes's law of inertia. He wrote out (in English) what he called a series of "Axiomes and Propositions," of which the first one reads: "If a quantity once move it will never rest unlesse hindered by some external caus." Another version reads as follows: "A quantity will always move on in the same streight line (not changing the determination nor celerity of its motion) unlesse some external caus divert it." He then started a new series of axioms, of which the first is labeled "Ax: 100." It reads: "Every thing doth naturally persevere in that state in which it is unlesse it bee interrupted by some externall caus, hence axiome 1st and 2nd." Note that, early on, he recognized the importance of Descartes's concept of uniform motion as a "state."[21]

An even more important reason why Newton had a separate Law 1 and Law 2 is that he was following the example set by Christiaan Huygens in his *Horologium Oscillatorium* of 1673, a work that Newton greatly admired. In the *Horologium*, Huygens axiomatized Galileo's rules for the motion of bodies such as projectiles, moving in the Earth's gravitational field. Huygens's first law (he calls these laws "Hypotheses") is that if there were no gravity and no resistance of air to motion, "any body will continue its motion with uniform velocity in a straight line."[22] Here is Newton's first law stated for a system in which the only possible forces are gravity and air resistance (and possibly some force that gets forward motions started, as in the firing of a projectile). That is, Huygens first considers a kind of inertial motion without falling. Then, in a second law, he allows such a moving body to be acted on by gravity so as to fall according to the laws of falling bodies. Although Huygens does not state his second law in the full generality found in the *Principia*, the model is structurally the same: first, an inertial motion in the absence of forces and then a new motion produced by the action of a force.

In the *Principia*, Newton added a statement about Galileo's discovery of the laws of projectile motion. According to Newton, Galileo did so by using the first two laws of motion. Thus Galileo would have been Newton's third source for a first and second law. There is no evidence, however, that Newton had ever read Galileo's *Two New Sciences* and his knowledge of Galileo's ideas must have come from secondary sources, such as the books of Kenelm Digby and John Anderson.

FROM IMPULSIVE FORCES TO CONTINUALLY ACTING FORCES

Newton's transition from the action of impulsive forces to the action of continuous forces occurs in the first proposition in the *Principia*. Here Newton's goal is to find the significance of Kepler's law of areas (which Newton does not attribute to Kepler).

Newton's proof starts out with a body (actually a mass point) moving freely with a component of linear inertial motion along a straight line. Newton shows (see Figure 2.2) that this motion is area-conserving, that is, a line drawn from the moving body to any point *P* (not on the line of motion) will sweep out equal areas in any equal times. Actually, this was a startling result. Here Newton revealed for the first time the link between the law of areas and the principle or law of inertia.

Next, after a time interval *T*, the body is given an impulsive blow directed toward the point *P*. The body will now move on a new linear path, with a new velocity, according to the second law. By simple geometry (see Figure 2.3), Newton proves that the area swept out in

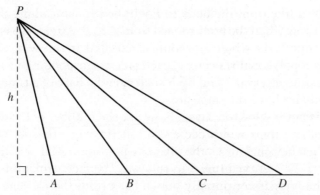

Fig. 2.2 The area law for uniform rectilinear motion. *A* body moves with uniform motion along the straight line *ABCD*...Then in equal times the distances *AB*, *BC*, *CD*...will be equal. Therefore, a line from the moving body to any point *P* (not on the line of motion) will sweep out equal areas in any equal time intervals, since the triangles *ABP*, *BCP*, *CDP*...have a common altitude *h* and equal bases.

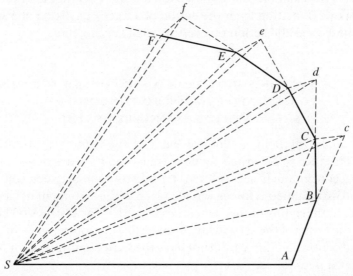

Fig. 2.3 Newton's polygonal path (from the first edition of the *Principia*, 1687). During the first equal time-interval *T*, the body moves from *A* to *B*. At *B* it receives a thrust toward *S*. Had there not been such a thrust, the body would have moved in the second time *T* from *B* to *c*, where *Bc* = *AB*. But, as a result of the thrust, the body moves from *B* to *C*. By the parallelogram rule and simple geometry, Newton shows that the area of triangle *BSC* equals the area of triangle *BSc*. In this way Newton constructs the polygonal path *ABCDEF*...

time T by a line from the body to P will be the same along the new path as it was when the body moved from A to B. After the passage of another time T, the whole procedure is repeated. In this way, Newton produces a polygonal trajectory, each side corresponding to motion during a time interval T and each such side the base of a triangle; all such triangles have the same area.

At this point, Newton says, "Now, let the number of triangles be increased and their width decreased indefinitely," that is, without limit. Then he continues, "the ultimate perimeter ADF will (by lem. 3, corol. 4) be a curved line." In this way, "the centripetal force by which the body is continually drawn back from the tangent of this curve will act uninterruptedly." Furthermore, "any areas described, SADS and SAFS, which are always proportional to the times of description, will be proportional to those times in this case." In other words, Newton has essentially proved that a centrally directed force will always produce (or is a sufficient condition for) the law of areas. This example shows how Newton used his method of limits to make a transition from the action of a force consisting of a series of impulses to the action of a continuously acting force.

NEWTON'S SHIFT FROM A SECOND LAW FOR IMPULSIVE
TO A SECOND LAW FOR CONTINUOUS
FORCES — NEWTON'S CONCEPT OF TIME

In analyzing Book 1, Proposition 1 of the *Principia*, attention has been called to Newton's mode of transition from a series of impulses to a continuously acting force. This distinction between continuous and instantaneous forces was also seen in the statement of Law 2. But a careful reading of the *Principia* shows that the distinction between these forms of the second law, and the distinction between impulsive and continuous forces, did not have the same significance for Newton that it does for us.

In Newton's system of dynamics, the two concepts of force – continuous and impulsive – are linked by Newton's concept of time. That this should be so is hardly surprising since the difference between the two forms of force lies in the factor of time of action: a finite time for a continuous force and an infinitesimal time for an impulsive force. We make a distinction between them but Newton could effect an easy transition from one to the other, conceiving (as in Book 1, Propositions 1 and 4) a continuous force to be the limit of a sequence of impulses. Newton's procedure is troubling to us because there is a difference in dimensionality between the impulsive force, which we measure by $d(mV)$, and the continuous force, measured by $d(mV)/dt$. Thus if we were to write these two forms of the law as algebraic statements of proportion,

$$F = k_1\, d(mV)$$
$$F = k_2\, d(mV)/dt$$

it becomes at once obvious that k_1 and k_2 have different dimensionality. It is for this reason that we would write the first of these equations as

$$F\,dt = k_1\, d(mV).$$

This was not a problem for Newton, however, since he did not write proportions as algebraic equations and so was not concerned by the fact that if the force F has the same dimensionality in both forms of the second law, then the constants of proportionality must have different dimensionality.

Newton generally compared one value of a quantity with another rather than make computations that involve the numerical value of the constant of proportionality. Thus, in Book 3, Proposition 12, he compares the quantity of matter in the Sun to the quantity of matter in Jupiter but does not compute either quantity in terms of some fixed set of units such as pounds. In the Scholium to Book 2, Section 6, he writes of a globe encountering a resistance which is to its weight as 61,705 to 121. But he also makes some computations that, in effect, involve evaluating a constant of proportionality (although he does not use this form of expression). But he did not ever compute numerical values (with units of dimensionality) in which he had to be concerned about the difference in dimensional units that arise because of the two forms of the second law.

It is well known that in Newton's mathematics, as in his physics, time is the primary independent variable, the one on which all other quantities depend. Newton does not have an entry for time in the section of definitions in the *Principia*, merely saying in a Scholium that "time, place, space, and motion are very familiar to everyone."

He then alerts the reader to "absolute, true, and mathematical time," which "without reference to anything external, flows uniformly."

It is, therefore, paradoxical that a consequence of Newton's concept of time as a uniform flow should be that it is composed of units (dt) which are essentially constant infinitesimal increments. And yet, in the *Principia*, Newton often writes of a "particle of time" ("particula temporis"). These are not finite atoms of time in the sense of tiny finite particles of matter. Rather, for Newton, time is finitely continuous and only infinitesimally discrete. Thus the "fluxional" character of the *Principia* depends in practice on a discrete kind of infinitesimal of time in which quantities do not really flow evenly or smoothly, but rather jerk, jerk along – to use a metaphor suggested by D. T. Whiteside. But this aspect of time appears only on an infinitesimal level so that to our finite eyes time appears to be flowing smoothly, as postulated by the method of first and ultimate ratios.

Thus, in Book 2, Proposition 2, Newton divides a time-interval into "equal particles" and eventually lets "the equal particles of time ... be diminished and their number increased without limit" ("in infinitum"). On first encounter, such a passage gives rise to many problems because we would ask how a continuous flow of time could possibly be composed of discrete units, even infinitesimal ones. This post-Newtonian problem may serve as an index of the difficulties that arise in the use of infinitesimals.

In considering the consequences of Newton's concept of time, we may anachronistically (that is, by using the Leibnizian algorithm of the calculus) consider dt as Newton's constant infinitesimal unit of time. Thus dt represents the Newtonian concept of a primitive or fundamental "time," flowing uniformly at a constant rate everywhere, at all times, and under all conditions. Then it will follow at once that there are a number of equivalent forms of the second law as follows:

(1) $F \propto dV$
(2) $F \propto dV/dt = d^2s/dt^2$, where $V = ds/dt$
(3) $F \cdot dt \propto dV$
(4) $F \cdot dt^2 \propto d^2s$

where F is taken as the accelerative measure of force. The only difference between eq. (1), the impact form of the second law, and eqs. (2)–(4), the continuous form, is that there is a different dimensionality in the constant of proportion (not shown). That is, the constant dt can be absorbed in the constant of proportionality at will. In these equations, if the force is itself a variable, then F must be the average value during the time dt.

In considering these equations for a "force" F, it must be kept in mind, as mentioned previously, that Newton did not write equations of motion but rather expressed his principles as statements of proportion. Hence the constant of proportionality did not need to appear explicitly, nor did Newton need to have any regard for the dimensionality of the various forces he was studying. This was especially the case since Newton tended to compare one force with another rather than compute numerical values in some given system of units – which would have required a consideration of the physical dimensions of the computed quantities. We may thus understand how it was possible to hold simultaneously the validity of a second law symbolized by eq. (1) and a second law symbolized by eq. (3), whereas we would encounter a problem with the quantity "F" in eq. (1) and would consider an impulsive force to be $F \cdot dt$ rather than F.

A FINITE OR INFINITESIMAL LEVEL OF DISCOURSE?

A critical study of the *Principia* reveals that much of the discourse is pitched on an infinitesimal level. For example, in Book 1, Proposition 41, Newton introduces a ratio of a distance to a time, "the line-element IK, described in a minimally small time." These, clearly, are not a finite distance and time, as is evident from the terms "line-element" and "minimally small." In the language of the calculus, Newton is invoking an infinitesimal distance ds and an infinitesimal unit or "particle" of time dt. Thus the ratio in question is Newton's way of expressing what we would write in Leibnizian terms as ds/dt.

An admirable exposition of the infinitesimal character of Newton's dynamics has been given by D. T. Whiteside,[23] who has made a careful analysis of the proof of the area law in Book 1, Proposition 1, of the *Principia*, essentially the proof given in the prior tract "De motu". In this proof, as we have seen, the continuous curved trajectory is the limit of a polygonal path. In this process, according to Whiteside, Newton replaces the continually acting central force by the limit of "a series of component discrete impulses, each acting instantaneously but separated from its predecessor by a measurable if indefinitely small time-interval." Under these circumstances, Whiteside finds, the elements of force must be "of a second order of the infinitely small." Whiteside then notes that since dt^2 is a constant (a consequence of dt being a constant), Newton's proof of Proposition 1 would accordingly make use of the second law in a form expressed by a variant of our eq. (4),

$$F \propto d^2 s$$

which would be another way of saying that the force impulse must be a second-order infinitesimal.[24]

A final example will show in a striking manner the importance of keeping in mind that much of the treatment of forces in the *Principia* is couched on an infinitesimal level. Newton's manuscripts show that in the early 1690s he was planning a new edition of the *Principia* in which he would revise his presentation of the second law. These attempts to alter the presentation of the second law are of special interest because there are no similar attempts to recast the presentation of Law 1 or Law 3.

In one set of these revisions, Newton writes of "a motion generated in a space either immobile or mobile," saying that such a motion "is proportional to the motive force impressed and occurs along the straight line in which that force is impressed." As the manuscript makes clear, Newton was thinking of a situation like Galileo's example of motion on a moving ship; Galileo compared the motion as seen by an observer on the ship with the motion as seen by an observer on the shore.

In the course of these revisions, Newton writes of the generated motion as follows:

[it] has the same determination [i.e., direction] as the impressed force and occurs from that place in which the body, before the force was impressed upon it, was at rest either truly or at least relatively. And, therefore, if the body was moving before the impressed force, the generated motion is either added to the original motion or is subtracted from it if contrary or is added obliquely to it if oblique and is compounded with it in accordance with the direction of both.

Newton then proceeds to examine the manner in which the two oblique motions are compounded, that is, combined according to the laws of composition of velocities. In the oblique case, the resulting

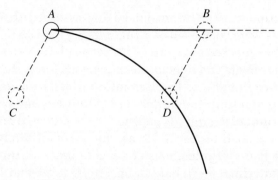

Fig. 2.4 The trajectory of a moving body that has received a blow or has been struck by an impulsive force. There can be no doubt that the force is a thrust, an instaneous force, a force of impact, or a force of percussion, since the text reads that the imparted motion "is proportional to the force."

motion, Newton says, "is neither parallel to, nor perpendicular to, the original motion to which it is added."

In this paragraph Newton will have anticipated Corollary 1 to the laws by giving a proof of the method of composition of two motions. But there is a major difference. In Corollary 1 to the laws, two impulsive forces act either separately or simultaneously on a body at rest, whereas in this revision a single impulsive force acts by giving an oblique blow to a body in uniform motion.

This manuscript presents a problem, however, because although the original motion is explicitly said to be uniform ("uniformiter continuato"), the trajectory resulting from the action of the impulsive force or blow is not a straight line as we would have expected. Rather (see Figure 2.4), the new trajectory AB is curved, seeming to imply that the action did not simply generate a new straight-line motion, as Newton's text might have led us to expect. Rather, the effect of the force seems to be to produce an acceleration, as if the force had been continuously acting rather than having been an impulse.

The trajectory AD, it should be noted, is the same parabola-like curve in three separate occurrences of the diagram. In none of these is the curve the result of a carelessly drawn free-hand diagram. AD is simply not the diagonal of a parallelogram of forces. Hence, the conclusion must be that Newton was thinking of a trajectory produced by a continuous force, even though the text indicates that the force is an impulse, an instantaneous blow.

Our bewilderment arises from our having assumed that these manuscript texts were conceived on a finite rather than an infinitesimal level. In the proposed revisions of the second law, Newton was dealing with the effects of a blow or instantaneous force, that is, an infinitesimal force-impulse acting in an infinitesimal time-unit δt. If we now divide that infinitesimal time-unit δt into sub-units or parts $(\delta t/n)$, then the limit of the initial condition of the proposed revisions of Law 2 (as $n \to \infty$) will correspond to a sequence of infinitely small quantities (which are infinitesimals of a higher order) of time. It is on such an infinitesimal level, but not on a finite level (and only on an infinitesimal level), that the two modes of action of an impulse – Newton's "simul et semel" and "gradatim et successive" – produce the effects illustrated by Newton within the framework of the stated Law 2 of the *Principia*.[25]

This analysis would accord with Newton's statement concerning the two ways in which a given force-impulse may act. Thus an impulse P may in an instant produce a change in motion (or momentum), acting – as Newton says – "altogether and at once." Alternatively, the impulse P can be considered as composed of a succession of infinitesimal force-impulses. This is the mode of action that Newton calls "by degrees and successively." The difference between the two lies in the mode of conceiving the actual production of the change in motion. In the first case, there is an instantaneous change that can occur in the direction and magnitude of the motion. In the second, there is a succession of infinitesimal blows that in the limit produce a curved motion, whose final direction and magnitude is the same as in the first case.

THE REALITIES OF FORCE – THE NEWTONIAN STYLE

Newton came to believe in the existence of forces that could produce curved or orbital motion without contact, thereby holding a drastically revised form of the then-current mechanical philosophy. In effect he now enlarged the basis of explanation from effects produced by matter and motion, adding the further concept of force. In the *Principia*, he avoided this issue as long as possible by starting out on a mathematical level in which he did not need to consider the physical aspects of his concepts. Thus the first ten sections of Book I explore a purely mathematical problem: the motions of bodies attracted to a mathematical point. These are mathematical bodies in so far as there are no considerations of mass, no physical dimensions, and no physical properties such as hardness. In the opening of Section 11 of Book 1, Newton states clearly that in the preceding sections he has "been setting forth the motions of bodies attracted toward an immovable center, such as, however, hardly exists in the natural world," where "attractions are always directed toward bodies." Newton, in other words, stated as clearly as possible that this opening part of Book 1 was a work of mathematics. Even though he had used the verb "to attract," he was not (in Book 1) concerned with a physical force of attraction, with an attractive force of gravity.

Some readers, especially on the Continent, did not take Newton at his word and did not read Book 1 as a work of "mathematical principles." In the early eighteenth century, Fontenelle argued that, no matter what Newton said, the word "attraction" implied a force of a kind that is unacceptable in discussions of physics, of "natural philosophy." This same charge has been repeated in our times by Alexandre Koyré.[26] The reviewer of the first *Principia* in the *Journal des Sçavans* could quite legitimately say that Newton had produced a work on "mechanics" but not "physics."

Since the primary difference between the subject of the first ten sections of Book 1 and the world of nature is that in the world of nature forces orginate in bodies, Newton – in Section 11 – introduces the mathematics of two-body systems. These, however, are not as yet "real" or physical bodies in the full sense. That is, they are not characterized by such physical properties as size, shape, degree of hardness, and so on. From a two-body system Newton next advances to a system of three mutually attracting bodies. Every reader would recognize that Newton's mathematical construct is getting more and more closely to resemble the physical universe. And indeed, in the twenty-two corollaries of Book 1, Proposition 66, Newton indicates how his study of three interacting bodies will eventually be related to the motion of the Moon. The diagram has a central body labeled T (for Terra or Earth), about which there moves in orbit a satellite or secondary planet P whose motion is being perturbed by a body marked S (Sol or Sun).

I have called this mode of studying successive mathematical constructs "the Newtonian style." Basically it consists of starting out with a simple mathematical "system," a mass point moving in orbit about a mathematical center of force toward which it is attracted.

Among the properties of this "system" developed mathematically by Newton are that Kepler's law of areas is a necessary and sufficient condition for motion in a central force field and that Kepler's law of elliptical orbits implies that the central force varies inversely as the square of the distance. Similarly, Newton shows that in a two-body system, each of the bodies will move around the common center of gravity.

Of course Newton's goal is eventually to get to the dynamics of the system of the world. But he makes it abundantly clear that in Book 1 he is primarily concerned with elaborating the properties of mathematical systems that have features resembling those found in nature. And here he makes an important distinction between mathematics and physics. In this way, Newton is free to develop the properties of mathematical forces of attraction without having to face the great problem of whether such forces can actually exist or can be considered an element of acceptable physics. This distinction is stressed by Newton in a concluding statement to Book 1, Section 11.[27]

As Newton proceeds step-by-step, he introduces into the mathematical system one-by-one such further properties as will make the system more and more closely resemble what we observe in the world of nature. Thus he considers the properties of bodies with physical shapes, for example bodies composed of a sequence of homogeneous spherical shells. Eventually, in Book 2, he will add another set of conditions found in the world of nature – various kinds of resisting mediums.

The essence of the "Newtonian style" is this sequence of adding one by one the conditions resembling those of the world of nature. The goal is to produce eventually a dynamics that will apply to the external world, to elaborate the properties of a mathematical system that will closely resemble the world of nature. This style has a number of advantages for Newton. The most important is that it permits him to explore the mathematical consequences of his assumptions one by one without having to face the impossible task of analyzing the properties of the complex physical world all at once. Furthermore, if we accept Newton's position, expressly stated in Book 1, Section 11, we can study the effects of forces of attraction without having to face the inhibiting fact that the reigning natural philosophy, the "mechanical philosophy," will not consider acceptable the concept of a force that is not the result of a material push or pull, that is not the result of some kind of contact between bodies.

Of course, it would have been obvious to every reader that Newton's goal was to display and analyze the physics of planetary motion. In the end, he would show that the celestial phenomena declare the action of an inverse-square force and he would boldly assert that this force is gravity, by which he means the force (whatever its cause) that produces weight here on Earth and that he can show must extend as far out as the Moon.

Newton himself was troubled by the idea of a universal gravitating force extending through space, and he tried again and again to find a way to account for its action. But, as he explained in the final General Scholium, he had no doubt that a force of universal gravity "really" exists. Newton did not disparage attempts to explain how gravity might act, but he believed that such considerations should not inhibit the use of the concept of universal gravity. His successors – including such giants as Euler, Clairaut, d'Alembert, Lagrange, and above all Laplace – were not inhibited by concerns about the nature of a force like universal gravity, and thus they found new principles and tremendously enlarged the subject that Newton had explored in the *Principia*.[28]

NOTES

1 All translations from the *Principia* in this chapter come from Isaac Newton, *The Principia, Mathematical Principles of Natural Philosophy: A New Translation*, trans. I. Bernard Cohen and Anne Whitman (Berkeley: University of California Press, 1999), containing a "Guide to Newton's *Principia*" by I. B. Cohen.

2 On Newton's concepts of force, see Richard S. Westfall, *Force in Newton's Physics: The Science of Dynamics in the Seventeenth Century* (London: Macdonald; New York: American Elsevier, 1971); Max Jammer, *Concepts of Force* (Cambridge, MA: Harvard University Press, 1957). On Newton's concept of force in the *Principia*, see Bruce Brackenridge, *The Key to Newton's Dynamics: The Kepler Problem and the* Principia (Berkeley: University of California Press, 1995); vol. 6 of D. T. Whiteside (ed.), *The Mathematical Papers of Isaac Newton*, 8 vols. (Cambridge: Cambridge University Press, 1967–81); François de Gandt, *Force and Geometry in Newton's* Principia, trans. Curtis Wilson (Princeton: Princeton University Press, 1995); and my "Guide to

Newton's *Principia*"; also my "Newton's Concept of Force and the Second Law," pp. 143–85 in Robert P. Palter (ed.), *The Annus Mirabilis of Sir Isaac Newton 1666–1966* (Cambridge, MA: MIT Press, 1970) and my *The Newtonian Revolution* (Cambridge: Cambridge University Press, 1980; a revised edition is in progress).

3   Here and there in the *Principia*, Newton introduces some other types of force, among them magnetic force (said in Book 3, Proposition 6, Corollary 5, to be as the inverse cube of the distance), a general force of attraction that is as the inverse cube of the distance (Book 1, Proposition 41, Corollary 3), and a hypothesized force of repulsion between particles of an "elastic fluid" (or compressible gas) inversely proportional to the distance between adjacent, proximate particles (Book 2, Proposition 23).

4   In his thinking about the forces of nature, Newton also developed the concept of "passive" and "active" forces. On this topic, see J. E. McGuire, "Force, Active Principles, and Newton's Invisible Realm," *Ambix* 15 (1968) 154–208, and "Neoplatonism, Active Principles and the Corpus Hermeticum," pp. 93–142 of Robert S. Westman and J. E. McGuire, *Hermeticism and the Scientific Revolution* (Los Angeles: William Andrews Clark Memorial Library, University of California, 1977). See, further, Betty Jo Teeter Dobbs, *The Janus Faces of Genius: The Role of Alchemy in Newton's Thought* (Cambridge: Cambridge University Press, 1991).

5   Alan Cook, *Edmond Halley: Charting the Heavens and the Seas* (Oxford: Clarendon Press, 1998), p. 151.

6   This translation was first proposed by Alexandre Koyré and later confirmed by I. B. Cohen.

7   Ernst Mach, *The Science of Mechanics: A Critical and Historical Account of Its Development*, trans. Thomas J. McCormack, 6th edn, with revisions from the 9th German edn (La Salle: The Open Court Publishing Company, 1960), ch. 2, §7: "As we can only define density as the mass of unit volume, the circle is manifest."

8   But such criticism ignores Newton's own statement. Newton does *not* say that mass "is proportional to" the product of density and volume. The verb, as we have seen, is "oriri" in the form "orta est," meaning "arises from." If Newton had intended to say that a body's mass is jointly proportional to its volume and density, he would have done so. Such statements of joint proportionality are not uncommon in the *Principia*.

9   Furthermore, in Newton's day, densities were usually given as relative numerical quantities rather than as independent values. Thus John Harris, in his *Lexicon Technicum* of 1704, follows Newton in giving relative densities of substances, for example "the Density of Water to Air" or "the Density of Quick-Silver to Water."

Newton himself, in Book 2, Part 3, Proposition 10, of the *Opticks* (1704), describes how density is to be determined. The "Densities of the Bodies," he writes, are to be "estimated by their Specifick Gravities." There follows a table in which one column gives "The density and specifick gravity of the Body."

10 See my *Introduction to Newton's "Principia"* (Cambridge, MA: Harvard University Press; Cambridge: Cambridge University Press, 1971), ch. 4, §3.

11 I have translated *vis insita* by "inherent force," which seems to be Newton's equivalent term in English, but others have rendered it as "innate force." See my *Introduction*, ch. 3, 5.

12 *Vis insita* also appears in the writings of Kepler, notably in the *Astronomia Nova* and in the *Epitome Astronomiae Copernicanae*, but we have no evidence that Newton had read either of these Keplerian works before composing the *Principia*. See, further, my *Introduction* and "Guide."

13 For details see my "Guide," pp. 101–2.

14 On the choice of "uniformly straight forward" rather than the traditional "uniformly in a straight line," see the new translation cited above.

15 On the identity of phrases used by Newton and Descartes, see my *Introduction*.

16 Although Newton's example is a sound one, in accord with the accepted principles of physics, it was willfully misunderstood by Clifford Truesdell, who alleged that Newton was here expressing a belief in a kind of "circular inertia."

17 For example, W. W. Rouse Ball, *An Essay on Newton's* Principia (London: Macmillan and Co., 1893), p. 77: "The rate of change of momentum [per unit of time] is always proportional to the moving force impressed." In order to indicate that he was giving a modern paraphrase of what Newton wrote, Rouse Ball enclosed his insertion in square brackets.

18 For details see my paper in the *Annus Mirabilis* volume, cited in note 2 *supra*.

19 In other words, a speed V is proportional to the force and time and inversely proportional to the mass of the body in question. If t is the time in which a velocity V is generated in a mass m by a force F, then

$$V = (1/k) \times Ft/m$$

where k is a constant of proportionality. In this case,

$$F = km(V/t)$$

where V/t is the acceleration A. Plainly, Newton knew the second law for continuous forces. As we shall see below, Newton showed how to get from the second law as stated for impulsive forces to the continuous form of the law.

20 See the notes by Whiteside in his edition of Newton's *Mathematical Papers*, vol. 6, pp. 98–9 (n. 16), 148–9 (n. 152).

21 Quoted in full in my *Newtonian Revolution*, pp. 183–4; see John W. Herivel, *The Background to Newton's* Principia: *A study of Newton's Dynamical Researches in the Years 1664–84* (Oxford: Clarendon Press, 1965), pp. 141, 153.

22 Christiaan Huygens, *The Pendulum Clock*, trans. Richard J. Blackwell (Ames: Iowa State University Press, 1986).

23 D. T. Whiteside, "Newtonian Dynamics," *History of Science* 5 (1966), 104–17.

24 For a different view, see this volume, p. 93, n. 30.

25 In my discussions of this question with D. T. Whiteside, he has pointed out that there are two possibilities which lead to "*exactly* the same theory of central forces." One, favored by Leibniz, is that on a finite level "the orbit is built up of a series of infinitesimal discrete force-impulses." The other, Newton's favored approach, is that there is a "series of infinitesimal arcs generated by a continuous force (composed of infinitesimal discrete force-impulses)." The first is what Newton in 1687 and afterwards called "simul et semel," the latter being "gradatim et successive."

26 Alexandre Koyré *Newtonian Studies* (Cambridge, MA: Harvard University Press; London: Chapman & Hall, 1965).

27 This concluding statement is examined in detail in George Smith's chapter in this volume.

28 At the time of the second edition of the *Principia* (1713), Newton had hopes that a physical cause of the action of gravity might be found in the study of electricity; see A. Rupert Hall and Marie Boas Hall, *Unpublished Scientific Papers of Isaac Newton* (Cambridge: Cambridge University Press, 1962), pp. 361–2 and my "Guide", pp. 280–7. Also see Henry Guerlac's studies on Newton and Francis Hauksbee's electrical experiments in his *Essays and Papers in the History of Modern Science* (Baltimore, Johns Hopkins University Press, 1977). In the 1717–18 edition of the *Opticks*, Query 21, Newton expressed the thought that the cause of gravity might be an "aetherial medium" of varying density.

3   Curvature in Newton's dynamics

INTRODUCTION

The first edition of Isaac Newton's *Principia* was published in 1687, followed by a second edition in 1713 and a third in 1726, the year before he died. The *Principia* is universally held to have been a major turning point in natural philosophy in the seventeenth century. That turning point is clearly reflected in the comparison of the title of Descartes's 1644 *Principles of Philosophy* with the title of Newton's *Mathematical Principles of Natural Philosophy*. Even though both men were noted mathematicians, Newton's book is distinguished from that of Descartes by virtue of being a *mathematical description of nature*. In the General Scholium of the second edition Newton sets out the difference quite clearly: "But hitherto I have not been able to discover the cause of those properties of gravity from phenomena, and I frame no hypotheses... And to us it is enough, that gravity does exist, and acts according to the [mathematical] laws which we have explained."[1] Although Newton was strongly influenced by the Cartesian mechanical philosophy during the first two decades of his scholarly work, he nevertheless expressed himself analytically from the very beginning of his work in 1664. By 1684, however, he had rejected Cartesian mechanical explanations for gravity, and in the *Principia* he emphasized the analytical expression of the inverse-square law for gravity. The final impetus for that rejection came from Newton's correspondence in 1679 with Robert Hooke,[2] which led Newton to derive Kepler's area law as a geometrical measure of time to employ in analyzing orbital motion. That same correspondence has shown that Newton's later work is an extension, not a revision, of his earlier work.[3,4]

In particular, the role of "curvature" in Newton's dynamics emerges as a major factor in the analysis of general curvilinear motion in both his early and mature work. As early as 1664, Newton had developed the concept of curvature as a measure of the rate of bending of curves:[5] that is, the change in the slope of the curve as a function of position on the curve. For example, a circle has a constant rate of bending and thus the curvature is the same at all points, while an ellipse has a changing rate of bending and thus the curvature is *not* the same at all points.[6] By 1671 curvature appeared as an important element in his *Method of Series and Fluxions*. The role of curvature in Newton's revised editions of the *Principia* was clearly recognized by eighteenth- and nineteenth-century commentators, and in fact was seen by many as the principal method of analysis despite Newton's representation of it in the revised *Principia* as an "alternate method."[7] Most twentieth-century commentators, however, have not been concerned with the role curvature played in Newton's dynamics.[8] Recently, however, it has been argued that curvature not only played a role in the *Principia*, but was the primary mathematical device employed by Newton in his *early* analysis of dynamical problems,[9] and it continued to serve him from his very first calculations as a student in 1665, through the initial 1687 edition of the *Principia*,[10] and into the revised editions of 1713 and 1726.[11, 12, 13]

The application of curvature to Newton's dynamics is linked to the analysis of *uniform circular motion*: circular because the path is a circle and uniform because the radius of the circle sweeps out equal arcs and angles in equal times. Such motion was seen by early Greek astronomers as central to the analysis of planetary motion. Plato is reported to have set the challenge for astronomers to find the set of uniform circular motions that would "save the phenomena"; that is, he wanted to find a way of using combinations of uniform circular motions to explain the apparent wandering motions of the planets. It is in this tradition of "celestial circularity" that astronomers from Hipparchus and Ptolemy to Copernicus and Kepler worked.[14] The role of circular motion in Newton's analysis of planetary motion is dramatically different from that of these early astronomers, but as John Herivel points out, that role is a critical one.

It is worth pausing for a moment to consider how fortunate the existence of uniform circular motion was for Newton, and how important his successful treatment of it for the whole future development of his dynamics. Apart from motion in a circle, the only relatively simple kinds of movement available for study by Newton were rectilinear, parabolic, and elliptical. The first two occurred in motion under gravity at the Earth's surface, and had already been fully explored, at least in their kinematical aspects, by Galileo. Both bulked large in the growth of Newton's dynamical thought, especially uniformly accelerated rectilinear motion, the paradigm case for all other more complicated motions. But neither of these motions admitted of any development of the concept of force. On the other hand, the elliptical motion discerned by Kepler in the unruly movements of the planet Mars was far too difficult and complex a case for Newton to treat first. In contrast, the problem of uniform circular motion was at once not impossibly difficult and yet of sufficient complexity to call for a real advance in his concept of force and his method of applying it to motion in a curved path.[15]

Herivel was not aware, however, that curvature provided Newton with an early method of extending the analysis of uniform circular motion to the analysis of curvilinear motion in general. It was not until after the 1679 correspondence with Robert Hooke,[16] which led Newton to the derivation of Kepler's area law, that he was able to obtain the solution for the problem of elliptical motion presented in the *Principia*. Between 1664 and 1684, however, Newton used curvature and the analytical expression for the force required to maintain uniform circular motion to address the more general problem of curvilinear motion.

UNIFORM CIRCULAR MOTION

Newton's first investigations into dynamics, appearing in his bound notebook, the *Waste Book*, were concerned with collisions. The only date among the dynamical entries in the *Waste Book* was the marginalia, "Jan. 20th, 1664" (1665 new style), that appeared in a section devoted to problems of collisions between two perfectly elastic bodies.[17] In this section, Newton developed and refined concepts and axioms of motion that Descartes had set out in 1644. For Descartes, the natural state of motion of a body is to remain at rest or, if set initially into motion by an external cause, to remain in uniform rectilinear motion. Thus, an object of and by itself will not move in a curved path unless it is acted upon by an external cause.[18] This basic principle of linear inertia appears implicitly in all of Newton's early work, and it appears explicitly in all editions of Newton's *Principia*.[19]

Herivel reports that the first discussion by Newton of the problem of circular motion is found at Axiom 20 of the *Waste Book*, in which a ball moves in a circular path on the interior of a hollow spherical surface.[20] Following Descartes, Newton observes that there is a constant tendency for the ball at any point to continue in the instantaneous direction of its motion along the tangent to the circle. Because the ball moves in a circle instead of along the tangent, Newton argues that a continuous force must act on it. This force can only arise from the pressure between the ball and the spherical surface. But if the surface presses on the ball, the ball must press on the surface, and Newton is led to the following axiom:

Axiom 21. Hence it appears that all bodies moved circularly have an endeavor from the center about which they move, otherwise the body . . . would not continually press upon . . . [the hollow sphere].[21]

In the *Principia*, Newton reproduced a version of this early analysis of circular motion. In 1664/5, he used the Cartesian terminology "outward endeavor," but he replaced it by Huygens's "centrifugal force" when it appeared as the last line of the Scholium to Proposition 4 in Book 1 of the revised 1713 and 1726 *Principia*:

Scholium. This is the centrifugal force, with which the body impels the circle: and to which the contrary force, wherewith the circle continually repels the body towards the center, is equal.[22]

It has been argued that in the 1664 version Newton held the opinion that the outward endeavor is an outward force that counterbalances the inward force and that he continued to hold this opinion until after 1679. Yet this early statement appears to be very similar to the later statement. In the *Waste Book* the body is said to press upon the sphere, and in the *Principia* the body is said to press upon the circle. In both cases the body is deflected from its natural tangential rectilinear motion by the action of an inward radial force. In the case of circular motion, as considered here, the two forces are equal and both lie along the radius. That condition, however, does not hold for general orbital motion. It is critical to note that for general orbital motion Newton never applied the term *centrifugal force* except when the radius is either a maximum or minimum, that is, at

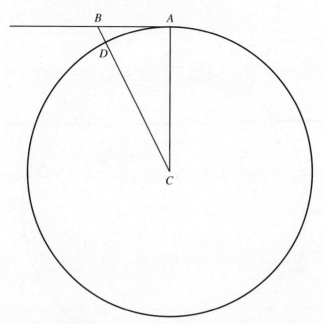

Fig. 3.1 A particle at *A* rotates uniformly in a circle *AD* constrained by a string attached to *C*, the center of the circle. The line *AB* is the tangent to the circle at the point *A*.

extreme points where the force does lie along the radius of the circle of curvature. This important distinction serves to clarify the specific role Newton assigned to centrifugal force in general orbital motion. Newton's careful restricted use of "centrifugal force," however, was lost as it evolved during the following centuries to the current view that centrifugal force is "fictitious."[23]

Central to all of Newton's analysis of curvilinear motion is the representation of the force by the displacement it produces in a given time. In Figure 3.1, the line *AB* is tangent to the circle *AD* at the point *A*. The distance *BD* between a nearby point *B* on the tangential displacement and the corresponding point *D* on the circle, to be called the *deviation*, is proportional to Newton's measure of the force required to maintain the uniform circular motion. In his *Two New Sciences*, Galileo demonstrated that the linear displacement down an inclined plane is directly proportional to the constant acceleration acting down the plane and to the square of the time.[24] Huygens, and independently Newton, demonstrated that the force (acceleration) required to produce the linear radial deviation *BD* from the tangent

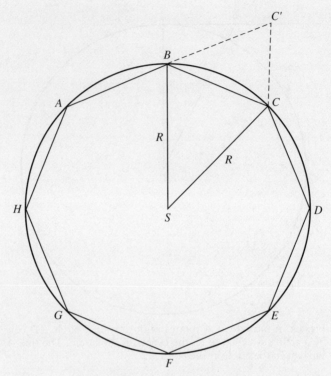

Fig. 3.2 A polygon *AB*, *BC*, etc. is inscribed in a circle of radius *R*. A particle moving with uniform velocity from *A* to *B* experiences an impulsive force at *B* and is then directed toward *C*. If the impulsive force had not acted, then the particle would have moved to *C′* in the same time that it moves to *C*.

in uniform circular motion is directly proportional to the square of the tangential speed and inversely proportional to the radius of the circle. Newton eventually applied this result for uniform circular motion to the analysis of general curvilinear motion by means of the circle of curvature.

Before he arrived at an expression for the force required for uniform circular motion, however, he recorded in the opening pages of the *Waste Book* a relatively less sophisticated study of uniform circular motion, one that uses a polygon as the initial representation of a circle.[25] In Figure 3.2 the polygon is inscribed in a circle of radius *R*, as in Newton's 1665 entry to the *Waste Book*. A particle travels with a constant velocity *V* from point *A* to point *B* along a linear portion *AB* of the polygon. At point *B* it 'collides' with the circle and experiences a change in velocity ΔV due to the impulsive action of the force at point B, which is directed toward the center of the circle S. The magnitude of velocity V is unchanged, but the direction is now along the linear portion BC. Newton first obtains a relationship for the polygon and then investigates that relationship as the number of sides of the polygon is increased until, in the limit of very small sides, the polygon approaches the circle. The limiting process is central to all of Newton's analysis; it is used, for example, in Proposition 1 of the *Principia* to obtain Kepler's area law.

Analysis

If the particle had not encountered the circle at B, then it would have traveled to the point C' in the same time interval T as it traveled to the point C. The distance $BC = BC' = V \times T$, and the distance $CC' = \Delta V \times T$ and is parallel to the radius BS (because the force at B was directed toward the center of the circle S). The distance CC' is the *deviation* of the particle from rectilinear motion due to the force at B and is thus the measure of the force imparted to the particle at point B. Newton then increases the number of sides of the polygon until it approaches the circle as a *limit*. In that limit, Newton demonstrates that a property of the motion is that "the force of all the reflections [the scalar sum of the impulses] is to the force of the body's motion [the scalar linear momentum] as the sum of the sides [of the inscribed polygon] is to the radius of the [circumscribed] circle." That property has no apparent application, but the two factors used in its derivation, the deviation as a measure of the force and the expansion to the limit, continue to be hallmarks of Newton's dynamics.[26]

Newton's first solution to the problem of uniform circular motion appeared in a manuscript written before 1669, now called *On Circular Motion*.[27] In contrast to the previous analysis, in which the path begins as a polygon, the path begins as a circle. Newton again used the deviation as a measure of the force and again called upon a limiting process. Figure 3.3 is from Newton's figure in that manuscript. A particle moves along a circular arc from P to Q under the influence of a force directed toward the center of the circle S.

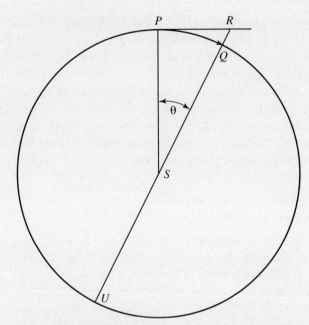

Fig. 3.3 A particle moves along a circular arc from P to Q under the influence of a force directed toward the center of the circle S. The line PR is the tangent to the circle at the point P and the line segment QR is the deviation from the tangent at point Q.

If no force acted upon the particle, it would continue along the tangent to point R. Because the force does act upon it, however, it moves instead to the point Q. Newton used the uniform angular rate and a version of a Euclidean theorem to solve the direct problem of uniform circular motion. He demonstrated that the force required to maintain uniform circular motion is constant, proportional to the given radius of the circle divided by the square of the constant period; or, what is the same, the square of the magnitude of the tangential velocity divided by the given radius, a result first published by Huygens.

Analysis

Referring to Figure 3.3, one has the following relationship from Euclid Book 3, Proposition 36:[28]

$RU/PR = PR/QR,$

which Newton applies to circular motion. In the limit as the point Q approaches the point P, Newton notes that the line RU approaches the diameter QU and the tangential displacement PR approaches the arc or chord QP. Hence, that limit is given as follows:

$$\text{limit } QR/QP^2 = 1/QU.$$

For uniform circular motion $QP = vt$, where v is the constant tangential velocity and t is a small time interval. Correspondingly in the limit as the time interval t vanishes

$$\text{limit } QR/t^2 = v^2 \text{ limit } QR/QP^2 = v^2/QU = (1/2)v^2/r$$

where $r = QU/2 = SP$ is the radius of the circle.[29]

Here, and in Lemma 10 of the *Principia*, Newton is applying the Galilean relation, $s \propto t^2$ "at the very start of motion." This relation applies to a displacement in a direction normal to the tangent of the orbit as well as to a displacement along the tangent. Hence, for uniform circular motion the radial acceleration or central force a_r is a constant given by the ratio v^2/r.[30]

CONIC MOTION

The types of problems in dynamics that initially challenged Newton were known in the late seventeenth and early eighteenth centuries as *direct problems*; that is, given the path of the particle and the location of the center of force, find the mathematical expression of the force required to maintain that motion. They are to be contrasted with *inverse problems*; that is, given the mathematical expression of the force as a function of distance, find the path of the particle relative to a given center of force. For direct problems with a single body in orbit about a fixed center of force, the mass of the body is not a factor, and the force is determined by the acceleration, or what Newton calls the *accelerative quantity* of the force (Definition 7, Book 1) in the *Principia*. Having solved the direct problem of uniform circular motion, the question then arose of how to extend this technique to evaluate acceleration or force for nonuniform motion along an arbitrary curve or orbit, and in particular for elliptical motion, as Kepler had proposed for the planets.

The primary challenge was to find a geometrical measure for the time interval. In uniform circular motion the radius sweeps out equal arcs and angles in equal times, and the time interval t can be obtained in terms of the fraction of the total period of revolution T given by the ratio $t/T = \text{arc}(QP)/\text{circumference}(\pi QU)$. The answer that Newton found after 1679 for any force directed toward a fixed center was that the radius sweeps out equal *areas* in equal times. It was fifteen years after his initial development of dynamics, however, before Newton discovered this justification for Kepler's area law. After he discovered it, he could measure the time interval by the area swept by the radius vector and apply it in a measure of force to a series of direct problems. Until that discovery, Newton had to seek other ways of treating direct and inverse problems.

The earliest reference to a method for treating elliptical motion appears in 1664/5 in Newton's journal, the *Waste Book*, immediately following his discussion of the polygonal technique applied to uniform circular motion. Newton states here that the force required to maintain elliptical motion can be found from the circle of curvature.

If the body b moved in an Elipsis, then its force in each point (if its motion in that point bee given) may bee found by a tangent circle of Equall crookednesse with that point of the Ellipsis.[31]

In his early work on mathematics, Newton had developed the circle of curvature as a measure of the bending or "crookednesse" of a curve, and as early as December of 1664 he had developed a method for finding centers of curvature along an ellipse.[32] In this statement from the *Waste Book* Newton claims that curvature can be employed to provide a solution to the direct problem of elliptical motion given the velocity, i.e., "the motion." *The Waste Book* does not contain such a solution, but later, after his discovery of the origin of the area law, it is given in detailed form in his unpublished 1690 revisions of the *Principia* and as the alternate measure of force in Proposition 6 of the revised 1713 *Principia*. The curvature measure of force is also used in the 1687 *Principia* in Proposition 15, Book 2, on the analysis of orbital decay caused by a resisting medium, and also in Proposition 28, Book 3, on the analysis of lunar motion perturbed by the gravitational force of the Sun. (See below, pp. 117–24.)

The question of when Newton first developed a curvature measure of force has received a new answer in recent years. The first published report of the cryptic curvature statement was by Herivel in 1965, but he observes only that "Newton is already pondering the more difficult problem of motion in an ellipse."[33] The cryptic curvature statement was published next by Whiteside in 1967, where he points out that the use of curvature is valid in arbitrary curves as well as in an ellipse.[34] In 1992, one of the authors of this chapter, Brackenridge, published a chapter in a *Festschrift* for Whiteside entitled "The Critical Role of Curvature in Newton's Developing Dynamics," in which he concluded that "the evidence is clear that such ideas [curvature] were in Newton's thoughts on dynamics as early as 1664, that they appeared in his solutions of 1684, and that they reached fruition in his unpublished revisions of the 1690's."[35] The reference to 1664 was to the cryptic curvature statement, the reference to 1684 was to an alternate solution employing curvature not included in the 1687 *Principia* (later sent to John Locke), and the reference to 1690 is to the unpublished revisions. Brackenridge did not have evidence of Newton's use of curvature in the solution of orbital problems in the two decades between 1664 and 1684. Nauenberg, the other author of this chapter, supplied the missing evidence on Newton's early computational methods for general orbital motion.[36, 37]

NEWTON'S EARLY COMPUTATIONAL METHOD FOR DYNAMICS

In 1679 Robert Hooke, who was then Secretary of the Royal Society, initiated a correspondence with Newton that is of considerable interest because it reveals the state of development of Newton's understanding of orbital dynamics at that time. In a letter of 13 December 1679, Newton discussed the orbits of a body under the action of general central forces.[38] In a corner of the letter is a drawing of an orbit for the case in which the force is constant, and in the text of the letter Newton discusses the changes that occur in such an orbit when the force is no longer constant. Newton's correct geometrical description of these orbits indicates that he had a much deeper understanding of orbital dynamics at this time than has generally been attributed to him. For example, he pointed out that these orbits have a maximum and minimum distance from the center, and that the angle subtended by these extremal points from the center increases as the force becomes "greater towards the center." In the past, however, most Newtonian scholars have underestimated Newton's understanding of this problem because his figure gives the magnitude of this angle in gross disagreement with the upper bound for a constant central force.[39] Newton did not reveal any details of the method by which he obtained this orbit except to indicate that it was an approximation, stating that

Your acute Letter having put me upon considering thus far the species of this curve, I might add something about its description by points *quam proxime*. But the thing being of no great moment. I rather beg your pardon for having troubled you thus far with this second scribble...

Newton did reveal, however, that he knew of other orbits beyond that due to a constant force. In particular, he wrote of the orbit due to a special force for which the body would *spiral* toward the center.

For the increase of gravity in the descent may be supposed such that the body shall by an infinite number of spiral revolutions descend continually till it cross the center by motion transcendently swift...

This remark is of great importance because an orbit with an *infinite number of spiral revolutions* cannot be obtained by any approximation method; thus, Newton must have used here an analytical method. The analytical proofs in the *Principia*, however, depend on the area law (to eliminate the time variable, reducing the problem to a geometrical one), and there is strong evidence that Newton did not discover the area law until after his 1679 correspondence with Hooke.[40] In his letter to Hooke, Newton did not give the radial dependence of this force, but he did give it in a canceled scholium to a revision of "De motu" (the short tract of late 1684 presaging the *Principia*) in which he effectively repeated the content of his letter.[41] Newton stated that the force required for a spiral orbit varies inversely with the cube of the distance.

It is of considerable interest to discover Newton's computational method by "points *quam proxime*" because it provides us with insight into how he developed orbital dynamics. The errors in Newton's drawing of the orbit for a constant central force have generally been attributed to some failure in his approximations.[42] A careful examination of Newton's figure, however, reveals that he made a substantial error only while *drawing* the figure representing the orbit, but not in its *calculation*. Moreover, the examination reveals that Newton's early computational method not only enabled him to calculate an orbit for a constant central force (after proper account has been taken of the drawing errors) but also to calculate orbits for forces that are not constant, but that increase with distance toward the center of force. Finally, Newton's early computational method does not depend upon the area law; this is an important historical constraint because at the time of the Newton–Hooke correspondence Newton, by his own account, had not yet discovered that the area law is a general consequence of central forces.

It is possible to employ curvature to obtain the correct angles and to account for Newton's figure without having recourse to the area law. Instead, a relation involving the change of velocity with distance, which depends on the component of the force tangential to the orbit, leads to an equation of motion based on Newton's fluxional approach to curvature. Moreover, for certain orbits, Newton could have solved the direct problem with this equation analytically. For example, the simplest non-trivial case is the spiral curve, which corresponds to the inverse-cube force (details to follow).

Since the publication of Newton's letter to Hooke, the large error (approximately 30°) in the angle between the successive apogees of the orbit in Newton's diagram has been noted by many scholars as evidence that Newton had not yet gained a proper understanding of orbital dynamics. This error is paradoxical, however, because the other features of the curve are correct; the orbit has approximate symmetries and it returns repeatedly to an apparent circumscribed circle. It is difficult to see, therefore, how an approximate method that gives such large errors in the angular position does not violate fundamental laws. Careful examination of the figure, however, indicates that the source of the angular error is not in the early computational method, but rather in certain features of the drawing itself. Figure 3.4 is Newton's diagram and it shows an orbit *AFOGHJKL* circumscribed by an apparent circle *ABDEA*, but the orthogonal axes *AD* and *BE* on this figure do not divide it into equal quadrants. Moreover, measurements of the distance of the crossing point *C* of these axes to the circumscribed curve reveal that this curve is not actually a circle; instead only the segment *KDHE* of this curve is part of a circle centered at *C*. Finally, the segment *AFOGH* displays mirror symmetry,

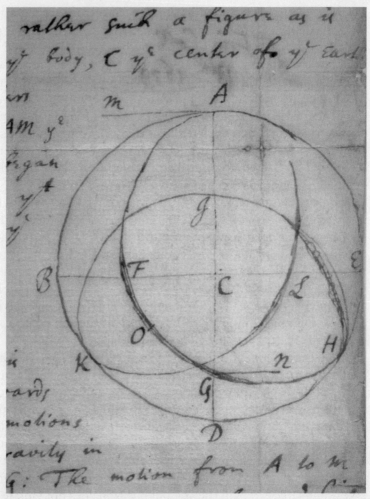

Fig. 3.4 Newton's drawing of the orbit for a constant radial force which appears on the upper right-hand corner of his letter to Hooke written on 13 December 1679.

but the rest of the figure does not. The property of mirror symmetry can be demonstrated by taking a transparency of Newton's diagram, reversing it, and putting it over the original diagram. If one aligns the reversed apogee H with the original apogee A, and vice versa, then the curve AFOGH and the reversed curve HGOFA will be identical, thus displaying mirror symmetry. Inspection of such a composite transparency shows that the segment $AFOGH$ does lie on its mirror image, but that the center C of the reversed mirror image (hereafter C_S) is *shifted up relative to the center C* of the original diagram and lies in the quadrant ACB. Measuring distances to the circumscribed curve $ABKDHEA$ from C_S, one finds that part of the curve BAE is a segment of a circle centered at C_S, with the same radius as the segment $KDHE$ measured relative to C.

These errors in the drawing reveal the graphical construction that Newton used to obtain his figure. Assuming that he had a method to calculate a segment AFO of the orbit, and that for this segment the force is centered at C_S, then he obtained the remaining segment OGH of the curve by a mirror reflection and rotation of the segment AFO. He evidently made an error in shifting the center C relative to C_S, however, and then he incorrectly adjusted the rotation in order to join these two segments of the orbital curve as smoothly as possible. This adjustment is also apparent in the section FOG of the drawing of this orbit where Newton uses multiple lines to patch up the break in the curve due to the incorrect rotation. In the text Newton refers to the point O as the "nearest approach of the body to the center C." This statement must be interpreted with some care, however, because the figure has not one center C, but two centers C and C_S. Indeed, while O is the point on the segment $AFOGH$ nearest to the center C, this center applies only to the segment OGH. Therefore, the appropriate angle subtended between the radial vectors along the maximum and minimum distances to C is the angle HCO between the radial lines HC and OC. This angle, when measured from the diagram, is found to be approximately $107°$, which is only about $3°$ larger than the maximum computed angle of $180°/\sqrt{3} \approx 103.9°$ for constant central force.[43] If one does not realize that the point C is not the actual center of force for this segment of the orbit, however, then the angle between apogee and perigee of this segment of the orbit appears to be the angle ACO. When measured from the diagram, that angle is found to be approximately $130°$, which is about $26°$ larger than the maximum computed angle of $103.9°$. That discrepancy is the source of much of the negative criticism of Newton's method, but it arises from an error in shifting the centers of the template when drawing the figure, and not from the curvature method of calculation.[44]

Newton's curvature method of computation

The preceding discussion has been largely concerned with Newton's construction of the diagram. We now turn to consideration of the computational method employing curvature by which Newton could have obtained the curve, and in particular how he calculated the segment AFO of the orbit between apogee and perigee.

Analysis

For a body moving on a circular orbit with radius ρ with a uniform velocity v, Newton had shown in 1665 that the force or acceleration f is directed toward the center of the orbit, with a magnitude[45]

$$f = v^2/\rho \tag{1}$$

This relation had also been obtained somewhat earlier by Huygens.[46] During this time Newton evidently had already started to think about the generalization of this result for an elliptical trajectory, as shown by the cryptic remark in his manuscript on circular motion. If the force is directed to a fixed center C, as in Figure 3.5, then the appropriate generalization of Eq. (1) for the acceleration, assumed to be proportional to the force, at a point P on the orbit is given by[47]

$$f_n = v^2/\rho \tag{2}$$

where $f_n = f \sin(\alpha)$ is the component of the force (acceleration) normal to the tangential velocity, $\rho = PQ$ is the radius of curvature at P, and α is the angle between the radius vector CP and the tangent to the curve at P. Given initially f and v, during a small interval of time δt the trajectory can then be approximated by the arc of circle obtained by rotating the radius of curvature vector through a small angle $\phi = v\delta t/p$ about Q. At the end of this time interval the magnitude of the velocity v changes by an amount

$$\delta v = f_t \delta t \tag{3}$$

where $f_t = a \cos(\alpha)$ is the component of force (acceleration) along the tangential velocity to the orbit at P. Thus, at the end

Curvature method

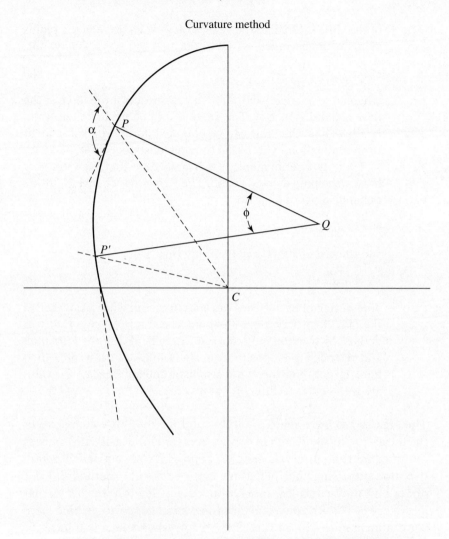

Fig. 3.5 Illustrating how a segment PP' of an orbit is obtained by rotating the radius of curvature vector PQ into $P'Q$ about its fixed center of curvature Q through an angle ϕ, while the center of force is located at C. The dashed lines PC and $P'C$ are the radial positions with respect to C, and the angle alpha is the angle between the tangent to the curve at P and the radial line PC.

of the time interval δt the velocity is $v' \approx v + \delta v$, and the radius of curvature becomes

$$\rho' \approx v'/f'_n \tag{4}$$

where $f'_n = f' \sin(\alpha')$ and f' is the magnitude of the force at the new radial distance r'. The angle α' can be evaluated geometrically. Thus, the orbit can be obtained during the subsequent time intervals δt by iterating the previous procedure.

There is a refinement in this procedure that Newton may have also applied at this time. The first-order change δr in the radial distance is given by

$$\delta r = -v\delta t \cos(\alpha) \tag{5}$$

and therefore Eqs. (3) and (5) imply that

$$v\delta v = -a\delta r \tag{6}$$

Integration of Eq. (6) leads to a special case of what is now called the law of conservation of energy; it is a relationship that was derived by Newton in Proposition 39 in Book 1 of the *Principia*, and extended in Proposition 40, along similar lines as presented here. Hence, Newton could also have applied this law to evaluate v' in Eq. (2) at different values of r.

The area law is only approximately valid for the finite step sizes of the curvature method, and in applications one finds that areas swept out in equal time intervals are only *approximately* equal. Therefore it is not surprising that Newton's early curvature method did not direct him to the area law for central forces. Newton was led to that discovery by Hooke's physical ideas on orbital dynamics, which were communicated to him in the 1679/80 correspondence. In a letter to Hooke, Newton remarked that

if its gravity be supposed uniform it will not descend in a spiral to the very center but circulate with an alternate ascent & descent by it's *vis centrifuga & gravity* alternatively overballancing one another...

This reference to "overballancing one another" has been taken to imply that "before 1679, Newton – like Descartes, Borelli, and Leibniz – believed that orbital motion depended on the imbalance between gravity and centrifugal force,"[48] where the centrifugal force acted upon the body in the same way as gravity. We here give quite a different meaning to the phrase as used by Newton in this curvature calculation in particular, and as used by Newton in orbital calculations generally.[49]

Newton first elected to consider motion under a constant central force function, that is, the motion depicted in the drawing in the letter to Hooke (see Figure 3.4).

I then took the simplest case for computation, which was that of gravity uniform in a medium not resisting...

Referring now to Figure 3.6, if the initial velocity v_0 is perpendicular to the initial radial distance $r_0 = AC$ (angle $\alpha_0 = \pi/2$) and if it has a magnitude such that the radius of curvature $\rho_0 = Aa$ is *less than AC*, where $\rho_0 = v_0^2/f_0$, then the radial distance will decrease, and the body will begin to descend toward the center of force. For a constant force, the radius of curvature ρ must increase monotonically until the curvature vector becomes parallel with the radius vector. Here at point O (F), as in the initial state at point A, the velocity vector is normal to the radius vector CF $(C_s O)$ (angle $\alpha = \pi/2$), and the radius of curvature MO is parallel to the radius vector CO and reaches an extremum value. Since the radius of curvature MO is now *greater than* the radial distance CO, the radial distance will increase, and therefore the body begins its "ascent" from the center of force as Newton indicated in his letter to Hooke. Newton could now apply a fundamental symmetry of the curvature method to deduce the subsequent evolution of the orbit. The continuation of this orbit by rotations of the curvature vector gives a curve that is just the reflection across the radial line CO of the orbit from A to O.

As Newton indicated in his letter to Hooke, he had found that orbits for central forces approach a minimum distance from the center of force, or may even pass through this center. The curvature method indicates that when r is a minimum or a maximum, the radius vector is perpendicular to the orbit (i.e., $\alpha = \pi/2$). In this case the radius of curvature vector becomes parallel to the radius vector. It is then clear from reflection symmetry that the iteration of the orbit past this minimum distance is the same as the original iteration, but in *reverse order*. It is evident from Newton's diagram (see Figure 3.4) that he made use of this symmetry, although it is only approximate for finite step size, to draw successive branches of the orbit. This is

Constant Central Force

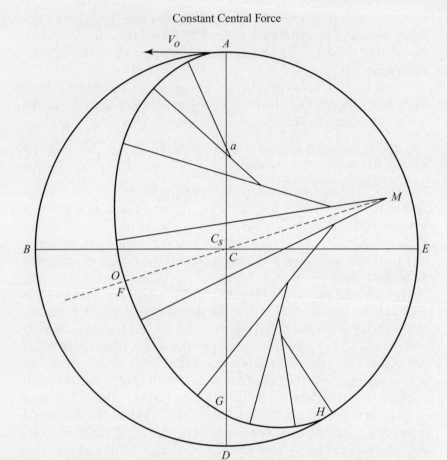

Fig. 3.6 The upper segment AO of the orbit for constant radial force as obtained by the iterations of the curvature method. The point O of closest approach to the center of force C is determined when the curvature vector MO crosses C. Then the lower segment OGH of the orbit is obtained by reflection symmetry of the segment AO about the axis OC.

shown explicitly in Figure 3.6, where the segment OGH of the orbit is obtained as the mirror reflection of the segment AO with the minimum distance OC as the axis of symmetry. This orbit is in good agreement with the exact orbit. If now the centers C_S and C are displaced by an amount corresponding to that mistakenly introduced in Newton's figure, and the lower segment OGH of the orbit is rotated

Constant Central Force

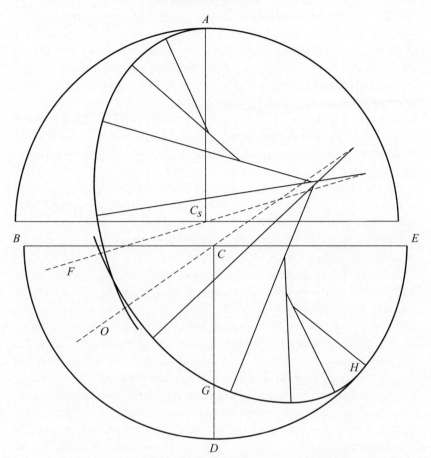

Fig. 3.7 A simulation which accounts for the angular error in Newton's drawing. The amount by which the center of force C, shown in Fig. 3.6, is shifted (relative to C_S) is obtained directly by reflection symmetry of Newton's diagram, Fig. 3.4.

by approximately 30', then Figure 3.7 is obtained. This figure gives a good approximation to Newton's diagram, as can be verified by superimposing Figure 3.7 on Newton's original diagram in Figure 3.4, after scaling it to the same size.

In the limit of small time steps, the curvature method (Eqs. 2 and 6) leads to equations of motion that can be solved analytically. Thus, Newton could have applied his curvature method to determine the relation between motion on a given curve and the radial dependence of the force, i.e., he could have solved some direct problems without being aware of the area law. The spiral orbit with a center of force at its pole is a particularly simple direct problem whose solution is an inverse-cube force.[50] In this way Newton could have discovered in a straightforward manner that for the inverse-cube force the orbit reaches the origin "by an infinite number of spiral revolutions," as he described it in his 13 December 1679 letter to Hooke. It is noteworthy that in "De motu" Newton quoted this result in a scholium without giving a geometrical demonstration as he did with his other propositions, and later on in the *Principia*, he applied the $1/r^3$ force law rather than the physically more interesting $1/r^2$ case, to solve explicitly the *inverse problem* (see Theorem 41, Corollary 3, Book 1).[51] Although Newton could also have applied his curvature method to solve the case of an elliptic orbit, there is no direct evidence that he actually carried out such a calculation.

The missing ingredient for a complete solution of the orbital problem, which must include the temporal as well as the spatial dependence of the motion, was provided by the fundamental idea of Hooke to view orbital motion as compounded by a tangential inertial velocity and a change of velocity impressed by the central force. This idea can be expressed in simple mathematical form for forces that act as periodic impulses for which the curvature method is not applicable, and it leads directly to the area law (see *Principia*, Proposition 1, Book 1). After the correspondence with Hooke, Newton evidently understood the equivalence of these two distinct physical approaches to orbital motion, but he never credited Hooke for his seminal contribution.

MEASURES OF FORCE IN THE *PRINCIPIA*: POLYGONAL, PARABOLIC, AND CURVATURE

The curvature method that Newton used to generate the curve in his 1679 correspondence with Hooke did not require the area law. In fact, Newton recounted to Halley in 1686 that it was following this correspondence with Hooke that he derived the area law in generating his solution to the direct problem of Kepler's ellipse. As remarked above (p. 90), in the opening pages of his 1664/5 *Waste Book*, Newton used a polygon as the initial representation of a circle, and a series of periodic impulsive forces of equal magnitude were directed toward the center of the circle. The final step was a limit-ing process in which the number of sides of the polygon increased until the polygon approached the circle, and a property of uniform circular motion was derived. Newton also used a generalized version of this polygonal technique to derive the area law in Theorem 1 of the 1684 "De motu," which appears with few revisions as Proposi-tion 1 of the 1687 *Principia*. A polygon was used to approximate an arbitrary smooth curve, and the motion was subject to a series of impulsive forces of variable magnitude that were directed toward a fixed center of force. The magnitude of this force is determined by the condition that after each impulse the body returns to the prescribed orbital curve. The final step again was a limiting process in which the number of sides of the polygon increased until it approached a general curve, demonstrating that in such motion the radius sweeps out equal areas in equal time: *uniform areal motion.*

The area law

Figure 3.8 is taken from the first proposition in the 1687 *Principia*, in which Newton derives Kepler's law of equal areas in equal time in-tervals. The path is a polygon described by a particle that experiences a periodic impulsive force directed toward a fixed center of force S in equal intervals of time T. The particle travels with constant ve-locity V_{AB} from point A to point B along a linear portion AB of the polygon. At point B it reaches the general curve and experiences a change in velocity ΔV due to the impulsive action of the force at B, which is directed toward the center of force S. In contrast to the circular motion, in this case the magnitude of the velocity generally changes, as well as the direction. Newton was able to use the same two factors, the deviation and limit, that he used previously in the analysis of circular motion to obtain a very important consequence for any force or force impulse directed toward a center S: the area law.

Analysis

If the particle had not received an impulse at B, it would have traveled to the point c in the same time T as it traveled to the point C. The distance $Bc = AB = V_{AB}T$ and the deviation Cc, which is due to the impulsive force at B, is parallel to SB.

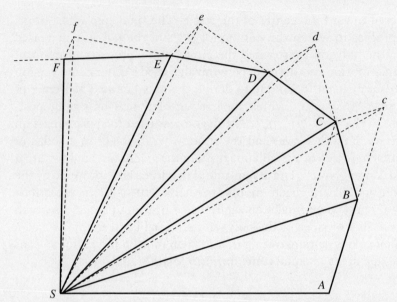

Fig. 3.8 Taken from Proposition 1, Book 1, 1687 *Principia*. At points *A*, *B*, *C*, etc., a particle is subject to a series of periodic impulsive forces of variable magnitude that are directed toward a given center of force *S*. A polygon *ABCDEF* is used to approximate an arbitrary smooth curve (not shown) that passes through each of the points. The magnitude of the force is determined by the condition that after each impulse the body returns to the prescribed curve (not shown in Newton's figure).

Figure 3.9(A) and 3.9(B) are taken from Figure 3.8; in Figure3. 9(A), triangles *SAB* and *SBC* have equal areas because they have equal bases *AB = Bc* and they have the same slant height *SX*. In Figure 3.9(B), the triangles *SBc* and *SBC* have equal areas because they have a common base *SB* and equal slant heights *cy = CY* (the deviation *Cc* is parallel to the impulsive force directed along *SB*). Thus, area *SAB* = area *ScB* = area *SBC*, and by extension this area is equal in turn to areas *SCD*, *SDE*, *SEE*, etc. Appealing to Corollary 4 of Lemma 3, which discusses the approximation of a curve by a polygon, Newton then increases the number of sides of the polygon which approaches a given general curve as a limit, and thus demonstrates that for any central force the radius sweeps out equal areas in equal times.[52] It is important to note that while Figure 3.8 does not show a curve associated with the vertices, Newton's reference to Lemma 3 indicates that

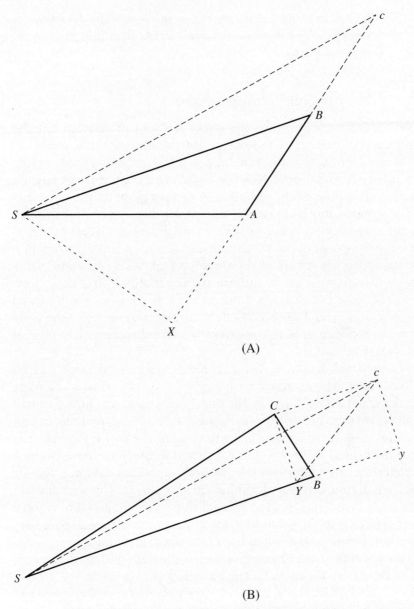

(A)

(B)

Fig. 3.9 Expanded from Fig. 3.8. (A) The triangles SAB and SBc have equal bases $AB = Bc$ and a common slant height SX. Thus, the triangles have equal areas. (B) The triangles SBC and SBc have a common base SB and equal slant heights $CY = cy$ (Cc is parallel to Yy). Thus, the triangles have equal areas.

he had in mind a curve that fixes the size of the deviations or impulses. There is considerable confusion on this point in the literature.[53]

The parabolic measure of force

Newton's first solution to the direct problem of uniform circular motion appeared before 1669 in a vellum manuscript now called *On Circular Motion*. In contrast to the polygonal technique used in 1664, in this later manuscript Newton began with a continuous circular path and considered the deviation between a point on the circle and the corresponding point on the tangent. He demonstrated that in the limit as the deviation becomes very small, the force (acceleration) is directly proportional to the rectilinear deviation and inversely proportional to the square of the time interval, where this interval is proportional to the arc in uniform circular motion. After 1679, however, Newton had developed the area law as a measure of time and so he could extend the technique to *any* central motion. The most famous application of this measure is to the direct problem of ideal planetary motion.

Galileo had demonstrated that motion under a constant gravitational force, when coupled with a projection velocity at some angle to the gravitational force, produces parabolic motion. During a small interval of time in Newton's measure of force, the instantaneous tangential velocity to a curve plays the role of the projection velocity; and the central force, which is a constant in the limit of vanishingly small time intervals, plays the role of the gravitational force. During that small time interval the orbital arc is represented by a parabola. In the 1687 *Principia*, Newton derived this parabolic measure of force and applied it to the solution of the direct problem of ideal planetary motion. Figure 3.10 is taken from Newton's figure for Proposition 6 of Book 1 of the 1687 *Principia* (which is the same as that in Theorem 3 of the 1684 "De motu"). The particle P moves along the general curve APQ under the action of a force centered at S. The force (acceleration) is proportional to the distance QR, divided by the square of the time interval, where QR is parallel to SP and the time interval δt is proportional to the triangular area $SP \times QT$. Thus, the parabolic measure of force $QR/\delta t^2$ is given by the ratio $QR/(QT \times SP)^2$.

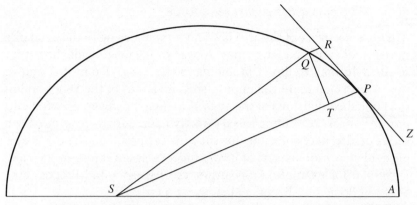

Fig. 3.10 Taken from Proposition 6, Book 1, 1687 *Principia*. The particle at *P* moves along the general curve *APQ* under the influence of a force center at *S*. The line *RPZ* is the tangent to the curve at *P* and the line *QR* is constructed parallel to the line *STP*.

Analysis

A particle moves along an arc *PQ* of a general curve *APQ* under the influence of a continuous force directed toward a center of force *S*. If no force acted upon the particle, it would continue along the tangent to point *R*. Because the force does act upon it, it moves instead along the arc *PQ*. Again, Newton obtains an appropriate measure for the force from the finite limit of the ratio of the "deviation" *QR* divided by the square of the time interval δ*t*, where the limit is taken as the time interval δ*t* vanishes and the point *Q* approaches the point *P*:[54]

Force $\propto$ acceleration $\propto$ Lim$[QR/\delta t^2] \propto$ Lim$[QR/(QT \times SP)^2]$

$\qquad = (1/SP^2)$Lim$[QR/QT^2]$.

To find the dependence of the force upon the radius *SP* for a given orbital curve and center of force, Newton expresses the ratio (QR/QT^2) in terms of the geometry of the orbital curve and then evaluates its limit as *Q* approaches *P*. In Proposition 11 Newton solved the direct problem of ideal planetary motion, an elliptical orbit with the center of force at a focus; he demonstrated that in the limit as *Q* approaches *P*, the ratio (QR/QT^2) approaches $1/L$, where *L* is the constant principal *latus rectum* of the ellipse. Thus, the force is proportional to the inverse square of the radius *SP*.

The curvature measure of force

After his discovery of the area law and its application to the parabolic measure of force, Newton may appear to have set aside curvature in the solutions to direct problems in the 1684 "De motu" and in the 1687 *Principia*. In the unpublished revisions of the 1690s and in the published revisions of the 1713 *Principia*, however, Newton employed a measure of force based directly upon curvature to provide a series of alternate solutions for these direct problems. There is ample evidence, moreover, that he did indeed use curvature in the 1687 *Principia*: for example, Proposition 15 of Book 2 and Propositions 26–29 of Book 3 as discussed below, pp. 117–24.[55]

Curvature is most evident in Lemma 11 of Book 1, which in the 1687 edition was only used in Proposition 4, Book 1 for the analysis of uniform circular motion and in Proposition 9, Book 1 for the analysis of spiral motion. In the revised editions, Newton gave a new solution for Proposition 4 that does not call upon Lemma 11. That lemma was given a central role, however, in the revised Proposition 6, Book 1 that provides the paradigm for analysis of all direct problems. Figure 3.11 is the diagram for Lemma 11 that appears in the 1687 *Principia* and in the revised editions that follow. The *general* curve *AbB* appears to be a circle, perhaps because the initial application was to the circular path in the figure in Proposition 4. In the revised editions, there is no figure in Proposition 4 and the first and major application of Lemma 11 is to the general curve in Proposition 6. There is no explicit mention of curvature in the text of Lemma 11 in the 1687 edition save for a reference to "the nature of circles passing through the points *A*, *B*, *G*; *A*, *b*, *g*," although curvature is implicit in the lemma. In the subsequent scholium, however, Newton specifies that Lemma 11 applies to curves where "the curvature is neither infinitely small nor infinitely large."[56] Figure 3.12 is an enhanced diagram for Lemma 11 with the general curve *AbB* no longer circular and with the addition of the two circles, *ABG* and *Abg*, that are explicit in Newton's text and the circle of curvature *AJ* that is implicit in the text.[57] Each circle is tangent to the general curve *AbB* at point *A*; circle *ABG* cuts the general curve at point *B* and circle *Abg* at point *b*; and they form their diameters at points *G*, *g*, and *J* respectively. Newton demonstrates that the square of the chord *AB* is equal to the product of the line *BD* (the subtense) and the diameter *AG*,

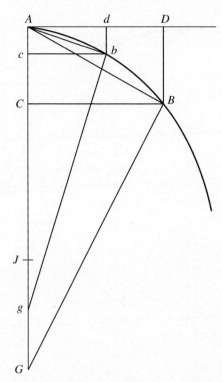

Fig. 3.11 Taken from Lemma 11, Book 1, 1687 *Principia*.

and therefore $AB^2/Ab^2 = (Bd \times AG)/(bd \times Ag)$. In the limit for curves of finite curvature at point A, as points B and b approach A, the diameters AG and Ag approach AJ, the diameter of curvature at point A, and the ratio AG/Ag approaches unity. Thus, the square of the chord AB or ab is ultimately proportional to the subtense BD or bd (where later the subtense is identified as being proportional to the force). Therefore, curvature is central to the demonstration of Lemma 11, and hence by extension to all the propositions that call upon it.

Figure 3.13 is taken from Newton's revised diagram for Proposition 6, Book 1 in the 1713 *Principia*, which is here enhanced by the addition of the circle of curvature PV. Comparison with the original diagram (in Figure 3.9 above) will show that the most obvious change is the addition of the dotted line YS, which passes through the force center S and is normal to the tangent YPZ. A more subtle but even more significant change in the figure is the extension of the line of force SP

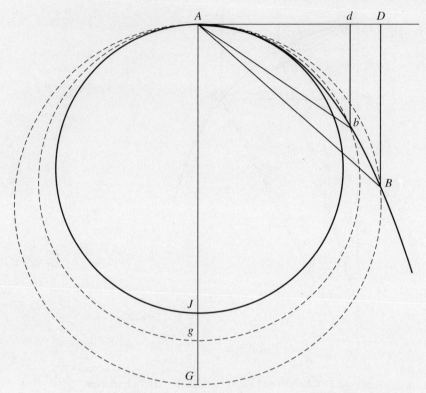

Fig. 3.12 Taken from Lemma 11, Book 1, 1687 *Principia*. In this enhanced version the general curve is no longer a circle, and circles *ABG*, *Abg*, and *AJ* have been added, where *AJ* is the circle of curvature at point *A*.

through the force center *S* to a point *V*, where the line *PV* is identified as the chord of curvature from *P* through the center of force *S*.[58] In this revised Proposition 6, Newton still derives the parabolic measure of force, $QR/(SP^2 \times QT^2)$, but in addition he shows that in the limit as *Q* approaches *P* it becomes equal to an alternate measure of force, $1/(SY^2 \times PV)$, which is clearly dependent upon curvature because *PV* is the chord of curvature through the point *S*, the center of force.

The relationship of the curvature measure to the parabolic measure can be seen by applying Lemma 11 to the revised diagram of Proposition 6. Figure 3.14 is an enhanced version of Newton's revised diagram for Proposition 6 with the addition of an auxiliary circle

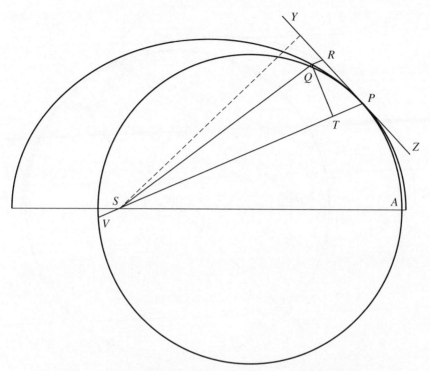

Fig. 3.13 Taken from Proposition 6, Book 1, 1713 *Principia*. In this revised diagram Newton has added the normal to the tangent through the
center of force *YS* and has extended the line *SP* to the point *V*, where
PV is the chord of curvature (the circle of curvature has been added to
Newton's diagram).

PUG and its diameter *PJG*. Following the argument from Lemma 11,
as the point *Q* approaches the point *P*, then the auxiliary circle *PUG*
approaches the circle of curvature *PVJ*. Thus, one can employ Euclidean relationships that are valid for the auxiliary circle to obtain
exact relationships for the general curve: that is, for the circle of
curvature. In particular, Proposition 36, Book 3 of Euclid's *Elements*
is directly applicable to Newton's revised diagram and, as was previously demonstrated for Figure 3.3, $RU/PR = PR/QR$. This Euclidean relationship is one that Newton employs elsewhere in the
Principia, often without any explicit reference.

In Book 1 of the revised edition of 1713, Newton provided solutions to the direct problems <orbit/force center> in Propositions 7

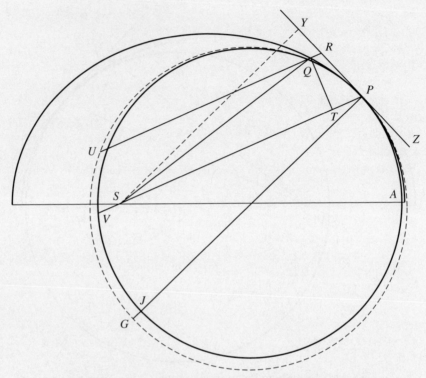

Fig. 3.14 An enhanced version of Newton's diagram shown in Fig. 3.13. An auxiliary circle *PUG* and its diameter *PJG* have been added to demonstrate the relationship of Lemma 11 to Proposition 6.

<circle/circumference>, 9 <spiral/pole>, 10 <ellipse/center> and 11 <ellipse/focus> using the alternate measure of force, $1/(SY^2 \times PV)$, as well as the solution using the parabolic measure of force, $QR/(SP^2 \times QT^2)$, found in the 1687 *Principia*. In the alternate solution for Proposition 10, Newton calculated *PV*, the chord of curvature through the center of the ellipse, and demonstrated that the force is directly proportional to the radius from the center of the ellipse to the point on the orbit. The alternate solution to Proposition 11, however, contains yet another measure of force, one that is clearly identified as a third measure in the unpublished revisions of the 1690s, but one that is not clearly outlined in the published revisions of 1713. In it, Newton employed a relationship from Proposition 7, Corollary 2 that relates the force for a given orbit (here an ellipse) and two different centers of force (here the center and focus of the ellipse). In the 1687 *Principia*,

Proposition 7 only gave the solution to the direct problem of a circular orbit with the center of force on the circumference – that is, a relatively simple application of the paradigm set out in Proposition 6. In the revised edition of Proposition 7, however, the force center is located at a general point, and in the first corollary the special case of a force center on the circumference is considered. In the second corollary, Newton obtains the expression for the forces directed toward any two points for an object that moves in a given circle. In the third corollary, Newton generalizes the result to any orbit in which the body revolves about the two centers in the same periodic time. In the closing line Newton uses curvature to relate the two corollaries: "For the force in this orbit at any point ... is the same as in a circle of the same curvature." This result permits Newton to use the force found in an elliptical path directed toward the center of the ellipse (Proposition 10) to find the force in an elliptical path directed toward a focus of the ellipse (Proposition 11). The role of curvature in the alternate solution of Proposition 11 is hidden, however, in a corollary of Proposition 7. Thus, even in the revised edition, which sets out alternate solutions to the direct problems that employ the chord of curvature PV, one must look carefully to find curvature.

APPLICATION OF NEWTON'S CURVATURE METHOD TO TWO DIFFICULT PROBLEMS: RESISTANCE FORCES AND LUNAR MOTION

Newton's curvature method first appeared as his cryptic statement of 1664 and is represented in this chapter by Eq. (2) (p. 100) as the generalization of uniform circular motion to the circle of curvature – that is, the curvature relationship in the central force $f = v^2/(\rho \sin(\alpha))$. In this section we describe the remarkable application of Newton's curvature method to two difficult problems in orbital dynamics: resistance forces and lunar motion. These applications appeared in the 1687 edition of the *Principia*, and thus provide clear evidence that Newton had developed his curvature approach to dynamics by that time, although he did not publish an exposition until the 1713 edition. Newton's geometrical constructions are difficult for the modern reader, and therefore we simplify our discussion by giving here an equivalent representation based on Newton's fluxional calculus. It is possible, moreover, that Newton may have made some of his discoveries in this manner, and then demonstrated them later in the geometrical language of the Ancients.

Resistance forces

One application of the curvature method is concerned with resistance forces, as found in Proposition 15, Book 2 of the 1687 *Principia*. Figure 3.15 is the diagram given in that proposition: a spiral curve centered at S with points P, Q, R, and r lying on the orbit. Here, Newton employs curvature to consider the effect of adding a resistance force in a direction opposite to the motion of a body revolving in a given orbit under the action of an inverse-square force. Newton expected that if the cause of gravity was Cartesian vortices, then the fluid forming these vortices must also give rise to a resistance force with properties which could be determined; this problem was beyond the capacity of his contemporaries.

In Propositions 15–17, Book 2, Newton considers a possible orbit, the equiangular spiral, for a body under the combined action of a given centripetal force F centered at the origin of the spiral, and an unknown resistance force, F_R. The orbital curve is given and the force is calculated: an example of a direct problem such as found in the first three sections of Book 1. Unlike the problems of Book 1, however, the unknown resistance force F_R is not centripetal, but acts along the tangent to the spiral. Thus, the area law is not valid, and Newton had to calculate the rate of change of area. What follows is an equivalent derivation of Newton's ingenious geometrical construction. This derivation is based on a differential form of the calculus, which is close to Newton's fluxional analysis.[59]

Analysis

The change of angular momentum δh during a small interval of time δt is determined by the component of force perpendicular to the radial direction r. In this case the rate of change is due entirely to the resistance force F_R, and therefore

$$\delta h = -r\, F_R \sin(\alpha)\delta t, \tag{1}$$

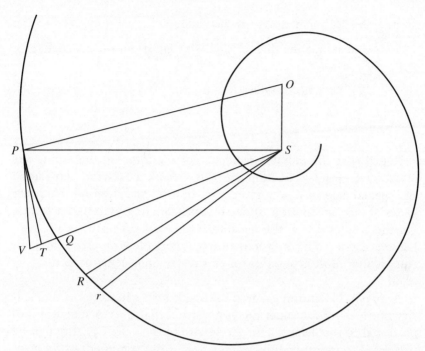

Fig. 3.15 Figure in Proposition 15, Book 2, describing an equiangular spiral curve $PQRr$ for an orbit under the action of a gravitational force centered at S and a resistance force (described in the text). The radius of curvature at P is the line PO.

where α is the angle between the radial and tangential directions at a point on the orbit. Since the component of the force normal to the orbit is due only to the centripetal force F, Newton's curvature relation depends only on this force. Newton had previously demonstrated that for an equiangular spiral $\rho \sin(\alpha) = r$,[60] and assuming the radial dependence for the central force $F = \mu/r^n$, given in Proposition 16, Book 2, the curvature relation can be written as

$$v = \sqrt{[F\rho \sin(\alpha)]} = \sqrt{[\mu/r^{n-1}]}, \tag{2}$$

and the angular momentum as

$$h = vr \sin(\alpha) = \sqrt{[\mu/r^{n-3}]} \sin(\alpha). \tag{3}$$

Hence, the change δh in a small interval δr, where $\delta r = v \cos(\alpha)\delta t$, is given by

$$\delta h = [(3 - n)/2] \sin(\alpha) \cos(\alpha) [\mu / r^{n-1}] \delta t, \tag{4}$$

and comparing this relation with Eq. (1) for the resistive force F_R gives

$$F_R = [(3 - n)/2] \cos(\alpha) \mu / r^n. \tag{5}$$

$$Q.E.D.$$

Recall that the radial dependence of the force on the radius r is given by $F = \mu / r^n$. In Proposition 15, Book 2 Newton considered the special case of $n = 2$, indicating that he had in mind the effect of resistance on motion under inverse-square gravitational forces. For the case of $n = 3$, the resistance force F_R, given in Eq. (5), vanishes as expected from Proposition 9, where Newton proved that an equiangular orbit is possible for an inverse-cube centripetal force by itself.

Actually, Newton presented his result for F_R in terms of the density of the medium under the assumption that the resistance is proportional to the density and the square of the velocity, although he neglected to mention this dependence in the statement of Propositions 15–17, Book 2. According to Eqs. (2) and (5), the ratio F_R/v^2 is proportional to $1/r$, which explains Newton's statement at the start of Propositions 15–17, that "if the density of a medium in each place thereof be inversely as the distance of the places from an immovable center..."[61]

Lunar motion

Another application of the curvature method is concerned with lunar motion, as found in Propositions 26–29, Book 3, of the 1687 *Principia*. Here Newton developed a special treatment of the influence of the gravitational force of the Sun on the Moon's motion around the Earth. Before Newton, geometrical models had been developed to account for the deviations of lunar motions from simple Keplerian elliptical motion, notably by Horrocks in 1641. The lunar deviations are considerable, as was well known to astronomers in Newton's time, but it was not realized that they are are caused primarily by the gravitational force of the Sun. In particular, Tycho Brahe had discovered a bi-monthly variation in the lunar speed after missing an expected lunar eclipse. From Proposition 29, entitled "To find the variation of the Moon," it is evident that the method developed by Newton in the two previous propositions was intended for the computation of this variation. Remarkably, in Proposition 28 Newton did not consider the actual motion of the Moon, which was known to be approximated by Horrocks's model of a precessing ellipse with the Earth at one focus. Instead, he considered an idealized model in which the Moon rotates in a circular orbit around the Earth in the absence of the solar perturbation. He then computed the change of the orbit due to this perturbation, and obtained results that were in good agreement with Brahe's observation. This was one of the great triumphs of Newton's gravitational theory; later it was developed further by Euler,[62] and by G. Hill.[63]

Newton's key idea was to assume a model in which the perturbed orbit of the Moon is an ellipse of small eccentricity with the Earth at the center rather than at one of the foci. The ellipse rotates in such a manner that one of the axes is always perpendicular to the Earth–Sun distance. He then calculated the curvature ρ at the two apses of the resulting rotating orbital curve, which depends on the unknown eccentricity of the ellipse and the observed ratio of the synodic and sidereal periods of the Moon. Since in his model the combined gravitational force of the Earth, f_{Earth}, and the Sun, f_{Sun}, on the Moon is perpendicular to the direction of the lunar motion at the apses, Newton could apply his curvature relation $\rho = v^2/f$ with $f = f_{Earth} + f_{Sun}$, to evaluate also the curvature of this orbit. Equating the resulting ratio of curvatures with his geometrical calculation then determines the eccentricity of the conjectured elliptical orbit. A complication occurs here because, except at the apses, the Sun also exerts a component of force on the Moon that is tangential to its motion. This implies that the area law (or conservation of angular momentum h) is not valid, and the velocity at the apses $v = h/r$ varies with h as well as with the radial distance r. Therefore, in Proposition 26, Newton computed the change in angular momentum between the two apses in the approximation that the orbit is circular, an approximation he announced in the title of this proposition, "To find the hourly increment of the area which the Moon, by a radius drawn to the Earth, describes in a circular orbit." In this manner he obtained a basically correct result, although his method does not give a complete solution. Such a solution requires that the geometrical curvature of the rotating elliptical curve be consistent with the solar gravitational perturbation at points other than the apses of the orbit. But, as Laplace remarked admiringly,[64] "These computational assumptions...are permitted to inventors in such difficult researches..." [*Ces hypothèses de calcul...sont permises aux inventeurs, dans des recherches aussi difficiles*...]

Figure 3.16 is the diagram used by Newton in Proposition 28, Book 3, where he states that

by computation, I find that the difference between the curvature $[\rho_a]$ of this orbit *Cpa* at *the vertex a*, and the curvature of a circle described about the center *T* with the interval *TA* is to the difference between the curvature $[\rho_A]$ of the ellipse at the vertex *A* and the curvature of the same circle, as the square of the ratio $[\xi]$ of the angle *CTP* to the angle *CTp*.

In mathematical form this statement implies that

$$(1/\rho_a - 1/TA)/(1/\rho_A - 1/TA) = \xi^2. \tag{8}$$

Newton does not tell us how he obtained this result except for a succinct remark that "All these relations are easily derived from the sines of the angles of contact, and of the differences of those angles." From this hint Newton's computation can be reconstructed by referring to Lemma 11, Book 1 and its accompanying figure (see Figure 3.11). This lemma gives a geometrical construction for the radius of curvature at a point *A* of a given curve in terms of a small arc *AB* of the curve, and the corresponding subtense of the angle of contact defined by the line *BD* normal to the tangent. Newton shows that the radius of curvature

$$\rho_A = AB^2/2DB, \tag{9}$$

in the limit that *B* approaches *A*.

Analysis

In Figure 3.16, let a point *T* on the vertical axis *AG* be the origin of a polar coordinate system, *r* the radial distance from *T* to a point on the curve *AB*, and $\delta\theta$ equal to the angle *ATB*. Then

$$AB \approx r_A \delta\theta \tag{10}$$

and

$$DB = r_A - r_B \cos(\delta\theta) \approx \delta^2 r + (r_A/2)\delta\theta^2, \tag{11}$$

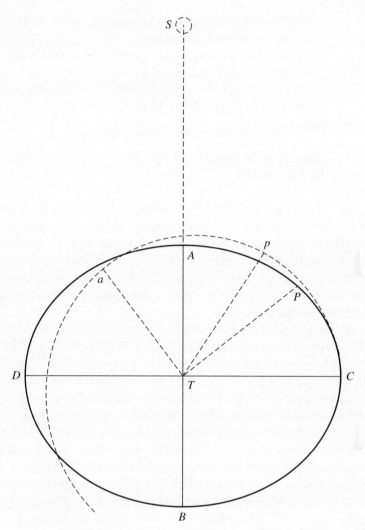

Fig. 3.16 Figure in Proposition 28, Book 3, for an ellipse $CPADB$ representing a hypothetical orbit of the Moon around the Earth at the center T of the ellipse in a frame rotating with the Earth around the Sun at S. The curve Cpa shown in dashed lines is the corresponding orbit in an inertial frame.

where the difference $\delta^2 r = (r_B - r_A)$ is a second-order differential. Hence, according to Eq. (9), the curvature $1/\rho_A$ at A can be written in the form[65]

$$1/\rho_A - 1/r_A = 2\delta^2 r/r_a^2 \delta\theta^2. \tag{12}$$

For the rotating elliptical orbit shown in Figure 3.16, which is obtained by the transformation $\theta \longrightarrow \theta' = (1/\xi)\theta$, the curvature ρ_a at the corresponding apse a is obtained by observing that at this vertex the angular interval $\delta\theta' = (1/\xi)\theta$, where $\xi = T_{syd}/T_{syn}$, while $r_a = r_A$ and $\delta^2 r' = \delta r^2$, because corresponding radial distances remain unchanged. Therefore,

$$1/\rho_a - 1/r_A = 2\xi^2(\delta^2 r/r_a 2\delta\theta^2),\tag{13}$$

and taking the ratio of Eqs. (12) and (13) gives Newton's result, Eq. (8). Q.E.D.

To evaluate ρ_a from Eq. (8), Newton had to obtain the curvature at the apse A for the stationary ellipse. This can be shown to be a straightforward application of Lemma 11 and Newton obtains "that the curvature of the ellipse in A is to the curvature of that circle [TA] as the square of the ratio of TA to TC." Likewise, the corresponding curvature ρ_c, at the rotated vertex c, not shown in the figure, can be obtained in this manner.[66]

At these two apses Newton also calculated the curvature by applying the dynamical relation $\rho = v^2/f$, where $v = h/r$ and f is the combined gravitation force of both the Earth and the Sun exerted on the Moon. In this case the angular momentum h is not a constant because the solar force has a component tangential to the orbit except at the two apses, and Newton evaluated the change in h (in Proposition 26, Book 3) by approximating the orbit by a circle. The details of this calculation have been discussed elsewhere[67,68] and will not be presented here. This calculation enabled Newton to equate the resulting ratio ρ_a/ρ_b obtained from dynamics with the corresponding ratio obtained from the geometry of the conjectured rotating elliptic orbit, to solve for the unknown eccentricity of the ellipse.

CONCLUSION

Two of the essential elements in Newton's dynamics are the concept of curvature and the area law for centripetal forces. Curvature, which is a measure of the rate of bending of a curve, was developed by Newton in the mid-1660s, but it was not until 1679, following his correspondence with Hooke, that he discovered that Kepler's area law was valid for central forces. Newton's early computational method lacked this crucial insight of the area law, and he was limited to the calculation of approximate orbits for general central forces. With the discovery of the area law, however, he was able to transform dynamical problems that depend on time into a purely geometric form by relating the time variable to the area of a sector of an orbit, and thus to go beyond approximate solutions. In modern terms the area law corresponds to conservation of angular momentum, which is proportional to the time rate of change of area swept by the radial line with its origin at the center of force. Newton gave the area law a very prominent part in the *Principia*, where it appears in the first two propositions of Book 1.

The area law also served to obscure the critical role that curvature played in Newton's dynamics. Following the substitution of equal areas as a measure of time for orbital motion, Newton was able to develop a purely geometrical measure of force (acceleration). This measure corresponds to Galileo's measure for force in the case of uniform accelerated rectilinear motion and leads to the parabolic measure of force $QR/(QT^2 \times SP^2)$. It was this meaure of force that appeared in the draft of "De motu" sent to Halley in 1684 and became the paradigm for the solution of direct problems in the 1687 *Principia*. Since it was the only measure published in the first edition, there exists a general, but mistaken, belief that Newton did not develop his curvature approach until after 1687. On the contrary, curvature plays a major role in Newton's unpublished works preceding and following the 1687 *Principia*, as well as in the work itself.

Newton's curvature method was based on an extension of the analysis of uniform circular motion to general orbital motion, which implies that the normal component of the force F_n at any point on the orbit is equal to the square of the tangential velocity v divided by the radius of curvature ρ, that is, $F_n = v^2/\rho$. Newton describes this curvature measure of force in his cryptic statement of 1664, employs it in his method *quam proxime* in the 1679 correspondence with Hooke, and applies it in the solution of the difficult problems of resisted motion and lunar inequalities in the 1687 *Principia*, as well as in some of his unpublished manuscripts. In some of these applications, he makes only limited reference to curvature, although we have demonstrated that it plays a major role. He may have been reluctant to refer to curvature because he had not yet published his mathematical work on curvature done almost two decades earlier, and he would have been well aware, therefore, that the concept of curvature was not known to most of his expected readers, with the exception of Huygens. Immediately following the publication of the 1687 *Principia*, however, Newton began work on a radical revision of the opening sections of Book 1 in which curvature is presented as the primary measure of force. He never published those revisions, although a version of them was included in Book 1 of the revised *Principia* as Corollaries 3–5 of Proposition 6, and as an alternate method of solution of the propositions of Sections 2 and 3. Some eighteenth- and nineteenth-century commentators did recognize the importance of curvature in Newton's revised editions of the *Principia*. The full role of curvature in the first edition (1687) has been made explicit only recently.

In summary, the essential point is that Newton's geometrical proofs in the first few sections of Book 1 and in some advanced problems in Books 2 and 3 are based on curvature and on area law (angular momentum) calculations. The task is to determine the chord of curvature $PV = 2\rho \sin(\alpha)$ and the normal to the tangent through the center of force $SY = r \sin(\alpha)$ for various orbits by whatever means the clever geometer can conjure, and thus to obtain the force from the curvature measure $1/(PV \times SY^2)$. This task can also be accomplished by combining these two calculations into a single one: that is, to calculate the limit of $QR/(SP^2 \times QT^2)$ as shown in Proposition 6, Book 1. This parabolic measure of force, however, does not have the direct geometrical significance of the curvature measure. Newton's first thoughts on a solution to the direct problem of elliptical orbital motion stem from considerations of curvature, and it is from curvature that we gain the deepest insights into his dynamics.

NOTES

1   Isaac Newton, *The Mathematical Principles of Natural Philosophy*, 3rd edn, 2 vols., trans. Andrew Motte [1729]. Facsimile reprint London: Dawsons of Pall Mall, 1968, vol. 2, p. 392. Hereafter, cited as Newton, *Principia*. There is an edition of Motte's 1729 translation of the *Principia* with some revisions by Florian Cajori published by the University of California Press in 1934 in a single volume and in 1971 in a two-volume paperback edition. Moreover, there is a new translation into English of the third edition: Isaac Newton, *The Principia, Mathematical Principles of Natural Philosophy: A New Translation*, trans. I Bernard Cohen and Ann Whitman, preceded by "A Guide to

Newton's *Principia*" by I. Bernard Cohen (Berkeley: University of California Press, 1999). No translation into English of the entire first or second edition of the *Principia* has been published, but an English translation by Mary Ann Rossi of Sections 1, 2, and 3 of Book 1 from the first (1687) edition of Newton's *Principia* is to be found in the appendix to J. Bruce Brackenridge, *The Key to Newton's Dynamics: The Kepler Problem and the* Principia (Berkeley: University of California Press, 1995). The references to the *Principia* in our chapter are to the facsimile reproduction of Motte's 1729 translation for the third edition, and to Rossi's 1995 translation for Sections 1, 2, and 3 of Book 1 of the first edition.

2 Michael Nauenberg, "Hooke, Orbital Motion and Newton's *Principia*," *American Journal of Physics* 62 (1994), 331–50, and "On Hooke's 1685 Manuscript on Orbital Mechanics," *Historia Mathematica* 25 (1998), 89–93.

3 J. Bruce Brackenridge, "The Critical Role of Curvature in Newton's Developing Dynamics," in P. M. Harman and Alan E. Shapiro (eds.), *An Investigation of Difficult Things: Essays on Newton and the History of the Exact Sciences* (Cambridge: Cambridge University Press, 1992), pp. 231–60, and pp. 238–9. Newton's early references to curvature as an analytical device are noted and its later uses are detailed, but his interim method and some early applications of curvature in the first edition of the *Principia* were unknown (see pp. 95–106 and 117–24).

4 Michael Nauenberg, "Newton's Early Computational Method for Dynamics," *Archive for History of Exact Sciences* 46 (1994), 212–52, at p. 227. Newton's interim method, which uses curvature as a central element and which was previously unknown (see note 2), was supplied by this paper; it is discussed in detail in pp. 95–106 of this chapter. The early applications of curvature in the first edition of the *Principia* are presented in pp. 112–17 of this chapter.

5 Michael Nauenberg, "Huygens and Newton on Curvature and its Application to Dynamics," *De Zeventiende Eeuw* 1 (1996), 215–34. In the study of mathematics, Newton was almost entirely self-taught. He attended a few lectures on the subject, but it was his acquisition of contemporary works on mathematics, in particular van Schooten's second Latin edition of Descartes's *Geometry*, that provided him with a point of departure. This second Latin edition contains extensive commentaries by van Schooten and some of his students, Jan Hudde, Hendrik van Heurat, Jan de Wit, and Christiaan Huygens, that extended Descartes's work and solved new problems. Newton makes use of their work as well as that of Descartes. The concept of curvature was developed independently by Huygens (about 1658–9) and by Newton (about 1664–5). Huygens published some of his results in 1673 in his

Horologium Oscillatorium (translated into English by R. J. Blackwell in Christiaan Huygens, *The Pendulum Clock*, Ames: Iowa State University Press, 1986), and sent a copy of his book to Newton, who acknowledged it in a response via Henry Oldenberg, then secretary of the Royal Society.

6   The curvature at a point on a general curve is defined by the inverse radius of the circle that best approximates a small arc of the curve at that point. This circle of curvature was introduced independently by both Newton and Huygens. Later, Leibniz called it the *osculating* circle (it just "kisses" the curve at that point). It is defined mathematically by taking a circle that is tangent to the curve at the chosen point, and that also intersects that curve at two nearby points. The radius of that tangent circle is then decreased until the two points of intersection approach the point of tangency and thus the tangent circle becomes the circle of curvature. An alternate definition requires taking two normals to the curve at nearby points and finding the point of intersection of the normals. When the two normals approach each other, the intersection of the normals approaches a limit point, and the radius of curvature is defined by the distance from the curve along the normal of this limit point.

7   For an eighteenth-century commentator on curvature, see John Clarke, *A Demonstration of Some of the Principal Sections of Sir Isaac Newton's Principles of Natural Philosophy* (London, 1730; Johnson Reprint Series with an introduction by I. Bernard Cohen, New York, 1972). In 1730, following the publication of the third edition (1726) and Newton's death in 1727, John Clarke published a translation of, and commentary on, a number of selected portions of the *Principia*, which were rearranged and ordered so as to give a coherent presentation of both the abstract dynamical principles and their practical astronomic application. Clarke also commented in some detail upon Newton's use of curvature in the qualification which was added to Lemma 11 in the revised editions of the *Principia*: "in all curves which have a finite curvature at the point of contact." Clarke even gave a reference for the reader to Milne's *Conic Sections* for a further discussion of curvature. For a nineteenth-century commentator on Lemma 11 and curvature, see Percival Frost, *Newton's Principia, First Book, Sections I., II., III., with Notes and Illustrations and a Collection of Problems*, 4th edn (Macmillan and Co., 1883), pp. 82–113. This excellent pedagogical guide for students preparing for the Mathematical Tripos first appeared in 1878 and was still being published into the twentieth century. Again, the role of curvature is clearly made manifest.

8   See Isaac Newton, *The Mathematical Papers of Isaac Newton*, 8 vols.,
    trans. and ed. D. T. Whiteside (Cambridge: Cambridge University Press,
    1967–81). The primary twentieth-century source of Newton's develop-
    ment of curvature is found in vols. 1, 3, and 6 of these monumental
    volumes of Newton's mathematical papers and in the extensive com-
    mentaries of the editor. In vol. 6, Whiteside, the editor, describes New-
    ton's application of curvature to dynamics in the proposed revisions of
    the *Principia*, which Newton wrote in the 1690s following the publi-
    cation of the first edition. Whiteside rejects any earlier explicit use of
    curvature by Newton, however, such as we find in the 1687 *Principia*.
    "In precise terms, if the orbital speed at the point be v and the ra-
    dius of curvature there be ρ, then v^2/ρ will measure the component
    [force] $f \sin \alpha$ normal to the orbit... No use of this corollary is made –
    explicitly so at least – either in the present '*De motu corporum*' or
    in the... *Principia*... (in 1687)" (Newton, *Mathematical Papers*, vol. 6,
    p. 131, note 86). In this chapter, however, we argue that Newton did
    make explicit use of this curvature relation in the 1687 *Principia* (see
    this chapter, pp. 117–24). See also Newton, *Mathematical Papers*, vol. 6,
    pp. 146–9, note 124 for Whiteside's additional commentary on this topic.
    For another excellent twentieth-century commentator on Newton's use
    of curvature in the *Principia*, see Bruce Pourciau, "Reading the Master:
    Newton and the Birth of Celestial Mechanics," *American Mathemati-
    cal Monthly* 104 (1997), 1–19.
9   Nauenberg, "Newton's Early Computational Method for Dynamics,"
    pp. 212–52.
10 Michael Nauenberg, "Newton's Perturbation Methods for the 3-Body
    Problem and Its Application to Lunar Motion," in Jed Buchwald and
    I. Bernard Cohen (eds.), *Issac Newton's Natural Philosophy* (Cambridge,
    MA: MIT Press, 2001).
11 Brackenridge, *The Key to Newton's Dynamics*. This book tracks New-
    ton's work on dynamics from its early stages at Cambridge before 1669,
    through its revival of interest ten years later, to its fruition in 1687 in
    the first edition of the *Principia*, and its revision and extension in the
    later editions. Throughout, Brackenridge stresses the role of curvature
    in all of Newton's dynamics. "If any single measure deserves the title
    of the key to Newton's dynamics, it is the curvature measure," p. 222.
12 S. Chandrasekhar, *Newton's* Principia *for the Common Reader* (Oxford:
    Clarendon Press, 1995). For a review of this book, see Michael Nauen-
    berg, in *American Journal of Physics* 64 (1996), 957–8.
13 Michael Nauenberg, "The Mathematical Principles Underlying the
    Principia Revisited," *The Journal for the History of Astronomy* 29

(1998), 286–300. This essay contains in part a review of Brackenridge's book, *The Key to Newton's Dynamics.*

14 J. Bruce Brackenridge, "Kepler, Elliptical Orbits, and Celestial Circularity: A Study in the Persistence of Metaphysical Commitment," *Annals of Science* 39 (1982), 117–43, 265–95. Kepler was working in this tradition early in the seventeenth century, even as he described the noncircular elliptical motion of the planets in his *New Astronomy* of 1609. He was concerned with the cause of celestial motion, however, as well as with its measurement and analysis. Despite his description of planetary motion as elliptical, the circle remained the primary element for Kepler in his understanding of God's plan of the universe.

15 John Herivel, *The Background to Newton's* Principia: *A Study of Newton's Dynamical Researches in the Years 1664–84*, (Oxford: Clarendon Press, 1965), p. 7.

16 *The Correspondence of Isaac Newton*, ed. H. W. Turnball, vol. 2 (Cambridge: Cambridge University Press, 1960), pp. 297–313.

17 Herivel, *Background to Newton's* Principia, pp. 133–5.

18 René Descartes, *Principles of Philosophy* (1644), trans. Valentine Roger Miller and Reese P. Miller (Dordrecht: D. Reidel Publishing Co., 1983), p. 59. "If it [a body] is at rest we do not believe that it will ever begin to move unless driven to do so by some external cause. Nor, if it is moving, is there any significant reason to think that it will ever cease to move of its own accord and without some other thing which impedes it."

19 Newton, *Principia*, 3rd edn, vol. 1, p. 19. "Every body perseveres in its state of rest, or of uniform motion in a right line, unless it is compelled to change that state by forces impressed thereon." It is interesting to note that both Descartes and Newton were anticipated by Aristotle, who in his *Physics* makes the following statement: "Hence, a body would either continue in its state of rest or would necessarily continue in its motion indefinitely, unless interfered with by a stronger force," Aristotle, *Aristotle's Physics* (c. 350 BC), trans. Richard Hope (Lincoln: University of Nebraska Press, 1961), p. 72. Aristotle, however, is arguing that a void cannot exist, for if it did then the above state of rest or uniform motion would be observed. Since such ideal states are not observed in nature, then Aristotle concludes that a void cannot exist.

20 Herivel, *The Background to Newton's* Principia, p. 7.

21 Cited in Herivel, *The Background to Newton's* Principia, p. 47.

22 Newton, *Principia*, 3rd edn, p. 67 and 1st edn, cited in Brackenridge, *The Key to Newton's Dynamics*, p. 250. The phrase "centrifugal force" does not appear in the first edition, but Newton inserts it into the text of the Scholium for the second and third editions.

23   Of interest are the commentaries of the continental scholars with re-
     spect to centrifugal force and the role that curvature plays in it. Bertoloni
     Meli attempts to sort out the multiple definitions of centrifugal force
     from Huygens in the mid-seventeenth century to Euler in the mid-
     eighteenth century. He selects five mathematicians to represent the
     wide range of opinions to be found among mathematicians in the early
     decades of the eighteenth century: John Keill (presumably representing
     Newton's position), Johann Bernoulli and Christian Wolff (defending
     Leibniz's position), and Pierre Varignon and Jakob Hermann. On the
     one hand, Leibniz refers to two types of *conatus*, or force, one of which
     is an outward *conatus* given by v^2/ρ, where the cause of the endeavor "is
     the rotation of the body and its tendency to escape along the tangent."
     Bertoloni Meli, "The Relativization of Centrifugal Force," *Isis* 81 (1990),
     23–43, at p. 31. On the other hand, Keill sees centrifugal force in terms
     of the third law: "A centrifugal force is the reaction or resistance which
     a moving body exerts to prevent its being turned out of its way, and
     whereby it endeavors to continue its motion in the same direction: and
     as re-action is always equal, and contrary to action, so in like manner
     is the centrifugal to the centripetal force. This centrifugal force arises
     from the *vis inertiae* of matter." John, Keill *An Introduction to Natu-
     ral Philosophy*, ed. Willem Jakob 'sGravesande (London, 1745), p. 286,
     cited in Bertoloni Meli, "The Relativization of Centrifugal Force,"
     p. 34.

24   Galileo found experimentally that the displacements of balls rolling
     down inclined planes were proportional to the square of the times, and
     deduced that the acceleration was uniform, where by uniform accelera-
     tion was meant equal increments of speed in equal intervals of time. The
     acceleration was attributed to the component of gravity acting down the
     incline of the plane.

25   Herivel, *The Background to Newton's* Principia, pp. 129–30. Herivel
     dates the entries to this folio on or after 20 January 1664 (OS) and he
     notes that "there can be no doubt that the first two dynamical entries
     on this folio must have been made later than the discussion of cir-
     cular motion beginning at AX.-Proposition 20." Thus, he conjectures
     that Newton had left the first few pages of the *Waste Book* blank, and
     later filled them in with this comparatively polished and complicated
     analysis.

26   In the Scholium to Proposition 4, Book 1 in all the editions of the *Prin-
     cipia* there is a revised version of this proof in which the relationship
     v^2/r is derived. Newton, *Principia*, 3rd edn, pp. 66–7 and 1st edn, cited
     in Brackenridge, *The Key to Newton's Dynamics*, p. 250.

27 First published in Rupert Hall, "Newton on the Calculation of Central Force," *Annals of Science* 13 (1957), 62–71 and then in vol. 1 (1959) of Newton, *Correspondence*, pp. 297–301. Herivel published the Latin text as well as a translation, and he dates the manuscript "before Newton's appointment to the Lucasian Chair of Mathematics in 1669." Herivel, *The Background to Newton's* Principia, pp. 193–8.

28 Euclid, *The Thirteen Books of Euclid's Elements*, with introduction and commentary by Sir Thomas L. Heath, 2nd edn (Cambridge: Cambridge University Press, 1956), pp. 73–5. Euclid's theorem can be demonstrated analytically in the following way, where θ is the angle between PS and QS as seen in Figure 3.3:

  1. $RU/PR = (RS + RS\cos\theta)/RS\sin\theta = (1 + \cos\theta)/\sin\theta$
  2. $PR/QR = RS\sin\theta/(RS - RS\cos\theta) = \sin\theta/(1 - \cos\theta)$
  3. Since $1 - \cos\theta^2 = \sin\theta^2$, then $RU/PR = PR/QR$.

29 Actually, Newton does not use the relationship $QP = vt$ explicitly in his demonstration. Rather, he demonstrates that the distance that would be traveled under the force that produces the deviation QR during a full cycle is equal to the square of the circumference divided by the diameter QU, i.e., $4\pi^2 QU$.

30 In an extended note, Whiteside discusses in considerable detail Newton's "unconsidered subtleties" of the conditions under which "the central force ... over the whole arc ... may be considered to be constant." Newton, *Mathematical Papers*, vol. 6, note 19, p. 37. We claim, however, that there are no "unconsidered subtleties" in Newton's argument, but rather that there is confusion about the nature of Newton's mathematical limits. The central force is not a constant over a *finite* arc, nor does Newton make such an incorrect assumption. Newton defines a ratio, e.g., $QR/(QT^2 \times SP^2)$, which varies with the location of both points Q and P, and then he defines its limit as Q approaches P. This limit exists for any curve with finite curvature. Newton defines the force to be proportional to this limit, which depends in general on the location of P. Therefore, for a general curve the force varies both in magnitude and in direction over any finite arc PQ. For further details, see Nauenberg, "The Mathematical Principles Underlying the *Principia* Revisited," pp. 284–300.

31 Newton, *Mathematical Papers*, vol. 1, p. 456. For a discussion of the source of this cryptic comment, see J. Bruce Brackenridge, "Newton's Mature Dynamics: A Crooked Path Made Straight," in Buchwald and Cohen (eds.), *Issac Newton's Natural Philosophy*.

32 Newton, *Mathematical Papers*, vol. 1, pp. 252–5.

33 Herivel, *The Background to Newton's* Principia, p. 132.

34 Newton, *Mathematical Papers*, vol. 1, note 3, p. 456. In a later volume, Whiteside expands his commentary and explains in detail how curvature is central to Newton's alternate measure of force. Newton, *Mathematical Papers*, vol.6, note 25, pp. 548–50.

35 Brackenridge, "The Critical Role of Curvature in Newton's Dynamics," p. 256.

36 Nauenberg, "Newton's Early Computational Method for Dynamics," pp. 212–52.

37 Nauenberg, "Newton's Perturbation Methods for the 3-Body Problem and Its Application to Lunar Motion."

38 *The Correspondence of Isaac Newton*, vol. 2, pp. 307–8.

39 For a discussion of such opinions, see Nauenberg, "Newton's Early Computational Method for Dynamics," p. 223.

40 Nauenberg, "Newton's Early Computational Method for Dynamics," note 30, p. 248.

41 Newton, *Mathematical Papers*, vol. 6, pp. 149–53.

42 V. I. Arnol'd, *Huygens & Barrow, Newton & Hooke* (Birkhauser, 1990), p. 19. Arnol'd states that "the letter contains among other mistakes an impossible picture of an orbit."

43 Newton, *Principia*, 3rd edn, vol. 1, pp. 182–3. See Corollary 2 of Proposition 44, Book 1.

44 Indeed, measuring the distance of this segment of the curve to the displaced center C_S, one finds that the closest distance lies nearer to F. Therefore, the correct angle between apogee and perigee is AC_SF and it is equal to HCO, as expected. In fact, Newton's computation of the segment of the orbit between apogee and perigee is remarkably good. Because of the drawing error, however, the circumscribed curve $ABKDEA$ is not a true circle and the additional segments HJK and KL of the orbit which touch or approach the circumscribed curve $ABKDEA$ cannot satisfy the reflection symmetry. Therefore these segments had to be partly sketched in and patched up by Newton, as is also quite evident in the segment HJ of the diagram in Figure 3.4.

45 Herivel, *The Background to Newton's* Principia, p. 130.

46 Christiaan Huygens, *De Vi Centrifuga, in Œuvres complètes de Christiaan Huygens*, vol. 16 (The Hague: Martinus Nijhoff 1929), pp. 253–301.

47 Newton, *Principia*, 3rd edn, vol. 1, pp. 68–70: Proposition 6, Corollary 3, Book 1.

48 Meli, "The Relativization of Centrifugal Force," p. 33.

49 For example, Bertoloni Meli claims that "in general, he [Newton] explained curvilinear motion in terms of centripetal force and inertia alone, without centrifugal force: why in this case centrifugal force could be neglected, however, was not clear." Meli, "The Relativization of

Centrifugal Force," p. 33. If one notes, however, that Newton always applies the concept of centrifugal force only to circular motion, or to the maximum and minimum points for general orbital motion (where the force lies along the radius of the circle of curvature), then the situation is clarified. Centrifugal force is not *neglected* in curvilinear motion as Bertoloni Meli claims; rather it is applied by Newton only under very *restricted* conditions. See Nauenberg, "Newton's Early Computational Method for Dynamics," p. 231.

50   Writing Eq. (2) in the form $\rho \sin(\alpha) = v^2/f$, where v^2 is given by conservation of energy, it is clear that both sides of this equation are functions of the radial distance r. By 1671 Newton had obtained an *explicit* expression in polar coordinates for the radial component of the curvature vector for any given curve. For a spiral curve Newton obtained the following relationship: $\rho \sin(\alpha) = r$, and therefore, $v^2 = fr$, according to Eq. (2). Taking differentials on both sides of this equation we have $2v\delta v = r\delta f + f\delta r$, and applying Eq. (6), the term $v\delta v$ can be eliminated to obtain $r\delta f + 3f\delta r = 0$, which gives that the force f is proportional to $1/r^3$.

51   Newton solves the *direct problem* for a logarithmic spiral orbit by an elegant self-similarity argument in Proposition 9, Book 1 of the *Principia*, giving the central force as $1/r^3$.

52   A problem still remains, however. It must be shown that the "impulsive" force divided by the side of the polygon squared approaches a limit when the side of the polygon becomes vanishingly small (evanescent). In this limit the deviation divided by the time interval squared corresponds to Newton's "accelerative" measure of force. Newton's proof of this property is essentially the content of Proposition 6, Book 1.

53   Nauenberg, "The Mathematical Principles Underlying the *Principia* Revisited," p. 298.

54   In Lemma 11, Newton shows that the limit of the ratio QR/QT^2 exists for curves of finite curvature. In the 1687 *Principia* Newton should have referred to this curvature lemma for the proof of Proposition 6, but instead he referred to Lemma 10, which has nothing to say about the existence of the limit of QR/QT^2. For a discussion of this point see Nauenberg, "The Mathematical Principles Underlying the Principia Revisited," pp. 289–92.

55   Other than the multiple references to curvature in Proposition 28, Book 3, which is concerned with lunar motion, the word "curvature" in the 1687 edition appears only in the following eight places: Book 1, Lemma 6, "in the middle of the continued curvature (*curvaturae*)" and "against the nature of curvature (*curvaturam*)"; Lemma 11, Scholium, "the curvature (*curvaturam*) at the point A"; Proposition 44. Corollary 4,

"the radius of curvature (*curvaturae*) which the orbit . . . "; Book 2, Proposition 52 Scholium, "the diminution of this curvature (*curvaturae*)"; Book 3, Lemma 4, "from the curvature (*curvatura*) . . . of the Comets"; and Proposition 41, "That this curvature (*curvatura*) is greater when the deviation is greater . . . for in the shorter tails, the curvature (*curvatura*) is hardly to be perceived." From an unpublished concordance of the words in the first three editions of Newton's *Principia*, which was compiled by I. Bernard Cohen.

56 Newton, *Principia*, 1st edn, cited in Brackenridge, "The Key to Newton's Dynamics," p. 243.

57 In the heavily annotated edition of the *Principia* edited by LeSeur and Jacquier and first published in Geneva in 1739–42, the diagram in the footnote to Lemma 11 has a revised diagram in which points A, B, and G lie on a semicircle identified as the "circuli osculantis." The chord AB is shown extended to a new point F, setting out a general curve. Isaac Newton, *Philosophiae Naturalis Principia Mathematica*, (reprinted: Glasgow 1822), vol. 1, p. 54.

58 For a full documentation of both the textual and graphical changes to Proposition 6, Book 1 in the first three editions of the *Principia* see *Isaac Newton's Philosophiae Naturalis Principia Mathematica*, 3rd edn (1726), ed. Alexandre Koyré and I. Bernard Cohen, with variant readings (Cambridge: Cambridge University Press, 1972), pp. 103–6.

59 We sketch here the main arguments in Newton's geometrical proof of Proposition 15, Book 2, which correspond to the calculus-based derivation given in Eqs. (1)–(5), pp. 118–20. Reference to Figure 3.15, which is from Proposition 15, Book 2, shows three nearby points P, Q, and r on a spiral curve centered at S, with corresponding radial lines SP, SQ, and Sr. The sectors PSQ and QSr have equal areas, corresponding to equal intervals of time δt, and for an equiangular spiral $Qr/PQ = SP/SQ$. Thus, P, Q, and r represent points along the spiral orbit traversed by a body under the action of a centripetal force alone. The additional point R between r and Q represents the position of the body when there is resistance. Hence, the change in area due to the resistive force F_R is given by the area of the sector $RSr = SP \times Rr \sin\alpha = \delta h \delta t$, where Rr is a second-order differential proportional to the magnitude of this force and to the square of the time interval. Substituting $Rr = F_R \delta t^2$ leads to Eq. (1), $\delta h = -SP \times F_R \sin(\alpha)\delta t$.

The location of R is determined by the relation $QR/PQ = \sqrt{(SP/SQ)}$, which follows from the condition that the velocity v of the body varies inversely as the square root of the radial distance. Newton derives this result by referring to Lemma 3, Book 2 and to Lemma 10, Book 1. It is clear, however, that Lemma 3 is based on a geometrical construction equivalent to Lemma 11, Book 1. The figure in Lemma 3 contains two lines perpendicular to the spiral at P and Q that intersect at O, and therefore in the limit that Q approaches P the line PO becomes the radius of curvature of the spiral at P. While Newton does not mention curvature in Lemma 3 or in Propositions 15–17, Book 2, nevertheless his geometrical derivation that v is proportional to $1/\sqrt{(SP)}$ makes explicit use of the curvature relation $PD = PQ^2/2PO$, where PD is the "subtense of the angle of contact" defined in Lemma 11, Book 1.

60   Newton had already obtained this result by his fluxional calculus by 1671. Later he demonstrated it geometrically in Proposition 9, Book 1, and implicitly in Section 4, Lemma 3, Book 2.

61   It should be pointed out that in his statement of Proposition 15, Book 2 Newton used the Latin words "gyrari potest," which when translated correctly as *"can revolve"* indicate that the equiangular curve is a *possible* orbit. See Isaac Newton, *The Principia*, trans. I. Bernard Cohen and Ann Whitman, p. 680. In the text of the proposition (although not in its statement), these words have been translated incorrectly by Motte, and subsequently by Motte–Cajori, as *"will* revolve" indicating that the equiangular curve is the *only* orbit. Unfortunately, these earlier translations have caused some confusion in the literature.

62   Leonhard Euler, *Opera Omnia* Series secunda, Opera Mechanica et Astronomica, vol, 23. ed. L. Courvoisier and J. O. Fleckenstein (Basel: Societatis Scientiarum Naturalium Helveticae), 1969, pp. 286–9.

63   *Collected Mathematical Papers of G. W. Hill* (Carnegie Institute of Washington, 1905), vol. 1, pp. 284–335.

64   P. S. Laplace, *A Treatise of Celestial Mechanics* trans. from the French by Henry H. Harte (Dublin, 1822), pp. 357–90.

65   This expression corresponds to the formula for the radius of curvature in polar coordinates that Newton had obtained already by 1671 with his fluxional calculus, evaluated at an extremal point of the curve where $dr/d\theta = 0$. In this case, $(1/\rho - 1/r) = (-1/r^2)d^2r/d\theta^2$. It appears from Newton's text, however, that he applied the curvature formula in the differential form, Eq. (12), obtained directly from geometry.

66   Newton presented his result for the ratio of these two curvatures as "the curvature of the figure Cpa at a to be to its curvature at C as $AT^3 + 16824/100000CT^2 \, AT$ is to $CT^3 + 16824/100000AT^2CT$; where the number $16824/100000$ represents the difference of the squares of the angles CTP and CTp divided by the square of the lesser angle CTP." Here the ratio $16824/1000$ corresponds to the numerical evaluation of $1/\xi^2 - 1$ with Newton's values for the sidereal and synodic period of the Moon. There is an error in the 1934 Motte–Cajori edition (p. 447) of the *Principia*, where the first plus sign in Newton's result is given

incorrectly as a minus sign, although it is correct in the original 1729 Motte edition (vol. 2, p. 270).

67 Curtis Wilson, "Newton on the Moon's Variation and Apsidal Motion: The Need for a Newer 'New Analysis'," in Jed Buchwald and I. Bernard Cohen (eds.), *Issac Newton's Natural Philosophy* (Cambridge, MA: MIT Press, 2001).

68 Nauenberg, "Newton's Perturbation Methods for the 3-Body Problem and Its Application to Lunar Motion."

4 The methodology of the *Principia*

In the Preface to the first edition (1687) Newton informs the reader straight off that he intends the *Principia* to illustrate a new way of doing what we now call empirical science:

And therefore our present work sets forth mathematical principles of natural philosophy. For the whole difficulty of philosophy seems to be to find the forces of nature from the phenomena of motions and then to demonstrate the other phenomena from these forces. It is to these ends that the general propositions in Books 1 and 2 are directed, while in Book 3 our explanation of the system of the universe illustrates these propositions ... If only we could derive the other phenomena of nature from mechanical principles by the same kind of reasoning! For many things lead me to have a suspicion that all phenomena may depend on certain forces by which the particles of bodies, by causes yet unknown, either are impelled toward one another and cohere in regular figures, or are repelled from one another and recede. Since these forces are unknown, philosophers have hitherto made trial of nature in vain. But I hope that the principles set down here will shed some light on either this mode of philosophizing or some truer one.[1]

Surprisingly, however, the main body of the first edition contains only two further comments about methodology: (1) a cryptic remark at the end of the opening discussion of space and time, announcing that the purpose of the work is to explain "how to determine the true motions from their causes, effects, and apparent differences, and, conversely, how to determine from motions, whether true or apparent, their causes and effects";[2] and (2) a scholium buried at the end of Book 1, Section 11 in which Newton proposes that his distinctive approach will make it possible to *argue more securely* in natural philosophy.

138

In the second edition (1713), clearly in response to complaints about his methodology, Newton introduces separate sections for the Phenomena and Rules for Natural Philosophy[3] involved in his derivation of universal gravity (adding a fourth rule in the third edition, 1726), and he adds at the end the General Scholium containing his most famous – and troubling – methodological pronouncement:

I have not as yet been able to deduce from phenomena the reason for these properties of gravity, and I do not feign hypotheses. For whatever is not deduced from the phenomena must be called a hypothesis; and hypotheses, whether metaphysical or physical, or based on occult qualities, or mechanical, have no place in experimental philosophy. In this experimental philosophy, propositions are deduced from the phenomena and are made general by induction.[4]

In a later (anonymous) work, Newton softened his renunciation of hypotheses by adding, "unless as conjectures or questions proposed to be examined by experiments."[5]

With or without this qualification, the thrust of the pronouncement remains mostly negative: Newton's new *experimental philosophy* does not proceed hypothetico-deductively, even under the supposedly safe constraint imposed by the then-prevailing *mechanical philosophy* that all hypothesized action arises strictly through contact of matter with matter. How, then, does theory construction proceed on Newton's approach? Vague talk of "deductions from phenomena" provided no more adequate an answer to this question then than it does now.

Newton leaves the task of extracting the answer from the *Principia* largely to the reader. Three centuries of disagreement give reason to think that the answer is far more complex than the hypothetico-deductive alternative, which Christiaan Huygens, the foremost figure in science at the time, managed to lay out in a single paragraph in his January 1690 Preface to his *Treatise on Light*, published thirty months after the *Principia*:

One finds in this subject a kind of demonstration which does not carry with it so high a degree of certainty as that employed in geometry; and which differs distinctly from the method employed by geometers in that they prove their propositions by well-established and incontrovertible principles, while here principles are tested by the inferences which are derivable from them. The nature of the subject permits of no other treatment. It is possible, however, in this way to establish a probability which is little short of certainty. This is the case when the consequences of the assumed principles are in perfect accord with the observed phenomena, and especially when these verifications are numerous; but above all when one employs the hypothesis to predict new phenomena and finds his expectations realized.[6]

Huygens's *Discourse on the Cause of Gravity*, which contains his critical evaluation of the *Principia*, was published in combination with his *Treatise on Light*, making this paragraph prefatory to both.

The nearest Newton ever comes to such a capsule summary of his approach is the one methodological pronouncement from the first edition from which I have yet to quote, the Scholium at the end of Book 1, Section 11:

By these propositions we are directed to the analogy between centripetal forces and the central bodies toward which those forces tend. For it is reasonable that forces directed toward bodies depend on the nature and the quantity of matter of such bodies, as happens in the case of magnetic bodies. And whenever cases of this sort occur, the attractions of the bodies must be reckoned by assigning proper forces to their individual particles and then taking the sums of these forces.

I use the word "attraction" here in a general sense for any endeavor whatever of bodies to approach one another, whether that endeavor occurs as a result of the action of the bodies either drawn toward one another or acting on one another by means of spirits emitted or whether it arises from the action of ether or of air or of any medium whatsoever – whether corporeal or incorporeal – in any way impelling toward one another the bodies floating therein. I use the word "impulse" in the same general sense, considering in this treatise not the species of forces and their physical qualities but their quantities and mathematical proportions, as I have explained in the definitions.

Mathematics requires an investigation of those quantities of forces and their proportions that follow from any conditions that may be supposed. Then, coming down to physics, these proportions must be compared with the phenomena, so that it may be found out which conditions of forces apply to each kind of attracting bodies. And then, finally, it will be possible to argue more securely concerning the physical species, physical causes, and physical proportions of these forces. Let us see, therefore, what the forces are by which spherical bodies, consisting of particles that attract in the way already set forth, must act upon one another, and what sorts of motions result from such forces.[7]

The goal in what follows is to describe the methodology of the *Principia* in the light of this too often neglected Scholium.[8]

First, however, the Scholium (which remained word-for-word the same in all three editions) should be put into context. Section 11 treats bodies moving under centripetal forces directed not toward a point in space, as in the preceding sections, but toward other moving bodies – so-called "two-body" and "three-body" problems. By far the largest portion of Section 11 presents Newton's limited, qualitative results for three-body effects on the motions of the planets and the Moon, results that he called "imperfect" in the Preface. The Scholium thus occurs just after it should have become clear to readers that the true orbital motions are so intractably complex as to preclude hope of exact agreement between theory and observation. To concede that theory can at best only approximate the real world, however, appears to concede that multiple conflicting theories can claim equal support from the available evidence at any time. Seventeenth-century readers would have been quick to note this, for equipollence of astronomical theories had been a celebrated concern for over a century,[9] and such leading figures as Descartes and Marin Mersenne had frequently called pointed attention to the limitations of experimental evidence.[10] Newton would have accordingly expected his readers to see his remark about *arguing more securely* as making a startling claim in the face of a concession that the real world is intractably complex.

Proposition 69, to which the Scholium is attached, lays the groundwork for Newton's law of gravity by asserting that in the relevant inverse-square case the forces directed toward the various bodies must be proportional to the masses of those bodies. Sections 12 and 13 examine the characteristics of forces directed toward bodies when these forces are composed out of forces directed toward the individual particles of matter making up the bodies. In other words, they lay the groundwork for Newton's claim that his law of gravity holds *universally* between individual particles of matter. Now, the mechanical philosophy did not bar "attractive" forces among macroscopic bodies, for intervening unseen matter could be hypothesized to effect these forces in the manner Descartes had proposed in the case of magnets, and also gravity.[11] As Newton well realized, however, no hypothetical contact mechanism seems even imaginable to effect "attractive" forces among particles of matter generally. The Scholium thus occurs at the point where adherents to the mechanical philosophy would start viewing Newton's reasoning as "absurd" (to use the word Huygens chose privately).[12] The Scholium attempts to carry the reader past this worry, but not by facing the demand for a contact mechanism head-on. Instead, Newton warns that he is employing mathematically formulated theory in physics in a new way, with forces treated abstractly, independently of mechanism. What we need to do first, then, is to understand how Newton is using mathematical theory and talk of forces in the *Principia*, and how he is departing from his predecessors. Then we can turn, in the last two sections of the chapter, to the questions of how Newton prefers to argue for theoretical claims and whether this way of arguing is more secure.

MATHEMATICAL THEORY IN NEWTON'S *PRINCIPIA*

The two most prominent books presenting mathematical theories of motion before the *Principia* were Galileo's *Two New Sciences* (1638)[13] and Huygens's *Horologium Oscillatorium* (1673).[14] Newton almost certainly never saw the former, but he knew the latter well, and it together with Galileo's *Dialogues on the Two Chief World Systems* (1632)[15] and various secondary sources[16] made him familiar with Galileo's results. Outwardly, the *Principia* appears to take the same mathematical approach as these two earlier books, proceeding from axioms to a series of rigorously demonstrated propositions. In fact, however, the approach to mathematical theory in Books 1 and 2 of the *Principia* differs from that taken by Galileo and Huygens in two important respects.

The first difference is subtle. Almost without exception, the demonstrated propositions of Books 1 and 2 of the *Principia* are of an "if-then" logical form, as illustrated by Propositions 1 and 2, restated in modern form: *if the forces acting on a moving body are all directed toward a single point in space, then a radius from that point to the body sweeps out equal areas in equal times, and conversely.*[17] So far as strict logic is concerned, the same can be said of the demonstrated propositions of Galileo and Huygens, as illustrated by the latter's celebrated isochronism theorem: *if a body descends along a path described by a cycloid, then the time of descent is the same regardless of the point along the path from which its descent begins.*[18] From the point of view of empirical science, however, this and the other demonstrated propositions of Galileo and Huygens are better described as having a "when-then" form, in which the antecedent describes an experimental situation and the consequent, a prediction of what will occur whenever that situation is realized. A primary aim of Galileo's and Huygens's mathematical theories is to derive observable consequences from their axioms that can provide evidence supporting these axioms, taken as hypotheses, or that can facilitate practical applications, such as the design of pendulum clocks.[19]

What lies behind this "when-then" form is the kind of quantities employed in the theories laid out by Galileo and Huygens. With the notable exception of the latter's theorems on centrifugal force, appended without proofs at the end of *Horologium Oscillatorium*, their axioms and demonstrated propositions make no reference to forces. Surprising as it may be, even the rate of acceleration in vertical fall – for us, g, and for them the distance of fall in the first second – enters nowhere into Galileo's propositions. This quantity does enter into the very last propositions of *Horologium Oscillatorium*, enabling Huygens to carry out a theory-mediated measurement of it to very high accuracy by means of pendulums; nonetheless, it plays no role in the development of his theory. The quantities central to the mathematical theories of motion under uniform gravity laid out by Galileo and Huygens were all open to measurement without having to presuppose any propositions of the theories themselves.

Unlike Galileo and Huygens, Newton takes his "axioms or laws of motion" to hold true from the outset of Books 1 and 2 of the *Principia*. His demonstrated "if-then" propositions amount to *inference-tickets*[20] linking motions to forces, forces to motions, and macrophysical forces to microphysical forces composing them. As Newton indicates in the quotation given earlier from the Preface to the first edition, the aim of the mathematical theories of Books 1 and 2 is first to establish means for inferring conclusions about forces from phenomena of motion and then to demonstrate further phenomena from these conclusions about forces. In Newton's hands *force* is a flagrantly theoretical quantity. The principal problem Newton's mathematical theories address is to find ways to characterize forces.

The second critical difference between Newton's mathematical theories and those of Galileo and Huygens concerns their respective scopes. Galileo offered a mathematical theory of uniformly accelerated motion, and Huygens extended this theory to curvilinear trajectories and uniform circular motion. Newton, by contrast, does not offer a theory of motion under inverse-square centripetal forces, much less under gravity, alone. Rather, Book 1 offers a *generic* theory of centripetal forces and motion under them. Inverse-square forces receive extra attention, but the theory also covers centripetal forces that vary linearly with distance to the force-center, that vary as the inverse-cube, and finally that vary as any function whatever of distance to the center. Similarly, while Book 2 emphasizes resistance forces that vary as the square of the velocity, it ultimately derives "if-then" propositions that allow resistance forces to vary as the sum of any powers of velocity whatever, including non-integer powers.[21] Book 2 thus strives to offer a generic theory of resistance forces, where these are characterized as arising from the velocity of a moving body in a fluid medium. The generic scope of these two theories is not simply a case of Newton displaying his mathematical prowess, as is sometimes suggested. The theories need to be generic in order to allow him to establish strong conclusions about forces from phenomena of motions, conclusions that exclude potential competing claims.

The propositions from Books 1 and 2 that become most important to the overall *Principia* are of two types. The first type consists of propositions that link parameters in rules characterizing forces to parameters of motion. The historically most significant example of this type is Newton's "precession theorem" for nearly circular orbits under centripetal forces.[22] It establishes a strict relationship between the apsidal angle θ – the angle at the force-center between, for example, the aphelion and the perihelion – to the square root of the index n, namely $n = (\pi/\theta)^2$, where the centripetal force varies as $r^{(n-3)}$. This relationship not only confirms that the exponent of r is exactly -2 when the apsidal angle is 180 degrees and exactly $+1$ when the angle is 90 degrees, but also yields a value of n and hence of the exponent for any other apsidal angle, or in other words for any rate at which the overall orbit precesses. This proposition and others of its type thus enable *theory-mediated measurements* of parameters characterizing forces to be made from parameters characterizing motions.[23] The propositions laid out earlier relating centripetal forces to Kepler's area rule, and their corollaries, provide another example of this type in which areal velocity yields a theory-mediated measure of the direction of the forces acting on a body.

As alluded to above, in his theory of motion under uniform gravity Huygens had derived propositions expressing the laws of the cycloidal and small-arc circular pendulums; and these results had enabled him to obtain from the periods and lengths of such pendulums a theory-mediated measure of the strength of surface gravity to four significant figures. This was a spectacular advance over prior attempts to measure the distance of vertical fall in the first second directly. Also, Huygens's theory of centrifugal force in uniform circular motion had allowed him to characterize the strength of these forces in terms of such motions, and from this to derive the law of the conical pendulum; and this result had enabled him to obtain a still further theory-mediated measure of the strength of surface gravity, in precise agreement with his other measures.[24] So, regardless of whether Newton first learned about propositions enabling theory-mediated measurements from Huygens, he at the very least had seen the utility of such propositions in *Horologium Oscillatorium*. Huygens, however, seems never to have seen any special evidential significance in his precise, stable measures of gravity. In Newton's hands, by contrast, theory-mediated measures became central to a new approach to marshaling evidence.

It is difficult to exaggerate the importance of measurement to the methodology of the *Principia*[25] or, for that matter, the sophistication with which Newton thought through philosophical issues concerning measurement. The importance is clear even in the definitions of key quantities with which the *Principia* opens, which are at least as much about measures of these quantities as they are about terminology. As the discussion of astronomical measures of *time* in the Scholium immediately following these definitions makes clear, Newton recognized that measures invariably involve theoretical assumptions, and hence remain provisional, even if not theory-mediated in the more restricted sense invoked above. He also seems to have appreciated that, because measurements in physics involve physical procedures and assumptions, a distinctive feature of this science is that it cannot help but include within itself its own empirically revisable theory of measurement. This insight may explain why Newton was so quick to view success in measurement as a form of evidence in its own right; here success includes (1) stability of values as a measure is repeated in varying circumstances – as illustrated by the stability of Huygens's measure of surface gravity by cycloidal pendulums of different lengths – and (2) convergence of values when the same quantity is determined through different measures involving different assumptions – as illustrated by the convergence of Huygens's cycloidal and conical pendulum measures. (Being open to increasingly greater precision appears to be a still further dimension of success in measurement for Newton.) Achieving success of this sort in determining values for forces is almost certainly what Newton had in mind with the cryptic remark at the end of the Scholium on space and time about the book explaining "how to determine the true motions from their causes, effects, and apparent differences."

The second type of proposition important to the *Principia* consists of combinations that draw clear contrasts between different conditions of force in terms of different conditions of motion. An historically significant example is the contrast between the simple form of Kepler's 3/2 power rule and the form requiring a specific small correction for each individual orbiting body; the latter holds if the orbiting and central bodies are interacting with one another in accord with the third law of motion, while the former holds if the orbiting body does not exert a force causing motion of the central body. Another historically significant example is the contrast between inverse-square celestial gravity acting to hold bodies in their orbits – a form of gravity that Huygens thought Newton had established – and inverse-square *universal* gravity between all the particles of matter in the universe: only under the latter does gravity vary linearly with distance from the center beneath the surface of a (uniformly dense) spherical Earth; and only under the latter does a particular relationship hold between the non-sphericity of a (uniformly dense) Earth and the variation of surface gravity with latitude. Combinations of propositions of this type thus provide contrasts that open the way to crossroads experiments – *experimenta crucis* – enabling phenomena of motion to pick out which among alternative kinds of conditions hold true of forces.

As these examples and the examples for the first type suggest, Newton prefers "if-and-only-if" results with both types. When he is unable to establish a strict converse, he typically looks for a result that falls as little short of it as he can find, as illustrated by the qualitative theorems on the "three-body" problem in Section 11.

Once these two types are identified, an examination of the overall development of the mathematical theories of Books 1 and 2 makes clear that the propositions Newton was most pursuing in these books are of these two types. His preoccupation with these explains why he included the propositions he did and not others that he could easily have added. Propositions that do not fall into these types generally serve to enable ones that do. By contrast, an examination of the overall development of the mathematical theories of Galileo and Huygens indicates that the propositions they were most pursuing are ones that make a highly distinctive empirical prediction, that provide an answer to some practical question, or that explain some known phenomenon. In other words, the mathematical theories of motion of Galileo and Huygens are primarily aimed at predicting and explaining phenomena. The mathematical theories of motion developed in Books 1 and 2 of the *Principia* do not have this aim. Rather, their aim is to provide a basis for specifying experiments and observations by means of which the empirical world can provide answers to questions – this in contrast to conjecturing answers and then testing the implications of these conjectures. Newton is using mathematical theory in an effort to turn otherwise recalcitrant questions into empirically tractable questions. This is what he is describing when he says:

Mathematics requires an investigation of those quantities of forces and their proportions that follow from any conditions that may be supposed. Then, coming down to physics, these proportions must be compared with the phenomena, so that it may be found out which conditions of forces apply to each kind of attracting bodies.

This initial picture of Newton's approach is too simple in one crucial respect: if only because of imprecision of measurement, the empirical world rarely yields straightforward univocal answers to questions. That Newton was acutely aware of this is clear from his supplementing key "if-then" propositions with corollaries noting that the consequent still holds *quam proxime* (i.e., very nearly) when the antecedent holds only *quam proxime*. Nothing adds to the complexity of Newton's methodology more than his approach to inexactitude. We will return to this subject after considering the way in which he talks of force.

NEWTONIAN FORCES: MATHEMATICAL AND PHYSICAL

The theories developed in the *Principia*, unlike the theory of uniformly accelerated motion developed by Galileo and extended by

Huygens, are first and foremost about forces. Book 1 develops a general theory of centripetal forces and motions under them, and the first two-thirds of Book 2, a general theory of resistance forces and motions under them; the last third of Book 2 then develops a theory of the contribution the inertia of fluid media makes to resistance forces, and Book 3, a theory of gravitational forces and their effects. Newton was not the first to employ talk of forces in theories of motion. As the warning in the Scholium at the end of Section 11 about how he uses "attraction" and "impulse" indicates, he saw his way of employing such terms as novel, threatening confusion he needed to obviate. Definition 8 at the beginning of the *Principia* includes essentially the same warning about these terms, and "force" as well, adding, "this concept is purely mathematical, for I am not now considering the physical causes and sites of forces."[26] The warnings themselves are clear enough: Newton wants to be taken as talking of forces in the abstract, as quantities unto themselves, totally without regard to the physical mechanisms producing them. Not so clear are the ramifications of talking in this way.

The prior work that comes closest to treating forces in the manner of Newton is Huygens's theory of centrifugal force arising from uniform circular motion.[27] Like Descartes, Huygens uses the contrapositive of the principle of inertia to infer that something must be impeding any body that is not moving uniformly in a straight line. He further concludes that the magnitude of the force acting on the impediment is proportional to the extent of departure from what we now call inertial motion, obtaining for uniform circular motion the familiar v^2/r result. What Huygens means by "centrifugal force," however, is the force exerted on the impediment – for example, the tension in the string retaining the object in a circle. Huygens's centrifugal force is thus a form of static force, expressly analogous to the force a heavy object exerts on a string from which it is dangling. Talk of static forces was widespread in accounts of mechanical devices during the seventeenth century. Huygens was reaching beyond such talk only in inferring the magnitude of the force from the motion.

As Newton's discussion of his laws of motion makes clear, he too intended his treatment of forces to be continuous with the traditional treatment of static forces. Unlike Huygens, however, he singles out the unbalanced force that acts on the moving body, making it depart from inertial motion. Where Descartes and Huygens used the contrapositive of the principle of inertia to infer the existence of an impediment in contact with the non-inertially moving body, Newton uses it to infer the existence of an unbalanced force, *independently of all consideration of what is effecting that force.* His second law of motion then enables the magnitude and direction of any such force to be inferred from the extent and direction of the departure from inertial motion. Unbalanced force as a quantity can thus be fully characterized in abstraction from whatever might be producing it. This is what Newton means when he speaks in Definition 8 of considering "forces not from a physical but only from a mathematical point of view."

Newton had reason to expect that this way of talking of forces would confuse many of his readers. In his writing on light and colors in the early 1670s he had adopted essentially the same strategy in talking of rays of light as purely mathematically characterizable, independently of the underlying physics of light and the process or mechanism of its transmission. His warnings notwithstanding, many readers had insisted on equating his rays of light with paths defined by hypothetical particles comprising light; they had then argued, to his consternation, that his claims about refraction had not been established because he had not established that light consists of such particles.[28] His warnings about considering forces "from a mathematical point of view" were scarcely any better heeded.

From the mathematical point of view any unbalanced force acting on a body is a quantity with magnitude and direction. The general theory of centripetal forces developed in Book 1 considers forces from this point of view, with the direction specified toward a center and the magnitude taken to vary as a function of distance from that center. The same is true of the general theory of resistance forces developed in the first two-thirds of Book 2, but with the direction specified opposite to the direction of motion and the magnitude varying as a function of velocity. An unbalanced force that is thus fully characterized by its direction and magnitude can be resolved into correspondingly fully characterized components in any way one wishes, without regard to the particular physical components that happen to be giving rise to it. This absence of constraint in resolving forces into components is important in several places in Books 1 and 2, perhaps most strikingly in Proposition 3 of the former:

Every body that, by a radius drawn to the center of a second body moving in any way whatever, describes about that center areas that are proportional to the times is urged by a force compounded of the centripetal force tending toward that second body and of the whole accelerative force by which that second body is urged.[29]

In principle – indeed, in practice – this situation can occur without there being any form of physical interaction, or physical forces, between the two bodies.

Still, as Newton's remark about "arguing more securely concerning the physical species, physical causes, and physical proportions of these forces" indicates, it does make sense according to his way of talking about forces to ask what *physical* forces a net unbalanced force results from. The theory of gravitational forces of Book 3 and the theory of the constituent of resistance forces arising from the inertia of the fluid at the end of Book 2 both treat forces from a physical point of view. Judging from the development of these two theories, Newton requires five conditions to be met for a component of a mathematically characterized force to be considered a physical force: (1) its direction must be determined by some material body other than the one it is acting on;[30] (2) all respects in which its magnitude can vary must be given by a general law that is independent of the first two laws of motion, such as the law of gravity, $F \propto Mm/r^2$; (3) some of the physical quantities entering into this law must pertain to the other body that determines the direction of the force; (4) this law must hold for some forces that are indisputably real, such as terrestrial gravity in the case of the law of gravity; and (5) if the force acts on a macroscopic body, then it must be composed of forces acting on microphysical parts of that body – this primarily to safeguard against inexactitude in the force law introduced by inferring it from macroscopic phenomena.

Notably absent from this list is anything about the mechanism or process effecting the force. Adherents to the "mechanical philosophy," such as Descartes and Huygens, and undoubtedly Galileo as well, would have required not just a mechanism effecting the force, but specifically a contact mechanism. Otherwise the putative force might be beyond explanation and hence occult. This is where Newton's new "experimental philosophy" departed most radically from the prevailing "mechanical philosophy."

The law characterizing a force from a physical point of view gives its "physical proportions" and assigns it to a "physical species." Two forces are of the same physical species only if they are characterized by the same law. Thus the inverse-square forces retaining the planets and their statellites in their orbits are the same in kind as terrestrial gravity, while (for Newton) the constituent of resistance forces arising from the inertia of the fluid is different in kind from that arising from its viscosity in so far as the former varies as velocity squared, and the latter does not. A theory of any physical species of force is required to give (1) necessary and sufficient conditions for a force to be present, (2) a law or laws dictating the relative magnitude and direction of this force in terms of determinable physical quantities, and (3) where relevant, an account of how it is composed out of microstructural forces.

Microstructural forces have a more fundamental status in the overall taxonomy of forces. In the *Principia* Newton identifies three species of microstructural force, gravity, pressure, and, percussion, where the theory of the latter had already been put forward by Huygens, Christopher Wren, and John Wallis.[31] The remark in the Preface to the first edition – "all phenomena may depend on certain forces by which the particles of bodies, by causes yet unknown, either are impelled toward one another and cohere in regular figures, or are repelled from one another and recede" – points to a program of pursuing theories of further species of microstructural force. This program is described in more detail in the unpublished portion of this Preface and an unpublished Conclusion, as illustrated by this passage from the former:

I therefore propose the inquiry whether or not there be many forces of this kind, never yet perceived, by which the particles of bodies agitate one another and coalesce into various structures. For if Nature be simple and pretty conformable to herself, causes will operate in the same kind of way in all phenomena, so that the motions of smaller bodies depend upon certain smaller forces just as the motions of larger bodies are ruled by the greater force of gravity. It remains therefore that we inquire by means of fitting experiments whether there are forces of this kind in nature, then what are their properties, quantities, and effects. For if all natural motions of great or small bodies can be explained through such forces, nothing more will remain than to inquire the causes of gravity, magnetic attraction, and the other forces.[32]

To his contemporaries, what seemed most confusing about Newton's way of talking about forces was his willingness to put forward a theory of gravitational "attraction" without regard to the causal mechanism effecting it. They generally concluded that he had to be committed to action at a distance as a causal mechanism in its own right. The outspoken opposition to the *Principia* in many quarters stemmed primarily from the inexplicability of action at a distance. Present-day readers, viewing the *Principia* in the light of 300 years of success in physics, are not likely to find the way Newton talks of forces from a physical point of view confusing. What most tends to confuse them is the distinction between considering forces from a physical point of view and considering them purely from a mathematical point of view. A symptom of this confusion is the tendency to read Book I as if its subject is gravitational forces, wondering why Newton bothered to include in it so many seemingly irrelevant propositions.

ARGUING FROM PHENOMENA OF MOTION TO LAWS OF FORCE

In the Scholium at the end of Section 11 Newton says, rather vaguely, that the transition from mathematically to physically characterized forces is to be carried out by *comparing* the mathematically characterized proportions with phenomena. As other methodological remarks in the *Principia* make clear, the specific approach he prefers is to use the "if-then" propositions of his mathematical theory to "deduce" the physical laws characterizing forces from phenomena[33] – most notably, to deduce the law of gravity from the phenomena of orbital motion specified by two of Kepler's rules,[34] along with Thomas Streete's conclusion that the planetary aphelia are stationary.[35] Serious difficulties stand in the way of any such deduction, however. Much of the complexity of Newton's methodology comes from his approach to these difficulties.

One difficulty, noted earlier, is that limits of precision in observation entail that statements of phenomena hold at most *quam proxime*. This limitation was evident at the time in the case of Kepler's rules. Ishmaël Boulliau had replaced Kepler's area rule with a geometric construction, yet had achieved the same level of accuracy relative to Tycho Brahe's data as Kepler – roughly the level of accuracy that Tycho had claimed for observations at Uraniborg; and Vincent Wing had done almost as well using an oscillating equant instead of the area rule.[36] Jeremiah Horrocks and Streete were the only orbital astronomers to claim that the lengths of the semi-major axes of the planetary orbits could be inferred more accurately from the periods using Kepler's 3/2 power rule than by classical methods that were known to be sensitive to observational imprecision.[37] Even in the case of the ellipse, which virtually all orbital astronomers were using, the question whether it is merely a good approximation or the true exact trajectory remained open.[38] In short, Kepler's rules were at best established only *quam proxime*, and any "deduction" from them would have to concede that other ways of stating the phenomena could not be eliminated on grounds of accuracy alone.

From Newton's point of view, however, imprecision was not the worst difficulty. In the brief "De motu" tracts that preceded the *Principia* he had concluded that there are inverse-square centripetal acceleration fields (to use the modern term) around the Sun, Jupiter, Saturn, and the Earth, with the strength of each given by the invariant value $[a^3/P^2]$ for bodies orbiting them, where a is the mean distance for any orbit and P is the period.[39] Presumably, the acceleration fields around Jupiter, Saturn, and the Earth extend to the Sun, putting it into motion. By a generalization of the principle of inertia to a system of interacting bodies – a generalization that is equivalent to the third law of motion of the *Principia* – the interactions among the bodies cannot alter the motion of the center of gravity of the system. From this Newton reached a momentous conclusion:

By reason of the deviation of the Sun from the center of gravity, the centripetal force does not always tend to that immobile center, and hence the planets neither move exactly in ellipses nor revolve twice in the same orbit. There are as many orbits of a planet as it has revolutions, as in the motion of the Moon...But to consider simultaneously all these causes of motion and to define these motions by exact laws admitting of easy calculation exceeds, if I am not mistaken, the force of any human mind.[40]

In other words, before he began writing the *Principia* itself (and, if I am right, before he had even discovered the law of gravity[41]), Newton had concluded that Kepler's rules can at best be true only *quam proxime* of the planets and their satellites, not because of imprecision of observation, but because the true motions are immensely more complicated than Kepler's or any other such rules could hope to capture.

Newton was not the first to conclude that real motions are exceedingly complex. Galileo had concluded that the multiplicity of factors affecting motion in resisting media preclude "fixed laws and exact description";[42] and, in a letter to Mersenne, Descartes too had denied the possibility of a science of air resistance.[43] Newton was most likely unaware of these remarks of Galileo and Descartes on resistance, but he definitely did know that Descartes, in his *Principia* (1644), had denied that the planetary orbits are mathematically exact, remarking that as "in all other natural things, they are only approximately so, and also they are continuously changed by the passing of the ages."[44] The response of Galileo, Huygens, and Descartes to the complexities of real-world motions and limits in precision of measurement was to employ the hypothetico-deductive approach to marshaling evidence, deducing testable conclusions from conjectured hypotheses and then exposing these conclusions to falsification. From the beginning of his work in optics in the 1660s, Newton had always distrusted the hypothetico-deductive approach, arguing that too many disparate hypotheses can be compatible with the same observations.[45] Inexactitude, whether from imprecision in observation or from the complexity of the real world, exacerbates this shortcoming. In saying that the approach illustrated by the *Principia* puts one in position to argue more securely about features of underlying physics, Newton was claiming to have a response to inexactitude that surmounts limitations of the hypothetico-deductive approach of his predecessors.

Because Newton never describes his approach in detail, we have to infer what it involves from the evidential reasoning in the *Principia*. A key clue is provided by what I. Bernard Cohen has called the "Newtonian style"[46] – proceeding from idealized simple cases to progressively more complicated ones, though still idealized. Thus, in the case of inverse-square centripetal forces, Book 1 first considers so-called "one-body" problems, for which Kepler's three rules hold exactly. Next are one-body problems in which inverse-cube centripetal forces are superposed on the inverse-square; Kepler's rules still hold exactly, but for orbits that rotate, that is, whose lines of apsides precess. Next are "two-body" problems subject to the third law of motion. The results for these show that two of Kepler's rules continue to hold, but the 3/2 power rule requires a correction. Last are problems involving three or more interacting bodies. For these Newton succeeds in obtaining only limited, qualitative results, yet still sufficient to show that none of Kepler's three rules holds. A distinctive feature of this sequence is the extent to which it focuses on systematic deviations from Kepler's simple rules that can serve as evidence for two-body and three-body interaction. Newton is putting himself in a position to address the complexity of real orbital motion in a sequence of successive approximations, with each approximation an idealized motion and systematic deviations from it providing evidence for the next stage in the sequence.

Here too Huygens had foreshadowed the Newtonian style, though again only up to a point. The initial theory of pendulum motion in *Horologium Oscillatorium* is for pendulums with idealized "point-mass" bobs.[47] Huygens then turns to the question of physical bobs with a distinctive shape and real bulk, solving the celebrated problem of the center of oscillation that Mersenne had put forward as a challenge decades earlier. The small-arc circular pendulum measurement of gravity presented near the end of the book incorporates a small correction to the length of the pendulum, corresponding to the distance between the center of gravity of the bob and its center of oscillation. This correction, however, holds only for the circular pendulum, not for the cycloidal pendulum that was the crowning achievement of Huygens's initial theory. For the correction depends not only on the shape of the bob, but also on the length of the string, and this length varies along the cycloidal path. (Indeed, it is this variation that makes the cycloid the isochronous path for a point-mass bob.) Huygens had tried to find the corrected path required for strict isochronism with a physically real bob, only to despair when the problem proved intractably complex. In the manner typical of pre-Newtonian science, the small residual discrepancies between idealized theory and the real world were dismissed as being of no practical importance. This is one more example of the way in which the complexity of the real world ended up being viewed as an impediment, limiting the quality of empirical evidence, and not as a resource for progressively higher-quality evidence that it became with Newtonian successive approximations.

Newton's "deductions" of the various parts of the law of gravity from phenomena of orbital motion reveal two restrictions, beyond mathematical tractability, that he at least prefers to impose on the successive approximations.[48] First, in every case in which he deduces some feature of celestial gravitational forces, he has taken the trouble in Book 1 to prove that the consequent of the "if-then" proposition licensing the deduction still holds *quam proxime* so long as the antecedent holds *quam proxime*. For instance, two corollaries of Proposition 3 show that the force on the orbital body is at least very nearly centripetal so long as the areas swept out in equal times remain very nearly equal. This, by the way, explains why Newton himself never deduced the inverse-square variation from the Keplerian ellipse even though he had proved in Book 1 that an exact Keplerian ellipse entails an exact inverse-square variation: an orbital motion can approximate a Keplerian ellipse without the exponent of r in the rule governing the centripetal force variation being even approximately minus 2.[49] Restricting the deductions to ones that hold *quam proxime* so long as the phenomenon describes the true motions *quam proxime* provides a guarantee: under the assumption that the laws of motion hold, the deduced feature of the physical forces holds at least *quam proxime* of the specific motions that license the statement of the phenomenon. In other words, thanks to this restriction, unless his laws of motion are seriously wrong, Newton's law of gravity is definitely true at least *quam proxime* of celestial motions over the century of observations from Tycho to the *Principia*.

Second, in every case in which Newton deduces some feature of celestial gravitational forces, mathematical results established in Book 1 allow him to identify specific conditions under which the phenomenon from which the deduction is made would hold not merely *quam proxime*, but exactly. For instance, the orbiting body would sweep out equal areas in equal times exactly if the only forces acting on it were centripetal, and its line of apsides would be stationary if the only forces acting on it were inverse-square centripetal forces. The choice of the subjunctive here is not mine, but Newton's: in Proposition 13 of Book 3, for example, he remarks, "if the Sun were at rest and the remaining planets did not act upon one another, their orbits would be elliptical, having the Sun at their common focus, and they would describe areas proportional to the times."[50] By imposing this restriction on the phenomena from which force laws are deduced, Newton is assuring that these phenomena are not just arbitrary approximations to the true motions; at least according to the theory of the "deduced" physical force, the true motions would be in exact accord with the phenomena were it not for specific complicating factors.

Let me here restrict the term "idealization" to approximations that would hold exactly in certain specifiable circumstances. If, as I have proposed, Newton is addressing the complexity of real orbital motion in a sequence of successive approximations, then he had profound reasons for preferring that each successive approximation be an idealization in this sense. For any deviation of the actual motions from a given approximation will then be physically meaningful, and not just a reflection of the particular mathematical scheme employed in achieving the approximation, as in curve fitting. Of course, omniscience is required to know whether any approximation really is an idealization in the requisite sense, and (as Book 2 attests) Newton was far from omniscient. The most he could demand is that the theory being "deduced" from the approximations entails that they be idealizations of this sort. At least from the point of view of the theory, then, any observed systematic pattern in the deviations from a given approximation would have the promise of being physically informative, and hence a promise of becoming telling evidence.

In sum, judging from details of Newton's "deductions" from phenomena, his approach to the complexities of real-world motions is to try to address them in a sequence of progressively more complex idealizations, with systematic deviations from the idealizations at any stage providing the "phenomena" serving as evidence for the refinement achieved in the next. Such systematic deviations are appropriately called "second-order phenomena" in so far as they are not observable in their own right, but presuppose the theory. Thus, for example, no one can observe the famous 43 arc-seconds per century discrepancy in the motion of the perihelion of Mercury that emerged in the second half of the nineteenth century and then became evidence for Einstein's theory of general relativity: they are the residual left over after subtracting the 531 arc-seconds per century produced by the other planets according to *Newtonian* theory from the 574 arc-seconds derived from observation once allowance is made for the 5600 arc-seconds associated with the precession of the equinoxes.

Attempting to proceed in *successive* approximations in this way involves restrictions on how second-order phenomena are to be marshaled as evidence. In the case of orbital motions, any systematic discrepancy from the idealized theoretical motions has to be identified with a specific physical force – if not a gravitational force, then one governed by some other generic force law. This restriction precludes inventing *ad hoc* forces to save the law of gravity. It thereby makes success in carrying out a program of successive approximations far from guaranteed.

A second, less familiar example shows this in a different way. In Propositions 19 and 20 of Book 3 Newton first calculates a 17 mile difference between the radii to the poles and to the equator of the Earth, and then a specific variation of surface gravity with latitude. These calculations presuppose *universal* gravity. Indeed, as Huygens was quick to notice (and Maupertuis and Clairaut forty years later), this is the sole result in the *Principia* amenable at the time to empirical assessment that differentiates *universal* gravity from macroscopic inverse-square celestial gravity. Newton's calculations also presuppose that the density of the Earth is perfectly uniform. Hence, his results are not straightforwardly testable predictions, for they apply only to an idealized Earth. In all three editions Newton pointed out that any deviation from the calculated results is a sign that the Earth's density increases from the surface to the core. In the first edition he went so far as to propose that a linear increase in density be assumed for the next idealized approximation.[51] This was not an *ad hoc* way of protecting the law of universal gravity from refutation because, as Huygens's efforts in his *Discourse on the Cause of Gravity* showed, different assumptions about gravity yield very different relationships between the Earth's oblateness on the one hand, and the variation of surface gravity with latitude on the other.[52] Therefore, a variation in density inferred from, say, an observed oblateness differing from Newton's 17 miles was not guaranteed to yield a corresponding improvement between the observed variation in surface gravity and Newton's calculated variation. (From Clairaut forward the field of physical geodesy has been inferring the internal density distribution of the Earth from features of its shape and gravitational field, always presupposing the law of universal gravity; the discrepancies between observation and current theory have grown continually smaller.[53])

Needless to say, Newton's theory of gravity provides an explanation of Kepler's rules and of each of the subsequent idealized orbital motions in the sequence of successive approximations. That is, the theory explains why these idealizations hold at least *quam proxime* and why they have claim to being preferred descriptions of the actual motions even though they are not exact and observation is not precise. Providing such explanations, however, is not the distinctive feature of the theory. As Leibniz showed in print within months after the *Principia* first appeared, a theory of a very different sort, one that meets the demands of the mechanical philosophy, can explain Kepler's rules too.[54] The distinctive feature of Newtonian theory is the spotlight it shines on discrepancies between theory and observation. In his "System of the World" in Book 3 Newton no sooner spells out the conditions under which, for example, Keplerian motion would hold exactly than he turns to the principal real-world respects in which it does not, such as the gravitational effect of Jupiter on the motion of Saturn and on the precession of the aphelia of the inner planets. In adopting his approach of successive approximations, with its focus on theory-dependent second-order phenomena, Newton was turning theory into an indispensable instrument for ongoing research. Exact science as illustrated by the *Principia* is thus not exact science in the sense of Newton's predecessors, an account of how the world would be if it were more rational. It is exact science in the sense that every systematic deviation from current theory automatically has the status of a pressing unsolved problem.

Even with the above restrictions, the "deduction" of the law of gravity, or any other force law, from phenomena of motion that hold only *quam proxime* shows at most that it holds *quam proxime*. When the restrictions are met, however, as they by and large are in the case of the law of gravity,[55] Newton views the derivation as authorizing the force law to be *taken*, provisionally, as exact. Specifically, his fourth Rule for Natural Philosophy says:

> *In experimental philosophy, propositions gathered from phenomena by induction should be considered either exactly or very nearly true notwithstanding any contrary hypotheses, until yet other phenomena make such propositions either more exact or liable to exceptions.*

This rule should be followed so that arguments based on induction may not be nullified by hypotheses.[56]

Taking the force law to be exact when the evidence for it shows at most that it holds *quam proxime* amounts to an evidential strategy for purposes of ongoing research. This strategy is transparently appropriate when the goal is to use systematic deviations from current theory as evidence in a process of successive approximations.

ARGUING MORE SECURELY

The preceding section has offered a detailed description of how Newton prefers to *argue* from phenomena to physically characterized forces. Nothing has yet been said, however, about why this way of arguing might have claim to yielding conclusions that are *more secure*.

One respect in which it offers more security is easy to see. The "if-then" propositions used in deducing the law, as well as their approximative counterparts ("if-*quam-proxime*-then-*quam-proxime*"), are rigorously derived from the laws of motion. The phenomena – that is, the propositions expressing Newton's phenomena – are inductive generalizations from specific observations, and hence they hold at least *quam proxime* of these observations. But then, unless the laws of motion are fundamentally mistaken, the force law too is guaranteed to hold at least *quam proxime* of these observations. By way of contrast, the fact that a consequence deduced from a hypothesized force law holds *quam proxime* of specific observations need not provide any such guarantee. A conjectural hypothesis can reach far beyond the observations providing evidence for it not merely in its generality, but in its content. In practice Newton's first Rule for Natural Philosophy – *no more causes . . . should be admitted than are both true and sufficient to explain their phenomena* – has the effect of confining the content of theory to no more than the data clearly demand. Calling for the force law to be deduced from phenomena is a way of meeting this Rule.

Put another way, Newton's demand for a deduction from phenomena is an attempt to confine risk in theorizing as much as possible to "inductive generalization." What Newton means by "made general by induction" and "propositions gathered from phenomena by induction" amounts to more than merely projecting an open-ended generalization from some of its instances. The Phenomena he lists at the beginning of Book 3 involve first projection from discrete observations to orbital rules that fill in the gaps among these observations, and then projection of these rules into the indefinite past and future. His second Rule for Natural Philosophy – *same effect, same cause* – authorizes inferences that Charles Saunders Peirce would have labeled *abductive* in contrast to inductive. Even his third Rule, which at first glance seems most akin to induction, authorizes inferences of much greater sweep than is customary in simple induction: it specifies conditions under which conclusions based on observations and experiments within our reach may be extended to the far reaches of the universe and to microphysical reaches far beyond our capacity to observe. The care Newton put into this third Rule,[57] which he formulated in the early 1690s when he was in close contact with John Locke, indicates that he was acutely aware of the risk in "propositions gathered from phenomena by induction." So too does his insistence on the provisional status of these propositions in the subsequently added fourth Rule.

Newton's further demand that the theory entail specific conditions under which the phenomena in question hold exactly provides some support for projecting these phenomena inductively beyond the available observations. Specifically, as noted earlier, such a "re-deduction" gives reason to take the phenomena as lawlike, and not just one among many possible curve-fits. The deduced force law itself, however, can hold *quam proxime* of these observations and still turn out not to be suitable for inductive generalization; the most that can be said is that its deduction and the subsequent re-deduction of the phenomena make it an exceptionally promising candidate for inductive generalization.

Over the long term, pursuit of refinements in a sequence of successive approximations can provide a further source of security. Any current approximation to, for example, orbital motions is an idealization predicated on the force law. Hence observed deviations from it continually, so to speak, put the law to test. Recalcitrant deviations point to deficiencies in the law. If, however, second-order phenomena emerge and the presence of further forces complicating the motions is successfully established from them, then new evidence accrues to the law. Such new evidence does more than just support the original inductive generalization. The process of successive approximations leads to increasingly small residual deviations from current theory, which in turn tighten the range over which the force law holds *quam proxime*. More important, because the process of successive approximations presupposes the force law, continuing success in it leads to progressively deeper *entrenchment* of the law, to use Nelson Goodman's term.[58] This, of course, is precisely what happened in the case of Newton's law of gravity, with continuing improvement over the last three centuries in the agreement between theory and observation not only for orbital motion within celestial mechanics, but also for the Earth's shape and gravity field within physical geodesy. Indeed, the process of successive approximations issuing from Newton's *Principia* in these fields has yielded evidence of a quality beyond anything his predecessors ever dreamed of.

Evidence from long-term success in pursuit of successive approximations, however, can in principle be achieved by a hypothetico-deductive approach as well. The most that can be said for Newton's approach in this regard is that its confining the risk to the extent it does to inductive generalization may enhance its prospects for achieving such success.

What form does the risk take with Newton's approach? His inductively generalized law of *universal* gravity is presupposed as holding exactly in evidential reasoning at each stage after the first in the process of successive approximations. The main risk is a discovery that would falsify this law in a way that nullifies all or part of the evidential reasoning that has been predicated on it. Suppose, for example, that a discovery entails that various second-order phenomena that had been crucial as evidence were not phenomena at all, but mere artifacts of a supposed law that just so happens to hold *quam proxime* under parochial circumstances. Then, to the extent the evidence for this discovery is predicated on advances based on these second-order phenomena, the discovery itself would, in a sense, be self-nullifying. The conclusion would have to be that the pursuit of successive approximations had been proceeding down a garden path, and the area of science in question would have to be restarted from some earlier point.

Newton's attempt to initiate successive approximations in the case of resistance forces was shown to be going down just such a garden path by Jean d'Alembert twenty-five years after the third edition of the *Principia* appeared.[59] Surprising as it may seem to many readers, however, this has yet to happen in the case of his theory of gravity. The large conceptual gap between Newtonian and Einsteinian gravitation notwithstanding, the theory of gravity in general relativity has not nullified the evidential reasoning predicated on Newton's theory. In particular, it has not nullified the evidential reasoning from which the phenomenon of the residual 43 arc-seconds per century precession of the perihelion of Mercury emerged; if it had, this phenomenon could not be used directly as evidence supporting it. The reason why evidential reasoning predicated on Newtonian gravity was not nullified is because general relativity entails that Newton's law holds in the weak-field limit, and virtually none of this reasoning, viewed in retrospect, required anything more of Newton's law than that it hold to very high approximation in weak gravitational fields.[60]

The risk of a garden path with Newton's approach, therefore, does not as such derive from the possibility that the force law deduced from phenomena at the outset is not exact. This law itself can be open to refinement as part of the process of successive approximations without undercutting the process and having to restart from some earlier point. The relativistic refinements to Newton's first two laws of motion show that the same can be said about the axioms presupposed in the deduction of the force law. Rather, the risk comes from the huge inductive leap, from a celestial force law that holds at least *quam proxime* over a narrow body of data to the law of *universal* gravity – a leap authorized by Newton's first three Rules governing inductive reasoning. More specifically, the risk comes from two "taxonomic" presuppositions entering into this leap. Newton's vision of a fundamental taxonomy based on physical forces – or, more accurately, interactions[61] – is largely beside the point so far as gravity alone is concerned. Nevertheless, his inductive generalization does presuppose (1) that there is a distinct species – or natural kind, to use our current term – of elementary motion and a distinct species of static force which are characterized at least to a first approximation by his deduced law of gravity. The risk lies in the possibility that subsequent research will conclude either that there are no such distinct species or that they are species of limited range, even artifacts of the data from which he was working. Further, his inductive generalization presupposes (2) that certain specific motions – primarily planetary motions – are pure enough examples of motions of a specific elementary species to typify this species as a whole.

The risks from both of these presuppositions are evident in the garden path formed by Newton's efforts on resistance forces. In the first edition of the *Principia* he thought that phenomena of pendulum decay would allow him to demarcate the different species of resistance force and their respective variation with velocity. Recognizing the failure of this,[62] in the second and third editions he assumed that vertical fall of ordinary-size objects is dominated by resistance forces arising purely from the inertia of the fluid – at least to a sufficient extent to allow a law to be established for this kind of resistance force. His announced plan was for the other kinds to be addressed using discrepancies between observations and this law.[63] The garden path arose because both of these taxonomic presuppositions were wrong. First, there are no distinct species of resistance force, but only one species governed by interaction between inertial and viscous effects in the fluid, interaction that is so complicated that we still have no law for resistance of the sort Newton was pursuing, but only empirically determined relationships for bodies of various shapes.[64] Second, as d'Alembert showed, resistance in an idealized inviscid fluid of the sort Newton had assumed in deriving his law for purely inertial resistance is exactly zero, regardless of shape and velocity. Newton's supposed "law" for the purely inertial effects of the fluid turns out to amount to nothing more than a very rough approximation to the total resistance on spheres for a limited combination of diameters, velocities, and fluid densities and viscosities – a mere curve-fit over a restricted domain.[65]

Newton's taxonomic presuppositions are best regarded as working hypotheses underpinning his inductive generalizations. As with all such working hypotheses, some immediate protection is afforded by demanding that the evidence developed out of the data be of high quality, without lots of loose ends. Newton's "deduction" of the law of gravity met this demand to a much greater extent than did his evidential reasoning on resistance.[66] Still, the "deduction" was based primarily on the motion of only five planets over an astronomically brief period of time. The danger of being misled by such limited data is always high.

I know of nowhere that Newton acknowledges the risk that such taxonomic working hypotheses introduce into inductive generalization. He does acknowledge the risk of inductive generalization in the most famous methodological passage in the *Opticks*, in the discussion of the methods of "analysis and synthesis" in the next to last paragraph of the final Query, which was added in 1706:

This Analysis consists in making Experiments and Observations, and in drawing general Conclusions from them by Induction, and admitting of no

Objections against the Conclusions, but such as are taken from Experiments, or other certain Truths. For Hypotheses are not to be regarded in experimental Philosophy. And although the arguing from Experiments and Observations by Induction be no Demonstration of general Conclusions; yet it is the best way of arguing which the Nature of the Thing admits of, and may be looked upon as so much the stronger, by how much the Induction is more general. And if no Exception occur from Phenomena, the Conclusion may be pronounced generally. But if at any time afterwards any Exception shall occur from Experiments, it may then begin to be pronounced with such Exceptions as occur. By this way of Analysis we may proceed from Compounds to Ingredients and from Motions to the Forces producing them; and in general, from Effects to their Causes, and from particular Causes to more general ones, till the Argument end in the most general.[67]

Perhaps Newton saw success in achieving unrestricted generality as the ultimate safeguard against the risk introduced by the unavoidable taxonomic hypotheses entering into induction.

This brings us to the last distinctive aspect of the approach to theory construction illustrated by the *Principia* – that is, illustrated in the case of gravity, though not in the case of resistance. After establishing the law of universal gravity and the conditions for Keplerian motion, Book 3 goes on to "applications" of the law in unresolved problems at some remove from the phenomena from which it was "deduced": (1) the non-spherical shape of the Earth and the variation of surface gravity with latitude; (2) the area-rule violation in the orbit of the Moon, the motion of its nodes, and its fluctuating inclination; (3) the tides; (4) the precession of the equinoxes; and (5) the trajectories of comets. The idea seems to be to protect against risks arising in the inductive leap by immediately pushing the theory for all it is worth, employing it as a tool of research on problems that *prima facie* have nothing to do with the original evidence for it. It goes without saying that, regardless of how far afield such "applications" may be, they still provide no *guarantee* against a garden path. Nevertheless, they do represent a concerted effort to expose limitations in the taxonomic presuppositions set out above. As already noted, the shape of the Earth and the variation of surface gravity directly involve the generalization from celestial to universal gravity, as does the precession of the equinoxes indirectly. The vagaries in the lunar orbit address the most glaring known counterexample to Keplerian motion and hence worries about generalizing beyond planetary motion. Both the tides and the precession of the equinoxes involve the generalization from simple centripetal forces to interactive gravity, as does a gravitational treatment of vagaries in the motions of Jupiter and Saturn. And finally the comets involve the extension of the law of gravity to bodies that appear to consist of matter very different from that of the planets and their satellites and that pass through the intermediate distances from the Sun between the orbits of the planets.[68] The fact that all of these address evidential worries in the original inductive generalization indicates that the process of comparison with phenomena, and hence the argument for securing universal gravity, extends across all of Book 3.[69]

The efforts occupying the rest of Book 3 were extraordinarily innovative. In this respect they are akin to predictions of novel phenomena of the sort Huygens singled out as the strongest form of evidence for empirical theories. None of them, however, is a truly straightforward prediction of the sort classically called for in hypothetico-deductive evidence. In every case some further, contestable assumptions were needed beyond Newton's theory, if only the assumption that no other forces are at work besides gravity. Still, Newton's inductive generalization to *universal* gravity clearly introduced a large conjectural element in his theory; and the applications of it beyond Keplerian motion put this element to the test, ultimately supplying the most compelling evidence for it. The key prediction put to the test in these applications was not so much that every two particles of matter interact gravitationally, but rather one that is more abstract: *every discrepancy between Newtonian theory and observation will prove to be physically significant and hence can be taken to be telling us something further about the physical world.* Contrast this with deviations from a curve-fit, which usually reflect nothing more than the particular mathematical framework that happened to have been used. Lacking omniscience, the only way we have of deciding whether a discrepancy is physically significant is from the point of view of ongoing theory. The issue of physical significance from this point of view turns most crucially on whether the taxonomic working hypotheses underlying Newton's inductive step to universal gravity remain intact as theory advances. Does the discrepancy give reason to conclude that a taxonomy of interactions is not fundamental or that gravitational interactions do not comprise a distinct kind within that taxonomy?

In part because of the further contestable assumptions, every one of the efforts occupying the rest of Book 3, as well as Newton's brief suggestions about the motions of Jupiter and Saturn, initiated its own historical sequence of successive approximations subsequent to the *Principia*. Moreover, even at the time the third edition appeared, almost forty years after the first, serious loose ends remained in the treatment of every one of these topics in the *Principia*. These loose ends may help to explain why so many capable scientists who came of age after the *Principia* were initially so cautious in accepting Newton's theory. A decade or so after Newton died, Clairaut, Euler, and d'Alembert began their efforts to tie up these loose ends, followed by Lagrange and Laplace over the last forty years of the eighteenth century.[70] In a very real sense, then, Newton's argument for universal gravity was not completed until a century after the publication of the first edition of the *Principia*. With its completion, the new approach to theory construction that the book was intended to illustrate – that is, the new type of generic mathematical theory, the contrast between mathematical and physical points of view, the roles of "deduced" theory and idealizations in ongoing research, and the insistence on pushing theory far beyond its original basis – became a permanent part of the science of physics.

NOTES

I thank Kenneth G. Wilson, Eric Schliesser, and I. Bernard Cohen for several useful comments on an earlier draft of this chapter.

1 Isaac Newton, *The Principia, Mathematical Principles of Natural Philosophy: A New Translation*, trans. I. Bernard Cohen and Anne Whitman (Berkeley: University of California Press, 1999), pp. 382f.

2 *Ibid.*, p. 415; see Robert DiSalle's chapter in this volume for a discussion of Newton's views on relative versus absolute motion.

3 In Latin, *Regulae Philosophandi*; see William Harper's chapter in this volume for a discussion of Newton's use of these Rules in his "deduction" of universal gravitation.

4 Newton, *Principia*, p. 943.

5 Isaac Newton, "An Account of the Book Entituled *Commercium Epistolicum*," reprinted in A. Rupert Hall, *Philosophers at War: The Quarrel between Newton and Leibniz* (Cambridge: Cambridge University Press, 1980), p. 312. Newton made much the same concession to hypotheses in 1672 in one of his exchanges with Pardies on his light and

colors experiments; see I. Bernard Cohen and Robert E. Schefield (eds.), *Isaac Newton's Papers and Letters on Natural Philosophy*, revised edition (Cambridge, MA: Harvard University Press, 1978), p. 106; see note 45 below.

6   Christiaan Huygens, *Traité de la Lumière*, in *Œuvres complètes de Christiaan Huygens*, vol. 19 (The Hague: Martinus Nijhoff, 1937), p. 454; the English translation is from Michael R. Matthews, *Scientific Background to Modern Philosophy* (Indianapolis: Hackett, 1989), p. 126. The hypothesis which Huygens had most in mind was the longitudinal wave theory of light.

7   Newton, *Principia*, pp. 588f.

8   A few Newton scholars have emphasized this Scholium, most notably I. Bernard Cohen in his *The Newtonian Revolution* (Cambridge: Cambridge University Press, 1980), Clifford Truesdell in "Reactions of Late Baroque Mechanics to Success, Conjecture, Error, and Failure in Newton's *Principia*," reprinted in his *Essays in the History of Mechanics* (New York: Springer-Verlag, 1968), and E. W. Strong in "Newton's 'Mathematical Way'," *Journal of the History of Ideas* 12 (1951), 90–110.

9   See N. Jardine, *The Birth of History and Philosophy of Science: Kepler's A Defence of Tycho against Ursus* (Cambridge: Cambridge University Press, 1984).

10 See Alexandre Koyré, "An Experiment in Measurement," in his *Metaphysics and Measurement* (Cambridge, MA: Harvard University Press, 1968).

11 René Descartes, *Principles of Philosophy*, trans. Valentine Rodger Miller and Reese P. Miller (Dordrecht: D. Reidel, 1983); gravity and magnetism are discussed in Part 4, the former in Propositions 20 through 27 and the latter in Propositions 133 through 183.

12 In a letter of 1690 from Huygens to Leibniz; see *Œuvres complètes de Christiaan Huygens*, vol. 9 (1901), p. 538.

13 Galileo Galilei, *Dialogues concerning Two New Sciences*, trans. Henry Crew and Alfonso de Salvio (Buffalo: Prometheus Books, 1991).

14 Christiaan Huygens, *The Pendulum Clock; or, Geometrical Demonstration concerning the Motion of Pendula as Applied to Clocks*, trans. Richard J. Blackwell (Ames: Iowa State University Press, 1986).

15 Galileo Galilei, *Dialogue concerning the Two Chief World Systems*, 2nd edn, trans. Stillman Drake (Berkeley: University of California Press, 1967). Newton read the English translation by Thomas Salusbury, published in 1661.

16 For example, Robert Anderson's *The Genuine Use and Effects of the Gun*; Kenelm Digby's "The Nature of Bodies" in his *Two Treatises*; and Walter Charleton's *Physiologia: Epicuro-Gassendo-Carltoniai, or*

A Fabrick of Science Natural, Upon the Hypothesis of Atoms. Newton either owned copies or copied out portions of each of these. I thank I. B. Cohen for this point.

17 See Newton, *Principia*, pp. 444 and 446.

18 See Huygens, *The Pendulum Clock*, Proposition 25, p. 69.

19 In his *Horologium Oscillatorium* Huygens expressly calls the three opening principles (the first of which is the principle of inertia) "hypotheses" (p. 33). Apparently following Huygens, Newton too called the forerunners of his laws of motion "hypotheses" in his tract, "De motu corporum in gyrum," the seed from which the *Principia* grew; the change to "laws" appears first as a correction to "hypotheses" in the revised version of this tract. See D. T. Whiteside (ed.), *The Preliminary Manuscripts for Isaac Newton's 1687 Principia: 1684–1686* (Cambridge: Cambridge University Press, 1989), pp. 3 and 13.

20 The term is Arthur Prior's.

21 See Newton, *Principia*, Book 2, Proposition 30 and 31, pp. 708–12.

22 Newton, *Principia*, Book 1, Proposition 45, pp. 539–45. This proposition is discussed in See Ram Valluri, Curtis Wilson, and William Harper, "Newton's Apsidal Precession Theorem and Eccentric Orbits," *Journal for the History of Astronomy* 28 (1997), 13–27.

23 Newton's use of such measurements has been discussed in several places by William Harper; see his chapter in this volume.

24 Huygens presents his simple pendulum measurement in Part 4 of his *Horologium Oscillatorium*, Proposition 26 (*The Pendulum Clock*, pp. 170–2), and he describes a conical pendulum measurement in Part v (pp. 173–5). See chapters 2–4 of Joella Yoder's *Unrolling Time: Christiaan Huygens and the Mathematization of Nature* (Cambridge: Cambridge University Press, 1988) for a discussion of the original measurements Huygens carried out in 1659.

25 E. W. Strong makes clear the indispensability of measurement to Newton's "mathematical way" in his "Newton's 'Mathematical Way'," cited in note 8 above. Unfortunately, the passage from the English translation of Newton's *System of the World* from which Strong develops his essay appears to be spurious, added by the translator; Strong's argument, however, requires no recourse to this passage.

26 Newton, *Principia*, p. 407.

27 Huygens lists 13 propositions on centrifugal force, a term he coined, at the end of his *Horologium Oscillatorium* (*The Pendulum Clock*, pp. 176–8). A full manuscript including proofs was published in 1703, in the edition of his posthumous papers prepared by de Volder and Fullenius. See *Œuvres complètes de Christiaan Huygens*, vol. 16 (1929), pp. 255–301.

28 This complaint was voiced most outspokenly by Robert Hooke; see
    p. 111 of *Isaac Newton's Papers and Letters on Natural Philosophy*,
    cited in note 5 above. Newton's mathematical treatment of rays of light
    is discussed in Alan Shapiro's chapter in this volume.

29 Newton, *Principia*, p. 448.

30 This requirement is met in the case of resistance forces because the
    velocity which determines their direction is the velocity of the resisted
    body *relative* to the fluid medium.

31 Papers summarizing the "laws of motion" by Wallis and Wren appeared
    in *Philosophical Transactions of the Royal Society* in the spring of 1669
    (pp. 864–8), followed shortly after (pp. 925–8) by a summary of the the-
    orems of Huygens, who had in effect refereed the papers by Wallis and
    Wren. Huygens's beautiful proofs of his account of impact did not ap-
    pear in print until his posthumous papers were published in 1703; see
    Œuvres complètes de Christiaan Huygens, vol. 16, pp. 29–91.

32 A. Rupert Hall and Marie Boas Hall (eds.), *Unpublished Scientific Papers
    of Isaac Newton* (Cambridge: Cambridge University Press, 1962), p. 307.

33 The word "phenomena" for Newton does not refer to individual obser-
    vations, but to inductively generalized summaries of observations, such
    as Kepler's area rule.

34 The word "rules" best describes Kepler's famous orbital claims at the
    time Newton was writing the *Principia*. They came to be called "laws"
    only after the *Principia* was published – first apparently in Leibniz's
    Illustrio Tentaminis de Motuum Coelestium Causis of 1689 (a transla-
    tion of which can be found in Domenico Bertolini Meli's *Equivalence
    and Priority: Newton versus Leibniz* [Oxford: Oxford University Press,
    1993], pp. 126–42).

35 Streete's *Astronomia Carolina*, from which Newton first learned his or-
    bital astronomy, was published in 1661. Streete's claim that the orbits
    are stationary was challenged in Vincent Wing's *Examen Astronomiae
    Carolinae* of 1665, and then defended anew in Streete's *Examen Exam-
    inatum* of 1667.

36 See Curtis Wilson, "Predictive Astronomy in the Century after Kepler,"
    in René Taton and Curtis Wilson (eds.), *Planetary Astronomy from the
    Renaissance to the Rise of Astrophysics, Part A: Tycho Brahe to Newton*
    (Cambridge: Cambridge University Press, 1989), pp. 172–85.

37 *Ibid.*, pp. 168 and 179.

38 Thus we find Robert Hooke, in the correspondence of 1679–80 with
    Newton that initiated his key discoveries on orbital motion, asking
    Newton to calculate the curve described by a body under inverse-square
    forces, and remarking, "this curve truly calculated will show the error of
    those many lame shifts made use of by astronomers to approach the true

motions of the planets with their tables." (*The Correspondence of Isaac Newton*, vol. 2, ed. H. W. Turnbull [Cambridge: Cambridge University Press, 1960], p. 309.)

39 Newton, "De motu corporum in gyrum," in D. T. Whiteside (ed.), *The Mathematical Papers of Isaac Newton*, vol. 6 (Cambridge: Cambridge University Press, 1974), pp. 30–74.

40 *Ibid.*, pp. 74–80. An English translation of the augmented version of "De motu" can be found in *Unpublished Scientific Papers of Isaac Newton*, cited in note 32 above, pp. 239–92. The English translation given here is from Curtis Wilson, "The Newtonian Achievement in Astronomy," in Taton and Wilson (eds.), *Planetary Astronomy*, p. 253.

41 See William Harper and George E. Smith, "Newton's New Way of Inquiry," in Jarrett Leplin (ed.), *The Creation of Ideas in Physics: Studies for a Methodology of Theory Construction* (Norwell: Kluwar, 1995), pp. 133–9.

42 Galileo, *Two New Sciences*, cited in note 13 above, p. 252.

43 René Descartes, *The Philosophical Writings of Descartes*, vol. 3, trans. John Cottingham, Robert Stoothoff, Dugald Murdoch, and Anthony Kenny (Cambridge: Cambridge University Press, 1991), pp. 9ff.

44 Descartes, *Principles*, cited in note 11 above, p. 98.

45 Thus, Newton remarked in a response to objections to his early publications in optics,

> For the best and safest method of philosophizing seems to be, first to inquire diligently into the properties of things, and establishing those properties by experiments and then to proceed more slowly to hypotheses for the explanation of them. For hypotheses should be subservient only in explaining the properties of things, but not assumed in determining them; unless so far as they may furnish experiments. For if the possibility of hypotheses is to be the test of the truth and reality of things, I see not how certainty can be obtained in any science; since numerous hypotheses may be devised, which shall seem to overcome new difficulties. (Cohen, *Isaac Newton's Papers and Letters on Natural Philosophy*, cited in note 5 above, p. 106)

Newton's attitude toward hypotheses in his work is optics in discussed in detail in Alan Shapiro's chapter in this volume.

46 Cohen, *The Newtonian Revolution*, cited in note 8 above, ch. 3; see his chapter in this volume as well.

47 The term "point-mass" is Euler's, not Newton's or Huygens's.

48 Newton's "deduction" of universal gravity from phenomena is examined in detail in William Harper's chapter in this volume.

49 For details, see my "From the Phenomenon of the Ellipse to an Inverse-Square Force: Why Not?," in David Malament (ed.), *Reading Natural Philosophy: Essays in the History of Science and Mathematics to Honor Howard Stein on his 70th Birthday* (La Salle: Open Court, 2002).

50 Newton, *Principia*, pp. 817ff.
51 Newton, *Principia*, textual note bb, p. 827.
52 See Huygens, *Discours de la Cause de la Pesanteur*, in *Œuvres complètes de Christiaan Huygens*, vol. 21 (1944), pp. 462–71, and pp. 476ff.
53 For a discussion of the current state of these discrepancies, see Kurt Lambeck, *Geophysical Geodesy: The Slow Deformations of the Earth* (Oxford: Oxford University Press, 1988).
54 See Leibniz, *Tentamen*, cited in note 34 above.
55 The one notable exception is the tacit assumption that the third law of motion holds between the Sun and the individual planets. This assumption has been pointed out by Howard Stein in his " 'From the Phenomena of Motions to the Forces of Nature': Hypothesis or Deduction?" (*PSA 2* [1990], 209–22); Dana Densmore in her *Newton's Principia: The Central Argument* (Santa Fe: Green Lion Press, 1995), p. 353; and before them by Roger Cotes, the editor of the second edition of the *Principia*, in correspondence with Newton (see *The Correspondence of Isaac Newton*, vol. 5, ed. A. Rupert Hall and Laura Tilling [Cambridge: Cambridge University Press, 1975], pp. 391ff). William Harper's chapter in this volume discusses this and the other details of Newton's "deduction" of universal gravity from phenomena.
56 Newton, *Principia*, p. 796.
57 The history of Newton's third Rule for Natural Philosophy is discussed in I. Bernard Cohen's *Introduction to Newton's "Principia"* (Cambridge, MA: Harvard University Press, 1978), pp. 23–6.
58 Nelson Goodman, *Fact, Fiction, and Forecast*, 3rd edn (Indianapolis: Bobbs-Merrill, 1973).
59 Jean d' Alembert, *Essai d'une Nouvelle Théorie de la Résistance des Fluides* (Paris: David, 1752).
60 Newton, by the way, took the trouble in Book 1, Section 10 to show that Galileo's and Huygens's results similarly hold in the limit in the case of *universal* gravity, namely the limit of the linear variation of gravity up to the surface of a uniformly dense Earth as the radius of this surface approaches infinity. This result authenticates Newton's use of Huygens's precise theory-mediated measurement of surface gravity in his crucial argument in Book 3, Proposition 4 that the Moon is held in orbit by terrestrial gravity.
61 See the chapter by Howard Stein in this volume for a discussion of the centrality of interactions in Newton's metaphysics.
62 See George E. Smith, "Fluid Resistance: Why Did Newton Change His Mind?," in Richard Dalitz and Michael Nauenberg (eds.), *Foundations of Newtonian Scholarship* (Singapore: World Scientific, 2000), pp. 105–36.
63 Newton, *Principia*, p. 749.

64 See L. D. Landau and E. M. Lifshitz, *Fluid Mechanics*, vol. 6 in *Course in Theoretical Physics* (Oxford: Pergamon, 1959), pp. 31–6, 168–79.

65 See George E. Smith, "The Newtonian Style in Book 2 of the *Principia*," in J. Z. Buchwald and I. B. Cohen (eds.), *Isaac Newton's Natural Philosophy* (Cambridge, MA: MIT Press, 2001), pp. 249–98, esp. p. 278, Fig. 9.7.

66 *Ibid.*, pp. 276–87.

67 Isaac Newton, *Opticks: or, A Treatise of the Reflections, Refractions, Inflections and Colours of Light* (New York: Dover, 1952), p. 404. The quotation continues: "This is the Method of Analysis: And the Synthesis consists in assuming the Causes discover'd, and establish'd as Principles, and by them explaining the Phenomena proceeding from them, and proving the Explanations." This passage was undoubtedly a direct response to Huygens's description of the hypothetico-deductive method quoted at the beginning of this chapter.

68 Extending gravity to comets was more important than first meets the eye. Hooke had expressed a general principle of celestial attraction in his *Attempt to Prove the Motion of the Earth* of 1674, but had denied that it extends to comets in his *Cometa* of 1678. See Curtis Wilson, "The Newtonian Achievement in Astronomy," p. 239.

69 Newton indicates as much in a letter to Leibniz in 1693 when he defends the *Principia* by remarking, "all phenomena of the heavens and the sea follow precisely, so far as I am aware, from nothing but gravity acting in accordance with the laws described by me." (*The Correspondence of Isaac Newton*, vol. 3, ed. H. W. Turnbull [Cambridge: Cambridge University Press, 1961], pp. 284 ff.)

70 See Curtis Wilson's chapter in this volume for a discussion of the development of celestial mechanics during the eighteenth century. This development culminates in the five volumes of Laplace's *Mécanique Céleste*, the first four of which appeared from 1798 to 1805, and the fifth in 1825. (All but the fifth volume are available in English in the translation of 1829–39 by Nathaniel Bowditch [Bronx, NY: Chelsea Publishing Company, 1966].)

5 Newton's argument for universal gravitation

The aspect of Newton's *Principia* that has provoked the most controversy within the philosophy of science, other than his invocation of absolute space, time, and motion, has been his claim to have "deduced" the law of universal gravity from phenomena of orbital motion. In particular, a tradition that began with Pierre Duhem[1] and continued with Karl Popper[2] and then Imre Lakatos[3] has argued that this claim is at best misleading (Duhem) and at worst a subterfuge (Lakatos). Among other reasons they have advanced against any such deduction is the objection that no deduction from consistent premises can yield a conclusion that entails one or more of these premises is false; yet one consequence of the law of universal gravity is that all the orbital phenomena from which Newton proceeds in his supposed deduction are, strictly, false. Duhem, Popper, and Lakatos insist, to the contrary, that only a hypothetico-deductive construal of Newton's evidence for universal gravity makes sense, Newton's outspoken objections to hypothetico-deductive evidence notwithstanding. More recently, Clark Glymour[4] has offered a "bootstrapping" construal of Newton's evidence, proposing that it captures the logical force of the reasoning for universal gravitation in the *Principia* better than a straightforward hypothetico-deductive construal can. Glymour too, however, sees no way around concluding that some of what Newton seems to think he is doing cannot be correct.

One issue this raises is understanding the reasoning Newton offers in arriving at the law of universal gravity and describes as a "deduction" from phenomena. Another is the extent to which such reasoning is cogent and illuminates scientific method. The simplest way to respond to these questions is to proceed step-by-step through Newton's reasoning. I will argue that his argument from phenomena to universal gravitation, which opens his system of the world in Book 3, illustrates a general methodology in which phenomena constrain theory to approximations established by measuring parameters. This methodology, which continues to guide research in gravitational physics, has not been as well appreciated by philosophers of science as it ought to be. Nevertheless, it becomes clear and easy to defend once attention is paid to the details of the argument in Propositions 1 to 8 of Book 3 in the third edition.

INFERENCES FROM PHENOMENA

Jupiter's Moons

Proposition 1. The forces by which the circumjovial planets [or satellites of Jupiter] are continually drawn away from rectilinear motions and are maintained in their respective orbits are directed to the center of Jupiter and are inversely as the squares of the distances of their places from that center.[5]

The first part of the proposition is evident from phen. 1 and from prop. 2 or prop. 3 of book 1, and the second part from phen. 1 and from corol. 6 to prop. 4 of book 1.

The same is to be understood for the planets that are Saturn's companions [or satellites] by phen. 2.

The cited phenomenon (Phenomenon 1) consists of two parts. The first part is that the moons of Jupiter, by radii drawn to the center of Jupiter, describe areas proportional to the times. This is what we call Kepler's "law" of areas for these moons with respect to that center.[6] The second part is that the periodic times of the orbits of these moons – the fixed stars being at rest[7] – are as the 3/2 power of their distances from the center of Jupiter. This is Kepler's harmonic law for these orbits.

Newton demonstrates that the law of areas carries the information that the force maintaining a body in an orbit which satisfies it is directed toward the center with respect to which it sweeps out equal areas in equal times. He also demonstrates that the harmonic law for a system of orbits carries the information that the accelerative forces maintaining bodies in those orbits are inversely as the squares of the distances from the center about which those orbits are described.

THE LAW OF AREAS AS A CRITERION FOR CENTRIPETAL FORCE. Propositions 1 and 2 of Book 1, together, yield a biconditional equivalence between the centripetal direction of the force maintaining a body in an orbit about an inertial center and the motion of that orbit being in a plane and satisfying Kepler's law of areas. According to Corollary 1 of Proposition 2, the rate at which areas are described is increasing only if the force is angled off-center toward the direction of motion, while a decreasing rate obtains only if the force is angled off-center in the opposite direction. These dependencies make the constancy of the rate at which areas are being swept out by radii to a center *measure* the centripetal direction of the force maintaining a body in an orbit about that center, provided the center can be treated as inertial.

Treating Jupiter's center as inertial ignores the substantial centripetal acceleration toward the Sun as the Jupiter system orbits it. To the extent that the Sun's actions on Jupiter and its moons approximate equal and parallel accelerations, the Jupiter system can be treated as unperturbed by the forces accelerating it toward the Sun.[8] To the extent that this approximation holds and the center of Jupiter approximates the center of mass of the Jupiter system, the center of Jupiter can be treated as inertial.[9]

Having the area rule hold, very nearly, for the orbits of these moons with respect to the center of Jupiter carries information that these approximations are not appreciably inaccurate.[10] In his discussion of Phenomenon 1, Newton pointed out that the orbits of Jupiter's moons so closely approximate uniform motion on circles concentric to Jupiter that no appreciable differences from such motions were detected in observations by astronomers. That good observations detected no appreciable departures from uniform motion on concentric circular orbits for Jupiter's moons indicates that no appreciable errors result from treating Jupiter's center as inertial for purposes of using the area rule as a criterion for the centripetal direction of the forces maintaining those moons in their orbits.

Newton's proofs of the theorems underwriting the area rule as a criterion for centers toward which orbital forces are directed make no assumptions about any power law for these forces. Given that the centripetal direction of the forces maintaining these moons in their orbits is inferred from the law of areas, Newton can appeal to his theorems about orbital motion under centripetal forces to argue that the harmonic law phenomenon, for the system of those orbits, carries the information that the accelerative forces are inversely as the squares of their distances from that center. This illustrates that Newton's inferences are not merely hypothetico-deductive.[11]

THE HARMONIC RULE AS A CRITERION FOR INVERSE-SQUARE FORCES. Corollary 6 of Proposition 4 of Book 1 states that the harmonic law for a system of circular orbits is equivalent to having the accelerative centripetal forces maintaining bodies in those orbits be inversely as the squares of the distances from the center. Corollary 7 is equivalent to the following universal systematic dependency

$$t \propto R^s \quad \text{iff} \quad f \propto R^{1-2s},$$

where f is the accelerative force maintaining a body in uniform motion in a circular orbit with period t and radius R. Corollary 6 follows when s equals $3/2$. For each of a whole range of alternative power law proportions of periods to orbital radii, Corollary 7 establishes the equivalent power law proportion to radii for the centripetal forces that would maintain bodies in those orbits. To have the periods be as some power $s > 3/2$ would be to have the centripetal forces fall off faster than the -2 power of the radii, while to have the periods be as some power $s < 3/2$ would be to have the centripetal forces fall off less fast than the -2 power of the radii. These systematic dependencies make the harmonic law phenomenon ($s = 3/2$) for a system of orbits *measure* the inverse-square (-2) power law for the centripetal forces maintaining bodies in those orbits. This constitutes a very strong sense in which the harmonic law carries the information that the forces maintaining bodies in those orbits satisfy the inverse-square power law.

As evidence for the harmonic law Newton offers a table citing periods agreed upon by astronomers and four distance estimates from astronomers for each of the four moons of Jupiter known at the time. The fit of the harmonic law to these data is quite good. He also offers more precise data from observations taken by Pound in 1718–20. The fit of the harmonic rule to these considerably more precise data[12] is very much better than the already good fit of the harmonic law to the earlier data.

Primary planets

Proposition 2. The forces by which the primary planets are continually drawn away from rectilinear motions and are maintained in their respective orbits are directed to the sun and are inversely as the squares of their distances from its center.

The first part of the proposition is evident from phen. 5 and from prop. 2 of book 1, and the latter part from phen. 4 and from prop. 4 of the same book. But this second part of the proposition is proved with the greatest exactness from the fact that the aphelia are at rest. For the slightest departure from the ratio of the square would (by book 2, prop. 45, corol. 1) necessarily result in a noticeable motion of the apsides in a single revolution and an immense such motion in many revolutions.

THE AREA RULE FOR THE PLANETS
Phenomenon 5. The primary planets, by radii drawn to the earth, describe areas in no way proportional to the times but, by radii drawn to the Sun, traverse areas proportional to the times.

That Newton considers radii drawn to the Earth as well as radii drawn to the Sun illustrates that he does not assume the Copernican system as a phenomenon to argue from. He points out that with respect to the Sun as center the angular motion is almost uniform and the departures from uniform motion – "a little more swiftly in their perihelia and more slowly in their aphelia" – are such that the description of areas is uniform.[13]

THE HARMONIC RULE FOR THE PLANETS. Newton provides a separate phenomenon stating that the orbits of the primary planets encircle the Sun. This phenomenon does not include the Earth as one of these planets.

Phenomenon 3. The orbits of the five primary planets – Mercury, Venus, Mars, Jupiter, and Saturn – encircle the Sun.

Tycho Brahe's geo-heliocentric system in which the other planets orbit the Sun, while the Sun together with those planets orbits the Earth, is compatible with this phenomenon. To every Copernican system a corresponding Tychonic system is defined by taking the center of the Earth rather than the center of the Sun as a reference frame.[14]

Newton's statement of the harmonic law is neutral between such Sun-centered and Earth-centered systems.

Log Period (years)

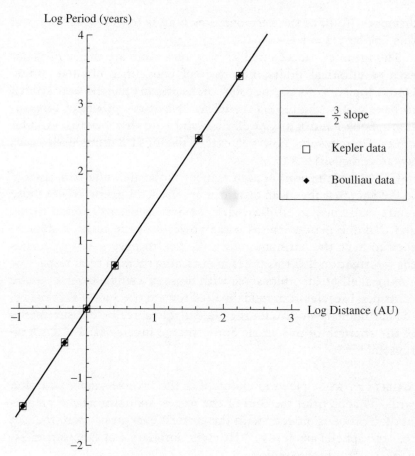

Fig. 5.1 Log mean distances versus log periodic times for the planets.

Phenomenon 4. The periodic times of the five primary planets and of either the sun around the earth or the earth around the sun – the fixed stars being at rest – are as the 3/2 power of their mean distances from the sun.

Newton cites periods agreed upon by astronomers and estimates of mean distances from Kepler and the French astronomer Boulliau which exhibit the excellent fit of the harmonic law to available data. This fit is nicely illustrated by plotting log periods against log distances, as in Figure 5.1.

That a straight line of some slope *s* fits the result of plotting Log*t* against Log*R* is to have the periods be as some power *s* of the distances. To have the harmonic law hold is to have the slope s of this line be $3/2 = 1.5$.

The mean distances cited in Newton's table are the semi-major axes of elliptical orbits, not radii of concentric circular orbits. Unlike Jupiter's moons, the orbits of the primary planets were known to have non-negligible eccentricities. Newton's proofs of Proposition 4, Book 1 and of its Corollaries 6 and 7 are for concentric circular orbits. These results, however, extend to elliptical orbits with forces toward a focus.[15]

Given that the orbit of each planet fits the area rule with respect to the Sun, that the mean distances are the semi-major axes of those orbits construed as ellipses with the Sun at their common focus, and that the periods are as some power s of the mean distances, then to have the harmonic law hold, i.e., to have $s = 3/2$, carries the information that the forces maintaining them in their respective con-focal elliptical orbits agree with those of a single inverse-square centripetal acceleration field directed toward the Sun.[16] This makes the harmonic law ratios for the planets into agreeing measurements of the strength of this single Sun-centered inverse-square acceleration field.[17]

APHELIA AT REST. Newton claims that the inverse-square variation with distance from the Sun of the forces maintaining the planets in their orbits is proved "with the greatest exactness" from the fact that the aphelia are at rest.[18] He cites Corollary 1 of Proposition 45, Book 1, according to which

Precession is p degrees per revolution	if and only if	The centripetal force f is as the $(360/360 + p)^2 - 3$ power of distance

If a planet in going from aphelion (the furthest point from the Sun) to return to it again makes an angular motion against the fixed stars of $360 + p$ degrees, then the aphelion is precessing forward with p degrees per revolution. According to this corollary, zero precession is equivalent to having the centripetal force be as the -2 power of distance; forward precession is equivalent to having the centripetal force fall off faster than the inverse-square; and backward precession is equivalent to having the centripetal force fall off slower than the inverse-square.

Newton's Proposition 45, Book 1 and its corollaries are proved for orbits that are very nearly circular. The results, however, can be extended to orbits of arbitrarily great eccentricity. Indeed, orbital eccentricity increases the sensitivity of absence of unaccounted for precession as a null experiment measuring inverse-square variation of a centripetal force.[19]

UNIFICATION AND THE MOON

The Moon

Proposition 3.
The force by which the moon is maintained in its orbit is directed toward the earth and is inversely as the square of the distances of its places from the center of the earth.

Newton claims that the first part (the centripetal direction) is evident from Phenomenon 6 (and Proposition 2 or 3 of Book 1).

Phenomenon 6. The moon, by a radius drawn to the center of the earth, describes areas proportional to the times.
   This is evident from a comparison of the apparent motion of the moon with its apparent diameter. Actually, the motion of the moon is somewhat perturbed by the force of the sun, but in these phenomena I pay no attention to minute errors that are negligible.

The comparisons of apparent diameter and apparent motion mentioned by Newton are in good rough agreement with the law of areas.[20]
   The observed motion of the apogee makes the argument for inverse-square variation more problematic than the corresponding argument for the planets. This apsidal motion is, Newton tells us, only about 3 degrees and 3 minutes forward in each revolution. According to Corollary 1, Proposition 45, Book 1, this is equivalent to a centripetal force varying inversely as the $2\frac{4}{243}$ power. As he also points out, this is $59\frac{3}{4}$ times closer to the square than to the cube.
   Newton claims that this motion of the lunar apogee is to be ignored because it arises from the action of the Sun. He appeals to Corollary 2 of Proposition 45, Book 1 to suggest that the action of the Sun to draw the Moon away from the Earth is roughly as $1/178.725$ of the centripetal force of the Moon.[21] Newton, however, does not

provide an account of how the lunar precession is due to the action of the Sun on the Moon's motion.[22]

Gravitation toward the Earth

Proposition 4. The moon gravitates toward the earth and by the force of gravity is always drawn back from rectilinear motion and kept in its orbit.

THE MOON-TEST. In the Moon-test, Newton cites six estimates by astronomers and assumes a mean Earth–Moon distance of 60 terrestrial semidiameters. He cites a lunar period established by astronomers and a circumference for the Earth according to measurements by the French, which, together with the assumption of 60 earth radii as the lunar distance, give 15.009 Paris feet as distance the Moon would fall in one minute if it were deprived of all its motion and let fall by the force by which it is maintained in its orbit.

Newton's assumption of 60 terrestrial semidiameters as the lunar distance, together with inverse-square variation, makes the one-minute fall corresponding to the strength of this force at the lunar distance exactly equal to the one-second fall corresponding to the increased strength this force would have at the surface of the Earth.

Huygens had used his experimentally established length of a seconds pendulum to measure the one-second fall produced on terrestrial bodies by the Earth's gravity. His determination of the length of a seconds pendulum was so stable over repetitions that his measured value for the one-second fall at Paris of 15.096 Paris feet could be trusted to about ±0.01 Paris feet.[23]

Newton's assumption of 60 earth radii as the lunar distance, together with his appeal to a correction factor to offset a supposed $1/178.725$ reduction due to the action of the Sun, leads to an extraordinarily close agreement with Huygens's measurement.[24] If we do not apply that correction and use all six (59, 60, 60, $60\frac{1}{3}$, $60\frac{2}{5}$, $60\frac{1}{2}$) of Newton's cited lunar distance estimates together with his cited circumference of the earth (123,249,600 Paris feet) and lunar period (39,343 minutes), we arrive at 15.041 ± 0.429 Paris feet as the measured value of the one-second fall at the surface of the Earth corresponding to the centripetal acceleration of the lunar orbit. That Huygens's value is well within these error bounds shows that the positive outcome of the Moon-test did not depend either upon the selection of 60 as the lunar distance[25] or upon Newton's assumed correction factor.

RULES 1 AND 2. Newton makes an explicit appeal to his first two rules for reasoning in natural philosophy to infer that the force maintaining the Moon in its orbit is terrestrial gravity.

And therefore that force by which the moon is kept in its orbit, in descending from the moon's orbit to the surface of the earth, comes out equal to the force of gravity here on earth, and so (by rule 1 and rule 2) is that very force which we generally call gravity.

The basic argument for Proposition 4 is the equality established in the Moon-test together with this appeal to Rules 1 and 2.

Rule 1. No more causes of natural things should be admitted than are both true and sufficient to explain their phenomena.

Rule 2. Therefore, the causes assigned to natural effects of the same kind must be, so far as possible, the same.

The statement of Rule 2 suggests that it is intended as a consequence or implication of Rule 1. We can read these two rules, together, as telling us to opt for common causes whenever we can find them. This seems to be exactly their role in the application we are considering.

We have two phenomena: the centripetal acceleration of the Moon and the length of a seconds pendulum at Paris. Each measures a force producing accelerations at the surface of the Earth. These accelerations are equal and equally directed toward the center of the Earth. Identifying the forces makes these phenomena count as agreeing measures of the very same inverse-square force. This makes them count as effects of a single common cause.

The identification of the centripetal force maintaining the Moon in its orbit with terrestrial gravity transforms the notion of terrestrial gravity by making it now count as varying inversely with the square of distance from the center of the Earth. This was acclaimed as an unexpected, and highly regarded, new discovery about gravity by such critics of universal gravitation as Huygens and Leibniz.[26]

INVERSE-SQUARE CENTRIPETAL ACCELERATION FIELD. Newton's Scholium[27] to Proposition 4 opens with a thought experiment which appeals to induction to extend Kepler's harmonic relation $(t \propto R^{3/2})$ to a hypothetical system of several moons revolving around the Earth. He explicitly calls this harmonic relation a "law" and backs up the inverse-square assumption in the Moon-test by appeal to the corresponding inverse-square $(f \propto R^{-2})$ relation among the centripetal forces that would maintain moons in orbits satisfying it.

Howard Stein[28] has argued that the scholium version of the Moon-test –

Therefore, since both forces – vis., those of heavy bodies and those of the moons – are directed toward the center of the earth and are similar to one another and equal, they will (by rule 1 and rule 2) have the same cause. And therefore that force by which the moon is kept in its orbit is the very one that we generally call gravity.

– should be interpreted in light of Newton's discussion (Definitions 5–8) of centripetal force and its three measures: absolute, accelerative, and motive. The motive measure of a centripetal force on a body is its mass times its centripetal acceleration – this is the measure of force familiar to students of Newtonian physics today. The accelerative measure is the acceleration produced and is referred to distances from the center. Stein[29] argues that Newton's discussion makes it clear that he intends this measure to be appropriate to a centripetal acceleration field – a centripetal force field that would produce equal centripetal accelerations on unsupported bodies at equal distances from the center. The harmonic law ratio for a system of orbits about a common center requires that the orbits exhibit centripetal accelerations corresponding to a single inverse-square centripetal acceleration field. The absolute measure of such a centripetal acceleration field is its strength. The ratio of the absolute measures of two such centripetal acceleration fields is the common ratio of the accelerations they would produce at any equal distances from their respective centers.

This suggests that, in the above passage from the Scholium Moon-test, the several forces – those of heavy bodies and those of the moons – are the motive forces exerted on those heavy bodies and moons. Their common cause is a single inverse-square centripetal acceleration field surrounding the Earth – the Earth's gravity. On this interpretation, all these motive forces directed toward the center of the Earth are the weights toward it of those moons and other bodies.

EMPIRICAL SUCCESS. This application of Rules 1 and 2 is backed by an ideal of empirical success exhibited in Newton's inferences from phenomena. According to this ideal, *a theory succeeds empirically by having its causal parameters receive convergent accurate measurements from the phenomena it purports to explain*. On the identification Newton argues for, we have a single inverse-square acceleration field the strength of which is given agreeing measurements by the length of a seconds pendulum at the surface of the Earth and by the centripetal acceleration exhibited by the orbit of the Moon.

Each of these counts as a phenomenon. The length of a seconds pendulum established by Huygens is a generalization that is backed up by a large and open-ended body of precise data. The centripetal acceleration exhibited by the orbital motion of the Moon is also a generalization backed up by a large and open-ended body of data. In this case the data are far less precise than those backing up Huygens's measurements. Even though they are less precise, their agreement in measured value of the strength of the common acceleration field makes the lunar data count as additional empirical support backing up Huygens's measurement of the acceleration of gravity at the surface of the earth.[30] It also makes Huygens's very precise data back up estimates of the centripetal acceleration of the lunar orbit.

Empiricists, who limit empirical success to prediction alone, would see the appeal to simplicity in Rules 1 and 2 as something extraneous to empirical success. According to such a view, these rules endorse a general commitment to simplicity imposed as an additional, pragmatic, requirement beyond empirical success. No merely pragmatic commitment to simplicity can do justice to the way in which identifying the force that maintains the Moon in its orbit with terrestrial gravity is empirically backed up by agreeing measurements. This gives reason to consider the richer notion of empirical success that informs Newton's methodology.

GENERALIZATION BY INDUCTION

Rule 4

Proposition 5. The circumjovial planets [or moons of Jupiter] gravitate toward Jupiter, the circumsaturnian planets [or satellites of Saturn] gravitate toward Saturn, and the circumsolar [or primary] planets gravitate toward the sun, and by the force of their gravity they are always drawn back from rectilinear motions and kept in curvilinear orbits.

This generalization is a unification – all these orbital phenomena are effects of gravitation of satellites toward primaries. On it, we can understand each of these phenomena as an agreeing measurement of such general features of gravitation toward primaries as centripetal direction and inverse-square accelerative measure.

Newton further generalizes centripetal forces of gravity (the first part of Corollary 1) that are inversely as the squares of distances from their centers (Corollary 2) to all planets universally. For planets without satellites there are no centripetal accelerations of bodies toward them to measure gravitation toward them.

The following Scholium is offered in support of this generalization to all planets.

Scholium. Hitherto we have called "centripetal" that force by which celestial bodies are kept in their orbits. It is now established that this force is gravity, and therefore we shall call it gravity from now on. For the cause of the centripetal force by which the moon is kept in its orbit ought to be extended to all planets, by rules 1, 2, and 4.

This appeal to Rules 1 and 2 is backed up by appeal to an additional rule.

Rule 4. In experimental philosophy, propositions gathered from phenomena by induction should be considered either exactly or very nearly true notwithstanding any contrary hypotheses, until yet other phenomena make such propositions either more exact or liable to exceptions.

This rule instructs us to consider propositions gathered from phenomena by induction as "either exactly or very nearly true"[31] and to maintain this in the face of any contrary hypotheses. We want to clarify what are to count as propositions gathered from phenomena by induction and how they differ from what are to count as mere hypotheses.

We have seen that the classic inferences from phenomena which open the argument for universal gravitation are measurements of the centripetal direction and the inverse-square accelerative quantity of gravitation maintaining moons and planets in their orbits. To extend attribution of centripetally directed inverse-square gravitational

acceleration to planets without moons is to treat such orbital phenomena as measurements of these quantifiable features of gravitation for planets universally.

What would it take for an alternative proposal to succeed in under-
mining this generalization of gravity to planets without moons? The
arguments we have been examining suggest that Newton's Rule 4
would have us treat such an alternative proposal as a mere "contrary hypothesis" unless it is sufficiently backed up by measurements from phenomena to count as a rival to be taken seriously.

Weight proportional to mass

Proposition 6. All bodies gravitate toward each of the planets, and at any
given distance from the center of any one planet the weight of any body
whatever toward that planet is proportional to the quantity of matter which
the body contains.

The centripetal forces that have been identified as gravitation toward
planets are acceleration fields. The ratio of weight to inertial mass
is the same for all bodies at any equal distances.[32] In arguing for this
proposition Newton backs up his earlier arguments by providing explicit measurements of the equality of these ratios of weight to mass.

GRAVITATION TOWARD THE EARTH. Newton begins with gravitation
toward the Earth. He describes pendulum experiments which measure the equality of the ratio of weight to inertial mass for pairs of
samples of nine varied materials. The equality of the periods of such
pairs of pendulums counts as a phenomenon which measures the
equality of these ratios for laboratory-sized bodies near the surface
of the Earth to a precision of 0.001.

A second phenomenon is the outcome of the Moon-test. The
agreement between the acceleration of gravity at the surface of the
Earth and the inverse-square-adjusted centripetal acceleration exhibited by the lunar orbit measures the further agreement between, on
the one hand, the ratio of the Moon's weight toward the Earth to
its mass and, on the other, the common ratio to their masses of
the inverse-square-adjusted weights toward the Earth that terrestrial
bodies would have at the lunar distance. The lunar distance data
Newton cites measure the equality of these ratios to < 0.03.

RULE 3. *Corollary 2* (Proposition 6, Book 3). All bodies universally that are on or near the earth are heavy [or gravitate] toward the earth, and the weights of all bodies that are equally distant from the center of the earth are as the quantities of matter in them. This is a quality of all bodies on which experiments can be performed and therefore by rule 3 is to be affirmed of all bodies universally.

Rule 3. Those qualities of bodies that cannot be intended and remitted [that is, qualities that cannot be increased and diminished] and that belong to all bodies on which experiments can be made should be taken as qualities of all bodies universally.

Those qualities of bodies that cannot be intended or remitted are those that count as constant parameter values. This rule, therefore, endorses counting such parameter values found to be constant on all bodies within the reach of experiments as constant for all bodies universally. In Corollary 2, the quality of bodies which is generalized is weight toward the Earth. To have gravitation toward the Earth count as an inverse-square acceleration field is to have the ratio between inverse-square-adjusted weight toward the Earth and inertial mass be a constant value for all bodies.

The equal periods of pairs of pendulums in Newton's experiments is a phenomenon established with sufficient precision to measure to 0.001 the equalities of ratios of weight to mass for terrestrial bodies.[33] Similarly, the outcome of the Moon-test counts as a rougher measurement bound (< 0.03) in agreement with the more precise measurement bound (< 0.001) that would result from extending the outcome of Newton's pendulum experiments to the equality of ratios to masses of the inverse-square-adjusted weights bodies would have at the lunar distance. These phenomena count as agreeing measurements bounding toward zero a parameter Δ_e representing differences between ratios of inverse-square-adjusted weight toward the Earth to mass for bodies.[34]

Rule 3 tells us to conclude that the ratio of mass to gravitation toward the Earth is equal for all bodies at any distance from the center of the Earth if that equality holds for all the bodies in reach of our experiments. The agreement exhibited by Newton among measurements of this equality by phenomena is an example of what he would take as sufficient to count the proposition that it holds for all bodies within reach of our experiments as gathered from phenomena by induction. This makes his Rule 4 tell us to put the burden of proof on a sceptic to provide evidence for bodies within reach of our experiments that would exhibit phenomena making this equality liable to exceptions.

THE ARGUMENT FOR PROPOSITION 6 CONTINUED. Newton follows up his argument for the Earth with an appeal to the harmonic law for Jupiter's moons as a phenomenon which measures, at the distance of each moon, the equality of the ratio of mass to inverse-square-adjusted weight toward Jupiter for bodies at that distance. Rule 3 would extend this equality to bodies at any distances. The data Newton cites from other astronomers measure the equality of these ratios to fair precision $(\Delta_j < 0.03)$, while Pound's more precise data do considerably better $(\Delta_j < 0.0007)$. Similarly, the data Newton cites for the harmonic law for the primary planets measure bounds $(\Delta_s < 0.004)$ on the equality of ratios between inverse-square-adjusted weight toward the Sun and mass for bodies at the mean distances of the planets.

For equality of ratios of mass to weight toward the Sun at equal distances Newton also appeals to three additional phenomena – absence of polarization toward or away from the Sun of orbits of respectively Jupiter's moons, Saturn's moons and the Earth's moon. If the ratio of mass to weight toward the Sun for a moon were greater or less than the corresponding ratio for the planet, then the orbit of that moon would be shifted toward or away from the Sun. Absence of such orbital polarization counts as a phenomenon measuring the equality of ratios of mass to weight toward the Sun at equal distances. The data on Jupiter's moons cited in Newton's table establish this phenomenon with sufficient precision to measure the equality of these ratios to a precision of $\Delta_s < 0.034$, while his data from Pound are precise enough to reach $\Delta_s < 0.004$.[35]

All these phenomena count as agreeing measurements bounding toward zero a single general parameter Δ representing differences between bodies of the ratios of their inertial masses to their inverse-square-adjusted weights toward planets.[36]

PARTS OF PLANETS. Newton concludes his argument for Proposition 6 by explicitly extending the argument to equal ratios between mass and weight toward other planets to individual parts of planets. Here, instead of direct measurements by phenomena, we have a thought experiment which makes salient that it would be very improbable to have parts differing in ratios of weight to inertial mass so exactly proportioned that whole planets had equal ratios. This is made especially implausible by the additional fact that the Moon-test establishes agreement between outer parts of the Earth (ordinary terrestrial bodies) and the whole of the Moon.

GRAVITATION IS A UNIVERSAL FORCE OF INTERACTION

Applying the third law of motion

Proposition 7. Gravity exists in all bodies universally and is proportional to the quantity of matter in each.

GRAVITATION TOWARD PLANETS

We have already proved that all planets are heavy [or gravitate] toward one another and also that the gravity toward any one planet, taken by itself, is inversely as the square of the distance of places from the center of the planet. And it follows (by book 1, prop. 69 and its corollaries) that the gravity toward all the planets is proportional to the matter in them.

In Proposition 69, Book 1, Newton considers a system of bodies A, B, C, D, etc. He argues that under the assumption that body A attracts all the others (including body B) with inverse-square accelerative forces and the assumption that body B, similarly, attracts all the others (including A), then the absolute force of A (the strength of the acceleration field toward A) will be to the absolute force of B as the mass of A is to the mass of B.

Newton's proof begins by pointing out that the supposition that each body attracts all the rest with inverse-square accelerative forces requires the ratios of accelerations produced by such forces at equal distances to be independent of distance. The distance of A from B equals the distance of B from A. Therefore,

$$\mathrm{acc}_A(B)/\mathrm{acc}_B(A) = \mathrm{abs}F_A/\mathrm{abs}F_B \tag{i.1}$$

The ratio of the magnitude of B's acceleration toward A to the magnitude of A's acceleration toward B equals the ratio of the strength of the attractive force toward A to the strength of the attractive force toward B.

The key step in Newton's proof is an application of his third law of motion to the motive force attracting B toward A and the motive force attracting A toward B.

Law 3. To any action there is always an opposite and equal reaction; in other words, the actions of two bodies one upon the other are always equal and always opposite in direction.

To have the motive forces of A on B, $f_A(B) = m(A)\mathrm{acc}_B(A)$, and of B on A, $f_B(A) = m(B)\mathrm{acc}_A(B)$, count as equal action and reaction makes

$$m(A)/m(B) = \mathrm{acc}_A(B)/\mathrm{acc}_B(A) \tag{i.2}$$

where $m(B)$ and $m(A)$ are the masses of B and A. Combining i.2 with i.1 yields Newton's conclusion,

$$m(A)/m(B) = \mathrm{abs}\,F_A/\mathrm{abs}\,F_B \tag{i.3}$$

In the assumption of the argument for Proposition 7, gravitation of any planets A and B toward one another is treated as an *interaction*, so that the equal and opposite reaction to the weight of B toward A is the weight of A toward B. This makes the argument of Proposition 69 apply, so the strengths of the centripetal attractions toward each are proportional to their masses.

GRAVITATION TOWARD PARTS OF PLANETS

Further, since all the parts of any planet A are heavy [or gravitate] toward any planet B, and since the gravity [weight toward B] of each part is to the gravity [weight toward B] of the whole as the matter of the part is to the matter of the whole, and since to every action (by the third law of motion) there is an equal reaction, it follows that planet B will gravitate toward all the parts of planet A, and its gravity toward any one part will be to its gravity toward the whole of the planet as the matter of that part to the matter of the whole. Q.E.D.

For any planets A and B, each part a of planet A is itself a body being accelerated toward planet B. Newton's supposition follows from proposition 6. We have

$$f_B(a)/f_B(A) = m(a)/m(A), \tag{ii.1}$$

where $f_B(a)$ and $f_B(A)$ are the weights of part a and planet A toward planet B.

As in the proof of Proposition 69, the third law of motion is applied to yield the conclusion. The weight, $f_a(B)$, of planet B toward part a is taken to be the equal and opposite reaction to the weight, $f_B(a)$, of part a to planet B, just as the weights $f_A(B)$ and $f_B(A)$ of the whole planets toward one another are taken to be equal action and reaction. This yields

$$f_a(B)/f_A(B) = f_B(a)/f_B(A). \qquad (ii.2)$$

Combining ii.2 with ii.1 gives Newton's conclusion,

$$f_a(B)/f_A(B) = m(a)/m(A). \qquad (ii.3)$$

The weight of planet B toward part a is to its weight toward the whole planet A as the mass of the part is to the mass of the whole planet.[37]

The extension of the argument to include, in addition to gravitation toward planets,[38] gravitation toward parts of planets would count, in Newton's day, as an extension to include gravitation toward all bodies within reach of experiments. This would make Rule 3 endorse extending to all bodies universal gravitation toward them proportional to their masses.

INVERSE-SQUARE GRAVITATION TOWARD PARTICLES
Corollary 2 (Proposition 7, Book 3). The gravitation toward each of the individual equal particles of a body is inversely as the square of the distance of places from those particles. This is evident by book 1, prop. 74, corol. 3.

Corollary 3 (Proposition 74, Book 1). If a corpuscle placed outside a homogeneous sphere is attracted by a force proportional to the square of the distance of the corpuscle from the center of the sphere, and the sphere consists of attracting particles, the force of each particle will decrease in the squared ratio of the distance from the particle.

The inference in this corollary is from inverse-square variation of the total force on a corpuscle outside a sphere toward its center to the inverse-square variation of the component attractions toward particles. Just as is the case with Newton's classic inferences from phenomena, this inference is backed up by systematic dependencies. Any difference from the inverse-square law for attraction toward the particles would produce a corresponding difference from the inverse-square for the law of attraction toward the center resulting from summing the attractions toward the particles.[39] These dependencies make phenomena measuring inverse-square variation of attraction toward the whole count as measurements of inverse-square variation of the law of attraction toward the particles.

Resolving the two chief world systems problem

In Proposition 8, Newton appeals to theorems on attraction toward spheres to extend his conclusions to gravitation toward bodies approximating globes made up of spherically homogeneous shells. Attraction between such bodies is directly as the product of their masses and inversely as the square of the distance between their centers.

Proposition 7 is applied to use harmonic law ratios to measure the masses of the Sun and planets with moons (Corollary 2, Proposition 8). The resulting convergent agreeing measurements of the masses of these bodies count as a significant realization of Newton's ideal of empirical success – a realization that is especially important because it adds support to his appeal to Law 3 in the argument for Proposition 7.[40]

These measurements lead to his surprising center-of-mass resolution of the two chief world systems problem.

Proposition 12 (Book 3). The sun is in continual motion but never recedes far from the common center of gravity of all the planets.

Both the Copernican and the Brahean systems are wrong; however, the Sun-centered system closely approximates true motions while the Earth-centered system is wildly inaccurate.

In this center of mass frame the separate centripetal acceleration fields toward solar system bodies are combined into a single system where each body undergoes an acceleration toward each of the others proportional to its mass and inversely proportional to the square of the distance between them.

General Relativity

Newton transformed the two chief world systems problem into a physically meaningful question that could be answered by analysis of relative accelerations and the information they carry about the distribution of mass. General Relativity incorporates the basic dependencies between acceleration fields and spherical mass distributions that inform Newton's account, even though it reinterprets gravitational free fall as motion along a shortest-distance path – "geodesic motion" – in a curved space-time.[41] Therefore, contrary to Reichenbach,[42] General Relativity does not undercut the objectivity of Newton's solution to the two chief world systems problem.[43]

Contrary to Kuhn,[44] the revolutionary change to General Relativity is in accordance with the evaluative procedures of Newton's methodology. The development and applications of perturbation theory, from Newton through Laplace at the turn of the nineteenth century and on through Simon Newcomb at the turn of the twentieth, led to increasingly accurate successive corrections of Keplerian planetary orbits. At each stage, departures from motion in accord with the model developed counted as higher-order phenomena carrying information about further interactions. These successive corrections led to increasingly precise specifications of solar system phenomena backed up by increasingly precise measurements of the masses of the interacting solar system bodies. The extra 43 arc-seconds per century of Mercury's perihelion precession was a departure from the Newtonian theory that resisted attempts to account for it by such interactions. The successful account of this extra precession, together with the Newtonian limit which allowed it to recover the empirical successes of Newtonian perturbation theory (including the account of the other 531 arc-seconds per century of Mercury's perihelion precession[45]), made General Relativity do better than Newton's theory on Newton's own ideal of empirical success. Since its initial development General Relativity has continued to improve upon what Newton's methodology counts as its clear advantage over Newtonian gravitation theory.[46]

NOTES

1 P. Duhem, *The Aim and Structure of Physical Theory*, trans. P. P. Wiener (Princeton: Princeton University Press, 1991), pp. 190–5.
2 K. Popper, "The Aim of Science", in *Objective Knowledge: An Evolutionary Approach* (Oxford: Oxford University Press, 1972).

3   I. Lakatos, "Newton's Effect on Scientific Standards," in J. Worrall and
    G. Curere (eds.), *The Methodology of Scientific Research Programmes*
    (Cambridge: Cambridge University Press, 1978), pp. 193–222.

4   C. Glymour, *Theory and Evidence* (Princeton: Princeton University
    Press, 1980), pp. 203–26.

5   The cited passages are from *The Principia, Mathematical Principles of
    Natural Philosophy: A New Translation*, trans. I. Bernard Cohen and
    Anne Whitman, preceded by "A Guide to Newton's *Principia*" by I. B.
    Cohen (Berkeley: University of California Press, 1999).

6   Curtis Wilson suggests that Leibniz in his "Tentamen de motuum
    coelestium causis" of 1689 (after reading the first edition of Newton's
    Principia) was the first author to call Kepler's rules "laws." C. Wilson,
    "From Kepler to Newton: Telling the Tale," in Richard H. Dalitz and
    Michael Nauenberg (eds.), *The Foundations of Newtonian Scholarship*
    (Singapore: World Scientific, 2000), pp. 223–42, at pp. 225–6.

7   Newton's clause – the fixed stars being at rest – tells us that the periods
    are calculated with respect to those stars. This treats a reference frame
    at the center of Jupiter with fixed directions with respect to the stars as
    non-rotating. Such non-rotating frames are also used to calculate areas
    in the areal law.

8   *Corollary 6* (Laws of Motion). If bodies are moving in any way whatsoever with
    respect to one another and are urged by equal accelerative forces along parallel
    lines, they will all continue to move with respect to one another as they would
    if they were not acted upon by those forces.

9   *Corollary 4* (Laws of Motion). The common center of gravity of two or more
    bodies does not change its state whether of motion or of rest as a result of the
    actions of the bodies upon one another; and therefore the common center of
    gravity of all bodies acting upon one another (excluding external actions and
    impediments) either is at rest or moves uniformly straight forward.

10 Newton explicitly gives corollaries (Corollaries 2 and 3 of Proposition 3,
    Book 1) to cover such approximations. These extensions show that the
    areal rule can be a quite general criterion for finding centers toward
    which forces maintaining bodies in orbits are directed.

11 Clark Glymour (*Theory and Evidence*) used these inferences as ex-
    amples of good scientific practice that could not be accounted for
    by hypothetico-deductive (H-D) methodology. The systematic depen-
    dencies backing up Newton's inferences make such inferences avoid
    the counterexamples put forward to challenge bootstrap confirmation,
    Glymour's proposed alternative to H-D confirmation. See W. L. Harper,
    "Measurement and Approximation: Newton's Inferences from Phenom-
    ena versus Glymour's Bootstrap Confirmation," in G. Weingartner,
    G. Schurz, and G. Dorn (eds.), *The Role of Pragmatics in Contempo-
    rary Philosophy* (Vienna: Hölder-Picher-Tempsky, 1998).

12   The mean error of Pound's observed estimates from today's values is only +0.135 of Jupiter's semi-diameter, while the average mean error for the other four astronomers cited by Newton is −1.098.

13   Newton also suggests that the area rule for Jupiter is "especially provable by the eclipses of its satellites." Each eclipse gives a heliocentric longitude (see D. Densmore, Newton's Principia: The Central Argument [Santa Fe: Green Lion Press, 1995], pp. 275–7). This allows triangulation of its heliocentric distance from observations of its angular position with respect to the Earth. The shortness of the time intervals between them compared to Jupiter's period allows sequences of such eclipses to afford sequences of triangles approximating areas swept out. The area law for Jupiter can be tested by checking that the areas of those triangles are proportional to the intervals of time.

14   In his Dialogue concerning the Two Chief World Systems, Galileo had appealed to the phases of Mercury and Venus and the absence of phases of Mars, Jupiter, and Saturn in concluding that the orbits of the first two encompass the Sun, but not the Earth, while the orbits of the last three encompass both. While ruling out Ptolemaic systems, this still left open the question of a Copernican versus a Tychonic system (or intermediates between them). See G. Galileo, Dialogue concerning the Two Chief World Systems, trans S. Drake (Berkeley: University of California Press, 1967), pp. 322ff.

15   See W. L. Harper, "The First Six Propositions in Newton's Argument for Universal Gravitation," The St. John's Review 45, no. 2 (1999), 74–93, at pp. 84–7.

16   Newton's orbital data can be fit as well or better by a higher-order curve that would not have the periods be any constant power s of the mean distances. On such a hypothesis, the application of Corollary 7 of Proposition 4 would be undercut. The orbits would, therefore, not carry information about any simple power law relating the accelerative forces to distances from the sun.

   Similarly, the orbital data are not precise enough directly to rule out an ellipse with the Sun slightly displaced toward the center from the focus so that the force is not directed exactly at that focus. As George Smith points out, Newton knew that any such orbit would be incompatible with an inverse-square power law. G. E. Smith, "From the Phenomenon of the Ellipse to an Inverse-Square Force: Why Not?," in David Malament (ed.), Reading Natural Philosophy: Essays in the History and Philosophy of Science and Mathematics to Honor Howard Stein on his 70th Birthday (La Salle: Open Court, 2002).

   These alternative hypotheses illustrate the fact that Newton's inferences from phenomena are not logically forced by the data, even together with mathematical theorems derived from the Laws of Motion.

17 Boulliau uses the same mean distances as Kepler for the Earth and Mars. For the ten distinct estimates cited by Newton, the ratio of sd^+ to the mean value of the harmonic law ratios $[R^3/t^2]$ is 0.007.

18 In his *System of the World*, an earlier version of Book 3 composed "in a popular method that it might be read by many" (Introduction to Book 3), Newton points out:

> But now, after innumerable revolutions, hardly any such motion has been perceived in the orbits of the circumsolar planets. Some astronomers affirm there is no such motion; others reckon it no greater than what may easily arise from causes hereafter to be assigned, which is of no moment to the present question. (F. Cajori [ed. and trans.], *Newton's* Principia, *Motte's Translation Revised* [Los Angeles: University of California Press, 1934], p. 561)

Any precession that can be accounted for by perturbation due to forces toward other bodies can be ignored in using stable apsides to measure inverse-square variation of the centripetal force toward the Sun maintaining planets in their orbits.

19 See S. R. Valluri, C. Wilson, and W. L. Harper, "Newton's Apsidal Precession Theorem and Eccentric Orbits," *Journal of the History of Astronomy* 27 (1997), 13–27.

20 See Densmore, *Newton's* Principia, p. 282.

21 Using $1/178.725$ in Corollary 2, Proposition 45 yields fairly close to what Newton cites as the lunar precession per revolution.

   In Proposition 26, Book 3, however, Newton shows that the average, over a lunar orbit, of the Moon–Earth radial component of the force of the Sun to perturb the Moon is a reduction of $1/357.45$ of the basic inverse-square centripetal force on the Moon. The result of using $1/357.45$ in Corollary 2, Proposition 45 shows that the radial component alone of the Sun's force on the Moon would account for only about half of the lunar precession. See G. E. Smith, "The Motion of the Lunar Apsis," in *The Principia*, ed. and trans. Cohen and Whitman, pp. 257–64.

22 It was not until 1749 that a solution showing how the lunar precession could be accounted for by the Sun's perturbation of the lunar orbit was achieved. See R. Taton and C. Wilson, *The General History of Astronomy*, vol. 2B (Cambridge: Cambridge University Press, 1995), pp. 35–46.

23 Huygens's one-second fall of 15.096 Paris feet corresponds to 980.7 cm/sec^2 for the acceleration of gravity at Paris. The modern value for q at Paris is 980.87 cm/sec^2. See G. E. Smith, "Huygens's Empirical Challenge to Universal Gravity" (forthcoming) for this comparison and for a detailed account of Huygens's achievement.

24 When the correction is applied we get 15.0935 Paris feet.

25 Newton's main text for Proposition 4 concludes with an appeal to the two-body correction which can defend using 60 in the Moon-test when the measured distance is somewhat greater.

26   See H. Stein, " 'From the Phenomena of Motions to the Forces of Nature':
     Hypothesis or Deduction?," *PSA 1990* 2 (1991), 209–22; also Taton and
     Wilson, *General History*, vol. 2B, pp. 7, 12 and Huygens's *Discourse
     on the Cause of Gravity*, trans. Karen Bailey, in George E. Smith (ed.),
     A Measure in Evidence: Huygens's Determination of Surface Gravity
     (forthcoming).
27   This Scholium was added in the third (1726) edition; see *Isaac
     Newton's Philosophiae Naturalis Principia Mathematica, the Third
     Edition with Variant Readings*, ed. A. Koyré, I. B. Cohen, and Anne
     Whitman (Cambridge, MA: Harvard University Press; Cambridge:
     Cambridge University Press, 1972), p. 569.
28   Stein, " 'From the Phenomena of Motions'," pp. 211–13.
29   Stein, " 'From the Phenomena of Motions'," p. 213, and H. Stein, "On
     the Notion of Field in Newton, Maxwell, and Beyond," in R. H. Stuewer
     (ed.), *Historical and Philosophical Perspectives of Science* (Minneapolis:
     University of Minnesota Press, 1970) pp. 264–87.
30   The lunar data will provide more epistemic resistance to conjectures
     that would make the acceleration of gravity at the surface of the Earth
     differ from Huygens's measure by enough to go outside the error bounds
     set by the Moon-test estimate than would have been provided by
     Huygens's data alone. Agreeing measurements by several phenomena
     contributes to increase the resiliency – resistance to large changes – of
     estimates of parameter values.
31   The provision for approximations fits with construing such propositions
     as established up to tolerances provided by measurements. This makes
     Rule 4 very much in line with the methodology guiding testing programs
     in relativistic gravitation today (Harper, "Measurement and Approxima-
     tion," pp. 284–5; W. L. Harper, "Isaac Newton on Empirical Success and
     Scientific Method," in J. Earman and J. D. Norton [eds.], *The Cosmos of
     Science* [Pittsburgh: University of Pittsburgh Press, 1997], pp. 55–86).
32   Where f_1/m_1 and f_2/m_2 are ratios of weights toward the center of a
     planet to inertial masses of attracted bodies while a_1 and a_2 are their
     respective gravitational accelerations toward it, it follows from $f = ma$
     that $a_1 = a_2$ if and only if $f_1/m_1 = f_2/m_2$.
33   These experiments extend to this, much greater, precision the many
     long-established, rougher but agreeing, observations that bodies fall at
     equal rates "at least on making an adjustment for the inequality of the
     retardation that arises from the very slight resistance of the air."
34   For any body x, let $Q_e(x) = (W_e(x)[d_e(x)]^2)/m(x)$, where $W_e(x)$ is the
     weight of x toward the earth, $d_e(x)$ is the distance of x from the cen-
     ter of the earth, and $m(x)$ is the inertial mass of x. For bodies x and y,
     $\Delta_e(x, y) = Q_e(x) - Q_e(y)$ is the difference in the ratios of their inverse-
     square-adjusted weights toward the earth to their inertial masses.

35 Newton does not provide the details of his calculation and the result he
    cites is incorrect. The 0.034 results from applying a modern calculation
    to the tolerances for distance estimates exhibited by the data cited by
    Newton from other astronomers and the 0.004 from applying it to tol-
    erances estimated from comparing Pound's data with current estimates
    of orbital distances for Jupiter's moons. See W. L. Harper, S. R. Valluri,
    and R. Mann, "Jupiter's Moons and the Equivalence Principle," forth-
    comming in *Proceedings of the Ninth Marcel Grossmann Meeting on
    General Relativity*, for discussion and references.

36 Bounds limiting this universal parameter toward zero are what count
    today as bounds limiting violations of the weak equivalence princi-
    ple – the identification of passive gravitational with inertial mass.
    The phenomena cited by Newton together with additional phenom-
    ena of far greater precision count today as agreeing measurements sup-
    porting this identification. (See Harper, "Isaac Newton on Empirical
    Success," and "Measurement and Approximation," for discussion and
    references.)

37 This extends the identification of gravitational and inertial mass to in-
    clude *active* as well as *passive* gravitational mass (see note 36).

38 The classic use of "planet" to refer to heavenly wanderers would in-
    clude the Sun, the Moon, and primary planets and their satellites. The
    argument for Proposition 6 includes gravitation toward the Earth, which
    suggests that Newton extends the classic use to count the Earth, also,
    as a planet.

    His thought experiment with terrestrial bodies raised to the Moon
    illustrates that a body can count as part of a planet just by falling on it.

39 S. Chandrasekhar (*Newton's* Principia *for the Common Reader* [Oxford:
    Clarendon Press, 1995], formula 9, p. 289) provides an integral formulat-
    ing the dependencies Newton provides in Lemma 29 and Propositions
    79–81, Book 1.

    According to Proposition 74, Book 1, inverse-square attraction to-
    ward the center of a uniform sphere on corpuscles outside, right down to
    the surface, results from summing the inverse-square attractions on the
    corpuscle toward the particles making up the sphere. This proposition
    follows from Chandrasekhar's integral when the law of attraction to-
    ward particles is the −2 power of distance.

    A power law differing even slightly from the inverse-square, e.g., a
    −2.01 power law, for the particles will approach the same power law for
    attractions to the whole at great distances but will yield attractions to
    the whole corresponding to differing non-uniform relations to distance
    for locations close to the surface of the sphere. The inverse-square case,
    and the simple harmonic oscillator case where attraction is directly as
    the distance, are special in that the law of attraction toward particles

yields the same law of attraction toward the whole all the way down to the surface of the sphere. These are the two cases Newton singles out for detailed treatment.

40 Howard Stein, in " 'From The Phenomena of Motions'," pointed out that Newton's application of Law 3 in his argument for Proposition 7 is not an inference from the phenomena cited in the argument for Propositions 1–7. This significant objection was anticipated by Cotes and responded to by Newton in letters to Cotes. For a discussion of how issues raised by this challenge illuminate Newton's methodology, see W. L. Harper, "Howard Stein on Isaac Newton: Beyond Hypotheses?," in David Malament (ed.), *Reading Natural Philosophy: Essays in the History and Philosophy of Science and Mathematics to Honor Howard Stein on his 70th Birthday* (La Salle: Open Court, 2002).

41 See DiSalle, this volume, for discussion and further references.

42 According to Hans Reichenbach (*The Philosophy of Space and Time* [New York: Dover, 1958], p. 217):

> The relativity theory of dynamics is not a purely academic matter, for it upsets the Copernican world view. It is meaningless to speak of a difference in truth claims of the theories of Copernicus and Ptolemy; the two conceptions are equivalent descriptions. What had been considered the greatest discovery of western science compared to antiquity, is now denied its claim to truth.

43 The mass of the Sun with respect to the masses of the planets is large enough to support geodesics approximating orbits of the planets about it, while the mass of the Earth (measured by the motion of the Moon) is far too small. These mass differences, together with the difficulties imposed on construing the irregularities of Brahean orbits as geodesics in a curved space-time generated by the Earth as a spherically symmetric mass distribution, make General Relativity agree with Newton in counting Earth-centered systems as wildly inaccurate. See DiSalle, this volume.

44 T. S. Kuhn, *The Structure of Scientific Revolutions*, 2nd edn (Chicago: University of Chicago Press, 1970), p. 94:

> Like the choice between competing political institutions, that between competing paradigms proves to be a choice between incompatible modes of community life. Because it has that character, the choice is not and cannot be determined by the evaluative procedures characteristic of normal science, for these depend in part upon a given paradigm, and that paradigm is at issue. When paradigms enter, as they must, into a debate about paradigm choice, their role is necessarily circular. Each group uses its own paradigm to argue in that paradigm's defense.

45 This 531 arc-seconds per century does not include the general precession of 5025.6 arc-seconds resulting from the precession of the equinoxes (see C. M. Will, *Theory and Experiment in Gravitational Physics* [Cambridge: Cambridge University Press, 1993], p. 4). The contrast between the approximately 531 + 43 arc-seconds per century that needs

to be dynamically accounted for and the general precession, which results merely from rotating coordinates, illustrates that General Relativity continues to distinguish between true and merely relative motion.

As Smith points out ("From the Phenomenon of the Ellipse"), General Relativity's solution to the Mercury perihelion problem requires that it be able to recover also the precession accounted for by Newtonian perturbations.

46 In addition to the famous three basic tests there are now a great many post-Newtonian corrections required by the more precise data made available by such new observations as radar ranging to planets and laser ranging to the Moon. These provide not just predictions but also measurements of parameters, such as those of the PPN testing framework, which support General Relativity. See Will, *Theory and Experiment*, and Harper, "Isaac Newton on Empirical Success," for discussion and references.

6   Newton and celestial mechanics

Newton's achievements in celestial mechanics tend in popular accounts to be underestimated in some respects, exaggerated in others. This chapter seeks to correct a number of misconceptions arising from inattention to the detailed history.

KEPLER'S FIRST TWO LAWS, SO-CALLED, AND NEWTON

The claim that the planets move in elliptical orbits, with the *radii vectores* from Sun to planet sweeping out equal areas in equal times, first appeared in Kepler's *Astronomia Nova* of 1609. Since the late eighteenth century the two parts of this claim have been referred to as Kepler's first two planetary "laws," understood as empirical laws. According to the popular account, Newton relied on these "laws" as thus established.

Writing to Halley on 20 June 1686, Newton stated: "Kepler knew ye Orb to be not circular but oval & guest it to be elliptical."[1] Whether Newton ever saw the *Astronomia Nova* is unknown.

The *Astronomia Nova* is an innovative work. It establishes important empirical results, such as the passage of the planet's orbital plane through the Sun's center and the orbit's oval shape. Was the orbit's ellipticity also a straightforwardly empirical result, say by means of triangulations of Mars, as sometimes asserted?[2] Kepler carried out many such triangulations, but they were subject to sizeable observational error, of which he was acutely aware.[3]

At the end of Chapter 58 we at last find him asserting that "no figure is left for the planetary orbit but a perfect ellipse." This chapter attempts to refute another oval orbit, the *via buccosa* or puffy-cheeked path. Kepler's whole effort, he tells us, has been to find a hypothesis yielding not only distances in agreement with observation, but also correct "equations" – "equation" here meaning the difference between the mean and the true heliocentric motions, measured from aphelion. To derive the true position at any time, Kepler used his area rule, in which area swept out is proportional to time. He had already found that this rule, when applied to a particular ellipse – the ellipse with the Sun at one focus – yielded the true positions with no more than expected observational error; but he was unable to explain why the planet should move in this ellipse. He turned to another hypothesis which he called the "libration," and which, so he supposed, implied a different orbit.

In the "libration," the planet oscillates sinusoidally along the radius vector. The cause of this oscillation, Kepler proposed, was a quasi-magnetic attraction and repulsion from the Sun. (In Kepler's preinertial physics, separate causes had to be assumed for the planet's forward motion about the Sun, and for its motion toward and away from the Sun.) The libration gave the Sun–planet distances correctly, agreeing with the triangulations to within the range of observational error. In another respect it was indeterminate: the radius vector started at the Sun's center, but where did the other end go? Kepler at first imagined he knew where it went, and his initial placement yielded the puffy-cheeked orbit (we omit details). Then he discovered that a different placement, just as plausible, would yield the Sun-focused ellipse. Thus the libration hypothesis could be combined with this ellipse to give both correct equations and correct distances.

But in his diagram he found the alternative *radii vectores* in the ellipse and puffy-cheeked orbit to be separated by observationally detectable angles, $+5'.5$ at $45°$ of anomaly and $-4'$ at $135°$ of anomaly. Since the ellipse gave correct equations, Kepler concluded that the puffy-cheeked orbit could not do so. Hence, "no figure is left for the planetary orbit but a perfect ellipse."

The conclusion is unwarranted. Motion on the puffy-cheeked orbit in accordance with the area rule, when calculated by integration throughout the orbit, differs at maximum from motion in the ellipse by about $1'$, a difference not observationally significant in Tycho's data.[4] (Of course, with the mathematics available to him Kepler would have been hard put to carry out an equivalent of the modern integration.)

If the ellipticity of the orbits was not empirically established by Kepler, then neither was the so-called second law: determination of areas presupposes orbital shape. For Kepler the area rule was the expression of a dynamical hypothesis, the idea of a motive virtue issuing from and rotating with the Sun so as to push the planets round, its strength varying inversely with distance from the Sun. Kepler's dynamics was Aristotelian, making speed proportional to force. His conception implied that the *component* of orbital speed at right angles to the radius vector varied inversely with distance.[5] The area rule, he belatedly realized, was a consequence.

Given his two rules, Kepler in his *Tabulae Rudolphinae* (1627) derived tables for calculating planetary and lunar positions. These proved more accurate than all earlier tables, and so confirmed the two rules *in combination*.

Newton was aware of the principal features of Kepler's causal account of planetary motion: he had read (probably in 1685 or 1686) the critique of it given by Ishmaël Boulliau (1605–94) in his *Astronomia Philolaica* (Paris, 1645). This astronomical treatise was the first after Kepler's *Rudolphine Tables* to take elliptical orbits as a basis for calculating planetary tables. But Boulliau entirely rejected Kepler's hypothetical physical causes, devoting the bulk of his Chapter xii to refuting them.[6] He preferred to believe that each planet is moved by its "proper form."[7] To Boulliau, Kepler's assumption of a *virtus movens* issuing from the Sun was mere conjecture.

Also, to Kepler's assumption of an inverse proportionality of the *virtus movens* to solar distance Boulliau objected that corporeal virtues issuing from a point source should vary inversely with the square of the distance from the source. Newton picked up on this assertion in a long postscript to his letter to Halley of 20 June 1686: "Bullialdus [Boulliau] wrote that all force respecting ye Sun as its center & depending on matter must be reciprocally in a duplicate ratio of ye distance from ye center."[8] Newton was here seeking to rebut Robert Hooke's claim to have furnished him originally with the idea of an inverse-square variation for gravity.

From Boulliau's critique Newton learned that Kepler's dynamics violated the principle of inertia, and that Kepler, in seeking to explain the planet's alternate approach to and recession from the Sun, had invoked a hypothetical magnetism in the Sun and planet – a hypothesis that Boulliau dismissed as merely conjectural. Newton, corresponding with Flamsteed in 1681, had argued that the Sun, being hot, could not be a magnet.[9]

In the inertial mechanics of Newton, equable description of area becomes equivalent to a centripetal force, a single cause for a single effect, namely the departure of the orbiting body from its instantaneous rectilinear path. His derivation of the ellipticity of the planetary orbits in Proposition 13, Book 3 of the *Principia* rested on the Laws of Motion announced at the beginning of the *Principia*, and on the inverse-square law of universal gravitation argued for in the first seven propositions of Book 3.[10] In contrast with Kepler's attempted derivation, it contained no bare conjectures.

Universal gravitation did not become the guiding idea in Newton's thinking on planetary motion till much later than was long supposed: not before 1685. How had Newton viewed the Keplerian rules in the years before the *Principia*?

In the mid-1660s Newton made notes on Thomas Streete's *Astronomia Carolina* (1661). In 1669 or 1670 he perused Vincent Wing's *Astronomia Britannica* (1669), and wrote notes on its endpapers.[11] Both authors took the orbits of the planets to be elliptical, without offering justification for the assumption. Neither mentioned or used Kepler's area rule. Instead, each proposed a different calculative procedure for passing from mean anomaly (angle from aphelion that would be traversed at the planet's mean rate) to true anomaly (the planet's actual angle from aphelion). The area rule did not admit of such a direct procedure, except by approximation. Both Wing's and Streete's procedures were corrections to a faulty procedure proposed in Boulliau's *Astronomia Philolaica* (we omit details[12]), and produced results differing by only small amounts from those derived by the area rule. Streete's procedure gives a maximum error for Mars of 1′51″. In Wing's procedure the corresponding error is 20″.

Newton's reaction to these hypothetical devices, as his notes on Wing's *Astronomia Britannica* attest, was to doubt both the ellipticity of the orbits and the accuracy of the calculative procedures. Both orbital shape and motion, he proposed, should be controlled empirically, and he showed in a construction how this could be done.[13]

Both Streete and Wing assumed that the planets are moved by a solar vortex. Newton in the 1660s, while rejecting the Cartesian identification of matter and extension (on which for Descartes the necessity of vortices rested), accepted planetary vortices. In his speculations about planetary motion during the 1670s, he again assumed such vortices. A document datable to 1681 shows him still doing so.[14] The supposition of vortices with their hydrodynamical complexities could hardly fail to give rise to doubts about the mathematical accuracy of the elliptical orbits accepted by his contemporaries.

KEPLER'S THIRD OR HARMONIC LAW, AND NEWTON

Streete differed sharply from Wing in asserting the strict accuracy of Kepler's third law – the law according to which the planetary periods are as the three-halves power of their mean solar distances. In a departure from Kepler's *Rudolphine Tables*, he used the law to derive the mean solar distances from the periods. The solar distances could be determined observationally only by imprecise triangulations, whereas the periods were precisely determinable from comparisons of ancient and modern observations. Hindsight tells us that, for the planets from Mercury to Mars (but not for Jupiter or Saturn), the new rule improved the accuracy of the solar distances by three orders of magnitude.

Streete took this procedure from the as yet unpublished *Venus in Sole Visa* of Jeremiah Horrocks (1618? – 3 January 1641). Horrocks had found empirical support for it in his observations of Mars and Venus.[15]

Newton, on reading about this rule in Streete's *Astronomia Carolina*, made a note of it. A few years later, perusing Wing's *Astronomia Britannica*, he found that Wing's values for the mean solar distances disagreed with this "regula Kepleriana." They would better agree with observations, he wrote in the endpapers of his copy, if they were reduced to the rule.

Newton's interest had a theoretical dimension. Probably in 1666 he had derived a formula for "the endeavor from the center of a body revolving in a circle," thus quantifying the Cartesian concept; in a not yet published work Huygens had given the name "centrifugal force" to the pull on a string that retains the body in the circle, counteracting this endeavor.[16] According to the formula, when bodies are moving in different circles, their endeavors from the centers of those circles are as the radii divided by the squares of the periodic times. Since by the "regula Kepleriana" the squares of the periods of the planets are as the cubes of their mean solar distances, their endeavors from the Sun will be reciprocally as the squares of their solar distances. Newton also compared the Moon's endeavor to recede from the Earth with gravity at the Earth's surface, and found the latter to be "4000 and more times greater" than the former – not $(60)^2 = 3600$ times, as an inverse-square relation would imply.

David Gregory on a visit to Newton in 1694 was shown a manuscript with these calculations, and wrote afterwards that here "all the foundations of his [Newton's] philosophy are laid: namely the gravity of the Moon to the Earth, and of the planets to the Sun."[17] From Henry Pemberton, writing in 1728,[18] and William Whiston, writing in 1749,[19] we have similar accounts. According to Whiston, the failed lunar calculation led Newton to suspect that the force on the Moon was due partly to gravity and partly to "Cartesius's Vortices."

These tales give us a Newton about to embark on the enterprise of the *Principia* in the 1660s, but delaying for twenty years on account of a computation's failing to match expectation. As Florian Cajori has pointed out, the computation could easily have been corrected. Newton had used an inaccurate value for the length of a degree of terrestrial latitude. Better values were readily available; Newton came to know of them by 1672.[20]

During these years Newton employed aethereal hypotheses to account for optical, electrical, chemical, and other phenomena. In the *Hypothesis Explaining ye Properties of Light* which he transmitted to the Royal Society in December 1675,[21] he assumed an elastic aethereal medium – not "one uniforme matter," but rather compounded of various "aethereall Spirits." These aethereal Spirits could be condensable, so that "the whole frame of Nature may be nothing but various Contextures of some certain aethereall Spirits or vapours condens'd as it were by precipitation." Terrestrial gravitation could be due to a certain aethereal Spirit which is condensed in the body of the Earth; in descending from above, it would "beare downe with it the bodyes it pervades with a force proportionall to the superficies of all their parts it acts upon." This aethereal matter, transformed alchemically within the Earth, would then slowly ascend to constitute the Earth's atmosphere for a time, before vanishing again into the aethereal spaces. "And as the Earth, so perhaps may the Sun imbibe this Spirit copiously to conserve his shineing, & keep the

Planets from recedeing further from him." This downward flux,
Newton supposed, was separate from the aethereal vortex carrying
the planets about the Sun; the two fluxes passed through one another
without mixing. He considered that the downward flux of aether into
the central body would lead to an inverse-square law.[22]

The dynamics that Newton here relied on was the Cartesian dynamics of an endeavor from the center – plausible for a stone twirled
in a sling or a planet carried about in a vortex. What if the planet
moves inertially in a straight line, and is simultaneously attracted
to a center? Robert Hooke proposed the latter conception to Newton
in a letter of 24 November 1679.[23]

The import of facts changes with the changing ideas in the light of
which they are viewed. Evidence for an inverse-square law of force
may be taken, in a universe of vortices, as evidence for a certain kind
of aethereal flux; but it hardly suggests an opening into an exact,
quantitative theory of planetary motion: unknown aethereal pres-
sures within and between vortices may be operative. In a universe
empty of aethereal matter, on the other hand, such evidence suggests
a force somehow acting across the space from Sun to planet, as the
predominant determinant of the planet's motion.

Newton in a tract "De motu" that he sent to Edmond Halley
in November 1684 proceeded along the lines of this latter conception. Centripetal force, he showed, implied equable description of
areas. Also, given a conic-section orbit about the Sun in a focus, the
force is inverse-square. Further, assuming inverse-square law implies
conic-section orbit, he showed how to find the conic section corresponding to any particular initial conditions of position and velocity.
"Therefore," he astonishingly claimed, "the major planets gyrate in
ellipses having their foci in the center of the Sun; and by radii drawn
to the Sun, describe areas proportional to the times, just as Kepler
supposed."[24]

What led Newton to pursue Hooke's conception we do not know.
Perhaps Comet Halley, appearing in 1682 in its retrograde orbit across
the sky, at last convinced him that vortices could not exist.[25]

At least as interesting is Newton's lack of conviction after November 1684 as to the exact truth of Hooke's conception or its sufficiency
to account for the phenomena. As he wrote Flamsteed on 12 January
1685, "Now I am upon this subject I would gladly know ye bottom
of it before I publish my papers."[26]

Newton had sought Flamsteed's help in December. From Flamsteed's letter of 27 December he learned that the maximum elongations of Jupiter's four satellites "are as exactly in sesquialte proportion to theire periods as it is possible for our sences to determine."[27] This was good news: "Your information about ye Satellits of Jupiter gives me very much satisfaction."[28] Flamsteed's determinations, made with the screw micrometer, were precise to one-thousandth of the semi-diameter of Jupiter's disk.

Whether the mean solar distances of the primary planets agreed with Kepler's harmonic rule was still a question. "The orbit of Saturn," Newton wrote Flamsteed on 30 December, "is defined by Kepler too little for ye sesquialterate proportion." He went on to explain how he thought the motion of Saturn might be perturbed by Jupiter. The idea astonished Flamsteed, but, responding on 5 January, he acknowledged that his determinations had not yet been strict enough to exclude "such exorbitation as you suggest of Saturn."[29] Newton replied:

Your information about ye error of Keplers tables for Jupiter & Saturn has eased me of several scruples. I was apt to suspect there might be some cause or other unknown to me, wch might disturb ye sesquialtera proportion . . . It would ad to my satisfaction if you would be pleased to let me know the long diameters of ye orbits of Jupiter & Saturn assigned by your self & Mr Halley . . . that I may see how the sesquiplicate proportion fills ye heavens together wth another small proportion wch must be allowed for.[30]

The "small proportion wch must be allowed for" is presumably the modification of Kepler's harmonic rule introduced in Propositions 57–60, Book 1 of the *Principia*.

Evidently Newton was now embarked on a program of substantiating a dynamical conception whose full reach was in doubt. He had yet to satisfy himself that the force between the planets and the Sun was solely gravitational, that terrestrial gravity like the solar and Jovial attractions was directly proportional to mass, that the gravitational attraction of a body arose from the gravitational attractions of all its least particles, etc.

The argument for universal gravitation is the crowning achievement of the *Principia*. The book abounds in mathematical triumphs as well. True, not all its demonstrations are valid; it does not achieve everything it attempts to achieve; it leaves unanswered questions that the idea of universal gravitation can raise. These judgments of a pioneering work should not surprise. Both by what it achieved and by what it failed to achieve, it set the agenda for the celestial mechanics of the next two centuries.

How Newton and his successors responded to this agenda will be our concern in the following sections.

NEWTON ON THE MOON'S MOTION

In Proposition 22, Book 3 of the *Principia* (all editions), with the aid of Corollaries of Book 1 66, Newton showed qualitatively how the known inequalities of the Moon arise from the varying difference between the accelerations that the Sun causes in the Moon and the Earth. These include the inequalities called "the Variation" and the "annual equation," the oscillations in the Moon's orbital eccentricity and apsidal line postulated in the lunar theory of Jeremiah Horrocks, the inequalities in the lunar latitudes detected by Tycho, and the general forward advance of the lunar apse.

Horrocks's lunar theory had first been published by Flamsteed in 1672, and then republished with Flamsteed's revised constants in 1681. It combined the Moon's unperturbed elliptical orbit with the second inequality due to the Sun (the "evection" as Boulliau called it) to obtain an ellipse with oscillating eccentricity and apse. The Horrocksian theory was the first lunar theory to admit in a direct way of a Newtonian analysis in terms of forces.

The *Principia* includes certain quantitative derivations with regard to the Moon's motions. Such are the derivations of the motions of the Moon's nodes (Propositions 30–33, Book 3) and of the changes in the Moon's orbital inclination (Propositions 34, 35, Book 3); these are valid and the results correct. Newton derives the Variation in Propositions 26, 28, and 29, Book 3, with an accurate result (it assumes without proof that the Sun has the effect of transforming an idealized circular lunar orbit into one that can be approximated by an ellipse with the Earth at the center).

In the first edition Scholium to Proposition 35, Book 3 of the *Principia*, Newton speaks of computing the motion of the Moon's apogee, and finding its annual mean motion to be 40°. "The computations, however, as being too complicated and impeded by approximations, and insufficiently accurate, it is better to omit." The manuscript in which these computations were made was discovered in the late nineteenth century, and has been published by Whiteside.[31] It shows Newton taking account of both the radial and transverse components of the Sun's perturbing force; the analysis is in many respects brilliant. It includes, however, an illegitimate step, and the final result, as Whiteside judges, is fudged. In later editions Newton omitted all reference to this computation.

In Corollary 2 of Proposition 45, Book 1 (all editions), Newton calculated the effect of the *radial* component of the solar perturbation in producing motion of the Moon's apse, but without identifying the calculation as having to do with the Moon. The calculated apsidal advance per revolution was $1°31'$ $28''$. In the third edition Newton added the remark: "The apse of the Moon is about twice as swift." To eighteenth-century readers, this appeared to be the sum total of what Newton had supplied in the way of a quantitative derivation of the Moon's apsidal motion. "Neither," wrote John Machin in 1729, "is there any method that I have ever yet met with upon the commonly received principles, which is perfectly sufficient to explain the motion of the Moon's apogee."[32]

On 1 September 1694 Newton visited Flamsteed at Greenwich. Flamsteed showed him about 150 observed places of the Moon, along with the corresponding places derived from his (Flamsteed's) lunar theory. The errors averaged to about 8 arc-minutes, but went as high as 20 arc-minutes. Now, a primary purpose of Flamsteed's appointment as "the King's Astronomer" (in 1675), and of the establishment of the Greenwich Observatory, was to obtain star positions and a lunar theory accurate enough to enable navigators to determine the longitude at sea. For determining the angular distance in longitude from a given meridian to within $1°$, the lunar theory had to be accurate to 2 arc-minutes. Newton, seeing that Flamsteed's theory was insufficiently accurate, undertook to develop a more accurate theory.

From Flamsteed Newton received a total of about 250 lunar observations, the most extensive and accurate database a lunar theorist had yet had to base a theory upon. Newton's new theory was published in 1702, first in Latin, then in English, as *A New and most Accurate Theory of the Moon's Motion; Whereby all her Irregularities may be solved, and her Place truly calculated to Two Minutes.*

The elements of the new theory are presented without explanation of their derivation. The core of the theory is (like Flamsteed's theory) Horrocksian but with revised numerical parameters. A few specifically Newtonian features are added: special annual equations in the mean motions of the lunar apsides and node, with coefficients of 20' and 9'30" respectively, and four new small terms whose origin is unexplained, although in the second edition of the *Principia* Newton asserted that they were derived from the theory of gravity.

Newton's theory is not as accurate as claimed in the title of the English version. But, when comparison is made with an historically accurate modern ephemeris, he is found to have determined the Moon's mean motion for the period 1680–1700 with greater accuracy than any of his contemporaries. And, when the small error in the mean motion is removed, the corrected theory proves to have a standard deviation of 1.9 arc-minutes; 95% of its values thus fall within 3.8 arc-minutes of the correct values. The errors in Flamsteed's theory of 1681 were about twice as large.[33] Not till 1753 would a lunar theory accurate to within 2 arc-minutes be devised.

ABERRATION, NUTATION, PRECESSION

In 1725 Samuel Molyneux and James Bradley undertook to replicate observations of the meridian transits of Gamma Draconis that Robert Hooke had made in 1669 – observations ostensibly confirming annual parallax in this star, and thus proving the Copernican hypothesis. Hooke's observations, they found, were mistaken: Gamma Draconis was moving in an annual cycle, but not the one that annual parallax implied. Later Bradley verified that other stars moved in such annual cycles. The pattern of motion could be explained by assuming that light has a finite velocity, and that the Earth is moving about the Sun, so that the direction of the light with respect to the moving Earth had a component in the direction of the Earth's motion. Thus all the stars move annually in ellipses, with a long axis of about 40"; the ellipses reduce to a straight line for stars on the ecliptic, and to circles for stars near the ecliptic North Pole. Bradley announced the discovery of this effect, which he named *the aberration of light*, to the Royal Society early in 1729.

Thereafter he discovered that, besides aberration, further stellar motions were occurring; and he was able to account for them as a kind of wobble in the precessional motion of the Earth's axis – a nutation – with a period of eighteen years, the period of revolution of the Moon's nodes. He announced this discovery to the Royal Society in January 1748, after verifying the hypothesis over a complete cycle.

For the attainment of an astronomy accurate to arc-seconds, these discoveries were crucial. Previously, aberration and nutation, unrecognized, had played havoc with attempts to found observational astronomy on a secure basis. As the astronomer Nicolas-Louis de Lacaille (1713–62) put it, "Many obscurities thus arose ... it finally seemed that hardly anything certain could be deduced from the heavens. Fortunately, to meet such evil, at length came Bradley."[34]

The nutation, which Newton had not predicted, required an explanation in terms of inverse-square gravitation, and in mid-1748 Jean le Rond d'Alembert (1717–83) set about deriving it. Nutation is a refinement of the precession of the equinoxes, and d'Alembert soon found that Newton's explanation of the precession (Proposition 66, Corollary 22, Book 1, and Proposition 39, Book 3 with the preceding lemmas) was deeply flawed.[35] Newton's basic error arose from his lack of an appropriate dynamics for the rotational motions of solid bodies, and his attempt to treat problems involving such motions in terms of linear momentum rather than angular momentum. D'Alembert now furnished the elements of the appropriate dynamics, and Leonhard Euler systematized it.

THE MOTION OF THE LUNAR APSE DERIVED FROM THE INVERSE-SQUARE LAW

The first to apply Leibnizian-style mathematics, that is to say differential equations, to the problem of the Moon's motions was Leonhard Euler. He published lunar tables in 1745, then revised them for his *Opuscula Varii Argumenti* of 1746. In the preface to the tables in the *Opuscula*, he stated that they were derived from Newton's theory of attraction, but gave no details.

In the spring of 1746 Alexis-Claude Clairaut (1713–65) and d'Alembert separately set out to derive differential equations for the three-body problem, and to apply them to the Moon's motions. By the summer of 1747 Clairaut knew that a first-order solution to his equations yielded reasonable values for the major perturbational terms, but only about half the observed motion of the Moon's apse. Meanwhile, Euler's essay on the perturbations of Jupiter and Saturn, submitted in the Paris Academy's prize contest for 1748, arrived, and

Clairaut, as a member of the prize commission, read it in September 1747. Therein Euler expressed doubt as to the accuracy of the inverse-square law of gravitation, and, in support of his doubt, stated that Newton's law led to but half the observed motion of the lunar apse.

Addressing the Paris Academy in November 1747, Clairaut proposed that Newton's law be altered by the addition of a small, inverse fourth power term, whereby the full motion of the lunar apse would become deducible. This proposal unleashed a storm of controversy.[36] Clairaut retracted his proposal in May 1749. In outline, the reversal came about as follows.[37]

From his differential equations, Clairaut had obtained by a double integration the result

$$\frac{f^2}{Mr} = 1 - g \sin v - q \cos v + \sin v \int \Omega \, dv \cos v - \cos v \int \Omega \, dv \sin v, \qquad (1)$$

where f, g, and q are constants of integration, M is the sum of the masses of the Earth and the Moon, v is the true anomaly, and Ω is a function of r and the perturbing forces. To solve this equation for r, it was necessary to substitute an approximate value of r into Ω on the right-hand side. It was known empirically that the Moon's apse moves, and Clairaut proposed using the formula $k/r = 1 - e \cos mv$, which represents a precessing ellipse. Here k, e, m are presumptive constants, determinable in terms of other constants in the equation. The resultant motion, Clairaut hoped, could be largely accounted for – small oscillations excepted – as motion on a precessing ellipse.

In the initial outcome, this hope appeared to be satisfied. Clairaut's modified equation took the form

$$\frac{k}{r} = 1 - e \cos mv + \beta \cos \frac{2v}{n} + \gamma \cos \left(\frac{2}{n} - m \right) v + \delta \cos \left(\frac{2}{n} + m \right) v, \qquad (2)$$

where n is the Moon's mean sidereal motion divided by its mean synodic motion, and β, γ, δ evaluated in terms of the other constants in the theory were found to be 0.007090988, −0.00949705, 0.00018361, hence small relative to e (known empirically to be about 0.05).

From the beginning, Clairaut had supposed that a second-order approximation was eventually to be carried out, to refine the coefficients of the several terms of the theory preparatory to constructing tables. In this second approximation, formula (2), with β, γ, δ retained as symbols, would be substituted back into Ω in (1), and the latter equation would again be solved for r. Before the spring of 1749, Clairaut had not supposed that this refinement could lead to other than minor improvements in the coefficients; certainly it could not result in a doubled value for m! The calculation proved him wrong. The contributions coming to m from the term with coefficient γ were especially sizeable. This term was proportional to the *transverse* perturbing force, whereas the initially computed contribution to m had been proportional to the *radial* perturbing force. Clairaut's final result for the apsidal motion per month was $3°2'6''$, just $2'$ shy of the empirical value he accepted.

Euler, learning of Clairaut's turnabout, tried to find the error in his own derivation. At last on 10 April 1751 he was able to tell Clairaut of his success.[38] Euler's unstinting praise for Clairaut's achievement overflows into another letter of 29 June 1751:

> the more I consider this happy discovery, the more important it seems to me, and in my opinion it is the greatest discovery in the Theory of Astronomy... For it is very certain that it is only since this discovery that one can regard the law of attraction reciprocally proportional to the squares of the distances as solidly established; and on this depends the entire theory of astronomy.[39]

THE 'GREAT INEQUALITY' OF JUPITER AND SATURN

The values for the mean motions of Jupiter and Saturn given in the *Rudolphine Tables* were early recognized to require correction. Jupiter was moving faster than Kepler's numbers implied, and Saturn slower. Flamsteed labored for nearly five decades to correct the theories of these planets, at first by simply refining their Keplerian elements. In the 1690s he asked Newton for help. Newton proposed taking as the focus of Saturn's orbit the center of gravity of Jupiter and the Sun, and introducing Horrocksian-style oscillations into Saturn's eccentricity and line of apsides (see Proposition 13, Book 3 of the *Principia*); his suggestions were not numerically specific. Flamsteed, left to his own devices, sought an oscillation in the motion of each of the two planets, such as might bring their theories into line with observations, but eventually gave up in despair.[40]

Edmond Halley (1656–1742), in planetary tables published posthumously in 1749, introduced a secular acceleration of Jupiter's mean motion of $+3°49'.4$ in 2000 years, and a secular deceleration of

Saturn's mean motion of $-9°16'.1$ in 2000 years. This proposal was widely accepted by astronomers.

In a paper completed in 1774, Pierre-Simon Laplace (1749–1827) demonstrated that, to the first order with respect to the masses, and to the second order with respect to the eccentricities and inclinations, mutual planetary perturbations could not produce secular variations of the mean motions. Joseph Louis Lagrange (1736–1813) in 1776 extended this result to all powers of the eccentricities and inclinations. In 1784 he showed that secular acceleration of the mean motions arising indirectly from secular accelerations in other orbital elements would be negligible for Jupiter and Saturn. Thus the anomalous motions of these planets remained unexplained. Laplace thought they might be due to perturbation by comets. Up to late 1785, they posed for Laplace the chief obstacle to asserting the stability of the solar system – its freedom from runaway variables.

At last, on 23 November 1785, Laplace announced to the Paris Academy that he had succeeded in resolving the anomalies. He had found that a periodic inequality of the third order with respect to the orbital eccentricities and inclinations of Jupiter and Saturn was large, with a coefficient of 49' for Saturn and 20' for Jupiter, and a period of some 900 years. A few shorter-term inequalities resulted from the combination of this long-term inequality with known inequalities, and all the inequalities taken together yielded a theory agreeing with both ancient and modern observations. Laplace's completed theory of Jupiter and Saturn appeared in 1786.

Inequalities of the third order in the eccentricities and inclinations had not been computed earlier because of the labor involved; only zeroth-order and first-order perturbations had been computed systematically. Laplace in attacking the higher-order inequalities proceeded by a species of sharpshooting, which left uncertain whether all terms to a given order of smallness had been accounted for. But his methods were empirically successful.

By December 1787 Laplace had an explanation for the one remaining major anomaly in the solar system, the secular acceleration of the Moon originally discovered by Halley in the 1690s. The secular decrease in the Earth's orbital eccentricity, Laplace showed, would lead to a secular diminution of the radial component of the Sun's perturbing force; consequently the Moon's mean motion would accelerate. (As we shall see later, this explanation was only partially correct.) To Laplace, it now appeared that Newton's law of gravitation was sufficient to account for all the motions in the solar system, and that the system was stable, like well-designed clockwork. This idea inspired his *Exposition du système du monde* (1796) and his *Traité de mécanique céleste* (first four volumes, 1798–1805).

ACCURATE LUNAR PREDICTION

The first three analytic theories of the Moon to be published, those of Clairaut (1752), Euler (1753), and d'Alembert (1754), proved accurate only to 4 or 5 arc-minutes, hence insufficiently accurate to meet the needs of navigation. But in 1753 Tobias Mayer (1723–62) published lunar tables which, compared with 139 lunar longitudes observed by Bradley from 1743 to 1745, deviated on average by only 27″, and at maximum by only 1′37″. In subsequent years Mayer refined his tables; his final version of them, submitted by his widow to the British Board of Admiralty in 1762, became the basis for the British *Nautical Almanac*. How did Mayer achieve such accuracy?

He had carried out an analytic derivation of the lunar inequalities from Newton's law in his *Theoria Lunae juxta Systema Newtonianum*, completed in 1754 but published only in 1767. In this he deduced forty-six perturbational corrections to the mean motion. They could be reduced, he then showed, to thirteen steps of progressive correction. In his preface he stated:

the theory has this inconvenience, that many of the inequalities cannot be deduced from it accurately, unless one should pursue the calculation – in which I have now exhausted nearly all my patience – much further. My aim is rather to show that at least no argument against the goodness of my tables can be drawn from the theory. This is most evidently gathered from the fact that the inequalities found in the tables, which have been corrected by comparison with many observations, never differ from those that the theory alone supplies by more than $\frac{1}{2}'$.

How did Mayer carry out his "comparison with many observations"? In all likelihood by applying a statistical procedure he had learned from Euler. Multiple equations of condition, derived from observation, were used in evaluating differential corrections to the elements of a theory; the equations were solved by neglecting small terms. (The invention of the more reliable method of least squares was still a half-century away.) The predictive accuracy of Mayer's tables rested on the empirical refinement of coefficients.

Revisions of Mayer's tables were carried out by Charles Mason in 1778 and by Johann Tobias Bürg a little later, in each case on the basis of large numbers of observations. "[Their tables] correspond with the observations made on the Moon," Laplace remarked, "with a degree of accuracy that it will be difficult to surpass."[41] In a few respects Laplace's lunar theory (published in 1802) improved on the empirically grounded tables; in other respects Laplace could aim only to match the accuracy of these tables. In 1811 Johann Karl Burckhardt (1773–1825) completed new lunar tables, based on Laplace's theory together with 4000 observations; they would serve as the basis for the French and British lunar ephemerides until 1861.

Not till 1862 did the national ephemerides come to be based on a lunar theory in which the inequalities (a very few excepted) were deduced from the Newtonian theory without resort to statistical correction. This was the lunar theory of Peter Andreas Hansen (1795–1874), elaborated by a method derived from the Lagrange–Poisson theory of variation of orbital constants. Hansen's theory was the first perfectly rigorous deduction of the lunar inequalities from Newton's theory. It would remain the basis of the national ephemerides until 1922.

Hansen's theory was numerical rather than literal: it did not give for each coefficient an algebraic formula that could be re-derived and so independently checked for accuracy. A literal theory, at least as accurate as Hansen's, was achieved by Charles Eugène Delaunay in the 1860s. The series giving the coefficients, however, converged all too slowly. The problem of slow convergence was at length overcome in a new and innovative theory whose foundations were laid by G. W. Hill in the 1870s. In 1888 E. W. Brown commenced the process of developing Hill's foundational ideas into a complete lunar theory. The resulting tables, demonstrably more accurate than all their predecessors, became the basis of the British and American ephemerides in 1923.

Nevertheless, small, long-term changes in the Moon's mean motion remained puzzling.

COMETARY ORBITS, UNPERTURBED AND PERTURBED

On 20 June 1686 Newton reported to Halley that "the third [book] wants ye Theory of Comets."[42] He had been hard put to discover a way of fitting an orbit to cometary observations. Sometime before

April 1687 when he sent the completed manuscript of Book 3 to Halley, he hit on a graphical method of fitting a parabolic trajectory to three observations. The longitude of the perihelion and node and the orbital inclination determined in this way are very nearly correct even if the orbit is elliptical rather than parabolic.

Edmond Halley used a partially arithmetized version of Newton's procedure to determine the parabolic orbital elements of some twenty-four comets, as presented in his *Synopsis Astronomiae Cometicae* (1705). The elements of the retrograde comets appearing in 1531, 1607, and 1682 were nearly identical, and Halley declared himself convinced that these three comets were one and the same. The two intervals between the three apparitions differed by nearly a year, but Halley believed the difference could be caused by perturbation due to Jupiter. In an expanded version of the *Synopsis* published posthumously with his *Tabulae Astronomicae* of 1749, Halley predicted that the comet would reappear toward the end of 1758 or the beginning of 1759.

For astronomers of the 1750s, Halley's prediction presented two challenges: to locate the returning comet as soon as possible and determine its parabolic elements; and to predict from Newton's theory and the previous apparitions the time of the new perihelion passage. The second task was undertaken by Clairaut, assisted by Lalande and Mme. Lepaute.

For his calculation Clairaut used the differential equations he had derived for the three-body problem. The new application was far more labor-intensive than the earlier application to the Moon. In the Moon's case, the integrands were approximated by trigonometric series and so rendered integrable. The goodness of the approximation depended on the rapidity of convergence of the series, which in turn depended on the orbit being nearly circular. The orbit of Halley's comet is very elongated. Trigonometric series could not be used, and Clairaut and his colleagues had to resort to numerical integration. This was the first large-scale numerical integration ever performed.[43]

In November 1758, Clairaut, in order not to be forestalled by the comet, announced preliminary results, predicting a perihelion passage in mid-April 1759, give or take a month. The comet was first detected by Johann George Palitzsch on 25 December, and then independently by Charles Messier on 21 January. In March it disappeared into the rays of the Sun, then reappeared on 31 March. Calculation showed that the perihelion had occurred on 13 March, a month earlier than Clairaut had predicted. This was the first proof that comets may indeed return, and move in accordance with the Newtonian law.

THE PROBLEM OF THE EARTH'S FIGURE AND THE PROBLEM OF THE TIDES

Newton addressed both these problems in his *Principia*; in both cases his attack on them proved inadequate, and further advances were made only after the introduction of new and more powerful mathematical techniques.

In Proposition 19, Book 3 Newton showed that for a homogeneous spherical Earth subject to inverse-square gravity and rotating diurnally, the downward acceleration at the Equator would be 288/289 of that at the Pole. Supposing the Earth to have been initially fluid, and assuming as its equilibrium shape an infinitesimally flattened ellipsoid of revolution, he claimed that all linear columns from center to surface would weigh the same, and inferred a flattening of 1/229. Could the assumptions be justified, and could Newton's conclusions be extended to cases (like Jupiter's) where the flattening was greater? Newton asserted without demonstration that, if the density increased toward the center, the flattening would be greater.

In analytical studies using partial differentiation and culminating in his *Théorie de la terre* of 1743, Clairaut showed that a homogeneous, rotating ellipsoid of revolution with infinitesimal flattening could be a figure of equilibrium. He showed further that for an Earth consisting of individually homogeneous ellipsoidal strata with infinitesimal flattening but with densities increasing toward the center, the Earth would be less flattened than in the homogeneous case, with a flattening between 1/576 and 1/230. He supplied a new necessary condition for a rotating figure to be in equilibrium: the work to take a unit mass round any closed path within the body must add to zero.

The discussion was taken up again by Adrien-Marie Legendre (1752–1833) and Laplace in the 1780s. Legendre introduced the Legendre polynomials for expressing the attraction, potential, and meridian curve of equilibrium figures of revolution. Laplace then generalized these results to 'spheroids', understood as any figures given by a single equation in r, θ, and φ.

A reconciliation of these mathematical results with practical geodetical measurements was effected only after F. W. Bessel's introduction of a sophisticated statistical understanding of the geodesist's task.

Newton's account of the tides appears in Propositions 24, 36, and 37, Book 3. Newton assumed that the waters would be raised in places directly underneath the Sun or the Moon, and also on the opposite side of the Earth, and would be depressed in places 90° distant. He supposed the height of the tide would be as the force raising it. He in effect assumed that the instantaneous figure of the waters raised by the Sun or the Moon would be a prolate ellipsoid with longer axis directed toward the attracting body. The height of the tide at any given place and time would be the sum of the *radii vectores* in the two ellipsoids at that place, minus the radius vector for the undisturbed sea. But the highest tide, Newton knew, did not occur at the syzygies, when the two ellipsoids combined to give a maximum height, but rather some forty-three hours later. He attributed this delay to the inertia of the waters.

Newton's theory leads to a number of predictions that are contradicted by observation. Thus it implies that two consecutive high tides at the time of the syzygies should differ greatly in height, especially when the difference in declination of the Sun and Moon is greatest; whereas these tides are known to be of nearly equal height. Laplace, stimulated by this and other anomalies, devised an analytical account of the tides based on the solution of partial differential equations; modern tidal theory has its starting point in his account. He showed that inertial maintenance of motion is negligible in the tides, and that the differences in linear speed of the waters at different latitudes owing to diurnal rotation play a significant role.

LIMITATIONS OF NEWTON'S THEORY OF GRAVITATION

In 1787, as we have seen, Laplace claimed to show that the Moon's secular acceleration arose from a secular decrease in the radial component of the Sun's perturbing force. The tangential component, he assumed, contributed nothing to the effect. In 1853 J. C. Adams showed that, in fact, the tangential component diminished the overall effect, reducing it to 6″ per century. Delaunay confirmed Adams's calculation in 1859.

In 1865 Delaunay suggested that the tidal protuberances raised by the Moon, being carried eastward of the Moon by the Earth's diurnal rotation, would be attracted backward by the Moon; friction between the tidal water and the solid Earth could then slow the Earth's rotation, making the Moon appear to accelerate. To the Moon's action on the tidal bulge must correspond a contrary force on the Moon, speeding it up so that it rises into a higher orbit with a reduced mean angular motion in longitude. This effect appeared to be confirmed in 1920 by J. K. Fotheringham in studies of ancient eclipses.[44] He found $10''.8$ for the secular acceleration of the Moon, and $1''.5$ for the secular acceleration of the Sun. The latter effect presumably arises solely from the retardation in the Earth's diurnal rotation. Because the Moon's mean motion is 13.4 times the Sun's, the acceleration of the Moon due to the same cause should be $13.4 \times 1''.5 = 20''T^2$. With the $6''T^2$ found by Adams added, the total result is $26''T^2$, exceeding the observed secular acceleration by about $15''$. The difference is attributable to the second half of the action–reaction pair in the interaction between the Moon and the terrestrial tides.

The Earth–Moon system is thus evolving in time, and so, it appears, are other satellite–planet pairs in the solar system. In our Moon's case, the effects of tidal friction appear to undergo irregular variations in rate. We have consequently to allow that the Moon's places are, to a small extent, subject to temporal changes in tidal friction.

Non-gravitational forces are now accorded a role in cometary motion. The second periodic comet to be discovered was Comet Encke, first located in 1818. It had a period of 3.3 years, but when Encke computed the perturbations he found a non-gravitational decrease of about 2.5 hours per period, which he attributed to aethereal resistance. Those who in the 1830s computed the perturbations of Halley's Comet to predict its perihelial passage in 1835 found its period to be increasing – a change not attributable to aethereal resistance. Current opinion assigns these non-gravitational accelerations to outgassing in the comet's near approach to the Sun; the comet is rotating, and the thrust it receives from the outgassing is a little delayed, so as to have a component accelerating or decelerating the comet's orbital motion.[45]

In 1859 U. J. J. Le Verrier discovered that some 38 arc-seconds per century of the precession of Mercury's perihelion could not be accounted for on the basis of Newton's inverse-square law.[46] (The total observed apsidal precession is about 5596" per century, of which over 5000" is due to the precession of the equinoxes, and over 500" to planetary perturbation.) In 1882 Simon Newcomb revised Le Verrier's value for the discrepancy upward to 43 arc-seconds per century. Asaph Hall in 1894 proposed accounting for the discrepancy by taking the exponent in the gravitational law to be −2.00000016.[47] In 1903, however, Ernest W. Brown showed this suggestion to be untenable: he had by this time developed the Hill– Brown lunar theory far enough to rule out an exponent differing from −2 by 0.00000016.[48] In 1915 Einstein showed that the anomalous apsidal precession could be derived from his Theory of General Relativity.[49]

Thus Newton's law of gravitation is not strictly correct. The basis of the national ephemerides remained essentially Newtonian till 1984, when a post-Newtonian basis, incorporating relativistic terms, was adopted. The measurement of time, derived from atomic clocks on a rotating Earth, also requires correction for relativistic effects.[50]

NOTES

1 *The Correspondence of Isaac Newton*, vol. 2, ed. H. W. Turnbull (Cambridge: Cambridge University Press, 1960), p. 436.
2 Some authors making this claim are referenced in my "Newton and Some Philosophers on Kepler's Laws," *Journal for the History of Ideas* 35 (1974), 231–58.
3 Curtis Wilson, "Kepler's Derivation of the Elliptical Path," *Isis* 59 (1968), 5–25. But see also A. E. L. Davis, "Grading the Eggs (Kepler's Sizing Procedure for the Planetary Orbits)," *Centaurus* 35 (1992), 121–42.
4 D. T. Whiteside, "Keplerian Eggs, Laid and Unlaid, 1600–1605," *Journal for the History of Astronomy* 5 (1974), 1–21, esp. 12–14.
5 See A. E. L. Davis, "Kepler's 'Distance Law' – Myth not Reality," *Centaurus* 35 (1992), 103–20.
6 Ishmaël Boulliau, *Astronomia Philolaica* (Paris, 1645), pp. 21–4.
7 On Boulliau's planetary theory, see Curtis Wilson, "From Kepler's Laws, So-called, to Universal Gravitation: Empirical Factors," *Archive for History of Exact Sciences* 6 (1970), 106–21.
8 *The Correspondence of Isaac Newton*, vol. 2, p. 438.
9 *Ibid.*, p. 360.
10 As to whether Newton in fact provided an adequate sketch of a derivation of the elliptical orbit from the inverse-square law in Corollary 1 of

Proposition 13, Book 1, see Bruce Pourciau, "On Newton's Proof that Inverse-Square Orbits Must Be Conics," *Annals of Science* 48 (1991), 159–72.

11 See Derek T. Whiteside, "Newton's Early Thoughts on Planetary Motion: A Fresh Look," *British Journal for the History of Science* 2 (1964), 117–29.

12 For a detailed account see René Taton and Curtis Wilson (eds), *Planetary Astronomy from the Renaissance to the Rise of Astrophysics, Tycho Brahe to Newton*, vol. 2, part A of *The General History of Astronomy* (Cambridge: Cambridge University Press, 1989), pp. 172–85.

13 D. T. Whiteside, "Newton's Early Thoughts," pp. 125–6.

14 See James Alan Ruffner, "The Background and Early Development of Newton's Theory of Comets" (Ph.D. dissertation, University Microfilms, 1966), pp. 308ff.

15 See my "Horrocks, Harmonies, and the Exactitude of Kepler's Third Law," in Erna Hilfstein, Pawel Czartoryski, and Frank D. Grade (eds.), *Science and History: Studies in Honor of Edward Rosen* (Studia Copernicana 16) (Warsaw: Ossolineum, 1978), pp. 235–59, esp. 248–55.

16 See John Herivel, *The Background to Newton's* Principia: *A Study of Newton's Dynamical Researches in the Years 1664–84* (Oxford: Clarendon Press, 1965), pp. 192–8; and Richard S. Westfall, *Force in Newton's Physics* (New York: American Elsevier, 1971), pp. 350–60.

17 See *The Correspondence of Isaac Newton*, vol. 3, ed. W. H. Turnbull (Cambridge: Cambridge University Press, 1961), p. 331.

18 H. Pemberton, *A View of Sir Isaac Newton's Philosophy* (Dublin, 1728), Preface.

19 W. Whiston, *Memoirs of the Life of Mr. William Whiston by himself* (London, 1749), vol. 1, pp. 35–6.

20 Florian Cajori, "Newton's Twenty Years' Delay in Announcing the Law of Gravitation," in *Sir Isaac Newton, 1727–1927: A Bicentenary Evaluation of His Work* (Baltimore: Williams and Wilkins, 1928), pp. 127–88, esp. 168–70.

21 *The Correspondence of Isaac Newton*, vol. 1, ed. W. H. Turnbull (Cambridge: Cambridge University Press, 1959), pp. 362ff.

22 *Ibid.*, vol. 2, pp. 446–7.

23 *Ibid.*, vol. 2, pp. 297–8.

24 A. Rupert Hall and Marie Boas Hall (eds.), *Unpublished Scientific Papers of Isaac Newton* (Cambridge: Cambridge University Press, 1962), p. 253.

25 Private communication from Nicholas Kollerstrom.

26 *The Correspondence of Isaac Newton*, vol. 2, p. 413.

27 *Ibid.*, p. 404.

28 *Ibid.*, p. 407.

29 *Ibid.*, p. 408.

30 *Ibid.*, p. 413.

31 D. T. Whiteside (ed.), *The Mathematical Papers of Isaac Newton*, vol. 6 (Cambridge: Cambridge University Press, 1974), pp. 508–37.

32 John Machin, *The Laws of the Moon's Motion According to Gravity* (London, 1729), p. 31.

33 Nicholas Kollerstrom, *Newton's 1702 "Theory of the Moon's Motion"* (based on a doctoral thesis at the University of London; University College, London, 1997), p. 155.

34 Lacaille, *Astronomiae Fundamenta* (Paris, 1757), p. 2.

35 See d'Alembert, *Recherches sur la précession des équinoxes, et sur la nutation de l'Axe de la terre, dans le système Newtonien* (Paris: David, 1749), pp. x–xxiii; Curtis Wilson, "D'Alembert versus Euler on the Precession of the Equinoxes and the Mechanics of Rigid Bodies," *Archive for History of Exact Sciences* 37 (1987), 238–42; G. J. Dobson, "Newton's Problems with Rigid Body Dynamics in the Light of his Treatment of the Precession of the Equinoxes," *Archive for History of Exact Sciences* 53 (1998), 125–45.

36 See Craig B. Waff, "Universal Gravitation and the Motion of the Moon's Apogee: The Establishment and Reception of Newton's Inverse-Square Law, 1687–1749" (Ph.D. dissertation, Johns Hopkins University, 1975), chapter 4.

37 *Ibid.*, chapter 5.

38 G. Bigourdan, "Lettres inédites d'Euler à Clairaut," *Comptes rendus du Congrès des sociétés savantes de Paris et des Départments tenu à Lille en 1928* (Paris: Imprimerie Nationale, 1930), p. 36.

39 *Ibid.*, pp. 38–9.

40 Francis Baily, *An Account of the Revd. John Flamsteed* (London, 1835), p. 327.

41 Laplace, *Celestial Mechanics*, vol. 3 (Boston, 1832; Chelsea Publishing Company reprint, 1966), p. 357.

42 *The Correspondence of Isaac Newton*, vol. 2, p. 437.

43 For a detailed account, see my "Clairaut's Calculation of the Eighteenth-Century Return of Halley's Comet," *Journal for the History of Astronomy* 24 (1993), 1–15.

44 John K. Fotheringham, "A Solution of Ancient Eclipses of the Sun," *Monthly Notices of the Royal Astronomical Society* 81 (1920), 104–26.

45 B. G. Marsden, Z. Sekanina, and D. K. Yeomans, "Comets and Nongravitational Forces," *Astronomical Journal* 78 (1973), 211–23.

46 U. J. J. Le Verrier, "Théorie du mouvement de Mercure," *Annales de l'Observatoire Impériale de Paris* 5 (1859), esp. 98–106.

47   A. Hall, "A Suggestion in the Theory of Mercury," *Astronomical Journal* 14 (1894), 49–51.

48   E. W. Brown, "On the Degree of Accuracy in the New Lunar Theory," *Monthly Notices of the Royal Astronomical Society* 64 (1903), 524–34, esp. 532.

49   A. Einstein, "Erklärung der Perihelbewegung des Merkur aus der allgemeinen Relativitätstheorie," *Königlich Preussische Akademie der Wissenschaften* [Berlin]: *Sitzungsberichte* (1915), 831–9.

50   See P. Kenneth Seidelmann (ed.), *Explanatory Supplement to the Astronomical Almanac* (Mill Valley, CA: University Science Books, 1992), pp. 41, 70, 96, 615.

7 Newton's optics and atomism

After his first optical publications in 1672 Newton was identified by his contemporaries and later generations as a supporter of the corpuscular or emission theory of light, in which light is assumed to consist of corpuscles, or atoms, emitted from a luminous source such as the Sun. While it is true that Newton believed in a corpuscular theory, utilized it in developing many of his optical experiments and theories, and argued vigorously against the wave theory of light, he never believed that it was a demonstrated scientific truth and considered it to be only a probable hypothesis. This distinction explains why, for example, he never set forth a synthetic account of the emission theory and eschewed it in his public accounts of his scientific theories. In order to understand Newton's advocacy and use of atomism in his optics it is necessary to understand his views on hypotheses and certainty in science.

HYPOTHESES IN NEWTON'S SCIENCE

From the beginning of his scientific career Newton was concerned with establishing a new, more certain science to replace contemporary science, which he felt was rife with "conjectures and probabilities."[1] He believed that he could establish a more certain science both by developing mathematical theories and by basing his theories on experimentally discovered properties. To establish a more certain science, Newton insisted that one must "not mingle conjectures with certainties."[2] To avoid compromising rigorously demonstrated principles by hypotheses, he developed the techniques of clearly labeling hypotheses as such and setting them apart, as with his "An hypothesis explaining the properties of light discoursed of in my severall Papers" in 1675, or with the queries appended to the *Opticks* in 1704 and in subsequent editions.

As part of his campaign to reform science, Newton continually railed against hypotheses, that is, conjectural causal explanations. His condemnations of hypotheses – the most famous being his "hypotheses non fingo" (I do not feign hypotheses) in the *Principia* (1687) – are always aimed at preserving the certainty of scientific principles rather than objecting to the use of hypotheses in themselves. Newton held that hypotheses without any experimental support whatever, such as Cartesian vortices, had no place in science, but those based on some experimental evidence, though insufficient to establish them as demonstrated principles, could be used to understand properties already discovered and to suggest new experiments. The corpuscular theory of light fell into the second category.

Newton believed that by formulating his theories phenomenologically, in terms of experimentally observed properties, or principles deduced from them, without any causal explanations (hypotheses) of those properties, he could develop a more certain science. While he considered causal explanations to be desirable, they never play an essential or necessary role in his science. As we shall see, however, in his private work Newton did use hypotheses to develop theories and predict new properties. When he used hypothetical causes such as light corpuscles and the aether in this way, he then purged them (or, at least, attempted to do so) from his public work and reformulated his theories in terms of experimentally discovered "properties" such as unequal refrangibility and periodicity. Newton appears never to have questioned the possibility of constructing an hypothesis-free science. To have denied such a possibility would have been tantamount to denying his conception of science.

By examining the role of atomism in Newton's theory of color and refraction and the colors of thin films, we will see how his attitude on the proper use of hypotheses in science played a fundamental role in the development and formulation of those theories. In investigating the colors of thin films, he introduced another hypothesis – a vibrating aether – in order to account for the periodicity of light. The hypothesis of a vibrating aether suffered a very different fate from that of light corpuscles, for the former – as "fits" devoid of the aether – was eventually raised to a demonstrated principle, while the latter always remained an hypothesis. We will examine the different fate of these two hypotheses. Although Newton's methodology can be considered to be very conservative, I shall argue that his refusal to accept the corpuscular theory as true was justified by the course of his own research program. Finally, we will consider Newton's theory of colored bodies, where he used an atomic theory of matter, but did not consider that to be an hypothesis.

THEORY OF LIGHT AND COLOR

Given this philosophical background, we should not expect Newton's use of the corpuscular theory of light to be readily evident in his published scientific works; rather we have to turn to his unpublished papers and his speculative writings. Optics was one of the subjects to which Newton devoted himself in his early years of discovery, 1664–6. In his commonplace book "Questiones quaedam philosophicae" (Certain Philosophical Questions) from this period Newton recorded, under the entry "Of Colours," his thoughts on optical subjects such as the nature of color and the cause of reflection and refraction. In all of his speculations he consistently worked with a corpuscular theory, though he seemed to be trying out a whole range of ideas for the physical interactions between bodies and light corpuscles, or, as he then called them, "globuli."[3] He considered the reflection of the light corpuscles variously to occur from the aether within the pores of bodies, from loose particles within the pores, and from the particles of the body. He also could not decide whether the color of light rays was due to their speed alone or their speed and mass (momentum), and he carried out a calculation of the change of momentum of light corpuscles of different size after colliding with particles of different size.

In the midst of these notes Newton made one of his most fundamental discoveries, namely, that rays of different color are refracted different amounts.[4] While his notes show that he made an attempt to explain this discovery in terms of the mechanical parameters of the particles, he soon largely abandoned such speculations to carry out a further series of experiments and develop a theory of the nature of sunlight and color. Newton worked out the essential elements of his theory by 1666. He formulated it in substantial detail in his *Optical Lectures* delivered at Cambridge University between 1670 and 1672, but he did not publish the theory until February 1672, when his

"New theory about light and colors" appeared in *Philosophical Transactions*. In order to see what role, if any, atomism or the corpuscular theory of light played in the development and formulation of that theory, I will briefly sketch its key elements.

Newton established his theory with a series of experiments with prisms that by the early eighteenth century became a model of an experimental science.[5] All of his optical investigations, which were gathered together in the *Opticks*, were founded on an extensive series of interlocking experiments, usually variants on a small number of fundamental experimental arrangements. His experiments play a variety of roles in his researches, for example determining the precise nature of the phenomenon and its causes, confirmation of them, and elimination of alternatives. Sometimes, as in the *Optical Lectures*, the large number of experiments with slight variations to establish various points may seem tedious, but Newton attempted to leave no room for objections.

The essential point of his theory of light and color is that sunlight or white light is a mixture of rays differing in degree of refrangibility and color. He found that, at the same angle of incidence, rays of different color are refracted different amounts and that there is a constant correspondence between color and degree of refrangibility; that is, the red rays are always least refracted, the violet most, and the intermediate colors intermediate amounts (Figure 7.1). Rays of each color apart obey Snell's law of refraction, but with a different index of refraction for each.

The color of a ray, he found, is immutable and cannot be changed by reflection, refraction, transmission, or any other means. In order to develop his new theory further, he introduced his new concepts of simple and compound colors. Though these two sorts of color appear identical to the eye, simple or primary colors consist of rays of a single degree of refrangibility and compound ones are a mixture of rays of different refrangibility. They can always be distinguished by refraction, which separates or decomposes the rays of different refrangibility that make up compound colors while leaving simple colors unchanged.

The colors of the spectrum – red, yellow, green, blue, and violet – together with their intermediate gradations, are primary colors. "But," Newton announced, "the most surprising and wonderful composition was that of Whiteness . . . 'Tis ever compounded." This

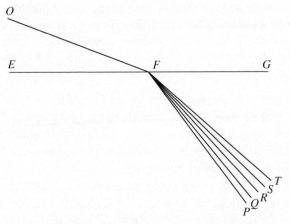

Fig. 7.1 Refraction at the surface *EG* decomposes a ray of sunlight *OF* into rays of different degrees of refrangibility and color.

was the most revolutionary part of the theory, for sunlight had universally been considered to be simple, homogeneous, and pure, whereas colors were assumed to be some modification of sunlight. "Colours are not *Qualifications of Light*," Newton concluded, "derived from Refractions, or Reflections of natural Bodies (as 'tis generally believed,) but *Original* and *connate properties*."[6] Whenever colors appear, they are only separated from sunlight; they are never created. The theory of color was the foundation for all of Newton's subsequent optical research.

The fundamental idea underlying Newton's theory, that light rays always preserve their identity – color and degree of refrangibility – whether they are isolated or mixed together, or whatever processes they undergo, certainly seems to be most naturally understood in terms of light rays as atoms. Indeed, the three early and eminent critics of Newton's theory – Robert Hooke, Ignace Gaston Pardies, and Christiaan Huygens – perceived that Newton supported an atomic theory of light and were concerned that his color theory was incompatible with a wave theory. In replying to Hooke's accusation, Newton did not deny that he believed in the emission theory, but insisted that it played no part in his theory of color. He replied that,

Had I intended any such Hypothesis I should somewhere have explained it. But I knew that the Properties wch I declared of light were in some measure capable of being explicated not onely by that, but by many other Mechanicall Hypotheses. And therefore I chose to decline them all, & speake of light in generall termes, considering it abstractedly as something or other propagated every way in streight lines from luminous bodies, without determining what that thing is.[7]

Newton's remarks illustrate many of the features of his optical science that I sketched in the introduction: its phenomenological formulation, which considers light "abstractedly" and describes properties and avoids hypotheses, and his clear declaration that the emission theory of light is an hypothesis.

To reassure his opponents that his theory does not depend on light corpuscles he then explained how the wave theory could be accommodated to it. If wave theorists considered sunlight to consist of a mixture of waves of various wavelengths ("depths or bignesses") each of which is refracted differently and excites a different color, then their theories would be compatible with his color theory without any need to adopt light corpuscles. After offering this pioneering suggestion, he then set out what would throughout his life be his principal objection to the wave theory, the violation of rectilinear propagation: "namely that the waves or vibrations of any fluid can like the rays of Light be propagated in streight lines, without a continuall & very extravagant spreading & bending every way into ye quiescent Medium where they are terminated by it. I am mistaken if there be not both *Experiment & Demonstration* to the contrary."[8] Of course, light rays conceived of as atoms would naturally move in a straight line when they were in a uniform medium.

It cannot be doubted that Newton fruitfully utilized the emission theory in devising his color theory or that it was easier to imagine his theory within a corpuscular theory where the light corpuscles retained their identity throughout, but there is insufficient evidence to conclude that it was an essential element in his thinking.[9]

EXPLAINING REFLECTION, REFRACTION, AND DISPERSION

Newton most systematically utilized the emission theory of light in his quest to explain refraction and chromatic dispersion (the amount that the rays of different color are separated by refraction, angle *PFT* in Figure 7.1). His aim was to derive quantitative measures of these effects for different substances by a strict mechanical approach, assuming that light corpuscles are deflected at the interface of different media.

The law of reflection had been known since antiquity and had been relatively easy to explain in a corpuscular theory by a simple collision model in analogy to the reflection of a ball from a hard surface. In his earliest notes Newton used collisions between the corpuscles of light and bodies to explain both reflection and refraction. However, he soon recognized that when matter was assumed to have an atomic structure, this model broke down. On an atomic scale the surface of a reflecting body is not smooth like a mirror but very rough, with corpuscles separated by pores. Reflection could not occur from the corpuscles of the body because this would require the fortuitous arrangement of all the corpuscles, whatever the angle of incidence, such that the rays were reflected from the body at an angle equal to their angle of incidence. This required reflection to occur from the aether or, later in the *Opticks*, "some power of the Body which is evenly diffused all over its Surface," namely, a force.[10] These solutions were hypothetical, though the experimental and observational evidence that he marshaled in the *Opticks* against reflection actually occurring from the corpuscles of bodies was overwhelming.

Newton moved beyond such qualitative physical models in an essay "Of Refractions," probably written between 1666 and 1668, and calculated a table for the index of refraction of the extreme rays (red and violet) in various media passing into air from water, glass, and "christall." From an entry in the table, "The proportions of y^e *motions* of the Extreamely Heterogeneous Rays," it is clear that he is considering the motion of corpuscles.[11] It is possible to reconstruct his table on this assumption, especially since he utilized the same model in his *Optical Lectures*, though he there suppressed any mention of corpuscles or motions.[12] Newton assumes (Figure 7.2) that when a light ray *IX* in air enters glass at the boundary *AB* at grazing incidence (i.e., parallel to the refracting surface), rays of each color receive the same increase of velocity perpendicular to the refracting surface. If *XC*, *XD*, *XE* represent the parallel component of the motion of the violet, green, and red rays in air, which is unchanged after refraction, then *XP*, *XR*, and *XT* represent the refractions of these rays. Each has had the identical quantity of velocity perpendicular

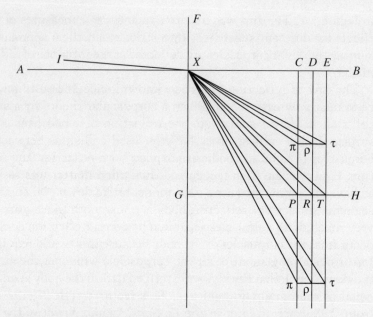

Fig. 7.2 Newton's dispersion model from his *Optical Lectures*.

to the surface, *CP, DR, ET*, added to its parallel component of velocity. The refractions at any other medium may be readily determined
by this model once the mean refraction *Xρ* is known. This model assumes that the projections parallel to the surface of all spectra are of
equal length and that the same colors always occupy equal portions
of it, that is, that chromatic dispersion is a property of light and not
of the refracting media.

In his *Optical Lectures* Newton left the origin of this dispersion
law totally mysterious, while conceding that "I have not yet derived
the certainty of this proposition from experiments . . . meanwhile being content to assume it gratuitously."[13] For much of the *Optical
Lectures* he pursued the implications of this law and derived numerous spurious properties of colored light, all with little or no concern
with reality. Meanwhile, he had deduced another dispersion law on
different grounds.[14] Newton was unable to choose between them on
the limited number of measurements that he made. Had he examined a greater range of substances, he would have found that neither is true.[15] Newton abandoned his plans to publish the *Optical
Lectures* for a number of reasons, but it is hard to believe that he

did not recognize that his dispersion law was an hypothesis that went nowhere. None the less, throughout his career he continued his quest to find a mathematico-mechanical explanation of refraction and dispersion, since the promised payoff was so high – namely, a mathematical foundation for a theory of color – and the models so tractable by the new science. He would return to it in the *Principia*.

Newton's dispersion model was inspired by Descartes's derivation of the law of refraction (Snell's law) in the *Dioptrique* (1637). The derivation was based on an analogy to a ball that has its velocity altered on crossing the boundary of two refracting media. In a mechanics that was based solely on contact action, it was difficult for Descartes to explain how the speed of the projectile was changed, especially when its speed increased in passing into an optically denser medium. In his "An hypothesis explaining the properties of light discoursed of in my severall Papers," which he sent to the Royal Society in December 1675, Newton explained how an aether could serve as the cause of refraction. He assumed that the aether permeates all space and is rarer in denser substances that have narrow pores, such as glass and water, than in free space such as air. When a light corpuscle moves through a region of aether of varying density, as near the boundary of two bodies, it is pressed by the denser aether towards the rarer, "& receivs a continuall impulse or ply from that side to recede towards the rarer, & so is accelerated if it move that way, or retarded if the contrary." If it is further assumed that the change of motion occurs perpendicular to the refracting surface, then Snell's law will follow.[16]

When Newton had developed the concept of force in the *Principia*, he concluded Book 1 with Section 14 on the analogy between the motion of corpuscles and light. By replacing the action of the aether in his earlier model of refraction by an intense short-range force between the corpuscles of the refracting body and light, he offered a powerful approach to optics and, more generally, to physics. In Figure 7.3 the force is assumed to act in the very small region between the refracting surfaces *Aa*, *Bb* and perpendicular to them. The motion of the particles in this field behaves exactly like that of a projectile "falling" in the earth's gravitational field. Newton demonstrated that its path *HI* in the region of the force field is a parabola ("from what Galileo demonstrated"), and that the angles of incidence *QMI* and refraction *MIK* obey Snell's law.[17] The derivation yielded

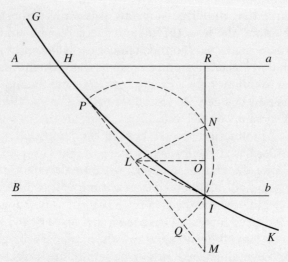

Fig. 7.3 Newton's derivation of Snell's law of refraction in the *Principia*, Book 1, Proposition 94.

an expression for the index of refraction n in terms of mechanical parameters. If we let $f(\rho)$ be the force per unit mass, where i and r are the angles of incidence and refraction, and ρ the distance from the refracting surface, then Newton's result in analytic form is:

$$n = \frac{\sin i}{\sin r} = \sqrt{1 - \frac{2\varphi}{v^2}},$$

where v is the incident velocity and $\varphi = \int_0^R f(\rho)d\rho$.

By at least 1675 in the "Hypothesis" Newton had recognized that if the change of motion of the light corpuscles occurs perpendicular to the refracting surface, then Snell's law will always follow. Thus, the aim of this demonstration was not to derive Snell's law, but rather to show that corpuscular optics could be brought into the realm of the new mechanics and to explore its physical implications and, in particular, to explain the cause of the different colors and refrangibility of light rays. The most natural explanation of the cause of the different refrangibility of rays of different color according to this model is that the velocity of the corpuscles varies. Four years after the publication of the *Principia*, Newton realized that this could be tested by observing the color of the eclipses of Jupiter's moons. When a satellite disappears behind the planet, the slowest color should be seen last, and when it reemerges, the fastest color should be seen first. In August 1691 Newton asked John Flamsteed if he had ever observed any color changes in eclipses of Jupiter's moons; the following February Flamsteed replied that he had not.[18] This was a serious blow to explaining refraction and dispersion by short-range forces, for it eliminated velocity as a cause of color and refraction. The model could be applied only with some radical assumptions that conflicted with the principles of terrestrial mechanics. Choosing mass instead of velocity would contradict the motion of projectiles, which is independent of their mass. Allowing the force to vary with the nature of the corpuscle and refracting substance would make the force a selective one like a chemical reaction, which was decidedly unlike any force in the new mechanics.[19] Newton's elegant demonstration based on his concept of short-range forces had to be restricted to monochromatic rays since color could not be explained with his new mechanics.

The model was not, however, without a notable success. In 1691 Newton used it to calculate the refraction of light rays entering the atmosphere and prepared a table of atmospheric refraction that was vastly superior to anything that then existed.[20] In a Scholium to this section of the *Principia* Newton also suggested that short-range forces acting on light corpuscles could explain diffraction. A few years later, as we shall see, he tried to carry out this program of applying short-range forces to diffraction before he hit a dead end. Newton concluded this Scholium by reminding his readers that he was proposing only an analogy and not arguing that light actually consists of corpuscles:

[B]ecause of the analogy that exists between the propagation of rays of light and the motion of bodies, I have decided to subjoin the following propositions for optical uses [namely, on geometrical optics], meanwhile not arguing at all about the nature of the rays (that is, whether they are bodies or not), but only determining the trajectories of bodies, which are very similar to the trajectories of rays.[21]

The two theorems that Newton added determined the surfaces, Cartesian ovals, that refracted light from a point to a point. Newton had in fact solved this problem more than fifteen years earlier in his *Optical Lectures* without the corpuscular theory of light.[22]

Newton attempted to provide a mechanical account of the actions of light corpuscles throughout his career, because it promised to unify optics as part of the mathematical science of mechanics and offered enough promising results to continue pursuing it. However, he did not limit himself to mechanical models in his speculations on the nature of light and always left his options open. For example, when he was writing the *Opticks* in the early 1690s, he briefly toyed with the idea that the force between light corpuscles and bodies might be selective like a chemical force: "If ye rays of light be bodies they are refracted by attraction [of] the parts of refracting bodies by some such principle as the parts of acids & alcalies rush towards one another & coalesce."[23] All these options remained hypothetical, since none of them had more than occasional experimental support.

AETHEREAL VIBRATIONS AND THE COLORS OF THIN FILMS

In his investigation of the colors of thin films, which he began while he was still developing his theory of color, Newton imaginatively expanded his corpuscular hypothesis to incorporate the aether and its interactions with light corpuscles in order to explain the periodicity of light. The essential feature of his aether is its vibrations, which reflect light corpuscles at condensations and transmit them at rarefactions. He was able to develop this qualitative, mechanical model into a relatively sophisticated mathematical one that agreed with his observations to a high degree of precision. Just as with the corpuscular model in his theory of color, Newton suppressed the vibrations in his formal accounts of his research on the colors of thin films. It was only in his speculative "Hypothesis" in 1675 that he chose to expound this model fully. Yet his aethereal vibrations differed in two significant ways from the light corpuscles that he used in his theory of color and refraction: (i) the vibrations were essential to the development of his explanation of the colors of thin films, and not just an heuristic; and (ii) he eventually elevated the vibrations – recast as "fits" in the *Opticks* – from an hypothesis to a confirmed scientific result, namely, the periodicity of light, whereas light corpuscles always remained hypothetical.

Newton learned about the colors of thin films from Hooke's account in the *Micrographia* (1665) of the colors seen in sheets of mica. Hooke had conjectured that the appearance of the colors was periodic, though he was unable to measure the thickness of such thin films in order to demonstrate this. Newton's key breakthrough was

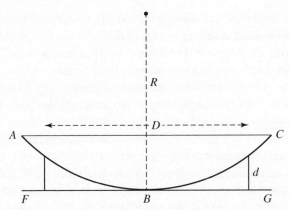

Fig. 7.4 Newton's method for determining the thickness d of a thin film of air formed between a spherical lens and a plane.

his insight that if he put a lens (which is really just a segment of a circle) on a flat plane, then by a principle from Euclidean geometry about tangents to circles he could readily determine the distance between them simply by measuring the circle's diameter. If (Figure 7.4) a convex lens ABC is placed on a glass plate FBG and illuminated and viewed from above, a set of concentric colored circles – now known as "Newton's rings" – produced by the thin film of air $ABCGBF$ will be seen through the upper surface of the lens. The circles will form an alternating sequence of bright and dark colored rings, and their common center, the point of contact B, will be surrounded by a dark spot. If the diameter of any of these colored circles be denoted by D, the thickness of the air film producing that circle by d, and the radius of the lens by R, then $d = D^2/8R$ by Euclid's *Elements*, Book 3, Prop. 36.

Newton apparently had this insight while reading the *Micrographia* and quickly carried out a rough and ready test in 1666 and entered it in his essay "On Colours." To establish that the circles do appear at integral multiples of some definite thickness, he simply had to measure the diameter of successive circles and see if their squares increased as the integers. For the first six circles he found that the thickness of the air between the lens and the plate increased by integral multiples of the thickness at the first ring, that is, as 1, 2, 3, 4, 5, 6. He then calculated that "y^e thickness of y^e aire for one circle was $\frac{1}{64000}$ inch, or 0,000015625. [wch is y^e space of a pulse of y^e vibrating medium.]."[24] His results, though quantitatively wide of the mark, as he later noted, were enough to demonstrate to his satisfaction that the appearance of the colors was a periodic phenomenon, and he succeeded in determining a measure of the periodicity. His method for determining the thickness of the film was in principle valid, and it later allowed him to develop a mathematical theory of the appearance of periodic colors. Moreover, from his remark in square brackets we can see that from the beginning of his research he was already utilizing vibrations in the aether as the physical cause of the rings.

Since one of Newton's immediate aims was to show that the colors of thin films are compatible with his recent discovery of the compound nature of sunlight, he would quite naturally have assumed that those colors in the incident sunlight that were not reflected by the film were transmitted. By examining the transmitted rings, he readily confirmed that the transmitted and reflected rings were complementary. And by examining the rings produced by rays of a single color, it was possible for him to understand their formation in white light when the colors are not separately visible because of their overlapping and mixing. Namely, he was able to see that at the same place some rays are reflected whereas the others are transmitted, and that rays of the same color are at some places reflected and at others transmitted. At this stage Newton had not fully elaborated these points, especially the second, which requires assigning a particular thickness or vibration length to each color.

Satisfied with this fundamental result and convinced that his method worked, Newton set it aside until he had fully worked out his theory of color. In about 1671 he undertook a serious investigation of the colors of thin films, and his record of this investigation, "Of ye coloured circles twixt two contiguous glasses," survives.[25] Newton's primary aim was to examine and describe Newton's rings quantitatively through a series of mathematical propositions and supporting measurements and observations; but he apparently also hoped to confirm his belief in the corpuscular constitution of light and its interactions with the aether. In the following year he wrote up his results for submission to the Royal Society, but because of the controversies over his theory of color he withheld it. When Newton once again felt sufficiently comfortable in revealing his works to the public, in 1675, he revised the "Observations" from 1672 and submitted it with a new companion piece, "An hypothesis explaining the properties of light," to the Royal Society.[26] The 1675 version of the "Observations," which also contains his theory of colored bodies, was later minimally revised to become the greater part of Book 2 of the *Opticks*. In the progression from the preliminary investigation in "Of Colours" through the "Observations" the variety of experiments carried out expanded significantly.

Before turning to Newton's model of corpuscles and aethereal vibrations, I will sketch his description of the conditions for the appearance of the rings and their periodicity. Although Newton did not write his results as an equation, they are equivalent to the following

$$d = \frac{D^2}{8R} = \frac{mI}{2},$$

where the first two terms of the equation express the Euclidean theorem cited above for the thickness of the film of air, and I is an interval such that for m odd the ring is a bright one and for m even a dark one. The interval I is the length of an aethereal vibration and, later, in the *Opticks* that of a fit.[27] However, in neither version of the "Observations" nor in the two parts of the *Opticks* does Newton introduce this physical interpretation, though it is apparent from "Of Colours" and "Of ye coloured circles" that he actually arrived at these results by working with the vibrations. He treats the interval solely as an experimentally determined property of the film – "the interval of the glasses, or thickness of the interjacent air, by which each colour was produced" – and not of light.[28] Although Newton did not calculate the value of the interval I in "Of ye coloured circles," in the "Observations" he adopted 1/80,000 of an inch – "to use a round number" – for the middle of white light (i.e., for a yellow).[29]

Only one other result from his investigation need concern us, his determination of the variation of the diameters of the rings when water was placed between the lenses. From his measurements he found that the diameters of the circles, and thus the thickness of the film, decrease in proportion to the index of refraction. Thus the earlier equation becomes

$$d = \frac{D^2}{8R} = \frac{mI}{2n},$$

where n is the index of refraction of the film. Newton was probably led to accept this as a general rule valid for any medium, because he was able to deduce it from his model of light particles and aethereal vibrations. In "Of y^e coloured circles" he had stated this law in Proposition 4 in terms both of the index of refraction (the "subtilty" of the medium) and "ye motions of ye rays in that medium."[30] Like all the other propositions in "Of ye coloured circles," no derivation was presented, but it is readily inferred. If the particles move faster in water in proportion to the increase of index of refraction (as the emission theory required), then they would more quickly reach the lower surface of the film and encounter the first aethereal condensation. The vibration length would then be shorter in the inverse proportion.

From his first effort at explaining the colors of thin films in "Of colours" Newton tried to derive their properties from the corpuscular theory. He set forth a law for the increase of the diameter of the colored circles as they are observed more obliquely to the surface as a proportion expressed in terms of the motion (momentum) and velocity of the incident light corpuscles. This passage is still not fully understood, but the proportion certainly does not agree with the phenomenon and Newton deleted it with a large $\times$.[31]

Newton later made one more attempt in "Of y^e coloured circles" to describe the variation of the circles in terms of the motion of the light corpuscles. The paper opens with six propositions to be confirmed in the subsequent observations. The properties of the circles are mathematically described, and many of them are interpreted in terms of the "motion," "force," and "percussion" of the corpuscles or rays, though no derivations are presented. The following two are typical:

Prop 2. That they [i.e., the colored circles] swell by ye obliquity of the eye: soe y^t the diameter of ye same circle is as y^e [co]secants of ye rays obliquity in ye interjected filme of aire, or reciprocally as ye sines of its obliquity; that is, reciprocally as y^t part of the motion of ye ray in ye said filme of aire wch is perpendicular to it, or reciprocally as ye force it strikes ye refracting surface wth all.

Prop 3. And hence ye spaces wch ye rays passe through twixt ye circles in one position to the said spaces in another position are as ye squares of ye said [co]secants or reciprocally as y^e [s]quares of ye sines, motion, or percussion.[32]

Both of these propositions were subsequently contradicted by the observations that follow in the manuscript. At this point Newton undoubtedly recognized that the phenomenon was simply not amenable to a description using corpuscles. In all his later quantitative work on the colors of thin films he worked only with the

vibrations set up by the corpuscles. However, in his physical thinking the encounter of the corpuscles with the compressions and rarefactions of the vibrations played a fundamental role, as we saw in
his deduction of the variation of the diameters of the rings with index
of refraction.

Newton submitted "An hypothesis explaining the properties of
light discoursed of in my severall Papers" to the Royal Society, because he hoped that revealing the hypotheses or physical models that
underlay his phenomenological theories would make them more intelligible. He insisted, however, "that no man may confound this
with my other discourses, or measure the certainty of one by the
other."[33] The "Hypothesis," which Newton did not allow to be published, is his most openly speculative work and – unlike the thirty-
one queries which roam over the scientific landscape – reveals how
he used his speculations to explore a single scientific theory. It shows
clearly how he was able to control and mathematize speculative mechanical models and arrive at experimentally confirmed laws.

The first two hypotheses assert that the aether exists and is capable of vibrating. This aether is almost without resistance, for it resists
the motion of light particles only initially, at their emission from a
luminous source, and at the boundaries of different bodies, where its
density changes. When light particles are emitted, they are accelerated "by a Principle of motion . . . till the resistance of the Aethereal
Medium equal the force of that principle." Henceforth the aether offers as little resistance as a vacuum. This is contrary to the principles
of Galilean mechanics, and Newton knew it: "God who gave Animals self motion beyond our understanding is without doubt able to
implant other principles of motion in bodies wch we may understand
as little. Some would readily grant this may be a Spiritual one; yet a
mechanical one might be showne, did not I think it better to passe it
by."[34] Although the problem of the aether's resistance would vanish
when Newton replaced the contact action of the aether with forces,
this shows how he was able to elide physical difficulties in order to
pursue the mathematical representation of a phenomenon. Newton
emphasizes that he considers the particles to be light and not the
vibrations, "I suppose Light is neither this Aether not its vibrating
motion," which is simply an effect of light.[35]

The aether has a stiff surface that is responsible for the reflec-
tive power of bodies. The constant bombardment of light particles

excites vibrations in the surface that are propagated throughout the aether. If a light corpuscle strikes the surface when it is compressed, it will be reflected because the surface is too stiff and dense to let the corpuscle pass; but if a corpuscle happens to strike the surface when it is expanded, it will pass through. This is the physical mechanism that Newton uses to introduce periodicity to a corpuscular theory of light. That he had failed in quantifying the relationship between the corpuscles and the magnitude of the excited vibrations did not hinder him from using it as the basis for describing the periodic colors of thin films. The corpuscles still play a fundamental, if less prominent, role in that one has to keep track of the location of both the corpuscles and the vibrations to determine the observed phenomenon.

The periodicity of Newton's rings is now readily explained (Figure 7.5). At the center A, where the glasses touch, the corpuscles will be transmitted because the aether in the two glasses is continuous, and a central dark spot will be seen. At a certain thickness BC (= $I/2$) away from the center the corpuscle will encounter the condensed part of the first overtaking vibration and be reflected, and a bright

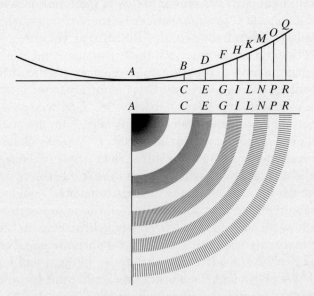

Fig. 7.5 One quadrant of Newton's rings produced with light of a single color.

ring will be seen; at double that thickness *DE*, it will encounter the rarefied part of that wave and be transmitted, and a dark ring will be seen; at triple the thickness *FG* it will encounter the condensed part of the second wave and be reflected; and so on in arithmetic progression, in agreement with observation. To extend this model to white light, Newton only had to introduce the idea that the rays or particles of different color vary in "magnitude, strength or vigour" and so excite vibrations of different size.[36] The red vibrations are assumed to be larger than the violet ones and thus to form larger circles, as is observed.

In the *Opticks* Newton transformed the aethereal vibrations into the "fits of easy reflection and transmission," and raised them to an established principle. The fits were now held to be a property of light, and not of the aether. Merely purging the vibrations of their hypothetical elements was insufficient ground for Newton to raise them to a demonstrated truth. More evidence for the periodicity of light was required. Newton found this in the new phenomenon of the colors of thick plates, which he set forth in Book 2, Part 4 of the *Opticks*. He was able to explain them with the same vibration lengths *I* and mathematical-physical theory as for thin plates, and he was able to predict the size of colored rings of thick plates with the same precision as those of thin films.[37] The existence of light corpuscles never achieved this level of generality or confirmation.

THE ATOMIC STRUCTURE OF MATTER
AND COLORED BODIES

If Newton always considered the existence of light corpuscles to be an hypothesis, he assumed the existence of corpuscles of matter in his explanation of the colors of natural bodies – the colors of all the things we see around us, like grass, cloth, and clouds. He was as certain of the existence of atoms as he was of the existence of God. Although the theory of colored bodies is an extension of his explanation of the colors of thin films and an integral part of his optical theory, it is as much a theory about the structure and properties of matter.

The essence of Newton's theory is the idea that the colors of bodies are produced in the same way as they are in thin films. He developed this theory in the early 1670s simultaneously with his account of the colors of thin films, and it forms the third part of the "Observations" of 1672 and 1675 and of Book 2 of the *Opticks*. In the more than thirty years between the time it was first developed and published in the *Opticks*, he abandoned the aether and developed the concepts of force and fits, but the theory of colored bodies scarcely changed.

Newton opens his theory by arguing that colored transparent and opaque bodies consist of transparent corpuscles and pores. The existence of aether in the pores is hypothetical, but he does not question the existence of corpuscles. His reasoning is straightforward: since reflection occurs only where there is a difference in optical density, for reflection to occur from the corpuscles composing bodies, the bodies must have pores that are of a different optical density from the corpuscles. Opacity is attributed to multiple reflections caused by the internal parts of the body. Newton's evidence for these claims comes almost entirely from macroscopic bodies, and it is then extended to the imperceptible corpuscles. For example, he argues that the "least parts" of bodies are transparent from observations that show that, when made sufficiently thin, bodies become transparent; and he argues that opacity arises from a multitude of internal reflections by observing that transparent substances like glass become opaque when they are shattered into tiny pieces. This can be a tricky mode of argument.[38]

The central proposition of Newton's theory establishes that: "The transparent parts of bodies, according to their several sizes, must reflect rays of one colour, and transmit those of another, on the same grounds, that thin plates or bubbles do reflect or transmit those rays: and this I take to be the ground of all their colours."[39] Newton demonstrates this by what would become his second Rule of Reasoning in the *Principia*, namely, that "the causes assigned to natural effects of the same kind must be, so far as possible, the same."[40] He presents evidence showing that the colors of natural bodies and thin plates are of the same kind, and therefore have the same cause. With this demonstrated, Newton estimated the size of the corpuscles composing various bodies from their color. He assumed that the corpuscles are of the same optical density as water or glass, "as by many circumstances is obvious to collect." In his account of the colors of thin films, Newton had prepared a table of the thicknesses of films of air, water, and glass that produce the various colors of each ring or order. For example, he deduced that the green of vegetation corresponds to the green in the third colored ring, and from his table he found that the corpuscles of vegetable matter are $17\frac{1}{2} \times 10^{-6}$ or about 1/60,000 inch in diameter, assuming that they had the same density as glass.[41] The corpuscles of black and colorless transparent bodies must be less than any of those producing colors, just as the central spot in Newton's rings is colorless and reflects no light.

While it is not possible to see light corpuscles, Newton anticipated actually seeing the corpuscles of bodies. He explained that he deduced the sizes of the corpuscles "because it is not impossible, but that microscopes may at length be improved to the discovery of the corpuscles of bodies, on which their colours depend." If their magnification could be increased five or six hundred times, we might be able to see the largest corpuscles, and if "three or four thousand times, perhaps they might be discovered but those, which produce blackness."[42]

A closer examination of the corpuscles responsible for the color of bodies reveals some characteristic features of Newton's theory of matter. Despite their apparent smallness, the corpuscles are none the less macroscopic, compound bodies. If we consider a thin sheet of colorless glass that is of this green color, or even one so thin (approximately 1/160,000 inch) that it exhibits a yellow of the first order, it must contain within that thickness a number of the corpuscles that make it glass. A segment of that glass as wide as it is thick is a small, albeit very small, piece of glass with all the properties of glass. Green glass (or grass) will be composed of corpuscles of the same size as these fragments, each of which is composed of the corpuscles that compose colorless glass. Thus, the corpuscles' composing bodies already have a structure and are themselves composed of parts; they are not atoms.

"And hence we may understand," Newton wrote in the *Opticks*, "that Bodies are much more rare and porous than is commonly believed."[43] If we recall his explanation of the colors of thin films and the model expounded in the "Hypothesis," a thin film or plate consists primarily of aether with some interspersed solid parts. The only function he assigns to the parts, besides defining the pores, is to stop and absorb any light particles that collide with them. The vibrations of the aether cause rays of some colors to be reflected while allowing others to be transmitted. Since colored bodies are composed of corpuscles the thickness of which is the same as a thin film of

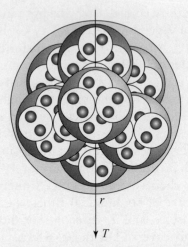

Fig. 7.6 A compound corpuscle of matter illustrating Newton's hierarchical conception of the structure of matter. A light ray T is transmitted through a corpuscle if it does not hit one of its parts.

that color, then those corpuscles must likewise primarily consist of aether and some parts. Consequently, for Newton matter actually consists mostly of aether or empty space.[44]

To explain how apparently solid matter could consist mostly of pores, Newton finally revealed his ideas on the hierarchical structure of matter in the Latin translation of the *Opticks*, though he had held this idea from almost the beginning of his scientific career. He had probably first encountered it in his reading of Boyle, and it was not an uncommon view in seventeenth-century (al)chemical works. If we imagine a body to consist of parts and pores and that the pores occupy as much space as the parts; and then imagine each of those parts to be similarly composed of much smaller pores and parts that occupy equal space; and then imagine this process to proceed until solid particles or atoms are reached, bodies would consist mostly of pores (Figure 7.6). A body, for example, with four such compositions would have fifteen times more pores than solid parts, and with ten compositions above one thousand times more pores than parts. It is important to recognize that Newton offered this particular structure only as a possibility, for "there are other ways of conceiving how Bodies may be exceeding porous. But what is really their inward Frame is not yet known to us."[45]

That Newton did not consider the existence of atoms to be an hypothesis becomes apparent from a preface that he drafted for the *Opticks* in 1703 but did not publish. He considered the possibility of deducing all phenomena from just four "general suppositions" or "principles." These principles were not hypotheses, but derived by induction, for "there is no other way of doing any thing with certainty then by drawing conclusions from experiments & phaenomena untill you come at general Principles." The first three principles are the existence of God, the impenetrability of matter, and the law of gravitational attraction. In describing the fourth principle, he announced that he intended to derive the theory of the colors of natural bodies from his hierarchical, corpuscular theory of matter:

A fourth Principle is that all sensible bodies are aggregated of particles laid together wth many interstices or pores between them ... As by the third Principle we gave an account heretofore of ye motions of the Planets & of ye flux & reflux of ye sea, so by this Principle we shall in ye following treatise give an acc^t of ye permanent colours of natural bodies, nothing further being requisite for ye production of those colours then that ye coloured bodies abound with pellucid particles of a certain size & density. This is to be understood of the largest particles or particles of ye last composition. For as bodies are composed of these larger particles with larger pores between them so it is to be conceived that these larger particles are composed of smaller particles with smaller pores between them.[46]

The corpuscular theory of matter was thus for Newton not an hypothesis but a demonstrated principle established with as much certainty as the existence of God or the theory of gravitation. He cites two principal sorts of evidence in its support: various substances penetrate the pores of bodies, like water into vegetable and animal matter, and quicksilver into metals; and transparency, which shows that light passes through the pores of a great variety of bodies (which, to be sure, assumes an emission theory of light). The theory of colored bodies was not only founded on the corpuscularity of matter; it was a theory of matter attributing specific properties and arrangements to the corpuscles that cause the transparency or opacity and colors of bodies. For Newton to have considered corpuscularity to be an hypothesis or a working assumption would have been to violate one of his most fundamental methodological principles.

ATOMISM AND HYPOTHESES

When Newton was completing the *Opticks* in the early 1690s, he undertook an investigation of diffraction and wrote it up as the last book of the *Opticks*. He took his usual phenomenological approach and described his observations and experiments while eschewing physical hypotheses. His unpublished papers show that as in his other investigations he fully used the corpuscular theory of light and – as this was carried out post-*Principia* – short-range forces. He assumed that diffraction occurred when light corpuscles pass very close to an edge of a body and are deflected by the short-range forces of the corpuscles of the body. He was able to develop this model mathematically and carried out measurements and calculations with it. He even derived some laws governing diffraction. After completing the manuscript, however, he carried out an experiment that showed conclusively that this model with forces and corpuscles could not possibly be correct. Newton removed this book from the manuscript of the *Opticks* with the intention of carrying out more experiments and revising it. It turned out that he was near the end of his scientific career and never carried out any more optical experiments. Shortly before he published the *Opticks* in 1704, he simply revised the book and eliminated the results that depended on the corpuscle-force model.[47]

If Newton had hoped that his investigation of diffraction would finally vindicate the corpuscular nature of light, this episode would have disabused him of that hope. The corpuscular theory of light would remain an hypothesis. This was by no means the first time that his efforts to establish that theory were stymied. His dispersion models could not be experimentally confirmed; his attempt to deduce the properties of the colors of thin films from the motion of the light corpuscles failed; the derivation of refraction in *Principia* was elegant, but it encountered serious problems when eclipse tests failed to confirm the velocity interpretation. Newton had some successes, especially with his qualitative models, such as in his interpretation of his theory of color, and the cause of Newton's rings, and the calculation of atmospheric refraction. This is not a sterling record, and we can understand Newton's conviction that the corpuscular theory of light was an hypothesis. It certainly was fruitful, guiding him through a series of major investigations by suggesting experiments and new laws, but it had not been confirmed in any generality, as had the periodicity of light. Newton was not acting out of method-ological fussiness in distinguishing certainties from conjectures, but rather exercising sound scientific judgment.

Because he judged the corpuscular theory of light to be an hypoth-esis, most of Newton's published writings on it are in the queries of the *Opticks*. Here Newton discusses such topics as the corpuscular theory and the cause of colors, fits, diffraction, and double refrac-tion, and also devotes substantial attention to refuting rival wave or continuum theories of light, not to mention sensation, heat, and es-pecially chemistry. In an anonymous review in 1715 Newton clearly described the hypothetical nature of the queries and explained why he set them apart from the rest of the *Opticks*. In the *Principia* and *Opticks*, he wrote, "Mr. Newton" adopted the "experimental phi-losophy," in which "Hypotheses have no place, unless as Conjec-tures or Questions proposed to be examined by Experiments. For this Reason Mr. *Newton* in his Optiques distinguished those things which were made certain by Experiments from those things which remained uncertain, and which he therefore proposed in the End of his Optiques in the Form of Queries."[48] In the eighteenth century the queries were widely interpreted as representing Newton's declared views on the topics discussed rather than as speculations. Our study of Newton's use of the corpuscular hypothesis in his optical inves-tigations, that is, his actual scientific practice, shows how mistaken this view was.[49]

NOTES

1   Alan E. Shapiro (ed.), *The Optical Papers of Isaac Newton, Volume 1: The Optical Lectures, 1670–1672* (Cambridge: Cambridge University Press, 1984), p. 89.
2   Newton, "New Theory about Light and Color," in *The Correspondence of Isaac Newton*, ed. H. W. Turnbull, vol. 1 (Cambridge: Cambridge University Press, 1959), p. 100.
3   John E. McGuire and Martin Tamny (eds.), *Certain Philosophical Ques-tions: Newton's Trinity Notebook* (Cambridge: Cambridge University Press, 1983), p. 432.
4   Newton did not think that light rays are colored; rather he held that they have a power or disposition to cause the perception of color: see the definition following Book 1, Part 2, Proposition 2, *Opticks: or, A Treatise of the Reflections, Refractions, Inflections and Colours of Light. Based on the Fourth Edition London, 1730* (New York: Dover Publications,

1952), pp. 124–5. None the less, to avoid cumbersome circumlocutions it is easier to refer to red rays, blue rays, and so on.

5   For the historical development of Newton's theory of color see Richard S. Westfall, "The Development of Newton's Theory of Color," *Isis* 53 (1962), 339–58; and A. Rupert Hall, *All Was Light: An Introduction to Newton's Opticks* (Oxford: Clarendon Press, 1993).

6   Newton, "New Theory," *Correspondence*, pp. 97, 98.

7   Newton to Oldenburg for Hooke, 11 June 1672, *Correspondence*, p. 174.

8   *Ibid.*, p. 175. Newton developed this objection in the *Principia*, Book 2, Propositions 41–2, and in the *Opticks*, Query 28.

9   See John Hendry, "Newton's Theory of Colour," *Centaurus* 23 (1980), 230–51.

10 *Opticks*, Book 2, Part 3, Proposition 8, p. 266.

11 See Newton, *Correspondence*, p. 103, n. 6, italics added; and D. T. Whiteside (ed.), *The Mathematical Papers of Isaac Newton*, 6 vols. (Cambridge: Cambridge University Press, 1967–81), vol. 1, pp. 559–74.

12 Newton, *Optical Lectures*, pp. 199–203; see also Zev Bechler, "Newton's Search for a Mechanistic Model of Colour Dispersion: A Suggested Interpretation," *Archive for History of Exact Sciences* 11 (1973), 1–37, esp. pp. 3–6.

13 Newton, *Optical Papers*, p. 201.

14 What I have called his linear dispersion law, which is based on the musical division of the spectrum; Shapiro, "Newton's 'Achromatic' Dispersion Law: Theoretical Background and Experimental Evidence," *Archive for History of Exact Sciences* 21 (1979), 91–128. Newton adopted this law in the *Opticks*, Book 1, Part 2, Proposition 3, Expt. 7.

15 In the eighteenth century it was discovered that there is no law relating dispersion to mean refraction, and that dispersion is a property of matter and not, as Newton had assumed, of light.

16 Newton, *Correspondence*, p. 371.

17 Newton, *The Principia, Mathematical Principles of Natural Philosophy: A New Translation*, trans. I. Bernard Cohen and Anne Whitman (Berkeley: University of California Press, 1999), Book 1, Part 1, Proposition 94, p. 622.

18 This episode is recounted in Alan E. Shapiro, *Fits, Passions, and Paroxysms: Physics, Method, and Chemistry and Newton's Theories of Colored Bodies and Fits of Easy Reflection* (Cambridge: Cambridge University Press, 1993), pp. 144–7. See also Bechler, "Newton's Search," p. 22; and Jean Eisenstaedt, "L'optique balistique newtonienne à l'épreuve des satellites de Jupiter," *Archive for History of Exact Sciences* 50 (1996), 117–56.

19   In fact, Newton did consider the possibility that the optical force be-
     haved like a chemical force; see note 23 below.
20   See D. T. Whiteside (ed.), *Mathematical Papers of Isaac Newton*,
     vol. 6 (1974), pp. 422–5, 431–4; D. T. Whiteside, "Kepler, Newton and
     Flamsteed on Refraction through a 'regular aire': The Mathematical and
     the Practical," *Centaurus* 24 (1980), 288–315; and Bechler, "Newton's
     Search," pp. 23–6.
21   Newton, *Principia*, Book 1, Part 1, Proposition 96, Scholium, p. 626.
22   Newton, *Optical Papers*, pp. 417–19.
23   Shapiro, *Fits, Passions, and Paroxysms*, p. 142, n. 16.
24   McGuire and Tamny (eds.), *Certain Philosophical Questions*, pp. 476–8.
     The square brackets here are Newton's way of setting off his speculative
     or interpretive comments. For a comprehensive account of Newton's
     investigations of the colors of thin films and the theory of fits see
     Shapiro, *Fits, Passions, and Paroxysms*, chs. 2 and 4; and for a philosoph-
     ical discussion, which historically is somewhat dated, Norwood Russell
     Hanson, "Waves, Particles, and Newton's 'Fits'," *Journal of the History
     of Ideas* 21 (1960), 370–91.
25   Richard S. Westfall, "Isaac Newton's Coloured Circles twixt Two Con-
     tiguous Glasses," *Archive for History of Exact Sciences* 2 (1965), 183–96.
26   Since Newton left what I call the "Observations" untitled, it has
     received various names. In I. Bernard Cohen (ed.), *Isaac Newton's
     Papers and Letters on Natural Philosophy and Related Documents*
     (Cambridge, MA: Harvard University Press, 1958) it was called
     "Newton's Second Paper on Color and Light"; and in Newton's *Cor-
     respondence*, "Discourse of Observations."
27   The thickness of air at which the first bright ring is produced is one
     half the physical vibration, or pulse length, that I call the interval I.
     All other rings, bright and dark, appear at integral multiples of this
     thickness. Newton's law for the appearance of rings is the same as that
     derived according to the modern wave theory except for a factor of 2,
     because his interval I turns out to be one half of the wavelength λ in
     the wave theory of light.
28   Observation 5, in Thomas Birch (ed.), *The History of the Royal Society of
     London, for Improving of Natural Knowledge, From Its First Rise*, 4 vols.
     (London, 1756–7; reprinted Brussels: Culture et Civilisation, 1968), vol.
     3, p. 274; which is reprinted in Cohen, *Newton's Papers and Letters*.
29   Observation 6, Birch, *History*, vol. 3, p. 275. In the *Opticks* Newton
     redetermined this value and found it to be a whopping 11% smaller
     or 1/89,000, which is very close to the modern value; see Shapiro, *Fits,
     Passions, and Paroxysms*, pp. 167–9.

30   Westfall, "Newton's Coloured Circles," p. 191.

31   Ibid., pp. 187–9.

32   Ibid., p. 191.

33   Newton, Correspondence, p. 364.

34   Ibid., p. 370.

35   Ibid., p. 370.

36   Ibid., p. 376.

37   See Shapiro, Fits, Passions, and Paroxysms, ch. 4.

38   For a discussion of Newton's theory of colored bodies and its mode of demonstration, see ibid., ch. 3.

39   Birch, History, vol. 3, p. 299.

40   Newton, Principia, p. 795.

41   Birch, History, vol. 3, p. 301.

42   Ibid., p. 303.

43   Newton, Opticks, Book 2, Part 3, Proposition 8, p. 267. This passage was not in the "Observations."

44   In the Opticks the aether is replaced by empty space and the vibrations by fits, but Newton's conviction that bodies contain little ponderable matter did not change. On Newton's theory of matter and atomism, see McGuire, "Body and Void and Newton's De mundi systemate: Some New Sources," Archive for History of Exact Sciences 3 (1966), 206–48.

45   Newton, Opticks, Book 2, Part 3, Proposition 8, p. 269. This particular example of continual halving is merely an example. In his unpublished papers Newton has calculations with other divisions, such as seven parts of matter and six parts of pores; see Newton's draft of an addition to the Principia, Book 3, Proposition 6, in A. Rupert Hall and Marie Boas Hall (eds.), The Unpublished Scientific Papers of Isaac Newton: A Selection from the Portsmouth Collection in the University Library, Cambridge (Cambridge: Cambridge University Press, 1962), pp. 314, 317.

46   J. E. McGuire, "Newton's 'Principles of Philosophy': An Intended Preface for the 1704 Opticks and a Related Draft Fragment," British Journal for the History of Science 5 (1970), 178–86, on pp. 183, 184.

47   For Newton's investigation of diffraction see Alan E. Shapiro, "Newton's Experiments on Diffraction and the Delayed Publication of the Opticks," in Jed Z. Buchwald and I. Bernard Cohen (eds.), Isaac Newton's Natural Philosophy (Cambridge, MA: MIT Press, 2001).

48   [Newton], "An Account of the Book Entituled Commercium epistolicum," Philosophical Transactions 29 (1714/15), 173–224, on p. 222.

49   On the reception of the queries in the eighteenth century see I. Bernard Cohen, Franklin and Newton: An Inquiry into Speculative Newtonian Experimental Science and Franklin's Work in Electricity as an Example Thereof, Memoirs of the American Philosophical Society 43

(Philadelphia: American Philosophical Society, 1956); Arnold Thackray, *Atoms and Powers: An Essay on Newtonian Matter-Theory and the Development of Chemistry* (Cambridge, MA: Harvard University Press, 1970); and Casper Hakfoort, *Optics in the Age of Euler: Conceptions of the Nature of Light, 1700–1795*, trans. Enid Perlin-West (Cambridge: Cambridge University Press, 1995).

8   Newton's metaphysics

When one speaks of Newton's "metaphysics," it should be noted that the word itself was rarely used by Newton; further, that in point of general philosophical usage, that word has not had in our own time a fixed and well-established acceptation. For the purposes of the present study, a rather broad view will be adopted – suggested on the one hand by Newton's most influential near predecessor, the previous author of a book called *Principia Philosophiae*,[1] Descartes, according to whom metaphysics treats of *the principles of* [all] *knowledge*, and serves as *the root* of the "tree of philosophy" (whose "trunk" is physics, and whose "branches" are what we should call the "applied sciences");[2] and on the other by the author of the article "Metaphysics" in the eleventh edition of the *Encyclopaedia Britannica*, Thomas Case, who summarizes the concern of this discipline in the two questions: "1. What is the world of things we know? 2. How do we know it?"[3] Thus metaphysics will here be understood to be the discussion of the most general features, *both* of the constitution of the world, *and* of the principles of human inquiry into the nature of the world.

It will be useful for our discussion to put Newton's position in comparison with that of Descartes; for the work of the latter was both enormously influential in general – in the seventeenth century, and also, so far as metaphysics (in contrast to natural philosophy) is concerned, right down to the present day – and of great moment for Newton in particular.

On the methodological side, Descartes's program for a reformation of knowledge – for the establishment of a science that should be both secure in its theoretical attainments and of unexampled power in its aid to the control of the natural conditions of human life[4] – was based upon the demand that every item of knowledge be either *immediately clear and certain beyond a doubt*, or be *connected* to such clear and certain foundations by clear and certain links. Both the guarantee of the truth of what the mind perceives clearly and with no possible doubt,[5] and the identification of the fundamental principles so perceived, come, according to Descartes, from metaphysics or "first philosophy"; therefore this science is indeed "first" in the order of investigation: as already remarked, metaphysics is the "root" of that tree of which physics – natural philosophy – is the "trunk."

It is important to emphasize that this radical position does *not* mean, as it has sometimes been taken to, that Descartes thinks all of physics can be *deduced* from principles known through "pure reason." In his program for the investigation of the natural world, *experiment* plays a central role. But to characterize that role, something must be said about the deliverances of Cartesian metaphysics on what one might call its "ontological" side. The chief points that are relevant here are these:

Descartes, like Aristotle and the scholastic tradition, takes "substance" to be the primary category of "being" in the world: the "things that are" are "substances." A central *innovation* by Descartes is his principle that there are two fundamentally distinct sorts of substance, each distinguished by its characteristic essential "attribute": "thinking things" (*res cogitantes*) or minds, and "extended things" (*res extensae*) or bodies. Bodies form the subject of natural philosophy. Since it is of the essence of these simply *to be extended*, the notion of empty space – extension void of body – is just contradictory; so the world is a plenum: body is everywhere. The only distinctions or diversities that are conceivable among bodies *as* extended things are diverse *motions*. Therefore, the processes of nature consist solely in the motions of bodies and the changes of those motions; and the foundations of physics consist in the principles that govern those motions and changes of motions. The task of natural philosophy, therefore, is to account for all natural phenomena by describing the motions and changes of motion in which they consist, and exhibiting those processes of motion and change of motion as consequences of such fundamental principles.

Now, at the very base of this conception lies a serious difficulty: namely, how to characterize "motion" *at all*, when it has been declared that there is nothing more to body than its attribute of *extension.* In his earliest treatise on physics, *The World*, Descartes takes for granted what one may call the "naive" conception of motion: it is "that by which bodies pass from one place to another and successively occupy all the spaces between"; and what *place* is, is a question not even raised. If, however, bodies are essentially just "what is extended," there is no real distinction between "bodies" and "spaces"; so one is baffled what to make of the notion of *the same body* successively occupying *different spaces*. It is in fact clear that in *The World* Descartes is taking it for granted that we possess – presumably as clear and innate ideas – two distinct notions of *identity* (over time) for "the extended": (1) identity of place, and (2) identity of body. On the other hand, since Descartes himself does not explicitly signalize this twofold notion of identity – which, as we shall see presently, Descartes drastically revises in his decisive work, the *Principles of Philosophy* – it seems impossible to acquit him of a *lack* of "clarity and distinctness" on this point.

The World was not published during Descartes's lifetime. In a letter to Mersenne of 22 July 1633, Descartes says that the treatise is nearly finished. In late November, he wrote again. This time he says that he had intended to give Mersenne a copy of the completed work as a New Year's present. But he has just learned that Galileo's *World System*[6] has been condemned in Rome; and the only reason he can think of for such a condemnation is the fact of its having "tried to establish that the earth moves" – on which issue, he continues: "I must admit that if the view is false, so too are the entire foundations of my philosophy, for it can be demonstrated from them quite clearly. And it is so closely interwoven in every part of my treatise that I could not remove it without rendering the whole work defective." Consequently, Descartes set the work aside, and – after a considerable lapse of time – proceeded to revise its foundations so far as the nature of motion is concerned.

The *Principles of Philosophy*, published in 1644, is repeatedly referred to by Descartes in his correspondence as a new version of "my World." In it he presents, in place of what has above been called the "naive" conception of motion, a new and sophisticated one. Motion "in the ordinary sense of the term" is still "the action by which a body travels from one place to another";[7] but *place* is now said to be an ambiguous, or relative, notion[8] and, "rightly taken," to be defined by *the surface of the surrounding body.*[9] Accordingly, "motion

in the strict sense of the term" is defined as "the transfer of one
piece of matter, or one body, from the vicinity of the other bodies
which are in immediate contact with it, and which are regarded as
being at rest, to the vicinity of other bodies." (This "sophisticated" –
and semi-relativist[10] – conception raises new problems of its own, as
Newton's critique will make plain.)

In any case, having posited the realm of "extended things" and
its character as a plenum, Descartes appeals to the testimony of the
senses (itself warranted as reliable on such an issue by God's necessarily non-deceptive character) to establish both that this realm
actually exists,[11] and that *it is in continual and very diversified
motion.*

The principles that govern such motion are on the other hand *not,*
according to Descartes, to be ascertained by means of, or with any
help from, empirical observation: these principles or rules he claims
to infer directly from God's immutability – from the *constancy of
his action* in preserving the world from moment to moment, which
implies (a) the conservation of all states which are not necessarily altered through the postulated fact of motion, and (b) the conservation
of the total "quantity of motion" itself (of all bodies together – not, of
course, of each individually), from moment to moment. The actual
rules stated by Descartes need not concern us (although it should
be remarked that they – and the arguments he gives for them – are
really bizarre); what is important is that these principles of motion
constitute, in Descartes's system, the analogue of what the physicists of our own time call the "fundamental forces" of nature. Thus
Descartes's position is (1) that a sound physics presupposes a (certain, indubitable) knowledge of the fundamental forces; (2) that such
knowledge – prior to the rest of physics – is indeed possible; and
(3) that this knowledge is possible through, and *only* through, un-
aided thought. In *this* sense, Descartes demands, and claims to have
achieved, a "purely rational" physics – more accurately, a purely rational *foundation* for physics. In his *Rules for the Direction of the
Mind,* this demand is expressed, in connection with the particular
example of a problem in optics, as the stipulation that for a satisfactory solution of the problem it must be traced back to a knowledge
of *what a natural power in general is* – "this last being the most
absolute term in [the] whole series" (of conditions upon which the
solution depends).[12]

The role of experiment in Cartesian method can now be briefly characterized as follows: by experiment we learn the existence of features of our natural environment, which pose *problems* for science. The *solution* of such problems, the very task of physics, consists in the tracing back of these observed natural phenomena to their *fundamental causes* – that is, the demonstration that the phenomena do (or would) result from the fundamental principles of physics, themselves derived as we have seen from first philosophy, when we have correctly attributed the phenomena we observe to underlying structures of Cartesian matter-in-motion: that is, when we have constructed (to use a later terminology) the appropriate *mechanical model* for each phenomenon. How *this* is to be done is certainly the most vexing problem in the interpretation of Descartes's scientific method; but what is most important in respect of Descartes's historical influence on later seventeenth-century investigators is the fact that the early attempts of Descartes to proceed *systematically and with certainty* from observed phenomena to their causes (that is, to mechanical models that represent the *true* nature of the processes underlying the observed phenomena) were abandoned – perhaps even in some degree by Descartes himself – in favor of a far more tentative procedure of seeking for *likely* models, that might "save" or "satisfy" the phenomena, and whose correctness could be rendered at least *highly probable* by their success in doing so.[13] In short, the method of investigation of nature that eventually came to complement Cartesian metaphysics – a method that grew out of the *failure* of his more stringent original prescription – was that of attempting to *invent mechanical hypotheses* that would explain, with the help of "rational" deduction from the fundamental principles of motion, whatever was discovered by experiment.

One other feature of the intellectual environment in which Newton developed should be mentioned: namely, that many adherents to some variety of the "new philosophy" came to reject Descartes's identification of matter with whatever is extended, in favor of the classical view of *atomism*: that (a) there is void space as well as occupied space – the world is not a plenum; and (b) the ultimate parts of matter are "corpuscles" or "atoms": *rigid* and *indivisible* bodies.[14] Within this "revisionist" conception – also known as the "corpuscular philosophy" – it was still maintained as a fundamental tenet that all the processes of nature consist in the motions of bodies, and that all natural *changes* of motion are occasioned by direct actions of one body *pushing* on another.[15] The features common to this position and Descartes's constituted the framework of the celebrated "mechanical philosophy." It is *from* the mechanical philosophy that the metaphysics, as well as the natural philosophy, of Newton *departed*: that philosophy was Newton's point of departure; and he indeed departed from it, in profound ways.

Taking Descartes as the first point of comparison, a radical difference between his view of metaphysics and Newton's lies in the fact that for Newton metaphysics is *not* the "root" or foundation of natural philosophy – the "beginning of wisdom." His position may rather be said to agree with that of Aristotle – a conception symbolized by the fact that the followers of Aristotle placed his treatises on first philosophy "after the physical ones."[16] Aristotle, distinguishing between what is "first and better known to nature" and what is "first and better known to us," regards the most basic principles – "prior," *in nature*, to those of the special sciences – as *to be known* only *after* the special sciences themselves have been established. An indication that Newton thought similarly is to be seen in the fact that his chief published discussions of the metaphysics of nature, and of his views concerning God in relation to nature, occur *at the end* of his two great treatises: in the General Scholium to the *Mathematical Principles of Natural Philosophy*, and at the end of the long concluding Query 31 in Book 3 of the *Opticks*. In his discussion of theological matters in the General Scholium, Newton says of God: "We know him only by his most wise and excellent contrivances of things, and final causes"; and concludes that discussion with the words: "And thus much concerning God; to discourse of whom *from the appearances of things*, does certainly belong to Natural Philosophy" (emphasis added). In Query 31 of the *Opticks*, after a long review of the most diverse phenomena (chiefly of chemistry), he says: "*All these things being consider'd*, it seems *probable* to me, that God in the Beginning form'd Matter in solid, massy, hard, impenetrable, moveable Particles, [etc.]" (again, emphases added here). In both places the views put forward are thus expressed as, in point of knowledge, *a posteriori*; and in the latter place, the view is explicitly described as *probable* (this is a lower degree of confidence than Newton attaches to his principal results in physics).[17] Further, it is not only man's knowledge of God, among doctrines one would call metaphysical, that Newton describes as deriving from experience rather than from pure reason. In the preface to the first edition of the *Principia*, and in the third of the "Rules of Philosophizing" at the beginning of Book 3 of that work,[18] Newton expresses the opinion that (a) *geometry* is founded in experience (in, as he says, "mechanical practice"), and (b) so is *everything* we know about *bodies* (in particular, their "extension, hardness, impenetrability, mobility, and *vis inertiae*"). This is a matter to which we shall return later; for the present, let it suffice to note that these statements leave little scope, in Newton's view of knowledge, whether in "first philosophy" or in natural philosophy, for the *a priori* or purely rational.[19]

Let us now turn to the content of Newton's metaphysical doctrine: what, according to him, is the basic constitution of the world – what are its constituents, and how are they interconnected?

The question does not have an entirely straightforward answer. In order to see why – and in order to arrive at as clear as possible a picture of his mature doctrine – it will be useful to pay some attention to the apparent development of Newton's view over time.

It is clear from Newton's early notebooks[20] that he moved rapidly, in his student years, towards adherence to the general views in natural philosophy represented by Galileo and – in part – Descartes, in opposition to the scholastic ("peripatetic") teachings; and also that he quickly became critical of some of the basic tenets of Descartes. For example, in a very early manuscript Newton discusses with evident skepticism various scholastic views about projectile motion;[21] argues against Aristotle's rejection of a vacuum;[22] and notes without comment Descartes's definition of motion in the strict sense of the term: "Cartes defines motion . . . to be the Transplantation of one part of matter or one body from the vicinity of those bodys which immediately touch it and seem to rest, to the vicinity of others."[23] Not long afterwards, in what is clearly an attempt (somewhat awkward) to sketch a systematic theory of motion, Newton states his own definition: "When a Quantity is translated/passeth from one parte of Extension to another it is saide to move"[24] – a definition not very remarkable, but which clearly deviates from the conception advocated by Descartes in his *Principles*. The result was a position that fell within the framework of the corpuscular philosophy. It is important to note, in particular, that in the manuscript last cited Newton offers a general characterization of force, as follows: "Force is the pressure or crouding of one body upon another."[25]

We come now to a crucial document, and what the present commentator regards as a crucial turn in the character and depth of Newton's thought on fundamental issues. The document – first published in 1962, in the original Latin followed by an (unfortunately defective) English translation[26] – is of a curious kind. It is an incomplete and untitled draft of what was evidently intended to be a treatment of hydrostatics, and begins with the statement: "De Gravitatione et aequipondio fluidorum et solidorum in fluidis scientiam duplici methodo tradere convenit"; that is: "It is fitting to treat the science of the gravitation [i.e., the "weighing down"] and equilibrium of fluids and of solids in fluids by a twofold method."[27] The opening phrase, "De gravitatione et aequipondio fluidorum," is the title by which the piece has come to be known.

What makes the fragment both odd and extraordinarily interesting is the fact that, after a brief introduction and four definitions, there occurs a digression into questions of metaphysics, taking up about two-thirds of the entire length of the manuscript; then the technical presentation resumes, with another fifteen definitions followed by two propositions (with five corollaries) – and breaks off. Thus in spite of the title under which it is known, and its evident original intent, the entire interest of the piece is as an essay in metaphysics – of a kind that is unique among Newton's writings.

The first four definitions are introduced and stated as follows:

Definitions

The terms quantity, duration, and space are too well known to be susceptible of definition by other words.

Def: 1. A place is a part of space that a thing fills adequately.
Def: 2. A body is that which fills a place.
Def: 3. Rest is remaining in the same place.
Def: 4. Motion is change of place.

Newton explains that in saying that a body *fills* (Latin: *implet)* a space, he means to imply "so fully occupies it as utterly to exclude other things of the same kind (other bodies) as if it were an impenetrable thing." Why, one may ask, "as if"? Does not a body's exclusion of other bodies mean that it *is* an "impenetrable thing"? The answer to this emerges later: Newton believes that *minds*, as well as bodies, have their definite places in space; and he believes that bodies and minds can occupy the same – or overlapping – places; so bodies are not absolutely impenetrable, but are so only to one another.

After a few further preliminary clarifications, Newton calls attention to the fact that in these definitions he has departed fundamentally from the doctrines of the Cartesians: both in *distinguishing* between space and bodies, and in that he has "determined motion with respect to the parts of that space, not with respect to the positions of the contiguous bodies." It is this remark that leads to the metaphysical digression, in which Newton is concerned, first, to refute the theory of space and motion of Descartes's *Principles of Philosophy*; then to present his own conception of the nature of space (and, with less elaboration, of time); finally – and with greatest originality – to present his conception of the nature of *body* – how it is related to, and how distinguished from, space.

The refutation of Descartes on place and motion has two main parts. In the first, Newton argues that Descartes himself, in the development of his physics in Parts 2 and 3 of his *Principles*, proceeds in a way that is inconsistent with his own theory of motion, and thus "seems to acknowledge" its inadequacy. Since we are not here primarily concerned with Descartes, one example may suffice – the one that is most directly connected with Newton's evidence for the view he himself favors. According to Descartes, the earth – and, indeed, each of the planets – is, "if we are speaking properly and according to the truth of the matter" (Newton paraphrases the second phrase as "according to the philosophical sense"), *not moved*, but rather *at rest*; since each of these bodies, according to Descartes's theory of the planetary system, is carried around the sun by a material vortex: each planet, then, is at rest *relative to the bodies that immediately surround it*, and is therefore at rest in the "proper" sense of the word.[28] This is the basis of Descartes's claim that his view in the *Principles* is immune to the charge of attributing motion to the earth. But, Newton points out, in his *dynamical theory* of the planetary system Descartes attributes to the planets *a tendency to recede from the Sun* on account of *their motion around it*. So in developing the principles *of his philosophy* Descartes makes use of a conception of motion that is *not* the one he puts forward as "proper and according to the truth of the matter"; or, again to use Newton's paraphrase, "according to the philosophical sense."[29]

In the second main part of his argument against the Cartesian theory of place and motion, Newton shows that the basic principles of the physics of motion generally agreed upon in his time cannot even be *formulated* within the conceptual framework provided by that Cartesian theory. (Thus we may say that whereas in the first part Newton had shown Descartes to be in contradiction with himself, in the second part he shows that the contradiction is not merely with some *special* features of *Cartesian* physics: rather, it is with the general principles – to which Descartes himself was a contributor – that underlie all of what for him is "modern" physics.) Again it will suffice here to consider one central point. Newton says it follows from Descartes's position "that a moving body has no determinate velocity and no definite line in which it moves. And," he adds, "what is much more, that the velocity of a body moving without resistance cannot be said to be uniform, nor the line straight in which its motion is accomplished." In other words, what is still called the "first law of motion" *does not make sense* in Cartesian terms. The reason is straightforward. In Descartes's terms, "according to the truth of the matter," a body's motion should be described in relation to bodies in immediate contact with it that "are regarded as at rest"; these define the body's "place" (at a given time). But over time, bodies that were once relatively at rest will in general no longer be so – they will disperse. Therefore, over time, these (former) "places" will no longer exist; so that it will be impossible to speak of the *distance a body has traveled* (the distance between its present and its former place) – and equally impossible to speak of the *path* it has followed (the ordered array of places through which it has passed).[30]

It is important to note that this argument of Newton's does not claim to rest on principles that are epistemologically *a priori*. When he claims that Descartes's concept of motion is *not the one needed for physics*, he is speaking of the *existing* physics of his time – and, indeed, of features of that physics that are *accepted* by the Cartesians as well as by himself. This physics had had some considerable success; therefore it was reasonable to make use of its principles, and to frame basic conceptions so as to be consistent with them. Objections should be considered out of order, unless (a) they are drawn from demonstrable inadequacies in the application of the accepted theory to phenomena, or (b) the objector has an alternative to offer that is at least as good as that theory, and better in respect of the points he objects to.[31]

Newton summarizes his results so far in the following words:

It follows indubitably that Cartesian motion is not motion, for it has no velocity, no direction, and hence there is no space or distance traversed by it. So it is necessary that the determination of places, and hence of local motion, be referred to some immobile being, such as extension alone, or space in so far as it is seen to be truly distinct from body. And this the Cartesian Philosopher may the more willingly acknowledge, if only he notices that Descartes himself had an idea of extension as distinct from bodies, which he wished to distinguish from corporeal extension by calling it "generic." Art. 10, 12, & 18, part 2 Princip. And that the whirlings of the vortices, from which he deduced the force of the aether in receding from the centers (and therefore his whole mechanical Philosophy), are tacitly referred to this generic extension.

He turns, then, to the question of what, in his own view, the nature is of the "immobile being" – *space* or *extension* itself, distinguished from body – to which places and motions are to be referred. He raises three possibilities, arising out of the philosophical tradition, as to how he might "now be expected" to define extension: either as itself a kind of *substance*; or as a kind of *accident* (note: this was the standard philosophical term for an *attribute*: anything that can be "predicated" of a substance); or, third, as "*simply nothing.*" The third alternative looks odd, but is undoubtedly meant to refer to the anti-establishment ancient tradition of atomism, in which the fundamental ontological contrast of atoms and the void was also expressed as that of "being" and "non-being." Newton repudiates all three answers, and offers instead something rather new: he says that extension "has a certain mode of existence of its own, which agrees neither with substances nor accidents." It is not substance for two reasons: (1) "because it subsists, not absolutely of itself, but as, so to speak, an emanative effect of God, and a certain affection of every being"; (2) because it is not something that *acts.*[32] The first point we must presently examine more closely. The second is of capital importance for Newton's view: he says that although philosophers do not traditionally define substance as "a being that can *act* upon something," they in fact all tacitly hold such a definition – "as for instance is plain from this, that they would easily concede extension to be a substance like a body if only it could move and could exercise the actions of a body; and on the other hand, they would by no means concede a body to be a substance if it neither could move nor arouse any sensation or perception in any mind whatever." To be noted well, then: (a) the definitive criterion of substantiality is the ability to act; (2) one of the characteristics that belongs to the essential nature of *bodies*, to their character as substances, is their ability to arouse perceptions in a mind. As to the question whether space is an "accident" – something that can exist only as "inhering in some subject" – Newton denies this emphatically: we can, he says, clearly conceive of empty space, and thus of "extension existing as it were without any subject"; "we believe it to exist wherever we imagine there to be no bodies; nor are we to believe that, if God were to annihilate some body, its extension [that is: the *place* of that body] would perish with it." This leads Newton to his repudiation of the third putative answer as well: so far is extension from being "nothing," that "it is more 'something' than is an accident, and rather approaches to the nature of substance" – namely, in that it needs no "subject" to "support" its existence. Further: "Of nothing, no Idea is given, nor has it any properties, but of extension we have an Idea the clearest of all, namely by abstracting the affections and properties of body so that there remains only the uniform and unlimited stretching out of space in length breadth and depth."[33]

But what does Newton mean by the statement quoted under (1) in the preceding paragraph, that space or extension "subsists . . . as, so to speak, an emanative effect of God, and a certain affection of every being"? There are a number of problems to be considered here: What are we to understand by an "emanative effect"? What *reason* can there be for Newton's statement that space is "an emanative effect of God"? And if space subsists as "a certain *affection*" – that is, a kind of "qualification" or "mode" – of every thing ("every being"), then how can it to be said *not* to be an "accident," but more like substance than accident? Of these questions, the first is very much clarified by what Newton goes on to say, in six numbered articles in which he proposes "to show not only that [space] is something, but what it is."

The fourth of these articles begins as follows:

Space is an affection of a being just as a being. No being exists or can exist that does not have relation in some way to space. God is everywhere, created minds are somewhere, and a body in the space that it fills; and whatever is neither everywhere nor anywhere is not. And hence it follows that space is an emanative effect of the first-existing being, for if I posit any being whatever I posit space. And the like may be affirmed of Duration: namely both are affections or attributes of a being in accordance with which the quantity of the existence of any individual is denominated, as to amplitude of presence and perseverance in its being. So the quantity of the existence of God, according to duration has been eternal, and according to the space in which he is present, infinite; and the quantity of the existence of a created thing, according to duration has been just so much as the duration since its first existence, and according to the amplitude of its presence, as much as the space in which it is.[34]

This paragraph sheds great light on the statement that extension is an emanative effect of God. In the first place, although Newton's theology is deeply involved in that statement, *and* in this paragraph, the latter actually makes it quite explicit that Newton does *not* derive his "Idea" of space – its ontological status included – *from* his theology (as has often been claimed); for he tells us that if *anything* is posited, space is posited. He infers – quite simply – that space (in some sense) "results from" *the existence of anything.* Now, in Newton's theology – which in some respects was heterodox, but certainly not on this point – the "first-existing being" was God, whom he regards as the creator of the universe; so space (in some sense) "results from" the existence of God. However, what follows from Newton's "metaphysics of space" is precisely the weaker statement he makes in this paragraph: that space is (some kind of) effect of the existence of anything; and therefore, of the first-existing thing.

But what kind of effect? What is here meant by an "emanative effect"? Here some historical consideration of the word is helpful. In the philosophical tradition of the neo-Platonic school, there was a quite elaborate doctrine of "emanations" from the godhead; and Newton was closely acquainted with members of the group at Cambridge University known as the Cambridge Platonists – most closely with Henry More. However, the neo-Platonist doctrine, in its ancient version, was concerned with the origin of the universe; whereas – as we shall presently see – Newton in the piece we are discussing sharply distinguishes between space, as an emanative effect of God, and both bodies and minds, as God's "creations." As for the Cambridge doctrines, it is instructive that the *Oxford English Dictionary*, under "emanation," 1.1, quotes the following from Henry More's philosophical *Poems*: "Man's soul's not by Creation...Wherefore let't be by emanation." On the one hand, this supports the view that "emanation," whatever it is, is to be *distinguished* from creation; on the other hand, it is clearly *not* in agreement with Newton's view – expressed in the very paragraph we are discussing – that human "souls" (or "minds") are *created*; indeed, that *all* minds save that of God are so[35] (for Newton writes, clearly intending a complete survey of *all* the kinds of "being" [or "beings"]: "God is everywhere, *created minds* are somewhere, and a body is in the space it fills"). So the grounds for thinking that Newton's theory of emanation is neo-Platonic, or "Cambridge Platonic," are very weak. On the other hand, the *OED* in the same entry, I.I.c, gives the definition (noted as obsolete): "Logical development from premises; inference" – with an illustrative quotation from the *Logic* of T. Spencer (1628); and gives in II.3.b the related definition *(not* designated obsolete): "A necessary consequence or result" – with two illustrative quotations, the first from Richard Steele in *The Tatler* (1710), the other the following phrase, from John Stuart Mill's *Utilitarianism* (1861): "A direct emanation from the first principles of morals."

But this sense of the word – simply *a necessary consequence*, with no connotation of "causal efficacy" or "action" – *exactly* fits the rest of what Newton says; indeed, this meaning might have been inferred directly from Newton's words: "[S]pace is an emanative effect of the first-existing being, for *if I posit any being whatever I posit space"*: the second clause tells us precisely what the first clause *means.*

For our second question – what reason Newton thought there was that justified this view of space as an "emanative effect" of whatever exists – it is to be noted that he describes the proposition as *inferred from* a preceding one: that "no being exists or can exist that does not have relation in some way to space"; and this in turn he founds upon an enumeration of all the kinds of "beings" he takes actually to exist, and their several relations to space. In the light of this, and of the fact that there is no suggestion – here or indeed anywhere the present writer knows of in Newton's writings – of an *a priori* epistemological ground for any item of knowledge, it appears reasonable to conclude that the reason in question is an empirical one: our experience affords no grounds for a conception of real existents – beings capable of acting – that do not have an appropriate relation to space.

It might well be asked how *experience* could be said to ground Newton's assertion that "God is everywhere." But first – although the claim that God is everywhere *present in space* was a controversial one, and even somewhat dangerous to advocate – Newton thought the doctrine of the *ubiquity* or *omnipresence* of God amply founded in the tradition of revealed truth; and second, he clearly thought experience shows that *minds* can act only *where they are*;[36] so the doctrine of God's omnipotence (likewise founded in revelation) itself entails his omnipresence. As to the possible outright heretical implications of the doctrine, Newton guards himself in the following passage (the second paragraph of the same fourth article as quoted above), which is of interest in its own right for its further elaboration of Newton's view both of space and of time ("duration"):

Moreover lest anyone imagine from this that God is extended and made of divisible parts like a body: it should be known that spaces themselves are not actually divisible, and furthermore that each being has its own proper mode of presence in spaces. Thus, the relation to space of duration is far different from that of body. For we do not ascribe different durations to the different parts of space, but say that they all endure together. A moment of the duration of Rome and of London is the same, as is one of the Earth and of [any] star in the entire heavens. And just as we understand any one moment of duration to be thus diffused through all spaces, in its own way, without any conception of its parts: so it is no more contradictory that a Mind can likewise, in its own way, be diffused through space without any conception of parts.

But this in turn calls for commentary. What does Newton intend by the statement that "spaces themselves are not actually divisible"? He certainly does *not* mean that, for instance, a line-segment is not, in the ordinary sense, "divisible into two equal parts." That space has parts is implied by Newton's definition of *place*, quoted earlier; and the first numbered article in the series enumerating the properties of extension begins with the assertion: "Space can be distinguished everywhere into parts whose common boundaries we are accustomed to call surfaces; and these surfaces can be distinguished everywhere into parts, whose common boundaries we call lines; and these lines in turn can be distinguished everywhere into parts that we call points." Newton means, rather, that this "distinguishing into parts" is not an "*actual*" division: the parts of space are not "divisible," or *separable* from one another, as the parts of a(n ordinary) body[37] are.

So we must say: *spaces* have *parts*, but are not "actually divisible";
God, furthermore, who is present everywhere in space, *not only* is
indivisible, but *does not have parts at all*: this is what the analogy
of "durations" emphasizes: moments of duration, too, are present
throughout space, but do not have spatial – or any – parts; just as,
again, on Newton's conception of ("absolute") space, *points of space*
are present throughout time, but do not have temporal – or any –
parts.

Finally (in this series of questions), as to the sense in which space
can be said to subsist "as a certain affection" of every being, and yet
not to be an "accident," but "more like substance than accident,"
Newton has already given a part of the answer explicitly: space is
not an accident because *we can conceive it to exist without any
subject.* But, says the objector, can we – on Newton's view – conceive space without *any* subject of which it is an "affection"? Can
we conceive space without God? We face again the question of the
relation of Newton's conception of space to his theology, on which a
view contrary to the one that has perhaps most often been held has already been stated above. But there is in fact explicit testimony from
Newton himself. Later in the piece under discussion, in reverting to
his objections to the Cartesian identification of body with extension,
Newton says the following (emphases added here):

If we say with Descartes that extension is body, do we not manifestly offer
a path to Atheism, both because extension is not a creature but has existed
eternally, *and because we have an absolute Idea of it without any relationship to God*, and therefore *we are able to conceive of it as existent while
feigning the non-existence of God?*[38]

That, surely, is decisive! Space, the existence of space, or extension,
follows from that of anything whatsoever; but extension does not
require a subject in which it "inheres," as a property; and it can
be conceived as existent without presupposing any *particular* thing,
God included. On the other hand, it is an "affection of every being."
We can perhaps understand this better with the help of another article in Newton's enumeration of the fundamental characteristics of
space – the third article:

The parts of space are immobile ... For just as the parts of duration are individuated by their order, so that (for example) if yesterday could change places
with today and become the later, it would lose its individuality and be no

longer yesterday but today: So the parts of space are individuated by their positions, so that if any two could interchange their positions, they would at the same time interchange their individualities, and each be converted numerically into the other. The parts of duration and of space are understood to be the same as they truly are solely by their order and mutual positions; nor have they any other principle of individuation beyond that order and those positions – which therefore cannot change.

This can be taken, in rather modern terms, as saying that space is a *structure*, or "relational system," which can be conceived of independently of anything else; its constituents are individuated just by *their relations to one another, as elements of this relational system*. But the system, or its constitutive elements, none the less can *and must* "affect," in the appropriate way, all things that exist: all existing things have spatial and temporal relations to one another by virtue of their having, each one of them, the appropriate kind of relation to the parts of space and of duration (again: *God is everywhere, created minds are somewhere, and a body is in the place it fills* – but, for the last two, we must add: *at each moment of its own duration*).

Having presented his view of the ontological status of space, Newton turns to the corresponding question about *bodies*. Before describing his answer, a comment about a rather curious historical connection seems in order – both for its intrinsic interest, and because it bears upon the question whether the views of this manuscript fragment can be taken to be those held by Newton in his mature years (opinion being divided as to the date of the fragment itself).[39]

In Locke's *Essay concerning Human Understanding* (Book 4, ch. x, §18) the following remark appears (but not in the first edition – 1690; it was introduced only in the second edition – 1694): "possibly, if we would emancipate ourselves from vulgar Notions... we might be able to aim at some dim and seeming conception how Matter might at first be made, and begin to exist by the power of [the] eternal first being"; but he immediately adds that to discuss this "would perhaps lead us too far from the Notions, on which the Philosophy now in the World is built," and so excuses himself from saying more about it. In his commentary on Locke's *Essay*, his *New Essays on Human Understanding* (in dialogue form), Leibniz's representative, Theophilus, responding to Philalethes, who presents the thoughts expressed by Locke, says of this: "You have given me real pleasure, sir, by recounting something of a profound thought of your able author, which his overscrupulous caution has stopped him from offering in its entirety. It would be a great pity if he suppressed it and, having brought us to a certain point with our mouths watering, left us standing there. I assure you, sir, that I believe there is something fine and important hidden under this rather enigmatic passage."[40] The second French edition of the *Essay* (1729 – after the deaths of all three concerned: Locke, who died in 1704; Leibniz, 1716; Newton, 1727) contained a note to this passage by the translator, Pierre Coste: "Here Mr. Locke excites our curiosity, without being inclined to satisfy it. Many persons, imagining that he must have communicated to me this mode of explaining the creation of matter" – Coste had served as Locke's amanuensis for several years, and had translated the work under Locke's supervision – "requested, when my translation first appeared, that I would inform them what it was; but I was obliged to confess that Mr. Locke had not made even me a partner in the secret. At length, long after his [Locke's] death, Sir Isaac Newton, to whom I was accidentally speaking of this part of Mr. Locke's book, discovered to me the whole mystery. He told me, smiling, that he himself had suggested to Mr. Locke this way of explaining the creation of matter; and that the thought had struck him one day, when this question chanced to come up in a conversation between himself, Mr. Locke, and the late Earl of Pembroke. He thus described to them his hypothesis:" – and there follows a brief statement of the same account of the creation of matter that appears in the present chapter.[41] It is clear, then, that the account we are about to consider, whenever it may have been written down, was in its general lines communicated by Newton to Locke at some time in the early 1690s. It is clear, also, that this account was considered by Locke to be a very radical philosophical departure – and that Leibniz thought that it must indeed be so, and was very eager to learn what it was.[42]

As all this has intimated, Newton's analysis of the fundamental nature of bodies takes the form of a discussion of *how bodies might have been created*. In one respect, this is of secondary importance; for one can reasonably see it as merely a vivid way of focusing attention on what bodies "fundamentally *are*" – to "create a body somewhere," God has to bring it to pass that *whatever* bodies "fundamentally are," by hypothesis not there before, *comes to be* there (for Newton is not going to tell us "how" God does this in the sense of analyzing his *power* to bring such-and-such to pass: this power he takes for granted, since he takes God to be omnipotent; he is going to tell us "how" a body is created, rather, in the sense of *exactly what has to be brought about* to achieve such a creation). To put the point another way: what "God creates" is simply "the fundamental constitution of corporeal nature"; we might leave God out of the story, and take it to be a description, or analysis, *of* the fundamental constitution of corporeal nature.

In another respect, however, there is something very important that this strategy of Newton implies – something that can be seen from the words with which this part of his discussion is introduced:

Extension having been described, for the other part the nature of bodies remains to be explained. Of this, however, since it exists not necessarily but by the divine will, the explanation will be more uncertain, because it is not at all given to us to know the limits of the divine power – namely, whether matter could have been created in one way only, or whether there are several ways by which other beings similar to bodies might have been produced. And although it hardly seems credible that God could create beings like bodies, that should perform all their actions and exhibit all their phaenomena, and yet in essential and metaphysical constitution should not be bodies: since nevertheless I do not have a clear and distinct perception of this matter, I should not dare to affirm the contrary, and accordingly I will not say positively what the nature of bodies is, but rather shall describe a certain kind of beings, in every way similar to bodies, whose creation we cannot fail to acknowledge to be within the power of God – and which thus we cannot certainly declare not to be bodies.

So Newton distinguishes between the epistemological status of his theory of space – which he has presented as something he regards as exceptionally clear in conception (or "Idea"), and as entirely convincing in its doctrine – and that of his theory of body, which is fundamentally *conjectural*, because bodies, unlike space, are *effects of God's will*;[43] and it is not given to us to know all the ways in which the exercise of that will might accomplish given observable effects. This, again, is a proposition that can be paraphrased non-theologically: "Our conception of the fundamental constitution of nature – that is, of the *substantial world* of *things capable of acting* – is a conception of how every phenomenon we observe *could be* effected; but since we have no epistemologically a priori knowledge of this, the possibility always remains that those phenomena *are* effected in some (perhaps even very) *different* way."

Newton's creation story starts by supposing that a corporeal world already exists; what, Newton asks, would God have to do to create a *new* body – or, rather, what *might* he do that would create a new entity *indistinguishable from the bodies we know*?

First, he says, "let us feign empty spaces scattered through the world, some one of which, defined by certain limits, by the divine power becomes impervious to bodies": bodies simply cannot enter this region, but are, let us say, constrained to bounce back from its boundary. Such a "region of impenetrability" will be like a body, except that (so far as we have gone) it will be immobile. Second, then, we may "feign that impenetrability not conserved always in the same part of space, but able to be transferred hither and thither according to certain laws, yet so that the quantity and shape of that impenetrable space are not changed."[44]

This is not the last step, but it is worth pausing over. First, one may ask whether, according to Newton, it is in some way a "conceptual necessity" that bodies be impenetrable. The answer to this question – at least, at the stage of the composition of the third of the "Rules of Philosophizing" in Book 3 of the *Principia*[45] – is unequivocally negative; for in the discussion of that Rule, Newton says: "That all bodies are impenetrable, we gather, not from reason, but from sensation." Second, we should note that in conferring mobility upon the new (quasi-)bodies – that is, in making the property of impenetrability "able to be transferred hither and thither" – it is essential that this "transfer" be regulated by suitable *laws*. Of these, all Newton specifies is that the transfer *preserve the size and shape* of the regions of impenetrability; this, in effect, gives to the new (quasi-)*particles* the distinguishing property of (rigid) *atoms*. It is, however, clear that the motion of these new things is to be governed by the "first law of motion": namely, that, in the absence of encounters with bodies (or with other "quasi-bodies"), a quasi-particle is propagated through space with uniform speed in a straight line (understood to include the case of *rest* – that is, no "transfer" at all); and that when encounters do occur, they are to be governed by the ordinary laws of impact (which, in turn, implies that each quasi-particle is characterized by a parameter corresponding – in "ordinary" particles – to their *mass*).

So far, we have a constitution for (quasi-)corporeal nature that looks very much like just what is needed for bodies, according to the corpuscular philosophy: rigid and indivisible ultimate particles, interacting only by impact – *"by impulse*, and nothing else," as Locke says: "It being impossible to conceive, that Body should operate on what it does not touch...or when it does touch, operate any other way than by Motion."[46] Yet Locke *also* tells us the following:

Another *Idea* we have of Body, is the power of *communication of Motion by impulse*; and of our Souls, the power of *exciting of Motion by Thought*. These *Ideas*, the one of Body, the other of our Minds, every days experience clearly furnishes us with: But if here again we enquire how this is done, we *are equally in the dark*. For in the communication of Motion by impulse, wherein as much Motion is lost to one Body, as is got to the other, which is the ordinariest case, we can have no other conception, but of the passing of Motion out of one Body into another; which, I think, is as obscure and unconceivable, as how our Minds move or stop our Bodies by Thought; which every moment we find they do...I think, we have as many, and as clear *Ideas* belonging to Spirit, as we have belonging to Body, the Substance of each being equally unknown to us; and the *Idea* of Thinking in Spirit, as clear as of Extension in Body; and the communication of Motion by Thought, which we attribute to Spirit, is as evident, as that by impulse, which we ascribe to Body. Constant Experience makes us sensible of both of these, though our narrow Understandings can comprehend neither. For when the Mind would look beyond those original *Ideas* we have from Sensation or Reflection, and penetrate into their Causes, and manner of production, we find still it discovers nothing but its own short-sightedness.[47]

In other words, according to Locke, the only way in which we can conceive bodies to act, is a way in which we *cannot* conceive bodies to act: it is a way that is *"obscure and unconceivable,"* and is beyond the capacity of "our narrow Understandings [to] comprehend."

Locke is here wrestling with a fundamental incoherence in the philosophical foundations of the corpuscular philosophy; the fact that he appears to contradict himself – that he *does* contradict himself! – is testimony to the basic honesty of his mind, and to his penetrating insight. For although he accepts the corpuscular philosophy as the most plausible hypothesis about nature, and accepts the widespread view that it represents the only basis on which we can *hope* to understand natural processes, he also sees (sometimes, at least) that the underpinnings of that philosophy are *not* "clear and distinct principles" such as the Cartesians thought they had, but principles whose *own* grounds are *obscure*. Partly for this reason, Locke draws very pessimistic conclusions concerning the possible advance of science; indeed, he thinks that a truly *systematic* knowledge of nature is beyond human capacity.[48]

Newton sees the very same impossibility of a "transparent" system of fundamental principles; but he faces it squarely, and it does not create for him a desperate predicament: the *fundamental* constitution of nature is simply not (directly) open to us; but we can nevertheless form perfectly clear conceptions of *what structures may underlie phenomena;* not *why* they do – nor even for certain *that* they do – but what structures *would suffice* as a basis for the constitution of the world we know, at the stage of knowledge we have reached. And what allows us to do this is a clear understanding of the *lawful relationships* that we have so far managed to discover among phenomena. Thus, first of all, we have "of extension an Idea the clearest of all." How did we obtain it? From experience – and, of course, *thought* (in particular, thought of the kind we call "mathematical") *based* upon experience: "geometry is founded in mechanical practice"; and "it is the glory of geometry that from [a] few principles, *brought from without*, it is able to produce so many things."[49] And in the second place, we have a perfectly clear conception of those attributes of bodies that the mechanical, corpuscular, philosophy has conceived as fundamental, including the laws governing the interactions of those bodies: the laws of impact. *That* means, in Newton's view, that we have a sufficiently clear conception of *what bodies are* if the mechanical philosophy is true.

To appreciate the clarifying power of this analysis, it is helpful to describe another perplexity in which Locke finds himself. In agreement with *both* the Aristotelian tradition *and* the Cartesian philosophy, Locke calls all "real existents" *substances;* and he asks what goes to make up our *"Ideas* of Substances."[50] His general answer is exemplified by one of his favorite examples: "the greatest part of the *Ideas,* that make up our complex *Idea* of *Gold,* are Yellowness, great Weight, Ductility, Fusibility, and Solubility in *Aqua Regia, etc.* all united together in an unknown *Substratum.*"[51] This "unknown substratum," the "idea" of which makes a part of *all* our ideas of particular substances according to Locke, he calls, simply, "substance" (or "substance in general"). At the same time, however, Locke tells us that we have of substance *no idea at all:*

I confess, there is [an] *Idea,* which would be of general use for Mankind to have ... and that is the *Idea of Substance,* which we neither have, nor can have, by *Sensation* or *Reflection*...We have no such *clear Idea* at all, and therefore signify nothing by the word *Substance*, but only an uncertain supposition of we know not what...which we take to be the *substratum*, or support, of those *Ideas* we do know.[52]

There has been much discussion of the precise nature of Locke's dilemma here – that of holding both that we *require* a certain "idea," and that we do not *have* it. If we "do not have" the idea, how can it be an *idea* at all – how can we know what it *is* that we need but do not have? The following is a passage that helps to clarify the issue: "[I]n Substances, besides the several distinct simple *Ideas* that make them up, the confused one of Substance, or of an unknown Support and Cause of their Union, is always a part."[53] What this suggests we "need" is an *answer* to the twofold question: "(1) *In what* do the qualities we attribute to a substance *exist together*? (2) What is the *cause* of their existing thus together?"

Newton's analysis may be said to separate these two questions. To the first, his answer is that the qualities that fundamentally constitute a body can be coherently and clearly conceived to *exist in*, or to have as their "logical subject" or the metaphysical "support" of their "being," simply *extension*: regions or "parts" of space. In the language of later natural philosophy, the distribution of bodies through space can be described as a kind of *field* on space: the "field of impenetrability," characterized, at each point of space, by the simple indication "filled" or "not filled."[54] Newton's own comment upon this part of the question (in his summing-up, later in the piece) is illuminating, both of his own view and for the possible light it sheds on the perplexity Locke felt – since Newton (quite independently of Locke's thoughts on the matter) names a perplexity that his account *removes*:

[F]or the existence of these beings [– that is, the beings whose creation by God he has imagined –] it is unnecessary to feign some unintelligible substance to be given in which as in a subject a substantial form should inhere: extension and an act of the divine will suffice. Extension takes the place of the substantial subject in which the form of the body is conserved by the divine will; and that effect of the divine will is the form or formal reason of the body, denominating as a body every region of space in which it is produced.

Newton goes on to assimilate the "unintelligible substance," the need for which he claims he has obviated, to the "materia prima" posited by the scholastics:[55] the notion of a totally "formless" ultimate "support" of all forms or attributes; and says the following (Articles (3) and (4) of his summary):

(3) Between extension and the form imposed upon it there is almost the same Analogy that the Aristotelians posit between the *materia prima* and substantial forms, namely when they say that the same matter is capable of assuming all forms, and borrows the denomination of numerical body from its form. For thus I suppose that any form may be transferred through any space, and everywhere denominate the same body.

(4) They differ, however, in that extension...has more reality than *materia prima*, and also in that it is intelligible, as likewise is the form that I have assigned to bodies. For if there is any difficulty in this conception, it is not in the form that God imparts to space, but in the way in which he imparts it. But that is not to be taken for a difficulty, since the same [point] occurs with respect to the way we move our limbs, and nevertheless we do believe that we can move them. If that way were known to us, by parity of reason we should also know how God can move bodies, and expel them from a certain space terminated in a given figure, and prevent the expelled bodies or any others from entering into it again – that is, cause that space to be impenetrable and to assume the form of a body.

Here, then, we have Newton's answer (in effect) to the second part of the above-posed twofold Lockean question: what *causes* the *coexistence* of the basic qualities of his "new" or "quasi-"bodies, as well as *the laws of propagation and interaction*, which form a part of the essential character of these entities, is just "God's action" itself; or, in our neutral paraphrase, this coexistence and these laws just *are*, on this view, *the fundamental constitution of corporeal nature*. This may indeed be wrong – it is possible that the phenomena we know are produced in a different way; but *if* it is right, it is *enough*: the demand for a further "explanation" of this constitutional fact stems from the Cartesian illusion that we must in principle have a "clear and distinct" apprehension of the necessity of the basic constitution of nature – precisely the illusion that Locke on the one hand shares when he speaks of "impulse" as *the only way we can conceive bodies to act*, and that he on the other hand *explodes* when he asks: "Have we indeed a clear conception of this mode of transfer of motion?"

But there still remains a step to be taken in the creation of the "new" bodies. Why so? If the "beings" so far described have all the fundamental properties posited by the corpuscular philosophy, why is that not sufficient? The reason is this: we must ask, *would* these beings have *all* the attributes required for us to take them for bodies of the sort we know? In particular, how could we detect the existence of these beings *at all*? So far, we have assumed that *"ordinary"* bodies *already* exist (including our own bodies!). Then we could detect the "new" bodies by the interaction of ordinary bodies with them: for instance, we should perceive that ordinary bodies bounce off the new ones, and so detect their presence; *light* might be reflected from them, so that we could *see* them; etc. But the metaphysical hypothesis Newton intends to suggest is that what we have been calling "new" or "quasi-"bodies are in fact just the bodies we know. And for *this*, he says, it is necessary to suppose that these beings are endowed, further, with the power to *interact with minds*: "[t]hat they be able to excite various perceptions in the senses and the fancy in created minds, and in turn to be moved by the latter" – most especially, that they are able, when they form part of what he calls our "sensorium" (the crucial region of our brain), to induce specific forms of *awareness* as a consequence of specific motions on their part; and, correspondingly, that our acts of will cause suitable motions in those that initiate activity in what we now call our motor neurons.

This is another rather original idea. Descartes placed the "essence" of bodies in extension alone; to this, Locke objects that impenetrability, which he calls "solidity," is equally essential to bodies;[56] and in an important summary passage, he suggests as the "primary and original" *ideas* we have of *anything* the following: "*Extension, Solidity, Mobility*, or Power of being moved; which by our Senses we receive from Body: *Perceptivity*, or the Power of perception, or thinking; *Motivity*, or the Power of moving: which by reflection we receive from our Minds."[57] But Newton points out (again, quite without any acquaintance with Locke's discussion) that just as "mobility" is correlative with "motivity," so must *perceptibility* be correlative with perceptivity; that, indeed, contrary to what the grammatical formation of the words might suggest, "perceptivity" is a *susceptibility* to being *affected*: a process in which it is *bodies* that "act on" *minds*. That such a power is essential to bodies is something he argues for rather strongly:

But should anyone object that bodies not united to minds cannot directly arouse perceptions in minds, and that hence . . . this power is not essential to them: it should be noted that there is no question here of an actual union, but only of a faculty in bodies by which they are capable of a union through the forces of nature. From the fact that the parts of the brain, especially the finer ones to which the mind is united, are in a continual flux, new ones succeeding to those which fly away, it is manifest that that faculty is in all bodies. And, whether you consider divine action or corporeal nature, to remove this is no less [a violation of the nature with which God has endowed bodies] than to remove that other faculty by which bodies are enabled to transfer mutual actions amongst one another[58] – that is, to reduce body to empty space.

Towards the end of this lengthy digression,[59] Newton makes the claim that "the usefulness of the described Idea of bodies shines forth most in that it clearly involves and best confirms and explicates the chief truths of Metaphysics." What he goes on to contend is that the conception of body in question provides a powerful argument against atheism. But the end of this passage has an importance beyond, and quite independent of, its theological claims. Having argued that the chief, or even the only, support of atheism is the "prejudice" or "notion" of bodies "as if having in themselves a complete absolute and independent reality," he adds:

Thus the prejudice just mentioned ought to be laid aside, and substantial reality rather ascribed to these kinds of Attributes which are real and intelligible in themselves and do not require a subject in which they inhere ... And this we can manage without difficulty if (besides the Idea of body expounded above) we reflect that we can conceive of space existing without any subject, when we think of a vacuum ... In the same way, if we should have an Idea of that Attribute or power by which God, through the sole action of his will, can create beings: we should perhaps conceive that Attribute as it were subsisting of itself, without any substantial subject, and involving his other attributes. But while we cannot form an Idea of this Attribute, nor even of our own power by which we move our bodies, it would be rash to say what is the substantial foundation of minds.

The boldness of this would be hard to exaggerate. In his rejection of the notion of "substance" as having reference to what he calls an "unintelligible" support or subject of attributes, in favor of a notion of "substantiality" *of the attributes themselves* (the criterion of substantiality being, as indicated by him earlier, the role played in *actions*), Newton goes so far as to suggest that even God might be conceived entirely in terms of his attributes, if only we could form clear "Ideas" of these. It is well known that Newton's theologico-religious convictions (which he kept carefully concealed from all but a few very trusted contemporaries)[60] were unorthodox; in particular, that he rejected the doctrine of the Trinity. Well, of course the view of substantial reality described here would make not so much false, as entirely unintelligible, the proposition that God is "three persons, but one substance"!

However, as has been remarked, the reach of Newton's suggestion is by no means only theological; it bears explicitly upon the so-called "mind–body problem" – or, perhaps better put as Newton put it: upon the problem of understanding "the substantial foundation of minds." Just as in the theological case, the suggestion sets aside the distinction of "kinds of substance": mind–body dualism or monism, in favor of the program: *to seek to understand mental attributes and their relation to corporeal ones*. When these relations are sufficiently understood, Newton implies, we may expect to know all that there is to know about the "substantial foundation of minds"; *before* they are sufficiently understood,[61] "it would be rash to say what is the substantial foundation of minds."

It remains now to discuss what consequences for Newton's metaphysics resulted from his greatest discovery in natural philosophy: that of the law of universal gravitation.

The short answer is that this discovery led Newton to a quite new conception of the nature of what Descartes had called "a natural power in general"; that is, to a new conception of how it *may be fruitful* – not, as for Descartes, how *it is necessary* – to conceive of the "actions" that characterize nature, with a view to the deeper understanding of natural phenomena. In the Preface to the *Principia*, Newton formulates this conception in the following way: having first remarked that, whereas the ancients cultivated mechanics as the science of *machines* – that is, as the "art" of *moving weights* – his design in the present work concerns "not arts but philosophy," and his subject is "not manual but natural powers," he goes on:

And therefore we offer this work as mathematical principles of philosophy. For all the difficulty of philosophy seems to consist in this, from the phaenomena of motions to investigate the forces of Nature, and then from these forces to demonstrate the other phaenomena ... In the third book we give an example of this in the explication of the System of the World. For by the propositions mathematically demonstrated in the first books, we there derive from the celestial phaenomena, the forces of Gravity with which bodies tend to the Sun and the several Planets. Then from these forces by other propositions, which are also mathematical, we deduce the motions of the Planets, the Comets, the Moon, and the Sea. I wish we could derive the rest of the phaenomena of Nature by the same kind of reasoning from mechanical principles. For I am induced by many reasons to suspect that they may all depend upon certain forces by which the particles of bodies, by some causes hitherto unknown, are either mutually impelled towards each other and cohere in regular figures, or are repelled and recede from each other; which forces being unknown, Philosophers have hitherto attempted the search of Nature in vain. But I hope the principles here laid down will afford some light either to that, or some truer, method of Philosophy.[62]

This is the new program for natural philosophy: deriving the phenomena of nature from "mechanical principles," not in the sense previously understood by the mechanical philosophy, but in the sense of *principles governing forces of attraction and repulsion* – themselves to be discovered by reasoning from the phenomena, as in Book 3 of the *Principia* itself. It is important to note that the program is put forward as *tentative* and *open to revision*. But what bearing does this change have on Newton's metaphysics?

For the answer to this, we must consider Newton's exposition of the general framework of his system of mechanical principles, both in the *Principia* and near the end of that thirty-first Query of the *Opticks* to which brief reference has already been made.

At the opening of the *Principia* we find first a section of "Definitions," and then one of "Axioms, or Laws of Motion." Among the eight definitions, six treat of concepts associated with the general notion of *force*. Definition 3 tells us that the "innate force of matter" is "a power of resisting, by which every body, as much as in it lies, endeavours to persevere in its present state, whether it be of rest, or of moving uniformly forward in a right line." The paragraph of discussion following this definition introduces the alternative expression *vis inertiae* – "force of inactivity" – for this same power; makes the important remark that this force is quantitatively measurable by "the [mass of the] body whose force it is"; and explains further that whenever a force is "impressed" upon one body, *A*, by another body, *B*, so as to tend to change the condition of *A*, the force of inactivity is *exercised* in a twofold way: (a) in the degree to which *A* "withstands" the force impressed – i.e., in the *smallness* of the change of velocity that results; and (b) in that A, "by not easily giving way," recipro-cally "endeavours to change the state" of B. Definition 4 is of a term already used in the passage just described: it says that an "impressed force" is an action exerted upon a body, tending to change its state of rest or motion. One might assume from this that "intrinsic force" and "impressed force" are, for Newton, correlative contrary terms; but as we shall see, this would be not quite correct. The paragraph of explanation following this definition remarks first that impressed force "consists in the action only; and remains no longer in the body, when the action is over." Thus, whereas the "force of inactivity" is a *permanent* attribute of a body – not always *exercised*, but always *present* – impressed force is by its nature *episodic*. The explanation ends with the remark, "Impressed forces are of different origins; as from percussion, from pressure, from centripetal force." The phrase-ology here – a force said to be "from" another (kind of) force as its "origin" – is rather odd. But the point is this: the "intrinsic force of matter" is, in Newton's terminology, one of the "natural powers" or forces of nature. The various "origins" of impressed forces, too, are natural powers: permanent features of material nature, not tran-sient episodes. An *impressed* force is the *action* upon a body of one of these natural powers.

Of the three kinds of "origin" instanced by Newton, two – percus-sion and pressure – are recognizably the ones assumed by the me-chanical philosophy. It is the third – "centripetal force" – that is the characteristic novelty of the *Principia*; and Definitions 5–8 are devoted to aspects of this notion.

Definition 5 tells us simply that a centripetal force is one directed towards a point as center. In the paragraph of discussion, Newton cites three characteristic examples – "Gravity by which bodies tend to the centre of the Earth; Magnetism, by which iron tends to the loadstone; and that force, whatever it is, by which the Planets are perpetually drawn aside from the rectilinear motions, which other-wise they wou'd pursue, and made to revolve in curvilinear orbits." These, it is clear, rightly count as "forces of nature"; and the main business of the *Principia* will be to establish that the first and third of them are the same, and to establish the fundamental law that char-acterizes this force. Unfortunately, with an uncharacteristic lapse in clarity, Newton adds a fourth example: that of the force by which a sling holds a stone in its orbit about the hand. In what sense this example obscures the concept Newton has chiefly in view, we shall soon see.

The remaining three definitions concern three "quantities," or "measures," of a centripetal force, which Newton calls the *absolute*, the *accelerative*, and the *motive* quantities; and it is in his characterization of these three measures – above all, in the second paragraph of discussion following Definition 8, which paragraph is devoted to a fuller explication of all three measures – that Newton gives us the deepest information about his conception of a centripetal force itself as a natural power. Of the three definitions taken by themselves, the first two are, in different ways, a little puzzling. Definition 6 says that the absolute quantity of a centripetal force is the measure of that force "proportional to the efficacy of the cause that propagates it from the centre, through the spaces round about"; and Newton adds by way of example that "the magnetic force is greater in one load-stone and less in another, according to their sizes and strength." This makes clear the general idea of what it is that the absolute quantity is supposed to measure; however, it fails to tell us *how* this is to be measured: the phrase "proportional to the efficacy of the cause" presupposes that we know how to express the efficacy of the cause in a quantitative way.[63] But in spite of this, when the issue arises concretely, in the case of the force of gravity, the appropriate quantitative measure is entirely clear. With Definition 7, on the other hand, the quantity is explicitly named – the "accelerative quantity" of a centripetal force is its measure, "proportional to the velocity which it generates in a given time": in other words, the accelerative quantity is in effect just what we call the *acceleration* produced by the force; what is puzzling is Newton's remark in explanation of this notion: "Thus the force of the same loadstone is greater at less distance, and less at greater: also the force of gravity is greater in valleys, less on tops of exceeding high mountains; and yet less (as shall be hereafter shown) at greater distances from the body of the Earth; but at equal distances, it is the same everywhere..." The puzzle is, why choose *acceleration* as the measure that varies in this sort of fashion with distance? But here, the puzzle vanishes upon a little reflection. In the case of a magnet, acceleration is indeed *not* an appropriate choice for the measure Newton really has in mind; for it is by no means true (nor does Newton say it is) of the acceleration produced by a magnet that "at equal distances, it is the same everywhere." But that *is* true of gravitational force. This is the centrifugal force Newton is chiefly concerned with in the *Principia*, and he has formulated his *general* definition in a way that strictly fits only this *special* case. Finally, Definition 8 presents us with the quantity that we normally associate with the word "force" in Newtonian mechanics: it defines the motive quantity of a centripetal force as its measure, "proportional to the motion which it generates in a given time." Since (1) according to Newton's Definition 2 the "quantity of motion" is jointly proportional to the mass and the velocity of a body, and since (2) the quantity generated "in a given time" means, in more modern language, the *rate, per unit time*, with which it is generated, the definition says that the motive quantity measures the force by the *rate of change of momentum* produced thereby; in other words, it measures the force impressed upon a body by the product of the mass of the body and the resulting acceleration.

Newton considers these interrelated notions important enough to devote a few paragraphs to their further clarification. Of these the most important part, for our concerns, is the following:

These quantities of Forces, we may for brevity's sake call by the names of Motive, Accelerative, and Absolute forces; and for distinction sake consider them, with respect to the Bodies that tend to the centre; to the Places of those bodies; and to the Centre of force towards which they tend: That is to say, I refer the Motive force to the Body, as an endeavour and propensity of the whole towards a centre, arising from the propensities of the several parts taken together; the Accelerative force to the Place of the body, as a certain power or energy[64] diffused from the centre to all places around to move the bodies that are in them; and the Absolute force to the Centre, as indued with some cause, without which those motive forces would not be propagated through the spaces round about; whether that cause is some central body, (such as is the Load-stone, in the centre of the force of Magnetism, or the Earth in the centre of gravitating force) or any thing else that does not yet appear. For I here design to give a Mathematical notion of those forces, without considering their Physical causes and seats.

This passage describes the conception of what in a later terminology is called a *field of force*, distributed about – and everywhere tending towards – a center.[65] The "absolute quantity" of this force (this field) is meant to characterize the strength of the field *as a whole* – the "efficacy of the cause" by which it is produced, or "propagated through the spaces round about"; again, in later terms, it is the "source-strength" at the center of the field. The "accelerative quantity" is *meant* to characterize the intensity of the field *at any given place* (and in the special case of gravitation, the "acceleration due to gravity" at the place in question successfully does so).[66] Finally, the "motive quantity" characterizes the action of the field upon an actual *body*: it measures, in other words, the force *impressed upon* a body by the field – the impressed force that has the given (field of) centripetal force as its "origin." In the case of gravity, the motive quantity of the force on a body is simply the *weight* of that body.[67]

When this array of concepts is juxtaposed with the passage quoted earlier from the preface to the *Principia*, in which the program is laid out of trying to account for the phenomena of nature as the effect of *forces of attraction and repulsion*, what emerges is the view that the natural powers – that of the *vis inertiae* of matter excepted – may all take the form of fields of force associated with the particles of matter; and, indeed, "central" fields (tending *either* toward *or away from* a center).[68]

One further essential point remains to be made – this derived from the Laws of Motion: namely, that the forces of nature constituted by the central fields are forces of *interaction*, governed by the third law of motion: that is, they produce *equal and opposite* motive forces between *pairs* of bodies. In Newton's argument in Book 3 culminating in the law of universal gravitation, this conception of a force of nature as an interaction subject to the third law plays a most crucial role.[69] Newton's awareness that there is in this a novel and important idea is clearly shown in a passage in the first version of Book 3, written (he tells us) "in a popular method,"[70] not published during his lifetime, but published both in Latin and in an English translation in 1728. The passage in question is striking in its iteration, which contrasts with Newton's usual conciseness of exposition (all emphases are added here, chiefly to highlight the main point – the one exception is explained in note 71):

Since the action of the centripetal force upon a body attracted is, at equal distances, proportional to the matter in this body, it accords with reason that it should be proportional also to the matter in the body attracting. For action is mutual, and (by the third Law of Motion) makes bodies by a mutual tendency approach one another, and hence must be conformable with itself in each body. *One body may be considered as attracting, another as attracted; but this distinction is more mathematical than natural. The attraction really is of each body towards the other*, and is thus of the same kind in each.

And hence it is that the attractive force is found in each. The Sun attracts Jupiter and the other Planets, Jupiter attracts the Satellites; and by parity of reason, the Satellites act among themselves reciprocally and upon Jupiter, and all the Planets mutually among themselves. *And though the mutual actions of two Planets may be distinguished from one another, and considered as two actions, by which each attracts the other: yet in so far as these [actions] are intermediate, they are not two, but a single operation between two terms.* By the contraction of a single interceding cord two bodies may be drawn each to the other. The cause of the action is twofold, indisputably [that cause is] the disposition of each body; the action is likewise twofold in so far as it is upon two bodies; but *as between two bodies it is sole and single. It is not one operation by which the Sun for instance attracts Jupiter, and another operation by which Jupiter attracts the Sun, but it is one operation by which the Sun and Jupiter mutually endeavor to approach one another.* By the action by which the Sun attracts Jupiter, Jupiter and the Sun endeavor to come nearer together (by the third Law of Motion) and, by the action by which Jupiter attracts the Sun, Jupiter and the Sun likewise endeavor to come nearer together: *but the Sun is not attracted towards Jupiter by a double action, nor Jupiter by a double action towards the Sun, but it is one intermediate action by which both approach nearer together.* Iron draws the loadstone as much as the loadstone draws the iron; for all iron in the neighborhood of the loadstone also draws other iron. *But the action between the loadstone and the iron is single, and is considered as single by the Philosophers* ... Conceive a single operation arising from the conspiring nature of both to be exerted in this way between two Planets; and this will be disposed in the same way *towards* both: hence being manifestly proportional to the matter in one of them, it will be proportional to the matter in the other.[71]

To repeat, then: the almost obsessive iteration in this passage seems clear evidence of Newton's intention to bring emphatically forward a new notion of the *unity* of interaction as the form of a force of nature. In terms of the fields already referred to, this means that exactly those bodies that are susceptible to the action of a given interaction-field are also the *sources* of the field; and that the measures of susceptibility and of source-strength (the "absolute quantity" of the body's force) are the same.

If all this is brought into relation to the metaphysical analysis in "De gravitatione et aequipondio fluidorum," it implies that in creating a body, God (or in the "constitution" of a body, *nature*) must impose, not only the field of impenetrability and the laws of motion appropriate thereto, but other fields as well, with their laws, characterizing forces of interaction of the kind that have been described – which fields, according to the Preface to the *Principia*, it becomes the presumed task of natural philosophy to discover.

And this is precisely the picture presented by Newton near the end of Query 31 of the *Opticks*. He there makes the explicit distinction, among natural powers or forces of nature, between the *vis inertiae*, as a "passive principle," and the other forces, which are "active principles"; but in both cases, he makes clear, what characterizes or identifies a particular such force is a *law* of nature (of the appropriate kind). Here are the principal relevant statements; they are preceded by a lengthy survey of physical and chemical phenomena, all tending to show that our understanding of nature depends upon the determination of forces of attraction and repulsion among particles:

And thus Nature will be very conformable to herself and very simple, performing all the great Motions of the heavenly Bodies by the Attraction of Gravity which intercedes those Bodies, and almost all the small ones of their Particles by some other attractive and repelling Powers which intercede the Particles. The *Vis inertiae* is a passive Principle by which Bodies persist in their Motion or Rest, receive Motion in proportion to the Force impressing it, and resist as much as they are resisted.[72]

We see, then, that Newton regards as *the law or principle* characterizing the intrinsic force of matter as a natural power, not what *we* call the "law of inertia," but the *conjunction of all three Laws of Motion*. This is quite in accord with what he has said in his discussion of Definition 3 of the *Principia*, where he describes the twofold manifestation or "exercise" of the force of inertia: in reducing the acceleration of the body acted upon by an impressed force (Law 2), and in the reciprocal "endeavor to change the state" of the body responsible for that impressed force (Law 3).

After some further discussion, which culminates in the statement: "All these things being consider'd, it seems to me probable that God in the Beginning form'd Matter in solid, massy, hard, impenetrable, moveable Particles, [etc.],"[73] mentioned earlier – a statement that in itself can be regarded as a pretty close counterpart of the creation story of "De gravitatione et aequipondio fluidorum," but with its deeper ontological analysis omitted – Newton goes on:

It seems to me farther, that these Particles have not only a *Vis inertiae*, accompanied with such passive Laws of Motion as naturally result from that Force, but also that they are moved by certain active Principles, such as is that of Gravity, and that which causes Fermentation, and the Cohesion of Bodies. These Principles I consider, not as occult Qualities, supposed to result from the specifick Forms of Things, but as general Laws of Nature, by which the Things themselves are form'd; their Truth appearing to us by Phaenomena, though their Causes be not yet discover'd. For these are manifest Qualities, and their Causes only are occult.[74]

We have, then, once again, the explicit distinction of the one passive principle and the several active principles; the explicit identification of such a principle with a "general Law of Nature"; and further, the indication that these principles, forces, or laws, are taken not to *result from* something like Aristotelian "substantial forms," which are "occult Qualities," but to *replace* them: it is *by* these "general Laws of Nature" that *"the Things themselves are form'd"* – just as, in "De gravitatione et aequipondio fluidorum," the *clear* attributes of impenetrability and laws of transference of the fields of impenetrability through the parts of space *replaced* the obscure notions of substance and substantial forms. The contrast is further drawn – and the *tentative* character of Newton's philosophic program further emphasized – in these words:

[O]ccult Qualities put a stop to the Improvement of natural Philosophy, and therefore of late Years have been rejected. To tell us that every Species of Things is endow'd with an occult specifick Quality by which it acts and produces manifest Effects, is to tell us nothing: But to derive two or three general Principles of Motion from Phaenomena, and afterwards to tell us how the Properties and Actions of all corporeal Things follow from those manifest Principles, would be a very great step in Philosophy, though the Causes of those Principles were not yet discover'd: And therefore I scruple not to propose the Principles of Motion above-mentioned, they being of very general Extent, and leave their Causes to be found out.[75]

Combining what Newton says here with the words previously quoted from the Preface to the *Principia*, one sees that – apart from the obvious openness to the future of a *program of investigation for physics* – the *metaphysics* that Newton presents is open and tentative in two respects: First, the words just cited imply that, although we are asked to consider the active principles as *candidates* to replace the old substantial forms as fundamental constitutional elements of nature, we are *not* to suppose, dogmatically, that whatever principles we have managed to discover are *necessarily* "the" fundamental ones: it will be a question for the future whether (yet deeper) *causes* of these principles may remain to be found out. In particular, this explains why Newton never claimed – and strongly denied holding – that gravity is "essential" to bodies. In the *Principia*, in the General Scholium to that work (added in the second edition, 1713), he says in a very celebrated passage:

Hitherto we have explain'd the phaenomena of the heavens and of our sea, by the power of Gravity, but have not yet assign'd the cause of this power. This is certain, that it must proceed from a cause that penetrates to the very centers of the Sun and Planets, without suffering the least diminution of its force ... But hitherto I have not been able to discover the cause of those properties of gravity from phaenomena, and I feign no hypotheses. For whatever is not deduc'd from the phaenomena, is to be called an hypothesis; and hypotheses, whether metaphysical or physical, whether of occult qualities or mechanical, have no place in experimental philosophy.[76]

And in the *Opticks* (in Query 21, added in its second edition, in 1717), Newton does actually sketch an hypothesis as to a possible "mechanical" cause of gravity by the action of a highly elastic aethereal medium (NB: a *possible* cause: one to be *considered*, not *adopted*; hence, although an hypothesis, not "feigned").

The second respect in which the metaphysics is left open to revision is more far-reaching (and commensurately vaguer). It is related to Newton's statement in "De gravitatione et aequipondio fluidorum" that we cannot know with certainty the ultimate constitution of things: namely, the general "probable" metaphysical conclusions Newton has reached on the basis of a comprehensive consideration of what has been discovered from phenomena are in the nature of the case open to possible *re*-consideration when *more* things have been learned; hence the form in which Newton expresses his hopes for the success of his program in the Preface to the *Principia*: "I hope the principles here laid down will afford some light either to that, or some truer, method of Philosophy."

In conclusion, it is worth considering briefly what the *actual* success has been of Newton's metaphysics, in the perspective of the natural philosophy of the present time. Of course, in our own physics, *all* the foundations of Newtonian physics have been radically modified: space and time, since the work of Einstein, are not conceived as Newton conceived them; finitely extended rigid and impenetrable ultimate particles have been replaced by far more exotic beings; fields that are *not* rigidly associated with particle sources, as Newton's were, but that are capable of existing to some degree independently, and that have their own internal structure and interaction among their parts (as in the propagation of *waves*), have come to have an "ontological" standing no less fundamental than "fundamental particles" themselves; and – especially since the advent of quantum mechanics – we have even had to abandon the notion of particles as having, at each instant of time, definite locations in space, and as interacting through Newtonian "impressed motive forces." On the other hand, in the developments that have led to the present state of physics, the conceptions introduced by Newton have played an indispensable role. And what are arguably his two most characteristic – and in his own time most sharply controverted – basic conceptions remain, *although* radically modified, as basic characteristics of the structure envisaged by our own science. The first of these is the structure of space-time. It was once thought that the development of the general theory of relativity had decided the issue of "absolute" versus "relative" space and motion against Newton and in favor of his strongest contemporary critic in this matter, Leibniz; but more careful consideration has shown that in spite of the very far-reaching changes wrought by Einstein – in spite of the fact that absolute space and absolute time have been abandoned, and the geometric structure of space-time has proved to be *interdependent with* the distribution of matter (or, rather, of "energy-momentum") – it remains necessary to regard space-time and its geometry as having a status as "real" as that of matter: the program of "reducing" the properties of space-time to properties and interrelations of "bodies" has not succeeded. So on this *general* score – although certainly *not* in *detail* – Newton was, in the eyes of our own science, "right" to take space and time as fundamental entities.[77]

The other characteristic notion of Newton's that has proved quite remarkably durable is that of a natural power, or force of nature. This statement may seem as surprising as the claim that Newton was "right" in a general sense about space and time: for (a) as has

been already remarked, Newtonian "motive force" has disappeared
from quantum mechanics, and (b) it *is* "motive force" – the "force"
of Newton's second law, $f = ma$ – that is usually taken as the characteristic notion of "Newtonian mechanics." But as we have seen,
as important as this concept is in Newton's *Principia*, it does not
express his most basic notion; for instance, whereas an impressed
force is not a natural power, the "force of inertia" – which is something entirely different from the force that is equal to ma – *is*
one. Newton's basic notion of a force of nature is, however, so far
from being antiquated that it is substantially the same – although
again, as in the case of space and time, with profound modifications in detail – as the notion used when physicists today speak
of the "four fundamental forces." Of these, the gravitational force
is the first to have been discovered; it was, of course, a great discovery of Newton's – and, on the analysis here offered, provided the
grounds on which Newton's general conception was based. Two of
the four fundamental forces – the weak and the strong nuclear force –
obviously could not have been foreseen in Newton's time. Of the remaining one – the electromagnetic force, whose classical definitive
form was discovered by Maxwell in the 1860s – we find some traces
in Newton's work. References to the loadstone have been quoted
above. In the long closing query of the *Opticks*, from which material occurring near the end has been cited as illuminating Newton's
general concept of a force of nature, there is also the following inci-
dental speculation about electrical force, in the midst of a more general consideration (itself showing again exactly the *tentative* view
of the "fundamental" that has been suggested as characteristic of
Newton):

What I call Attraction may be perform'd by impulse, or by some other means
unknown to me. I use that Word here to signify only in general any Force
by which Bodies tend towards one another, whatsoever be the Cause. For
we must learn from the Phaenomena of Nature what Bodies attract one
another, and what are the Laws and Properties of the Attraction, before we
enquire the Cause by which the Attraction is perform'd. The Attractions of
Gravity, Magnetism, and Electricity, reach to very sensible distances, and
so have been observed by vulgar Eyes, and there may be others which reach
to so small distances as hitherto escape Observation; and perhaps electrical
Attraction may reach to such small distances, even without being excited
by Friction.[78]

When we remember that electrical attractions, in Newton's time, constituted a rather isolated phenomenon, observed only when certain bodies were suitably rubbed – and when we recall that the "attractions [and repulsions as well] extending to small distances *within* bodies" that Newton had in mind were the ones that should eventually account for cohesion and for chemical processes – this glimmering of a suspicion that electricity might not be merely a special effect of rubbing, but might exist and be responsible for forces at short range as a general fact of nature surely deserves to be considered a remarkable one. In our own science, it is the electromagnetic force that is in fact seen to be responsible (but only in the light of quantum mechanics, not of Newtonian mechanics) for the physical and chemical properties of ordinary bodies.

"To derive *two or three* general Principles of Motion from Phaenomena, and afterwards to tell us how the Properties and Actions of all corporeal Things follow from those manifest Principles, would be a very great step in Philosophy, though the Causes of those Principles were not yet discover'd." Such is the great step in philosophy that Newton's metaphysics was conceived to facilitate: "I hope the principles here laid down will afford some light either to that, or some truer, method of philosophy." It seems fair to say that that hope has been amply realized.

NOTES

1 "The previous author" of a book with that title: for the title Newton used – *Philosophiae Naturalis Principia Mathematica* – is clearly a deliberate allusion to Descartes's work.

2 René Descartes, *Principles of Philosophy*, trans. Valentine Rodger Miller and Reese P. Miller (Dordrecht: D. Reidel Publishing Company, 1983), p. xxiv (in the "Letter from the Author to the Translator of this Book [into French], which can serve here as a Preface").

3 *Encyclopaedia Britannica*, 11th edn, vol. 18, p. 253.

4 Descartes hoped that his goals for a new science would be achieved *entirely* in his *own lifetime*, and indeed by his own efforts – aided only by the work of artisans and trained technicians he needed to construct equipment for experiments and to help in carrying out the experiments. The most ambitious of these goals was the establishment, on sound principles, of a science of medicine that should succeed in prolonging human life to a term measured in centuries.

5 The guarantee, that is, of what we should call the "objective validity" of those principles that carry complete "subjective" conviction. (Descartes's terminology, following that of the medieval philosophers, is the reverse: for him, "subjective" means what characterizes the proper *subject of knowledge* – the "real things"; whereas "objective" means characteristic of the "object of the mind," *as* mental object, whatever it may be in reality – or indeed whether or not it exists in reality.) The guarantee of truth is obtained by the famous argument of Descartes's *Meditations*, a crucial turn in which is the (alleged) demonstration (a) of the existence of God as a "perfect being," and (b) of the consequence that, since a perfect being cannot be a deceiver, everything we perceive as true beyond the possibility of doubt must be true in reality.

6 That is, the *Dialogue concerning the Two Chief World Systems.*

7 *Principles of Philosophy*, Part 2, §24.

8 *Ibid.*, §13.

9 *Ibid.*, §15. In the *Rules for the Direction of the Mind*, in stark contrast, "place" is offered as an example of those "simple natures" which are self-evident in themselves, and cannot be defined or "explained" in terms of something even more evident; and Descartes adds: "And when told that 'place' is the surface of the surrounding body, would anyone conceive of the matter in the same way? For the surface of the 'surrounding body' can change, even though I do not move or change my place; conversely, it may move along with me, so that, although it still surrounds me, I am no longer in the same place." (Quoted from *The Philosophical Writings of Descartes*, ed. John Cottingham, Robert Stoothoff, and Dugald Murdoch, vol. 1 [Cambridge: Cambridge University Press, 1985], p. 45.) So here Descartes has ridiculed, as a bizarre doctrine of the scholastic philosophy he is attacking, the very notion he puts forward in his *Principles* as the scientifically "correct" one. (We shall later see that Newton makes mincemeat of this way of conceiving place and motion.)

10 "*Semi-*"relativist, because some bodies are singled out – or *partially* singled out – as the ones to which motion *in the strict sense* should be referred; but only partially singled out because of the arbitrariness implied by "and which are regarded as being at rest."

11 Both in his *Meditations on First Philosophy* and in his *Principles of Philosophy*, what Descartes claims to establish by thought without the aid of sensation is the *essential attribute* of material things, in the sense of "what they would be if they *did* exist"; then sensory experience is called upon to show that such things *do* exist.

12 Quoted from the fourth paragraph in the discussion of *Rule Eight*; edition of Cottingham *et al.*, p. 29.

13   In the *Rules for the Direction of the Mind*, Descartes deprecates in the strongest terms any reliance upon hypotheses ("conjectures") and any "merely probable cognition"; and at least as late as 1637, in replying to an objection of Fermat to the argumentation of Descartes's *Dioptrics* (which was published in that year in the same volume as his *Discourse on the Method of Rightly Conducting One's Reason and Seeking the Truth in the Sciences*), he says "I consider almost as false whatever is only a matter of probability" (letter of 5 October 1637, to Mersenne). At the end of his *Principles of Philosophy* (1644), he says, in contrast to that: "With regard to the things which cannot be perceived by the senses, it is enough to explain their possible nature, even though their actual nature may be different" (Part 4, §204) – certainly an endorsement of the value of "hypotheses," even of ones that may in the end not be true. He goes on, however (in the next two articles), to claim (a) that his explanations "appear to be at least morally certain"; and (b) that his explanations possess "more than moral certainty"; indeed that "perhaps even these results of mine will be allowed into the class of *absolute* certainties" (emphasis added).

14   It is of course possible to maintain proposition (a) while rejecting (b); but hardly the reverse: for if space is *full* of *rigid, indivisible* bodies, the possibilities for motion are extremely restricted – the kinds of motion we encounter in the world would be quite impossible on such an assumption. It should be added that one important philosopher, slightly younger than Newton, who came to reject Descartes's metaphysical characterization of matter, nevertheless *also* rejected *both* (a) and (b): namely, Leibniz, in whose view empty space was not a *contradictory* notion, but who claimed to derive the proposition that the world is a plenum from his metaphysical principle of "sufficient reason."

15   A characteristic expression of this view, late in the century, by a philosopher who was certainly *not* a Cartesian, is to be found in Locke; cf. his *Essay concerning Human Understanding*, Book 2, ch. viii, §11, which reads as follows in the first edition (1690): "The next thing to be consider'd, is how *Bodies operate* one upon another, and that is manifestly *by impulse*, and nothing else. It being impossible to conceive, that Body should operate on what it does not touch, (which is all one as to imagine it can operate where it is not) or when it does touch, operate any other way than by Motion." Quoted from John Locke, *An Essay concerning Human Understanding*, ed. Peter H. Nidditch (Oxford: Clarendon Press, 1979), p. 135 *(via* the apparatus at the foot of the page – the passage having been drastically revised in the fourth edition).

16 This, as is well known, is the origin of the very word "metaphysics" (which is quite foreign to Aristotle himself): the collection of Aristotle's treatises on first philosophy was labeled – as if by a call-number – τὰ μετὰ τὰ φυσικά: "the [writings] after the physical [ones]."

17 The point needs to be emphasized, because there is a tradition that sees the basic conceptions of Newton's natural philosophy, most especially his conceptions of space and time, as derivative from, or grounded in, his theology. Thus, J. E. McGuire claims "that the basic concepts of Newton's natural philosophy can be ultimately clarified only in terms of the theological framework which guided so much of his thought" (see his "Force, Active Principles, and Newton's Invisible Realm," *Ambix* 15 [1968], 154). McGuire goes on to remark that the thesis is not original with him, and gives the following citations:

See the fundamental studies of H. Metzger, *Attraction universelle et religion naturelle chez quelques commentateurs anglais de Newton*, Paris, 1938, and A. Koyré, *From the Closed World to the Infinite Universe*, Harper edition, 1958. Also see H. Guerlac, "Newton et Epicure," *Conf[é]rences du palais de la découverte*, no. 91, Paris, 1963: an excellent study by David Kubrin, "Newton and the Cyclical Cosmos: Providence and the Mechanical Philosophy," *J.H.I.*, 1967, XXVIII, 325–46; J. E. McGuire and P. M. Rattansi, "Newton and the Pipes of Pan," *Notes and Records of the Royal Society of London*, 1966, 21, 108–43; J. E. McGuire, "Body and Void and Newton's *De Mundi Systemate*: some new sources," *Archive for History of Exact Sciences*, 1966, 3, 206–48; an important lengthy study by A. Koyré and I. B. Cohen, "Newton and the Leibniz–Clarke correspondence," *Archive[s] Internationales d'histoire des Sciences*, 1962, 15, 63–126; and A. R. and M. B. Hall, *Unpublished Scientific Papers of Isaac Newton*, Cambridge, 1962, part 3.

The evidence cited in the text above, preceding and immediately following the place to which this note is attached, does not show that this opinion is wrong, so far as concerns either the psychological connections of Newton's thought or the logical or conceptual connections among his principles; but it does at least strongly suggest that the opinion is at variance with what Newton himself thought about these connections, and therefore at variance with at least the epistemological side of Newton's own metaphysics. To discuss the controversy implied with any pretence to thoroughness is beyond the scope of a chapter like the present one; but further evidence will be given, tending to show that on the objective or ontological side, too, Newton's doctrine about space and time, in the light of his explicit statements, did not teach that space and time *per se*, or their attributes, depend upon the nature of God.

On the degree of confidence attached by Newton to his main results in physics, in both his optical work and that on the solar system and the theory of gravity, cf. Shapiro's and Smith's chapters in this volume.

18   This rule, with the statement referred to in the text above, first appeared in the second edition of the *Principia*, 1713.

19   To avoid a possible wrong inference, it should be added that besides knowledge of God "from the appearances of things," which "belongs to Natural Philosophy," Newton holds that there is knowledge of God through *revelation*. This, too, of course, would be through *experience*; and what is more important so far as concerns Newton's own efforts in the domain of "revealed" theology (efforts that occupied no small part of his whole intellectual career), the deliverances of revelation are, for Newton, accessible *only through historical documents* (Newton does not subscribe to any claim of immediate religious authority – nor does he claim access to revelation through personal inspiration), and therefore demand a very arduous historical-critical investigation of such documents. In any event, there is nowhere in Newton a suggestion that our knowledge of anything pertaining to *natural philosophy* can be derived from revealed truths. (He does *relate* some aspects of his views about space, for example, to passages in ancient writings, both pagan and Judeo-Christian; but this is far from ascribing evidentiary or conceptually binding force to such relations.)

20   See the specimens given in John Herivel, *The Background to Newton's Principia: A Study of Newton's Dynamical Researches in the Years 1664–84* (Oxford: Clarendon Press, 1965).

21   Herivel, *Background to Newton's* Principia, p. 123.

22   *Ibid.*, p. 124.

23   *Ibid.*, p. 125.

24   *Ibid.*, p. 136.

25   *Ibid.*, p. 138.

26   See A. Rupert Hall and Marie Boas Hall (eds.), *Unpublished Scientific Papers of Isaac Newton* (Cambridge: Cambridge University Press, 1962), pp. 89–121 (Latin), 121–56 (English). In the present text, translations from this work are my own.

27   Mistranslation begins with this first sentence, which the Halls render as: "It is proper to treat the science of gravity and of the equilibrium of fluid and solid bodies in fluids by two methods." This version has been used as the basis of a claim that the manuscript actually represents an abortive draft of an introduction to Newton's *Principia*, "[s]ince the two studies mentioned – of gravitation and of the equilibrium of fluids and of solid bodies in fluids – bear a strong resemblance to Books I and II of the published *Principia*," and since the two methods Newton describes

also have a correspondence to the *Principia*. (See Betty Jo Teeter Dobbs, *The Janus Faces of Genius: The Role of Alchemy in Newton's Thought* [Cambridge: Cambridge University Press, 1991], p. 141.) But Newton's phrase has nothing to do with a "science of gravity": he is speaking of the *weight* of fluids and of solids in fluids, which is the exact subject of the classic treatise "On Floating Bodies" of Archimedes; and, on the other hand, Book 2 of the *Principia* is concerned with the *motions*, not the *equilibrium*, of fluids and of solids in fluids – an entirely *new* subject at the time of its publication.

28 For these statements, see Descartes, *Principles of Philosophy*, Part 3, §27.

29 It is important to bear in mind that for Newton – and for *all* seventeenth-century thinkers – the word "philosophy" was used for all *systematic knowledge* or *systematic inquiry*. Thus, when Newton speaks of "philosophical" usage, he means *exact*, or *systematic*, or *technical* usage; and so does Descartes. So Newton's criticism is that *in Descartes's technical discussion of motion, he does not use that conception of motion which he had put forward as technically correct*; and so he has implicitly acknowledged that the conception he calls "proper" is in fact unsuitable for technical purposes.

30 On the particular issue of the "straightness" of the path, an important argument of Galileo's is relevant, and may be clarifying. Galileo considered an object dropped from high up on the mast of a ship that is sailing, in a smooth sea, with uniform speed. To an observer on shipboard, the object will appear to fall vertically downward – that is, in a straight line – alongside the mast, with a speed that increases proportionally to the time of fall. To an observer on the shore – who of course also sees the object as falling directly alongside the mast, but who also sees the mast itself as moving uniformly forward – the object will appear to traverse a parabolic arc. Therefore – even setting aside the issue of the *dispersal* of surrounding bodies – whether, in general, a path is straight or not will depend upon *which* bodies one chooses to "regard as at rest."

31 The force of Newton's argument is great. In a famous polemic that came to a head late in the lives of both men, Leibniz took up the cudgels against Newton on behalf of a "relational" view of space and motion – not, indeed, that of Descartes, but one that was still open to Newton's criticism that on that view neither straightness of a path of motion nor constancy of speed is a concept that makes sense. Yet Leibniz – in the same polemic – in arguing against Newton's theory of gravitation, says that for one body to move in a *curved line* about the other without something that *pushes* on the first "could not be done without a miracle; since it cannot be explained by the nature of bodies" (because

a body of itself tends to move uniformly in a straight line) (Leibniz's third letter, in his correspondence with Samuel Clarke of 1715–16, §17; in, e.g., H. G. Alexander [ed.], *The Leibniz–Clarke Correspondence* [Manchester: Manchester University Press, 1956], p. 30.) It is unfortunate that Clarke – Newton's representative in this discussion – did not point out to Leibniz the incoherence that Newton had long ago noted in a position that simultaneously maintains that principle about the motion of bodies and regards motion as having a meaning *only* as "relative," *among bodies*. This *might* have led to a clarification by Leibniz of his own relational theory. For further discussion of the issues involved, in which Newton's own position – although much stronger than it was once thought to be among philosophers – is by no means the last word (so far as the foundations of "Newtonian mechanics" itself are concerned), see Howard Stein, "Newtonian Space-Time," *The Texas Quarterly* 10 (1967), 174–200; also (with correction of an important typesetting error in a quotation) in Robert Palter (ed.), *The* Annus Mirabilis *of Sir Isaac Newton* 1666–1966 (Cambridge, MA: MIT Press, 1970), pp. 258–84. For further discussion of the views of Leibniz, and also those of Huygens, on the relativity of motion, see also Howard Stein, "Some Philosophical Prehistory of General Relativity," in John Earman, Clark Glymour, and John Stachel (eds.), *Foundations of Space-Time Theories*, Minnesota Studies in the Philosophy of Science 8 (Minneapolis: University of Minnesota Press, 1977), pp. 3–49 (§§1 and 2, with relevant Notes, and Appendix). Cf. also DiSalle's chapter in the present volume.

32   Newton's words here – quite scholastic in cast – are: "it does not stand under the kind of characteristic affections that denominate substance, namely actions, such as are thoughts in a mind and motions in a body."

33   The use of the word "idea" – unusual for Newton – is striking; and so is its capitalization (here, and in similar contexts later in the piece). One is reminded of Locke's *Essay concerning Human Understanding*, in which the word is also uniformly capitalized (and italicized as well). There can be no question of influence, in either direction: whatever the date of this fragmentary piece of Newton's, it certainly antedates Locke's *Essay*; and, as certainly, Locke had never seen it when he wrote the *Essay*.

34   Some words are necessary here concerning the translation, since this passage is one of those in which the published version is badly at fault. There, the first sentence reads: "Space is a disposition of being *qua* being." Newton's Latin is: "Spatium est entis quatenus ens affectio." Now, the word *affectio* is standard in philosophical Latin, and is regularly translated by its English cognate, "affection"; "disposition" has a rather different connotation. But this is a minor point. The major one is how

to translate – and how to understand – the phrase *entis quatenus ens.*
Latin "ens" and English "being" are precisely synonymous; and "entis"
is the genitive of "ens"; so "an affection of being as being" – or "of being *qua* being" – that is, "of being as such" – is linguistically warranted.
Further, the phrase is borrowed directly from the Aristotelian tradition,
in which "being *qua* being" is the standard definition of the subject-
matter of first philosophy or metaphysics. So far, therefore, the Halls'
rendering seems justified. However, one must also note two things: first,
that the Latin word "ens" like the English word "being" is susceptible
of a concrete meaning (as when we call *ourselves* "human beings") as
well as an abstract one; second, that in Latin there are no articles, definite or indefinite; and therefore the reading given in the text above
is, on purely linguistic grounds, equally eligible. Two considerations
may be thought to favor the Halls: first, the point just made about the
formula in the Aristotelian tradition; second, the fact that the phrase
"being *qua* being," understood to mean "being *in the highest sense*,"
had the special connotation of "*[the] divine Being*" (cf. God's answer to
Moses, Exodus 3.14, in response to the question what Moses shall tell
the people is the name of the one who has sent him: "I AM THAT I AM");
this would seem to agree with Newton's former statement that space is
an emanative effect of God. However, these considerations are clearly
overborne by what follows – in particular, by Newton's statement, "*If
I posit any being whatever, I posit space.*" The word "being" – *ens* –
in *this* assertion can only be taken in its concrete sense. And since this
statement is given to ground the clause immediately preceding it, there
too "being" must be used in the concrete sense; indeed, in any case,
only the concrete sense – "the first-existing *thing* – or *entity*" – fits that
clause at all. (The translation of that phrase by the Halls – "the first
existence of being," rather than "the first-existent being" – not only
makes its sense obscure, but is incompatible with the grammar of the
Latin. To discuss this in detail here would take us too far into purely
linguistic matters.)

35 Newton, of course, under the rubric "all minds," would have included
the minds of *angels*.

36 On this point it is instructive to compare what Locke says about the relation of mind ("spirit" or "soul") to place and motion: "[F]inding that
Spirits, as well as Bodies, cannot operate, but where they are; and that
Spirits do operate at several times in several places, I cannot but attribute
change of place to all finite Spirits... Every one finds in himself, that his
Soul can think, will, and operate on his Body, in the place where that
is; but cannot operate on a Body, or in a place, an hundred Miles distant
from it. No Body can imagine, that his Soul can think, or move a Body

at *Oxford*, whilst he is at *London*; and cannot but know, [*sic*] that being united to his Body, it constantly changes place all the whole Journey, between *Oxford* and *London*, as the Coach, or Horse does, that carries him [etc.]."

37   The qualification, "ordinary," is needed to distinguish the case from the special one of an *atom*, which on Newton's (and the traditional) conception is precisely an *indivisible* body.

38   Another case of mistranslation in the published version: the latter reads, not "and therefore we are able [etc.]," but (emphasis added): "and so *in some circumstances* it *would be possible* for us to conceive of extension while imagining the non-existence of God." This suggests that only on Descartes's conception would we be able – "in some circumstances" – to conceive extension while "imagining the non-existence of God." But this is not what Newton says: (1) There is nothing in the Latin that corresponds to the phrase "in some circumstances." (2) The verb is *possumus*: indicative – *"we are able"*; not the subjunctive *possimus*: *"we should be able."* Newton asserts unqualifiedly that we *are* able to conceive of space without any reference to God ("we have an absolute Idea of it without any relationship to God"); his point against Descartes is that on the identification of extension with body the same thing would hold of body: (a) it would be uncreated; (b) we could conceive of it *"as existent"* while "feigning" the non-existence of God. (This criticism would of course be rejected by Descartes; the point here is merely to be clear about what Newton's doctrine is.)

39   The Halls, in first publishing "De gravitatione et aequipondio fluidorum," expressed uncertainty about its date, but described the handwriting as characteristic of Newton's youth, and – although they noted the important fact that it has affinities with the General Scholium to Newton's *Principia* (introduced in the second edition of that work, thus in 1713, when Newton was seventy years old) – they characterized its general style as labored, and some of its thought as immature (see *Unpublished Scientific Papers*, pp. 89–90); on these grounds, they leaned toward an early date. The present writer, in a paper presented at a conference in 1969 and published in 1970, while not contesting the early date assigned, suggested two reasons for caution about it: first, a disagreement with the Halls' assessment of the thought; second, the testimony of Coste about to be discussed in the text of the chapter (see Howard Stein, "On the Notion of Field in Newton, Maxwell, and Beyond," in Roger H. Stuewer (ed.), *Historical and Philosophical Perspectives of Science*, Minnesota Studies in the Philosophy of Science 5 [Minneapolis: University of Minnesota Press, 1970], p. 274, n. 11). More recently, Dobbs, who gives a survey of opinions on the question (Dobbs, *The Janus*

Faces of Genius, pp. 139–40), has argued for a date close to that of the *Principia* – namely, late in 1684 or early in 1685; but it must be noted that an important part of her case rests upon the mistakes noted earlier (note 27 above). It seems fair to say that uncertainty remains about the date of "De gravitatione," and evidence based upon handwriting may after all be decisive.

40 Gottfried Wilhelm Leibniz, *New Essays on Human Understanding*, trans. Peter Remnant and Jonathan Bennett (Cambridge: Cambridge University Press, 1981), p. 442.

41 Coste's account is quoted in A. C. Fraser's edition of Locke's *Essay*; see Locke, *An Essay concerning Human Understanding*, ed. Alexander Campbell Fraser (reprinted New York: Dover Publications, 1959), vol. 2, pp. 321–2.

42 In their edition of Leibniz's *New Essays*, Remnant and Bennett cite a letter from Leibniz to Locke's friend Lady Masham in 1704, containing "an urgent request that she ask Locke to elucidate"; but it arrived after Locke's death. (See Leibniz, *New Essays*, ed. Remnant and Bennett, p. xxxix, near the end of the volume.)

43 Latin, *arbitrarius*: "depending on the will."

44 Newton's repeated use of the expression "let us feign" – Latin, *fingamus*: the same verb that occurs in Newton's famous declaration, in the General Scholium to the *Principia*, "Hypotheses non fingo": "I do not feign hypotheses" – is reminiscent of language used by Descartes in his own "creation fable," both in *The World* and in his *Principles of Philosophy*. For the former, see René Descartes, *Le Monde, ou Traité de la lumière*, parallel edition (French and English), trans. Michael Sean Mahoney (New York: Abaris Books, 1979), pp. 50 (French), 51 (English); the phrase in French is "Or puisque nous prenons la liberté de *feindre* cette matière à nostre fantaisie ..." (emphasis added) – "Now since we are taking the liberty of feigning this matter to our fancy ..."; "la liberté de feindre" is rendered by Mahoney as "the liberty of imagining." As to the *Principles*, the verb *fingere* occurs in Part 4, §2: "Fingamus itaque Terram hanc [etc]" – "Let us therefore feign this earth [etc]." (Again, in the translation by Miller and Miller cited earlier, the verb is translated "Let us imagine.") The phrase "fingamus itaque," in this last place, is exactly the same as that used by Newton in the opening sentence of *his* creation story: "Fingamus itaque spatia vacua ... " – "Let us therefore feign empty spaces... " In view of the fact that this whole metaphysical discussion has the character of an anti-Cartesian polemic, the parody of Descartes is most probably intentional.

45 See note 18 above.

46 Cf. note 15 above.

47 Locke, *Essay concerning Human Understanding*, Book 2, ch. xxiii, §28;
    Nidditch edition, pp. 311–12.

48 These pessimistic views about the possibility of systematic science
    were strikingly ameliorated by Locke's reflections on what Newton had
    achieved, but he did not allow his changed assessment to have any effect
    on the later editions of the *Essay*. The point is discussed in Howard Stein,
    "On Locke, 'the Great Huygenius, and the incomparable Mr. Newton',"
    in Phillip Bricker and R. I. G. Hughes (eds.), *Philosophical Perspectives
    on Newtonian Science* (Cambridge, MA: MIT Press, 1990), pp. 17–47;
    see esp. pp. 30–3.

49 Both quotations are from the Author's Preface to the first edition of the
    Principia. They are quoted in an order the reverse to that in which they
    occur there; and the emphasis (in the second passage) is added here.

50 The subject of Book 2, ch. xxiii of the *Essay concerning Human Under-
    standing*.

51 *Ibid.*, §37; Nidditch edn, p. 317.

52 *Ibid.*, Book 1, ch. iv, §18; Nidditch edn, p. 95.

53 *Ibid.*, Book 3, ch. vi, §21; Nidditch edn, p. 450.

54 This characterization of Newton's theory of bodies as a theory of *fields
    of impenetrability* was first given in Stein, "On the Notion of Field
    in Newton, Maxwell, and Beyond" (cited in note 39 above); there fol-
    low immediately in the same volume some critical comments by Gerd
    Buchdahl and by Mary Hesse, with responses by the author defending
    his view.

55 Whether Aristotle himself believed in such a thing is a debatable
    question.

56 See *Essay concerning Human Understanding*, Book 2, ch. iv.

57 *Ibid.*, ch. xxi, §73; Nidditch edn, pp. 286–7.

58 Newton's wording is a little odd, in its reference to "removing"
    the power in question; he has in mind Descartes's famous thought-
    experiment with a lump of wax, of which he attempts to strip away,
    in thought, whatever properties can be removed from the wax without
    destroying its "essential" character as bodily substance. Descartes con-
    cluded that only extension cannot be removed; Newton argues that to
    remove impenetrability, and the laws of transfer of motion, from his
    mobile impenetrable regions would be to reduce them to empty space;
    and he adds, here, that to remove the power to produce perceptions in
    minds would be an equally serious derogation from their substantial
    nature.

59 (But before the passage quoted immediately above.)

60 (Locke was prominent among these.)

61 (A condition in which it would seem we remain to this day.)

62 This and subsequent passages are quoted from the (unemended!) trans-
    lation of Andrew Motte: Isaac Newton, *The Mathematical Principles of
    Natural Philosophy*, trans. Andrew Motte (1729) (reprinted in two vol-
    umes, London: Dawsons of Pall Mall, 1968). See "The Author's Preface"
    (prefatory material is on unnumbered pages).

63 More precisely, for the expression "proportional to the efficacy of the
    cause" to have a well-defined meaning, one would have to have the
    conception of the *ratio* of the efficacy of one cause to that of another.

64 The Latin phrase here rendered as "a certain power or energy" is *effica-
    ciam quandam*: that is, simply, "a certain efficacy."

65 Again, cf. Stein, "On the Notion of Field in Newton, Maxwell, and
    Beyond," cited in note 39 above.

66 For other fields, quite different measures of the field intensity are ap-
    propriate: e.g., for magnetism, the "force per unit pole"; for electricity,
    the "force per unit charge." (For a fuller discussion of the role of the
    concept of field in Newton's investigation, see Stein, "On the Notion
    of Field in Newton, Maxwell, and Beyond," cited in note 39 above.)

67 One sees, then, how far the example of the sling is from illustrating the
    intended pattern: here, there is indeed an impressed motive force toward
    the hand as a center; but no good sense can be made of the conception
    of "a certain efficacy diffused from the center *to all the places around*,"
    with a definite magnitude or measure *at each point* (whether or not
    there is an actual body there to be acted upon).

68 In the *Opticks*, on the basis of a wide survey of phenomena – both
    optical and *chemical* phenomena figuring largely among them – Newton
    concludes that there must be some forces that are *attractive at certain
    distances, repulsive at others*. See Isaac Newton, *Opticks* ("based on the
    fourth edition, London, 1730"; New York: Dover Publications, 1952),
    pp. 395ff.

69 That Newton's special use of the third law, crucial to his argument,
    involves a risky assumption, was briefly mentioned in Stein, "On the
    Notion of Field in Newton, Maxwell, and Beyond" (cited in note 39
    above), p. 269; the point is discussed more fully in Howard Stein, "'From
    the Phenomena of Motions to the Forces of Nature': Hypothesis or
    Deduction?" *PSA 1990* 2 (1991), 209–22, and also in Dana Densmore,
    Newton's Principia: *The Central Argument* (Santa Fe: Green Lion Press,
    1995), p. 353.

70 See *Principia*, introductory paragraph to Book 3.

71 Translated by the present author from Newton, *De Mundi Systemate
    Liber* (London, 1728), pp. 24–6. Matter in square brackets has been
    added to help to show in clear English the sense of the Latin. Besides
    the emphases added to highlight the main point, the word "towards"

in the last sentence has been italicized; this has been done to indicate a contrast Newton is making, perhaps somewhat subtly, by the way he manages his prepositions: that between how the "operation" arises *from* the bodies, on the one hand, and how it "behaves *towards* them" on the other (if it arises from them in the same way, it will affect them in the same way).

The author has had the advantage of consulting both the excellent English translation of 1728 (anonymous, but presumably by Andrew Motte, whose translation of the *Principia* was published the following year) *A Treatise of the System of the World* (London, 1728), and a draft of a forthcoming translation by I. B. Cohen and Anne Whitman. The old translation was reissued with revisions in the volume: *Sir Isaac Newton's Mathematical Principles of Natural Philosophy and his System of the World*. Translated into English by Andrew Motte in 1729. The translations revised... by Florian Cajori. (2nd printing; Berkeley: University of California Press, 1946). In that edition the sections (distinguished in the original Latin publication and in the 1728 English version by marginal section-headings) are numbered (these numbers do not appear in the 1728 English or in the 1728 or 1731 Latin editions); the paragraphs quoted are, with a small elision, §§20–21 there (pp. 568–9). Unfortunately, the revisions made in that publication introduce a serious error into the text of §21; the author is therefore particularly grateful to Benjamin Weiss, Curator of Rare Books at the Burndy Library of the Dibner Institute for the History of Science and Technology at the Massachusetts Institute of Technology, for making available photostatic copies of the 1728 English and Latin versions of those sections (and of the 1731 Latin edition as well); and to George Smith for obtaining those copies, as well as a copy of the Cohen and Whitman draft mentioned above. (See editors' additional note, p. 307.)

72 *Opticks* (Dover edn), p. 397.
73 *Ibid.*, p. 400.
74 *Ibid.*, p. 401.
75 *Ibid.*, pp. 401–2.
76 *Principia* (edition cited in note 62 above), vol. 2, p. 392. (One emendation has been made of the Motte translation: "I feign no hypotheses" for "I frame no hypotheses." It was pointed out by Alexandre Koyré – cited in I. Bernard Cohen, *Introduction to Newton's "Principia"* [Cambridge, MA: Harvard University Press, 1978], p. 241, n. 9 – that this is the English version of his Latin phrase "hypotheses non fingo" used by Newton himself in the *Opticks*, in Query 28; see Dover edn, p. 369.)
77 Cf., for fuller discussion of these matters, Stein, "Newtonian Space-Time" and "Some Philosophical Prehistory of General Relativity" (sections 1–3), both cited in note 31 above.

78 *Opticks* (Dover edn), p. 376.

Editors' note. In note 71 above, Professor Stein calls attention to the
section numbers in Cajori's version of the English translation of *A Treatise of the System of the World* and their absence in both the English
and Latin editions of 1728. The history of these section numbers
is complicated. The manuscript from which the Latin edition was
printed, entitled "De motu corporum liber secundus," is in the hand of
Humphrey Newton (Isaac's amanuensis at the time), with modifications
in Isaac's hand. This manuscript contains eighty section-headings in
the margins, with the first twenty-eight numbered in Roman numerals,
precisely in the manner of Descartes's published *Principia*; the remaining fifty-two sections, however, are not numbered. In every edition of
the English translation before Cajori's, and in all Latin editions save one,
the section-headings are placed in the margin without numbers. The exception is Samuel Horsley's Latin edition in his *Isaaci Newtoni Opera
Quae Exstant Omnia* of 1779–85. Horsley, who had gained access to the
"De motu corporum liber secundus" manuscripts, kept the eighty
section-headings in the margins, but placed Arabic numerals at the
beginning of the text of seventy-eight of the sections, electing to omit
a number in the case of the seventy-fifth section-heading (introducing
Table II) and the eightieth (introducing the lemmata near the end). In
his German translation, attached to his 1872 translation of Newton's
Principia, Jakob Phillipp Wolfers put numbered section-headings in
the text rather than the margins, and he dropped the seventy-fifth
and eightieth section-headings entirely. Cajori, who acknowledged his
use of this German translation, followed Wolfers save for putting the
numbers in brackets, presumably to signify their absence in the English
translation that he was modifying.

9 Analysis and synthesis in Newton's mathematical work

The opposition between analytical and synthetic proof methods has an intriguing and complex role in the history of Western mathematics. In Antiquity analytical method (in brief, analysis) was conceived of as a method of discovery, or problem solving: it starts from what is sought as if it had already been achieved, and, working step by step backwards, it eventually arrives at what is known. This and similar rather vague definitions were aimed at describing in a general way a whole apparatus of geometric problem solving procedures developed by the Greeks. Synthesis goes the other way round: it starts from what is known and, working through the consequences, it arrives at what is sought. The axiomatic and deductive structure of Euclid's *Elements* was the model of the synthetic method of proof. Analysis (or *resolutio*) was often thought of as a method of discovery preliminary to the synthesis (or *compositio*), which, reversing the steps of the analytical procedure, achieves the true scientific demonstration. Analysis was thus the working tool of the geometer, but it was with synthesis that one could demonstrate things in an indisputable way. In the Middle Ages this pattern of definitions became bound up with the philosophical and logical tradition. A question which was often raised concerned the relationship between the mathematical proof methods and other accepted forms of deductive proof, typically those codified in Aristotle's *Organon*.[1]

Publication in the sixteenth century of new editions of the Greek classics sparked new interest in the analytical method. Most notably, in 1588 Federico Commandino published his Latin translation of the *Mathematicae Collectiones*, a synopsis of Greek geometry compiled by the fourth-century mathematician Pappus. The attitude of Renaissance culture towards the classics, whether in sculpture, architecture, music, or philosophy, was characterized by admiration and a desire to recover the forgotten achievements of the ancients. The works of Euclid, Apollonius, and Archimedes were considered unsurpassable models. How could the Greeks have achieved such a wealth of results? Pappus' *Collectiones* offered not only geometrical theorems, but also, in the seventh book, a method of analysis, described in vague terms, which would have permitted the ancients to discover their extraordinary results. The books containing full descriptions of this method of analysis referred to by Pappus had been lost. This was the starting point for a deeply rooted, and widely accepted, belief that the ancient geometers were in possession of a powerful method of discovery which they kept hidden, either because it was a secret to be revealed to a handful of adepts, or because they deemed it a method not suitable for public demonstration.

In the decades following the publication of the *Collectiones*, this belief in the existence of a lost or hidden "treasure of analysis" prompted many attempts to "restore" the ancients' method of discovery. Not everybody trod in the steps of Commandino, however. Many promoters of the new symbolic algebra were proud to define themselves as innovators, rather than as restorers. Still, it was common even among creative algebraists such as François Viète, John Wallis, and Isaac Newton to relate symbolic algebra to the ancient analysis, to the hidden problem solving techniques of the ancients.[2] In fact symbolic algebra could be seen as "analysis" since it solves problems by means of equations in which names are given to all quantities – known and unknown. When we state an equation, as Descartes observed, "we first suppose the solution already effected."[3] The equation, linking known and unknown quantities, is the starting point of a process which ends with the expression of the unknown in terms of quantities which are given. Viète's main work, significantly entitled *In Artem Analyticem Isagoge*, published in 1591, opens with a reference to the ancients' knowledge of analysis. Such references to the remote past have often been used (Copernicus in *De Revolutionibus* [1543] is another example) to validate theories which appear to be extremely innovative. Ascertaining the rhetorical role of such declarations is always a difficult historiographic matter. Did Viète genuinely believe himself to be a rediscoverer of past truths, or was he merely invoking the authority of the ancients in order to render new ideas acceptable? It often happens that

reference to the lost ancient tradition is used in different ways by the
same author, sometimes even in the same work. Identifying algebra
with the analytical methods of discovery of the ancients became
common currency, finding a place in the widely circulated, late-
seventeenth-century mathematical dictionary by Ozanam (1690).[4]
However, as the seventeenth century progressed, the rapid advances
in mathematical techniques made this form of reference to the ancients less and less plausible, since the results that mathematicians
were then obtaining were obviously beyond the grasp of the ancient
geometers.

A work that forcefully displayed this idea of modernity, this
awareness of having superseded the venerated ancients, was René
Descartes's *Géométrie* (1637). In this little tract Descartes showed
how symbolic algebra could be applied to the study of plane curves.
Algebra had been developed by mathematicians such as Girolamo
Cardano and Rafael Bombelli in order to deal in a general way with
problems concerning numbers; its object was the solution of algebraic equations. Thanks to the work of Viète, Pierre de Fermat, and
Descartes, it became possible to unite algebra with geometry. According to Descartes, given a coordinate system, a curve can be defined as the locus of points which satisfy an algebraic equation of the
form $f(x, y) = 0$, and the study of the algebraic equation defining a
curve allows one to study the properties of the curve. In *Géométrie*
Descartes did not stress continuity with past tradition: his tract could
be read as a deliberate proof of the superiority of the new analytical
methods, uniting symbolic algebra and geometry, over the purely geometrical ones of the ancients. (At least this is how the *Géométrie*
was read by many seventeenth-century mathematicians; recent research has shown that Descartes's ideas on the relationships between
algebra, geometry, and ancient analysis were actually much more
complex than this.[5]) Descartes began the *Géométrie* with a problem stated in Pappus' *Collectiones*. According to Descartes, it could
be inferred from Pappus' text, which he cited at length, that Euclid
and Apollonius were not able to solve this problem, at least in its
general form, yet Pappus' problem, as it became known, received a
general solution in *Géométrie*: could there have been better proof of
the superiority of the moderns over the ancients?

Descartes's *Géométrie* was introduced in England in a Latin translation prepared by the Dutch mathematician Frans van Schooten.

Two editions of this Latin *Geometria* were published, in 1649 and 1659–61, both with a series of appendices written by van Schooten and other Dutch mathematicians. The second of these editions was known to the young Isaac Newton during his early mathematical studies in Cambridge. He had on his desk a limited, very well chosen, set of mathematical books, which included Viète's works (1646), William Oughtred's *Clavis Mathematicae* (1631), and John Wallis's *Arithmetica Infinitorum* (1655). Oughtred was one of the most outspoken English supporters of Viète's analytic art. His *Clavis* was a small, symbol-laden introduction to algebraic equations, and his preference for the symbolic style was backed by a number of English mathematicians, including Thomas Harriot, John Pell, John Kearsey, John Collins, and Wallis. These authors, in their efforts to promote the acceptance of symbolic algebra, often underscored the advantages of the terse language of modern mathematics when compared with the verbose style of geometry. Such major figures of the scientific revolution as Francis Bacon and Robert Hooke had the same view of the requirements for scientific prose.[6]

The two books which made the strongest impact on Newton's mathematical mind were Descartes's *Geometria* and Wallis's *Arithmetica Infinitorum*. In Descartes's work Newton could study the connection between algebraic equations and curves and learn about the Cartesian algebraic method for drawing a tangent to a curve. He could also acquaint himself with the recent results on maxima and minima of the Dutch school, as laid out in the commentaries by van Schooten, Johann Hudde, and René F. Sluse. Wallis's work went a step further. Where Descartes, Viète, and Oughtred had concerned themselves with finite algebric procedures – the equations which they handled consisted of a finite number of terms – Wallis had employed infinitary approximation procedures, typically infinite products and infinite series, in dealing with "quadratures" (i.e., with the problem of determining the area bounded by a curve). Wallis's infinitary techniques belong to what historians of mathematics often call pre-calculus. In the first half of the seventeenth century, mathematicians tackled problems such as finding tangents and curvatures of curves, or finding areas, volumes, and arc-lengths. Bonaventura Cavalieri, Evangelista Torricelli, James Gregory, Fermat, Blaise Pascal, Gilles Personne de Roberval, and Isaac Barrow, among many others, felt the need to make recourse to the infinite and the infinitesimal. For instance, a tangent to a curve could be conceived as a straight line which intercepts two infinitely close points on the curve, and an area bounded by a curve could be calculated by summing an infinite number of infinitesimally small areas composing it. Newton termed the finitary algebraic methods which he learned in Descartes and Oughtred "common analysis," and he termed "new analysis" the methods that he learned from reading Wallis and from personal contacts with Isaac Barrow, who held the Lucasian Chair of Mathematics when Newton was a student at Cambridge.[7]

Newton was able, during the winter of 1664–5, to establish his first mathematical discovery, the binomial theorem, which can be expressed in somewhat modernized notation as follows:

$$(a + b)^n = a^n + na^{n-1}b + \frac{n(n-1)}{2}a^{n-2}b^2 + \frac{n(n-1)(n-2)}{3 \times 2}a^{n-3}b^3 + \cdots$$

where n can be a positive or negative fraction, such as $-3/2$. Newton obtained this result by generalizing Wallis's interpolation techniques. Starting from a table of the binomial coefficients for positive integer powers, he interpolated for fractional powers and extrapolated for negative powers through complex and rather shaky guesswork.

Newton employed the binomial theorem in order to find the area bounded by curves. This can best be illustrated by an example. A circle with unit radius and center coinciding with the origin of a rectangular coordinate system has equation $x^2 + y^2 = 1$, from which we get $y = (1 - x^2)^{1/2}$. Here is a classic question: what is the area of the circle? Applying the binomial theorem to this formula for y gives the following infinite series:

$$y = 1 - \frac{x^2}{2} - \frac{x^4}{8} - \frac{x^6}{16} - \frac{5x^8}{128} + \cdots$$

Now the areas bounded by the curves of equations $y = 1$, $y = -x^2/2$, $y = -x^4/8$, etc., are easy to calculate by techniques well known to Newton's predecessors. The area of the circle will be obtained by summing all these easily obtainable areas. In practice one can approximate the area under the curve $y = (1 - x^2)^{1/2}$ over the interval $[0,x]$ by summing a finite number of terms. The intuitive idea, not yet substantiated by a theory of convergence as nowadays would be required, was that the greater the number of terms, the better the approximation.

Newton systematized his findings on quadratures via infinite series in a little tract entitled "De analysi per aequationes numero terminorum infinitas"; it was written in 1669, but not published until 1711.[8] As its title suggests, it deals with analysis: it is based on algebraic symbolism derived from Viète and Oughtred, while curves are represented by equations as in Descartes's *Géométrie*. However, these equations are "infinite equations" (i.e., infinite series), something that Descartes would not have accepted. Infinite series were understood by Newton and his contemporaries as "infinite equations," symbolic objects to which the rules of algebra could be straightforwardly applied. This rather free, algebraic handling of infinite series was common until the beginning of the nineteenth century, when concerns over rigor in dealing with infinites began to take hold. According to Newton, the realm of the "common analysis," restricted to "finite equations," could thus be extended to all known curves. Newton wrote: "From all this it is to be seen how much the limits of analysis are enlarged by such infinite equations: in fact by their help analysis reaches, I might almost say, to all problems."[9]

During 1670–1, Newton wrote one of his greatest mathematical works, the *Method of Fluxions and Infinite Series* (the title with which it first appeared in an English translation in 1736).[10] In this long treatise, he presented the rules and the applications of a "method" which he had devised in the *anni mirabiles* 1665–6, the period in which he also performed experiments with prisms and speculated on gravitation. The central idea of his method is the introduction of quantities which are "infinitely" or "indefinitely" small in comparison with finite quantities. Such infinitesimal quantities had already been widely used in seventeenth-century pre-calculus. For these infinitely small quantities a principle of cancellation holds: if a is infinitely small and A is finite, then $A + a = A$.

The objects to which Newton's algorithm is applied are quantities which "flow" in time. For instance the motion of a point generates a line; the motion of a line generates a surface. The quantities generated by "flow" are called "fluents," and their instantaneous speeds are called "fluxions." The "moments" of the fluent quantities are "the infinitely small additions by which those quantities increase during each infinitely small interval of time."[11] Thus, consider a point which flows with variable speed along a straight line. The distance covered at time t is the fluent; the instantaneous speed is the fluxion; the "infinitely" (or "indefinitely") small increment acquired after an "infinitely" (or "indefinitely") small period of time is the moment. Newton further observed that "the moments of the fluent quantities . . . are as their speeds of flow" (i.e., as the fluxions).[12] His reasoning is based on the idea that during an "infinitely small period of time" the fluxion remains constant, and therefore the moment is proportional to the fluxion.

The notation Newton developed for this was rather awkward; it was not until the 1690s that he introduced a now standard notation: the moment of time is o, the fluxion of x is denoted by $\dot{x}$, and the moment of x by $\dot{x}o$. The fluxions themselves can be considered fluent quantities, and hence they too have fluxions. In the 1690s Newton denoted the "second" fluxion of x by $\ddot{x}$.

Newton gives the basic algorithm for calculating fluxions by means of an example. He considers the equation:

$$x^3 - ax^2 + axy - y^3 = 0. \tag{1}$$

He substitutes $x + \dot{x}o$ in place of x and $y + \dot{y}o$ in place of y and expands the powers. Deleting $x^3 - ax^2 + axy - y^3$ as equal to zero and dividing through by o, he obtains an equation from which he cancels the terms which have o as a factor. In fact, these terms "will be equivalent to nothing in respect to the others," since "o is supposed to be infinitely small."[13] At last Newton arrives at:

$$3\dot{x}x^2 - 2a\dot{x}x + a\dot{x}y + a\dot{x}x - 3\dot{y}y^2 = 0, \tag{2}$$

a relation from which the ratio $\dot{y}/\dot{x}$ defining the tangent to the curve expressed by equation (1) can be obtained.

This result is achieved by employing the rule of cancellation of infinitesimals. In fact, Newton assumes that during the infinitesimal interval of time o the motion is uniform, so that when x flows to $x + \dot{x}o$, y flows to $y + \dot{y}o$. He then applies the principle of cancellation of infinitesimals, so in the last step the terms in o are dropped. His justification for this procedure is not much more rigorous than that offered for similar algorithms earlier in the century, such as those by Hudde and Sluse in the commentaries to Descartes's *Geometria*. As we will see, Newton was soon to face some serious foundational questions.

In the *Method*, Newton gives the solution of a series of problems "in illustration of this analytical art," mainly problems of maxima and minima, tangents, curvatures, areas, surfaces, volumes, and arc lengths. With quantities represented as generated by continuous flow, all of these problems can be reduced to the following two (one the inverse of the other):

1. Given the length of the space at every time, to find the speed of motion at any proposed time.
2. Given the speed of motion at every time, to find the length of the space described at any proposed time.[14]

This is among the greatest generalizations in the history of mathematics, reducing the great majority of problems faced by mathematicians of the time to two basic problems. Today's students are accustomed to tackling an impressively large class of problems through the differential and integral calculus. They also know that differentiation and integration are inverse operations, a fact established in the second half of the seventeenth century by Newton and Gottfried Wilhelm Leibniz independently.

In 1671 Newton was thus in possession of a mathematical method which allowed him to supersede all his contemporaries. Just after completing the *Method of Fluxions and Infinite Series*, Newton drafted an *addendum*[15] in which a "more natural approach" was presented, based on axioms "as is customary with the synthetic method."[16] In this short appendix he seems to have been influenced by the mathematical style of his predecessor in the Lucasian Chair, Barrow. Barrow is one of the main representatives – the other, for different reasons, being Thomas Hobbes – of what has been described as a "geometric backlash" in English seventeenth-century mathematics.[17] Barrow and Hobbes were vocal in their support of geometry and took a critical stance toward what they saw as an excessive reliance on symbolism. As indicated earlier, the case for symbolic algebra tied in well with the general move toward simple scientific prose which was characteristic of the English scientific revolution; the defense of geometry, meanwhile, tied in with another equally important aspect of the Baconian methodology then in vogue, empiricism.[18] Questions often asked were whether the symbols employed by the practitioners of the new analysis correspond to existing entities and what the referents are of such new symbols

as the roots of negative numbers (the "imaginary" numbers) and the
infinitesimals. In his unfinished *addendum* to the *Method of Fluxions and Infinite Series*, Newton began to reformulate his method in
purely geometric terms, avoiding the symbolism which had allowed
him to advance so far.

Neither the *addendum* nor the *Method of Fluxions and Infinite
Series* was published during Newton's lifetime. Indeed, one of the
most striking aspects of Newton as a mathematician is how little
and how late he published his results. Soon after completing the
addendum he was drawn into a bitter dispute concerning his optical theory. Some scholars think that his reluctance to publish in
mathematics originated from this sad experience. But other interests, rather than optics or mathematics, were to dominate Newton's
attention during the 1670s, and study of these new interests can
help us to understand Newton's changing approach to mathematical
methodology, revealing other reasons which might have led him not
to publish his early mathematical discoveries.[19]

In the 1670s Newton devoted a great deal of effort to the study
of alchemy, theology, and chronology. Some of his correspondents
observed that he had almost abandoned the study of mathematics
and natural philosophy.[20] These new interests were driven in part by
a deep concern about the theological consequences of the new mechanical philosophy, whose champion was Descartes. Like many of
his English contemporaries, most notably Henry More, Newton felt
that the reduction of natural phenomena to matter and motion was
the first step toward a view of nature which left little room for God's
providential action. By contrast, all his life Newton held to the idea
that God was continuously intervening in the course of natural and
historical events. He turned to the tradition of alchemy and natural
magic, therefore, in order to decipher, behind the figurative language
of the hermetic literature, a truth about Nature and its relation to
God deeper than the image offered by the mechanical philosophy.

In his many alchemical and theological manuscripts Newton
simply repeated themes, rhetorical figures, and myths from the
neo-Platonic tradition. His interest in topics such as the prophecies,
the Kabbala, the chronologies of ancient kingdoms, and alchemy are
typical of a philosophical tradition that was pervasive in the Renaissance, and still alive in Newton's England. It is from this tradition
that Newton derived his idea of history as a process of corruption.

On this view, the ancients – the Jews, but also the Egyptians, the Chaldeans, the Phoenicians, the Greeks, and the Romans – were in possession of the true religion (an uncorrupted form of Christianity), and of the true philosophy as well. As is well known, in the 1690s Newton attributed to the ancients a knowledge of the heliocentric planetary system, of atoms and the void, and of the law of gravitation.[21] In Newton's writings the religion and the natural philosophy of the moderns are always depicted as inferior to, or even a distorted corruption of what the ancients knew. In the neo-Platonic tradition the wisdom of the ancients is often associated with mathematics. A typical example is the myth that Pythagoras revealed to his adepts a secret philosophy based on the mathematical understanding of the harmonies of the world, a myth endorsed by Newton.[22]

During the 1670s Newton developed a great admiration for the geometrical writings of the ancients, leading him into outspoken criticism of the symbolical mathematics pursued by the moderns. His target was often Descartes, whom he criticized with a vehemence illustrated by the following comment on Descartes's solution of Pappus' problem:

To be sure, their [the ancients'] method is more elegant by far than the Cartesian one. For he [Descartes] achieved the result by an algebraic calculus which, when transposed into words (following the practice of the Ancients in their writings), would prove to be so tedious and entangled as to provoke nausea, nor might it be understood. But they accomplished it by certain simple propositions, judging that nothing written in a different style was worthy to be read, and in consequence concealing the analysis by which they found their constructions.[23]

Similar statements can be found in the polemic works of Hobbes, for instance his criticism of the algebraist Wallis in the following terms:

You show me how you could demonstrate the ... articles a shorter way. But though there be your symbols, yet no man is obliged to take them for demonstration. And though they be granted to be dumb demonstrations, yet when they are taught to speak as they ought to do, they will be longer demonstrations than these of mine.[24]

Newton's close study of the seventh book of Pappus' *Collectiones* and his work on the restoration of lost books by Apollonius undoubtedly influenced him in his reassessment of geometry. He devoted particular attention to Pappus' problem, to which his own geometric solution – clearly framed in opposition to Descartes's solution – exhibits "not an [analytical] composition but a geometrical synthesis, such as the ancients required"; it was to appear in print in Section 5, Book 1, of the *Principia*.[25] In manuscripts, Newton characterized the geometry of the ancients as simple, elegant, concise, fitting for the problem posed, and always interpretable in terms of existing objects. In particular, he held, geometrical demonstrations have a safe referential content. By contrast, he stressed the mechanical character of the algebraical methods of the moderns, their utility only as heuristic tools and not as demonstrative techniques, the lack of referential clarity of the concepts employed, and their redundance.[26]

This admiration for the geometrical methods of the ancients and critical view of the algebraical methods of the moderns have their roots in the 1670s, becoming stronger as the years passed. Henry Pemberton, a privileged witness (as editor of the third [1726] edition of the *Principia*) of Newton's last years, wrote:

I have often heard him censure the handling of geometrical subjects by algebraic calculations . . . Of their [the ancients'] taste and form of demonstration Sir Isaac always professed himself a great admirer: I have heard him even censure himself for not following them yet more closely than he did; and speak with regret of his mistake at the beginning of his mathematical studies, in applying himself to the works of Des Cartes and other algebraic writers before he had considered the elements of Euclide with that attention, which so excellent a writer deserves.[27]

In a manuscript dating from the early 1690s, Newton quotes Pappus' definition of the methods of analysis and synthesis, and then directs his attention to algebra, which seems to "differ from their [the ancients'] analysis except in the mere manner of its expression." He then considers a few geometrical problems, remarking that "neither Hercules' patience nor Methuselah's years would . . . suffice" in order to solve them by algebra alone.[28]

It would certainly be overstatement to say that Newton completely abandoned the "new analysis" that he had developed in his *anni mirabiles*. Some of his mathematical achievements in algebra that date from the 1670s were published in 1707 as *Arithmetica Universalis*, and in his later years he continued to be interested in the algebraic classification of cubic curves, in integration techniques, and in power series. However, it is fair to say that after the 1670s he set out to contrast geometrical methods with algebraical ones with the purpose of showing the superiority of the former to the latter, and that he emphasized this superiority on a number of occasions. The circumstances surrounding the publication of the *Arithmetica Universalis* of 1707 are interesting in this regard. This work appeared anonymously, and Newton made it clear that he was compelled to publish it in order to obtain the support of his Cambridge colleagues in the election to the 1705 Parliament.[29] In the preamble "To the Reader" it was stated that the author had "condescended to handle" the subject, and the work ended with oft-quoted statements in favor of pure geometry and against the "moderns" who had lost the "Elegance" of Geometry.[30] In his later years Newton did continue to publish analytical works, but he always emphasized to the reader that these works were not solely representative of his mathematical activity and that geometrical works were superior.

Another way in which Newton distanced himself from his early work in mathematics was the preference he gave to a new method, the "synthetic method of fluxions," which he contrasted with his earlier "analytical method of fluxions."[31] This new synthetic method was first presented in a treatise entitled "Geometria curvilinea," written around 1680.[32] He called this new method "synthetic" because it was based on a number of definitions, axioms, and postulates concerning continuous motion,[33] and its deductive structure was modeled on that of Euclid's *Elements*. The "Geometria curvilinea" opens with the following declaration:

Men of recent times, eager to add to the discoveries of the ancients, have united specious arithmetic [i.e., algebra] with geometry. Benefiting from that, progress has been broad and far-reaching if your eye is on the profuseness of output, but the advance is less of a blessing if you look at the complexity of its conclusions. For these computations, progressing by means of arithmetical operations alone, very often express in an intolerably roundabout way quantities which in geometry are designated by the drawing of a single line.[34]

Newton's purpose in this work was to reformulate the results concerning fluents and fluxions from his early analytical method in geometric terms that were compatible with the methods of the ancients. In the first place he had to avoid symbolic algebra, which he did by referring directly to geometric figures and their properties. Second, he

had to avoid infinitesimals. In the Preface of the "Geometria curvilinea" Newton wrote:

Those who have taken the measure of curvilinear figures have usually
viewed them as made up of infinitely many infinitely-small parts. I, in fact,
shall consider them as generated by growing, arguing that they are greater,
equal or less according as they grow more swiftly, equally swiftly or more
slowly from their beginning. And this swiftness of growth I shall call the
fluxion of a quantity.[35]

In the synthetic method of fluxions Newton considers geometrical
figures not as composed by infinitesimals, but as generated by continuous motion. Furthermore, instead of making recourse to a rule
of cancellation of infinitesimals, he deploys limit procedures. A typical limit procedure consists in the determination of a ratio of two
geometrical flowing quantities (i.e., two "fluents") which "vanish"
in the same instant. For example, given a plane curve, the "ultimate ratio" – when points A and B "come together" – of the chord
and arc terminated by points A and B is equal to 1.[36] Such geometric limit procedures are extensively employed in Newton's *Principia*
(1687).[37] By means of this method, he achieved an improvement on
the "Geometria curvilinea" in explicitly avoiding infinitesimals, replacing them with limits, though he still needed to justify the limits
themselves.

Berkeley was to observe in the *Analyst* (1734) that the "limits of
vanishing quantities" employed in the *Principia* are as mysterious as
the infinitesimals, since the "ultimate ratio of two vanishing quantities," when the quantities are "vanished," is o/o, and before they
have vanished the ratio is not the "ultimate." It is worth quoting
from Section 1 of the *Principia* on this point, where Newton invokes
intuitions concerning continuous motion:

It may be objected that there is no such thing as an ultimate proportion
of vanishing quantities, inasmuch as before vanishing the proportion is not
ultimate, and after vanishing it does not exist at all. But by the same argument it could equally be contended that there is no ultimate velocity of a
body reaching a certain place at which the motion ceases; for before the body
arrives at this place, the velocity is not the ultimate velocity, and when it
arrives there, there is no velocity at all.[38]

The synthetic method of first and ultimate ratios is not the only
mathematical tool employed in the *Principia*:[39] the book draws on a

considerable repertoire of mathematical techniques. The analytical method of fluxions plays a role in Book 2 of the *Principia*,[40] a fact that Newton emphasized in the heated context of the famous priority dispute in which he and Leibniz, who had discovered the calculus independently, accused each other of plagiarism. Clearly Newton was trying to use the *Principia* as proof that his knowledge of analytic methods was equivalent to Leibniz's calculus prior to the first publication of the differential calculus in 1684. Speaking of himself in the third person, he wrote:

By the help of this new Analysis Mr. Newton found out most of the Propositions in his *Principia Philosophiae*. But because the Ancients for making things certain admitted nothing into Geometry before it was demonstrated synthetically, he demonstrated the Propositions synthetically that the systeme of the heavens might be founded upon good Geometry. And this makes it now difficult for unskillful men to see the Analysis by which those Propositions were found out.[41]

Clearly such statements have to be regarded with some caution since they were aimed at proving Leibniz's plagiarism. However, there are a number of Newton's manuscript notes in existence that give demonstrations of the *Principia* which show the analytical method of fluxions being deployed. Newton is quite right in stating that the "synthetic method of fluxions [notably, the method of first and ultimate ratios] occurs widespread" in the *Principia*. There is abundant evidence that he is also right in maintaining that in the *Principia* there are also "specimens of the analytical method."[42] Most notably, in many demonstrations of the *Principia* Newton used his highly symbolic algorithms for quadratures which he had developed in the *Method of Fluxions and Infinite Series*.

There are propositions in the *Principia* which begin with phrases such as "granting the quadratures of curvilinear figures." These propositions reduce the problem to the quadrature of (i.e., the determination of the area subtended by) a curve. Newton does not explain to the reader how these quadratures can be achieved, but he sometimes states the results which follow from them. So it is true that specimens of the analytical method occur in the *Principia*, but in a rather oblique, veiled way. The following points provide further evidence of this: (i) there are results in the *Principia* which can be achieved only by application of quadrature techniques (in Leibnizian jargon, integral calculus), (ii) these results are preceded, or followed, by statements in which the analytical method of quadratures is referred to, (iii) all these quadratures are included in the *Method of Fluxions and Infinite Series*, and (iv) when David Gregory asked Newton to complete missing steps alluded to in the *Principia*, Newton replied by expressing the dynamical quantities (such as velocity and acceleration) in the geometric diagrams in symbolic terms and then formed a fluxional equation and solved it. The analytical method of fluxions thus did occur in the *Principia*, but it occurred implicitly.[43]

There are many reasons why Newton might have chosen not to be open about his use of the analytical method of fluxions. One of these is his classicism, the methodological turn in favor of the ancient geometry which had led him to distance himself prior to the composition of the *Principia* from modern symbolical methods; but this provides only one cultural reason for his adopting the geometric style of the *Principia*. There were other reasons behind his choice of the *Principia*'s mathematical style: the readers whom he had in mind, his ideas on the relationship between mathematics and nature, and the problems that his cosmology implied.

When Newton wrote the *Principia*, he was addressing himself to readers who did not know the calculus, which during this period, the 1680s and 1690s, was practiced by only a handful of initiates. In the late 1710s Newton showed awareness that the competence of his readers had changed:

To the mathematicians of the present century, however, versed almost wholly in algebra as they are, this [i.e., the *Principia*'s synthetic style of writing] is less pleasing, whether because it may seem too prolix and too akin to the method of the ancients, or because it is less revealing of the manner of discovery. And certainly I could have written analytically what I had found out analytically with less effort than it took me to compose it. I was writing for philosophers steeped in the elements of geometry, and putting down geometrically demonstrated bases for physical science.[44]

While the "philosophers" of 1687 were "steeped" in geometry, the generation of mathematicians formed under the Bernoullis in Paris and Basel, who began their studies in higher mathematics reading L'Hospital's *Analyse des infiniment petits* (1696), found the *Principia* obscure.

Furthermore, Newton insisted that his mathematical methods be ontologically well founded. While the algebraical, symbolical methods were merely heuristic tools, the method of fluxions, especially in its synthetic, geometric version, dealt with objects, fluents, and fluxions, which "take place in the reality of physical nature and are daily witnessed in the motion of bodies."[45] According to the Galilean tradition the Book of Nature is written in geometric terms. Newton endorsed this tradition and resisted the idea of representing motion, acceleration, and force in symbolic terms. The geometric diagrams of the *Principia* exhibit real trajectories and represent real accelerations and forces in terms of visualizable geometric magnitudes: "for fluxions are finite quantities and real, and consequently ought to have their own symbols; and each time it can conveniently so be done, it is preferable to express them by finite lines visible to the eye rather than by infinitely small ones."[46] A late Newtonian, John Colson, went so far as to describe the fluxional geometrical procedures as "ocular demonstrations."[47]

One further reason lies behind the preference given to geometry in the *Principia*: Newton's cosmology of universal gravitation and the problems it implied. According to this cosmology, mathematizing Nature means dealing in mathematical terms with universal gravitation: mathematizing all the effects caused by the gravitational force, e.g., tides and planetary shapes. The possibility of mathematically predicting these effects was crucial for Newton, and the acceptance of universal gravitation depended on the success of such a mathematization. However, the analytical method of fluxions was not yet sufficiently powerful to cope with these problems, and Newton and his followers found on their agenda a set of problems which could not be tackled with the calculi which he and Leibniz had created. Recent research carried on by Subrahamyan Chandrasekhar and Michael Nauenberg has shown us how far Newton could go in dealing in analytical terms with lunar motion.[48] It seems clear to me, however, that in advanced topics such as these the analytical method could be employed only with sporadic success. In several passages of his demonstrations Newton had no choice but to fall back on the rich traditional arsenal of geometry.

After the *Principia*, Newton's creativity as a mathematician somewhat declined. He was busy, however, editing his mathematical works, forming a school of proselytes, and arguing with Leibniz. He also devoted a great deal of time to his project of reinstating the work of the ancient geometers. As the century progressed, this project appeared more and more old fashioned, but Newton was adamant in championing the ancients against the moderns. In the 1690s he wrote: "and if the authority of the new Geometers is against us, nonetheless the authority of the Ancients is greater."[49] He also succeeded in communicating his interest in classical mathematics to some of his disciples, which resulted in, for example, the editions of Apollonius' *Conics* by Gregory and Edmond Halley and the restoration of Euclid's *Porisms* by Robert Simson and Matthew Stewart.

Newton's concern for the foundations of his method is evident in the editing for publication of his "Tractatus de quadratura curvarum" (composed in the early 1690s and published in 1704) and the "De analysi per aequationes numero terminorum infinitas" (composed in 1669 and published in 1711). He revised his original manuscripts in an effort to avoid reference to infinitesimals.[50] He also made it clear in the Preface to the "De quadratura" and in the anonymous *Account of the Commercium Epistolicum* (1715) that the algorithmic techniques of the analytical method of fluxions were nothing more than an heuristic tool, employed when "not demonstrating but only investigating a Proposition, for making dispatch," which could and should be translated into the rigorous geometric form of the synthetic method.[51] He viewed Leibniz's calculus in this way, as an heuristic tool, devoid of scientific character: "Mr. Leibnitz's [method] is only for finding it out."[52] His analytical fluxional algorithm, by contrast, was truly demonstrative since it could always be interpreted in geometric terms:

This approach agrees basically with that of Leibniz, yet is, however, but a small part of a more general method... analytical mathematicians attempt to bring everything down to equations. In the present method equations are hardly handled at all.[53]

The values that Newton promoted among his disciples – continuity with the past geometrical tradition, an interest in the representability of mathematical symbols, and a distrust of algorithmic techniques – were in sharp conflict with the values enthusiastically adopted by the Leibnizian school. Leibniz thought of his calculus as an example of universal characteristic, a universal symbolic language able to express all forms of reasoning. Indeed, he praised the *cogitatio caeca*, the blind use of reasoning, which frees the mind from the burden of imagination.[54] In his view the geometry of the ancients was inferior to the new calculus. Writing to Huygens in September 1691, he affirmed with pride:

It is true, Sir, as you correctly believe, that what is better and more useful in my new calculus is that it yields truths by means of a kind of analysis, and without any effort of the imagination, which often works as by chance, and it gives us the same advantages over Archimedes, which Viète and Descartes gave us over Apollonius.[55]

This highly abstract, proudly innovative and de-geometrized calculus, which was to dominate eighteenth-century mathematics, found little favor with Newton and his British disciples.[56]

NOTES

1   See Michael Otte and Marco Panza (eds.), *Analysis and Synthesis in Mathematics: History and Philosophy* (Dordrecht: Kluwer, 1997) for a recent collection of studies devoted to the changing meaning of the methods of analysis and synthesis.
2   See Katherine Hill, "Neither Ancient nor Modern: Wallis and Barrow on the Composition of Continua. Part one: Mathematical Styles and the Composition of Continua," *Notes and Records of the Royal Society of London* 50(2) (1996), 165–78 (p. 171).
3   René Descartes, *The Geometry of René Descartes*, trans. David E. Smith and Marcia L. Latham (New York: Dover, 1954), p. 6.
4   Jacques Ozanam, *Dictionnaire mathématique* (Paris, 1690).
5   Henk J. M. Bos, "On the Representation of Curves in Descartes' *Géométrie*," *Archive for History of Exact Sciences* 24 (1981), 295–338; Giorgio Israel, "The Analytical Method in Descartes' *Géométrie*," in Otte and Panza (eds.), *Analysis and Synthesis*, pp. 3–34.
6   See Wilbur S. Howell, *Eighteenth-Century British Rhetoric and Logic* (Princeton: Princeton University Press, 1971), pp. 481, 486, and 494; Helena M. Pycior, *Symbols, Impossible Numbers, and Geometric Entanglements: British Algebra through the Commentaries on Newton's Universal Arithmetick* (Cambridge: Cambridge University Press, 1997), pp. 46–7.
7   See Richard T. W. Arthur, "Newton's Fluxions and Equably Flowing Time," *Studies in History and Philosophy of Science* 26 (1995), 323–51, and Mordechai Feingold, "Newton, Leibniz, and Barrow Too: An Attempt at a Reinterpretation," *Isis* 84 (1993), 310–38 for recent work on the much disputed topic of Barrow's influence on Newton.

8   D. T. Whiteside (ed.), *The Mathematical Papers of Isaac Newton*, 8 vols., (Cambridge: Cambridge University Press, 1967–81), vol. 2, pp. 206–47.

9   *The Correspondence of Isaac Newton*, vol. 2, ed. H. W. Turnbull (Cambridge: Cambridge University Press, 1960), p. 39.

10 Whiteside (ed.), *Mathematical Papers*, vol. 3, pp. 32–329. *The Method of Fluxions and Infinite Series* (London: H. Woodfall and J. Nourse, 1736).

11 Whiteside (ed.), *Mathematical Papers*, vol. 3, pp. 80–1.

12 *Ibid.*, pp. 78–9.

13 *Ibid.*, pp. 80–1.

14 *Ibid.*, pp. 70–1.

15 *Ibid.*, pp. 328–53.

16 *Ibid.*, pp. 328–31.

17 Pycior, *Symbols, Impossible Numbers, and Geometric Entanglements*, p. 6.

18 On Barrow's defense of mathematics as a science dealing with "things … exposed to senses," see *ibid.*, p. 156.

19 For a masterful study on the interaction between Newton's studies in theology, chronology, alchemy, and mathematics see Richard S. Westfall, *Never at Rest: A Biography of Isaac Newton* (Cambridge: Cambridge University Press, 1980), ch. 9.

20 See John Collins's letter to James Gregory of October 1675 in *The Correspondence of Isaac Newton*, vol. 1, ed. H. W. Turnbull (Cambridge: Cambridge University Press, 1959), p. 356.

21 See J. E. McGuire and P. M. Rattansi, "Newton and the 'Pipes of Pan'," *Notes and Records of the Royal Society of London* 21 (1966), 108–43.

22 Paolo Casini, "The Pythagorean Myth: Copernicus to Newton," in Luigi Pepe (ed.), *Copernico e la questione copernicana in Italia* (Florence: Olschki, 1996), pp. 183–99.

23 Whiteside (ed.), *Mathematical Papers*, vol. 4, pp. 276–7.

24 *The English Works of Thomas Hobbes*, ed. William Molesworth (London: Longman, Brown, Green and Longmans, 1985), vol. 7, pp. 281–2.

25 Newton, *Principia*, Book 1, Lemma 19.

26 Whiteside (ed.), *Mathematical Papers*, vol. 8, pp. 449–51.

27 Henry Pemberton, *A View of Sir Isaac Newton's Philosophy* (London: S. Palmer, 1728), Preface (pages unnumbered).

28 Whiteside (ed.), *Mathematical Papers*, vol. 7, pp. 251, 254n.

29 Westfall, *Never at Rest*, pp. 648–9.

30 Whiteside (ed.), *Mathematical Papers*, vol. 5, p. 429.

31 *Ibid.*, vol. 8, pp. 454–5.

32 *Ibid.*, vol. 4, pp. 420–521.

33 *Ibid.*, pp. 424–9.

34 *Ibid.*, p. 421. I have departed at one point from Whiteside's translation.
35 *Ibid.*, p. 423.
36 Newton, *Principia*, Book 1, Lemma 7.
37 The relationship between Newton's method of first and ultimate ratios, as presented in Section 1 of Book 1 of the *Principia*, and the differential and integral calculus is discussed in Bruce Pourciau, "The Preliminary Mathematical Lemmas of Newton's *Principia*," *Archive for History of Exact Sciences* 52 (1998), 279–5.
38 Newton, *Principia*, Book 1, Scholium to Lemma 11.
39 The method of first and ultimate ratios is defined by Newton as part of the synthetic method of fluxions in Whiteside (ed.), *Mathematical Papers*, vol. 8, pp. 446–7.
40 Specifically, in Lemma 2 and the sequel. See also Michael Nauenberg, "Newton's Portsmouth Perturbation Method for the Three-Body Problem and Its Application to Lunar Motion," in R. Dalitz and M. Nauenberg (eds.), *The Foundations of Newtonian Scholarship* (Singapore: World Scientific, 2000), for discussion of another place in which Newton relies on the analytic method of fluxions in the *Principia*.
41 This quotation comes from the anonymous review of the *Commercium Epistolicum* which appeared in the *Philosophical Transactions* for the year 1715. See Whiteside (ed.), *Mathematical Papers*, vol. 8, pp. 598–9.
42 *Ibid.*, pp. 455–7.
43 See Niccolò Guicciardini, *Reading the* Principia: *The Debate on Newton's Mathematical Methods for Natural Philosophy from 1687 to 1736* (Cambridge: Cambridge University Press, 1999).
44 Whiteside (ed.), *Mathematical Papers*, vol. 8, pp. 450–1. I have slightly altered Whiteside's translation from the Latin.
45 *Ibid.*, pp. 122–3.
46 *Ibid.*, pp. 112–15.
47 See Niccolò Guicciardini, *The Development of Newtonian Calculus in Britain, 1700–1800* (Cambridge: Cambridge University Press, 1989), p. 57.
48 Subrahamyan Chandrasekhar, *Newton's* Principia *for the Common Reader* (Oxford: Clarendon Press, 1995) and Nauenberg "Newton's Portsmouth Perturbation Method."
49 Whiteside (ed.), *Mathematical Papers*, vol. 7, p. 185n.
50 In the published "De quadratura" (1704) Newton changed "infinite parva" into "admodum parva." See Whiteside (ed.), *Mathematical Papers*, vol. 7, p. 512n. In the published "De analysi" (1711) the editor William Jones, most probably after Newton's instruction, changed "esse infinite parvam" into "in infinitum diminuui & evanescere." See *ibid.*, vol. 2, pp. 242–3.

51 Whiteside (ed.), *Mathematical Papers*, vol. 8, p. 572.
52 *Ibid.*, vol. 8, p. 598.
53 *Ibid.*, vol. 4, pp. 570–1.
54 See Enrico Pasini, *"Arcanum artis inveniendi*: Leibniz and Analysis," in Otte and Panza (eds.), *Analysis and Synthesis*, pp. 35–46.
55 Gottfried Wilhelm Leibniz, *Leibnizens mathematische Schriften*, 7 vols., ed. C. I. Gerhard (Berlin: Weidmannische Buchhandlung, 1875–90; reprinted Hildesheim: Olms, 1978), vol. 2, p. 104.
56 Three other important works consulted while preparing this chapter were C. H. Edwards, *The Historical Development of the Calculus* (New York and Berlin: Springer, 1979), and D. T. Whiteside, "Patterns of Mathematical Thought in the Later Seventeenth Century," *Archive for History of Exact Sciences* 1 (1961) 1, 180–388 and "The Mathematical Principles underlying Newton's *Principia Mathematica*," *Journal for the History of Astronomy* 1 (1970), 116–38.

10 Newton, active powers, and the mechanical philosophy

Among the notable eighteenth-century expositions of Newton's achievements were Henry Pemberton's *A View of Sir Isaac Newton's Philosophy* (1728), Willem Jacob 'sGravesande's *Mathematical Elements of Natural Philosophy confirm'd by experiments: or, an introduction to Sir Isaac Newton's Philosophy* (6th edn, 1747), and Colin Maclaurin's posthumous *An Account of Sir Isaac Newton's Philosophical Discoveries* (1748). To the modern eye, there is something puzzling about these titles. We note the terms "philosophy," "natural philosophy," and "philosophical," and we wonder what they mean in this setting. Take Maclaurin's *Account*, the best of the genre, and written by one of the leading Newtonians of the day. Newton made great scientific discoveries, and we can learn what most of them are from reading *An Account*, but what *philosophical* discoveries did he make? Maclaurin describes Newton's work in mechanics, rational and celestial, and in physics, theoretical and experimental (though not optics). But Newton the *philosopher*? To answer these questions requires a preliminary disentanglement of the disciplinary classifications that clustered around the business of "philosophy" in the seventeenth and eighteenth centuries.

In Newton's day the predominant framework of university instruction in philosophy was that of the Peripatetic or scholastic tradition, adapted to local religious and cultural requirements (Protestant in Germany, Holland, and Britain; Catholic in France, Spain, and Italy). In that tradition, *Philosophy* divides into *speculative* and *practical* philosophy. Speculative philosophy divides in turn into three principal *sciences* (*scientiae*): *metaphysics* or *first philosophy*, *natural philosophy*, and *mathematics*; to which are added the *middle sciences* (*scientiae mediae*), which include theoretical mechanics, optics, and astronomy. Loosely speaking, science (*scientia*) is knowledge of virtually anything, or a *habitus*, an intellectual disposition enjoyed by the possessor of scientific knowledge. Properly speaking, science results from demonstration with respect to "the why" of something, and is knowledge (*cognitio*) of things through their proximate causes.[1] Mathematics is the science of number, extension, and measure, in abstraction from material things. Natural philosophy, also called physics (*physica*) or sometimes physiology (*physiologia*), is the science of the causes of change and stasis in the natural world; the middle or mixed sciences combine mathematics and physics. In its widest acceptation, *metaphysics* is the science of being *qua* being, in abstraction from particular beings, but for some, metaphysics is the science of beings that are other than physical, that is, God, angels, and separated souls or minds, though some argued that to treat of God, angels, and souls is not the business of metaphysics,[2] and others that it is not the business of physics.[3] For yet others, metaphysics is the universal science of concepts that apply transcendentally to beings in general. *Practical* philosophy divides into *active* or *moral* philosophy (ethics, home economics, and politics), and the *mechanical arts* (*artes mechanicae*), which are concerned with the production of artificial objects for human use. Some writers included logic as a branch of philosophy, though it was more commonly seen as an art or instrument of reason.[4] Another important classification of philosophy was that of the Stoics, or more generally of the Hellenistic philosophers, who divided philosophy into physics, ethics, and logic. This taxonomy shaped Locke's "Division of the Sciences" at the end of Book 4 of the *Essay concerning Human Understanding* (1690),[5] and is reflected in Newton's proposal, which dates from the early 1690s, for university reform, "Of Educating Youth in the Universities." The philosophy professor is to begin with "things introductory to natural philosophy" (space, time, laws of motion, circular motion, mechanical powers, laws of gravity, hydrostatics, projectiles), and then move to natural philosophy in the wider sense (cosmology, meteors, minerals, vegetables, animals, anatomy). "Also to examin in Logicks & Ethicks."[6]

Viewing them within a disciplinary perspective (as distinct from the revolutionary changes in their theoretical content), mathematics and natural philosophy retained the same core identity throughout the seventeenth and eighteenth centuries. Mathematics maintained its special autonomy. Natural philosophy continued to be defined in eighteenth-century dictionaries and encyclopedias as the science of natural bodies, and its topical range underwent no substantial change from the late sixteenth to well into the eighteenth century. When Newton began the study of natural philosophy in his second year at Trinity College, Cambridge, in June 1661, the textbook was Johannes Magirus's *Physiologia Peripatetica*. Magirus dealt with the full sweep of topics proper to *physiologia*: the principles of natural things, place, vacuum, motion, time; the planets, fixed stars, eclipses; the elements, primary, secondary and occult qualities, mixed bodies; meteors, comets, tides, winds; metals, minerals, plants, spirits, man, zoophytes; the soul, the senses, dreams, the intellect, the will. This was the broad agenda for natural philosophy throughout Newton's lifetime, unimpaired in his case by a possible inclination toward the Stoic classification of philosophy.[7] He wrote on many of these topics, though not in equal measure. In particular, he wrote and experimented in great measure on alchemical questions. As a speculative inquiry into the manifold reactions between metals, acids and alkalis, minerals and other substances, alchemy was part of natural philosophy. As an art (*ars*), wielding crucible and furnace for the prize of transmutation in accordance with the precepts of speculative theory, alchemy was distinguished from natural philosophy by Peripatetic encyclopedists. As for metaphysics, there were varying senses of the term in Newton's day, as we have seen, and its career in Britain, from Locke through Newton and Berkeley to Hume, was markedly at variance with its career across the English Channel, from Descartes, Spinoza, and Leibniz through Wolff to Kant.

Evidently, Newton was a natural philosopher and mathematician in the traditional senses. But he was also a metaphysician in one or other of the senses mentioned above, and to be one he did not have to have published a metaphysical discourse in the *Acta Eruditorum* or a treatise on first philosophy. In the unpublished manuscript "De gravitatione" (mid-1680s), metaphysics deals with God and his management of his Creation, doctrines of substance, the nature of mind and body and their interaction and union.[8] In the *Principia* (1687), written shortly after "De gravitatione," we find what seems a shift in perspective that is all the more significant because it appears in a public setting. The "General Scholium," which first appeared in the second edition, contains the famous passage on God, Lord over all. He is eternal, infinite, absolutely perfect, omnipotent and omniscient, and substantially omnipresent. His substance is unknown to us; we know God only through his attributes and the excellency of the natural order, and through the final causes of things. He is the God of providence: "no variation in things arises from blind metaphysical necessity, which especially is always and everywhere the same." Newton rounds off the passage with the remark: "And thus much concerning God, to reason about whom, at least from phenomena, is a concern of Natural Philosophy."[9] The study of God *qua* Author of Nature (of souls too, by implication), or rather the study of Christ's vice-regency in the world, in keeping with Newton's Arianism,[10] has become part of natural philosophy, as allowed by Locke's division of the sciences. On this view, metaphysics would be restricted to such topics as freedom and necessity, causality, and (presumably) being *qua* being. Again, the evidence of some manuscript drafts (*c.* 1705) relating to Query 23 of the Latin *Optice* (1706), which became Query 31 of the second English edition (1717–18), is that "metaphysical" describes non-empirical inquiries into the occult non-inertial powers, and associated laws of motion hitherto undiscovered, that might activate the interacting realms of the spiritual and the corporeal.[11] Yet part of Query 28 in the printed *Opticks* (3rd and 4th English editions, 1721, 1730) reads as though the metaphysician inquires into the divine ground of physical process, a view in keeping with that in "De gravitatione." The ancient atomists rejected a universal fluid medium for the propagation of light,

tacitly attributing Gravity to some other Cause than dense Matter. Later Philosophers banish the Consideration of such a Cause out of natural Philosophy, feigning Hypotheses for explaining all things mechanically, and referring other Causes to Metaphysicks: Whereas the main Business of natural Philosophy is to argue from Phaenomena without feigning Hypotheses, and to deduce Causes from Effects, till we come to the very first Cause, which certainly is not mechanical.[12]

Taken together, these representative passages suggest ambiguities in Newton's position on the identity of metaphysics, or reveal tensions arising from an awareness of creeping unsettlement on these taxonomic matters among his philosophical peers. Perhaps the issue can be stated in another way: how much of the study of God, *qua* Author of Nature, is to belong to natural philosophy, how much to metaphysics?

Leaving the general question of how Newton understood the discipline of metaphysics, there are metaphysical aspects of his natural philosophy that are crucial to an adequate understanding of two specific issues on which I want to concentrate. These are (1) Newton's engagement with the mechanical philosophy, and (2) his account of the causal interventions of mind and soul in the physical world. As it happens, a convenient bridge to these issues is provided by Maclaurin's *Account*, of which Book 1 is a survey of previous philosophical systems designed to silhouette the superiority of Newton's system. Maclaurin's closeness to the Newtonian legacy wins him a measure of ostensible authenticity which I shall exploit for my purposes in this chapter.

Maclaurin sees natural philosophy as "the firmest bulwark against Atheism," securing natural religion equally "against the idle sophistry of *Epicureans*, and the dangerous refinements of *modern metaphysicians*."[13] He attacks those philosophers, ancient and modern, whose transgressions have compromised the firmness of that bulwark. In every case, and on nearly every issue, the paragon of all virtues philosophical, whether natural, metaphysical or mathematical, is Sir Isaac Newton.[14] Newton unmasks the monstrous Lucretian system, reborn in the extravagant system of Descartes, who banished final causes, referring all explanations to "mechanism and metaphysical or material necessity." It was Newton's delight, "as I have heard him observe," notes Maclaurin, that his philosophy called attention to final causes. Among Descartes's errors was a principle of conservation of motion, based on an "extraordinary" inference from the constancy of God's action. Yet nothing is more at odds with experience, because perfectly elastic bodies do not exist, the only circumstance that would make the principle plausible. Some motion is always lost when bodies collide, so the universe *per se* cannot be a mechanical perpetual motion. The conservation principle is the cornerstone of the mechanist's universe, whether in the Cartesian, Leibnizian, or Spinozan form. In Spinozism, "un Cartésianisme outré" (Maclaurin expediently quoting Leibniz), substance exists necessarily, all happens with absolute necessity, there are no final causes, there is no vacuum, the account of good and evil is a perversion, and the same quantity of motion, or at any rate the same proportion of motion to rest, is conserved in the universe. The absurdities of Spinozism illustrate the nonsense to which Cartesianism leads, and for those coming fresh to the Spinozan system, in trusting innocence, they reveal its source, "which is no other than the *Cartesian* fable; of which almost every article has been disproved by Sir *Isaac Newton* or others."

A philosopher who "ridiculed the metaphysics of the *English*, as narrow, and founded on unadequate notions,"[15] was responsible for "a far-fetched uncommon stretch of metaphysics" according to which there cannot be atoms or a vacuum, because a principle of the identity of indiscernibles stipulates that not even God can choose between two identical states of affairs. Leibniz's claim that "the material system is a machine absolutely perfect," a consequence of "an excessive fondness for necessity and mechanism," is refuted by Newton's observation that "the fabrick of the universe, and course of nature, could not continue for ever in its present state, but would re-quire, in process of time, to be re-established or renewed by the same hand that formed it." Descartes's beast-machine doctrine is as noth-ing compared with Leibniz's preestablished harmony, or with his pre-tense "that the soul does not act on the body, nor the body on the soul; that both proceed by necessary laws, the soul in its perceptions and volitions, and the body in its motions, without affecting each other; but that each is to be considered as a separate independent machine."

In short, almost everybody is found wanting. Witness the absurd schemes of Plato, Aristotle, Epicurus, the Sceptics, the alleged clear ideas of Descartes, the fictitious metaphysics of Leibniz, the crazy notions of Spinoza. The obsession with mechanism has led some to exclude from the universe everything but matter and motion (pre-sumably Hobbes); others (meaning Berkeley) admit only perceptions and what perceives; others (presumably the Occasionalists) "impair the beauty of nature" by denying intermediate causal links between God and the world. "Many who suffered themselves to be pleased with *Des Cartes*'s fables, were put to a stand by *Spinoza*'s impi-eties. Many went along with Mr. *Leibnitz*'s scheme of absolute ne-cessity, but demurred at his *monads* and *pre-established harmony*. And some, willing to give up the reality of matter, could not think of giving up their own and other minds." Such a medley of philosophies has induced scepticism in certain quarters about the ability of philosophy to furnish any knowledge at all (presumably Locke and Hume).

But it has appeared sufficiently, from the discoveries of those who have consulted nature and not their own imaginations, and particularly from what we learn from Sir *Isaac Newton*, that the fault has lain in the philosophers themselves, and not in philosophy. A compleat system indeed was not to be expected from one man, or one age, or perhaps from the greatest number of ages; could we have expected it from the abilities of any one man, we surely should have had it from Sir *Isaac Newton*: but he saw too far into nature to attempt it. How far he has carried this work, and what are the most important of his discoveries, we now proceed to consider.

Allowing for Maclaurin's hagiographical intemperance, we are intrigued that he sends the knight of Woolsthorpe to battle against Descartes, Spinoza, Leibniz, and, though he is shy about naming them, Locke, Berkeley, and Hume. The author of the *Principia* and the *Opticks* seems not to belong in the same intellectual arena as the opposing triumvirates of what some now call "Rationalism" and "Empiricism." But that is not how Maclaurin saw the situation. Looking at it through his eyes, without kneeling with him at the Newtonian altar, we discover a Newton who is not a dabbler in metaphysical matters, but a mathematician and natural philosopher whose theorizing is inseparable from metaphysical concerns he shared with his contemporaries and predecessors.[16]

For those working within "the new philosophy," the most striking limitation of Peripatetic natural philosophy was its inability to provide what they took to be properly explanatory schemes for dealing with natural phenomena. The Peripatetics had constructed impressive arrays of divisions and subdivisions for *describing* the bewildering variety of principles, qualities, relations, motions, and quantities revealed by natural bodies, but for the protagonists of the new philosophy these classificatory proliferations were absurdly complex and, more to the point, were useless for *explaining* natural phenomena. They welcomed the possibility of explaining nature by recourse to three or four fundamental attributes and modes of body.[17] The undergraduate Newton would have quickly spotted the explanatory ineffectiveness of the Peripatetic system, and would have appreciated the contrasting attractions of the new ways of philosophizing that he found in the writings of Galileo, Charleton, Hobbes, Boyle, Hooke, More, Glanvill, Digby, and Descartes, when he began to study them on his own (they were not in the curriculum!) a couple of years after entering Trinity College.

However, Newton also quickly understood that the new physics promised more than it could ever deliver, seducing many into believing that its explanatory simplicities would be able to cope with the endlessly complex real worlds of (al)chemist, metallurgist, experimental philosopher, pharmacist, physiologist, or physician. The mechanical philosophy, of whatever stripe, was by no means an unqualified success in explaining all natural phenomena. There is much truth in Stahl's observation (1723) that "mechanical philosophy, though it vaunts itself as capable of explaining everything most clearly, has applied itself rather presumptuously to the consideration of chemico-physical matters ... it scratches the shell and surface of things and leaves the kernel untouched."[18] Or rather, it purported to reveal the reality of the kernel though it was incapable of reaching it through experimental inquisition. No one understood that better than Isaac Newton.

Newton's engagement with the mechanical philosophy is therefore an intractable issue. There are two immediate difficulties. The first concerns the term "mechanical." In the early modern period it enjoyed a wide range of meanings, the shared central sense being "concerned in some way with manual activity," that is, with artisanal operations, practical skills, the construction and working of machines, physical conditions and objects and the interactions between them, chemical manipulations, and experiments. By extension, since Antiquity, "mechanical" had connoted the theory of machines and more generally mechanics *qua* the science of bodies in motion and rest.[19] But proper usages of "mechanical" in the "artisanal sense" and in the "theoretical sense" did not depend on or assume any perceived necessary relation between them. Writing in 1594, Henry Percy extolled "the doctrine of generation and corruption," which "unfoldeth to our understandings the method generall of all attomycall combinations possible in homogeneall substances, together with the wayes possible of generating of the same substance," a part of philosophy that "the practisse of Alkemy doeth mutche further, and it selfe [is] incredibely inlarged, being a meere mecanicall broiling trade without this phylosophicall project."[20] Clearly, this mechanical trade is far removed from anything in Pseudo-Aristotle's *Mechanica* or Book 8 of Pappus' *Collectiones*. When Thomas Sprat in 1667 asked whether it would not be better for children to learn through seeing and touching sensible things – "In a word, Whether a Mechanical Education would not excel the Methodical?"[21] – he was not referring to the theory of machines or to the laws of motion. Nor was Henry Power when in 1664 he looked to the day when the microscope would reveal magnetic effluvia, the atoms of light and of fluids, and air particles. "And though these hopes be vastly hyperbolical," he conceded, "yet who can tel how far Mechanical Industry may prevail; for the process of Art is indefinite, and who can set a *non-ultra* to her endeavours?"[22] Robert Boyle understood "mechanical" in both the artisanal and theoretical senses, and had a sharper insight into their relations than most of his contemporaries.[23] Shortly before the publication of Newton's *Principia* his friend Fatio de Duillier informed the Abbé Nicaise that: "They are publishing a Latin work by Monsieur Newton in which he deals with the general mechanics of the world. This work concerns mainly the system of astronomy, but it is filled with a large number of very interesting things about rather another subject and which concerns at the same time physics and mathematics."[24] The phrase "the general mechanics of the world" might be thought to refer to mechanics in the theoretical sense. But even here the substantive "the mechanics" refers to "the general workings or mechanism of the world," not to a body of mechanical laws that apply to that mechanism, though of course Fatio de Duillier knew that the *Principia* contained those as well. Newton himself wrote in the *Opticks* that one of the tasks of natural philosophy is "to unfold the Mechanism of the World" (quoted below); these are virtually the same terms used by Fatio de Duillier to describe the *Principia*.

The second difficulty is how to characterize "the mechanical philosophy." A theory of explanation of phenomena in the non-qualitative terms of the configurations and motions of atoms or corpuscles, or other homogeneous matter individuated into bodies? A theory characterized by the notion that the universe and every system within it is a machine? Or characterized by the ideal of mathematizing the world picture? Or by the belief in necessary laws of nature and of motion? A theory in which the spiritual and the immaterial have been banished from the domain of investigation? Each of these is distinct from the others, yet each of them is a candidate for inclusion under the umbrella of "the mechanical philosophy."[25] Robert Boyle seems to have been the first to coin the term, in 1661. Pairing the philosophies of Gassendi and Descartes, Boyle noted their shared wish to explain phenomena intelligibly "by little bodies diversely figured and diversely moved." Searching for a suitable name for this species of natural philosophy, Boyle suggests "the corpuscular philosophy," though sometimes he calls it the "the Phoenician philosophy," because of the believed origin of corpuscularianism. But because "it is evident and efficacious in the domain of mechanical engines, sometimes I call it also the mechanical hypothesis or philosophy."[26] Boyle's sense of the mechanical philosophy centered on its intelligible ontological content and on its marked advantages over the tautologous explanations of Peripatetic natural philosophy.

These considerations must be borne in mind when we ask to what extent Newton can be described as a proponent of "the mechanical philosophy." If there is a coherent answer to the question, it will not be easy to come by. In the first place, Newton used "mechanical" (English and Latin) in both the theoretical and artisanal senses. There are several occurrences of "mechanical" ("mechanics") in the Principia, the Opticks, and certain manuscript drafts, where it is clear that Newton has in mind either the theory of machines or rational mechanics, a division within mechanics in the theoretical sense that creates problems of its own.[27] However, his use of the artisanal sense creates problems too. In the important alchemical draft manuscript "Of natures obvious laws & processes in vegetation" (c. 1672), natural processes are either "mechanicall" or "vegetable," corresponding to the distinction between "common" and "vegetable" chemistry (alchemy). Mechanical processes are sensible interactions between chemical bodies, whereas vegetation is the result of an enlivening, universal aether working in a "subtile secret & noble way" in all animal, vegetable, and alchemical activity. So Newton can write:

All these changes thus wrought in the generation of things so far as to sense may appear to be nothing but mechanism, or several dissevering & associating the parts of the matter acted upon, & that because several changes to sense may be wrought by such ways without any interceding act of vegetation...Nay all the operations in vulgar chemistry (many of which to sense are as strange transmutations as those of nature) are but mechanical coalitions or separations of particles, as may appear in that they return into their former natures if reconjoined or (when unequally volatile) dissevered, & that without any vegetation.[28]

Here Newton is talking about "mechanism" in the artisanal sense, not about some version of "the mechanical philosophy." Elsewhere in this manuscript, and indeed as a general rule, when Newton describes a process as "mechanical" (English or Latin), we cannot assume without further ado that he is using the term in the theoretical sense. To ignore the distinction is to risk misinterpretation. Earlier in the same manuscript Newton declares that "Natures actions are either vegetable or purely mechanicall (grav. flux. meteors. vulg. Chymistry)."[29] For Dobbs this is explicit evidence that at the time of the composition of "Of natures obvious laws" Newton "still thought...that his gravity was mechanical in its operation."[30] That would be so if all the bracketed examples were of the "purely mechanicall," but the operations of "vulgar chemistry" are not at all the same sort of thing as gravity (the "gravitating flux") or meteorological phenomena, and in such a disorganized draft it is just as likely that the bracketed examples refer *respectively* to the vegetable and the purely mechanical. That is (taking meteorological phenomena to be in a doubtful category), gravity is a vegetable action, and common chemistry is purely mechanical, in the artisanal sense.

Newton's employment of the term "mechanical" in the artisanal sense tells us nothing about his involvement with "the mechanical philosophy." His employment of the term (or the cognate substantive) in the theoretical sense points to the ideal of mathematizing the world picture, as is evident from the early studies on motion, the Definitions, Laws of Motion, Corollaries and their applications in the *Principia*, and the Preface to the first edition. But for Newton the mathematical way went hand-in-hand with a denial of mechanistic necessity, a denial of a purely corporeal world and an insistence on the existence of non-corporeal active powers at work in nature under God's stewardship, and a deep antipathy to the dogmatic assurance of the Cartesians and others who claimed that in a mechanical universe the causes of phenomena are already known, or are readily accessible to human inquiry.

One wonders if Newton ever was a mechanical philosopher of "the canonical" sort. The editors of the student manuscript "Questiones quaedam philosophicae" (1664–5) rightly note that there is nothing in the text that shows unqualified support for either Boyle's program or the action-by-contact condition characteristic of Descartes's mechanical philosophy.[31] Often Newton's tone is hypothetical rather than declarative. For example, he begins the section "Of Gravity & Levity" with the words: "The matter causing gravity must pass through all the pores of a body. It must ascend again, (1) for either the bowels of the Earth must have had large cavities and inanities to contain it, (2) or else the matter must swell the Earth."[32] It would be a mistake to infer from these "must"s that Newton is affirming gravity to be corporeal in nature. Rather, he means that *if* gravity is corporeal, then "the matter causing gravity must pass through all the pores of a body," but we cannot tell from the text what Newton's own views on gravity were at that time. After all, these were *quaestiones*, not *postulata*. Still, the "Questiones" does show "a unity of outlook," as the editors conclude, that of Newton as an atomist, a commitment that remained with him throughout his life.

Newton's alchemical papers of the 1660s were not expressed or conceived in mechanist terms. His first attempts to interrelate his alchemical thinking and mechanist doctrines date from 1672–5. In "An Hypothesis explaining the Properties of Light discoursed of in my severall Papers" (read to the Royal Society in 1675), Newton sought to explain these properties in terms of "an aethereall Medium much of the same constitution with air, but far rarer, subtiler & more strongly Elastic." This aether was denser outside bodies than within their pores, and its pressure deflected light corpuscles in varying directions. But it had to explain a wide range of phenomena, such as surface tension, the cohesion of solids, animal motion, the phenomena of static electricity and magnetism, and "the gravitating principle," and so was non-homogeneous, being "compounded partly of the maine flegmatic body of aether partly of other various aethereall Spirits."

Newton's aether hypothesis, of neo-Platonic origin, was a revision of the doctrine of the Universal Spirit from which embodied specific forms are born. "Perhaps the whole frame of Nature may be nothing but aether condensed by a fermental principle," wrote Newton in the initial version of his 1675 paper. For his Royal Society audience he expanded this idea in terms less redolent of the alchemical origin of the aether hypothesis: "Perhaps the whole frame of Nature may be nothing but various Contextures of some certain aethereall Spirits or vapours condens'd as it were by praecipitation ... and after condensation wrought into various formes, at first by the immediate hand of the Creator, and ever since by the power of Nature." So forms change into forms through unending cycles, "for nature is a perpetual circulatory worker, generating fluids out of solids, and solids out of fluids, fixed things out of volatile, & volatile out of fixed, subtile out of gross, & gross out of subtile."[33]

The transformability of matter was one of Newton's abiding beliefs, as was the corresponding unity of matter implied by the notion of nature as a "perpetual circulatory worker." Both doctrines therefore fall under the umbrella of the mechanical philosophy, as indicated earlier, so they form a link between Newton's alchemy and his inclinations toward mechanism. Furthermore, despite its neo-Platonic origins, Newton's aether, here and in his later writings, is material, so when employed to explain natural phenomena, its role was indistinguishable from that of analogous material media in other mechanical philosophies.

Yet because of the materiality of this aether, Newton had a serious problem. Do the aether's actions themselves have material causes, or are they the effects of a non-material active source? Are the ultimate sources of alchemical and mechanical activity material or non-material? In "Of Natures obvious laws & processes in vegetation" the principles of (al)chemical activity are material. On the other hand, in "An Hypothesis" Newton invokes non-material "secret principles of (un)sociableness" that account for (im)miscibility between certain fluids.[34] The vitalizing magnetic principles in "the star regulus of antimony" (the crystalline star formation that appears when antimony is prepared from antimony ore – stibnite – using a non-metallic reducing agent under controlled conditions), called "magnesia" by Newton, are also non-material. In short, Newton can never quite say if the natural changes he analyzes are the effects of purely material causation or of vital causation acting through the matter undergoing change.

In the decade following "An Hypothesis" and "Of Nature's obvious laws," Newton became temporarily disenchanted with aether hypotheses. In addition to the difficulties just mentioned, he surmised that an aether ought to retard the heliocentric motions of the planets, but no retardation had ever been observed. So the general concept of forces seemed to offer a way of explaining natural phenomena, and coupled with this idea was a developed account of chemical and physical composition. All Newton's aethers, from whatever stage in his thinking, were particulate, so it was a relatively comfortable transformation from the concept of an aethereal medium to that of conglomerations of particles under the influence of attractive and repulsive inter-particulate forces acting across the pores or other spaces separating the particles. The best-known application of this idea is Newton's account of bodies in terms of hierarchies of increasingly complex aggregations of particles held together by short-range attractive forces, as detailed in his "De natura acidorum" ("On the nature of acids," 1692, published in 1710).[35] The idea of hierarchical composition appears in Query 31 of the second English edition (1717) of the *Opticks*, where, in addition, longer-range repulsive forces (at the micro-level) explain the emission, reflection, and refraction of light, and where too the aether stages a comeback (as it did in the General Scholium of the *Principia*) in the tentative hope that it might after all account for gravity and optical phenomena.

In later life Newton did take a view on the ultimate causes of corporeal activity that seemed like a decision between material or non-material, or, more accurately, seemed to reveal the ultimate ground of every cause, of whatever corporeal kind. In Query 31 of the *Opticks* (1717–18) we read:

The *Vis inertiae* is a passive principle by which bodies persist in their motion or rest, receive motion in proportion to the force impressing it, and resist as much as they are resisted. By this principle alone there could never have been any motion in the world. Some other principle was necessary for putting bodies into motion; and now they are in motion, some other principle is necessary for conserving the motion. For from the various composition of two motions, 'tis very certain that there is not always the same quantity of motion in the world. For if two globes joined by a slender rod, revolve about their common centre of gravity with an uniform motion, while that centre moves on uniformly in a right line drawn in the plane of their circular motion; the sum of the motions of the two globes, as often as the globes are in the right line described by their common centre of gravity, will be bigger than the sum of their motions, when they are in a line perpendicular to that right line. By this instance it appears that motion may be got or lost. But by reason of the tenacity of fluids, and attrition of their parts, and the weakness of elasticity in solids, motion is much more apt to be lost than got, and is always upon the decay. For bodies which are either absolutely hard, or so soft as to be void of elasticity, will not rebound from one another. Impenetrability makes them only stop. If two equal bodies meet directly *in vacuo*, they will by the laws of motion stop where they meet, and lose all their motion, and remain in rest, unless they be elastic, and receive new motion from their spring... Seeing therefore the variety of motion which we find in the world is always decreasing, there is a necessity of conserving and recruiting it by active principles, such as are the cause of gravity, by which planets and comets keep their motions in their orbs, and bodies acquire great motion in falling; and the cause of fermentation, by which the heart and blood of animals are kept in perpetual motion and heat; the inward parts of the earth are constantly warm'd, and in some places grow very hot; bodies burn and shine, mountains take fire, the caverns of the earth are blown up, and the sun continues violently hot and lucid, and warms all things by his light. For we meet with very little motion in the world, besides what is owing to these active principles. And if it were not for these principles the bodies of the earth, planets, comets, sun and all things in them, would grow cold and freeze, and become inactive masses; and all putrefaction, generation, vegetation and life would cease, and the planets and comets would not remain in their orbs.[36]

This is a far cry from the materialist universe of metaphysical necessity that Maclaurin ridiculed in the writings of Descartes and Spinoza. However, the magnificence of Newton's vision in this fine passage should not deflect us from asking a few troubling questions. Do these active principles act according to mathematical law? If not, what becomes of the mathematical architecture that informs the *Principia Mathematica*? If they do, has metaphysical necessity not just returned by the back door?

Newton was a dualist and, on the question of human volition, a libertarian. He was in no doubt whatever about the mind's freedom to create new motion in the corporeal world, though he confesses his ignorance as to how this causal transaction takes place. We learn from Query 28 of the second English edition (1717/18) of the *Opticks* that this is one of the great problems that the natural philosopher should aim to unravel:

the main Business of natural Philosophy is to argue from Phaenomena without feigning Hypotheses... and not only to unfold the Mechanism of the World, but chiefly to resolve these and such like questions... How do the Motions of the Body follow from the Will, and whence is the Instinct in Animals?[37]

There is abundant textual evidence of Newton's belief in the motive powers of the will. For example, in a draft variant (c. 1705) of Query 23 of the 1706 Latin edition of the *Opticks*, that is, of Query 31 of the later English editions, Newton stipulates that:

the first thing to be done in Philosophy is to find out all the general laws of motion (so far as they can be discovered) on wch the frame of nature depends... in this search metaphysical arguments are very slippery... We find in o^r selves a power of moving our bodies by o^r thoughts (but the laws of this power we do not know) & see ye same power in other living creatures but how this is done & by what laws we do not know. And by this instance & that of gravity it appears that there are other laws of motion (unknown to us) than those wch arise from Vis inertiae (unknown to us) wch is enough to justify & encourage o^r search after them. We cannot say that all nature is not alive.[38]

In the second edition (1713) of *Principia Mathematica*, the final paragraph of the General Scholium of Book 3 reads:

And now we might add something concerning a certain most subtle spirit which pervades and lies hid in all gross bodies; by the force and action of which spirit the particles of bodies attract one another... and electric bodies operate to greater distances... and light is emitted, reflected... and heats bodies; and all sensation is excited, and the members of animal bodies move in accordance with the will, namely, by the vibrations of this spirit, mutually propagated along the solid filaments of the nerves, from the outward organs of sense to the brain, and from the brain into the muscles. But these are things that cannot be explained in few words, nor are we furnished with that sufficiency of experiments which is required to an accurate determination and demonstration of the laws by which this electric and elastic spirit operates.[39]

A few years later, in Query 24 of the second (and subsequent) English edition (1717/18) of the *Opticks*, Newton returned to his aethereal vibrations, asking a question that was to inspire the associationist David Hartley's "doctrine of vibrations": "Is not animal motion perform'd by the vibrations of this medium [aether], excited in the brain by the power of the will, and propagated from thence through the solid, perlucid, and uniform capillamenta of the nerves and the muscles, for contracting and dilating them?"[40]

The general reading public would have got enough hints from the General Scholium and the editions of the *Opticks*. For readers of *Philosophical Transactions*, there was Newton's 1715 anonymous review of the *Commercium Epistolicum*, which he rounds off with an explicit recognition of the opposing views he and Leibniz took on the question of volitions and their physical effects:

It must be allowed that these two Gentlemen differ very much in Philosophy. The one proceeds upon the Evidence arising from Experiments and Phaenomena, and stops where such Evidence is wanting; the other is taken up with Hypotheses, and propounds them, not to be examined by Experiments, but to be believed without Examination... The one doth not affirm that animal Motion in man is purely mechanical: the other teaches that it is purely mechanical, the Soul or Mind (according to the Hypothesis of an *Harmonia Praestabilita*) never acting upon the body so as to alter or influence its Motions.[41]

Those in the know would have had the full picture. Newton explained to Antonio Conti, ultimately for Leibniz's edification, that Leibniz

colludes in the significations of words, calling those things miracles w[ch] create no wonder & those things occult qualities whos causes are occult tho the qualities themselves be manifest, & those things the souls of men w[ch] do not animate their bodies, His Harmonia praestabilita is miraculous & contradicts the daily experience of all mankind, every man finding in himse[l]f a power of seeing with his eyes & moving his body by his will.[42]

As we have seen from the draft for Query 23 of the 1706 Latin *Opticks*, and as we would have expected from these anti-Leibnizian sallies, the will in Newton's universe is not shackled by the impositions of any universal conservation principle. That too carried a Newtonian seal of approval. Query 31 of the *Opticks* shows that a principle of the universal conservation of something equivalent to *vis viva* or "energy" was wholly foreign to Newtonian natural philosophy:

The *Vis inertiae* is a passive principle by which bodies persist in their motion or rest, receive motion in proportion to the force impressing it, and resist as much as they are resisted. By this principle alone there could never have been any motion in the world. Some other principle was necessary for putting bodies into motion; and now they are in motion, some other principle is necessary for conserving the motion. For from the various composition of two motions, 'tis very certain that there is not always the same quantity of motion in the world . . . by reason of the tenacity of fluids, and attrition of their parts, and the weakness of elasticity in solids, motion is much more apt to be lost than got, and is always upon the decay . . . Seeing therefore the variety of motion which we find in the world is always decreasing, there is a necessity of conserving and recruiting it by active principles . . . And if it were not for these principles the bodies of the earth, planets, comets, sun and all things in them would grow cold and freeze, and become inactive masses; and all putrefaction, generation, vegetation and life would cease, and the planets and comets would not remain in their orbs.[43]

In creating the world, evidently, God opted not to follow Leibnizian recipes. It is not surprising that Maclaurin denounced the conservation principles of Descartes, Leibniz, and (as he misreads him) Spinoza.

I conclude with a couple of issues on which we find Newton and Descartes in intriguing counterpoise. The first concerns the roles of the divine and human will. For Descartes, the only idea we have of the way God can move bodies is our consciousness of the power of our own minds to move our bodies.[44] Newton takes a similar line in his discussion of the nature of body in "De gravitatione," but reaches an anti-Cartesian conclusion. He does not know what the real nature of body is, so he substitutes an entity which it is within God's power to create, and which will be indistinguishable from body as known empirically:

Since each man is conscious that he can move his body at will, and believes further that all men enjoy the same power of similarly moving their bodies by thought alone; the free power of moving bodies at will can by no means be denied to God, whose faculty of thought is infinitely greater and more swift. And by like argument it must be agreed that God, by the sole action of thinking and willing, can prevent a body from penetrating any space defined by certain limits.

If he should exercise this power, and cause some space projecting above the Earth, like a mountain or any other body, to be impervious to bodies and thus stop or reflect light and all impinging things, it seems impossible that we should not consider this space to be truly body from the evidence of our senses (which constitute the sole judges in this matter); for it will be tangible on account of its impenetrability, and visible, opaque and coloured on account of the reflection of light, and it will resonate when struck because the adjacent air will be moved by the blow.[45]

One lesson to be drawn from this speculation is "that the analogy between the Divine faculties and our own is greater than has formerly been perceived by Philosophers. That we were created in God's image holy writ testifies." Some might prefer the supposition that God entrusts the task of "solidifying" space to "the soul of the world," but Newton does not see why he should not do it directly, without any intermediary, thereby creating bodies empirically on all fours with Cartesian *res extensae*. Furthermore, this account of body is useful in that "it clearly involves the chief truths of metaphysics, and thoroughly confirms and explains them. For we cannot postulate bodies of this kind without at the same time supposing that God exists, and has created bodies in empty space out of nothing, and that they are beings distinct from created minds, but nevertheless able to unite with minds."[46]

Cartesian *res extensa* fails this test. It leads to atheism, because extension is uncreated and can be conceived together with the imagined non-existence of God. It makes the mind–body distinction unintelligible, unless we say that mind is unextended and therefore exists nowhere, which is to say it does not exist at all, or at least that its union with body is completely unintelligible, if not impossible.[47] Furthermore, the Cartesian real distinction between body and mind implies that God does not contain extension *eminenter* and so cannot create it, so God and extension are two quite independent substances. On the other hand, if extension is contained in God *eminenter*, "the idea of extension will be eminently contained within the idea of thinking, and hence the distinction between these ideas will not be so great but that both may fit the same created substance, that is, that bodies may think or thinking things be extended."[48] This could be an allusion to Spinoza's doctrine of Thought and Extension as the two (known) attributes of infinite substance.[49] If it is, it is also a misunderstanding of Spinoza, who does not claim that "bodies may think." That is the well-known speculation of Locke, but that seems not to be the allusion Newton has in mind here.[50]

The second issue takes the form of a puzzling incongruity in Newton's natural philosophy that matches an incoherence at the heart of Descartes's doctrine of mind–body causal relations. Descartes claims that the freely acting mind can increase or diminish motions in the body to which it is united, from which it follows that each time I kick a ball or stop something in motion, I violate Descartes's principle of conservation of motion.[51] Descartes was aware of the difficulty, which it seems he tried to side-step by separating the jurisdiction of human volitional activity in the corporeal world from that of the divinely maintained conservation principle and the laws of nature, but this leads to difficulties in explaining how the conservation law can be applied with assurance in given cases.[52] Newton did not have a principle of conservation that might have conflicted with the consequences of the mind's actions on body, but he did share with Leibniz the principle of conservation of momentum (as I call it for the sake of convenience) in the form of the third law, which states that action and reaction are equal and opposite. However, it is unclear if and how the third law applies to corporeal actions caused by human will. If I move my finger, causing directly at least one part of my physiology to begin a new motion, on what does that part *react*, as it must do, according to the third law? Does my mind suffer in reply a reaction quantitatively equal to the action received by the part I will into motion? If so, why am I never aware of any such reaction each time I decide to move my body? The problem seems to have been recognized, though confusedly, by two Newtonians, the idiosyncratic Roger Boscovich, and the less idiosyncratic Colin Maclaurin. In the Appendix to his *A Theory of Natural Philosophy* (1763) Boscovich writes that motion

can never be produced by the mind in a point of matter, without producing an equal motion in some other point in the opposite direction. Whence it comes about that neither the necessary nor the free motions of matter produced by our minds can disturb the equality of action and reaction, the conservation of the same state of the centre of gravity, & the conservation of the same quantity of motion in the Universe, reckoned in the same direction.[53]

Far from resolving the difficulty, Boscovich has deftly multiplied it by two. Maclaurin offers a similar and equally unavailing resolution in his *Account*. He insists the third law is so general that

Even in the motions produced by voluntary and intelligent agents, we find the same law take place; for tho' the principle of motion, in them, be above mechanism, yet the instruments which they are obliged to employ in their actions are so far subject to it as this law requires. When a person throws a stone, for example, in the air, he at the same time reacts upon the earth with an equal force; by which means the centre of gravity of the earth and stone perseveres in the same state as before.[54]

For one Newtonian experimentalist in the domain of moral subjects, the consequence seems to have been taken as read, without any apparent puzzlement. At one point in the *Dialogues concerning Natural Religion* (1779), Hume has Philo argue for the causal fit between the parts of an organism and its environment, explaining that "thought has no influence upon matter, except where that matter is so conjoined with it, as to have an equal reciprocal influence upon it. No animal can move immediately any thing but the members of its own body; and indeed, the equality of action and re-action seems to be an universal law of nature."[55] Hume's causal match in the ecological economy of organisms might be important in the context of the emergence of Lamarckian or Darwinian evolution theory, but it does nothing to clarify how matter interacts with mind according to Newton's third law.

Newton did nothing to clarify the issue either. According to the hypothesis in "De gravitatione" that bodies are the effects of God willing that regions of space be endowed with impenetrability, a corpuscle created in this way would lack no empirically known property of body.

It would have shape, be tangible and mobile, and be capable of reflecting and being reflected, and constitute a part of the structure of things no less than any other sort of corpuscle, and I do not see that it would not equally operate upon our minds and in turn be operated upon, because it is nothing other than the product of the divine mind realized in a definite quantity of space. For it is certain that God can stimulate our perception by his own will, and thence apply such power to the effects of his will.[56]

I sense Berkeley waiting in the wings. But apart from that, Newton evidently takes mind–body interactions to be unproblematic. There is no evidence that he was aware of the mismatch between his third law and his inviolable belief in the power of the human

mind to intervene in the mechanism of the world. This parallel between Descartes and Newton points to the incompatibility between
the doctrine of human freedom of action and the doctrine of the in-
violate rule of physical law.

The *Principia* and the *Opticks* were formative influences on
eighteenth-century discussions of mind–body interaction and their
physiological background, providing much of the methodological
and conceptual backcloth. The impact of these great works, the absence of a conservation principle in Newton's natural philosophy,
the work of Locke, and the anti-Leibnizian ethos of the Newtonian
Age in England – all of these help to explain why eighteenth-century
British physiologists, psychologists, and theorists of mind discussed
the mind's action on the body without feeling the need to address
– perhaps in some cases without being aware of – the purely mechanical or dynamical considerations that had energized Leibniz's
critique of Cartesian mind–body causality. There were good reasons
not to pay much attention to Leibniz anyway, not only because of the
vis viva controversy and the priority dispute over the calculus, but
also because any general conservation law, whether Cartesian or
Leibnizian, could be discounted on the authoritative Newtonian
ground that "motion is much more apt to be lost than got, and is
always upon the decay." In those circumstances, it is not surprising that mind–body interrelations could be analyzed without anyone having to confront their physiology of action with a principle of
universal conservation of motion or force (however quantified).

So, rather unexpectedly, it turns out that Isaac Newton merits a
recognized place in the twin histories of psychology and philosophy
of mind.

NOTES

1   Rudolphus Goclenius, *Lexicon Philosophicum* (Frankfurt, 1613);
    reprinted in same volume with Goclenius, *Lexicon Philosophicum
    Graecum* of 1615 (Hildesheim: Olds, 1964), p. 1010. See Goclenius,
    Lexicon Philosophicum, pp. 623–5, 1012; Adriaan Heerboord, *Meletem-
    ata Philosophica* (Leiden, 1659), "Collegium logicum, Positionum logi-
    carum disputatio quarta, de Qualitate," p. 6; Bartholomew Keckermann
    Operum Omnium quae Extant tomus primus (Geneva, 1614), cols.
    871–5, Lib. 1, Cap. 6 "(De explicatione qualitatum), Exemplum primae
    speciei qualitatis nempe *Habitus*." See also Charles Lohr, "Metaphysics

and Natural Philosophy as Sciences: The Catholic and Protestant View
in the Sixteenth and Seventeenth Centuries," in Constance Blackwell
and Sachiko Kusukawa (eds.), *Philosophy in the Sixteenth and Seventeenth Centuries: Conversations with Aristotle* (Aldershot: Ashgale
Publishing, 1999), pp. 280–95.

2 For example, Etienne Chauvin, in his *Lexicon Philosophicum*, 2nd edn
(Leeuwarden, 1713; first edn, *Lexicon Rationale*, 1692). Chauvin's article on *metaphysics* gives a useful summary of differing conceptions of
metaphysics in vogue in the early eighteenth century.

3 Magirus claimed that spirits, including God, being instances of pure
act and immaterial form, do not have a "nature" in that they are not
subjects of motion or rest, and cannot therefore be the subject of inquiries in physics. Furthermore, "since God is above nature [*supra nat-
uram*], he cannot be part of the subject of physics." Johannes Magirus,
Physiologiae Peripateticae libri sex, cum commentariis (Cambridge,
1642), p. 8. The atomist Johann Sperling excluded the doctrine of angels from physics, and Alsted argued that divine action is neither physical nor metaphysical *motus*, but *motus hyperphysicus*. Johann Sperling,
Institutiones Physicae (Frankfurt and Wittenberg, 1664), p. 25. Johann-
Heinrich Alsted, *Theologia Naturalis Exhibens Augustissimam Naturae Scholam* (Hanover, 1623), pp. 150–1.

4 For Toletus's division into *speculative, practical,* and *factive* philosophy, see William J. Wallace, "Traditional Natural Philosophy," in
Charles B. Schmitt, Quentin Skinner, Eckhard Kessler, and Jill Kraye
(eds.), *The Cambridge History of Renaissance Philosophy* (Cambridge:
Cambridge University press, 1988), pp. 209–13. For the disciplinary divisions and subdivisions common in Germany, see Joseph S. Freedman,
*Deutsche Schulphilosophie im Reformationszeitalter (1500–1650):
ein Handbuch für den Hochschulunterricht.* Arbeiten zur Klassifika-
tion 4 (Münster: Münsteraner Arbeitskreis für Semiotik E. V., 1985),
pp. 65–105. On the three-way division of moral philosophy, see Jill
Kraye, "Moral Philosophy," in Schmitt *et al.* (eds.), *Cambridge History
of Renaissance Philosophy,* pp. 303–6.

5 Locke divides the sciences into Natural Philosophy ("the Knowledge of
Things . . . whereby I mean not only Matter, and Body, but Spirits also"),
Ethics, and the Doctrine of Signs (Logic). On Newton and Locke, see
G. A. J. Rogers, "The System of Locke and Newton," in Zev Bechler
(ed.), *Contemporary Newtonian Research* (Dordrecht: Reidel, 1982),
pp. 215–38.

6 Cambridge University Library (CUL), MS Add. 4005, fols. 14–15. A.
Rupert Hall and Marie Boas Hall (eds.), *Unpublished Scientific Papers of Issac Newton: A Selection from the Portsmouth Papers in the*

University Library, Cambridge (Cambridge: Cambridge University Press, 1962), p. 370. Note also (pp. 372–3): "All students who will be admitted to Lectures in naturall Philosophy to learn first Geometry & Mechanicks. By mechanicks I mean here the demonstrative doctrine of forces & motions including Hydrostaticks. For without a judgment in these things a man can have none in Philosophy."

7 On Newton's involvement with Stoic natural philosophy, see B. J. T. Dobbs, "Newton and Stoicism," *The Southern Journal of Philosophy* 23 (1985, Supplement), 109–23.

8 Hall and Hall (eds.), *Unpublished Scientific Papers*, pp. 105, 108–9 (Latin), 139, 141–3 (translation). On Newton's status as a metaphysician (or "philosopher" in the modern sense), I stand corrected by Robert Palter, "Saving Newton's Text: Documents, Readers, and the Ways of the World," *Studies in History and Philosophy of Science* 18 (1987), 434–5.

9 *Isaac Newton's Philosophiae Naturalis Principia Mathematica, the Third Edition with Variant Readings*, ed. A. Koyré and I. B. Cohen with the assistance of Anne Whitman (Cambridge, MA: Harvard University Press; Cambridge: Cambridge University Press, 1972), vol. 2, pp. 763–4 (my translation). In an interleaf belonging to Newton's own interleaved and annotated copy of the second edition of the *Principia* (1713), *caeca* (blind) is omitted. More strikingly, in an interleaf belonging to Newton's interleaved copy, and in the second edition itself, *experimentalem* replaces *naturalem*: "to discourse of God, at least from the phenomena, belongs to experimental philosophy."

10 B. J. T. Dobbs, *The Janus Faces of Genius: The Role of Alchemy in Newton's Thought* (Cambridge: Cambridge University Press, 1991), pp. 81–8.

11 See J. E. McGuire "Force, Active Principles, and Newton's Invisible Realm," *Ambix* 15 (1968), 154–208, at pp. 170–1.

12 *Opticks*, p. 369.

13 Colin Maclaurin, *An Account of Sir Isaac Newton's Philosophical Discoveries, in Four Books* (London, Printed for the Author's Children, 1748; Johnson Reprint, 1968), pp. xix–xx. In *An Enquiry concerning Human Understanding*, published by fellow-Scotsman David Hume the same year as *An Account*, "our modern metaphysicians" are criticized for their doctrine of God's direct management of creation without subordinate powers or secondary causes, just as Newton is praised for having recourse, though laudably in hypothetical terms, "to an etherial fluid to explain his universal attraction." David Hume, *Enquiries concerning Human Understanding and concerning the Principles of Morals*, ed. L. A. Selby-Bigge, 3rd edn rev. P. H. Nidditch (Oxford: Oxford University Press, 1975), p. 73, n. 1. Hume's

"modern metaphysicians" seem to be the occasionalists, or possibly Berkeley.

14 To avoid a clutter of references and footnotes, I list here the range of pages in Book 1 of Maclaurin's *Account* where the reader can find the material that follows: pp. 4–5, 14–15, 29–30, 65–6, 76–7, 78, 79, 82–4, 86, 89–90, 94–6.

15 For the only comprehensive commentary on the Leibniz–Clarke correspondence, see Ezio Vailati, *Leibniz and Clarke: A Study of Their Correspondence* (Oxford: Oxford University Press, 1997).

16 There is strong support for this claim, grounded on other considerations, in James E. Force, "The God of Abraham and Isaac (Newton)," in James E. Force and Richard H. Popkin (eds.), *The Books of Nature and Scripture* (Dordrecht: Kluwer, 1994), pp. 179–200, esp. p. 180.

17 Steven Nadler, "Doctrines of Explanation in Late Scholasticism and in the Mechanical Philosophy," in Daniel Garber and Michael Ayers (eds.), *The Cambridge History of Seventeenth-Century Philosophy* (Cambridge: Cambridge University Press, 1998), pp. 513–52.

18 G. E. Stahl, *Fundamenta Chymiae Dogmaticae & Experimentalis* (Nuremberg, 1723), Preface, quoted in J. R. Partington, *A History of Chemistry* (London: Macmillan, 1961–70), vol. 2, p. 665. Georg Ernst Stahl (1660–1734) was the principal architect of the phlogiston theory.

19 For more on this background and on the tricky problem of Newton's conception of the discipline of "mechanics," see my "Newton's *Mathematical Principles of Natural Philosophy*: A Treatise on 'Mechanics'?," in P. M. Harman and Alan E. Shapiro (eds.), *The Investigation of Difficult Things* (Cambridge: Cambridge University Press, 1992), pp. 305–22.

20 "Advices to his Son," Petworth House MS, HMC 24/2, fols. 30–31. I am indebted to Stephen Clucas for this quotation and reference.

21 Thomas Sprat, *The History of the Royal Society* (London, 1667), p. 329.

22 Henry Power, *Experimental Philosophy* (London, 1664), "The Preface to the Ingenious Reader." Newton too hoped for a time when improved microscopes would show all of the ultimate corpuscles on which the colors of bodies depend, "but those which produce blackness." *Opticks* (1730), Book 2, Part 3, Proposition 7, p. 261. The passage first appeared in the "Discourse of Observations," which Newton enclosed with "An Hypothesis explaining the Properties of Light discoursed of in my severall Papers" in his letter to Oldenburg of 7 December 1675: *The Correspondence of Isaac Newton*, vol. 1, ed. H. W. Turnbull (Cambridge: Cambridge University Press, 1959), p. 391.

23 See for example *The Origin of Forms and Qualities* (1666): Robert Boyle, *Selected Philosophical Papers* (Manchester: Manchester University

Press and New York: Barnes and Noble, 1979), pp. 74–9. Also my "Newton's *Mathematical Principles of Natural Philosophy*," pp. 313–15.

24 Fatio de Duillier to Abbé Nicaise, 5/15 June 1687. Bibliothèque Nationale, Fds fr. nouv. acq. 4218, ff. 26r–27v: f. 27r.

25 For a full-scale study of the problem of "the mechanical philosophy," see Sophie Roux, "La philosophie mécanique (1630–1690)," Thèse de Doctorat, préparée sous la direction d'E. Coumet, Centre A. Koyré, EHESS, 2 vols. (Paris: EHESS, 1996), vol. 1, pp. 30–2.

26 *Some Specimens of an Attempt to make Chemical Experiments useful to Illustrate the Notions of the Corpuscular Philosophy* (1661), Preface, in *The Works of the Honourable Robert Boyle*, ed. Thomas Birch, 5 vols. (London, 1744. Facsimile reprint, Hildesheim: Olms, 1966), vol. 1, p. 355. On the question of the origins and nature of the mechanical philosophy, and of its relations to mechanics, see the important preliminary discussion ("Introduction générale") in Roux, "La philosophie mécanique," vol. 1, pp. 3–39.

27 See my "Newton's *Mathematical Principles of Natural Philosophy*," pp. 316–22.

28 Smithsonian Institution Libraries, Dibner MSS 1031 B, fol. 5v. Quoted from the transcription in Dobbs, *The Janus Faces of Genius*, Appendix A, p. 268. To improve readability of this extended quotation without altering the meaning, I have ignored deletions, incorporated the interlineations, inserted a few commas, and modernized the spelling.

29 Smithsonian Institution Libraries, Dibner MSS 1031 B, fol. 5r. Quoted from the transcription in Dobbs, *The Janus Faces of Genius*, Appendix A, p. 267.

30 Dobbs, *The Janus Faces of Genius*, p. 99.

31 J. E. McGuire and Martin Tamny (eds.), *Certain Philosophical Questions: Newton's Trinity Notebook* (Cambridge: Cambridge University Press, 1983), pp. 323–4.

32 *Ibid.*, pp. 362, 363.

33 "An Hypothesis Explaining the Properties of Light" (1675), in I. Bernard Cohen and Robert E. Schofield (eds.), *Isaac Newton's Papers and Letters on Natural Philosophy and Related Documents* (Cambridge: Cambridge University Press, 1958), pp. 178–235, at pp. 179–81. See also Betty Jo Teeter Dobbs, *The Foundations of Newton's Alchemy, or "The Hunting of the Greene Lyon"* (Cambridge: Cambridge University Press, 1975), pp. 175–93, 205–6; *The Janus Faces of Genius*, pp. 102–04.

34 Dobbs, *The Janus Faces of Genius*, pp. 267, 268, 269. Richard S. Westfall, *Never at Rest: A Biography of Isaac Newton* (Cambridge: Cambridge University Press, 1980), pp. 307–8.

35 "De natura acidorum" (1692), in Cohen and Schofield (eds.), *Papers and Letters*, pp. 256–58.

36 Isaac Newton, *Opticks: or, A Treatise of the Reflections, Refractions, Inflections and Colours of Light*. Foreword by Albert Einstein, introduction by Edmund Whittaker, preface by I. Bernard Cohen, analytical table of contents prepared by Duane H. D. Roller (New York: Dover Publications, 1952 [1st English edn 1704, 1st Latin edn 1706]), pp. 397–400.

37 *Ibid.*, pp. 369–70.

38 CUL, Add. MS 3970, fol. 620r. Transcribed in J. E. McGuire, "Force, Active Principles, and Newton's Invisible Realm," p. 171.

39 *Principia*, ed. Koyré and Cohen, vol. 2, pp. 764–5. Translation by Motte and Cajori

40 *Opticks*, pp. 353–4. For Hartley's doctrine of vibrations, see David Hartley, *Observations on Man, His Frame, His Duty, And His Expectations (1749)*, facsimile reproduction, introduction by Theodore L. Huguelet, 2 vols. in 1 (Gainesville, FL: Scholars' Facsimiles & Reprints, 1966).

41 "*An Account of the Book entitled* Commercium Epistolicum Collinii & aliorum, De Analysi promota; *published by order of the* Royal-Society, *in relation to the Dispute between Mr.* Leibnitz *and Dr.* Keill, *about the Right of Invention of the Method of* Fluxions, *by some call'd* the Differential Method," *Philosophical Transactions* 29 (342) (1715), 224. Also in A. R. Hall, *Philosophers at War: The Quarrel between Newton and Leibniz* (Cambridge: Cambridge University Press, 1980), Appendix.

42 Newton to Conti [for Leibniz], 26 February 1716. *Correspondence*, vol. 6, p. 285. It is perhaps significant that in one of the drafts of this letter there is a different order of words in the last couple of lines: "For all men find by experience that they can move their bodies by their will, & that they see heare & feel by means of their bodies." A. Koyré and I. B. Cohen, "Newton & the Leibniz–Clarke Correspondence with Notes on Newton, Conti, & Des Maizeaux," *Archives Internationales d'Histoire des Sciences* 15 (1962), 63–126, at pp. 73–4.

43 *Opticks*, pp. 397–400.

44 See for example Descartes to Henry More, 15 April 1649. René Descartes, *Œuvres de Descartes*, ed. Charles Adam and Paul Tannery, Nouvelle présentation, en co-édition avec le Centre National de la Recherche Scientifique, ed. P. Costabel, J. Beaude, and B. Rochot, 11 vols. (Paris: Vrin, 1964–74), vol. 5, p. 347.

45 Hall and Hall (eds.), *Unpublished Scientific Papers*, pp. 105–6 (Latin), 138–9 (translation); pp. 105, 108–9 (Latin), 139, 141, 142, 143 (translation).

46 *Ibid.*, p. 109 (Latin), 142 (translation, slightly modified).

47 This is basically the same criticism of Descartes's account of spiritual substance that the Cambridge Platonist Henry More made in his *Divine Dialogues* (1668) and *Enchiridion Metaphysicum* (1671). If spirits are not extended, then neither is God, which means he is nowhere, though he exists. More ridiculed the Cartesians on this issue by calling them the "Nullibists," the "Nowhere-men." See my "Philosophia Cartesiana Triumphata: Henry More (1646–1671)," in Thomas M. Lennon, John M. Nicholas, and John W. Davis (eds.), *Problems of Cartesianism*, McGill–Queen's Studies in the History of Ideas 1 (Kingston and Montreal: McGill–Queen's University Press, 1982), pp. 171–250, at pp. 238–9.

48 Hall and Hall (eds.), *Unpublished Scientific Papers*, p. 109 (Latin), 143 (translation, modified and corrected).

49 As far as I can tell, nowhere does Newton mention Spinoza's name or refer to any of his works. No work of Spinoza's is listed as having been in Newton's library (John Harrison, *The Library of Isaac Newton* [Cambridge: Cambridge University Press, 1978]), but I find it hard to believe that he never read Spinoza or did not hear about his ideas from others. At any rate, it is utterly impossible to believe that he (would have) found Spinoza to his liking.

50 Hall and Hall (eds.), *Unpublished Scientific Papers*, pp. 105, 108–9 (Latin), 139, 141, 142, 143 (translation).

51 "That God is the primary cause of motion and conserves always the same quantity of motion in the universe." *Principia Philosophiae*, Part 2, Article 36, in *Œuvres de Descartes*, ed. Adam and Tannery, vol. 8(i), p. 61.

52 The separation of human and divine spheres of volitional activity has been argued in Daniel Garber, "Mind, Body and the Laws of Nature in Descartes and Leibniz," *Midwest Studies in Philosophy* 8 (1983), 105–33; Garber, "Descartes and Occasionalism," in Steven Nadler (ed.), *Causation in Early Modern Philosophy: Cartesianism, Occasionalism, and Preestablished Harmony* (University Park: Pennsylvania State University Press, 1993), pp. 9–26; and in Peter McLaughlin, "Descartes on Mind–Body Interaction and the Conservation of Motion," *The Philosophical Review* 102 (1993), 155–82. Garber and McLaughlin see this separation as a reason for preserving the coherence of Descartes's position; I see it as a reason to conclude that it is ultimately incoherent. Cf. my "The Mechanical Philosophy and Its Problems: Mechanical Explanations, Impenetrability, and Perpetual Motion," in J. C. Pitt (ed.), *Change and Progress in Modern Science* (Dordrecht: Reidel, 1985), pp. 9–84, at pp. 19–28.

53 Roger Boscovich, *A Theory of Natural Philosophy* (Cambridge, MA: MIT Press, 1966), p. 190.

54 Maclaurin, *An Account*, pp. 144–6.

55 David Hume, *Dialogues concerning Natural Religion*, ed. Norman Kemp Smith (London: T. Nelson, 1947), p. 186.

56 Hall and Hall (eds.), *Unpublished Scientific Papers*, p. 106 (Latin), 139 (translation, slightly modified).

11   The background to Newton's chymistry

To those who are unfamiliar with the history of alchemy, the image of Isaac Newton poring over manuscripts illuminated strangely with dragons, sceptered gods, and couples copulating within flasks cannot fail to educe a strikingly discordant tone. How could such a great mathematical mind, the father of modern physics, concern himself with such seemingly unintelligible gibberish? Must we simply throw up our hands at the "superstitious" *Zeitgeist* of the age, as Newton's nineteenth-century biographers did, and conclude that he was deluded by the work of "a fool and a knave"?[1] Should we conclude, with more recent scholars of Newton's alchemy, that he was engaged in a fundamentally religious quest in which alchemy would provide the key by which God's immaterial activity could be linked to the phenomenal world of matter?[2] Or is there yet another answer – that Newton's alchemical research was primarily an investigation of the microstructure of matter, the forces of chemical affinity, and the ability of material substances to undergo radical transformation in the laboratory?[3] Needless to say, the matter is not easy to decide, given that Newton copied, abstracted, commented upon, and composed about a million words of manuscript material on the subject of alchemy, over a period spanning more than thirty years.[4] One thing, however, is sure: in order to understand Newton's fascination with alchemy, we must not consider the enterprise from an anachronistic viewpoint that equates alchemy with the irrational, the mystical, or the anti-mechanical. If we wish to comprehend Newton's deep involvement in this subject, we must have a firm grounding in the subject of alchemy as it existed in the seventeenth century.

Despite the image of gold-making and charlatanry that alchemy may conjure up in the minds of modern readers, the term "alchemy" to most seventeenth-century writers was synonymous with "chymistry." Chymistry was a multi-faceted discipline that included such diverse practices as the production of mineral acids, distilling of alcholic beverages, manufacture of dyes and perfumes, extraction and use of pharmaceuticals, and of course "chrysopoeia" and "argyropoeia," the attempt to make artificial precious metals, also known as *alchemia transmutatoria* or "transmutatory alchemy." But chymistry was not merely an industrial pursuit. In the previous century, the founder of "chymiatria" (chymical medicine), Paracelsus, had emphasized the power of chymical techniques, such as distillation, and products, such as the mineral acids, as tools of analysis. Hence chymistry acquired the cognomen "spagyria," which was widely interpreted in the seventeenth century to be fused from the Greek terms for "analysis" and "synthesis."[5]

Seventeenth-century England was fully alive to the industrial and scientific promise of chymistry, and in the period of the Interregnum the subject experienced wide popularization by the medical followers of the Belgian iatrochemist Joan Baptista van Helmont.[6] Among the most prolific of the English commentators on van Helmont were two authors who would form the object of Newton's intense scrutiny: Robert Boyle and George Starkey, who together supply over one hundred pages of extracts in Newton's most important chymical laboratory notebook.[7] As the author of *The Sceptical Chymist* (1661) and *The Origine of Forms and Qualities* (1666), Boyle hardly needs an introduction. Yet the full involvement of Boyle in chrysopoeia – a quest that occupied some forty years of his life – has only recently come to light.[8] Surprisingly, it was the obscure American chymist George Starkey (1628–65) who introduced Boyle to the experimental pursuit of this subject, supplying him with a recipe for a "sophic mercury" – a substance that was supposed to reduce gold into its first principles and stimulate it into becoming the "philosophers' stone" or agent of metallic transmutation.[9] A graduate of Harvard College who immigrated to London in 1650, Starkey soon began a dual career of writing Helmontian works under his own name while also composing a series of works devoted to transmutatory alchemy under the *nom de guerre* of "Eirenaeus Philalethes" (a peaceful lover of truth).[10] While Newton's chymical notebook is filled with extracts from Starkey's works on chymical medicine, such as *Pyrotechny* (1658), it was the Philalethan *œuvre* that he returned to throughout his career in his ongoing attempt to decipher the veiled processes of the alchemical *magnum opus*.

Although some have maintained that van Helmont exercised little influence on Newton, it is quite clear that Newton's most fundamental positions in chymistry were of Helmontian origin, even if partially mediated by Starkey, Boyle, and other Helmontians such as John Webster.[11] This emerges not only from explicitly alchemical papers in Newton's *Nachlass*, but also from his works on physics. Hence the chymical treatise entitled "Of natures obvious laws & processes in vegetation" (Dibner MS 1031 b) employs such Helmontian concepts as that of the "Alkahest," a marvellous dissolvent and analytical tool that could supposedly resolve all bodies into their primitive constituents, and the notion of "Gur" (or "Bur"), a half-formed metallic substance that was thought to be the immature substance of metals within their mines.[12] More importantly, one finds here and in Newton's unfinished *Conclusio* to the *Principia*, an explicit adherence to the idea that all material things are made, ultimately, from water.[13] The *Conclusio* passage is striking for its open acceptance of van Helmont's position:

that rare substance water can be transformed by continued fermentation into the more dense substances of animals, vegetables, salts, stones and various earths. And finally by the very long duration of the operation be coagulated into mineral and metallic substances. For the matter of all things is one and the same, which is transmuted into countless forms by the operations of nature, and more subtle and rare bodies are by fermentation and the processes of growth commonly made thicker and more condensed.[14]

This remarkable passage not only affirms van Helmont's theory that the source of the phenomenal world is water, but also adopts the Helmontian belief that the transmutation of water into other substances is brought about by fermentation. Newton's laboratory notebooks are filled with attempts to make various mineral and chemical products ferment and "putrefy."[15] Although fermentation was an idea dear to the heart of many an alchemist, the particular notion of fermenting water in order to produce the specified materials of the world perceived by the senses is at heart Helmontian. In the following it will therefore be useful to give a brief overview of van Helmont's matter-theory.

HELMONTIAN MATTER-THEORY

As Walter Pagel, the leading modern scholar of van Helmont, has noted, the Belgian iatrochemist was eager to explain chemical and physical processes in terms of immaterial powers.[16] At the same time, however, van Helmont employed many explanations that resorted to the displacement and rearrangement of corpuscles which were invisibly small. The most striking example of van Helmont's corpuscularism lies in the *Supplementum de Aquis Spadanis*, published in 1624, and then integrated into the voluminous *Ortus Medicinae* of 1648.[17] In the *Supplementum*, van Helmont correctly describes the plating of iron by the copper found in naturally occurring springs of "vitriol" (mostly copper sulfate). Unlike most previous authors, van Helmont did not attribute this striking change to a transmutation of iron into copper, but argued that atoms (*atomi*) of copper were being deposited on the surface of the iron, which itself was losing corpuscles by gradually going into solution.[18] Van Helmont's *Ortus Medicinae* presented many other corpuscular explanations as well, some of them going so far as to describe the internal structure of the corpuscles at the micro-level. These micro-structural ruminations led van Helmont to devise what I (following the lead of Karin Figala) have elsewhere called the shell-theory of matter, whose fullest explanation appears in the *Ortus Medicinae*'s description of water.[19] In an attempt to explain how water can both vaporize upon boiling and sublime upon freezing, van Helmont argues that water is composed of complex corpuscles made up of layers. The layers correspond to the three Paracelsian principles, mercury, sulfur, and salt, although van Helmont is careful to point out that water cannot be analyzed into its constituent principles.[20] When liquid water is vaporized, its particles are separated and forced upward. It can be converted to "gas," however, by a further attenuation, which also "extraverts" the particles by rearranging the order of their shells. The sulfur, which had formed the central kernel of the "atom," is now forced to the exterior, where it provides a hard shell. Van Helmont seems to have thought that this further extenuation and reordering of the water particles could account for the facts that ice is less dense than water and that ice can sublime.[21]

Van Helmont's corpuscular theory also played a part in his treatment of metals. Like water, metals were composed of particles made up of shells corresponding to the Paracelsian principles. Van Helmont argued that ordinary acids worked on metals by attacking their sulfur and separating their corpuscles from one another.[22] Such corrosives eventually ceased their operation on a given metal because they were "exantlated" – that is, exhausted – by their own action.[23] The mysterious universal dissolvent, or Alkahest, was supposed to operate on metals by subjecting them to a much finer division than the mineral acids could achieve, ultimately reducing them to water. The Alkahest, unlike acids, worked *sine repassione* – it suffered none of the exhaustion that caused ordinary corrosives to lose their acidity. Once a metal had been reduced to its minimal particles by the Alkahest, it could then be transmuted into another metal, or indeed any other substance. All that was necessary was that the atoms of the erstwhile metal absorb a "ferment," which could impress a new "seed" (*semen*) on them.[24] The *semina* acquired through fermentation were the agents, therefore, by which water was transmuted into the multifarious substances of the physical world.

One can see, then, that van Helmont's work provided a vitalistic corpuscular theory: the "atoms" and corpuscles of which he speaks were endued with powers and forces which could cause them to "ferment" and "vegetate." This vitalistic corpuscularism was developed further by the seventeenth-century English Helmontians such as George Starkey. In his treatment of alchemical theory, the *De Metallorum Metamorphosi* composed in the early 1650s, Starkey presents an elaborate corpuscular theory combining elements of Helmontianism with the theory of the Polish alchemist Michael Sendivogius, who claimed that the *semen* of every substance was a "spark of light" (*scintilla lucis*) making up 1/8200 of its total substance.[25] Starkey adopted the shell-theory of van Helmont, and argued that the Sendivogian *scintilla lucis* was the genuine minimal part into which matter could be divided. At the center of every metallic corpuscle, within the shells provided by van Helmont's corpuscular theory, one could therefore find the active *semen* which provided the "fermentative force" (*vis fermentativa*) to that metal.[26] If one could only find a means of dividing metals into their minimal parts, then, he would free the tiny, active particles that lay "in fetters," chained within the center of each metallic corpuscle.[27] Such radical division would serve as the necessary precursor to metallic transmutation.

CORPUSCULARISM IN NEWTON'S CHYMISTRY

Since Newton had already begun transcribing the works of Eirenaeus Philalethes in the late 1660s, and his massive collation of alchemical writers, the *Index Chemicus* composed in the 1680s, contains over 300 references to Philalethes, we should not be surprised to see the Helmontianism of the Philalethan corpus reappear in Newton's writings.[28] This influence is already apparent in Newton's 1675 "Hypothesis of light" written to Henry Oldenburg. In this letter, Newton stresses the role of "mediation," by which two substances normally incapable of undergoing mixture can be made to fuse together.[29] This emphasis on chymical mediation was probably stimulated by Newton's reading of the Philalethan corpus, where great emphasis is placed on the making of eutectic alloys. In a letter that Starkey wrote to Boyle in 1651, which Newton transcribed fairly early in his alchemical career, the American alchemist describes the manufacture of a sophic mercury from the "star regulus" of antimony (crystalline metallic antimony), silver, and quicksilver. The silver acted as a mediator, allowing the mercury and antimony to amalgamate.[30] Newton used the concept of mediation to explain "how some things unsociable are made Sociable." Among the examples that he provides one finds regulus of antimony, which allows the mixture of molten copper and lead.

The same emphasis on mediation appears in a well-known letter that Newton sent to Boyle in February 1679, with many of the same examples. Here, however, Newton adds a corpuscular model intended to explain how water can be made to mix with metals by the mediation of "saline spirits." Like most seventeenth-century chymists, Newton at this time envisioned the mineral acids as highly active and subtle salts dissolved in water. The acid particles congregated around metallic ones because of their "sociability" with them, and worked their way into the pores between the corpuscles of metal. Breaking the metallic corpuscles loose, the saline particles then encompassed the metallic ones "as a coat or shell does a kernell." If a base, such as salt of tartar, was then added, it would attract the saline particles away from the metal, which would then precipitate to the bottom of the vessel.[31] What is truly striking about this explanation is its use of the shell/kernel terminology already employed by the Helmontian Philalethes. In his *Marrow of Alchemy*, a work intensely studied by Newton from the late 1660s onward, Philalethes said that the "metalline sulfur" of gold "like to a Coat/the *Mercury* encloseth."[32] Now one could argue that Newton was not talking here about sulfur and mercury, but rather about salts enclosing particles of metal. This objection quickly disappears, however, if we consult Newton's treatise on acids, "De natura acidorum," first published in 1710 as part of John Harris's *Lexicon Technicum*, but composed in or before 1692.

The "De natura acidorum" covers much the same ground as the 1679 letter to Boyle, but with different emphases. Here Newton places great importance on the relative sizes of water, acid, and metallic corpuscles, the last of which he now refers to as "earthy" particles. Water is composed of extremely minute corpuscles, acid of bigger ones, and earthy particles are bigger yet. As in the letter to Boyle, Newton envisions the dissolution of metals in acid as a process that results in the coating of a central kernel with an acidic shell. Here, however, he views the combination of acid and earthy particles as making up a salt, rather than thinking of the salt as resident only in the "saline spirits" of the acid. Newton also adds that acid particles can in some circumstances eventually penetrate into the earthy core to compose "sulphureous" or "fatty bodies" that are difficult to mix with water.[33] The conversion of salts into sulfurous oils was a theme dear to the heart of Helmontians, and Newton's laboratory notebooks contain passages excerpted from George Starkey on this very subject.[34] What cements Newton's debt to the Helmontian shell-theory, however, is a passage where Newton affirms that "what is said by chemists, that everything is made from sulphur and mercury, is true, because by sulphur they mean acid, and by mercury they mean earth."[35] Hence Newton's image of acid particles surrounding earthy ones as a shell does a kernel was another way of saying – as Philalethes did – that the sulfurous shell encloses the mercurial one. And since Newton here affirmed that "everything" is made of sulfur and mercury, the shell-theory was applicable to the material world as a whole. As if to underscore his Helmontian allegiances, Newton then apparently dictated to his scribe that "all things can be reduced into water."[36]

A final point at which the shell-theory emerges in Newton's published work can be found in Query 31 of the *Opticks*. Here Newton develops an analogy already suggested in passing in "De natura acidorum," between a particle of salt and the globe of the earth. Since many of the themes touched upon up to now are developed further in the *Opticks* passage, it is worth inspecting *in toto*:

As Gravity makes the Sea flow round the denser and weightier Parts of the Globe of the Earth, so the Attraction may make the watry Acid flow round the denser and compacter Particles of Earth for composing the Particles of Salt. For otherwise the Acid would not do the Office of a Medium between the Earth and common Water, for making Salts dissolvable in the Water; nor would Salt of Tartar readily draw off the Acid from dissolved Metals, nor Metals the Acid from Mercury. Now, as in the great Globe of the Earth and Sea, the densest Bodies by their Gravity sink down in Water, and always endeavor to go towards the Center of the Globe; so in Particles of Salt, the densest Matter may always endeavor to approach the Center of the Particle: So that a Particle of Salt may be compared to a Chaos; being dense, hard, dry, and earthy in the Center; and rare, soft, moist, and watry in the Circumference.[37]

Here we may see the full flowering of Newton's corpuscular speculations, along with the associated concept of mediation. As in "De natura acidorum," Newton here stresses that the acid particles serve as a mediator between the water and the metallic earth at the kernel of a particle of salt. The attraction that holds the acid particles in place around this earthy core is similar to the gravity that retains the sea around the earth. Interestingly, Newton now emphasizes the qualitative differences between the kernel and the shell of the salt corpuscle. The corpuscle is hard and dry at its earthy center, and moist and rare at its watery circumference. A quasi-metaphorical terminology of opposed "centers" and "circumferences" was the daily bread of seventeenth-century chymists, and it is highly likely that Newton is replaying the language of Eirenaeus Philalethes or earlier alchemists. In his commentaries to the fifteenth-century English alchemist George Ripley, Philalethes had spoken of the hidden and manifest parts of metals, which can be internally hot and dry while externally cold and moist.[38]

In addition, Newton's reference to a particle of salt as a "chaos" deserves comment. In his *Telluris Theoria Sacra* of 1681, Thomas Burnet speaks of the primordial earth, already layered into strata of earth, water, and air, as a chaos.[39] Newton was keenly interested in Burnet's theory, as witnessed by a letter from Newton written in 1681.[40] Burnet is a likely candidate, then, for Newton's peculiar terminology of the layered earth as a chaos. At the same time, another source may have been in Newton's mind at the time of writing Query 31. Eirenaeus Philalethes frequently refers to mineral antimony as a "chaos," and, unlike Burnet, Philalethes stresses the opposed qualities at the center and the surface of the antimony, apparently a reference to the shell-theory. Newton paraphrased a Philalethan passage to this intent in his chymical dictionary, the *Index Chemicus*, under the entry "Chaos."[41] In some sheets preceding his alchemical composition *Praxis*, written in the 1690s, Newton explicitly associates mineral antimony with the sphere of the world, probably because he believed that antimony was close to the primordial substance of the metals. Significantly, both the terrestrial globe and antimony-ore shared the same graphic symbol – a circle surmounted by a cross. Here too, as in Query 31, Newton stresses the opposed characteristics of the antimony-globe: "It is hot and dry, wet and cold. It is a watery fire and a fiery water. It is a corporeal spirit and a spiritual body. It is the condensed spirit of the world; it is the noblest quintessence of all things, and therefore it is customarily depicted by the symbol for the world."[42]

From the brief overview given here, it should be clear that there is a close integration between Newton's corpuscular matter-theory and his researches in chymistry. This should not be surprising, given the prevalence of corpuscular explanations for material change among early modern chymists, both those who actively engaged in a search for the philosophers' stone and those who focused on more mundane aspects of chymical technology. Like most of his contemporaries, Newton distinguished between a "vulgar chymistry" that concerned itself only with interactions between gross particles and a more sublime chymistry that could penetrate between the smallest corpuscles of bodies by means of processes such as fermentation and putrefaction, and by doing so, work marvelous transmutations.[43] We must not see this as equivalent to the modern distinction between "chemistry" and "alchemy," however, for it was a dichotomy erected by the alchemists themselves, in common use from the Middle Ages onward. Newton, like other Helmontians, was both "alchemist" and "chemist" at the same time, and it does damage to the historical record to distinguish the two pursuits. Once we acknowledge the fact that Newton's "alchemy" and "chemistry" were inseparable, an answer to the questions posed at the beginning of this chapter begins to emerge. Newton's chymistry was certainly not a product of delusion, and no more dominated by religiosity than any other part of his scientific endeavor. The precise observations that he made of chemical affinity and his speculations about the invisible structure of matter are as "scientific" as any other part of his work. Only if one wishes to label Newton's work as a whole as some sort of natural theology may one argue that the goal of his chymistry was primarily spiritual. It is no longer acceptable to single out Newton's alchemical endeavors as a rearguard rebellion against the mainstream of seventeenth-century science.

NOTES

1 Sir David Brewster, *Memoirs of the Life, Writings, and Discoveries of Sir Isaac Newton* (Edinburgh: T. Constable, 1855), p. 375.

2 Betty Jo Teeter Dobbs, *The Janus Faces of Genius: The Role of Alchemy in Newton's Thought* (Cambridge: Cambridge University Press, 1991), pp. 12–13, 18, 19–52, 114–17, *et passim*; Dobbs, *Alchemical Death and Resurrection: The Significance of Alchemy in the Age of Newton* (Washington, DC: Smithsonian Institution Libraries, 1990); Richard S. Westfall, *Never at Rest: A Biography of Isaac Newton* (Cambridge: Cambridge University Press, 1980), pp. 20–2, 299–301.

3 William R. Newman, *Gehennical Fire: The Lives of George Starkey, an American Alchemist in the Scientific Revolution* (Cambridge, MA: Harvard University Press, 1994), p. 228; Karin Figala, "Die exakte Alchemie von Isaac Newton," *Verhandlungen der Naturforschenden Gesellschaft in Basel* 94 (1984), 157–227.

4 Westfall, *Never at Rest*, p. 290.

5 William R. Newman and Lawrence M. Principe, "Alchemy vs. Chemistry: The Etymological Origins of a Historiographical Mistake," *Early Science and Medicine* 3 (1998), 32–65.

6 Charles Webster, *The Great Instauration* (London: Duckworth, 1975); P. M. Rattansi, "The Helmontian–Galenist Controversy in Restoration England," *Ambix* 12 (1964), 1–23; Harold J. Cook, *The Decline of the*

Old Medical Regime in Stuart London (Ithaca: Cornell University Press, 1986).

7   Cambridge University Library Add. MS 3975. The bulk of Newton's excerpts from Boyle occur on pp. 25–80, 90–100, 160–1, 163–73 and 177–207; most of Starkey's occur on pp. 162, 174, and 209–23.

8   Lawrence M. Principe, *The Aspiring Adept: Robert Boyle and his Alchemical Quest* (Princeton: Princeton University Press, 1998); Principe, "Boyle's Alchemical Pursuits," in Michael Hunter (ed.), *Robert Boyle Reconsidered* (Cambridge: Cambridge University Press, 1994), pp. 91–105; Principe, "Robert Boyle's Alchemical Secrecy: Codes, Ciphers, and Concealments," *Ambix* 39 (1992), 63–74; Michael Hunter, "Alchemy, Magic and Moralism in the Thought of Robert Boyle," *British Journal for the History of Science* 23 (1990), 387–410.

9   Principe, "Boyle's Alchemical Pursuits," pp. 96–7; Newman, *Gehennical Fire*, p. 76.

10 Newman, *Gehennical Fire*, pp. 58–78, 171–96.

11 Westfall, *Never at Rest*, p. 292. Dobbs, *The Janus Faces of Genius*, p. 51, suggests that a reading of Webster's 1671 *Metallographia* may have been the "immediate stimulus" behind "Of natures obvious laws & processes in vegetation." For Boyle as a follower of van Helmont, see Antonio Clericuzio, "A Redefinition of Boyle's Chemistry and Corpuscular Philosophy," *Annals of Science* 47 (1990), 561–89.

12 Dobbs, *The Janus Faces of Genius*, pp. 259–60, 262.

13 *Ibid.*, pp. 262–3.

14 A. Rupert Hall and Marie Boas Hall (eds.), *Unpublished Scientific Papers of Isaac Newton* (Cambridge: Cambridge University Press, 1962), p. 341.

15 Cambridge University Library Add. MSS 3975, 3973.

16 Walter Pagel, *Joan Baptista van Helmont* (Cambridge: Cambridge University Press, 1982).

17 Joan Baptista van Helmont, *Supplementum de Spadanis Fontibus* (Liège: Leonardus Streel, 1624).

18 Joan Baptista van Helmont, *Ortus Medicinae* (Amsterdam: Elzevir, 1648), p. 691.

19 Newman, *Gehennical Fire*, pp. 162–8; Karin Figala, "Newton as Alchemist," *History of Science* 25 (1977), 123–4.

20 Van Helmont, *Ortus Medicinae*, p. 74.

21 *Ibid.*, pp. 78–9.

22 *Ibid.*, p. 70.

23 *Ibid.*, p. 333.

24 *Ibid.*, p. 115.

25 Michael Sendivogius, *Novum Lumen Chemicum*, in J. J. Manget (ed.), *Bibliotheca Chemica Curiosa* (Geneva, 1702), vol. 2, p. 466.

26 Eirenaeus Philalethes, *De Metallorum Metamorphosi*, in Manget, *Bibliotheca Chemica Curiosa*, vol. 2, p. 681.

27 Eirenaeus Philalethes, *The Marrow of Alchemy* (London: Edward Brewster, 1654), Part 1, p. 17.

28 Westfall, *Never at Rest*, pp. 286–8; Richard S. Westfall, "Isaac Newton's Index Chemicus," *Ambix* 22 (1975), 174–85.

29 Isaac Newton, *The Correspondence of Isaac Newton*, vol. 1, ed. H.W. Turnbull (Cambridge: Cambridge University Press, 1959), p. 369.

30 William R. Newman, "Newton's *Clavis* as Starkey's *Key*," Isis 78 (1987), 564–74; *Gehennical Fire*, pp. 67–71, 229–31.

31 Isaac Newton, *The Correspondence of Isaac Newton*, vol. 2, ed. H.W. Turnbull (Cambridge: Cambridge University Press, 1960), pp. 292–3.

32 Eirenaeus Philoponos Philalethes, *The Marrow of Alchemy* (London: Edward Brewster, 1655), Part 2, p. 21.

33 Isaac Newton, *The Correspondence of Isaac Newton*, vol. 3, ed. H.W. Turnbull (Cambridge: Cambridge University Press, 1960), pp. 205–12.

34 Cambridge University Library, Add. MS 3975, p. 65.

35 Newton, *Correspondence*, vol. 3, p. 210.

36 *Ibid.*, p. 207. This passage is found in the notes appended by Archibald Pitcairne to the "De natura acidorum." See Westfall, *Never at Rest*, p. 527.

37 Isaac Newton, *Opticks* (London: G. Bell, 1931), p. 386.

38 Eirenaeus Philalethes, *Ripley Reviv'd* (London: William Cooper, 1678), p. 261. See also pp. 203 and 255.

39 Thomas Burnet, *Telluris Theoria Sacra* (London: G. Kettilby, 1681), pp. 34–6.

40 Westfall, *Never at Rest*, p. 391.

41 Cambridge University Library, MS Keynes 30, fol. 22r. For the passage, see Newman, *Gehennical Fire*, p. 335 n. 36.

42 Babson College MS 420, p. 2: "Est calidus et siccus [*deletion*] humidus et frigidus. Est ignis aquosus et aqua ignea [*deletion*] Est spiritus corporalis et corpus spirituale. Est condensatus spiritus mundi et rerum omnium quintessentia nobilissima ideoque charactere mundi [*deletion*] insigniri solet."

43 William Newman, review of Betty Jo Teeter Dobbs, *The Janus Faces of Genius*, in *Isis* 84 (1993), 578–9. See also Newman and Principe, "Alchemy vs. Chemistry," pp. 56–9.

12   Newton's alchemy

NEWTON'S ALCHEMICAL MANUSCRIPTS[1]

It may seem suprising to present Isaac Newton, the founder of modern mathematical natural science, as a serious student of alchemy. He himself must have felt this anomaly, since at all stages of his life he was concerned to hide his occult interests from the public. Until very recently his large collection of alchemical manuscripts was hardly looked at, much less systematically sorted or studied, in contrast to his better-understood manuscripts dealing with mechanics or the theory of matter. Yet Newton dedicated at least as much time to alchemical and theological studies as to his mathematical and physical ones.

The process of dating his manuscripts has shown that Newton worked on alchemy at all periods of his productive life, in parallel with his scientific work. This evidence proves that his occult studies were not the aberrations of senility. Newton would hardly have devoted so much time to such "absurdities" if he had not been convinced that some deeper knowledge lay hidden, which he eventually believed that he had at least in part discovered.

Newton attempted to make a synthesis of his occult-alchemical and exact-scientific research. For him a means of attaining this goal was the study of the so-called "prisca sapientia," a tradition of ancient wisdom. Newton considered that the original wisdom of the ancients, which had been gradually lost through the ages, was most fully retained in the writings of the Hermetic tradition. He saw himself as endeavoring to explain, by means of experimental science, this "sapientia," which had grown unintelligible.

The combination of exact science and magical thinking, which to-day can only be seen as schizophrenic, corresponds to a seventeenth-century mode of thinking. The tension evident in Newton's personality and work is also characteristic of an era which tried to combine tradition and progress in science with mystical revelation and metaphysics.[2] For Newton such philosophical teaching, explaining the first cause and the relationships between all creation, was not a modern pale abstract philosophical system, but was clearly visible in nature and had been handed down from the beginning of time in spiritual alchemy.

One can safely assume that if this great mathematician, for whom the Bible was the highest authority, stressed that God created all things in wonderful and harmonious proportions, he was thinking about a fundamental universal law. In what follows, I shall argue that we can understand Newton's goal by considering as central his only fragmentarily published "composition theory of matter." In this way we shall be able to represent important characteristic assumptions of the alchemical tradition in formulae: the "golden hierarchical chain of being," the relation of the above (heaven) and below (earth) of the legendary Hermes Trismegistus, and the continuing dispersing movement from the original "divine unity."

Newton also succeeded in expressing mathematically, with the help of this seemingly static model for the construction of matter, the most important symbol of alchemy, the "three-fold acting Mercury of the philosophers." The mediating function of this "divine messenger," which combines the opposites of matter – that is, sulfuric male earth and vacuum or female mercurial heaven – on all levels of the "living" pyramid of being, is precisely described in the generally valid "recurrence relation" of the theory of composition.

Although the hierarchical theory of matter, which was briefly presented in the *Opticks* of 1717, is nowhere mentioned explicitly in the great number of alchemical manuscripts, it may be deduced from Newton's choice of texts, and especially those from his favorite authors.[3] In this study it will only be possible to show this by examples primarily from a single alchemist, one whom Newton particularly valued throughout his life: Michael Maier (1569–1622).

NEWTON'S COMPOSITION THEORY OF MATTER

Newton may have had in mind a specific model for the internal structure of matter when writing his *Principia* (1687).[4] He may have been referring to this model in Definition 1: mass ("quantitas materiae"). This definition, in terms of the product of density ("densitas") and volume ("magnitudo"), has often been criticized as tautological. This formulation seems circular because density is defined as the relation of mass to volume. In the *Principia* Newton did not define density but was using this concept in the generally understood sense. The criticism of circularity does not, however, take into account the background of Newton's theory of matter. In the seventeenth century the experimental way of comparing masses was by measuring densities, that is, specific gravities.[5] But such measured densities give no indication of the inner structure of bodies, that is, of the distribution of matter and vacuum (pores). Some law is required about the inner structure of bodies that defines this relationship.

A variety of sources provide evidence of Newton's having such a law concerning the "inner structure of matter." Newton mentioned it to his younger friend David Gregory (1661–1710) in 1705, and to his confidant and favorite pupil in alchemy, Nicolas Fatio de Duillier (1664–1753), at least a decade earlier.[6] It was mentioned in print by Newton considerably later, in the second English edition of his *Opticks* of 1717–18.

we conceive these Particles of Bodies to be so disposed amongst themselves, that the Intervals or empty Spaces between them may be equal in magnitude to them all; and that these Particles may be composed of other Particles much smaller, which have as much empty Space between them as equals all the Magnitudes of these smaller Particles; And that in like manner these smaller Particles are again composed of others much smaller, all which together are equal to all the Pores or empty Spaces between them; and so on perpetually till you come to solid Particles, such as have no Pores or empty Spaces within them; And if in any gross Body there be, for instance, three such degrees of Particles, the least of which are solid; this Body will have seven times more Pores than solid Parts. But if there be four such degrees of Particles, the least of which are solid, the Body will have fifteen times more Pores than solid Parts. If there be five degrees, the Body will have one and thirty times more Pores than solid Parts. If six degrees, the Body will have sixty and three times more Pores than solid Parts. And so on perpetually.[7]

It appears from various remarks that Newton held the opinion that originally absolute matter is completely pure and homogeneous. Its separate, smallest, yet already structured particles, which do not differ in extension, hardness, impenetrability, mobility, and inertia – that is, in the characteristics of matter – seem to correspond to the "elementary particles" which can be no further divided through any natural, physical process. It is notable that although Newton calls the smallest particles of matter by a variety of names, he generally avoids the term "atom."

These original minute particles, which are themselves combinations of equal parts of matter and vacuum, are characterized by the strongest attractive force. Called first-order forms, they combine to make new "compositions" of the second order ("particulae secundae compositionis"), in which the elementary particles are surrounded by equally large spaces. The width of these "vacuoles" or pores corresponds to the diameter of the fundamental particles. Particles of a lower order provide building blocks for those of a higher order, while the width of the pores always corresponds to the diameter of the smaller element. From this pattern, one can construct particles of the first, second, third order, and so on, up to the biggest particles of the "ultimae compositionis." These build perceptible bodies held together only by weak forces of attraction on which depend the normal chemical reactions and colors of natural matter.[8]

Although Newton in his *Opticks* referred specifically to the two main elements of the old atomist theory, the atom and the vacuum,[9] his philosophy of the atom was fundamentally different from that of the ancient authors. On the one hand, he introduced opposing forces in the form of the passive inherent power (*vis inertiae*) and the active forces of gravitation, fermentation, and cohesion; and on the other, he presupposed this hierarchical structure within the formed particles.

The unchangeable, inherent "inertia" or *vis insita*[10] seems to have corresponded in Newton's alchemy to the "immutable seeds" which can be formed only by God. Newton attributed the active, "external" forces to a "spirit" which can nurture and bring to fruition the seeds which only God can create. Similarly, he equated the "matter-seed" with the "sulphuric principle" of alchemy, while the "alchemical Mercury" symbolizes the originally completely "matter-less spirit-vacuum." Through this "theory of structure" one can visualize quantitatively the alchemical sulfur seed as the material part and the alchemical spirit of Mercury as the vacuum.

NEWTON'S SOURCE FOR THE "PRISCA SAPIENTIA"

In what follows, besides a short glimpse of the alchemy of the Polish alchemist Michael Sendivogius (1556–1636), one author who was undoubtedly influential in Newton's alchemical work will be considered, the German Rosicrucian Michael Maier. Sendivogius's work inspired a kind of alchemical school in London whose activities can be traced at least to the beginning of the eighteenth century. The spiritual leader of this alchemical group, who published under the pseudonym Eirenaeus Philalethes, was George Starkey (died 1665?), whose influence on the young Newton has been shown by Westfall and Dobbs, and more recently by the findings of William Newman.[11]

With regard to Newton's later alchemical interests, Cleidophorus Mystagogus (the likewise pseudonymous successor of Philalethes) and the medical doctor William Y–Worth (or Yarworth), both members of this school, should be mentioned.

Newton's library contained works of both authors.[12] A recent discovery has demonstrated that they were one and the same man. A letter from Y–Worth to Newton, written about 1702, indicates a close, personal relationship between the two unevenly matched "adepts"[13] and contradicts Westfall's opinion that Newton's interest in alchemy ceased when he moved to London.[14]

For both Maier[15] and Sendivogius,[16] alchemy was the greatest science of principles, in a sense a metaphysics. Maier's alchemy, presented symbolically through ancient myths, represented to him an all-embracing universal science. Newton may have been interested in Maier's genealogical interpretation of heathen mythology, since Newton in his philosophical as well as in his theological and alchemical works always held that time and history unfold according to law. Sendivogius's alchemy, on the other hand, offered to Newton a natural philosophy with underlying universal dynamic principles characterized by internal forces and a mutual relation between reacting bodies. Two of the earliest of Newton's manuscripts, from about 1669, contain extracts from Maier's *Symbola Aureae*

Mensae (Keynes MS 29) and Sendivogius's *Novum Lumen Chymicum* (Keynes MS 19).[17]

Further influences on Newton's philosophical concepts, less marked than those of the alchemists, can be attributed to Joan Baptista van Helmont (1579–1644), who advocated vitalism, and Pierre Gassendi (1592–1655), who represented atomism.[18] One may wonder why Newton preferred the apparently occult and unintelligible works of the alchemists Sendivogius and Maier to those of enlightened rational philosophers such as van Helmont and Gassendi.

MICHAEL MAIER AND THE ROSICRUCIAN TRADITION

As already mentioned, the German Rosicrucian Michael Maier was besides Sendivogius one of the first alchemical authors Newton read and copied extracts from;[19] throughout his life Newton numbered them both among the "authores optimi" and the "magis utiles."[20] Most of Maier's works, heavily annotated, are still to be found in Newton's library;[21] they must have fascinated him all the more since the German Rosicrucian also saw that an intensive study of chronology and alchemy, as well as the Bible, was the best way of resolving experimentally God's Revelation and the secrets of the "composition" of matter. Newton's interest in Maier's writings also supports the view, expressed above, that his alchemy cannot be seen solely in connection with his chemical experiments but was also a link between his religious beliefs and his scientific aims.

Even in one of Maier's earliest works, the *Arcana Arcanissima* of 1614, there are clear parallels to Newton's ideas. Although Maier dismissed the worship of false gods of ancient civilizations as the falling away from the Truth of the one God, he believed in a hidden deeper meaning which must be surmised from the myths of gods and demons as well as from the Egyptian hieroglyphs. Accordingly, the aim of his research and work was to detect the philosophical, the scientific, and particularly the chemical truths in the allegories and adventures of the gods. Wars, battles, and deeds of the gods were for him exact symbols of natural laws, that is, the laws which regulate matter and the structure of the universe.[22] Throughout his life, Newton also believed that mankind originally worshipped one God and received one law from him. The worship of false gods led to an estrangement which became greater as more objects were worshipped.[23] Like Maier, Newton considered that we can understand the worship of these gods as the symbol of an exact scientific truth.[24]

Although Newton did not blindly follow Maier, he usually agreed with the ideas of the German Rosicrucian and saw him as one of the true philosophical "magi" who had theoretical as well as practical knowledge. The rich alchemical bibliography in Maier's works shows that he had read widely on alchemy. Since most of the works named by Maier can still be found in Newton's library, it is possible that Newton based his alchemical studies to a large degree on this author, whom he had discovered early in his career.[25]

It is also possible that some ideas in Newton's color theory may have been influenced by Maier, who believed that Saturn corresponds to the black out of which comes light. In the *Opticks* the smallest particles are described as black and invisible – even through better microscopes – on account of their transparency.[26] In alchemy black matter under the rule of Saturn corresponds to chaos and to the "materia prima" for which Newton set out more than forty names in his long handwritten "Index chemicus" (c. 1680–1700).[27] Through putrefaction this black matter becomes completely shapeless and therefore capable of assuming new forms. In Newton's composition-theory the blackness of Saturn, that is, the "materia prima," belongs to the first level of order which is characterized by equal parts of matter and vacuum.

The God Jupiter, whose realms are light and air, can be classed in a relatively primal "celestial" region, and in Maier's alchemy light and air are associated with him. This could have led Newton to pay greatest attention to this element, the metal tin, in his chemical experiments, particularly in those involving volatization. In Newton's chemical and alchemical writings after 1681, we find the myth of the dethroning of Saturn, and the assumption of power by Jupiter, together with his peace-making function through the scepter and the eagle which carries him to the throne.[28] Following Maier, Newton named Jupiter as the father of Mars and the other planets, which shows the importance and original position Newton gave to Jupiter, to the equivalent light-mediator-function in optics, and to the corresponding metal in chemistry.

In many places Maier implied a model of an increasingly split, structured, and specialized "pyramid of composition." The four chemical gods of the Egyptians – the female–male original principle of Osiris (male Sun) and the corresponding Isis (wife–sister, female Moon), as well as Mercury and Vulcan – become eight and finally twelve gods, who are later taken over by the Greeks. The death and resurrection of Osiris were used by Maier and by Newton as a symbol for the alchemical process. Osiris is killed and dismembered by his brother Typhon; this corresponds to death, putrefaction, and a return to primary matter; his body, which is collected by Isis, symbolizes the renewed circle of life and death.

The special position of the "incestuous couple" Isis and Osiris in Newton's alchemical chronology, or chronological chemistry, may be understood if one looks at Maier's dark symbols through Newton's clear mathematician's eyes. His careful and at the same time formalizing drawings in early extracts from Maier (Keynes MS 29), around 1668, and in the late manuscript (Keynes MS 32) seem to indicate that he found his composition-theory in Maier's "Arbor genealogica metallorum."

The relationships in Maier's genealogical tree seem to indicate that Newton in his composition-theory identified the valued last offspring of alchemy with the absolute, filled matter-particle (without vacuum) which on its own is completely immobile, cold, and dead. In the pyramid which reflects "life," the last offspring characteristically corresponds to the relative, sulfuric matter-particles. In his diagram Newton graphically presents these confusing alchemical symbols for the incestuous relationships which intermingle the generations, and the increasingly complicated mixed particles typical of this model.

The model of Maier's god–metal genealogy can also be detected in the mature alchemical *Praxis* manuscript,[29] written by Newton not earlier than 1693. The text of this manuscript was revised several times, indicating that it was not merely a copy but an original composition by Newton. Right at the beginning are various versions of a model that combines planets, metals, and elements. A notable feature is the "old-fashioned," markedly Pythagorean order.[30] Although Maier is quoted only among other authors in the subsequent text of *Praxis*, the chronological ordering suggests that it was based on his concept, one to which Newton devoted long study. Newton took this concept found in the works of the German Rosicrucian[31] and further developed it, made it more "scientific," and included it in his chronological system. In the *Praxis* manuscript an unsuccessful (that is, crossed-out) attempt and a less extensive scheme are followed by one which is introduced with the words: "In Aegyptiorum philosophia Dij erant duodecim quibus menses anni et signa Zodiaci dicabantur [sic]. Hi erant: 'Planetae septem', 'Elementa quatuor', 'Quintessentia...' " This mode of ordering the presentation can also be found in Newton's published Chronology, where even indications of relationships are shown,[32] starting with the four elements ("Elementa quatuor") and their correspondence to countries; three elements carry the names (Misraim, Phut, Canaan)[33] of the sons of Ham, who was the son of Noah. A second line of elements contains purely Egyptian gods, while the seven planet-metals cannot in this case be attributed to particular nations. The following third line gives the corresponding Roman gods, and the fourth and fifth lines contain the alchemical symbols and the Latin names of metals and chemicals. In his first draft, the first line, except "Thot," was missing, but the chemical classification of the four elements and of chaos was done more carefully. (That Newton was not sure about this classification can be seen from the fact that he entered different ideas in the same manuscript as well as in Keynes MS 48.) In an additional list he added to his ideas on the four peripatetic elements by distinguishing the "elements" of the metals from the minerals that form them.[34]

In what follows I will try to point out some aspects of the genealogy of the gods in Newton's (al)chemical system whose sequence of generations, in accordance with the Chronology, starts with the descendants of Noah in the period when – according to Newton – the turning away from monotheism began. It led via hero worship to polytheism, to downfall and corruption, and eventually to complete estrangement from God. The special position of Jupiter in Newton's alchemy, mentioned earlier, is indicated here in the dual position of "Ham" ("Cham") who as planet-metal ♃ (= Jupiter, tin) is the father of the planet-metal ♂ (= Mars, iron) as well as of the three elements of fire, water, and earth, or the corresponding mineral- and metal-elements. Newton's working laboratory notes show that this is not just the result of theoretical reflection but also of experiments.[35]

According to Praxis the "Spiritus Mundi" works on the completely undifferentiated chaos gradually to separate the four elements. Chaos and "Spiritus Mundi" differ only in their degree of condensation, so that each chaos can be termed "condensatus spiritus mundi," "spiritus corporalis," or "corpus spirituale."[36] In Newton's diagram, chaos corresponds to antimony and is equated with "Quintessentia," while in the text he distinguishes between the chaos of the "four elements" of the imperfect metals and the "Quintessentia" of bismuth.[37] The more specific term, "hollow oak," applied to the amalgamated metal-chaos, was often used in Newton's chemical laboratory notes.[38] For Newton, antimony is the microcosmic mineral-metal correspondence of the macrocosmic globe. Just as the earth presents the most intense homogeneous mixture of the four "peripatetic" elements, antimony corresponds to the amalgam of the four elements of the imperfect metals. In the *Praxis* scheme as found in Babson MS [420], the separation of elements from the chaos is presented in the same order as in Newton's exact natural philosophy, as found in the early Burndy MS 16 manuscript[39] and perhaps in the *Principia*.

In *Praxis*, both Typhon[40] and the Sea-God Neptune[41] are classed as "aqua pontica." The importance which Newton attributed throughout his life to the Egyptian Typhon is already clear in his earliest Maier manuscripts. This wild, fiery, sulfur-mercurial spirit, which can break up a coherent mass into its smallest elements, is also compared to the dragon. That the snake which was killed by the Greek Cadmus is called a descendant of Typhon seems to indicate the active acid character of its Egyptian ancestor. Newton's laboratory notes of about 1680 show how much importance he attached to the "aqua pontica" even in exact chemical experiments. Here the corresponding Sea-God Neptune is called "menstruum aqueum minerale." His power is symbolized by the trident which is equated with the ferment and compared to the "caduceus mercurii."[42]

In his theory of acids, Newton attributed to all acid particles, because of their ability to dissolve or dilute, a relatively strong attractive force resulting from their high content of spirit. Small quantities, which are hidden in earthy, that is, passive substances, can be gradually recognized by their being "Fat and Fusible Bodies."[43] In quantitative chemistry, the proportion of acid (= force of attraction), equivalent to the alchemical fire-sulfur in each substance, can be determined.

The parallel between chemical acid and alchemical fire-sulfur becomes clear in Query 31 of the *Opticks*, where the "acid vapours," which are best suited to fermentation in the mineral as well as the animal kingdom, generate heat and eventually, acting as a "very potent Principle," set fire to bodies.[44] Although one could quote many more examples from Query 31 for the analogy with the alchemical models in *Praxis*, I want only to point out that their general arrangement clearly distinguishes between the two attracting poles – the earthy, alkaline, fixed, passive, and the fiery, acid, volatile.

Although in his later excerpts, made about 1700, Newton concentrated particularly on the alchemical–arithmetical–astronomical aspects of Maier's definition of sulfur, earlier in his life he had been stimulated by other aspects of its definitions. One can almost assume that in the *annus mirabilis*, after his first reading of Maier's works, he orientated himself on this model, and then, during the following years, never lost sight of its "encircling" method. Only when the "innermost hidden sulphur" has been precisely defined in all disciplines can its "innermost, hidden," absolute (that is, pure, separate, independent) character be known and defined according to the same laws.

There is no doubt that Newton accepted Maier's physical-biological definition of sulfur as the "foetus" just born into light.[45] He succeeded in transferring the alchemical symbolism to physics by defining light as the "corporeal emanation" of the aether-spirit. Maier's alchemical foetus corresponds to Newton's light in optics, and the mercurial, fruit-bearing womb becomes the aether, the carrier of the sun-tinder.

Maier's tendency to look for repeated, ordered relationships also permeated Newton's scientific works. He established a relationship between optics and music by applying the Doric mode to define the diameter of the colored rings of thin films as well as to the intervals of consecutive "fits of easy reflexion and easy transmission." Newton strengthened this relationship between optics and music when, in his apparently arbitrary division of light into the seven colors of the spectrum, he arranged the spectrum so as to agree with the divisions of the monochords. Another indication of the influence of the German Rosicrucian on his optical theories can be seen in the late manuscript (Keynes MS 32), where, in an excerpt of around 1700, he deals with the "mythological" connection between colors and music which is associated with Apollo, God of Light, who leads the nine Muses.[46] Newton's attempt to establish a relationship between musical notes and optical colors has often been criticized by historians of science. In spite of this criticism, so far no research has been carried out into why Newton assumed the same law for the thickness of air in the bands that produce color in thin films and for the intervals between single "fits."[47] It is possible that this idea was influenced by Maier's definition of sulfur.

NOTES

This chapter is an abridgement of Karin Figala, "Die exakte Alchemie von Isaac Newton," *Verhandlungen der Naturforschenden Gesellschaft Basel* 94 (1984), 155–228. For the author's findings concerning Newton's exact alchemy, see K. Figala, "Newton as Alchemist," *History of Science* 15 (1977), 102–37; also K. Figala, "Newton's Alchemical Studies and His Idea of the Atomic Structure of Matter," Appendix A (pp. 381–6) of A. Rupert Hall's *Isaac Newton: Adventurer in Thought* (Oxford: Blackwell, 1992).

1 Some major writings on alchemy, notably by Betty Jo Teeter Dobbs, are listed in the Bibliography.

2 For Robert Boyle's attitude toward alchemy see Lawrence M. Principe, *The Aspiring Adept: Robert Boyle and His Alchemical Quest* (Princeton: Princeton University Press, 1998), and "Robert Boyle's Alchemical Pursuits," in Michael Hunter (ed.), *Robert Boyle Reconsidered* (Cambridge: Cambridge University Press, 1994), pp. 91–105; Michael Hunter, "Alchemy, Magic and Moralism in the Thought of Robert Boyle," *British Journal of the History of Science* 23 (1990), 387–410; William R. Newman, "Boyle's Debt to Corpuscular Alchemy," in Hunter (ed.), *Boyle Reconsidered*, pp. 107–18.

3 A presentation of my mathematical analysis may be found in the works cited in note 1.

4 Isaac Newton, *Philosophiae Naturalis Principia Mathematica* (London, 1687).

5 On this point see the chapter by William Newman in this volume.

6 W. G. Hiscock (ed.), *David Gregory, Isaac Newton and Their Circle: Extracts from David Gregory's Memoranda 1677–1708* (Oxford: printed for the editor, 1937), pp. 29ff. See also Bernard Gagnebin, "De la cause de la pesanteur, mémoire de Nicolas Fatio de Duillier présenté à la Royal Society le 26 février 1690," *Notes and Records of the Royal Society* 6 (1949), 117ff.

7 Isaac Newton, *Opticks: or, A Treatise of the Reflections, Refractions, Inflections and Colours of Light* (London 1717/18); all quotations are taken from the reprint edition, New York: Dover Publications, 1952, pp. 268ff.

8 *Ibid.*, p. 394.

9   *Ibid.*, p. 369

10 On Newton's use of the term *vis insita*, see pp. 96–102 of I. B. Cohen,
    "Guide to Newton's *Principia*," part of *The Principia, Mathematical
    Principles of Natural Philosophy: A New Translation*, trans. I. Bernard
    Cohen and Anne Whitman, Preceded by "A Guide to Newton's
    Principia" by I. B. Cohen (Berkeley: University of California Press, 1999).

11 See William Newman, *Gehennical Fire: The Lives of George Starkey,
    an American Alchemist in the Scientific Revolution* (Cambridge, MA:
    Harvard University Press, 1994).

    Ronald Sterne Wilkinson, "The Problem of the Identity of Eirenaeus
    Philalethes," *Ambix* 12 (1964), 24–33; also "A Further Note on Eire-
    naeus Philalethes," *Ambix* 13 (1965), 53–4, and "Further Thoughts
    on the Identity of Irenaeus Philalethes," *Ambix* 19 (1972), 204–8, and
    "Some Bibliographical Puzzles Concerning George Starkey," *Ambix* 20
    (1973), 235–44.

    Richard S. Westfall, "The Role of Alchemy in Newton's Career," in
    M. L. Righini Bonelli and W. R. Shea (eds.), *Reason, Experiment and
    Mysticism in the Scientific Revolution* (New York: Science History
    Publications, 1975), pp. 189–231; "Alchemy in Newton's Library,"
    Ambix 31 (1984), 97–101; and "The Influence of Alchemy on Newton,"
    in Marsha P. Hanen, Margaret J. Osler, and Robert G. Weyant (eds.),
    Science, Pseudo-Science and Society (Waterloo, Ontario: Wilfrid Laurier
    University Press, 1980), pp. 145–69.

    Betty Jo Teeter Dobbs, *The Foundations of Newton's Alchemy or
    "The Hunting of the Greene Lyon"* (Cambridge: Cambridge University
    Press, 1975); "Newton's Copy of 'Secrets Reveal'd' and the Regimens of
    the Work," *Ambix* 26 (1979), 145–69; and *The Janus Faces of Genius:
    The Role of Alchemy in Newton's Thought* (Cambridge: Cambridge
    University Press, 1991).

12 John Harrison, *The Library of Isaac Newton* (Cambridge: Cambridge
    University Press, 1978), p. 198 (no. 1138), p. 216 (no. 1301), p. 264
    (no. 1760).

13 K. Figala, "Zwei Londoner Alchemisten um 1700: Sir Isaac Newton
    und Cleidophorus Mystagogus," *Physis* 18 (1976), 245ff. The letter
    from Yarworth to Newton is reprinted in *The Correspondence of Isaac
    Newton*, vol. 7, ed. A. Rupert Hall and Laura Tilling (Cambridge: Cam-
    bridge University Press, 1900), p. 441, no. x. 704. The other manuscript is
    Keynes MS 65, "Processus Mysterii Magni Philosophicus." (The desig-
    nation "Keynes MS" refersk to manuscripts in the Keynes collection in
    the library of King's College, Cambridge.) See also K. Figala and Ulrich
    Petzold, "Alchemy in the Newtonian Circle: Personal Acquaintances
    and the Problem of the Late Phase of Isaac Newton's Alchemy,"

in J. V. Field and F. A. J. L. James (eds.), *Renaissance and Revolution: Humanists, Scholars, Craftsmen, and Natural Philosophers in Early Modern Europe* (Cambridge: Cambridge University Press, 1993), pp. 173–92.

14 Westfall, "The Role of Alchemy," pp. 231ff; see, further, Westfall's *Never at Rest: A Biography of Isaac Newton* (Cambridge: Cambridge University Press, 1980), pp. 530ff.

15 On Maier see Ulrich Neumann, "Maier, Michael," in Claus Priesner and Karin Figala (eds.), *Alchemie, Lexikon einer hermetischen Wissenschaft* (Munich: Verlag C. H. Beck München, 1998), pp. 232–5; Karin Figala and Ulrich Neumann, "Author Cui Nomen Hermes Malavici: New Light on the Bio-Bibliography of Michael Maier (1569–1622)," in P. Rattansi and A. Clericuzio (eds.), *Alchemy and Chemistry in the 16th and 17th Centuries* (Dordrecht: Kluwer Academic Publishers, 1994), pp. 121–47.

16 On Sendivogius see Karin Figala, "Sendivogius, Michael," in *Alchemie, Lexikon einer hermetischen Wissenschaft*, pp. 332–4.

17 The reader is reminded that such references as "Keynes MS 19" refer to manuscripts in the Keynes collection in the library of King's College, Cambridge.

18 See the chapter in this volume by William Newman. Newton seems to have read van Helmont's works in his younger days. His library contains only the main work, *Ortus Medicinae* (Lyons, 1667), but a number of quotations and excerpts from van Helmont are to be found in Newton's alchemical–chemical manuscripts, often with very critical remarks. See Keynes MS 16, Babson MS [416], B, no. 2, and Westfall, *Never at Rest*, p. 292; also Harrison, *The Library of Isaac Newton*, no. 751. (The Babson manuscripts are now on permanent deposit at the Burndy Library, Cambridge, MA.)

19 Newton's interest in Maier is mentioned by Frances A. Yates, *The Rosicrucian Enlightenment* (London and Boston: Routledge and Kegan Paul, 1972), pp. 201, 204ff. See also J. E. McGuire and P. M. Rattansi, "Newton and the Pipes of Pan," *Notes and Records of the Royal Society of London* 21 (1966), 108–43; Frank E. Manuel, *A Portrait of Isaac Newton* (Cambridge, MA: Harvard University Press, 1968), pp. 163, 171, 424; and Westfall, *Never at Rest*, pp. 22, 293, 305, 358, 363, 524, 529, and esp. 193, 291–2.

20 Keynes MS 29. Excerpts from Michael Maier's *Symbola Aureae Mensae Duodecim Nationum* (Frankfurt, 1617), quoted below from the reprint (Graz: Österreich. Verlagsanstalt, 1972) (written about 1668/9); Keynes MS 12, "Alchemical Propositions," written about 1670, which contains many quotes from Maier's work; Keynes MS 13, fol. 2r. Newton here

gives a list of the dates of publication of Maier's works without naming the titles: 1610 (fol. 2r), 1617 (fols. 3v, 4v), 1620 (fol. 3v), and 1637 (fols. 3v, 4v) (written about 1696); Keynes MS 49, fol. 1r (written about 1685–90). The date of 1610 for one of Maier's books seems to indicate that Newton used either manuscripts or until very recently lost works of this author; see also note 15.

21 Harrison, *The Library of Isaac Newton*, pp. 188ff, nos. 1044–52.

22 Michael Maier, *Arcana Arcanissima, hoc est, Hieroglyphica Aegyptio-Graeca* (London, 1614). See James B. Craven, *Count Michael Maier* (London: Dawsons, 1968), pp. 32ff.

23 Frank E. Manuel, *Isaac Newton Historian* (Cambridge, MA: Harvard University Press, 1963), pp. 113ff.

24 Yahuda Papers: Jewish National and University Library, Jerusalem, MS var. 1, Newton papers 15.3, fol. 47v: "that we may thank him God for our being & for all the blessings of this life, & forbear to take his name in vain or worship images or other Gods. We are not forbidden to give the name of Gods to Angels & Kings, but we are forbidden to have them as Gods in our worship."

25 See also Karin Figala, John Harrison, and Ulrich Pefzold, "De Scriptoribus Chemicis: Sources for the Establishment of Isaac Newton's (Al) chemical Library," in P. M. Harman and Alan E. Shapiro (eds.), *The Investigation of Difficult Things: Essays on Newton and the History of the Exact Sciences* (Cambridge: Cambridge University Press, 1992) pp. 135–79.

26 Newton, *Opticks*, 261ff.

27 Keynes MS 30; see also Richard S. Westfall, "Isaac Newton's Index Chemicus," *Ambix* 22 (1975), 174–85.

28 See for example Cambridge University Library (CUL) Add MS 3975; fol. 121ff.

Fol. 123: "June 1682 Saturn destilled per se in a red heat sent up 60g & there remained in ye bottom 90gr. This spirit carries not up ♃ [tin] nor tinglass."

Fol. 149: after experiments in sublimation with "tin regulus" Newton notes: "ffriday May 23 [1684] Jovem super aquilam volare feci."

CUL Add MS 3975 and Add MS 3973 are located in the Cambridge University Library. Here Newton's own chemical experiments are recorded.

29 Babson MS [420] seems to be Newton's own draft in five chapters with the following titles:

Cap. 1 De materiis spermaticis
Chap. 2 De materia prima

Cap. 3 De Sulphure Ph[ilosoph]orum
Cap. 4 De agente primo
Chap. 5 Praxis

Newton's text is partially reproduced, without all of the schemata, in Dobbs, *The Janus Faces of Genius*, Appendix E, pp. 293–305.

30 The graph in the alchemical Babson MS [420] corresponds to one in a later, chronological draft (Yahuda MS var. 1, Newton papers MS 17, fol. 19). In arranging the planets Newton chooses the system of "Pythagoras" in which the order is arranged according to the harmonic proportions of notes and half-notes.

31 Keynes MS 29, fol. 2r (about 1669) and Keynes MS 32, fol. 4 (about 1700) contain relevant excerpts from Maier's *Symbola*, lib. iv, p. 154.

32 Isaac Newton, "The Chronology of Antient Kingdoms Amended," ed. S. Horsley, in *Isaaci Newtoni Opera quae exstant omnia*, commentariis illustrabat Samuel Horsley, LL. D.R.S.S. Reverendo admodum in Christo Patri Roberto Episcopo Londinensi a Sacris, i–v (London 1779–85; reprinted Stuttgart–Bad Cannstadt, 1964) v, pp. 1–291; see also Oxford, Bodleian Library, New College MS 2, fol. 89.

33 Yahuda MS var. 1; Newton papers MS 16, fol. 19.

34 Keynes MS 30; MS 35, fol. 16r; MS 32, fol. 23ff.

35 CUL Add MS 3975, fol. 123ff, in particular fol. 129/30. In these experiments tin (Jupiter), antimony, bismuth and ammoniac NH_4Cl ("vulgar" and "our" [ammoniac salt]) are the main substances used; the latter is also attached to Jupiter because of its volatile character and its origin.

36 Babson MS [420], B, fol. 2.

37 Babson MS [420], B, fol. 15.

38 For example CUL Add MS 3975, fol. 133.

39 The Burndy MS 16 was originally located in the Burndy Library, Norwalk, CT. A generous gift to the nation from the "old" Burndy Library in 1976 placed it in the Dibner Library, Smithsonian Institution, Washington, DC as Dibner MS 1031B.

40 See also Keynes MS 30, "Index chemicus," heading: Typho.

41 Keynes MS 30, heading: Neptunus.

42 CUL Add MS 3975, fol. 12b.

43 "De natura acidorum," written in 1692 and first published in 1710 in the "Introduction" to vol. 2 of the *Lexicon Technicum* of John Harris, now reprinted in *Isaac Newton's Papers and Letters in Natural Philosophy and Related Documents*, ed. I. Bernard Cohen (Cambridge, MA: Harvard University Press, 1958), pp. 256–8.

44 Newton, *Opticks*, Query 31, p. 380. A difficulty in comparing the *Opticks* with the alchemical manuscripts often lies in the fact that they

attribute different names to the same substances so that any similarity is only detected on closer scrutiny of the texts. For example in Babson MS [420], B, fol. 1 an ore of zinc is called "Tutia" which in the *Opticks* is "Lapis Calaminaris."

45 Michael Maier, *Atalanta Fugiens, hoc est, Emblemata Nova de Secretis Naturae Chymica* (Oppenheim, 1618), Emblema v, 14. In Newton's library this book is found in a slightly altered edition of Frankfurt, 1687 (see Harrison, *The Library of Isaac Newton*, no. 1045).

46 Keynes MS 32, fol. 18.

47 Newton, *Opticks*, pp. 126ff, 212, 225ff, 284.

13 Newton on prophecy and the Apocalypse

THE INTELLECTUAL BACKGROUND OF A NATURAL PHILOSOPHER OF THE SEVENTEENTH CENTURY

Newton's theological manuscripts are concerned principally with two subjects: the interpretation of the prophecies of the Apocalypse and Daniel, and the history of the early Church. These two subjects are linked, but it was as a consequence of his interpretation of the Apocalypse that Newton undertook his study of the history of the Church. The study of prophetic literature was firmly rooted in Cambridge, where this subject was taught by Joseph Mede, author of a *Clavis Apocalyptica* (or Key to the Apocalypse), a work much used by Newton.

Newton's interest in the prophecies is already documented in the "Quaestiones" of the Trinity Notebook (1664–5).[1] In "Of Earth" (c. 1664) Newton made deductions about physics, "in rerum natura," directly from the Scriptures: the final conflagration of the earth, and the probable succession of worlds. This last affirmation was supported by a passage of the Book of Revelation which referred to days and nights after the Last Judgment, which would have made no sense had the world finished for ever. In "Of the Creation" (c. 1664) Newton made use of a passage from Genesis to prove that God had created time.[2] From these entries it is evident that Newton used biblical texts to determine the truth of a philosophical proposition. Strange or ingenuous as this approach of Newton's might seem, given that the trial and condemnation of Galileo had shown the difficulty of reconciling philosophy and religion, it was one he maintained in subsequent years.[3]

Newton's theological and scientific interests not only manifested themselves almost contemporaneously, but always remained connected. Shortly before matriculating at Cambridge on 8 July 1661, Newton had acquired a Greek–Latin dictionary and an edition of the New Testament in Greek and Latin.[4] In his first year at Cambridge, Newton acquired only one book from the curriculum, the *Logicae Artis Compendium* (Summary of Logical Art) by Robert Sanderson, which exerted, as we shall see, a notable influence upon Newton's methodological ideas. Yet he bought as many as four theological books.[5] In a pocket book, Newton also noted the purchase, for a shilling, of a second-hand edition of *De Quatuor Monarchiis* (The Four Kingdoms) by J. Sleidan.[6]

Sleidan interpreted the dream of the king of Babylon (Daniel 2): a colossal statue was broken into four pieces, each made of a different metal. The four kingdoms (Babylonian, Persian, Greek, and Roman) would correspond to the four parts of the statue. Sleidan, drawing upon arguments in Luther, held that the fourth kingdom had not yet ended, and that it would endure until Christ's return, represented by the rock which, independently of man, detached itself from the mountain, destroyed the colossus, and became in its turn a great mountain. Newton's reading of Sleidan probably served to strengthen his interest in the relations between prophecies and history.

The Trinity Notebook indicates that in 1664–5 other intellectual passions took their places firmly alongside Newton's interest in the Bible. The entries on light and colors occupied more and more space in the notebook, and there one finds the first draft of the "New Theory of Light and Colors" which Newton presented to the Royal Society in 1672. From 1664, having obtained a scholarship to Trinity College, Newton studied mathematics intensively. During the two plague years (1665 and 1666), Newton withdrew to Woolsthorpe, claiming later that he was "in the prime of my age for invention & minded Mathematicks & Philosophy more then at any time since."[7]

The results of this extraordinary creative explosion are well known: the method of fluxions, the theory of light and colors, and the law of an inverse-square force, necessary for the stability of planetary orbits. These achievements have sustained the myth of the creative genius, struck by sudden illuminations. Newton's manuscript papers tell a different story, no less deserving of admiration. The expression that Newton applied to himself of seeing further by virtue of standing on the shoulders of giants[8] was a particularly apt metaphor.

Many indeed stood upon those shoulders, but no one else saw as far. The method of fluxions was at first a generalization and application of Wallis's method, as the theory of colors was a felicitous combination of Cartesian explanations and Boylean experiences.[9] The inverse-square law was only a theorem – based on Galileo's law of falling bodies and on Kepler's rule of the periodical times – which as yet had not been verified with reference to the orbit of any of the planets. Much work was to be done – work which would occupy almost the rest of Newton's life – before these brilliant results would acquire the significance they have in the *Principia*, in the *Opticks*, and in the mathematical writings.

These discoveries came into being together with criticism of the methods used by the authors Newton was reading (Descartes, Galileo, Boyle, Wallis, etc.), and from the effort to establish a more reliable method for the investigation of nature.

Having returned to Cambridge in 1667, Newton continued to work on optics until at least 1670, when he drafted the manuscript of the *Lectiones Opticae*, which contained his lectures as Lucasian Professor of Mathematics for the year 1669/70. Here Newton indicated a new approach that united geometry and experimental research, taking as an example his own discoveries of the refractions of light and the explanation of colors.[10] It was probably in the same years that Newton began to compose an essay on physics, the "De gravitatione."[11] This work begins with a brief exposition of the methods that Newton intended to adopt, but which also serves to illustrate the manner by which he had arrived at the brilliant discoveries of the years 1665 and 1666.

Newton asserts that:

it is proper to treat the science of gravity and of the equilibrium of fluid and solid bodies in fluids by two methods. To the extent that it appertains to the mathematical sciences, it is reasonable that I largely abstract it from physical considerations. And for this reason I have undertaken to demonstrate its individual propositions from abstract principles, sufficiently well known to the student, strictly and geometrically. Since this doctrine may be judged to be somewhat akin to natural philosophy, insofar as it may be applied to making clear many of the phenomena of natural philosophy, and in order, moreover, that its usefulness may be particularly apparent and the certainty of its principles perhaps confirmed, I shall not be reluctant to illustrate the propositions abundantly from experiments as well, in such a way, however, that this freer method of discussion, disposed in scholia, may not be confused with the former which is treated in Lemmas, propositions and corollaries.[12]

"De gravitatione" also contains a long metaphysical discussion of the concept of space, in open disagreement with the ideas of Descartes. In this discussion, Newton used subjects drawn from the Bible in a characteristic manner.

Space – Newton contended – is not the essence of matter, but a property of being as such. Taking motifs similar to those of Gassendi and More, Newton upheld the idea of the real presence of God in space; he not only denied that extension is the essence of matter, but also suggested that matter in and of itself had no essence. Matter depended for its existence on God. Thus "we cannot postulate bodies... without at the same time supposing that God exists."[13] It is evidence – argued Newton – that God created the world by the action of will alone, as man, by the same action, has the power to move his own body. To justify this affirmation Newton added, the "analogy between the Divine faculties and our own is greater than has formerly been perceived by Philosophers. That we were created in God's image holy writ testifies."[14] The Scriptures, therefore, completed and corrected philosophy.

By the beginning of the 1670s Newton had to his credit an experience of study which ranged from mathematics to theology, from physics to metaphysics, from optics to alchemy. Without doubt, however, his principal interests in the preceding years had been mathematics and physics, areas of research in which he had demonstrated considerable open-mindedness, a strong critical sense, and the tendency to unify these two fields of knowledge. In 1672, after the publication in the *Philosophical Transactions* of the theory of the colors, and the disputes which followed, Newton abruptly abandoned his research into mathematics and physics, and dedicated himself with the same passion to the interpretation of the Apocalypse along with his study of alchemy. However one accounts for this new direction, which, as Westfall stated, "absorbed virtually all of his time for the following fifteen years before a visit from Edmond Halley started the investigation that resulted in the *Principia* and altered the tenor of his existence,"[15] Newton never abandoned his search for a method by which truth could be established no matter what the field of knowledge. Whatever interests exercised him, there was always one central question that Newton tried to resolve: how is it possible to arrive at certain knowledge?

It is therefore misleading to ask – as many interpreters have done – what influence Newton's theology had upon his science. In his search for a criterion of the truth, Newton made no distinction between science and theology. It was the same approach that had led him to break down the boundaries between mathematics and physics, between geometric optics and philosophy, between matter and spirit. In this sense, the anachronistic debate between those who would have Newton preeminently a theologian, and those who would have him preeminently a scientist, can be resolved only by the assertion that, like Descartes, Hobbes, and Leibniz, Newton was a philosopher in the seventeenth-century sense of the term.

TO METHODIZE THE APOCALYPSE

A book Newton acquired at the same time as the one by Sleidan, and which was set by the university curriculum, helped Newton to "methodize" the Apocalypse, in other words to render his interpretation univocal. The book was Sanderson's manual of logic, in which were listed the laws common to every method of arranging or discovering in all sorts of knowledge. This manual, as we shall see, was the main source for Newton's rules for interpreting the Apocalypse.

Why was it necessary to have a method for understanding the Apocalypse? The obscurity of the Apocalypse presents its interpreter with a problem: either it expresses God's plans – the wisest and most suitable for his purpose – or it is entirely without sense.[16] According to Newton, no one had successfully tried to understand its visions; therefore the Book of Revelation had been neglected by every Church. But in that case – Newton insisted – what was the reason why God had given the prophetic Scriptures? Was it in jest? If the prophecies were not supposed ever to have been understood, to what end had God revealed them?

Newton used the argument from design to affirm the perfect comprehensibility of the Apocalypse. The design, the purpose, constituted the first condition of interpretation itself. If God spoke, he spoke to be understood. The prophecies therefore must contain an ascertainable significance, straightforward and comprehensible to the intellect, appropriate for all men, without requiring the mediation of the learned. Why then were they so obscure that Newton himself held that not even the most learned men could ever have understood them? The simplest solution to the problem was that of making the obscurity itself relevant to God's plans. The obscurity was God's way of prolonging the revelation in time and of distinguishing true Christians from apostates.

The true Christian is therefore characterized by his "understanding," which is distinct from the mere natural gift of intelligence, and requires also humility and impartiality:

And for this end it is that they are wrapt up in obscurity, & so framed by the wisdom of God that the inconsiderate, the proud, the self-conceited the presumptuous the sciolist, the sceptic, they whose judgments are ruled by their lusts, their interest, the fashions of the world, their [opinions] esteem of men, the outward shew of thing or other prejudice; & all they who, of how pregnant natural parts soever they be, yet cannot discern the wisdom of God in the contrivance of the creation: that these men whose heads are thus hardened in seeing should see & not perceive & in hearing should heare & not understand.[17]

Newton affirmed that "God who best knows the capacities of men does hide his mysteries from the wise & prudent of this world" and reveals them to the children and "the inferiour people."[18] This account never became socially subversive, because its real function was to underline the clarity of the prophecies and the possibility of arriving at certainty in interpreting them.

The "understanding" to which Newton referred was that capable of perceiving the wisdom of God, the unity of his design, in nature and in Scripture. It is an "understanding" common to all men, one which is characterized in a positive sense by the activity of the individual search for truth, and which acquires a strong ethical connotation from its contrast with the state of being blinded by prejudice.

Everyone therefore can and must understand the "substance" of the prophecy with absolute certainty.

But what is the substance of the prophecy? The prophecy has a content, and a function or purpose. The content of the prophecy is history, nothing other than the history of the things which must occur.[19] The identity of content between prophecy and history demands that one interpret the first according to the same criteria as one reconstructs the second. This is why Newton speaks of the construction of the Apocalypse, which is the proper outcome of his idea of a method of interpretation. The term "construction" is reminiscent also of the grammatical and rhetorical tradition that Newton had learnt from Sanderson's manual. To understand the Apocalypse it is necessary to fix rules for constructing it. These will be preceded by general rules for interpreting the words and language of the Scriptures, and followed by specific rules for interpreting the Apocalypse.

Besides a content, prophecy has a function or purpose. For what reason did God reveal the future to men? Undoubtedly because he deemed it useful that it should be known by those who were to live in the future. There is, therefore, in the history of the final events a content the knowledge of which is necessary to men and to the Church. In fact:

All sacred Prophesies are given for the use of the Church, & therefore they are all to be understood by the Church in those ages for whose use God intended them. But these prophesies were never understood by the Church in the former ages: they did not so much as pretend to understand them, nor thought that they concerned their times, but with one universall consent delivered down to posterity the famous Tradition of the Antichrist described therein to come in the latter ages. And therefore since they were never yet understood, & God cannot be disappointed, we must acknowledg that they were written & shall prove for the benefit of the present & future ages, & so are not yet fulfilled. Wherefore let men be carefull how they indeavour to divert or hinder the use of these scriptures, least they be found to fight against God.[20]

The purpose of the prophecies of the Apocalypse is the edification of the true Church, which will come to fulfillment at the end of time. The churches of history are not yet the true Church. On the contrary. The necessity of the degeneration of the churches is, for Newton, not only clearly written in the Apocalypse, but a conclusion to be drawn by common sense when one considers their multiplicity. The true Church is constituted not by all those who "call themselves Christians, but a remnant, a few scattered persons which God hath chosen, such as without being [bended] led by interest, education or humane authorities can set themselves sincerely and earnestly to search after truth."[21] This virtual Church will become real only at the end of time.

If this is the purpose of the Apocalypse, then its content becomes clear: in these prophecies there is told the story of the Antichrist in as much as true believers can recognize him, and, by not adhering to his kingdom, save themselves. Newton largely accepts Sleidan's interpretation of the four Kingdoms of Daniel's visions, of which the last, the Roman Empire, corresponds to the ten-horned Beast of the Apocalypse. The two-horned Beast corresponds to the little horn of Daniel's Fourth Beast. The two-horned Beast is identified by Newton with other figures: the False Prophet and the Whore of Babylon. The two-horned Beast receives the power of the first Beast (that is of Rome, in the age of Constantine) by deception, using portents and miracles (an allusion to the Catholic Church). The whore Church bids its believers construct an image of the first Beast (an allusion to the Caesarism of the Popery). The Woman Fled into the Wilderness is the primitive evangelical Church sent into exile (after the Council of Nicaea). The mystery or the blasphemy written on the forehead of the Whore are probably the Trinity, introduced by Athanasius as a new form of polytheism. We come to the Grand Apostasy, to the seventh seal, which represents one and the same, continual apostasy, which ceases at the onset of the seventh trumpet. With the seventh trumpet we are already in the future. The Grand Apostasy cannot be overthrown without the intervention of the Savior, the second coming of Christ, announced by the Book of Revelation. A new monarchy that would put an end to apostasy is not possible because it is not part of God's plans. Hence the reformed Churches are also necessarily apostate.

The mystery of iniquity is at the center of the Apocalypse, epitomized in the figure of the man of sin, the Antichrist. The Antichrist is the type of deception rather than a person. To be truly effective, deception must be seductive, and present itself in the trappings of truth.

But what if the hour of the Antichrist has not yet arrived? Newton foresaw this objection, and his response showed that his conception of the Antichrist was not purely eschatological. As he is the prince of deception, he is preceded by whatever deception is perpetrated to man's cost, and the very multiplicity of religions renders deception ever possible:

Antichrist was to seduce the whole Christian world & therefore he may easily seduce thee if thou beest not well prepared to discern him. But if he should not be yet come into the world yet amidst so many religions *of which there can be but one true* & perhaps none of those that thou art acquainted with it is great odds but thou mayst be deceived & therefore it concerns thee to be very circumspect.[22]

The possibility of deception is explained by the argument that there can be only one truth, an affirmation which corresponds almost *verbatim* with a passage from *Discours de la méthode* by Descartes.[23] For this reason Newton denounces the errors of learned interpreters. Where had these interpreters gone wrong? Fundamentally from excess of imagination. Newton called it, to underline its negativity, private imagination, in other words subjective and arbitrary imagination. It was the source of heresy. Not truly understanding the word of God, they superimposed their own. Private imagination corrupted the interpretation of the Scriptures as the hypotheses and rash dreams of conjecturing philosophers did sane philosophy.

Among the interpreters who had preceded him, Newton absolved only, and in part, Joseph Mede, attributing to him the merit of having begun to methodize the Apocalypse:

all that I have seen besides the labours of Mr Mede have been so botched & framed without any due proportion, that I [could heartily wish those Authors] fear some of those Authors did not so much as beleive their own interpretations.[24]

The natural order, the internal characters, the due proportion were the new interpretive criteria that Newton wanted to introduce. If no one could arrive at certainty in understanding the Scriptures, then there was a reason "which is to make the scriptures no certain rule of faith, & so to reflect upon the spirit of God who dictated it."[25]

Thus we arrive at the heart of Newton's hermeneutic method: to reduce prophecy to its univocal meaning in the same way in which phenomena could be reduced to a single law. The univocity of the prophecy and the univocity of the laws of nature were the sign of their truth: "Tis true that an Artificer may make an Engin capable of being with equal congruity set together more ways then one, & that a sentence may be ambiguous: but this Objection can have no place in the Apocalyps, because God who knew how to frame it without ambiguity intended it for a rule of faith."[26]

Newton's hermeneutic method envisaged three phases. The first phase consisted of sixteen rules of interpretation, moving from the general to the particular, such that "the judgment of the Reader be prepared by considering well the following Rules for inabling him to know when an interpretation is genuine & of two interpretations which is the best."[27]

The second phase of the method was the elaboration of definitions. The prophetic language had to be understood in terms of the figurative language that was its distinguishing feature and the most appropriate way to communicate revealed truth because it was that best understood by all. In fact the definitions constituted the vocabulary of the prophetic language: "By which means the Language of the Prophets will [appear] become certain & the liberty of wresting it to private imaginations be cut of. The heads to which I reduce these words I call Definitions."[28]

The third phase consisted of the elaboration of propositions. Given the rules and the definitions, the Apocalypse was divided into comparable, and thus ordered, parts. The "substance" of the prophecy was drawn out in propositions, to each of which was added the reason of truth, in other words, the proof.

THE INTERPRETIVE RULES OF THE APOCALYPSE AND THE EXPERIMENTAL METHOD

According to Frank Manuel, the interpretive rules of the Apocalypse were a copy of the *Regulae Philosophandi* of the *Principia*, but this conclusion is chronologically impossible – the rules of the *Principia* were written almost forty years after those of the *Trattato*.[29] Obviously the inverse must be the case. But how can it be that the Rules of Reasoning of the *Principia*, considered the foundation of the experimental method, are a copy of the interpretive rules of the Apocalypse? If we bear in mind Newton's intellectual development, the answer is clear. Even before he was concerned with the interpretation of the Apocalypse, Newton had developed many of his methodological ideas. Both in his studies in optics and in the unfinished "De gravitatione" Newton had proposed a method by which to arrive at a greater degree of certainty in understanding. In any case Newton did not apply to optics – at least for the time being – the method described in a letter to Oldenburg of 1672:

I drew up a series of such Experiments on designe to reduce the Theory of colours to Propositions & prove each Proposition from one or more of those

Experiments by the assistance of common notions set down in the form of Definitions & Axioms in imitation of the Method by which Mathematitians are wont to prove their doctrines.[30]

In fact the method sketched here, which represented a notable step forward with respect to "De gravitatione," in which Newton still spoke of two distinct methods, was applied to the interpretation of the Apocalypse. And it was precisely here that Newton introduced the rules for the first time with a goal of reconciling the understanding of particulars with the definitions. Finally, the proof or demonstration of the propositions was obtained both with the help of the definitions and with recourse to particulars, ordered according to the rules. For example, the eighth proposition ("The Dragon & Beast are the Kingdome whose symptomes are declared in the Seales & Trumpits, whereof the Dragon begins with the Seales and the Beast with the Trumpets"[31]) is proved by eight particulars, and the meaning of each particular is referred to the definitions with the aid of the rules.

These rules, as has been pointed out, are largely a reworking of those contained in Sanderson's manual, as one can see from the table on pp. 398–9 in which the *regulae* of the *Principia* are also cited.[32]

As can be seen, Newton's hermeneutic method did not differ formally from his scientific method, even if the subject matters were very different. The principal risk of Newton's hermeneutic method was dogmatism:

He that without better grounds then his private opinion or the opinion of any human authority whatsoever shall turn scripture from the plain meaning to an Allegory or to any other less naturall sense declares thereby that he reposes more trust in his own imaginations or in that human authority then in the Scripture [& by consequence that he is no true beleever]. And therefore the opinion of such men how numerous soever they be, is not to be regarded.[33]

With his deprecation of the private imagination Newton intended to reduce arbitrary interpretation to the minimum, but at the same time his method impeded the exercise of criticism and discussion. Following the construction, the truth of the Apocalypse was fully disclosed and evident. In fact "a meer naturall man, how wicked soever, who will but read it, may judg of it & perceive the strength of it with as much perspicuity & certainty as he can a demonstration in Euclide."[35] The justification for Newton's dogmatism was without

Rules of method: a comparison

Sanderson's Compendium	Rules of the *Treatise on Apocalypse* (c. 1672)	*Regulae Philosophandi* [Rules of Reasoning in Philosophy][34]
Law of brevity: "Nothing should be left out or be superfluous in a discipline."	"2. To assign but one meaning to one place of scripture." "3. To keep as close as may be to the same sense of words."	Rule 1 (1687) "We are to admit no more causes of natural things than such as are both true and sufficient to explain their appearances." Comment to Rule 1 "Nature is pleased with simplicity, and affects not the pomp of superfluous causes."
Law of harmony: "The individual parts of each doctrine should agree among themselves."	"1. To observe diligently the consent of Scripture." "8. To choose those constructions which ...reduce contemporary visions to the greatest harmony of their parts." "9. To choose those constructions which ...reduce things to the greatest *simplicity*."	
Law of unity or homogeneity: "No doctrine should be taught that is not homogeneous with subject or end."	Rules 4, 6, 7, 10, 12, 14, 15	Rule 2 (1687) "Therefore to the same (*eiusdem generis*) natural effects we must, as far as possible, assign the same causes."
Law of connection: "The individual parts of a doctrine ought to be connected by opportune transitions."	"5. To acquiesce in that sense of any portion of Scripture as the true one which results most freely & naturally from the use & propriety of the Language & tenor of the context in that & all other places of Scripture to that sense."	Rule 3 (1713) "The qualities of bodies, which admit neither intension nor remission of degrees, and which are found to belong to all bodies within the reach of our experiments, are to be esteemed

the universal qualities of all bodies whatsoever."

Rule 4 (1726)
"In experimental philosophy we are to look upon propositions inferred by general induction from phenomena as accurately or very nearly true, notwithstanding any contrary hypotheses that may be imagined, till such time as other phenomena occur, by which they may either be made more accurate, or liable to exceptions."

11. To acquiesce in that construction of the Apocalyps as the true one which results most naturally & freely from the characters imprinted . . . for insinuating their connexion."

"[2] If two meanings seem equally probable he is obliged to believe no more then in general the one of them is genuine untill he meet with some motive to prefer one side."

"Induction, by which we make a universal conclusion summoning any experiences."

doubt the strong sense he attributed to the notion of truth, which in all cases originated in God. All error was implicitly heresy. It was for this reason that Newton did not countenance objections:

Hence if any man shall contend that my Construction of the Apocalyps is uncertain, upon pretence that it may be possible to find out other ways, he is not to be regarded unless he shall show wherein what I have done may be mended. If the ways which he contends for be less natural or grounded upon weaker reasons, that very thing is demonstration enough that they are fals, & that he seeks not [after] truth but [labours for] the interest of a party. And if the way which I have followed be according to the nature & genius of the Prophecy there needs no other demonstration to convince it.[36]

Pressed by Hooke's objections to his theory of colors, Newton had already replied to Oldenburg with the tone and almost the same words used in the *Trattato*:

And therefore I could wish all objections were suspended, taken from Hypotheses or any other Heads then these two; Of showing the insufficiency of experiments...; Or of producing other Experiments which directly contradict me, if any such may seem to occur.[37]

Throughout the 1670s, Newton revised and enlarged the text of his first treatise, including modifications to the method of interpretation, but only in verbal details (for example, calling "Positions" that which he had called "Propositions"). After Halley's visit in 1684, Newton returned to his first passions, natural philosophy and mathematics, with a far more precise idea of the method to follow in the construction of the system of the world than he had had in 1665–6. After Newton's death, his nephew Benjamin Smith published the *Observations upon the Prophecies of Daniel, and the Apocalypse of St John* (1733). As Westfall observed, this was "a work of surpassing tedium,"[38] compiled provisionally by Newton in his old age. None the less it sold very well. In it, the methodological apparatus of the first work on the Apocalypse was omitted. There are only a few pages, inserted after the introduction, given to the figurative style of the Prophets, which summarized the section dedicated to the Definitions in the early treatise. If Newton's interest in the figurative language endured so long, it is likely that it constituted a cultural component of primary importance, which interpreters have hitherto underestimated.

THE FIGURATIVE LANGUAGE OF THE PROPHETS
AND THE LANGUAGE OF DREAMS

In his early interpretation of the Apocalypse Newton is also concerned with dreams. His exegesis views the dream as a fundamental metaphor. The dreams of Joseph and of the king of Babylon, as disclosed by Daniel, testify that to reveal the future God prefers oneiric language. Thus, the Apocalypse is like a dream; decoding the Book of Revelation is the same as interpreting a dream. Oneiric language is composed of figurative expressions. It is likely that Newton's remarks on the language of the prophecies were deeply influenced by the visual culture of the Baroque, in keeping with the Renaissance tradition of emblems and devices. Moreover, as we shall see, the metaphors, medieval in origin, of the theatre of the world (*theatrum mundi*) and of the "book of nature" (*liber naturae*) become the foundation itself of mystical language.

The seventy definitions that form the dictionary of the prophetic language according to Newton are inspired in particular by an (alleged) medieval Arab writer, Achmet,[39] who dealt with the events and meanings of dreams. Newton provides the following reasons for his choice:

Now although these interpretations by their analogy with one another & resemblance to the things signified, may seem plain enough, yet that nothing be wanting to establish them, I shall further show their consent with the scriptures, & also with the translation of the Chalde Paraphrast & with the ancient doctrin of the Eastern Interpreters (of Dreams & [visions]) as it is recorded by Achmet an Arabian out of the ancient monuments of Egypt Persia & India...For the Prophets without doubt spoke in a dialect then commonly known to the more understanding sort of men, & many of their types & figures which are unusual & difficult to us appear by these records of Achmet to have been very familiar to those Eastern nations; at least among their interpreters.[40]

Newton's personal library contained the *De Symbolica Aegyptiorum Sapientia* (Cologne, 1631) by Nicolas Caussin, the well-known author of Baroque eloquence.[41] There was also a copy of Valeriano's Hieroglyphica, a famous book of sacred emblems, and a work by Emanuele Tesauro, one of the theorists of the new oratorical, lapidary, and symbolic art. It is noteworthy that Tesauro compares the skill of man in producing metaphors and symbols with the creative action of God.[42] A similar idea, not necessarily taken from Tesauro, is clearly expressed in the "De gravitatione."[43] I think that this idea, which enhances the creative aspect of the mystical language, guided Newton in his choice of the true interpreters of the Apocalypse. The human talent and the revelation of God share the same language: "And therefore since God gave the sacred Prophesies to be interpreted by humane skill, we cannot next after the Scriptures have a better guide then the established doctrin of the ancient Interpreters."[44]

For according to the ancient interpreters – like Daniel, the magicians, and the wise men of the Pharaoh – the gift of prophecy is the same as the talent of understanding visions and dreams. Nevertheless, as we have seen, Newton does not credit the private imagination but the collective one, founded upon the precise agreement of the testimonies.

The salient value of the metaphors is historical rather than literary. Through their figurative language, they bring us nearer to the time in which God revealed himself to men. Thus what is difficult and unusual to us acquires a cognitive significance. This will be made clear by some examples. The fundamental postulation of the figurative language of the prophets is the correspondence of the features of heaven and earth to those of a kingdom. Newton found the same correspondence in Achmet, the interpreter of dreams: "The Sun immutably represents the King, the moon the next in power to the King, the Planet Venus the Queen, the rest of the greater stars the great men of the Kingdom. Achmet. chap. 167. Ind. Pers. Eg."[45]

Prophecy is similar to dream not because the latter discloses the future, but because the prophet is using the same language as that of dreams: "If a King dream that he sits upon the Clouds carried whither he will he shall rule over his enemies, & obtein victories & unexpected joy."[46]

The correspondence between the images of dream and reality is established in detail. Analogy also conveys mathematical proportionality:

Achmet in c 151 affirms:...If a King dream that he plants trees he shall institute new Magistrates. And if a plebeian dream that he gathers into his hous the leaves of trees, he shall obtein riches from great men proportionall to the leaves.[47]

Newton combined the biblical images with those of the inter-preters of dreams in order to get new meanings. The emblems are founded upon analogy, and there is often a reason for their meaning:

If one dream that he builds a merchant ship he shall gather an assembly of men to celebrate religious mysteries. The reason of this Emblem I suppose is that a Temple brings profit to a Priest as a ship to a Merchant & is also separate from other buildings as ships are from one another.[48]

The emblem of the apocalyptic dragon contains various meanings in one:

A Dragon signifies the person of a *hostile* King, & serpents according to their bignes the persons of other greater or lesser enemies Achm: c 288. According to which doctrin the Apocalyptic Dragon is a very proper emblem as well of the Roman Kingdom which was so great an enemy to the Church, as of the Devil that arch-enemy to mankind. But there seems to be in this emblem a further mystery: namely to insinuate a comparison of the oppression of the Church under the Roman Empire to the Egyptian Bondage, as if that were a type of this.[49]

It can be noticed that the emblem linking dreams to reality has various degrees of realization: the Egyptian bondage, the Roman Empire, the devil. A single emblem – the dragon – unites several events at once, attributing to each of them a further symbolic value: the Egyptian bondage is the type of the Roman Empire as the Antichrist is the type of the Devil. Newton is willing to use these constant products of imagination (emblems and types) as if they were univer-sal definitions, and on this presumed universality he establishes the possibility of unambiguous interpretation of the Apocalypse. The emblems become a universal type because of analogy.

So the hermeneutic method of Newton cannot be well understood without understanding the literature of emblems, so deeply rooted in Baroque culture. The Newtonian iconography of the Apocalypse is vivid and intense like the colors produced by the prism. How-ever, the figures are not external accessories. Newton stresses the unifying function of the emblems, because of their reasonableness as against the excessive liberty of "a luxuriant ungovernable fansy" which "borders on enthusiasm."[50]

The mechanism of the Baroque metaphor is carefully analyzed by Newton. Since the emblem links together different sorts of par-ticular events with no ambiguity, it is thereby possible to achieve a construction of the Apocalypse's content according to the laws of prophetic language. In order to discover these laws, Newton searches for an hermeneutic method in which every emblem is exactly defined:

To prepare the Reader also for understanding the Prophetique language I shall lay down a short description thereof, showing how it is borrowed from comparing a kingdom either to the Universe or to a Beast: So that by the resemblance of their parts the signification of the figurative words & expressions in these Prophesies may be apprehended at one view & limited from the grownd thereof.[51]

As we have said, the rules for interpreting the words and language in Scripture were later to become, in the *Principia*, the Rules of Reasoning (*Regulae Philosophandi*). At the heart of the scientific rules we again find analogy as the key for reading the book of nature. The analogy of nature corresponds entirely to the analogy of the prophetic style, because God is the same author of the infinite world and of the eternal prophecy.

Newton's successors (and Newton himself) call the use of analogy in the scientific enterprise "induction." Nothing is more misleading than this term, borrowed from Aristotelian logic, in pointing out the concrete use that Newton made of analogy. For example, Newton compares the spectrum of colors with the tonal scale, and he is able to find in it numerical correspondences.[52] In the classical *scholia* Newton is convinced that the ancients caught sight of the law of gravitation through the harmony of the celestial spheres.[53] The harmony of heavens is the type of the gravitation just as the Babylonian bondage is the type of the Roman Empire. In the same manner, he interprets the Pythagorean discovery of the *direct* proportion between the weights hung from strings of equal length and the resulting sounds as a type of the *inverse* proportion between gravity and the square of the distance.[54] Analogy is not enumerative induction, but a search for types. It becomes an alternative way of explaining why an apple falls!

Therefore it is not too surprising, as we have already seen, to find Newton's assertion of the similarity between the creative powers of man and of God in the unpublished "De gravitatione," being the extreme outcome of his Baroque mentality:

Holy writ testifies that we were created in God's image. And his image would shine more clearly in us if only he simulated in the faculties granted to us the power of creation in the same degree as his other attributes.[55]

It is the same concept we have found in Tesauro, the theorist of Baroque eloquence. For Newton this similarity, neither a literary ornament alone nor a rhetorical effect, was to be the groundwork of his conception of matter, since God is to matter as man is to his body. The human will is the *type* of the divine one.

Newton goes even further. Every difficulty that concerns the nature of bodies may be reduced to our faculty of moving our bodies, that is, by virtue of analogy, to God's will:

Thus I have deduced a description of this corporeal nature from our faculty of moving our bodies, so that all the difficulties may at length be reduced to that.[56]

The similarity between man and God occurs as well in the General Scholium of the *Principia*.[57] Man is a type of God.

To give further weight to this likeness, Newton researched into the properties of an immaterial aether for many years. The aethereal spirit would have been a way of explaining gravity, animal movement, and such forces acting in the microcosm as electric and magnetic attractions. It may be the intermediary between the thinking soul and the unthinking body,[58] between God and the world. Newton's Baroque science is the theatre of divine manifestations, since the world is like a dream of God.

.

NOTES

1   See J. E. McGuire and M. Tamny (eds.), *Certain Philosophical Questions: Newton's Trinity Notebook* (Cambridge: Cambridge University Press, 1983), pp. 375–7.

2   *Ibid.*, p. 449.

3   In the *Principia* (1687), Newton refers to the Sacred Scriptures to support his conception of absolute space and time. See *Isaac Newton's Philosophiae Naturalis Principia Mathemathica, the Third Edition with Variant Readings*, ed. A. Koyré and I. B. Cohen (Cambridge, MA: Harvard University Press; Cambridge: Cambridge University Press, 1972), p. 52. In "An Account of the Book entituled Commercium

Epistolicum" (1714–15) Newton, outlining the differences between his philosophy and that of Leibniz, cites St. Paul (Acts 17:27, 28).

4   See J. Harrison, *The Library of Isaac Newton* (Cambridge: Cambridge University Press, 1978), p. 2.

5   *Ibid.*, p. 3.

6   *Ibid.*, p. 7.

7   Cambridge University Library (CUL), Add. MS 3968, 1, 85. See I. Bernard Cohen, *Introduction to Newton's 'Principia'* (Cambridge, MA: Harvard University Press; Cambridge: Cambridge University Press, 1971), pp. 290–2.

8   *The Correspondence of Isaac Newton*, vol. 1, ed. H. W. Turnbull (Cambridge: Cambridge University Press, 1959), p. 416.

9   See M. Mamiani, *Il prisma di Newton* (Rome and Bari: Laterza, 1986), pp. 49–93.

10 See M. Mamiani, *Isaac Newton filosofo della natura* (Florence: La Nuova Italia, 1976), p. 65. See also the introduction to Alan E. Shapiro (ed.), *The Optical Papers of Isaac Newton* (Cambridge: Cambridge University Press, 1984), p. 1.

11 A. Rupert Hall dates "De gravitatione" between 1664 and 1668. See A. R. Hall and Marie Boas Hall (eds.), *Unpublished Scientific Papers of Isaac Newton* (Cambridge: Cambridge University Press, 1962), p. 90. B. J. T. Dobbs, on the other hand, suggests a much later date, 1684 or the beginning of 1685. See B. J. T. Dobbs, *The Janus Faces of Genius: The Role of Alchemy in Newton's Thought* (Cambridge: Cambridge University Press, 1991), pp. 143–8. Considering the arguments presented in this chapter, I would suggest that it should be dated to between 1667 and 1670/1.

12 See Hall and Hall (eds.), *Unpublished Scientific Papers*, p. 121.

13 *Ibid.*, p. 142.

14 *Ibid.*, p. 141.

15 R. S. Westfall, "Newton and Christianity," in I. Bernard Cohen and R. S. Westfall (eds.), *Newton: Texts, Backgrounds, and Commentaries* (New York and London: W. W. Norton & Company, 1995), pp. 361–2.

16 Isaac Newton, *Trattato sull'Apocalisse*, ed. M. Mamiani (Turin: Bollati Boringhieri, 1994), p. 35.

17 *Ibid.*, p. 34. (Bracketed words deleted in manuscripts.)

18 *Ibid.*, p. 14.

19 *Ibid.*, p. 32.

20 *Ibid.*, pp. 16, 18.

21 *Ibid.*, p. 2.

22 *Ibid.*, p. 6.

23 "Et que considerant combien il peut y avoir de diverses opinions touchant une mesme matiere, qui soient soustenues par des gens doctes, sans

qu'il y en puisse avoir iamais plus d'une seule qui soit vraye, ie reputois presque pour faux tout ce qui n'estoit que vraysembable," R. Descartes, *Discours de la méthode* (Leiden: Maire, 1637), p. 10.

24 Newton, *Trattato sull'Apocalisse*, p. 16. (Brackets around deletions.)
25 *Ibid.*, p. 24.
26 *Ibid.*, p. 30.
27 *Ibid.*, p. 18.
28 *Ibid.* (Brackets around deletions.)
29 F. E. Manuel, *The Religion of Isaac Newton* (Oxford: Clarendon Press, 1974), p. 98.
30 *Correspondence of Isaac Newton*, vol. 1, p. 237.
31 Newton, *Trattato sull'Apocalisse*, p. 128.
32 Cf. M. Mamiani, "To Twist the Meaning: Newton's 'Regulae Philosophandi' Revisited," in Jed Buchwald and I. B. Cohen (eds.), *Isaac Newton's Natural Philosophy* (Cambridge, MA: MIT Press, 2001).
33 Newton, *Trattato sull'Apocalisse*, p. 24.
34 Translation by A. Motte, revised by F. Cajori.
35 *Ibid.*, p. 36.
36 *Ibid.*, pp. 28, 30. (Brackets around deletions.)
37 *Correspondence of Isaac Newton*, vol. 1, p. 210.
38 Westfall, "Newton and Christianity," p. 363.
39 *Apomasaris Apotelesmata, sive de significatis et eventis somniorum, ex Indorum, Persarum, Aegyptiorumque disciplina* (Frankfurt, 1577). Newton identifies the author correctly, who is not Apomazar [= Abu Masar al-Falaki], died in AD 886, but Achmet, son of Sereim. This suggests that Newton was perhaps acquainted with the Greek edition of Achmet's work, edited by N. Rigault together with that of Artemidorus, *Artemidori Daldiani & Achmetis Sereimi F. Oneirocritica* (Paris, 1603).

Achmet, believed to have been an Arabic physician, lived in the court of the Caliph Mamun (AD 813–833), and little is known of him. F. Drexl, in the foreword to the critical edition of *Achmetis Oneirocriticon* (Leipzig: Teubner, 1925), suggests that Achmet's work is a compilation from Arabic sources, arranged by a Christian Syriac author and then translated into Greek. His dating is from the year 813 (beginning of the kingdom of the Caliph Mamun) to 1176 (date of the first Latin translation of Leo Tuscus). Henry More and Joseph Mede utilized Achmet's book. Cf. P. C. Almond, "Henry More and the Apocalypse," *Journal of the History of Ideas* 54 (1993), 192.
40 Newton, *Trattato sull'Apocalisse*, p. 50. (Brackets around deletions.)
41 Harrison, *The Library of Isaac Newton*, p. 116.
42 "Si come Dio di quel che non è produce quel che è, così l'ingegno di un non ente, fa ente, fa che il leone diventa uomo e l'aquila una città, innesta una femmina sopra un pesce e fabbrica una sirena per simbolo

dell'adulatore," E. Tesauro, *Il cannocchiale aristotelico* (Turin, 1670), p. 82.

43 See *infra*, note 55.

44 Newton, *Trattato sull'Apocalisse*, p. 52.

45 *Ibid.*, pp. 52, 54.

46 *Ibid.*, p. 54.

47 *Ibid.*, pp. 66, 68.

48 *Ibid.*, p. 72.

49 *Ibid.*, p. 78.

50 *Ibid.*, p. 22.

51 *Ibid.*, p. 18.

52 Cf. P. Gouk, "The Harmonic Roots of Newtonian Science," in J. Fauvel, R. Flood, M. Shortland, and R. Wilson (eds.), *Let Newton Be! A New Perspective on His Life and Works* (Oxford: Oxford University Press, 1988), pp. 101–26.

53 Isaac Newton, "Gli scolii classici," ed. P. Casini, *Giornale Critico della Filosofia Italiana* Gennaio–Aprile (1981), 7–53.

54 *Ibid.*, pp. 40–1.

55 Hall and Hall (eds.), *Unpublished Scientific Papers*, p. 141.

56 *Ibid.*

57 "Omnis homo, quatenus res sentiens, est unus et idem homo...Deus est unus et idem deus," Isaac Newton, *Philosophiae Naturalis Principia Mathematica*, 2nd edn (Cambridge, 1713), p. 762.

58 "This spirit therefore may be the medium of sense & animal motion & by consequence of uniting the thinking soul & unthinking body", CUL, Add. MS 3970, fol. 241r.

14 Newton and eighteenth-century Christianity

You will be very able to deal with Sr Isaac, and I shall be glad to leave Him in such good hands. He is a man of such scope, and his Authority so justly celebrated in some things, that his name is of great weight in other matters, where He was plainly out of his element, and knew little of what He was talking about. Besides his countenancing Arianism, in the piece referred to, He has given too much encouragement to Popery by his large concessions, such as our best Protestant writers, att the time of K[ing]. James as well as before, would never make.[1]

Isaac Newton's *Observations upon the Prophecies of Daniel, and the Apocalypse of St. John,* prepared for the press from his manuscripts by his nephew Benjamin Smith, was published in two editions in London and Dublin in 1733.[2] According to Richard S. Westfall, Newton's finest twentieth-century biographer, the author "had cleansed his *Observations*" and his heirs "could publish the manuscript without concern."[3] Yet one might be permitted to wonder whether either the actual or the intended reception of Newton's posthumous work was as uncontroversial as it has seemed to late-twentieth-century eyes. The book was dedicated to Peter King, baron of Ockham, the lord chancellor, who had defended Newton's sometime disciple, William Whiston, during his trial for heresy in July 1713.[4] Although Whiston later fell out with King, he nevertheless continued to maintain that King's youthful writings on the primitive Church supported the Arian position for which he had himself been condemned.[5] King was also the dedicatee of other works of dubious theological orthodoxy, such as Daniel Mace's attempted revision of the New Testament. Mace showed little respect for the authenticity of the two New Testament texts that most clearly upheld the orthodox doctrine of the Trinity, 1 John 5.7 and 1 Timothy 3.16.

Listing ancient manuscripts which gave non-Trinitarian readings, he hinted strongly that their modern, orthodox variants were the product of interference with the primitive text of scripture.[6]

The young King's most significant friendship had been with his second cousin, John Locke. He was one of the philosopher's closest confidants toward the end of his life and an executor of his will, by which he inherited half of Locke's library and all of his manuscripts. He was also charged with "a little packet sealed up and directed to Mr Newton."[7] King had acted as an occasional intermediary between Newton and Locke, passing on information between the two men about matters concerning the Mint and about the interpretation of scripture. He conveyed chapters of the draft of Locke's *A Paraphrase and Notes on the Epistles of St. Paul* to Newton for comment.[8] Locke informed King that Newton was "really a very valuable man not onely for his wonderfull skill in Mathematicks but in divinity too and his great knowledge in the Scriptures where in I know few his equals."[9] As an acquaintance of Newton and a prominent whig politician, King may therefore have been a natural choice as the dedicatee of the *Observations*. But, as his earlier doctrinal sympathies, his knowledge of suspicions that had been voiced about Locke's orthodoxy on the matter of the Trinity, and his later patronage of heterodox Presbyterians such as Mace make clear, King was not a theologically neutral choice as a patron of a work of biblical interpretation.[10] Moreover, as the owner of Locke's manuscripts, King had access to evidence of Newton's heterodox beliefs about the Trinity, in the letters that passed into his keeping at Locke's death.[11] It is tempting to speculate that the "little packet" that King had been charged with returning to Newton may have contained a more incriminating piece of correspondence, sent by Newton to Locke in 1690 but no longer extant among Locke's papers: Newton's initial letters comprising "An Historical account of two Notable Corruptions of Scripture," 1 John 5.7 and 1 Timothy 3.16.[12] King was not displeased by the dedication of *Observations*, granting Smith a mediety of the rectory of Linton in Craven, Yorkshire.[13]

Smith had been ordained by a friend of Newton's twilight years, William Stukeley. Stukeley himself had been inspired by Newton to "[study] the Mosaic cosmogony seriously," suggesting that "Here is the Original Source of True Philosophy The Oracle of Nature, The Springhead of knowledge where Those that thirst after the

Newtonian Draughts may drink largely at the Fountain."[14] He seems to have been only one of a group of those who met and were influenced by Newton who undertook to defend the accuracy of Moses' natural philosophy at one time or another.[15] His affection for Newton's theology extended to attempts to reconstruct the plan of Solomon's Temple, itself the setting for many of the prophetic events that Newton tried to elucidate.[16] However, Stukeley, like many of Newton's erstwhile disciples, doubted the accuracy of the calculations to be found in *The Chronology of Ancient Kingdom's Amended*, published by Newton's heirs from his manuscripts in 1728.[17]

The *Chronology* had been dedicated to Queen Caroline, an admirer of Newton who had encouraged his chronological writing and protected his closest theological disciple, Samuel Clarke, throughout the 1710s and 1720s. Even the Queen, however, was powerless to prevent debate about the historical accuracy and religious orthodoxy of Newton's writings. This had begun with criticism of the *Chronology*, but soon spilled over into more serious attacks on *Observations*. Remarking on the plans for the publication of the *Chronology*, Stukeley's friend and Newton's physician, Richard Mead, commented that Newton "was a christian, believed revelation, though not all the doctrines which our orthodox divines have made articles of faith."[18] Following its publication, others were less generous to Newton's beliefs and intentions. The Bristol clergyman, orientalist, and moral reformer Arthur Bedford observed that:

When Sir Isaak Newton's Chronology was printed and extolled by many, which must absolutely have destroyed all the Scripture History, [I] first printed an Octavo against it, and afterward a Folio intituled, The Scripture Chronology demonstrated by Astronomical Observations, a Work recommended by Archbishop Usher in his Annals, but never attempted 'til then; the Consequence of which was the Establishing the Authority of the Hebrew Chronology, in somuch that the other notions are now intirely disregarded.[19]

Bedford's work was sponsored by the Society for Promoting Christian Knowledge, with which many of the hierarchy of the Church of England were associated.[20] His initial criticisms were directed at the astronomical methods of dating that Newton's chronology had deployed. He pointed out that Newton's findings disagreed with those of the most prominent orthodox writers on chronology –

James Ussher, William Lloyd, Richard Cumberland, and William Beveridge – all of whom were in agreement about the major dates in secular and sacred history.[21] But he soon identified his real target: "we live in an Age, when we cannot be too cautious... The *Divinity* of our blessed SAVIOUR is struck at by the Revivers of ancient and modern Heresies; especially that, which destroyed all the eastern Nations, and introduced *Mahometism* among them."[22]

Bedford was perceptive in noticing that Newton's conclusions about sacred history created doubts over the authority and antiquity of scripture.[23] He felt these were reminiscent of the beliefs of Newton's disciples, Whiston and Clarke, and therefore raised the specter of Arianism. This heresy had swept through the eastern Church in the early fourth century, weakening it both theologically and politically. Its beliefs about Christ's nature as the first of God's creations, rather than as God himself, seemed to people like Bedford the most blasphemous of the primitive heresies that were currently being revived by Whiston and, more cautiously, Clarke.[24]

In the months following Newton's death, speculation was rife that he had shared the heterodox beliefs for which Whiston and Clarke were pilloried. The Presbyterian minister and historian Robert Wodrow, who was a friend of a number of Scottish Newtonians, received frequent reports about the publication of Newton's *Chronology*. As early as 1711, Wodrow had recorded rumours concerning Newton's influence on Whiston: "It is said he has not only much of his Mathematicks, but severall of his other errours from Sir Isaack Neuton, which I incline not to belive."[25] He was thus relieved to be informed in November 1727 that Newton's unpublished papers appeared at first to contain nothing about the doctrine of the Trinity. Wodrow's composure was shattered in May 1729 when he learned that Newton had agreed with Clarke about the subordination of Christ to God the Father and had had peculiar notions about the interpretation of the prophecies of Daniel.[26]

In the following year, Whiston excited speculation by writing that Clarke's interpretation of the prophecy of the seventy weeks (Daniel 9.24–7) was "only a Conjecture of Sir *Isaac Newton*'s, and I think a Conjecture not well grounded neither." This prophecy was widely believed to have predicted the birth of Christ, the Crucifixion, or the destruction of Jerusalem by the Romans as marking the end of a period of captivity for God's people. Whiston mischievously looked forward to the publication of "*Sir Isaac's* own great work *upon the Scripture Prophecies*...which we expect this Summer," confident that it would provide information about Newton's unusual belief that the entire prophecy had not yet been fulfilled.[27] Others of Newton's former acquaintances also began to reveal details of his heterodox beliefs. John Craig privately observed that Newton's thoughts about religion "were some times different from those which are commonly receiv'd."[28] The Chevalier Ramsay was less discreet, suggesting to Joseph Spence that "Sir Isaac Newton and Dr. Clarke endeavoured to clear it [the doctrine of the Trinity] from its corruptions, but in their way 'tis as difficult and embarrassed as it was before." Ramsay had once been a pupil of Newton's closest friend of the early 1690s, Nicolas Fatio de Duillier, and shared his faith in the orthodox doctrine of the Trinity.[29] Once Newton's *Observations* was published in 1733, therefore, it was bound to become the subject of scrutiny from orthodox divines, whatever protection might be provided for it by dedication to a prominent member of the ministry.

Daniel Waterland, Master of Magdalene College, Cambridge was perhaps the most indefatigable upholder of Trinitarian orthodoxy of the time. He was a veteran of numerous controversies, notably with Samuel Clarke, the deist Matthew Tindal, and Conyers Middleton. At first glance, Waterland's attitude toward Newton's posthumous publications seems to have been ambivalent. His second in the duel with Middleton, Zachary Pearce, found Newton's *Chronology* a ready weapon in an argument about the relative antiquity of Egyptian and Israelite religious practices and hence about the reliability of the literal sense of the Bible as a historical source.[30] In this context, Newton was presumably one of the "men as learned and honest as *Spencer*, or *Marsham*" who had answered their arguments about ancient Egyptian religion.[31] Waterland advised Pearce in this opportunistic use of Newton's work: "And though I do not myself follow Sir Isaac Newton's Chronology, yet I am very well pleased to see it so strongly pressed upon one who perhaps does."[32]

Middleton, however, soon turned the use of Newton against Waterland and his ally: "I must take the liberty to dissent from you, and to declare, that for a thorough knowledge of Antiquity, and the whole compass of *Greek and Ægyptian* Learning, there have been, in my Opinion, and now are, many Men as far superior to him, as he within his proper Character is superior to everybody else." To hold Newton up as an authority on chronology was simply rash.[33] Yet this did not deter Waterland from again invoking Newton's authority, in the preface published with the final part of his attack on Tindal, *Scripture Vindicated*. Here, Waterland referred admiringly to Newton's *Observations*, which, he claimed, "has given us some useful Hints for the better explaining such *symbolical* language."[34] It is, however, tempting to presume that this was a knowing attempt to set a thief to catch a thief.[35] Waterland and his allies were concerned to use the strong literalism and respect for the Hebrew Bible to be found in Newton's posthumous writings to combat the tendency of deist authors to read the Bible allegorically and to offset historical and critical concerns about the reliability of the Hebrew text as a source. They wished to do this not because they were convinced of Newton's own orthodoxy but because so many of their opponents either cited the work of Newton or his followers in some way or could be expected to be awed by his example as a natural philosopher.[36]

Elsewhere, Waterland expressed much more straightforward opinions about Newton's theological writings and those of his allies. He attacked Clarke's duplicity with regard to the thirty-nine articles of the Church of England and the ambiguous language deployed in *The Scripture-Doctrine of the Trinity*.[37] He was equally damning about what he took to be Newton's lack of candor about the intentions and implications of his arguments in his *Chronology* and *Observations*. He thus wrote to Zachary Grey that he was "sorry that no one yet has undertaken a just *Answer* to *Sir Isaac Newton's 14th. Chapter* relating to the *Prophecies of Daniel*: in which he slily abuses the *Athanasians*... That *Prophetical* Way of managing this Debate on the Side of *Arianism*, is a very silly one, & might be easily retorted. But besides that, what *Sir Isaac* has said, is most of it *false History*. I have scribbled the *Margin* all the way."[38] A particular excitement for Waterland and Grey was the possibility provided by Newton's *Observations* of catching the great mathematician out in his own calculations.[39] Since Waterland claimed he was too busy and too unwell for the task, Grey duly took up the cudgel on his behalf, thus enhancing his growing reputation as an apologist for the Church of England.[40]

The resulting attack on the fourteenth chapter of the *Observations* was unforgiving in its criticism of Newton's argument and intentions and unpleasantly insightful about his methods as a theologian and historian. Grey confronted Newton's chronology, logic, and use of sources and found all of them wanting. His target was particularly well chosen, since the chapter under review presented Newton's case for the growth of idolatry in the early Christian Church, itself a sign of Newton's broader point that the incarnation of Christ had not marked the fulfillment of Daniel's prophecies. Grey cannot have known that these had been the principal themes of Isaac Newton's theology since the 1670s, and it was only an inspired guess on his part to identify this passage as the key to the underpinning of Newton's Arian Christology in his interpretation of prophecy.[41] He argued that Newton had suppressed evidence demonstrating that respect was given to saints and martyrs in the primitive Church which was inconvenient to his prophetic scheme. He showed that Newton had distorted the Greek Fathers, to make it appear that the early cult of martyrs' graves constituted a form of idolatry and that the first monks had perverted true Christianity. He suggested that the accusations of furthering idolatry which Newton leveled at the orthodox, Trinitarian Athanasians ought properly to be directed at the Arians themselves.[42] An earlier attack on the *Chronology* by the Cambridge divine Arthur Young had also pointed out that Newton had placed the origins of the worship of saints too early. Whereas Grey and Waterland were content to imply that Newton's work might give comfort to the deists, Young explicitly associated his publications with those of Tindal. He also argued that Newton's comments on figurative language and the preservation of the text of the Hebrew Bible, which had been disingenuously admired by Waterland, in fact "[could] not [be] more prejudicial to Christianity."[43]

For both Young and Grey, the commentaries of Symon Patrick, Bishop of Ely, and the *Connection* of Humphrey Prideaux, Dean of Norwich, provided the definitive treatments of the meaning of Hebrew prophecy.[44] They thus both upheld the authority of the classic biblical commentators of the time, whose works appealed to a broad spectrum of ecclesiastical opinion. Moreover, both critics argued that the only real beneficiary of Newton's attack on the reputation of the Fathers was the Roman Catholic Church. Grey suggested that Newton assisted its polemicists by falsely attributing corrupt Catholic doctrines to the pure, primitive Fathers.[45] Given Newton's own powerful history of anti-Catholicism, this was a remarkable conclusion. Because of the reputation of the theology of the early

Church in English Protestant writing from the time of the Reformation, however, it was also justifiable.

Intellectually, one of the most powerful of Grey's criticisms of
Newton's theological writings was that they distorted the meaning of the Greek Fathers. Grey noticed that Newton's quotations
from writers like St. Cyril of Jerusalem, St. Cyril of Alexandria, or
St. Gregory of Nazianzus were often selective and that he was prone
to making errors in citations (for example, confusing Sozomen with
one of his sources, Socrates). Above all, the problem was that Newton
often seemed to be using translations rather than the original text.
This was most extreme in the case of St. Ephraem Syrus, where
Newton appeared to be using a Latin translation made from a Greek
version of the original Syriac text.[46] Grey had realized that Newton's
method for his theological writings depended largely on the assimilation of works in English and Latin, many of which already seemed
dated. Although he possessed several editions of patristic texts,
Newton's Greek was probably not good enough to allow him to cope
easily with the original versions of many of the sources on which he
ought to have been most dependent for a history of the early Church.
Where Newton did own the relevant Greek works, he did so in editions which also gave the text in Latin.[47] This tendency was even
more marked with Newton's use of Hebrew works, where he quite
shamelessly marked passages in the Latin parallel texts that later
appeared as quotations in Hebrew in his own writings.[48] Newton's
theological writings frequently appear to be little more than compen-
dia of quotations; what is less apparent is that their copious citations
were often constructed largely out of the compilations of previous
critics.[49] Newton was not unusual among humanist scholars in employing this method of study, in which selective reading was rapidly
converted into the appearance of mammoth erudition in pursuit of
a particular, clearly defined goal. However, this technique worked
best when the ideology informing it was an orthodox one, since, by
definition, it was likely to be vulnerable to scrutiny.[50] Given the
unusual nature of the case that Newton was trying to prove, it was
unlikely that scholarly habits such as his would bear up well under
examination.

Waterland, Grey, and Young were not the only churchmen
to criticize Newton's posthumously published theological works.
Both Samuel Shuckford and William Warburton attacked Newton's

Chronology and his attitude to ancient Egyptian history.[51] George Berkeley, engaged in controversy over the metaphysical implications of Newton's mathematics, found it necessary to deny that he wrote out of annoyance that "Sir *Isaac Newton* had presumed to interpose in Prophecies and Revelations, and to decide in religious affairs." Like Grey or Waterland, he also asserted that "there are too many that deride Mysteries, and yet admire Fluxions; who yield that Faith to a mere Mortal, which they deny to *Jesus Christ*, whose Religion they make it their Study and Busines to discredit."[52] Although some authors defended Newton's writings in the course of the eighteenth century, they tended to be drawn either from the ranks of enlightened dissent, or from a noisy but embattled group of churchmen who were sympathetic to Newton's Arianism. The latter included writers like Arthur Ashley Sykes, a client of the Conduitt family, and the renegade Bishop of Clogher, Robert Clayton.[53] During the whole of the eighteenth century, Newton's *Chronology* and *Observations* were not reprinted separately after their original publication. When the unsold sheets of the first edition of the *Chronology* were reissued in 1770, a letter was appended to them that had been written in 1754 by Zachary Pearce to Thomas Hunt, Regius Professor of Hebrew at Oxford and a friend of Arthur Bedford. This contained an account of Newton's revision of the *Chronology* in the weeks before his death which made it clear that sections of the published *Chronology* had never been revised and that some of the problems which later authors had exposed were a product of confusion on the part of its editors.[54]

That Newton's reputation as an author who favored Christian belief grew during the eighteenth century depended largely on three things. The first was the steadfast maintenance of the story of Newton's own simple piety by friends like William Stukeley. This concealed the fact that Newton was only an occasional conformist for whom attendance at the worship of the Church of England was made considerably easier during his later years by life in Samuel Clarke's parish, where accommodations in the public liturgy could be made to ease his tender conscience.[55] Second, the general reception of Newton's natural philosophy, as presented by Richard Bentley's Boyle lectures, by Newton's own General Scholium to the *Principia*, and by the published correspondence of Leibniz and Clarke, was that it tended to promote Christianity and support the Church. This was perhaps more a reflection of a belief among Low Church divines that natural philosophy itself might be conducive to religion, and of the popularity of Locke's epistemology, rather than a wholesale endorsement of Newtonianism, but nevertheless it had powerful effects.[56] It was also the way in which the cautious Newton had intended to present his system, apparently shorn of most of its clandestine heterodoxy. Even so, its appearance required the prompting of Bentley in 1692 and the careful direction given to the reader by Roger Cotes's preface to the *Principia* in 1713. Nor were the works in question, particularly the General Scholium, in fact completely free of theological controversy.[57] Finally, there was the revival in eschatological prophecy in the last two decades of the eighteenth century, in whose vanguard came Unitarian readers of Newton's theology such as Joseph Priestley. This also paved the way for the widespread interest in Newton's *Observations* among nonconformists in the nineteenth century.[58] This movement, however, returned Newton's theological works to controversy rather than saving them from it. Thus, Samuel Horsley, the High Church editor of Newton's *Opera Omnia* (1779–85), which reprinted the *Chronology* and the *Observations* and provided the first reliable edition of Newton's letters on the corruption of scripture, took Priestley to task:

It is probable too, that after the pains which I have taken to examine the writings and authorities on which [Newton's] ancient chronology was founded, I am as well qualified, as Dr. Priestley, to judge of his talents in . . . subjects, which are not capable of demonstration. Now in these, I scruple not to say . . . that the great Newton went out like a Common Man.[59]

For Horsley, as for many other orthodox divines, the printing of Newton's theological works was a way to reveal their inadequacy and thus to snatch away a weapon from anti-Trinitarian critics of the Church.

It was therefore unnecessary for eighteenth-century critics of Newton's theology to take refuge in the natural philosophy and scriptural exegesis of John Hutchinson, whose tenets seemed laughable to those, like Arthur Bedford, who had a competent knowledge of Hebrew. The Hutchinsonians, in any case, were more concerned with overthrowing Newton's natural philosophy than with bothering about his divinity, and their arguments in favor of the Trinity were often less than incisive.[60] For many of Newton's readers, however, the principal attraction of his writings both in natural philosophy and in theology lay in their anti-Trinitarianism. These included several leading figures in the Church of England, notably Edmund Law, Bishop of Carlisle, who themselves had doubts about the doctrine of the Trinity and for whom Newton's letters on "Two Notable Corruptions of Scripture," eventually published in 1754, provided irresistible ammunition in the campaign to institute a fresh translation of the Bible as part of the doctrinal improvement of the Church.[61]

Yet neither Newton nor Clarke ever risked his career for such a reformation of the Church. According to Whiston, who was himself less cautious, the reason for this was that they believed that the prophecy of Daniel's seventy weeks remained unfulfilled.

However, it is not impossible that such a Notion of a long future corrupt State of the Church soon coming on, according to the Scripture Prophecies, might be one Discouragement to Sir *Isaac Newton*'s and Dr. *Clarke*'s making publick Attempts for the Restoration of Primitive Christianity: as I confess my Expectation of the near approach of the Conclusion of the corrupt State, and by Consequence of the Commencement of the State when Primitive Christianity is, by those Prophecies, to be restored, greatly encourages me to labour for its Restoration.[62]

The reticence which led Newton to keep secret his views about the doctrine of the Trinity indeed did not derive principally from anxiety concerning publication of his ideas about the two notable corruptions of scripture. Other more orthodox critics also doubted the authenticity of the verses examined by Newton. Thus John Mill, to whose massive attempt to gather up variant readings of the text of the New Testament Newton had himself contributed during the 1690s, noted the paucity of authentic manuscript witnesses to 1 John 5.7 and rehearsed more briefly the problems associated with 1 Timothy 3.16.[63] Richard Bentley, who perhaps knew of Newton's discussion of 1 John 5.7, also questioned the authenticity of the received reading of that verse without casting doubt on the doctrine of the Trinity that it underpinned: "Arianism in its height was beat down without the help of that verse: and, let the *fact* prove as it will, the *doctrine* [of the Trinity] is unshaken."[64] Newton's concerns arose from the fact that for him the corruption of the text of the Bible was one aspect of a much broader perversion of the Christian religion, perpetrated by Athanasius and his followers in the fourth century. They had spread

calumnies against other theologians, notably Arius, fomented sedi-
tion, and distorted the true meaning of the Nicene Creed:

this Council [Nicaea] allowed the interpretation of homousios by similitude
& the fathers by way of caution exprest this interpretation in their sub-
scriptions yet by the clamours of Athanasius & his party it is since grown y^e
semiarrian heresy for any man to make this interpretation. Whether Athanasius therefore & his friends have not done violence to this Council I leave
to be considered.[65]

The false religion and idolatry introduced during the fourth century
had been perpetuated by the Catholic Church and survived even
in the reformed Church of England of Newton's day. The Reformation had swept away many of the aspects of Catholic religion that
Newton most distrusted. These included the invocation of saints and
the institution of monasticism, which seemed to him to have fos-
tered many of the errors of the Church. But the critical elements of
Athanasian corruption, in particular the failure to acknowledge the
full extent of God's dominion by attributing divinity to Christ and
the Holy Ghost, persisted in the Church of England. The exercise of
political power by the priesthood, which Newton argued had helped
to corrupt the early Church,was also one of the distinguishing characteristics of the contemporary English Church.[66] Yet, despite the
need for further reformation, Newton believed that the lives of the
faithful had to be governed by the times of prophecy, not by personal
whim. This may explain why he waited for signs that the prophecy
of the seventy weeks was being fulfilled before taking action that
might undermine lawful authority.[67]

Through his belief that he belonged to a remnant singled out to
preserve the truth about the Church and his distrust of sacerdotal
power, Newton revived concerns which were expressed earlier in
the seventeenth century by numerous Independent divines, especially in the tumultuous years of the 1640s and 1650s. His suspicion
of set forms in religion and his reluctance to subscribe to any of the
accepted creeds of the Church are again reminiscent of the writing
of that time, as are his convictions that the primitive Church had
not practiced infant baptism and had worshipped God on a Satur-
day sabbath.[68] Like many writers of the mid-seventeenth century,
Newton approached issues of ecclesiastical and doctrinal history
through the prism of a strict biblical literalism. One aspect of this

attitude to the Bible was that the text of scripture both confirmed and interpreted itself.[69] These hermeneutical principles were borne out in the synchronism of the prophecies of Daniel and the Apocalypse which Newton proposed. They also helped to cast doubt on the authenticity of the doctrine of the Trinity, which depended for its scriptural authority largely on two verses, 1 John 5.7 and 1 Timothy 3.16.

For Newton, the notion of the divine Trinity represented the culmination of the human tendency to corrupt religion into idolatry. The survival of the true Church depended on the correct understanding of God, who ruled through his servants with undivided dominion over the created world, and its manifestation in an appropriate form of worship.[70] Much of Newton's unpublished theological scholarship was devoted to elucidating the history of that Church, from its reestablishment by Noah to its most recent corruption by Athanasius and his papal successors.[71] Traces of his conclusions about the pure, primitive religion of Noah can also be found in the published and unpublished queries to the *Opticks*.[72] It is possible that Newton derived some of his ideas about the corruption of scripture and the true nature of God from reading contemporary heterodox writings, in particular those of Socinian authors, yet it is equally likely that he reached his conclusions largely by himself, through the application of a sharp mind, intolerant of ambiguity, to the complexities of the Bible. He was certainly unwilling to accept anyone as his master in the study of scripture and was thus representative of the most defiantly independent tradition of nonconformist biblical scholarship.[73] Newton's belief that the Christian religion consisted in a few fundamental truths (the worship of God and love of one's neighbor) found expression in his distrust of creeds that seemed to impose more than these essentials on the believer.[74] His concern to avoid excessive prescription in matters of faith may have been a reflection on his first experiences at Trinity College, Cambridge, where, within little more than a year of his arrival as an undergraduate, he would have witnessed bitter argument over the liturgy to be used in chapel and the expulsion of one fellow, the natural philosopher John Ray, for refusing to take the oaths under the Act of Uniformity in 1662.[75] Perhaps it was also a consequence of these events that Newton wanted to confine suffering for his faith to the private experience of his closet, even though his personal beliefs were quite different from those of ordinary members of the Church to which he nominally belonged.

Yet the burden of the prophecy of the seventy weeks may have forced Newton to intervene publicly in debate about the doctrines of the Church at two moments, in 1687–91 and in 1709–13. These were both times of tribulation for God's people when it seemed that the captivity of the Church might begin again.[76] In 1687, Newton broke cover to defend the legality of the University of Cambridge's refusal to admit the Benedictine monk Alban Francis to an MA without taking the oaths. This was Newton's first public act of defiance to the regime of James II and its policy of advancing the rights of Catholics. Following James's deposition in 1688, Newton took up a university seat in the Convention Parliament, which considered not only the succession but the right of the Church of England to persecute dissenters. Less than nine months after the dissolution of the Convention, when fears were already mounting about the religious and theological disorder that might result from the Toleration Act that it had passed, Newton sent the first of his letters to Locke about two notable corruptions of scripture, 1 John 5.7 and 1 Timothy 3.16. For a brief few months, Newton dared to think of allowing Locke's friend Jean Le Clerc to publish a Latin or French translation of the work, before retreating under the mounting anxieties of the time.[77] Le Clerc's copy of Newton's work, written in Locke's hand, was never returned. Versions of it circulated after Le Clerc's death in 1736, by which time the manuscript was incomplete.[78] One of these later became the basis for the first, inaccurate publication of the letters in 1754.[79]

Newton again considered publishing the letters in around 1709, when he commissioned Hopton Haynes, an employee at the Mint who shared his anti-Trinitarian sentiments, to translate what he had written about 1 John 5.7 into Latin. The manuscript title-page of this work bore the putative imprint "Amsterdam. 1709."[80] The years around the end of the first decade of the eighteenth century were difficult ones for Newton and his closest disciples. After the tory election victory of 1710, the liberties that had been won for religious dissenters in 1689 seemed to be under increasing threat. Moreover, from 1708, Whiston began to draw attention to himself as a critic of the orthodox doctrine of the Trinity and a proponent of further reformation in the Church.[81] Whiston attempted to involve both Samuel Clarke and Newton in the debate that he conducted with Archbishops Tenison and Sharp and Bishop Lloyd during 1708 and 1709.[82] It seems likely that this exchange prompted Newton to reconsider the publication of his letters on the scriptural authority for the doctrine of the Trinity. Haynes later remarked of his translation that "I know Sr Isaac intended them for the Press, and only waited for a good opportunity."[83] Yet Newton hesistated. Both Whiston and Clarke knew of Newton's attack on the authenticity of 1 John 5.7 by 1719.[84] But although Whiston had obtained a copy of the letters by 1738, it seems unlikely that he had extensive physical evidence of Newton's beliefs during his mentor's lifetime.[85] Newton did reveal hints of his heterodox ideas about God in the General Scholium that he added to the second edition of the *Principia* in 1713, in the process supporting Clarke's arguments, published in *The Scripture-Doctrine of the Trinity* during the preceding year.[86] Controversial though Newton's published views were, they stopped short of spelling out the implications for the Church of his beliefs about the nature of God.[87] Newton therefore chose to keep his own counsel about the past and future of true religion, despite the dangers that confronted his friends and the threat of a return to the persecution of dissent. Curiously, the exposure of his genuine opinions was thus left to the divines of the eighteenth-century Church of England.

NOTES

I am grateful to Rob Iliffe, Tabitta van Nouhuys, and Steve Snobelen for their help with this chapter.

1 Daniel Waterland to Zachary Grey, c. 1735, British Library (hereafter BL), MS Add. 6396, fol. 14r.

2 See Richard S. Westfall, *Never at Rest: A Biography of Isaac Newton* (Cambridge: Cambridge University Press, 1980), pp. 815–20, 872–3; Jewish National and University Library, Jerusalem, MS Yahuda Var. 1/ (Yah. MS) 7.2b, fols. 1–9 and 7.2j, fols. 1–139; Yah. MSS 7.1, 7.2, and parts of 7.3 contain drafts which relate to the preparation of the book, see also Cambridge University Library (CUL), Add. MS 3989 (3); some surviving proof sheets can be found in the Hampshire County Record Office, Winchester, MS NC 10.

3 Westfall, *Never at Rest*, p. 817.

4 William Whiston, *Memoirs of the Life and Writings of Mr. William Whiston*, 2 vols. (London, 1749), vol. 1, p. 227; Eamon Duffy, "Whiston's Affair: The Trials of a Primitive Christian 1709–1714," *Journal of Ecclesiastical History* 27 (1976), 129–50.

5 Whiston, *Memoirs*, vol. 1, pp. 35, 362, 484; James E. Force, *William Whiston: Honest Newtonian* (Cambridge: Cambridge University Press, 1985), p. 99; cf. [Peter King], *An Enquiry into the Constitution, Discipline, Unity and Worship of the Primitive Church* (London, 1691) and King, *The History of the Apostles Creed* (London, 1702).

6 [Daniel Mace], *The New Testament in Greek and English*, 2 vols. (London, 1729), vol. 1, pp. iii–vii; vol. 2, pp. 772–3, 917, 921–35.

7 E. S. de Beer (ed.), *The Correspondence of John Locke*, 8 vols. (Oxford: Clarendon Press, 1976–89), vol. 8, pp. 412–17, 419–27 (quotation at p. 415); John Harrison and Peter Laslett, *The Library of John Locke* (Oxford: Oxford University Press, 1965), pp. 54–6; Maurice Cranston, *John Locke* (Oxford: Oxford Bibliographical Society, 1985), pp. 438–9, 449–82.

8 De Beer (ed.), *Correspondence of Locke*, vol. 8, pp. 404–6; John Locke, *A Paraphrase and Notes on the Epistles of St Paul*, ed. Arthur W. Wainwright, 2 vols. (Oxford: Clarendon Press, 1987), vol. 1, pp. 6–11; John Marshall, *John Locke* (Cambridge: Cambridge University Press, 1994), pp. 390–2.

9 De Beer (ed.), *Correspondence of Locke*, vol. 7, p. 773. For exchanges of information on the prophecies of Daniel and Revelation between Newton and Locke, see Bodleian Library, Oxford, MS Locke c. 27, fol. 88; MS Locke f. 32, fol. 143v; *The Holy Bible* (London, 1648) [Bodleian Library, Locke 16.25], pp. 859, 866; *The Holy Bible* (London, 1654) [Locke 10.59–60], vol. 2, fifth interleaved page.

10 See de Beer (ed.), *Correspondence of Locke*, vol. 6, p. 522.

11 Peter, seventh Lord King (ed.), *The Life of John Locke* (London: Henry Colburn, 1829), pp. 215–33.

12 New College, Oxford, MS 361.4, fols. 2–41; printed in *The Correspondence of Isaac Newton*, vol. 3, ed. H. W. Turnbull (Cambridge: Cambridge University Press, 1961), pp. 83–122; Newton had attempted to reclaim these papers as early as 26 January 1692, see *Correspondence of Isaac Newton*, vol. 3, pp. 192–3.

13 John Nichols, *Illustrations of the Literary History of the Eighteenth Century*, 8 vols. (London, 1817–58), vol. 4, pp. 33–4.

14 William Stukeley, *Memoirs of Sir Isaac Newton's Life*, ed. A. Hastings White (London: Taylor Francis, 1936), p. 78; Library of Freemasons' Hall, London, MS 1130, p. 5.

15 For example, William Whiston, *A New Theory of the Earth* (London, 1696) or various comments by Nicolas Fatio de Duillier, in Bibliothèque Publique et Universitaire, Geneva (BPU), MSS Français 602, fol. 85r; 605, fol. 12r.

16 See W. C. Lukis (ed.), *The Family Memoirs of the Rev. William Stukeley*, 3 vols. (Durham: Surtees Society, 1880–7), vol. 1, p. 78. Cf. Freemasons' Hall, MS 1130, pp. 73–120; Isaac Newton, *The Chronology of Ancient Kingdoms Amended* (London, 1728), pp. 332–47; Yah. MS 14; Grace K. Babson Collection, Burndy Library, Cambridge, MA, MS 434; Matt Goldish, *Judaism in the Theology of Isaac Newton* (Dordrecht: Kluwer Academic, 1998), pp. 85–107.

17 Lukis (ed.), *Family Memoirs*, vol. 2, pp. 262–3; for Whiston's reaction, see Frank E. Manuel, *Isaac Newton, Historian* (Cambridge: Cambridge University Press, 1963), pp. 171–7, and Whiston to Fatio, 5 December 1734, BPU, MS Français 601, fols. 270–1.

18 Lukis (ed.), *Family Memoirs*, vol. 1, pp. 424–5.

19 Wiltshire Record Office, Trowbridge, MS 1178/631. On Bedford, see Jonathan Barry (ed.), "The Society for the Reformation of Manners 1700–5," in Barry and Kenneth Morgan (eds.), *Reformation and Revival in Eighteenth-Century Bristol*, Bristol Record Society's Publications 45 (Stroud: Alan Sutton, 1994), pp. 1–62; William Weber, *The Rise of Musical Classics in Eighteenth-Century England* (Oxford: Clarendon Press, 1992), pp. 47–56.

20 Archives of the Society for Promoting Christian Knowledge (formerly held by the Society in London, recently deposited in CUL), Minute Book 12 (1726–8), p. 106; Abstract Letter Book 14 (1727–9), letters 9271 and 9288.

21 Arthur Bedford, *Animadversions upon Sir Isaac Newton's Book, Intitled the Chronology of Ancient Kingdoms Amended* (London, 1728), p. 5; see also Bedford, *The Scripture Chronology demonstrated by Astronomical Calculations* (London, 1730), pp. v–vi. Cf. James Ussher, *Annales Veteris Testamenti* (London, 1650); the chronological information which had been provided in large-format English Bibles since an edition published by Lloyd at Oxford in 1701; Benjamin Marshall, *Chronological Tables*, 2 parts (Oxford, 1712–13), which were based on more detailed work by Lloyd; Richard Cumberland, *Sanchoniatho's Phoenician History*, ed. S. Payne (London, 1720); William Beveridge, *Institutionum Chronologicarum libri II*, 2nd edn (London, 1705). Newton's copies of these works, with the exception of Marshall, survive in the library of Trinity College, Cambridge, shelfmarks Tr/NQ.10.1; Tr/NQ.9.16; Tr/NQ.8.96; see John Harrison, *The Library of Isaac Newton* (Cambridge: Cambridge University Press, 1978). Cf. Marshall, *A Chronological Treatise upon the Seventy Weeks of Daniel* (London, 1725), which is highly critical of Newton's preferred source, Sir John Marsham, *Canon Chronicus Ægyptiacus, Ebraicus, Graecus, et Disquisitiones* (Leipzig, 1676).

22 Bedford, *Animadversions*, p. 143.
23 Manuel, *Isaac Newton*, pp. 171–7.
24 See Samuel Clarke, *The Scripture-Doctrine of the Trinity* (London, 1712); William Whiston, *Primitive Christianity Reviv'd* (London, 1712); Eamon Duffy, "Primitive Christianity Revived: Religious Renewal in Augustan England," *Studies in Church History* 14 (1977), 287–300.
25 Robert Wodrow, *Analecta*, ed. Matthew Leishman, 4 vols. (Glasgow, 1842–3), vol. 1, p. 325.
26 Wodrow, *Analecta*, ed. Leishman, vol. 3, pp. 205–6, 461–2; vol. 4, p. 59. For contemporary Scottish interest in Newton's religious beliefs, see also National Library of Scotland, Edinburgh, MS Wodrow Letters Quarto xxi, fols. 75r–77v (Andrew Grey to Wodrow, 20 March 1725); Stella Mills (ed.), *The Collected Letters of Colin MacLaurin* (Nantwich: Shiva, 1982), pp. 179–80 (Robert Simson to MacLaurin, 6 November 1727).
27 William Whiston, *Historical Memoirs of the Life of Dr. Samuel Clarke* (London, 1730), pp. 156–7; cf. Newton, *Observations*, pp. 128–43. For the more orthodox interpretation, that the prophecy was completely fulfilled at the death of Christ, see Humphrey Prideaux, *The Old and New Testament Connected in the History of the Jews and Neighbouring Nations*, 2 parts (London, 1726–8), part 1, pp. 262–4; H. H. Rowley, *Darius the Mede and the Four World Empires in the Book of Daniel* (Cardiff: University of Wales Press, 1935), p. 135.
28 King's College, Cambridge, Keynes MS (KMS) 132, fol. 2r (Craig to John Conduitt, 7 April 1727).
29 Joseph Spence, *Observations, Anecdotes, and Characters of Books and Men*, ed. James M. Osborn, 2 vols. (Oxford: Clarendon Press, 1966), vol. 1, p. 464; Bibliothèque Méjanes, Aix-en-Provence, MS 1188, pp. 8–9, 33–9, 81–104; cf. G. D. Henderson, *Chevalier Ramsay* (London: Nelson, 1952) and D. P. Walker, *The Ancient Theology* (London: Duckworth, 1972), pp. 231–63; Fatio's views on the Trinity may be found in BPU, MS. Français 602, fol. 24r.
30 [Zachary Pearce], *A Reply to the Letter to Dr. Waterland* (London, 1731), pp. 42–50, citing Newton, *Chronology*, pp. 186, 197 especially; cf. [Conyers Middleton], *A Letter to Dr. Waterland* (London, 1731), pp. 21–35. See also Pearce, *A Sermon Preached at the New Parish Church of St. Martin in the Fields* (London, 1727), which urged Newton to publish his revisions to ancient chronology in full.
31 The quotation comes from one of Waterland's annotations in his copy of [Middleton], *A Letter* [Bodleian Library, Oxford: Rawl. 8°437, p. 27]; for Marsham, see note 22 above; cf. John Spencer, *De legibus Hebraeorum*

ritualibus et earum rationibus, libri III (Cambridge, 1683–5) (Newton's copy is Tr/NQ.17.18).

32 Edward Churton (ed.), *Supplement to Waterland's Works: Fourteen Letters from Daniel Waterland to Zachary Pearce* (Oxford: James Parker, 1868), p. 7.

33 [Conyers Middleton], *A Defence of the Letter to Dr. Waterland* (London, 1732), p. 70; cf. [Conyers Middleton], *Some Remarks on a Reply to the Defence of the Letter to Dr. Waterland* (London, 1732), p. 7.

34 [Daniel Waterland], *Scripture Vindicated*, 3 parts (London, 1730–3), p. xii; cf. Matthew Tindal, *Christianity as Old as the Creation* (London, 1730).

35 [Waterland], *Scripture Vindicated*, p. xii.

36 Tindal, *Christianity as Old as the Creation*, pp. 352–432, for example, is structured around a discussion of passages from Clarke's writings.

37 Daniel Waterland, *The Case of Arian-Subscription Considered* (Cambridge, 1721); BL, MS Add. 5831, fols. 173r–174r.

38 Waterland to Grey, 5 February 1735, BL, MS Add. 5831, fols. 172r–173r.

39 B. W. Young, *Religion and Enlightenment in Eighteenth-Century England: Theological Debate from Locke to Burke* (Oxford: Clarendon Press, 1998), pp. 37–8.

40 BL, MS Add. 6396, fols. 7–9, 14r; cf. MS Add. 5831, fols. 173r, 182r–183r; Zachary Grey, *An Impartial Examination of the Second Volume of Mr. Daniel Neal's* History of the Puritans (London, 1736); Grey, *The Spirit of Infidelity, Detected*, 2nd edn (London, 1735).

41 Zachary Grey, *An Examination of the Fourteenth Chapter of Sir Isaac Newton's Observations upon the Prophecies of Daniel* (London, 1736) (CUL, 7100 d.46, is Grey's own copy with his additions interleaved). Many of Newton's unpublished theological manuscripts relate to these issues, most importantly: KMS 5 and 10; Yah. MSS 1, 2, 8.2, 15; Fondation Martin Bodmer, Geneva, MS 'Of the Church' (Bodmer MS); William Andrews Clark Memorial Library, Los Angeles, MS 'Paradoxical Questions concerning yᵉ morals & actions of Athanasius & his followers' (Clark MS).

42 Grey, *Examination*, pp. 7–25, 35–58, 72–85, 103–17.

43 Arthur Young, *An Historical Dissertation on Idolatrous Corruptions in Religion*, 2 vols. (London, 1734), vol. 2, pp. 265–70, quotation at p. 269.

44 Young, *Dissertation*, vol. 2, p. 269; Grey, *Examination*, p. 3; cf. Symon Patrick, *A Commentary upon the Historical Books of the Old Testament*, 3rd edn, 2 vols. (London, 1727); Prideaux, *The Old and New Testament Connected*.

45 Young, *Dissertation*, vol. 2, p. 268; Grey, *Examination*, p. 1.

46 Grey, *Examination*, pp. 35, 56, 85, 109, 137, for example.

47   See Harrison, *Library of Isaac Newton*, pp. 128 (St. Cyril of Jerusalem), 153 (St. Gregory of Nazianzus).

48   Thus Newton's copy of Moses Maimonides, *De Idololatria Liber*, ed. Dionysius Vossius (Amsterdam, 1641) [Tr/NQ.8.46^1], at p. 168.

49   For example, Gerardus Joannes Vossius, *De Theologia Gentili* (Amsterdam, 1641) [Tr/NQ.8.46^2], in which Newton has frequently chosen to mark Vossius' Latin paraphrases rather than the original Greek.

50   Anthony Grafton, "The Humanist as Reader," in Guglielmo Cavallo and Roger Chartier (eds.), *A History of Reading in the West*, trans. Lydia G. Cochrane (Cambridge: Polity Press, 1999), pp. 179–212.

51   Samuel Shuckford, *The Sacred and Profane History of the World Connected*, 2nd edn, 3 vols. (London, 1731–40), vol. 2, pp. i–iv; William Warburton, *The Divine Legation of Moses*, 2 vols. (London, 1738–41), vol. 2, pp. 206–81; both works criticized Newton's *Chronology*.

52   [George Berkeley], *A Defence of Free-Thinking in Mathematics* (London, 1735), quotations from pp. 67 and 7.

53   Arthur Ashley Sykes, *An Examination of Mr. Warburton's Account of the Conduct of the Antient Legislators* (London, 1744), pp. 222–364; Robert Clayton, *The Chronology of the Hebrew Bible Vindicated* (London, 1747); Nigel Aston, "The Limits of Latitudinarianism: English Reactions to Bishop Clayton's *An Essay on Spirit*," *Journal of Ecclesiastical History* 49 (1998), 407–33.

54   "An Account of what related to the Publishing of Sir Isaac Newton's Chronology of Antient Kingdoms, in 1728," in Newton, *The Chronology of Ancient Kingdoms Amended*, 2nd edn (London, 1770).

55   See Stukeley, *Memoirs*, ed. Hastings White, pp. 69–71; Whiston, *Historical Memoirs*, pp. 98–9; Stephen D. Snobelen, "Isaac Newton, Heretic: The Strategies of a Nicodemite," *British Journal for the History of Science* 32 (1999), 381–419, esp. pp. 396–412.

56   See John Gascoigne, *Cambridge in the Age of the Enlightenment* (Cambridge: Cambridge University Press, 1989); [Daniel Waterland], *Advice to a Young Student* (London, 1730), pp. 22–8.

57   *Correspondence of Isaac Newton*, vol. 3, pp. 233–40; Larry Stewart, "Seeing through the Scholium: Religion and Reading Newton in the Eighteenth Century," *History of Science* 34 (1996), 123–65.

58   See Clarke Garrett, *Respectable Folly* (Baltimore: Johns Hopkins University Press, 1975); John Arthur Oddy, "Eschatological Prophecy in the English Theological Tradition c. 1700–c. 1840," unpublished Ph.D. thesis, London University, 1982; David S. Katz and Richard H. Popkin, *Messianic Revolution: Radical Religious Politics to the End of the Second Millennium* (London: Allen Lane, 1999), pp. 107–204.

59 [Samuel Horsley], *Remarks upon Dr. Priestley's Second Letters to the Archdeacon of St. Alban's* (London, 1786), p. 20; cf. F. C. Mather, *High Church Prophet* (Oxford: Clarendon Press, 1992), pp. 45–8, 55–60.

60 For example, George Horne, *A Fair, Candid, and Impartial State of the Case between Sir Isaac Newton and Mr. Hutchinson* (Oxford, 1753); Bristol Central Library, MS B 26063, correspondence of A. S. Catcott and John Hutchinson, letter 2; cf. Wiltshire Record Office, MS 1178/631.

61 See Law's annotations interleaved in a copy of the Geneva Bible (London, 1606) [BL, c.45.g.13], especially vol. 3, facing sig. Mmm5v; Young, *Religion and Enlightenment*, pp. 45–119.

62 Whiston, *Historical Memoirs*, p. 157.

63 John Mill (ed.), Ἡ Καινὴ Διαθήκη *Novum Testamentum cum lectionibus variantibus* (Oxford, 1707), pp. 624, 738–49; *Correspondence of Isaac Newton*, vol. 3, pp. 289–90, 303–4, 305–8 (Newton's "Spicilegia Variantium lectionum in Apocalypsi," whose whereabouts are described as unknown (p. 308), may be found at The Queen's College, Oxford, MS 326, fols. 2r–4v).

64 *The Correspondence of Richard Bentley, D.D.*, ed. Christopher Wordsworth, 2 vols. (London: John Murray, 1842), vol. 2, p. 530; cf. Whiston, *Historical Memoirs*, p. 101.

65 Clark MS, fol. 73r and questions 1, 3, 9, 14, 15; cf. KMS 10 and Yah. MSS 1.4, fols. 53–106; 1.5; 1.6; 15.1.

66 For these beliefs, see especially Bodmer MS, fols. 36–40, 62–8, 98–102, 155–228, 260–367; cf. Yah. MSS 17.2, fols. 20v–21; 41, fol. 26.

67 Yah. MS 1.1, fols. 1–3r.

68 KMS 3, fols. 1–3; Yah. MS 15.4; Bodmer MS, fols. 36–40; Clark MS, fol. 2r; cf. Bryan W. Ball, *The Seventh-Day Men* (Oxford: Clarendon Press, 1994); J. C. Davis, "Against Formality: One Aspect of the English Revolution," *Transactions of the Royal Historical Society*, 6th series, 3 (1993), 265–88.

69 Yah. MS 1.1, fols. 12–18r.

70 Yah. MSS 14, fols. 25, 173; 15.5, fol. 90r; cf. Isaac Newton, *The Principia, Mathematical Principles of Natural Philosophy: A New Translation*, trans. I. Bernard Cohen and Anne Whitman (Berkeley: University of California Press, 1999), pp. 940–1.

71 KMS 146, fols. 1–4; Yah. MSS 15.5; 15.7; 16; 17; 41; Bodmer MS, chapter 1, fols. 5–30.

72 Isaac Newton, *Opticks: or, A Treatise of the Reflections, Refractions, Inflections and Colours of Light*, 4th edn (London, 1730; reprinted New York: Dover, 1979), pp. 405–6; Manuel, *Isaac Newton*, plate facing p. 117.

73 Yah. MS 1.1, fols. 1–10r; cf. Snobelen, "Isaac Newton, heretic," pp. 383–91, 406–7; Martin Mulsow, "Orientalistik im Kontext der sozinianis-chen und deistischen Debatten um 1700," *Scientia Poetica* 2 (1998), 27–57; Richard A. Muller, *Post-Reformation Reformed Dogmatics*, 2 vols. (Grand Rapids, MI: Baker Book House, 1985–93), vol. 2, pp. 465–543.

74 KMS 3.

75 See James Fawket, *An Account of the late Reverend and Worthy Dr. George Seignior* (London, 1681), pp. 4–13; Charles E. Raven, *John Ray: Naturalist*, 2nd edn (Cambridge: Cambridge University Press, 1950), pp. 57–61; East Sussex Record Office, Lewes, MSS Dan. 346–59.

76 Cf. Yah. MS 10.2, especially fol. 14v.

77 Jean Le Clerc, *Epistolario*, ed. Maria Grazia and Mario Sina, 4 vols. (Florence: Olschki, 1987–97), vol. 2, pp. 50–2.

78 BL, MS Add. 32, 415, fol. 388, Hopton Haynes to Rev. C[aspar] Wetstein, 17 August 1736; Leicestershire Record Office, Conant MSS, Barker correspondence, vol. 2, letter 123A (Samuel Crell to William Whiston, 28 September 1736); a copy made from Crell's copy of the manuscript survives at Bibliotheek der Rijksuniversiteit, Leiden, MS Semin. Remonstr. Bibl. 12; Sir David Brewster, *Memoirs of the Life, Writings, and Discoveries of Sir Isaac Newton*, 2 vols. (Edinburgh: Thomas Constable and Co., 1855), vol. 2, p. 338.

79 *Two Letters of Sir Isaac Newton to Mr. Le Clerc* (London, 1754), pp. 13–14.

80 Yah. MS 20.

81 BL, MS Add. 24, 197; Gloucestershire Record Office, Lloyd-Baker MSS [D 3549], box 74, bundle 9; Northamptonshire Record Office, Finch-Hatton MSS 2623–5.

82 Whiston, *Historical Memoirs*, pp. 15–17.

83 BL, MS Add. 32, 415, fol. 388.

84 Whiston, *Historical Memoirs*, p. 100.

85 Whiston, *Memoirs*, vol. 1, p. 365; see also Isaac Newton, *Ecrits sur la religion*, ed. Jean-François Baillon (Paris: Gallimard, 1996), pp. 21–2.

86 Stewart, "Seeing through the Scholium."

87 See Newton, *Principia*, trans. Cohen and Whitman, pp. 940–1.

15 Newton versus Leibniz: from geometry to metaphysics

In the course of a long life Isaac Newton made many enemies: Francis Linus (or Hall), Robert Hooke, John Flamsteed, Gottfried Wilhelm Leibniz, Johann I Bernoulli. Of these Leibniz was by far the greatest intellect and above all an outstanding mathematician and philosopher. Newton defeated them all and outlived them all except the last, twenty-five years his junior.

It was a sad chronology that brought two such inventive mathematicians as Newton and Leibniz to live in the same age; never were temperaments and intellectual characters more at odds. Almost the only feature that they had in common was Protestant piety, yet even in appealing to God the Creator they could not agree. In mathematics and its applications to celestial mechanics, and more particularly in the development of the calculus, though the methods promulgated by the two men were equivalent, they had been reached and were justified by wholly distinct arguments. Newton was by choice a geometer, Leibniz an algebraist; the difference does not of course imply that they could not tackle the same problems. J. E. Hofmann has written that Leibniz's "first major [mathematical] discovery in Paris [in 1673] originated in thoughts strongly influenced by considerations of logic and philosophy – and as so often with Leibniz, was not fully established but came as the fruit of a particular insight observed in simple examples and generalised by a stroke of genius."[1] At this stage Leibniz was working with numerical series, for example:

$$1 + \frac{1}{5} + \frac{1}{15} + \frac{1}{35} + \frac{1}{70} + \cdots = \frac{4}{3};$$

a particular case of his general theorem that even infinite series of numbers can be summed. Later of course Leibniz would extend his technique to include the approximate summation of the infinite series which could be used to express the magnitude of areas bounded by curved lines, that is, problems in geometry; thus he found that

$$1 - \frac{1}{3} + \frac{1}{5} - \frac{1}{7} + \cdots = \frac{\pi}{4}$$

Other series which he developed – in some cases having been anticipated (unknown to him at this time) by other mathematicians – expressed $\sin x$, $\tan x$, etc. Moreover, in his approach to his far greater discovery of the methods of calculus, Leibniz relatively early (in 1675) developed a new algebraic symbolism in which to express them. The outline of his invention that he wrote for Newton on 21 June 1677 (N.S.) is wholly algebraic even though the object of the operation may be to define the tangent to a curve or its quadrature. We have to remember, however, that in contemporary terms to effect the quadrature or rectification of a curve demanded (where possible) the expression of the result in a definite algebraic expression, whereas the method of series – first developed by Newton and then used by others – employed for the same purpose could only afford an approximation because such a series could not be exactly summed.[2]

With Newton it was far otherwise. The undergraduate who (according to a familiar anecdote) had failed to master Euclid because it seemed to him a trifling book, became the mathematician who regarded algebra as bungling. It is no coincidence that Newton's only set of lectures on algebra was published under the title *Arithmetica Universalis*. Or we may contrast the relative fullness of our knowledge of Leibniz's relations with his mentor, Christiaan Huygens, with the complete absence of any facts bearing on Newton's relations with *his* mentor and patron, Isaac Barrow (also a geometer), before Newton was 27 years of age in 1669.[3] In later life, in the course of the long dispute with Leibniz and the continental mathematicians, Newton sought to maintain that (like the ancient geometers) after having found the propositions in the *Principia* by analysis (that is, algebra) he had *demonstrated* them to the reader by means of geometry; thus at one and the same time asserting his mastery of the supreme modern analysis, calculus or fluxions, and the superiority in certainty of his work over that of others who relied entirely on discovery by analysis, without geometrical demonstration.[4]

This contention of Newton's, developed as a consequence of the calculus dispute in order to buttress his claim that in composing the *Principia* he had employed the method of fluxions for the solution of intricate problems in mechanics, has been discussed by D. T. Whiteside. Its complete factual truth is at least debatable. I have myself long accepted the view that he has advanced that the *Principia* was in large part drafted in the form in which, after considerable revision, we now have it. The earliest precursors of the book, including the tract(s) "De motu," are of the same mathematical form.[5] We do not find many analytical attacks upon *Principia* propositions. We only know that in the case of just one recalcitrant problem, the determination of the form of the solid of least resistance (Proposition 34, Book 2, in the third edition), Newton left a sound analytical demonstration of the result, which was published without proof. In other cases (for example, in Proposition 10 of the same book) it is possible that a prior analysis might have preceded the printed geometrical proof. But there is no evidence, and this was certainly not Newton's usual procedure.

When we consider also Newton's own early researches into analysis, which brought him to the fluxional calculus, perhaps it may seem that his later insistence upon geometrical demonstration was contrary to the tenor of his mathematical work during his most creative years. D. T. Whiteside has reminded us that though in youth Newton critically annotated a copy of Descartes's *La Géometrie* with *Error* and *Non Geom*, as well as writing a paper on *Errores Cartesii Geometriae*, they are nowhere "connected to form any imputation that Descartes errs because he adopts an algebraic method of geometrical analysis."[6] On the other hand, Newton commended Huygens's use of geometry in proving the propositions of *Horologium Oscillatorium* (1673). Further, at a late date indeed (the mid-1690s), Newton drafted a major work on geometry amounting to more than 150 of D. T. Whiteside's large pages.[7] In the last revision of Book 2 is an abbreviated version of the still unpublished "De quadratura curvarum" (written in 1691–2). In an early draft of his *Geometry* Newton expressed his opinion that our algebra seems not to differ from the ancients' process of analysis

except in the manner of its expression. But they in composing the resolved [that is, synthetic] proof used to shape demonstrations of their findings in a [geometrical] form adapted to the common capacity to comprehend; whereas we exhibit the [algebraic] analysis of the findings and are less solicitous about its [synthetic] composition.[8]

Elsewhere, post-1698, Newton wrote an opinion of a book *Analysis Geometrica* (Cadiz, 1698) by Hugo de Omerique:

therein is laid [he wrote] a foundation for restoring the Analysis of the Ancients wch is more simple, more ingenious & more fit for a Geometer than the Algebra of the Moderns. For it leads him more easily and readily to the composition [synthetic demonstration] of Problems and the Composition which it leads him to is usually more simple and elegant then that wch is forct from Algebra.[9]

These passages were all written before the poison of the priority dispute had infected the mathematical writings of Newton's old age. Newton had long been attached to the idea of the "prisca theologia": the Renaissance belief that the ancients had been far wiser and more inventive than the moderns, that their wisdom had therefore exceeded ours, and that the best endeavors of the moderns should be devoted to recovering what the ancients had possessed. We may guess that as such a philosophy matured in Newton's mind during his middle years it penetrated even his thoughts on mathematics.

The story of the calculus dispute may conveniently begin with Newton's admission in the first edition of the *Principia* that Leibniz had in 1677 sent to him "a method of determining maxima and minima, of drawing tangents, and performing similar operations, serving for irrational terms as well as rational ones … which hardly differed from my own except in words and notation"; Newton's method of fluxions (of which he now gave a terse algebraic outline) had of course been in existence by then for more than a decade without reaching print. Nor did Newton ever freely open it to Leibniz, in response to the latter's frankness. The whole Scholium in the *Principia*, this limited disclosure of the method of fluxions (which went not beyond what Leibniz had disclosed in 1677), has to be seen as Newton's response to Leibniz's first (difficult) paper on *his* new calculus in the *Acta Eruditorum* of 10 October 1684.[10]

As yet there were no claims for priority nor assertions of bad faith. The first unpleasantness occurred after the senior English mathematician, John Wallis, published a fuller account of Newton's method of fluxions (derived from its author) in his own *Opera Mathematica* (vol. 2, 1693).[11] On this Leibniz merely remarked again the equivalence of Newton's method with his own, and expressed some disappointment that Newton had discovered no newer method of quadrature (integration) than that offered by the summation of infinite series. His younger friend Johann I Bernoulli, however, in a letter to Leibniz (of 15 August 1696) said he did not know "whether or not Newton, having seen your calculus, did not thereupon fabricate his own method, especially as I see that you had imparted your calculus to him before he published his method."[12] This was of course a private expression of opinion, not a public accusation. Neither Newton nor Leibniz was inflamed against the other. Indeed, an exchange of letters between the two men after a silence of many years was conducted in formally affable terms, each man praising the other for his contributions to mathematics and Leibniz assuring Newton that "above all things, I desire you, who are a perfect geometer, to continue as you have begun to treat Nature mathematically, in which kind of investigation you have certainly accomplished something very worthwhile."[13]

Meanwhile, it must be added, Leibniz had published another paper in the *Acta* which was in subsequent years further to sour Newton's unexpressed thoughts about him. This was Leibniz's essay *Tentamen de Motuum Coelestium Causis* ("An Essay on the Causes of the Celestial Motions"), appearing only two years after the publication of the *Principia*. In this essay (also obscure to its readers) Leibniz took care to explain that he had not yet seen a copy of the *Principia* when he wrote it, being stimulated to do so by a review of that book in the *Acta Eruditorum*. Domenico Bertoloni Meli has convincingly shown this account to be untrue;[14] notes on the *Principia* made in Vienna by Leibniz are clearly to be placed at a time before Leibniz wrote the essay in Italy. Its object was to show how the motions of the Moon and planets calculated by Newton on the basis of his law of universal gravitation might be mechanically produced by a "harmonic" aethereal vortex, divided into five layers so that each might have a speed appropriate to the planet which it propelled. To account for the ellipticity of the orbits, Leibniz proposed (following G. A. Borelli in 1665) that each planet oscillated on a solar radius, thrust outwards to aphelion by the force of rotation and equally drawn inwards to perihelion by the force of a *second* aether acting independently of the first.

Since the *Acta Eruditorum* were little read in England, it was perhaps only after other incidents had begun to set Newton against

Leibniz, during the early years of the eighteenth century, that
Newton became aware of Leibniz's complicated theory of celestial
mechanics, in which he at once discovered a numerical error (in
Leibniz's computation of the central forces acting on the planets),
an error that Leibniz was impelled to correct when it was privately
brought to his notice by the French mathematician Pierre Varignon
in 1704. Newton was not impressed by Leibniz's vortical theory, finding this and all Leibniz's excursions into physics contorted, unnecessary, and geometrically unsound; he held the private opinions that
Leibniz's claim of ignorance of the *Principia* at the time of writing the
Tentamen was false, and that the vortical theory of the *Tentamen*
was more closely modeled on his own book than Leibniz cared to admit. The incident was seen by him as another instance of Leibniz's
questionable candor.

This was an opinion that Newton's friends were eager to confirm.
Apart from Fatio de Duillier they were mostly Scots, of whom the
first to become acquainted with Newton was John Craige (d. 1731),
an able mathematician, who spent some time in 1685 in Cambridge
with Newton (who called it "an extended stay").[15] Craige brought
with him a draft work on the quadrature of geometric figures which
he asked Newton to comment upon before having it printed. Continuing with Craige's narrative, "this with great kindness Newton
did" and then acquainted him with the quadrature of two curves
$(m^2y^2 = x^4 + a^2x^2)$ and $(my^2 = x^3 + ax^2)$ "and assured me that he
could show innumerable others of the same kind, by means of an
infinite series."[16] In fact, it seems that Newton permitted Craige
to study some of his own early manuscripts and *Principia* drafts, as
Craige had formerly studied works by Barrow and Leibniz already
in print. In his ensuing revised book, however, Craige used Leibniz's
calculus notation, changing only in later years to fluxions; he expressed indebtedness to both Leibniz and Newton.[17] After his return
to Scotland, Craige brought Newton's achievements to the attention
of David Gregory in Edinburgh, who in turn imparted them to his
students Cheyne, Keill, and Pitcairne.

These Scottish Newtonians, most of whom established themselves either in Oxford or in London, in later years offered strong
support to Newton in diffusing his innovations and in supporting
him against the continentals. The first author to print an accusation
against Leibniz tantamount to a charge of plagiary was, however,

Nicolas Fatio de Duillier. For about ten years
to Newton's mathematical papers of the 1660s a
ous essays, and correspondence with other mather
even have received from Newton some hint that
ungenerous in forgetting the kindness he had recei
in 1676, when Leibniz had been allowed to look th
massive correspondence and even Newton's tract "D
Analysis"} and so to scan a great deal of British mat ......cs. The
immediate occasion of Fatio's attack was the challenge issued to "the
finest mathematicians of Europe" by Johann I Bernoulli to solve a
pair of problems in mechanics. Newton first saw the challenge on
29 January 1697; he solved the problems that night after a hard day's
work at the Mint, though much out of practice in analysis. Almost
certainly Bernoulli had expected him to master the problems – as was
done only by the challenger himself, his own elder brother Jakob, and
Leibniz. At any rate, he correctly guessed that an anonymous solution from England came from Newton, "as the lion [is known] by his
claw."

Contrary to Fatio's supposition, the challenge can hardly have
been posed in order to expose Newton's weakness in calculus; rather,
the continentals perceived and respected Newton's ability. Fatio,
anxious to leap to Newton's defense and piqued because he himself
had not been sent a copy of the challenge, now declared in print:

I recognise that Newton was the first and by many years the senior inventor
of the calculus . . . as to whether Leibniz, the second inventor, borrowed anything from him, I prefer to let those judge who have seen Newton's letters
and other manuscripts, not myself.[18]

Leibniz's eagerness, he went on, "in ubiquitously attributing the calculus to himself would deceive no one familiar with the documents
I have myself examined."

As happened to Newton in the opposite sense, this attack made
Leibniz sensitive to the Newtonians' hostility, but he was too much
occupied in bringing to a successful conclusion his grand scheme
for an Academy at Berlin to pay much attention to a mere "fish-
wives' quarrel." In a published reply to Fatio of May 1700 Leibniz
merely claimed that Newton himself would not be taken in by such
nonsense as Fatio had printed and (correctly) that only Newton and
himself were original founders of the calculus, as Newton had stated

7. This last point was made in opposition to Fatio's assertion that he was himself an inventive mathematician, having "since 1687 acquired by his own self-tutored efforts a working proficiency with the basic methods and procedures of elementary calculus" and indeed imparted to Newton a useful integration process.[19]

In his next intervention Leibniz became more severe. In 1703 George Cheyne, both physician and mathematician like (later on) Newton's editorial assistant Henry Pemberton, published the third or fourth treatise on fluxions to appear in print, *Fluxionum Methodus Inversa* ("The Inverse Method of Fluxions," that is, integration) based on the work of Newton and David Gregory; the latter noted that this book provoked Newton into publishing "On the quadrature of curves" with his *Opticks* in 1704.[20] Abraham de Moivre wrote against Cheyne's book; no Newtonian thought well of it. Cheyne's marked Anglophilia and use (without acknowledgment) of Leibniz's published work irritated the continentals. In one passage Cheyne wrote that everything published about methods of quadrature during the previous twenty-four years "relating to these methods of [Newton], *or to other not dissimilar methods,* is only a repetition or an easy corollary of what Newton long ago communicated to his friends *or the public*" (my emphasis). Although Johann Bernoulli thought Cheyne's book "stuffed with clever discoveries," Leibniz was sufficiently provoked to comment in one of his letters to Bernoulli:

it may be the case that just as Mr Newton discovered some things before I did, so I discovered others before him. Certainly I have encountered no indication that the differential calculus *or an equivalent to it was known to him before it was known to me.* (My emphasis)[21]

It seems that privately Leibniz was beginning to lose his earlier willingness to accept Newton as a co-discoverer of the calculus, which after all rested only on his belief that Newton – whom he never met – was an honorable man.

The death of Robert Hooke (3 March 1703) enabled Newton to publish *Opticks*, begun more than fifteen years before; indeed, he had promised his friends even before the end of the year 1702 that he would publish this work together with "The quadrature of curves" and his "Enumeration" of the cubic curves.[22] There was no great triumph, alas, to be won by this first public appearance of Newton, now past 60 years of age, as a pure mathematician. The first textbook of Leibnizian calculus, adapted by the Marquis de L'Hospital from the lessons he had received from Johann I Bernoulli, was now eight years old; intensive work by Leibniz himself, the Bernoulli brothers, and others had brought their mathematics up to, perhaps beyond, the accomplishment of Newton, single-handed, twenty years earlier. Newton's suppression of "Quadrature" was twelve years too long. In the words of D. T. Whiteside:

> Newton's historical importance as the author of "De Quadratura Curvarum" is the minimal one of a lone genius who was able, somewhat uselessly in the long view, to duplicate the combined expertise and output of his contemporaries in the field of calculus. What is not communicated at its due time to one's fellow-men is effectively stillborn.[23]

Newton's achievements might stand as a model and inspiration for Britons and a few continentals – such as the Comte de Buffon whose translation, *La méthode des fluxions*, appeared in 1740 – but there was nothing new in "Quadrature" for those at the forefront of mathematics, who (moreover) were busy expressing Newton's own science of rational mechanics in the new analytical form.[24] All this of course is not to deny the essay ingenuity and depth of thought.

Not surprisingly, "Quadrature" figured largely in Leibniz's unsigned review of the *Opticks* volume in the *Acta Eruditorum*;[25] five whole pages were devoted to the two mathematical treatises. Leibniz was naturally particularly attentive to a very early passage in which Newton gave a reasonably exact summary of how "in the years 1665 and 1666 I gradually hit upon the method of fluxions, which I have here employed in the quadrature of curves." The fluxion, he continued – in one of his only partially successful attempts at the definition of his fundamental and unchanging concept – is the velocity with which a [geometrical] quantity increases or diminishes according to some law, while the fluent is the quantity generated.

> Mathematical quantities I here consider not as consisting of least possible parts [infinitesimals] but as described by a continuous motion. Lines are described, and generated by being described, not by the addition of parts but by the continuous motion of points, surfaces by the motion of lines, solids by the motion of surfaces, angles by the motion of sides, and times by [their] continuous flow and so for the rest.[26]

It is very relevant that Newton did not at this point plunge at once into algebra, as Leibniz had done in his letter to Newton of 11 June

1677, but defined and explained his procedure in geometrical terms, treating of geometrical figures defined by lines and areas. Leibniz commented not at all on the geometry/algebra contrast between the two methods; instead, he insinuated (with only a veneer of politeness) that Newton's calculus was derived by imitation from his own antecedent model:

instead of the Leibnizian differences Mr Newton employs, and has always employed, *fluxions which are almost the same as the increments of the fluents generated in the smallest equal portions of time.* He has made elegant use of them both in his *Principia Mathematica* and in other publications. (Emphasis in original)[27]

Leibniz then went on: "just as Honoré Fabri in his *Synopsis Geometrica* substituted the advance of movements for the method of [Evangelista] Cavalieri." The sense of these last words, as they appeared to Newton after they had first been kindly brought to his attention by John Keill in 1711, was stated by Newton himself:

The sense of the words is that Newton substituted fluxions for the differences of Leibniz, just as Honoré Fabri substituted the advance of movements for the [infinitesimal] method of Cavalieri. That is, that Leibniz was the first author of this method and Newton had it from Leibniz, substituting fluxions for differences.[28]

There were, however, compliments to Newton in this review, and when *Arithmetica Universalis* was brought out by William Whiston in 1707 Leibniz wrote in the *Acta* that things missing from large tomes on algebra were to be found in this little book.

While Leibniz's reviews were still unread by Newton, John Keill in 1708 repeated Fatio de Duillier's accusation of Leibniz's plagiarism. Printing as his first contribution to the *Philosophical Transactions* an article on "The Laws of Force," Keill declared that:

All these things follow from the nowadays highly celebrated arithmetic of fluxions, which Mr Newton beyond any shadow of doubt first discovered, as anyone reading his letters published by Wallis [in 1693] will readily ascertain, and yet the same arithmetic was afterwards published by Mr Leibniz in the *Acta Eruditorum* having changed the name and the symbolism.[29]

Here there is an obvious *suggestio falsi* that Newton had published his fluxions before Leibniz had made the calculus known. Since there is no evidence that Keill was familiarly acquainted with Newton at this time, it is possible that his words only paraphrase those of Fatio in 1699. Before considering Leibniz's rebuttal, one must note that in the first years of the eighteenth century Leibniz's attitude to Newton's concept of universal gravitation as an immaterial (or at least, indefinable) force in the universe had become more hostile; he now judged that it was time to refute the foolish "English philosophy" in the *Acta Eruditorum*, a periodical very much under his control. Its reviews inveighed against George Cheyne's *Philosophical Principles of Natural Religion* (1705) and John Freind's *Chymical Lectures* (1709) for teaching Newtonian concepts of gravitational and chemical forces, with the accusation that these writers were reverting to the "occult qualities, such as sympathy and antipathy were in the [medieval] schools of philosophy." To attack the writings of Cheyne and Freind was in effect to attack Newton's works. Only recently, in *Optice* (1706), in Query 23, Newton, while admitting that "what I call Attraction may be perform'd by impulse, or by some other means unknown to me" had (after this gesture toward metaphysical neutrality) questioned whether "the small Particles of Bodies" do not have "certain Powers, Virtues or Forces, by which" matter affects light, "but also upon one another for producing a great Part of the Phaenomena of Nature," instancing gravity, magnetism, and electricity as making "it not improbable that there may be more attractive Powers than these."[30] To such neo-Cartesians as Leibniz Newtonian forces betrayed all the advances made by Francis Bacon and Gassendi, Galileo, and Desartes, the modern reformers of philosophy. As for the personal accusation, Leibniz had been a Fellow of the Royal Society since 1673 (Keill only since 1700); he now wrote to its Secretary, Hans Sloane, to protest against Keill's accusations. Sloane in turn sought the advice of the President, Sir Isaac Newton (as he now was), who demanded an explanation from Keill. The latter had no difficulty in showing how Newton, his mathematics and his philosophy had been criticized in the *Acta Eruditorum*, so that Newton now thought himself more sinned against than sinning.[31]

Accordingly, clearly with Newton's help, Keill composed a substantial letter to Leibniz, withdrawing nothing but rather affirming that in his two letters to Leibniz of 1676 Newton "had given pretty plain indications to that man of most perceptive intelligence, whence Leibniz derived the principles of [his] calculus, or at least could have derived them." Newton, he declared, had advanced further in calculus by 1671 than anyone else had done to the present day.[32] By the time that this letter had been approved by the Royal Society (24 May 1711) and sent to Berlin, Newton's position had been slightly reinforced by the publication – from the papers of the long-deceased John Collins which had passed into the hands of William Jones, a teacher of mathematics – of Newton's "De analysi" (written forty-two years before), together with a more recent treatise, *Methodus Differentialis*, and the pair of essays already printed with *Opticks*, and correspondence. Leibniz's second demand for an apology from Keill reached London in January 1712, prompting Newton for the first time to make a verbal statement before the Royal Society: in this he pointed out that though himself the "first author" of the new calculus he was not the first aggressor in the dispute that had arisen. No doubt at the President's instigation a committee was appointed to report on the issues at stake, a committee consisting of ten Fellows (mostly mathematicians, among whom William Burnet was well acquainted with Leibniz) and the Prussian Ambassador in London.[33]

The report of this committee, appointed on 6 March, was ready by 24 April 1712. Newton himself had in effect done its work; he had made a *dossier* of the relevant documents and drafted a report which was in all essentials adopted by the committee; its judgment was that "Mr Newton was the first inventor [of the calculus] *and are of opinion that Mr Keill in asserting the same has been noways injurious to Mr Leibniz.*"[34] The Society ordered the immediate printing of both the report and selected documents (in Latin for international circulation). So appeared at the end of 1712 – to Anglicize its long title – *The Correspondence of Mr John Collins and Others concerning the Promotion of Analysis.*[35]

As long ago as 1855, Newton's biographer Sir David Brewster, overwhelmed by the published investigations of Augustus De Morgan, confessed: "It is due to historical truth to state that Newton supplied all the materials for the *Commercium Epistolicum* and... was virtually responsible for its contents." Whiteside repeats the same needless adverb: "It was in fact Newton who, virtually single-handed, elicited and annotated the volume of letters which was not quite a year later printed off and privately circulated."[36] Further, a decade later and six years after Leibniz's death, Newton carefully doctored a second edition of this book to make his own priority still more evident. To the Victorians this revelation of Newton's duplicity – he who had told Leibniz that no man should stand as a witness in his own cause! – was very shocking. In our more cynical age it is still deplorable and, as we now know, it was pointless. Newton was a powerful and a very great man: few cared to oppose him. Of him it may be said – to revise Shakespeare's words – that the good he did lived on and the evil was inter'd with his bones. Many of the claims made for the *Commercium* were true (the Committee was international in that de Moivre was born in France, the Ambassador Bonet in Prussia), the documents were faithfully printed, and so on. But Leibniz was allowed no hand in activating Newton's puppets. Only the evidence from one side was heard and judged.

Not surprisingly, many of the elections to the Royal Society from about 1690 onwards were of men already, or soon to be, Newton's admirers, from Joseph Raphson in 1690 to Henry Pemberton in 1720. When Newton became President in 1705 the Society accorded him solid support. William Jones's publication of Newton's mathematical essays from 1669 initiated a series of Newtonian publications: the *Commercium Epistolicum* was followed by the second edition of the *Principia* (1713) – with a Preface by Roger Cotes strongly attacking Leibniz's criticisms of universal gravitation – reprinted at Amsterdam in the following year. Raphson's *History of Fluxions* appeared in 1715 to be followed two years later not only by the third edition of *Opticks* with further Queries but by the *Leibniz–Clarke Correspondence* (see below), in which, by Leibniz's death toward the end of 1716, Clarke was given the last word. These various authors were not at all conscious of defending a weak cause; rather they were fully convinced of its strength.

The spread of Newton's reputation on the Continent was limited for a time by the *Commercium Epistolicum* affair. To the Leibnizians the book revealed the British as enemies of truth and progressive mathematics; all their mathematicians were tainted by Newton's false conduct. A damaging rift was created, isolating the British mathematicians from the Continent for a century, even though in time cordial personal relations were restored. Only slowly, beginning with *Opticks*, first the Italians, then the French, accepted and adopted Newtonian science, while the Germanic school, represented by men of the highest talent such as Johann Bernoulli and Leonhard Euler, continued to reject its more speculative aspects. In the last years of his life continental rejection caused Newton not a little distress, hence his particular cordiality toward those like Pierre Varignon and Willem 'sGravesande who showed intelligent appreciation of his enormous achievements in mechanics and also personal esteem.

From about 1710 Newton or his friends kept a close eye on the *Acta Eruditorum*. Early in 1713 Newton drafted a letter (the addressee is not stated, and the letter was never sent) protesting against a review of William Jones's *Analysis per Quantitatum Series, Fluxiones et Differentias* (1711); in his own method of first and last ratios, he protested, quantities are never considered as infinitely little.[37] By now the *Commercium Epistolicum* had reached Germany, to the great affront of Johann Bernoulli who in May 1713 sent Leibniz a detailed account of its iniquities: "you are at once accused before a tribunal consisting, as it seems, of the participants and witnesses themselves, as if charged with plagiary, then documents against you are produced, sentence is passed; you lose the case, you are condemned." Bernoulli assured his friend that Newton's understanding of differentiation was imperfect – a charge to be repeated later by him in several places, but unjustified; it was his incomprehension of Newton's processes that was at fault.[38] This was to be the basis for the oft-repeated charge that Newton did not understand how to obtain second differentials, which was urged in a particular context. In September 1712 Nikolaus Bernoulli, Johann's nephew and an able mathematician, had made a visit to London, bringing news of an error in Newton's investigation of resisted motion in *Principia*, Book 2, Proposition 10. This had been discovered by Johann in 1710; by Bernoulli's calculations Newton's printed result was in error by a factor of three to two. No one, however, had identified the flaw in Newton's reasoning, which he was left to find out for himself within two or three days of first being told of the discrepancy, when he gave a dinner to Nikolaus and his host Abraham de Moivre. Newton's review of his old work was long and difficult, filling some fifty pages;[39] he satisfied himself of the error of his original result and the accuracy of his new one (agreeing with Bernoulli) in five different ways. Then he had to construct a proof of the new result that would more or less exactly fill the same space in the already printed text of the second edition. All this he successfully did. Three months had passed, however, before Newton could send his draft of the necessary rewritten pages to Roger Cotes at Cambridge, eagerly awaiting them for the second edition of the *Principia*. Neither Cotes, Newton's patient editor who corrected many blemishes in the new text, nor the Bernoullis (in relation to Proposition 10 of Book 2) ever received a word of public acknowledgment.[40]

Meanwhile, Leibniz had been inflamed by what he read of the new English philosophy of attraction, in the originals or reviews in the *Acta*, not least by the rejection of his own vortex hypothesis in the *Tentamen* and by suggestions of his own plagiarism from Newton, all suggestions he dismissed as "idiotic...[Newton] no more knew our calculus than Apollonius knew the algebraic calculus of Viète and Descartes...He knew fluxions but not the calculus of fluxions" which he had fashioned later upon Leibniz's model.[41] The English, Leibniz believed, were inveterate thieves of German inventions, as with Boyle whose air-pump had been taken from Otto von Guericke. On 18 July Leibniz, now living in Vienna, had his *Acta Eruditorum* friends in Leipzig publish anonymously a flysheet (the *Charta Volans*), based on letters from Johann Bernoulli and others, designed to set Newton's iniquities and injustice to himself before a wide European public.[42] After discovering the "unnatural xenophobia of the English," which had led them not only to include Newton among the discoverers of the calculus but to exclude Leibniz himself from their number, he had begun to suspect "that the calculus of fluxions had been developed in imitation of the differential calculus":

having undeservedly obtained a share in this, through the kindness of a foreigner [that is, Leibniz], he [Newton] longed to have deserved the whole – a sign of a mind neither fair nor honest. Of this Hooke too has complained, in relation to the hypothesis of the planets, and Flamsteed because of the use of his observations.

Leibniz, not mincing his words, was looking for allies. More interesting, in the passage immediately before that just quoted, is his remark that he had discovered the differential calculus "first in numbers [arithmetic] and then transferred it...to Geometry." Newton's method of fluxions was from the first geometrical, conceived from the generation of lines by moving points and areas by moving lines.

The flysheet was widely distributed in continental journals, with some "Remarks" added by Leibniz, and probably Keill had no great difficulty in convincing Newton (during the autumn of 1713) that it must be refuted. Keill had already printed a Newtonian account of fluxions in the *Journal Litéraire de la Haye*; he now wrote an "Answer" to Leibniz that appeared in the same journal during July/August 1714.[43] From this time, for about five years (that is, until after the death of Leibniz in 1716) there was a frequent exchange of alternate accusations and rebuttals between the young champions on either side, neither Newton nor Leibniz contributing much directly to the debate. Each side continued to accuse the other of stealing the principles of calculus, and (as proof of this) lacking the knowledge to apply second differentials correctly in the solution of the more difficult problems in mechanics.[44] Both sides attempted to invoke the support of parties unconcerned in the original dispute about events that had occurred forty years before. Two vain attempts at mediation between the principals were made: one by a journalist, John Chamberlayne (who possibly put copies of the *Charta Volans* into Newton's hands), the other by a curious international amateur of philosophy, the Abbé Conti; both failed. Newton's principal late intervention was the printing in the *Philosophical Transactions* for 1715 of *An Account of the Book entituled Commercium Epistolicum*, purporting to be an impartial review but in fact written by Newton himself. Here, employing much the same kind of scholastic argument that he used in writing history and theology, Newton "proved," plausibly enough, that Leibniz by his own admissions could not possibly have known the differential method before 1677, that is, *after* he had read Newton's two long letters of the previous year. Newton's reconstruction was distorted by his own self-interest and by his inability to appreciate how partial and idiosyncratic Leibniz's knowledge of recent mathematics had then been. Further, he insisted on the superiority of the concept of fluxions: "We have no ideas of infinitely little quantities, and therefore Mr Newton introduced fluxions into his method, that it might proceed by finite quantities as much as possible."

Here he contrasted the fluxion, "the first ratio of nascent quantities, which have a being in geometry" with the differences, or first nascent quantities "which have no being either in geometry or nature." Moreover, the Leibnizian calculus requires "a summing of indivisibles to compose an area or solid ... never yet admitted into geometry," and so that process afforded only analysis, not demonstration, while his own method of fluxions admitted of synthetic demonstration. Even as a technique of analysis Leibniz's calculus was defective, Newton argued, without the use of the method of infinite series to which Leibniz could lay no possible claim. One statement in the *Account* has caused confusion through the years:

By the help of the new [fluxional] analysis Mr Newton found out most of the Propositions in his *Principia philosophiae*, but because the Ancients for making things certain admitted nothing into geometry before it was demonstrated synthetically, he demonstrated the propositions synthetically that the system of the heavens might be founded on good geometry. And this makes it now difficult for unskilful Men to see the Analysis by which those Propositions were found out.

As already remarked, this process of double work seems rarely to have been used, or at any rate recorded.[45]

Perhaps Newton hoped to end the dispute by the publication of this detailed history of mathematics from the 1660s onwards and the exposure of Leibniz's iniquities. If so, he failed. Little that was new about the mathematical issues was to be brought out in subsequent papers, but considerable attention was to be paid to criticisms of Newton's philosophy by Leibniz. We may start from the Preface to the second edition of the *Principia* composed by Roger Cotes (to whom Newton deliberately refused any hints or guidance), the purpose of which was to defend the theory of universal gravitation formulated by Newton and refute vortex theories such as that of Leibniz. Cotes explained the superior character of experimental philosophy as compared with that which enjoys purely rational foundations: "This is that incomparably best way of philosophizing, which our renowned author most justly embraced" when he deduced the system of the world from the theory of gravity. Some persons of great name, Cotes went on, "too much prepossessed with certain prejudices, are unwilling to assent to this new principle, and are ready to prefer uncertain [hypothetical] notions to certain."[46] In the remainder of the Preface he developed the argument that the science of rational mechanics, applied to the question of the system of the world with the aid of the law of universal gravitation, yielded a far more certain philosophy than did such vortex theories as that expounded by Leibniz and was fully in accord with true religious principles.

Leibniz seems not to have greatly concerned himself with the errors of the metaphysical foundations of Newton's natural philosophy, as he saw them, until late 1715.[47] True, he had some long time before noted the two curious passages in *Optice* (1706, pp. 315 and 346; Queries 20 and 23) in which Newton twice invoked the notion that space is the *sensorium* of God, which Leibniz chose to interpret in the absurd sense of space's constituting the sense-organs of God.[48] Moreover, his *Essais de théodicée* (1710) had made clear his opposition to the way in which – as Leibniz saw it – Newton as well as non-mathematicians like Richard Bentley and the philosopher John Locke, who followed Newton's example, attributed universal gravitation to the arbitrary will of the Creator. In Leibniz's opinion it was incumbent upon philosophers to find out the logical links or mechanisms whereby phenomena might duly appear from the unchanging structure of the world. Bentley, under Newton's guidance, had indeed written that gravitation is above all mechanism and mechanical causation; that in fact "it cannot be innate and essential to matter"; consequently "it could never *supervene* to it, unless impress'd and infused into it by an immaterial and divine Power" (perhaps a last vestige of Henry More's Spirit of Nature?).[49] We know that Newton did not disdain the notion that since the fabric of the world could not endure for ever as he had described it, without change, its long continuance would require occasional divine interventions. Leibniz thought such a divine intervention a miracle, and that universal gravitation should arise from the divine power seemed to him a miracle also. In his "First Paper" answered by Samuel Clarke, Leibniz famously appealed to the analogy of the Clockmaker:

Nay, the machine of God's making [the universe] is so imperfect, according to [the Newtonians]; that he is obliged to clean it now and then by an extraordinary concourse, and even to mend it, as a clockmaker mends his work.

This letter led to a series of five exchanges between Leibniz and Samuel Clarke, theologian, metaphysician, and friend of Newton; Leibniz's death on 14 November 1716 prevented his reading Clarke's Fifth Reply.[50]

This correspondence, of which Newtonian science was the passive subject, began with a letter written in November 1715 by Leibniz to Caroline, Princess of Wales, in London; she was later George II's Queen. Caroline's friendship with Leibniz had begun during a visit she made to the Electoral Court at Berlin and was renewed after her marriage to the Electoral Prince of Hanover (later George II). She and Leibniz maintained a correspondence until the latter's death. In this letter of November 1715 Leibniz deplored Newton's influence upon English philosophy; the Princess, being already acquainted with Dr. Clarke, and knowing that he had adopted Newton's metaphysical opinions, invited him to read Leibniz's letter and respond to it,[51] For herself, she declared, she was "in a dispute with" Dr. Clarke because he was "too much of Sir Isaac Newton's opinion" and rejected those favored by Leibniz. The latter responded to Clarke's First Reply, and so on.

The volume in which Clarke, in 1717, printed his exchanges with Leibniz is a small one, but the various matters on which Leibniz found Newton at fault while Clarke defended him were neither few nor trivial. One controversy, on the correct definition of mechanical force, was settled (when shown to be founded on inadequately defined terms) only after two generations of debate, by d'Alembert in 1743. Another – is there an absolute space and an absolute time? – was settled only by Einstein in 1905. Other matters in debate, such as the application of the principle of sufficient reason to the actions of God, were not and perhaps are not capable of decision. In the extreme form, Leibniz's confidence that God must always act for the best was later mocked by Voltaire and others. However, on the first specific criticism by Leibniz, touched on in all the letters, whether or not Newton had attributed to God the possession of sense-organs, the debate turned essentially on the meaning of Newton's word *sensorium* – was it an organ or a place? – and again no decision was possible. In general, the points at issue have since been settled – without in general one party or the other being better vindicated – where they were matters of physics; when they were metaphysical they may still be debated. Time has not spoken decisively on either side save in the matter of the vacuity of space: celestial vortices have been dead for over 200 years. Most authorities judge Leibniz to have been a sounder metaphysician than either Newton or Clarke, yet the latter presumably thought well of his own performance since he put the letters into print so quickly.

Leibniz clearly believed that Newton directed Clarke's pen. It may have been so; but there is no firm evidence that Newton did not isolate himself as completely from Clarke as he had previously from Cotes and would later attempt to do from Des Maizeaux. For the death of Leibniz, while it ended the philosophical discussions, by no means brought a cessation of mathematical irritation. Exchanges between the antagonists continued until at least 1720; some of them were published in the literary journals. In the final years of his life Leibniz began a documentary statement of his own mathematical evolution, *Historia et Origo Calculi Differentialis*, unfinished and unpublished till the nineteenth century. Newton wrote a last important letter on the issues to the Abbé Conti, in February 1716; the original is lost.[52] In this Newton, besides rehearsing many familiar points in dispute, drew attention to Leibniz's admission in the *Acta* (1700) that no one before Newton and himself had original knowledge of the calculus, and that Newton was the first to prove his knowledge by example, in the *Principia*. Challenge problems continued to be directed against the English: Leibniz's "orthogonals" problem of November 1715[53] was followed by Keill's challenge (1717) to Johann Bernoulli to solve the general problem of ballistics: what is the trajectory in a resisting medium such as air?[54] This was an unfair problem in that Keill had not solved it, and never did; Bernoulli published appropriate differential equations in the *Acta Eruditorum* of May 1719. The equations do not admit of an exact integration. After this humiliation of the English, whose honor was partly redeemed by Brook Taylor, it remains only to note the penultimate major publication bearing on the quarrel between Newton and Leibniz, Pierre Des Maizeaux's *Recueil de diverses pièces sur la philosophie, la religion naturelle, l'histoire, les mathématiques etc.* (Amsterdam, 1720).[55] The editor was a Huguenot refugee, in England from 1699, who (like Newton) won the patronage of Charles Montagu, earl of Halifax. His plans for the book were never fully realized: he published only the *second* edition of the Leibniz–Clarke correspondence (in French) and Newton only gave him small help (and some hindrance) in printing the selection of correspondence in the second volume. Newton was pleased subsequently to declare (not quite truthfully!) that he had had no hand in the book.

While Newton's star rose slowly on the Continent from about 1706 with the publication of the Latin *Opticks*, Leibniz's chief shield-bearer, Johann I Bernoulli, never yielded his position. To the end he supported Leibniz's invention of calculus and his planetary vortices. Yet, with the eager encouragement of Pierre Varignon, Bernoulli made an effort to effect a personal reconciliation with Newton by clearing himself of false accusations. If only flattery were all! He addressed Newton as "a man of divine genius of whom our age has no equal"; Newton's optical discovery was "more enduring than any bronze, and one to be more greatly prized by posterity than it is now."[56] But Newton was never more than formally correct in return. He could never forgive the "eminent mathematician" who had so strongly buttressed Leibniz's false claims (as he saw them). Perhaps in this volume Newton may be given the last word, from a draft written for Des Maizeaux in 1718:

> If Mr Leibnitz could have made a good objection against the Commercium Epistolicum, he might have done it in a short letter without writing another book as big. But this book being matter of fact & unanswerable he treated it with opprobrious language & avoided answering it by several excuses, & then laying it aside by appealing to the judgment of his friend Mr Bernoulli & by writing to his friends at Court, & by running the dispute into a squabble about a Vacuum, & Atoms, & universal gravity, & occult qualities, & Miracles, & the Sensorium of God, & the perfection of the world, & the nature of time & space, & the solving of Problemes, & the Question whether he did not find the Differential Method *proprio marte*: all of which are nothing to the purpose... The proper question is: Who was the first Inventor?[57]

To that question at least there is now a clear answer.

NOTES

This chapter is based on the material provided in A. Rupert Hall and Laura Tilling (eds.), *The Correspondence of Isaac Newton*, vol. 5 (Cambridge: Cambridge University Press, 1975) and D. T. Whiteside (ed.), *The Mathematical Papers of Isaac Newton*, vol. 8 (Cambridge: Cambridge University Press, 1981), esp. pp. 469–697.

1   J. E. Hofmann, *Leibniz in Paris, 1672–1676* (Cambridge: Cambridge University Press, 1974), pp. 14–19.

2   *Ibid.*, p. 187.

3   Whiteside (ed.), *Mathematical Papers*, vol. 8, p. 427 n. 6.

4   "The Propositions in the following Book [the *Principia*] were invented by Analysis; but considering the Ancients... admitted nothing into Geometry before it was (for greater certainty) demonstrated by composition [synthesis] I composed what I invented by Analysis, to make it Geometrically authentick and fit for the public." From a draft Preface to the *Principia*, c. 1716, *ibid.*, pp. 647–8.

5   *Ibid.*, p. 443 n. 1.

6   John Harrison, *The Library of Isaac Newton* (Cambridge: Cambridge University Press, 1978), pp. 14–15 and no. 507. Whiteside (ed.), *Mathematical Papers*, vol. 7 (1976), p. 194 n. 46.

7   Whiteside (ed.), *Mathematical Papers*, vol. 7 (1976), pp. 248–561: I divide 313 by two (to allow for the English translations and extensive notes).

8   *Ibid.*, p. 251.

9   *Ibid.*, p. 198; *The Correspondence of Isaac Newton*, vol. 7, ed. Hall and Tilling (Cambridge: Cambridge University Press, 1977), pp. 412–13 for the full text of this draft.

10 *Principia* (1687), Scholium to Lemma 2, Book 2, pp. 250–4; much modified in subsequent editions. G. W. Leibniz in *Acta Eruditorum* (1684), pp. 467–73 and *ibid.* (June 1686), pp. 292–300.

11 Whiteside (ed.), *Mathematical Papers*, vol. 7, pp. 170–80; the matter had been borrowed by Newton from his own draft of *De Quadratura Curvarum* (a tract unpublished till 1704).

12 A. Rupert Hall, *Philosophers at War: The Quarrel between Newton and Leibniz* (Cambridge: Cambridge University Press, 1980), p. 117. These words were first printed in the *Commercium Epistolicum* of Leibniz and Bernoulli in 1745, vol. 1, p. 191).

13 Hall, *Philosophers at War*, p. 109; *The Correspondence of Isaac Newton*, vol. 3, ed. H. W. Turnbull (Cambridge: Cambridge University Press, 1961), pp. 257–8, 7 March 1693.

14 Domenico Bertoloni Meli, *Equivalence and Priority: Newton versus Leibniz* (Oxford: Oxford University Press, 1993).

15 Others of this group were David Gregory, Professor of Mathematics at Edinburgh 1683–91 (whose correspondence with Newton began in 1691 also), George Cheyne, John Keill, and Archibald Pitcairne.

16 John Craige, *De Calculo Fluentium* (London, 1718), Craige's third mathematical publication. A fourth was posthumously published.

17 *Methodus . . . Quadraturas Determinandi* (London, 1685).

18 Hall, *Philosophers at War*, pp. 100–1, 106–7. Fatio would never know that Leibniz was to write in 1708 of his "love for Mr Fatio, for he is a man excellent in mathematics." Fatio had made similar criticisms of Leibniz in letters to Huygens in 1692 (*Œuvres complètes* [The Hague, 1905], pp. 257–8; *Correspondence of Isaac Newton*, vol. 3, pp. 193–4). The quoted accusation was made in *Lineae Brevissimi Descensus Investigatio Geometrica* (London, 1699); cf. D. T. Whiteside (ed.), *Mathematical Papers*, vol. 6 (1974), p. 466 n. 25. This was Fatio's belated response to the challenge problems. He added the following scornful words: "[Leibniz] has acquitted himself in a way so remote from Mr Newton's that in comparing the two I feel strongly that the difference between them is that between a finished original and a spoiled and very imperfect copy."

19 The quoted words are Whiteside's from *Mathematical Papers*, vol. 7, p. 12 n. 4; cf. also pp. 78–9 n. 68.

20 W. G. Hiscock, *David Gregory, Isaac Newton and Their Circle* (Oxford, 1937), p. 15.

21 25 March 1704; first printed in the *Commercium Epistolicum* of Bernoulli and Leibniz, vol. 2 (1745), p. 111.

22 Hiscock, *David Gregory*, p. 14, 15 November 1702. This memorandum contradicts Gregory's later remark, p. 15, 1 March 1704.

23 Whiteside (ed.), *Mathematical Papers*, vol. 7, p. 20.

24 I think of Jakob Hermann's *Phoronomia* (Amsterdam, 1716) – a book favorably reviewed by Leibniz in the *Acta Eruditorum* – and Pierre Varignon's papers on dynamics published by the Académie Royale des Sciences, Paris.

25 January 1705.

26 "De quadratura curvarum" (1704) with *Opticks* (1704), p. 165; Whiteside (ed.), *Mathematical Papers*, vol. 8, pp. 122–3.

27 *Acta Eruditorum* (January 1705), pp. 30–6; *Commercium Epistolicum* (1712), p. 108.

28 Hall, *Philosophers at War*, p. 139; from *Commercium Epistolicum*, p. 108n.

29 *Philosophical Transactions* 26 (1708), 185. This 1708 volume was actually issued in 1710. See also Whiteside (ed.), *Mathematical Papers*, vol. 8, p. 473.

30 I quote the English of Query 31 in the later English editions of *Opticks*.

31 Newton was particularly angered by the implication in the *Acta*'s 1705 account of *Opticks* and its appendages that "Quadrature" was patched together from publications by Leibniz, Craige, and Cheyne.

32 *Correspondence of Isaac Newton*, vol. 5, pp. 142, 145.

33 The British members were Arbuthnot, Aston, Burnet, Halley, Hill, Jones, Machin, de Moivre, Robarts, and Brook Taylor.

34 The italicized words are absent from Newton's draft.

35 The finished Report, as found in the Society's Journal-Book, is printed (with indications of Newton's contribution) in *Correspondence of Isaac Newton*, vol. 5, pp. xxvi–xxvii. Newton's draft is in Whiteside (ed.), *Mathematical Papers*, vol. 7, pp. 545–7.

36 A. Rupert Hall, *Isaac Newton: Eighteenth Century Perspectives* (Oxford: Oxford University Press, 1999), p. 187. Whiteside (ed.), *Mathematical Papers*, vol. 8, 1981, p. 485. The draft of the "Ad lectorem" ("To the Reader") introducing the correspondence, in Newton's holograph English, is at pp. 558–60.

37 *Correspondence of Isaac Newton*, vol. 5, pp. 383–4; cf. Whiteside (ed.), *Mathematical Papers*, vol. 2, pp. 263–273.

38 Whiteside (ed.), *Mathematical Papers*, vol. 8, pp. 59–61.

39 *Ibid.*, pp. 312–424.

40 *The Correspondence of Isaac Newton*, vol. 5, Letters 952, 961.

454   A. RUPERT HALL

41 *Ibid.*, vol. 6, ed. Hall and Tilling (Cambridge: Cambridge University Press, 1976), pp. 8–9, 17 June 1713.
42 It was printed and circulated by Christiaan Wolff, editor of the *Acta Eruditorum*; there was also a French translation.
43 It was completed by May: *Correspondence of Isaac Newton*, vol. 6, Letter 1069. Newton had drafted an (abandoned) reply, Letter 1053a.
44 For the 'flow' of the various pieces, see the chart we printed in *Correspondence of Isaac Newton*, vol. 5, p. xxviii.
45 The *Account* is reprinted in A. Rupert Hall, *Philosophers at War*; quotation here p. 296.
46 *Principia Mathematica*, Motte–Cajori translation, p. xxi (Cohen–Whitman translation, p. 386). At this time rigorous observations, such as those in astronomy, were often called 'experimental'.
47 I omit any consideration here of Johann Bernoulli's second challenge problem presented by Leibniz to the "English analysts" in December 1715. See Whiteside (ed.), *Mathematical Papers*, vol. 8, pp. 425–41.
48 A. Rupert Hall, *All was Light: An Introduction to Newton's Opticks* (Oxford: Oxford University Press, 1993), pp. 136–8. The corresponding Queries in the second English edition are nos. 28 and 31. Newton's late awareness of the doubtful sense of his words enforced the reprinting of one gathering in Query 20; copies in both states exist.
49 Richard Bentley, *A Confutation of Atheism* (London, 1693), p. 29.
50 Samuel Clarke (1675–1729), too unconventional a theologian for his own good, translated *Opticks* into Lation for Newton, and was otherwise closely associated with him. See H. G. Alexander, *The Leibniz–Clarke Correspondence* (Manchester: Manchester University Press, 1955).
51 *Ibid.*, pp. ix–xii.
52 *Correspondence of Isaac Newton*, vol. 6, Letter 1187; there are seven holograph drafts and two printed versions.
53 See Hall, *Philosophers at War*, pp. 216–17, n. 12; Whiteside (ed.), *Mathematical Papers*, vol. 8, pp. 425–41.
54 Supposing gravity uniform and the resistance of the air proportional to the square of the velocity. Newton had given an approximate solution to this problem in *Principia*, Book 2, Proposition 10, Scholium.
55 The last was Newton's second edition of the *Commercium Epistolicum* (1722).
56 *Correspondence of Isaac Newton*, vol. 7, pp. 45, 220.
57 *Ibid.*, vol. 6, p. 461 n. 8.

16 Newton and the Leibniz–Clarke correspondence

INTRODUCTION

Between 1715 and 1716 Gottfried Wilhelm Leibniz and Samuel Clarke were engaged in a theological and philosophical dispute mediated by Caroline, Princess of Wales. Ten letters were exchanged, five on each side, before the controversy was brought to an end by Leibniz's death in November 1716. During the controversy those involved agreed to publish the texts, which were edited in 1717 by Clarke, who also translated Leibniz's letters into English. His *editio princeps* is considered to be both fair and excellent, and contains Leibniz's original French on facing pages, as well as a useful selection of additional explanatory materials. This extraordinarily influential controversy is among the most famous and heavily studied philosophical disputative texts of all times, and, in the words of a recent interpreter, its intellectual intricacies are reserved only for the very learned or the foolhardy.[1]

Despite the extent of interest and studies the correspondence has attracted,[2] however, we still lack a comprehensive critical edition taking into account all the relevant texts, including Caroline's and Clarke's. Interestingly, eighteenth-century editions did not include the private correspondence between Caroline and Leibniz, which was first made available in the nineteenth century, notably by Onno Klopp in the most complete form.[3] The private correspondence of the Princess of Wales was probably not available to Clarke and, even if it had been, publishing it at the time would have been highly inappropriate. That correspondence, however, provides interesting perspectives on the exchange between Leibniz and Clarke. At times interpreters have assumed that Leibniz was writing to Clarke and

Clarke to Leibniz, without taking sufficiently into account all levels of the exchange. Paying attention to Caroline's role and to the genre of the correspondence will help shed light on what was at stake.[4]

Besides the lack of a complete critical edition, some areas are still relatively unclear and little explored. For the purposes of this chapter, I wish to examine briefly two topics, namely the character of the exchange in terms of literary genre, and the level of Newton's involvement alongside Clarke in both defending his world-view and attacking Leibniz's. Although in the final section I will survey some of the main themes of the correspondence, this chapter should be read as an invitation to study it afresh.

THE GENRE OF THE CORRESPONDENCE

The correspondence between Leibniz and Clarke originated when Caroline, Princess of Wales, passed to Clarke an extract of a letter she had just received from Leibniz, an extract not originally intended for Clarke. She claimed that she was having a dispute with the English divine, gave him Leibniz's extract, and then passed on Clarke's reply to Leibniz. Caroline remained the mediator throughout the controversy. The documents that have survived consist of two parallel sets of exchanges, one between Leibniz and Clarke, and one between Caroline and Leibniz. In addition, we have records of Clarke's discussions with Caroline and Newton's visits to her, as well as her witnessing several experiments on colors and the void. Other parallel exchanges too have been considered relevant, such as that between Leibniz and Newton mediated by the Abbé Conti.[5]

Why did Leibniz and Clarke proceed inexorably, month after month, to exchange ever longer letters on the nature of space and time, the notion of miracle, and the cause of gravity? Are there literary precedents for such types of exchange? I shall start with the second question.

The first examples which spring to mind are the Leibniz–Arnauld and Leibniz–Pellisson correspondences, both dealing with theological and philosophical issues. The correspondence between Leibniz and French theologian and philosopher Antoine Arnauld was mediated by the Landgrave of Hesse-Rheinfels, a Catholic convert interested in Church reunion. The correspondence between

Leibniz and Paul Pellisson, which also involved Church reunion, was instigated by, and conducted through, an interested aristocratic intermediary, Sophia, Duchess of Hanover. In both cases philosophical themes were interwoven with theological ones.[6] Incidentally, the issue of Church reunion was raised in the correspondence between Leibniz and Caroline early in 1716, at the time of the election of William Wake as Archbishop of Canterbury. In the dispute between Leibniz and Clarke, however, Church reunion was not mentioned, and the tone was more confrontational. Thus we need to look for a more appropriate precedent.

Another episode from earlier in the seventeenth century looks helpful, namely the affair involving scripture and Copernicanism at the Tuscan court in the mid-1610s. The exchanges between Benedetto Castelli and Galileo on one side, and the philosopher Cosimo Boscaglia on the other, with Grand Duchess Christina of Lorraine as patron and intermediary, share some analogies with the Leibniz–Clarke correspondence. Castelli had lunch with Christina, mother of Grand Duke Cosimo II, the Grand Duke himself, Boscaglia, and others. Apparently, Boscaglia had Christina's ear for a while. When Castelli left, he barely managed to get out of the palace before he was called back inside by Christina's porter. There, he was asked to reconcile passages from scripture with Copernicanism – notably where Joshua invoked God, asking him to stop the sun – a task Castelli accomplished brilliantly. This was a crucial episode in the attack against Galileo and Copernicanism, leading to his Copernican letters to Castelli, Piero Dini, and eventually Christina. Galileo's letter to the Grand Duchess was, at one and the same time, a continuation of the prior discussion after lunch when Copernicanism had been attacked and an appeal to an influential family member of Galileo's patrons.[7]

In the cases of both Christina and Caroline, one party used its contacts with a high-ranking female patron in order to launch an attack on the opposite side. In both cases the female patrons were not just spectators, but were known for their religious interests and orthodoxy, Christina on the Catholic side, Caroline on the Lutheran. Christina is described by the sources as a bigot in the hands of the papacy and, following Cosimo II's death in 1621, a regent possessed by religious zeal against state interests. By contrast, Caroline is depicted as an intellectual woman with a mind of her own. In her early twenties she showed sufficient independence of judgment to refuse to convert to Catholicism, thus renouncing marriage to the Emperor's son, in order to retain her Lutheran confession. Writing to a female patron, moreover, enabled Galileo, as well as Clarke and Leibniz, to reach a wider audience by addressing philosophical and theological issues in an intelligent, but not excessively technical fashion.[8]

On the philosopher's side, of course, Leibniz was a far more interesting and sophisticated thinker than Boscaglia, and his arguments are of incomparably greater philosophical import than the Joshua quotation from the Bible. Despite these important differences, however, the structure of the two events shows revealing similarities.

By appealing to such high-ranking patrons with such accusations as the claim that the Joshua passage in the Bible contradicted Copernicanism, or that Newton's and Locke's philosophies were detrimental to natural religion, philosophers were not just engaging in an intellectual debate. They were launching potentially devastating attacks with very serious consequences. Although Leibniz was not aiming at having Newton tried for heresy, he was certainly attempting to reduce him, together with his philosophical system, to the status of an intellectual pariah. Unable to reach an honorable settlement in the priority dispute over the invention of the calculus, Leibniz tried to undermine Newton and his allies through his contacts with the recently installed Princess of Wales.

Seen from this perspective, the correspondence between Leibniz and Clarke appears in a rather dramatic light. Leibniz's accusation of Socinianism, a discredited religious sect, launched against Clarke, Locke, and Newton was an important step in this strategy.[9] The contenders were trying not just to explain their philosophies to each other, but to undermine the very credibility of each other's system. This partly explains the very selective nature of the exchange, the inclusion of some topics, and the exclusion of others. Readers of Clarke's dedication to Caroline will not fail to realize the high stakes involved, as well as how astutely Clarke used his theological prowess and proximity to Caroline against his rival.

By reflecting on the genre of the correspondence, we are drawn into paying more attention to Caroline's role. After the early events in her life mentioned briefly above, she became very close to Leibniz, whose *Théodicée* was one of her favorite readings. It is certainly not by accident that Leibniz referred to it so frequently in his dispute with Clarke. In the absence of a queen, since George I's wife remained in Germany relegated to the Castle of Ahlden, Caroline was the highest female royal.[10] Her role and theological interests made her particularly influential on religious matters. Some said that the election of the new Archbishop of Canterbury, William Wake, in December 1715 was due to her good offices. It is not difficult to grasp from this perspective a dimension of the dispute that would have been obvious in its significance to contemporaries.

NEWTON'S ROLE

The role Newton played in the correspondence has been a matter of debate. It seems appropriate here briefly to review both sides of the argument, assessing their significance in relation to the circumstantial and documentary evidence.

Manuscript evidence indicating Newton's involvement in the exchange does exist, but it is scanty, especially bearing in mind how obsessively he drafted and redrafted his works. Alexandre Koyré and I. Bernard Cohen forcefully stated that they had found no drafts of Clarke's replies in Newton's hand, no suggestions as to what those replies should be, and not even versions of Clarke's replies with Newton's emendations. There is, however, a copy in Newton's hand of Leibniz's "Apostille" to his fourth letter on atoms and the void, where Newton wrote "received of the Princess May 7th 1716, and copied May 8." The Princess must have made the text available to Newton immediately upon its arrival, and with good reason.[11] At that time, between April and May 1716, Caroline witnessed several experiments on colors and the void. The king set a special room aside so that they could be performed in front of his daughter-in-law. This may have been necessary for the optical demonstrations, requiring a space sufficiently long and which could be suitably darkened. It is difficult to imagine that Newton was not involved in these experiments, especially since Caroline referred to them as "les expérimens du chevalier Newton." Moreover, in the same letter where Caroline announced that she was going to witness the experiments, she referred to a visit by Newton and Clarke with Conti.[12]

Thus, despite the relative lack of manuscript evidence, what we have does suggest that Newton was kept abreast of the developments not just by Clarke, but by Caroline as well. In addition, Clarke and Newton were neighbors, and Clarke served at Newton's parish, St. James's, and was rector of the chapel in Golden Square, of which Newton was a trustee. Circumstances for meeting and discussing the exchange, without the need to pass written documents, would have been plentiful, and indeed we know that Caroline herself warned Leibniz that Clarke's letters were not written "without the advice of the Chevalier Newton." Moreover, we know from the diary of Mary Cowper, Lady of the Bedchamber to Caroline, that on 11 February 1716 "Sir Isaac Newton and Dr Samuel Clarke came this afternoon to explain Sir Isaac's System of Philosophy to the Princess."[13] Thus historians looking for signs of Newton's involvement exclusively among Newton's manuscripts may have cast their nets too narrowly. Evidence from a broader set of sources strongly points to his having been involved in the dispute.

Alongside these remarks, one should not forget that Clarke was a powerful intellect in his own right and an able controversialist. His views were broadly, though not completely, in agreement with Newton's. Although he was clearly the material author of the letters on the English side of the dispute, his replies to Leibniz can be seen to some extent as the result of the collaboration between two minds working on the same wavelength.[14]

THE CORRESPONDENCE

These preliminary reflections are a useful springboard for a historicist reading of the correspondence, one taking into account circumstances of composition and authorship in conjunction with a number of themes interwoven with the religious and political events and debates of the day.

Unfortunately, we do not know what Leibniz wrote to Caroline in November 1715 in the letter that started the exchange. We know only the extract communicated by Caroline to Clarke, which seems to be cut out from a larger canvas, as the opening sentence and especially the word "itself" suggest: "Natual religion itself seems to decay." In the previous letter to Caroline of 10 May 1715, for example, Leibniz had outlined a sophisticated and effective argument on the doctrine of gravity and the Eucharist to embarrass the Newtonians. Topics related to other aspects of the decay of religion in England would thus have been at hand. Moreover, the extract from Leibniz's letter was selected by Caroline, and this is a significant feature. It seems at least plausible that Caroline selected for Clarke a portion she deemed suitable for an exchange. The fact that all subsequent exchanges went through her reinforces the importance of her role.

The opening words, "Natural religion," set the tone of the entire exchange. There was widespread belief in several quarters that the recent advancements of knowledge and the development of the experimental philosophy were going hand in hand with the strengthening of true religion. Leibniz's attack tried to put a devastating wedge between crucial points in Locke's and Newton's philosophies, on the one hand, and religious orthodoxy, on the other. This was a line of attack particularly suited to gaining Caroline's approval, and one Clarke had to reject thoroughly point by point. In his dedication to the Princess of Wales, he stated that "*Christianity* presupposes the Truth of *Natural Religion*. Whatsoever subverts Natural Religion, does consequently much more subvert Christianity: and whatsoever tends to confirm Natural Religion, is proportionably of Service to the True Interest of the Christian."[15]

The themes of the correspondence evolved from letter to letter. In some cases, such as Leibniz's attack on Locke's alleged opinion that the soul is material and perishable, Clarke did not see fit to mount a defense. In other cases, such as God's role in the universe, the exchange proceeded through all ten letters. Leibniz argued that in the Newtonian system God had to intervene from time to time in the mechanisms of the universe in order to repair it, as if God lacked foreknowledge to arrange them perfectly from the beginning. Clarke argued that Leibniz's system introduced materialism and fatality, in that the world continues by itself without any role for a deity. Other themes in the correspondence follow a similar pattern: for example, Leibniz's God has preordained the future course of events in the universe in the most perfect way, whereas Clarke's and Newton's God has to intervene every now and then to reach his purposes. Polemically, Clarke argued that Leibniz's God was *intelligentia supramondana*, emphasizing his detachment from the affairs of the world. The notion of miracle too is linked to this issue in that alterations to the normal course of nature were seen differently by the contenders. Clarke relied on the notion of what commonly happens in order to define a miracle. By contrast, Leibniz relied on the notion of laws of nature and what is not explicable by them in his definition. Thus attraction is obviously not miraculous according to Clarke, because it acts at each instant, whereas for Leibniz it is, because it transcends the power of bodies, which cannot act without being present.[16]

Probably the most heavily studied topic in the entire correspondence is the nature of space and time. The issue was raised in the first letter, when Leibniz accused Newton of having made space the *sensorium* of God. Indeed, Newton had unguardedly let this notion slip through his pen in two passages of his 1706 *Optice*, only one of which was removed in some copies, with an awkward cancel.[17]

The crucial point of the debate about space and time concerned again God's actions. In his attack Leibniz was able to construct an argument he had not previously put forward, although a similar line of reasoning can be found in the *Théodicée*.[18] He posited the principle of sufficient reason, namely that nothing happens without a reason, and argued that if space and time were something absolute and uniform, as Newton believed, the principle of sufficient reason would be violated. God could have created the universe in space, preserving the mutual situations among bodies, but changing for example West into East; similarly, he could have created the universe at a different instant. There could be no reason, however, why God could have chosen between two qualitatively identical situations, and thus in his act of creation he would have acted without a sufficient reason. Clarke's reply was that God's will was in itself a sufficient reason for his actions.

The existence of atoms too was attacked by Leibniz on the basis of a principle derived from that of sufficient reason, namely the identity of indiscernibles. Leibniz argued that if two qualitatively identical atoms existed, there would be no reason to place one of them here and the other there. God's wisdom would not allow him to create a world where he would have to make choices without reason, and therefore atoms do not exist. Later Leibniz argued that the existence of atoms would directly violate the other principle as well, because God would lack a sufficient reason to stop the divisibility of matter at one point rather than another.[19]

Caroline's presence as an arbiter between the contenders provided implicit guidelines for their correspondence, but his does not make the historian's task easier. Rather, it adds a dimension to the already complex field of Leibniz's, Clarke's, and Newton's theological and philosophical views.

NOTES

I wish to thank Daniel Garber, Andrew Janiak, Massimo Mugnai, and Richard Sorrenson for their help.

1   S. Shapin, "Of Gods and Kings: Politics and the Leibniz–Clarke dispute," *Isis* 72 (1981), 187–215, on 187. The most recent comprehensive account is E. Vailati, *Leibniz and Clarke: A Study of their Corresondence* (Oxford: Oxford University Press, 1997).

2   The main editions are the following: S. Clarke, *A collection of papers, which passed between the late learned Mr. Leibnitz and Dr. Clarke in the years 1715 and 1716: relating to the principles of natural philosophy and religion: with an appendix to which are added, letters to Dr. Clarke concerning liberty and necessity, from a gentleman of the University of Cambridge, with the doctor's answers to them: also, remarks upon a book, entituled, A philosophical enquiry concerning human liberty by Samuel Clarke* (London: James Knapton, 1717); H. G. Alexander, *The Leibniz–Clarke Correspondence* (Manchester: Manchester University Press, 1956); A. Robinet, *Correspondance Leibniz–Clarke présentée d'après les manuscrits originaux des bibliothèques de Hanovre et de Londres* (Paris: Presses Universitaires de France, 1957); V. Schüller, *Der Leibniz–Clarke Briefwechsel* (Berlin: Akademie Verlag, 1991), pp. 566–70. For editions of the private correspondence between Leibniz and Caroline see E. Ravier, *Bibliographie des œuvres de Leibniz* (Paris: F. Alcan, 1937).

3   O. Klopp, *Die Werke von Leibniz: Erste Reihe*, 11 vols. (Hanover: Klindworth, 1864–84), vol. 11.

4   The following reflections develop some of the themes explored in D. Bertoloni Meli, "Caroline, Leibniz, and Clarke," *Journal of the History of Ideas* 60 (1999), 469–86.

5   A. Koyré and I. B. Cohen, "Newton and the Leibniz–Clarke Correspondence," *Archives Internationales d'Histoire des Sciences* 15 (1962), 63–126.

6   E. J. Aiton, *Leibniz: A Biography* (Bristol and Boston: Hilger, 1985), pp. 171–2 and 180–6; R. C. Sleigh, *Leibniz and Arnauld: A Commentary on Their Correspondence* (New Haven: Yale University Press, 1990).

7   Joshua 10.12–13; S. Drake, *Galileo at Work* (Chicago: University of Chicago Press, 1978), p. 222. The critical edition of the letter to Christina is in *Le opere di Galileo Galilei*, ed. A. Favaro, 20 vols. in 21 (Florence: Le Monnier, 1890–1909), vol. 5, pp. 263–78 and 308–48. See also J. Dietz

Moss, "Galileo's *Letter to Christina*: Some Rhetorical Considerations," *Renaissance Quarterly* 36 (1983), 547–76; and E. McMullin, "Galileo on Science and Scripture," in P. Machamer (ed.), *The Cambridge Companion to Galileo* (Cambridge: Cambridge University Press, 1998), pp. 271–347.

8   On Caroline see Bertoloni Meli, "Caroline, Leibniz, and Clarke," pp. 471–4. On Christina see *Dizionario Biografico degli Italiani*.

9   This issue will be discussed below. On Socinianism see Nicholas Jolley, *Leibniz and Locke: A Study of the New Essays on Human Understanding* (Oxford: Clarendon Press, 1984), ch. 2.

10 Aiton, *Leibniz: A Biography*, pp. 177–8. For a discussion of Wake's election and its possible links to the dispute between Leibniz and Clarke see Bertoloni Meli, "Caroline, Leibniz, and Clarke," pp. 483–5.

11 Cambridge University Library, Add. MS 3968.36, fol. 517; Koyré and Cohen, "Newton and the Leibniz–Clarke Correspondence," p. 67; Richard S. Westfall, *Never at Rest: A Biography of Isaac Newton* (Cambridge: Cambridge University Press, 1980), p. 778.

12 Caroline to Leibniz, 24 April, 15 May, and 26 May 1716, in Klopp, *Leibniz*, vol. 11, pp. 90–1, 93 and 112, respectively. On 24 April Caroline wrote: "Après demain nous aurons les expérimens du chevalier Newton. Le Roy a donné une chambre pour celà. Je vous y souhaite comme aussi pour samedi, où le chevalier Newton, l'abbé Conti et Mr Clarke seront avec moy."

13 *Diary of Mary Countess Cowper, Lady of the Bedchamber to the Princess of Wales, 1714–1720* (London, 1864), p. 74.

14 Vailati, *Leibniz and Clarke*, pays attention to Clarke's intellectual abilities. On Clarke see *Dictionary of Scientific Biography, Dictionary of National Biography*, and L. Stewart, *The Rise of Public Science* (Cambridge: Cambridge University Press, 1992), ch. 3; M. C. Jacob, *The Newtonians and the English Revolution, 1689–1720* (Ithaca, NY: Cornell University Press, 1976), ch. 4.

15 S. Clarke, dedication, p. vi. On Leibniz and the Eucharist, see Robert Merrihew Adams, *Leibniz: Determinist, Theist, Idealist* (New York: Oxford University Press, 1994), pp. 349–60.

16 See especially Leibniz, iii, 17 and Clarke, iii, 17.

17 The details of this typographic and philosophico-theological case are reconstructed in A. Koyré and I. B. Cohen, "The Case of the Missing *Tanquam*: Leibniz, Newton and Clarke," *Isis* 52 (1961), 555–66.

18 Bertoloni Meli, "Caroline, Leibniz and Clarke," pp. 482–3.

19 Leibniz, iv, 1ff. See also the "Apostille" to Leibniz's fourth paper.

BIBLIOGRAPHY

The first part of this bibliography lists Newton's writings in three groups: those published in his lifetime, works published posthumously during the first decades after he died, and edited collections of his papers. Although the works Newton published in his lifetime were monumental in their impact, after the initial flurry provoked by his first two papers on optics, they were few in number both by our standards and by those of his time, comprising a small fraction of his surviving writings. Extensive publication of his remaining papers and manuscripts began only in the 1950s and is still continuing. Through the extraordinary effort of D. T. Whiteside, Newton's mathematical papers, including work in mathematical physics, have been gathered into eight volumes, stretching from his undergraduate years in Cambridge until his final decade. One volume of his optical writings is now in print, and the second volume will soon appear. Efforts continue on compiling and publishing his writings in chemistry and alchemy, almost none of which has ever been put into print; these include detailed recordings of a vast array of experiments Newton personally conducted. Efforts are also under way on his theological manuscripts, the majority of which became available only after they were deposited as the Yahuda Papers in the Jewish National and University Library in Jerusalem. Beyond these efforts, with Cambridge University's purchase now completed, the Earl of Macclesfield Collection of Newton's papers should soon be open to general scholarly examination for the first time. The next few decades will therefore be adding significantly to the list of Newton's printed works.

The second part of the bibliography provides a selection of notable writings on Newton, separated into groups corresponding to the major areas of his intellectual endeavors. Our selection is limited to works in English, omitting many outstanding studies in French and German. It also concentrates on comparatively recent works. One reason for this is the thorough listing in *Newton and Newtoniana 1672–1675: A Bibliography* published by Peter Wallis and Ruth Wallis in 1977, to which readers can turn to survey earlier writings. A second reason is the transformation in Newton scholarship that has resulted from the continuing publication of his papers and manuscripts (see the Introduction to *Isaac Newton's Natural Philosophy*, edited by Jed Buchwald and I. Bernard Cohen). The literature on Newton is so vast and so constantly growing that it is not possible to list in a small compass all the works that might be of use to readers of this volume, even all those published in the last few decades. Limitations of space have forced us to remove from our preliminary list many works of great merit. Their absence should not be taken as a negative judgment concerning their worth. The works we list under Handbooks and Bibliographies contain further listings of secondary sources, as do the individual chapters in this book.

PART I NEWTON'S WORKS

A list of Newton's more important works, published and unpublished, along with details of their becoming available and published, can be found in Derek Gjertsen, *The Newton Handbook*, pp. 614–23.

1a. Published in his lifetime (plus editions and reprints)

Papers on light and colors

Appearing in *Philosophical Transactions of the Royal Society*, 1672–6; facsimile reprints are in I. Bernard Cohen and Robert E. Schofield (eds.), *Isaac Newton's Letters and Papers on Natural Philosophy*.
"A Letter of Mr. Isaac Newton, Professor of the Mathematics in the University of Cambridge; containing his New Theory about Light and Colors," *Phil. Trans.* 80 (February 1671/2), 3075–87.
"An Account of a New Catadioptrical Telescope invented by Mr. Newton," *Phil. Trans.* 81 (March 1672), 4004–10.
"Mr. Newton's Letter to the Publisher of March 26, 1672, containing some more suggestions about his New Telescope," *Phil. Trans.* 82 (April 1672), 4032–4.
"An Extract of another Letter of the same to the Publisher, dated March 30, 1672, by way of Answer to some Objections, made by an Ingenious French Philosopher [A. Auzout] to the New Reflecting Telescope," *Phil. Trans.* 82 (April 1672), 4034–5.
"Mr. Isaac Newton's Considerations upon part of a Letter of Monsieur de Bercé printed in the Eighth French *Memoire*, containing the Catadioptrical Telescope, pretended to be improv'd and refined by Mr. Cassegrain," *Phil. Trans.* 83 (May 1672), 4056–9.
"Some Experiments proposed in relation to Mr. Newton's Theory of light, printed in Numb. 80; together with the Observations made thereupon by the Author of that Theory," *Phil. Trans.* 83 (May 1672), 4059–62.

"Mr. Newton's Letter of April 13, 1672 ... being an Answer to the foregoing Letter of P. Pardies," *Phil. Trans.* 84 (June 1672), pp. 4087–93.

"A Series of *Quere's* propounded by Mr. Isaac Newton, to be determined by Experiments, positively and directly concluding his new Theory of Light and Colours," *Phil. Trans.* 85 (July 1672), pp. 5004–7.

"Mr. Newtons Answer to the foregoing [second] Letter [of P. Pardies]," *Phil. Trans.* 85 (July 1672), pp. 5012–18.

"Mr. Isaac Newtons Answer to some Considerations [of Robert Hooke] upon his Doctrine of Light and Colors," *Phil. Trans.* 88 (November 1672), 5084–103.

"Mr. Newtons Answer to the foregoing Letter [of Christiaan Huygens] further explaining his Theory of Light and Colors, and particularly that of Whiteness; together with his continued hopes of perfecting Telescopes by Reflections rather than Refractions," *Phil. Trans.* 96 (July 1673), 6087–92.

"An Extract of Mr. Isaac Newton's Letter, written to the Publisher from Cambridge April 3, 1673, concerning the Number of Colors, and the Necessity of mixing them all for the Production of White, [in further response to Huygens]," *Phil. Trans.* 97 (October 1673), 6108–11.

"An Answer to this Letter [of Franc. Linus]," *Phil. Trans.* 110 (January 1674/5), 150.

"Mr. Isaac Newton's Considerations on the former Reply [to Linus]; together with further Directions, how to make Experiments controverted aright," *Phil. Trans.* 121 (January 1675/6), 500–2.

"An Extract of another Letter of Mr. Newton, written to the Publisher the 10th of January 1675/6, relating to the same Argument," *Phil. Trans.* 121 (January 1675/6), 503–4.

"A particular Answer of Mr. Isaak Newton to Mr. Linus his Letter, printed in Numb. 121, p. 499, about an Experiment relating to the New Doctrine of Light and Colours," *Phil. Trans.* 123 (March 1676), 556–61.

"Mr. Newton's Answer to the precedent Letter [of Anthony Lucas]," *Phil. Trans.* 128 (September 1676), 698–705.

The *Principia*

Philosophiae Naturalis Principia Mathematica (London, 1687; 2nd edition, Cambridge, 1713; 3rd edition, London, 1726). The second edition was reprinted in Amsterdam in 1714 and again in 1723. The third edition was reprinted in Geneva in 1739–42 (with an extensive commentary) and again in 1760, as well as in Prague in 1780–5; the third edition was also reprinted in Samuel Horsley's edition of Newton's *Opera* (London, 1779–82), 5 vols. Bibliographical details of these, the several *Excerpta* in Latin and in English, and translations into other languages are given in the Variorum edition of Koyré and Cohen, listed below, Appendix VIII, pp. 851–83.

Isaac Newton's Philosophiae Naturalis Principia Mathematica, the Third Edition with Variant Readings, ed. A. Koyré and I. B. Cohen, with the assistance of Anne Whitman (Cambridge, MA: Harvard University Press; Cambridge: Cambridge University Press, 1972).

The Principia, Mathematical Principles of Natural Philosophy: A New Translation, trans. I. Bernard Cohen and Anne Whitman, with the assistance of Julia Budenz, preceded by "A Guide to Newton's *Principia*" by I. B. Cohen (Berkeley: University of California Press, 1999).

The *Opticks*

Opticks: or, A Treatise of the Reflexions, Refractions, Inflexions and Colours of Light (London, 1704; Latin edition, London, 1706; third edition, London, 1717/18).

Opticks: or, A Treatise of the Reflections, Refractions, Inflections and Colours of Light. Based on the Fourth Edition London, 1730, with a preface by I. B. Cohen, a forward by Albert Einstein, an introduction by E. T. Whittaker, and an analytical table of contents by Duane H. D. Roller (New York: Dover Publications, 1952).

Other publications in Newton's lifetime (in chronological order)

[Anonymously] "Epistola missa and praenobilem virum D. Carolum Montague Armigerum, Scaccarii Regii apud Anglos Cancellarium, & Societatis Regiae Praesidium, in qua solvuntur duo problemata mathematica à Johanne Bernoullo Mathematico celeberrimo proposita," *Phil. Trans.* 224 (January 1696/7), 348–9. Reports Newton's solution to the problem of the curve of fastest descent. (Reprinted in Whiteside [ed.], *The Mathematical Papers of Isaac Newton*, vol. 8.)

"Scala graduum Caloris," *Phil. Trans.* 270 (March and April 1701), 824–9. (Reprinted in Cohen and Schofield [eds.], *Isaac Newton's Letters and Papers on Natural Philosophy*.)

"Theoria Lunae," an Appendix to David Gregory, *Astronomiae Physicae & Geometricae Elementa* (Latin edition, Oxford, 1702; English edition, London, 1715); English version published as a pamphlet in 1702 and reprinted in facsimile in *Isaac Newton's Theory of the Moon's Motion (1702)*, introduction by I. B. Cohen (Folkestone: Dawson, 1975).

"Tractatus de quadratura curvarum" and "Enumeratio linearum tertii ordinis," published as Appendices to the first edition of the *Opticks*, 1704; an English translation of the "Tractatus" appeared in John Harris, *Lexicon*

Technicum in 1710. (Reprinted in Whiteside [ed.], *The Mathematical Papers of Isaac Newton*, vols. 7 and 8.)

Arithmetica Universalis, ed. William Whiston (Cambridge, 1707; first English translation, 1720; second Latin edition, edited by John Machin, 1722). (Reprinted in Whiteside [ed.], *The Mathematical Papers of Isaac Newton*, vol. 5.)

"De natura acidorum" and "Some Thoughts about the *Nature* of *Acids*," in John Harris, *Lexicon Technicum: Or, An Universal English Dictionary of ARTS and SCIENCES: explaining Not only the TERMS of ART, but the ARTS Themselves*, vol. 2, Introduction (London, 1710). (Reprinted in Cohen and Schofield [eds.], *Isaac Newton's Letters and Papers on Natural Philosophy*.)

"De analysi per aequationes numero terminorum infinitas," in William Jones, *Analysis per Quantitatum Series Fluxiones ac Differentias: Cum Enumeratione Linearum Tertii Ordinis* (London, 1711). (Reprinted in Whiteside [ed.], *The Mathematical Papers of Isaac Newton*, vol. 2.)

"Methodis differentialis," in William Jones, *Analysis per Quantitatum Series Fluxiones ac Differentias: Cum Enumeratione Linearum Tertii Ordinis* (London, 1711). (Reprinted in Whiteside [ed.], *The Mathematical Papers of Isaac Newton*, vol. 4.)

[Anonymously] "Problematis mathematicis anglis nuper propositi Solutio Generalis," *Phil. Trans.* 347 (January–March 1716), 399–400. (Reprinted in Whiteside [ed.], *The Mathematical Papers of Isaac Newton*, vol. 8.)

[Anonymously] "An Account of the Book entituled *Commercium Epistolicum Collinii & aliorum, De Analysi Promota*; published by order of the Royal Society, in relation to the Dispute between Mr. Leibnitz and Dr. Keill, about the Right Invention of the Method of Fluxions, by some call'd the Differential Method," *Phil. Trans.* 342 (1715), 173–224. (Reprinted in facsimile in A. R. Hall, *Philosophers at War: The Quarrel between Newton and Leibniz*, pp. 263–314.)

"Tabula refractorum," *Phil. Trans.* 368 (1721), 172.

[Anonymously] "Ad lectorem," in *Commercium Epistolicum Collinii & aliorum, De Analysi Promota*, 2nd edition, ed. John Keill (London, 1722).

A Short Chronicle from the First Memory of Things in Europe to the Conquest of Persia by Alexander the Great, first published in a French translation in 1725 and then in English, edited by John Conduitt (London, 1728).

[Anonymously] "Remarks upon the Observations made upon a Chronological Index of Sir Isaac Newton," *Phil. Trans.* 389 (1726), 315–21.

1b. Published for the first time in the decades after Newton died

The Chronology of Ancient Kingdoms Amended, edited by John Conduitt (London, 1728).

A Treatise of the System of the World, a translation (published first) of "De motu corporum liber secundus," Newton's original concluding book of the *Principia,* retitled by the translator (London, 1728).

De Mundi Systemate Liber, retitled publication of "De motu corporum liber secundus," Newton's original concluding book of the *Principia* (London, 1728). A new translation by I. B. Cohen and Anne Whitman is scheduled for publication by the University of California Press.

Optical Lectures read in the Public Schools of the University of Cambridge, Anno Domini, 1669, translated from the Latin (London, 1729).

Lectiones Opticae, annis MDCLXIX, MDCLXX, MDCLXXI (London, 1729).

The Mathematical Principles of Natural Philosophy, translated into English by Andrew Motte; to which are added, *The Laws of the Moon's Motion, according to Gravity,* by John Machin (London, 1729). (Facsimile reprint [London: Dawsons of Pall Mall, 1968]; reprinted without Machin's appendix as *The Principia* [Amherst, NY: Prometheus, 1995].)

Observations upon the Prophecies of Daniel and the Apocalypse of St. John, edited by Benjamin Smith (London and Dublin, 1733). (Reprinted in W. Whitlaw, *Sir Isaac Newton's Daniel and the Apocalypse with an Introductory Study... of Unbelief, Miracles and Prophecy* [London: John Murray, 1922].)

The Method of Fluxions and Infinite Series; with its Application to the Geometry of Curve-Lines, translated from the Latin (London, 1736).

A Treatise of the Method of Fluxions and Infinite Series, with its Application to the Geometry of Curve Lines, translated from the Latin (London, 1737). (Reprinted in Whiteside [ed.], *The Mathematical Papers of Isaac Newton,* vol. 1.)

A Dissertation upon the Sacred Cubit of the Jews, edited by Thomas Birch in *Works of John Greaves,* vol. 2 (London, 1737), pp. 405–33.

"A Description of an Instrument for Observing the Moon's Distance from the Fixt Stars at Sea," *Phil. Trans.* 465 (October 1742), 155–6. (Reprinted in Cohen and Schofield [eds.], *Isaac Newton's Letters and Papers on Natural Philosophy.*)

"An Hypothesis Explaining the Properties of Light" [Newton's second paper on color and light], read to the Royal Society in December 1675/6, printed in Thomas Birch, *The History of the Royal Society of London* (London: A. Millar, 1757), pp. 247–305. (Reprinted in Cohen and Schofield [eds.], *Isaac Newton's Letters and Papers on Natural Philosophy.*)

Four Letters from Sir Isaac Newton to Doctor Bentley concerning Some Arguments in Proof of a Deity, a pamphlet (London: R. and J. Dodsley, 1756). (Reprinted in Cohen and Schofield [eds.], *Isaac Newton's Letters and Papers on Natural Philosophy.*)

1c. Edited collections of Newton's papers

Cohen, I. Bernard and Schofield, Robert E. (eds.), *Isaac Newton's Letters and Papers on Natural Philosophy*, revised edition (Cambridge, MA: Harvard University Press, 1978).

Edleston, J., *Correspondence of Sir Isaac Newton and Professor Cotes, including letters of other eminent men, now first published from the originals in the Library of Trinity College, Cambridge; together with an appendix, containing other unpublished letters and papers by Newton* (London: John W. Parker; Cambridge: John Deighton, 1850).

Hall, A. Rupert and Hall, Marie Boas (eds.), *Unpublished Scientific Papers of Isaac Newton: A Selection from the Portsmouth Papers in the University Library, Cambridge* (Cambridge: Cambridge University Press, 1962).

Herivel, John, *The Background to Newton's* Principia: *A Study of Newton's Dynamical Researches in the Years 1664–84* (Oxford: Clarendon Press, 1965).

McGuire, John E. and Tamny, Martin (eds.), *Certain Philosophical Questions: Newton's Trinity Notebook* (Cambridge: Cambridge University Press, 1983).

Rigaud, Stephen Peter, *Correspondence of Scientific Men of the Eighteenth Century...in the Collection of...the Earl of Macclesfield*, 2 vols. (Oxford: Oxford University Press, 1841).

Shapiro, Alan E. (ed.), *The Optical Papers of Isaac Newton, Volume 1: The Optical Lectures 1670–1672* (Cambridge: Cambridge University Press, 1984).

The Correspondence of Isaac Newton, edited by Herbert. W. Turnbull, John F. Scott, A. Rupert Hall, and Laura Tilling, 7 vols. (Cambridge: Cambridge University Press, 1959–77).

Whiteside, D. T. (ed.), *The Mathematical Works of Isaac Newton*, 2 vols. (New York: Johnson Reprint Corporation, 1964, 1967). Contains facsimile reprints of the translations into English of works that enabled Newton's contemporaries and successors to learn his mathematical methods.

The Mathematical Papers of Isaac Newton, 8 vols. (Cambridge: Cambridge University Press, 1967–81).

The Preliminary Manuscripts for Isaac Newton's 1687 Principia, *1684–1686* (Cambridge: Cambridge University Press: 1989). Contains facsimiles of the handwritten manuscripts.

PART 2 SELECT WRITINGS ON NEWTON

Handbooks, bibliographies, and collections of documents

Gjertsen, Derek, *The Newton Handbook* (London and New York: Routledge and Kegan Paul, 1986).

Gray, George J., *Sir Isaac Newton: A Bibliography, together with a List of Books Illustrating His Works* (Cambridge: Bowes and Bowes, 1907).

Harrison, John, *The Library of Isaac Newton* (Cambridge: Cambridge University Press, 1978).

Hiscock, W. G. (ed.), *David Gregory, Isaac Newton, and Their Circle: Extracts from David Gregory's Memoranda* (Oxford: printed for the editor, 1937).

Wallis, Peter and Wallis, Ruth, *Newton and Newtoniana 1672–1975: A Bibliography* (London: Dawsons, 1977).

Biographies (in chronological order)

Hall, A. Rupert (ed.), *Isaac Newton, Eighteenth-Century Perspectives*, a collection of early biographical memoirs (Oxford: Oxford University Press, 1999).

Fontenelle, Bernard le Bovier de, *The Elogium of Sir Isaac Newton: by Monsieur Fontenelle, Perpetual Secretary of the Royal Academy of Sciences at Paris* (London: J. Tonson, 1728). (Reprinted in Cohen and Schofield [eds.], *Isaac Newton's Letters and Papers on Natural Philosophy.*)

Stukeley, William, *Memoirs of Sir Isaac Newton's Life, 1752: Being some account of his family and chiefly of the junior part of his life*, edited by A. Hastings White (London: Taylor & Francis, 1936).

Brewster, Sir David, *Memoirs of the Life, Writings, and Discoveries of Sir Isaac Newton*, 2 vols. (Edinburgh: Thomas Constable and Co., 1855). (Photo-reprint with a new introduction by R. S. Westfall [New York and London: Johnson Reprint Corporation, 1965].)

More, Louis Trenchard, *Isaac Newton: A Biography* (New York and London: Charles Scribner's Sons, 1934). (Reprint edition, New York: Dover Publications, 1962).

Keynes, John Maynard, "Newton, the Man," in *Essays in Biography* (New York: W. W. Norton & Company, 1963), pp. 310–23.

Manuel, Frank E., *A Portrait of Issac Newton* (Cambridge, MA: Belknap Press of Harvard University, 1968). (Reissued as a Da Capo Press paperback.)

Cohen, I. Bernard, "Newton, Isaac," *Dictionary of Scientific Biography*, vol. 10 (New York: Charles Scribner's Sons, 1974), pp. 41–103.

Westfall, Richard Samuel, *Never at Rest: A Biography of Isaac Newton* (Cambridge: Cambridge University Press, 1983). (The premier intellectual biography.)

Christianson, Gale E., *In The Presence of the Creator: Isaac Newton and His Times* (New York: Free Press, 1984).

Hall, A. Rupert, *Isaac Newton: Adventurer in Thought* (Oxford: Blackwell, 1992).

Westfall, Richard Samuel, *The Life of Isaac Newton* (Cambridge: Cambridge University Press, 1993). (A condensed version of *Never at Rest*.)

Collections of studies

Bechler, Zev (ed.), *Contemporary Newtonian Scholarship* (Dordrecht: D. Reidel Publishing Company, 1982).

Bricker, Phillip and Hughes, R. I. G. (eds.), *Philosophical Perspectives on Newtonian Science* (Cambridge, MA: MIT Press, 1990).

Buchwald, Jed and Cohen, I. Bernard (eds.), *Isaac Newton's Natural Philosophy* (Cambridge, MA: MIT Press, 2001).

Cohen, I. Bernard and Westfall, Richard S. (eds.), *Newton: Texts, Backgrounds, and Commentaries*, A Norton Critical Edition (New York: W. W. Norton & Company, 1995).

Dalitz Richard H. and Nauenberg, Michael (eds.), *The Foundations of Newtonian Scholarship* (Singapore: World Scientific, 2000).

Durham, F. and Puddington, R. D. (eds.), *Some Truer Method: Reflections on the Heritage of Newton* (New York: Columbia University Press, 1990).

Fauvel, John, Flood, Raymond, Shortland, Michael, and Wilson, Robin (eds.), *Let Newton Be! A New Perspective on his Life and Works* (Oxford: Oxford University Press, 1988).

Greenstreet, W. J. (ed.), *Isaac Newton, 1642–1727: A Memorial Volume Edited for the Mathematical Association* (London: G. Bell and Sons, 1927).

King-Hele, D. G. and Hall, A. R. (eds.), *Newton's* Principia *and its Legacy*, Proceedings of a Royal Society Discussion Meeting of 30 June 1987 (London: The Royal Society, 1988).

Palter, Robert (ed.), *The Annus Mirabilis of Sir Isaac Newton 1666–1966* (Cambridge, MA: MIT Press, 1970).

Theerman, P. and Seef, A. F. (eds.), *Action and Reaction* (Newark: University of Delaware Press, 1993).

Beyond Hypothesis: Newton's Experimental Philosophy, Proceedings of a Conference at St. John's College, Annapolis, *The St. John's Review* 45, no. 2 (1999).

Sir Isaac Newton, 1727–1927: A Bicentenary Evaluation of His Work, a series of papers prepared under the auspices of the History of Science Society (Baltimore: The Williams and Wilkins Company, 1928).

Newton Tercentenary Celebrations, the Royal Society (Cambridge: Cambridge University Press, 1947).

Some general works

Blay, Michel, *Reasoning with the Infinite: From the Closed World to the Mathematical Universe*, trans. M. B. DeBevoise (Chicago: University of Chicago Press, 1998).

Cohen, I. Bernard, *The Newtonian Revolution* (Cambridge: Cambridge University Press, 1980).

The Birth of a New Physics, revised and updated edition (New York: W. W. Norton & Company, 1985).

Dobbs, Betty Jo Teeter and Jacob, Margaret C., *Newton and the Culture of Newtonianism* (Atlantic Highlands, NJ: Humanities Press, 1995).

Gabbey, Alan, "Force and Inertia in Seventeenth-Century Dynamics," *Studies in History and Philosophy of Science* 2 (1971), 1–67.

Guerlac, Henry, *Essays and Papers in the History of Modern Science* (Baltimore: Johns Hopkins University Press, 1977). (Includes a major section on Newton, including important studies on experiments by Newton and Hauksbee.)

Newton on the Continent (Ithaca, NY: Cornell University Press, 1981).

Harper, William and Smith, George E., "Newton's New Way of Inquiry," in Jarrett Leplin (ed.), *The Creation of Ideas in Physics: Studies for a Methodology of Theory Construction* (Dordrecht: Kluwer Academic Publishers, 1995).

Hesse, Mary B., *Forces and Fields: The Concept of Action at a Distance in the History of Physics* (London: Thomas Nelson and Sons, 1961; Totowa, NJ: Littlefield, Adams & Co., 1965).

Koyré, Alexandre, *Newtonian Studies* (Cambridge, MA: Harvard University Press; London: Chapman & Hall, 1965).

McMullin, Ernan, *Newton on Matter and Activity* (Notre Dame, IN: University of Notre Dame Press, 1978).

Westfall, Richard S., *Force in Newton's Physics: The Science of Dynamics in the Seventeenth Century* (London: Macdonald; New York: American Elsevier, 1971).

The Construction of Modern Science: Mechanisms and Mechanics (Cambridge: Cambridge University Press, 1977).

Wilson, Curtis, "From Kepler's Laws, So-called, to Universal Gravitation," *Archive for History of Exact Sciences* 6 (1970), 89–170.

Studies of the Principia and related topics

Ball, W. W. Rouse, *An Essay on Newton's* Principia (London and New York: Macmillan and Co., 1893). (Reprinted New York and London: Johnson Reprint Corporation, 1972.)

Bertoloni Meli, Domenico, "The Relativization of Centrifugal Force," *Isis* 81 (1990), 23–43.

Brackenridge, J. Bruce, *The Key to Newton's Dynamics: The Kepler Problem and the* Principia, with English translations from the Latin by Mary Ann Rossi (Berkeley: University of California Press, 1995). Contains English versions of the first edition of initial sections of the *Principia*.

Chandrasekhar, S., *Newton's* Principia *for the Common Reader* (Oxford: Clarendon Press, 1995).

Cohen, I. Bernard, "Hypotheses in Newton's Philosophy," *Physis* 8 (1966), 163–84.

Guide to Newton's Principia (part of the new English translation of the *Principia*, listed above).

Introduction to Newton's "Principia" (Cambridge, MA: Harvard University Press; Cambridge: Cambridge University Press, 1971).

de Gandt, François, *Force and Geometry in Newton's* Principia, trans. Curtis Wilson (Princeton: Princeton University Press, 1995).

Densmore, Dana, *Newton's* Principia: *The Central Argument*, with translations and illustrations by William Donahue (Santa Fe, New Mexico: Green Lion Press, 1995).

DiSalle, Robert, "Space-Time Theory as Physical Geometry," *Erkenntnis* 42 (1995), 317–37.

Dobson, Geoffrey J., "Newton's Problems with Rigid Body Dynamics in the Light of his Treatment of the Precession of the Equinoxes," *Archive for History of Exact Sciences* 53 (1998), 125–45.

Earman, John, *World Enough and Space-Time: Absolute versus Relational Theories of Space and Time* (Cambridge, MA: MIT Press, 1989).

Earman, John and Friedman, Michael, "The Meaning and Status of Newton's Law of Inertia and the Nature of Gravitational Forces," *Philosophy of Science* 40 (1973), 329–59.

Ehrlichson, Herman, "The Visualization of Quadratures in the Mystery of Corollary 3 to Proposition 41 of Newton's *Principia*," *Historia Mathematica* 21 (1994), 145–51.

Guicciardini, Niccolò, *Reading the* Principia: *The Debate on Newton's Mathematical Methods for Natural Philosophy from 1687 to 1736* (Cambridge: Cambridge University Press, 1999).

Harper, William, "Isaac Newton on Empirical Success and Scientific Method," in John Earman and John D. Norton (eds.), *The Cosmos of Science: Essays of Exploration* (Pittsburgh: University of Pittsburgh Press, 1997), pp. 55–86.

"Measurement and Approximation: Newton's Inferences from Phenomena versus Glymour's Bootstrap Confirmation," in P. Weingartner, G. Schurz, and G. Dorn (eds.), *The Role of Pragmatics in Contemporary Philosophy* (Vienna: Hölder-Pichler-Tempsky, 1998), pp. 65–87.

Herivel, John, *The Background to Newton's* Principia: *A Study of Newton's Dynamical Researches in the Years 1664–84* (Oxford: Clarendon Press, 1965).

Kollerstrom, Nicholas, *Newton's Forgotten Lunar Theory: His Contribution to the Quest for Longitude* (Santa Fe, New Mexico: Green Lion Press, 2000).

Lakatos, Imre, "Newton's Effect on Scientific Standards," in *The Methodology of Scientific Research Programmes, Philosophical Papers*, vol. 1 (Cambridge: Cambridge University Press, 1978), pp. 193–222.

Nauenberg, Michael, "Newton's Early Computational Method for Dynamics," *Archive for History of Exact Sciences* 46 (1994), 221–52.

"Hooke, Orbital Motion and Newton's *Principia*," *American Journal of Physics* 62 (1994), 331–50.

"Newton's Portsmouth Perturbation Method and its Application to Lunar Motion," in Dalitz and Nauenberg (eds.), *The Foundations of Newtonian Scholarship*, listed above, pp. 167–94.

Rigaud, Stephen Peter *Historical Essay on the First Publication of Sir Isaac Newton's* Principia (Oxford: Oxford University Press, 1838). (Reprinted New York and London: Johnson Reprint Corporation, 1972.)

Rynasiewicz, Robert, "By Their Properties, Causes and Effects: Newton's Scholium on Time, Space, Place and Motion," *Studies in History and Philosophy of Science* 26 (1995), 133–53, 295–321.

Smith, George E., "The Newtonian Style in Book II of the *Principia*," in Buchwald and Cohen (ed.), *Isaac Newton's Natural Philosophy*, listed above, pp. 249–313. An appendix includes English translations of the passages from the first edition replaced or removed in the second and third.

"From the Phenomenon of the Ellipse to an Inverse-Square Force: Why Not?," in David Malament (ed.), *Reading Natural Philosophy: Essays in the History and Philosophy of Science and Mathematics to Honor Howard Stein on his 70th Birthday* (La Salle: Open Court, 2002).

Stein, Howard, "Newtonian Space-Time," *Texas Quarterly* 10 (1967), 174–200; reprinted in Palter (ed.), *The Annus Mirabilis of Sir Isaac Newton 1666–1966*, listed above.

"'From the Phenomena of Motions of the Forces of Nature'; Hypothesis or Deduction?" *PSA 1990*, Proceedings of the 1990 Biennial Meeting of the Philosophy of Science Association, vol. 2 (East Lansing, MI: Philosophy of Science Association, 1991), pp. 209–22.

Taton, René and Wilson, Curtis (eds.), *Planetary Astronomy from the Renaissance to the Rise of Astrophysics, Tycho Brahe to Newton*, vol. 2, part A of *The General History of Astronomy* (Cambridge: Cambridge University Press, 1989). Especially noteworthy is Curtis Wilson's "The Newtonian Achievement in Astronomy," pp. 273–4.

Planetary Astronomy from the Renaissance to the Rise of Astrophysics, The Eighteenth and Nineteenth Centuries, vol. 2, part B of *The General History of Astronomy* (Cambridge: Cambridge University Press, 1995).

Weinstock, Robert, "Inverse-Square Orbits in Newton's *Principia* and Twentieth-Century Commentary Thereon," *Archive for History of Exact Sciences* 55 (2000), 137–62.

Whiteside, D. T., *The Mathematical Principles Underlying Newton's Principia* (Glasgow: University of Glasgow, 1970); reprinted in *The Journal for the History of Astronomy* 1 (1970), 116–38.

"The Prehistory of the *Principia* from 1664–1686," *Notes and Records, The Royal Society* 45 (1991), 11–61.

Whiteside, D. T. (ed.), *The Mathematical Papers of Isaac Newton*, vol. 6, listed above.

Wilson, Curtis, *Astronomy from Kepler to Newton: Historical Studies* (London: Variorum Reprints, 1989). Of special interest to philosophers is "Newton and Some Philosophers on Kepler's 'Laws'," which originally appeared in *Journal for the History of Ideas* 35 (1974), 231–58.

Mathematics

Guicciardini, Niccolò, *The Development of Newtonian Calculus in Britain, 1700–1800* (Cambridge: Cambridge University Press, 1989).

Pourciau, Bruce, "On Newton's Proof that Inverse-Square Orbits must be Conics," *Annals of Science* 48 (1991), 159–72.

"The Preliminary Mathematical Lemmas of Newton's *Principia*," *Archive for History of Exact Sciences* 52 (1998), 279–95.

"The Integrability of Ovals: Newton's Lemma 28 and its Counterexamples," *Archive for History of Exact Sciences*, 55 (2001), 479–99.

Turnbull, Henry Westren, *The Mathematical Discoveries of Newton* (London and Glasgow: Blackie & Son, 1945).

Whiteside, D. T., "Patterns of Mathematical Thought in the Later Seventeenth Century," *Archive for History of Exact Sciences* 1 (1961), 179–388.

Whiteside, D. T. (ed.), *The Mathematical Papers of Isaac Newton*, 8 vols., listed above. The editor's introductions and annotations in these volumes provide detailed, step-by-step analyses of Newton's mathematics and place Newton's efforts in their historical context.

Newton and Leibniz

Aiton, Eric J., *Leibniz, a Biography* (Bristol: Adam Hilger, 1985).

Alexander, H. G. (ed.): *The Leibniz–Clarke Correspondence* (Manchester: Manchester University Press, 1956).

Bertoloni Meli, Domenico, *Equivalence and Priority: Newton versus Leibniz* (Oxford: Clarendon Press, 1993), including Leibniz's unpublished manuscript notes on the *Principia*.

Hall, A. Rupert, *Philosophers at War: The Quarrel between Newton and Leibniz* (Cambridge: Cambridge University Press, 1980).

Vailati, Ezio, *Leibniz and Clarke: A Study of Their Correspondence* (Oxford: Oxford University Press, 1997).

Whiteside, D. T. (ed.), *The Mathematical Papers of Isaac Newton*, vol. 8.

Optics

Hall, A. Rupert, *And All Was Light: An Introduction to Newton's Opticks* (Oxford: Clarendon Press, 1993).

Laymon, Ronald, "Newton's *Experimentum Crucis* and the Logic of Idealization and Theory Refutation," *Studies in History and Philosophy of Science* 9 (1978), 51–77.

Sabra, A. I., *Theories of Light from Descartes to Newton*, 2nd edition (Cambridge: Cambridge University Press, 1981).

Schaffer, Simon, "Glass Works: Newton's Prisms and the Use of Experiment," in David Gooding, Trevor Pinch, and Simon Schaffer (eds.), *The Use of Experiment: Studies in the Natural Sciences* (Cambridge: Cambridge University Press, 1989), pp. 67–104.

Sepper, Dennis L., *Newton's Optical Writings: A Guided Study*. (New Brunswick, NJ: Rutgers University Press, 1994).

Shapiro, Alan E., "The Evolving Structure of Newton's Theory of White Light and Color: 1670–1704," *Isis* 71 (1980), 211–35.

Fits, Passions, and Paroxysms: Physics, Method, and Chemistry and Newton's Theories of Colored Bodies and Fits of Easy Reflection (Cambridge: Cambridge University Press, 1993).

"The Gradual Acceptance of Newton's Theory of Light and Color," *Perspectives on Science* 4 (1996), 59–104.

Steffens, Henry John, *The Development of Newtonian Optics in England* (New York: Science History Publications, 1977).

Alchemy, chemistry, and theory of matter

Dobbs, Betty Jo Teeter, *The Foundations of Newton's Alchemy, or "The Hunting of the Greene Lyon"* (Cambridge: Cambridge University Press, 1975).

The Janus Faces of Genius: The Role of Alchemy in Newton's Thought (Cambridge: Cambridge University Press, 1991).

Figala, Karin, "Newton as Alchemist," *History of Science* 15 (1977), 102–37.

"Die exakte Alchemie von Isaac Newton," *Verhandlungen der Naturforschenden Gesellschaft Basel* 94 (1984), 155–228.

"Newton's Alchemical Studies and His Idea of the Atomic Structure of Matter," Appendix A (pp. 381–6) of A. R. Hall's *Isaac Newton, Adventurer in Thought*, listed above.

Golanski, Jan, "The Secret Life of an Alchemist," pp. 146–67 of John Fauvel *et al.* (eds.), *Let Newton Be!*, listed above.

McGuire, J. E., "The Origin of Newton's Doctrine of Essential Qualities," *Centauris* 12 (1968), 233–60.

"Atoms and the 'Analogy of Nature': Newton's Third Rule of Philosophizing," *Studies in the History and Philosophy of Science* 1 (1970), 3–58.

Newman, William R., *Gehennical Fire: The Lives of George Starkey, an American Alchemist in the Scientific Revolution* (Cambridge, MA: Harvard University Press, 1994).

Priesner, Claus and Figala, Karin (eds.), *Alchemie: Lexicon einer hermetischen Wissenschaft* (Munich: Verlag C. H. Beck München, 1998).

Thackray, Arnold, *Atoms and Powers: An Essay on Newtonian Matter-Theory and the Development of Chemistry* (Cambridge, MA: Harvard University Press, 1970).

Westfall, Robert S., "Newton and the Hermetic Tradition," in Allen G. Dubus (ed.), *Science, Medicine and Society in the Renaissance: A Festschrift in Honor of Walter Pagel*, vol. 2 (New York: Neale Watson Academic Publications, 1972), pp. 183–92.

"The Role of Alchemy in Newton's Career," in Maria Luisa Righini Bonelli and William R. Shea (eds.), *Reason, Experiment and Mysticism in the Scientific Revolution* (New York: Science History Publications, 1975), pp. 189–232.

"The Influence of Alchemy on Newton," in Marsha P. Hanen, Margaret J. Osler, and Robert G. Weyant (eds.), *Science, Pseudo-Science and Society* (Waterloo, Ontario: Wilfrid Laurier University Press, 1980), pp. 145–69.

Westman, Robert and McGuire, J. E., *Hermeticism and the Scientific Revolution* (Los Angeles: William Andrews Clark Memorial Library, University of California, 1977), esp. J. E. McGuire's "Neoplatonism, Active Principles and the Corpus Hermeticum," pp. 93–142.

Religion and chronology

Force, James E. and Popkin, Richard H. (eds.), *Newton and Religion: Context, Nature, and Influence* (Dordrecht: Kluwer Academic Publishers, 1998).

Iliffe, Rob, "'Making a Shew': Apocalyptic Hermeneutics and the Sociology of Christian Idolatry in the Work of Isaac Newton and Henry More," in James E. Force and Richard H. Popkin (eds.), *The Books of Nature and Scripture* (Dordrecht: Kluwer Academic Publishers, 1994).

Jacob, Margaret C., *The Newtonians and the English Revolution 1689–1720* (Hassocks, Sussex: The Harvester Press; Ithaca, NY: Cornell University Press, 1976). (Reprinted New York: Gordon and Breach, 1991.)

McGuire, J. E. and Rattansi, P. M., "Newton and the 'Pipes of Pan'," *Notes and Records of the Royal Society* 21 (1996), 118–43.

McLachlan, Herbert, *Sir Isaac Newton's Theological Manuscripts* (Liverpool: Liverpool University Press, 1950).

Mamiani, Maurizio (ed.), *Trattato sull'Apocalisse* (Turin: Bollati Botinghieri, 1994), with the complete text (in English) of Newton's "Treatise on the Apocalypse," together with an Italian translation.

Mandelbrote, Scott, "'A Duty of the Greatest Moment': Isaac Newton and the Writings of Biblical Criticism," *British Journal for the History of Science* 26 (1993), 281–302.

Manuel, Frank, *Isaac Newton, Historian* (Cambridge, MA: Harvard University Press, 1963).

The Religion of Isaac Newton (Oxford: Clarendon Press, 1973).

Westfall, Robert S., "Newton's Theological Manuscripts," in Bechler (ed.), *Contemporary Newtonian Research*, listed above, pp. 129–43.

INDEX

Abbé Conti, 450, 456, 459
abduction, 161
aberration, 212–13
absolute motion, 33–6, 174; see also
    motion
absolute quantity, 64
absolute space, 33–6, 40–1, 174; see also
    space
absolute time, 40–1
    controversies over, 33–6, 174
    Newton's context and, 36–8
    see also time
acceleration, 12, 64
    absolute time/space and, 40–1
    conic motion and, 93–5
    great inequality and, 215–17
    harmonic rule and, 180
    impulsive to continuous forces and,
        74–5
    mathematical to physical
        characterization and, 153
    unification of Moon and, 183–4
Account of Sir Isaac Newton's
    Philosophical Discoveries, An
    (Maclaurin), 329, 348–9
Account of the Commercium
    Epistolicum (Newton), 324
Achmet, 401
Acta Eruditorum, 435, 440–1, 444–5, 450
action at a distance, 152
Act of Uniformity, 421
Adams, J. C., 221–2
ad hoc reasoning, 158
aether, 207–8
    mechanical philosophy and, 340–2,
        344

optics and, 235, 238–45
    refraction and, 235
Alchemist, The (Jonson), 25
alchemy, 11–12, 17, 23, 27–9, 316,
    382–6, 390
    composition theory and, 372–4
    criticism of, 25–6
    Maier and, 374–81
    Newton's manuscripts and, 370–1
    prisca sapientia, 370–1, 374–5
    religion and, 24, 378–81
    see also chemistry
algebra, 11, 309, 311, 323
    ancient wisdom and, 433–4
    attacks on, 317
    geometry and, 431–2, 439–40
    Newton vs. Leibniz and, 439–40
    see also mathematics
Analyse des infiniment petits
    (L'Hospital), 322
Analysis per Quantitatum Series,
    Fluxiones et Differentias (Jones),
    444
analysis, see dynamic analysis
Analyst, The (Berkeley), 22
ancient wisdom, 370–1, 374
    algebra and, 433–4
    Rosicrucianism and, 375–81
angular momentum, 121
Antichrist, 393–5
antimony, 363
aphelia, 178–80
Apocalypse, 387, 390, 421
    argument from design and, 391–2
    construction of, 393
    experimentalism and, 396–400

481

Apocalypse (*cont.*)
  interpretive rules of, 396–400
  methodization of, 391–6
apogee, 210–11
  curvature method of computation,
    100–6
Apollonius, 309, 324
approximations, 157–8, 161–3
Archbishop Sharp, 422
Archbishop Tenison, 422
Archimedes, 309
area law, *see* Kepler's area law
arguing more securely, 141, 150, 160–7
Arianism, 412, 414–15, 417
Aristotle, 1–3, 10, 60, 204, 334
Arithmetica Infinitorium (Wallis), 311
Arithmetica Universalis (Newton),
    318–19, 432
Arius, 23
Arnauld, Antoine, 1, 456
astrology, 23
Astronomia Britannica (Wing), 205–6
Astronomia Carolina (Streete), 205
Astronomia Nova (Kepler), 202–3
Astronomia Philolaica (Boulliau), 204–5
astronomy, 15, 330
  aberration and, 212–13
  aether and, 207–8, 235, 238–45, 340–2,
    344
  Earth, 81; *see also* Earth
  geometry and, 317–18; *see also*
    geometry; Kepler's area law
  great inequality and, 215–17
  group effort of, 15
  Jupiter and, 153; *see also* Jupiter
  lunar apse and, 213–15
  Moon-test and, 182–3; *see also* Moon
  Mercury and, 194, 206, 222–3
  Newton's place in, 7–8
  planetary motion and, 193–4; *see also*
    planetary motion
  reflecting telescope and, 11
  Sun and, 203–5; *see also* Sun
  uniform circular motion and, 86–93,
    143–4
  van Schooten and, 310–11
  see also celestial mechanics; orbital
    motion
Atalanta Fugiens (Maier), 24
Athanasius, 394

atomism
  color and, 245–9
  hypothesis and, 250–1
  see also optics

Bacon, Francis, 1, 3
ballistics, 450
Barrow, Isaac, 10–11, 311, 315, 432
Barton, Catherine, 13
Beast of the Apocalypse, 394
Bedford, Arthur, 411–12
Bentley, Richard, 417, 419, 448
Berkeley, George, 1, 22–3, 334, 417
  absolute space/time and, 33, 46
  metaphysics and, 331, 335
Bernoulli, Jakob, 437
Bernoulli, Johann, 322
  Charta Volans and, 445
  Leibniz controversy and, 431, 435,
    437, 439, 443–4, 450
  reconciliation of, 450–1
Bernoulli, Nikolaus, 444
Beveridge, William, 412
biblical studies, 11, 28
  Antichrist, 393–5
  Book of Daniel, 24, 387–8, 394, 412,
    414–15, 419, 421–2
  Book of Nature, 323
  Book of Revelation, 24, 387, 390–400,
    421
  correct philosophy and, 390
  corruption of scripture and, 409–10,
    419
  False Prophet, 394
  Genesis, 387
  idolatry, 420
  infant baptism, 420
  I John 5:7, 409–10, 419, 421–3
  Joshua, 457–8
  literalism and, 420–1
  Mace and, 409
  monotheism and, 378
  Moses, 410–11
  prophecy and, 387–405
  rejection of Trinity, 10–11, 23–4,
    409–10, 412–15, 419–23
  Rosicrucianism and, 376
  I Timothy 3:16, 409–10, 419, 421–2
  truth and, 390–1
  understanding and, 392

universal law and, 371
Whore of Babylon, 394
see also God
binomial theorem, 312
Bishop Lloyd, 422
Book of Daniel, 24, 387–8, 394
  eighteenth-century Christianity and,
    412, 414–15, 419, 421–2
  prophecy of Seventy Weeks and, 412,
    419, 422
Book of Nature, 323
Book of Revelation, 24, 421
  Apocalypse and, 387, 390–400
bootstrapping, 174
Borelli, G. A., 15, 435
Boscaglia, Cosimo, 457–8
Bouillau, Ishmaël, 15, 152, 179, 204–5
Boyle, Robert, 16, 25, 338
  alchemy and, 26
  chemistry and, 359–60, 363
  density and, 59
  theft and, 445
Brackenridge, J. Bruce, xi, 6, 85–137
Bradley, James, 212–13, 217
Brahe, Tycho, 15–16
  absolute time/space and, 37
  accuracy of data and, 152–3
  harmonic rule and, 178–80
  lunar motion and, 120–1
  mathematical to physical
    characterization and, 156
  puffy-cheeked orbit and, 203
Brewster, David, 25, 442–3
bright-idea myth, 6–8
British Board of Admiralty, 217
Brown, Ernest W., 223
Buffon, Comte de, 439
Bur, 360
Burckhardt, Johann Karl, 218
Burg, Johann Tobias, 218
Burnet, Thomas, 366
Burnet, William, 442

Cabalieri, Bonaventura, 311
Cadmus, 379
Cajori, Florian, 207
calculus, 10–11, 21, 117, 388–9
  Charta Volans and, 445–6
  dynamic analysis and, 313–16,
    319–20, 324

lunar motion and, 120–4, 213–15
Newton vs. Leibniz and, 13–14, 432,
  439–40, 445–7
"Quadrature" and, 439
resistance forces and, 118–20
see also mathematics
Cambridge, 9–13
Caroline, Princess of Wales, 411,
  448–9
  Leibniz–Clarke correspondence and,
    455–63
Cartesian ovals, 237
Case, Thomas, 256
Castelli, Benedetto, 457
Catholic Church, 415–16, 420, 422
causal interactions, 37
  absolute time/space and, 38–49
  gravity and, 152
  greater certainty and, 228
  Kepler and, 204
Caussin, Nicolas, 401
celestial circularity, 86
celestial mechanics, 224–6
  aberration and, 212–13
  aether and, 207–8; *see also* aether
  comets and, 208, 218–20, 222
  Earth's figure and, 220–1
  gravitation theory limitations and,
    221–3
  harmonic rule and, 206–10
  inverse-square law and, 213–15
  Jupiter/Saturn inequality and,
    215–17
  Kepler's laws and, 202–10
  Moon and, 213–18; *see also* Moon
  nutation and, 212–13
  precession and, 212–13
  problem of the tides and, 220–1
  vortices and, 205–7
  see also astronomy
Celestial Mechanics (Laplace), 7, 217
center of force, 12, 125
  conic motion and, 93–5
  curvature method and, 100–6
  early computational methods and,
    95–106
  harmonic rule and, 206–7
  Kepler's area law and, 107–10
  spiral motion and, 96
  uniform circular motion and, 87–93

centrifugal force, 88–9
  absolute time/space and, 44–5
  curvature method and, 100–6
  Huygens and, 145, 206
centripetal force, 6, 12, 57, 62–3
  First Law of Motion and, 64–5
  harmonic rule and, 180
  induction and, 187–9
  infinitesimals and, 75–8
  mathematical to physical
    characterization and, 153
  Newtonian style and, 144, 148, 156
  theory-mediated measurement and,
    144
  three measures of, 64
  unification of Moon and, 181–5
Chambers, Ephraim, 29
Charles II, 9
Charleton, Walter, 16
Charta Volans, 445–6
Chaucer, Geoffrey, 25
chemistry, 11–12, 17, 24, 358–60, 368–9
  corpuscularism and, 363–7
  Helmontian matter-theory and, 361–3
  Paracelsian principles and, 362
  vitriol and, 361
  see also alchemy
Chevalier Ramsay, 413
Cheyne, George, 438, 441
Christianity, 394, 424–30
  anti-Catholicism and, 415–16
  Bedford and, 411–12
  Berkeley and, 417
  Chronology and, 411
  Greek Fathers and, 416
  historical accuracy and, 412
  Hutchinsonians and, 418–19
  literalism and, 420–1
  Moses and, 410–11
  Observations and, 409–10
  rejection of Trinity and, 10–11, 23–4,
    409–10, 412–15, 419–23
  Shuckford and, 416–17
  Warburton and, 416–17
  Whiston and, 412–13
  see also biblical studies
Chronology of Ancient Kingdom's
  Amended, The (Newton), 411, 417
Church of England, 10, 411, 414, 417,
  420, 422–3

Chymical Lectures (Freind), 441
circular motion, see orbital motion
Civil War, 9
Clairaut, Alexis-Claude, 158, 167
  comets and, 219–20
  Earth's figure and, 220
  lunar motion and, 213–15, 217
Clarke, Samuel
  Leibniz correspondence and, 455–63
  Newton vs. Leibniz and, 448–50
  religion and, 411–13, 417, 422–3
"Clavis," 24–5
Clavis Apocaliptica (Mede), 387
Clavis Mathematicae (Oughtred), 311
cogitatio caeca, 325
Cohen, I. Bernard, xi, 1–32, 57–84, 154
Collins, John, 11, 14, 311, 442
collisions, 87–93
color, 10–11, 389
  aether and, 238–45
  atomism and, 245–9
  Hooke's objections and, 400
  reflection and, 230
  refraction and, 230, 237
  theory of, 229–32
  see also optics
Comet Encke, 222
Comet Halley, 208, 222
comets, 208, 218–20, 222
Commandino, Federico, 308
Commercium Epistolicum, 324, 442–4,
  450–1
common analysis, 312; see also dynamic
  analysis
composition theory, 372–4
Conclusio (Newton), 360
Conduitt, John, 13
conic motion, 93–5, 208
Conics (Appolonius), 324
continuous forces
  First Law of Motion and, 64–5
  impulsive forces and, 70–5
controversies, 11–12
  Commercium Epistolicum and, 442–4
  gravity and, 174–5
  Leibniz and, 455–63; see also Leibniz,
    Gottfried Wilhelm
  Observations and, 409–10
  publishing dates, 439–41
  religious, 412; see also Christianity

space, time, motion, 33–6
Trinity and, 10–11, 23–4, 409–10,
    412–15, 419–23
Convention Parliament, 422
Copernican theory, 37, 86, 457
    Gamma Draconis and, 212
    geocentrism vs. heliocentrism, 51
    system of, 178
copper sulfate, 361
corpuscular theory
    Helmontian theory and, 361–3
    Newton's chemistry and, 363–7
    see also optics
Coste, Pierre, 273
Cotes, Roger, 418, 443, 445, 447
Craig, John, 413, 436
"Critical Role of Curvature in Newton's
    Developing Dynamics, The"
    (Brackenridge), 95
Cumberland, Richard, 412
curvature, 21, 85, 125–7
    area law and, 107–10
    computational methods and, 95–106
    conic motion and, 93–5
    force measurement and, 106–17
    lunar motion and, 120–4
    major role of, 86
    Newton's methodology and, 143–4
    parabolic, 110–11
    resistance forces and, 118–20
    uniform circular motion and, 87–93
    see also geometry
Cyclopaedia (Chambers), 29

d'Alembert, Jean le Rond, 29, 167, 213,
    217
Daniel, Book of, 24, 387–8, 394
    eighteenth-century Christianity and,
    412, 414–15, 419, 421–2
    prophecy of Seventy Weeks and, 412,
    419, 422
"De analysis per aequationes numero
    terminorum infinitas" (Newton),
    11, 313
deduction, 139, 155–7, 174–5
"De gravitatione et aequipondio
    fluidorum" (Newton)
    metaphysics and, 263
    prophecy and, 390, 397
    space/time and, 45–6

Delaunay, Charles Eugene, 218, 221–2
De Metallorum Metamorphosi
    (Starkey), 362
"De motu corporum in gyrum"
    (Newton), 6, 12
    curvature and, 106
    force/mass concepts and, 59–60, 75
    harmonic rule and, 208
    Newton's methodology and, 153
density, 58–9, 158, 372
Densmore, Dana, 172
De Quatuor Monarchiis (Sleidan), 388
De Revolutionibus (Copernicus), 309
Descartes, René, 1–3, 10, 15
    absolute time/space and, 37, 41, 43,
    46–8
    analysis vs. synthesis and, 310, 313
    causal interactions and, 38
    centripetal force and, 63
    errors of, 433
    God and, 333
    impulsive force and, 66–7
    inverse-square law and, 141
    mass and, 59
    mechanical philosophy and, 346–50
    metaphysics and, 256, 331, 335;
        see also metaphysics
    methodology and, 141, 147–52
    motion and, 154
    Newton's attack and, 317
    refraction and, 235
    scientific reform and, 228
    truth and, 395
    vortices and, 43, 205, 207
De Symbolica Aegyptiorum Sapientia
    (Caussin), 401
Dialogue concerning Natural Religion
    (Hume), 349
Dialogues on the Two Chief World
    Systems (Galileo), 1, 142
Diderot, Denis, 29
Dini, Piero, 457
Dioptrique (Descartes), 66–7, 235
direct problems, 106
    uniform circular motion, 10, 86–93,
    143–4
DiSalle, Robert, xi, 5, 33–56
Discours de la méthode (Descartes), 395
Discourse on the Cause of Gravity
    (Huygens), 140, 158

dispersion, 232–8
Dobbs, Betty Jo Teeter, xiv, 26–8
dot-notation, 13, 21
dreams, 401–5
Duhem, Pierre, 174
Duillier, Nicolas Fatio de, 337, 372, 413
  plagiarism charges and, 436–8
dynamic analysis, 37, 125–6
  aberration and, 212–13
  absolute time/space and, 38–49
  aether and, 207–8
  Arithmetica Universalis and, 319
  curvature and, 86; *see also* curvature
  early computational method, 95–9
  elliptical motion and, 93–5
  error and, 97–9
  Euclid and, 308–9
  fluxions and, 313–15, 319–22, 324
  geometry and, 317–20, 322–5
  impulsive to continuous forces and,
    72–5
  Leibniz dispute and, 321
  Newton's calculus and, 433–5
  symbolic algebra and, 309, 311, 317,
    323
  uniform circular motion and, 87–93
  Viète and, 309–11

Earl of Pembroke, 273
Earth, 81
  aether and, 207–8
  density and, 158
  entrenchment of law and, 162
  figure of, 220–1
  gravity and, 182–5, 187–9; *see also*
    gravity
  harmonic rule and, 207
  Kepler's area law and, 178
  limitations of gravitational theory
    and, 221–3
  lunar motion and, 120–4, 182–5,
    213–15
  mathematical to physical
    characterization and, 153
  Moon-test and, 182–3
  tide problem and, 220–1
eccentricities, 215–17
Egyptians, 375–9, 413, 417
Einstein, Albert
  absolute space/time and, 33–6, 44

geocentrism vs. heliocentrism, 51
  gravity and, 5, 223
elastic bodies, 87–93
Elements (Euclid), 308, 319
elliptical motion, 12, 86, 93–5
  harmonic rule and, 180
  Kepler and, 202–6
emission theory, *see* optics
empiricism, 16–19
  absolute time/space and, 51–3
  gravity and, 185
  Kepler and, 202–6
  Newtonian style and, 166–7
Encyclopédie (Diderot and d'Alembert),
    29
entrenchment of the law, 161–2
Epicurus, 334
equinox, 213
Errores Cartesii Geometriae (Newton),
    433
*Essay concerning Human
    Understanding* (Locke), 272, 330
Euclid, 92, 308–9, 319, 324
Euler, Leonhard, 5, 167, 443
  lunar motion and, 121, 213–15, 217
experimental philosophy, 2, 139, 150
experimentation
  absolute time/space and, 42
  Apocalypse and, 396–400
  commitment and, 16–19
  geometry and, 389
  spiritual areas and, 24

False Prophet, 394
false religion, 420
Fermat, Pierre de, 310–11
Figala, Karin, xi, 24–7, 370–86
figmenta, 2, 13, 228
first-order forms, 373
Flamsteed, John, 15, 205, 208–9
  great inequality and, 215
  Moon and, 210–11
  Newton and, 431
  refraction and, 237
fluents, 21
fluxions, 21, 117, 388–9
  Charta Volans and, 445–6
  dynamic analysis and, 313–16,
    319–20, 324
  lunar motion and, 120–4

Newton vs. Leibniz and, 439–40, 445–7
  "Quadrature" and, 439
  resistance forces and, 118–20
  see also calculus
Fluxionum Methodus Inversa (Cheyne), 438
forces, 6
  composition theory and, 372–4
  contrapositive of inertia and, 148–9
  curvature measurement of, 100–6, 112–17
  geocentrism vs. heliocentrism, 49–51
  impressed, 62
  impulsive to continuous, 70–5
  infinitesimals and, 75–8
  Kepler's area law, 107–10; see also Kepler's area law
  mathematics and, 147–60; see also mathematics
  metaphysics and, 283–8, 292–4
  microstructural, 151
  motion propositions, 144
  Newtonian style and, 78–81, 154–60
  parabolic measurement of, 110–11
  physical characterization of, 147–60
  resistance, 8, 118–20, 144, 163–4
  separate laws for, 68–70
  universal interaction and, 190–4
  varieties of, 57
Fotheringham, J. K., 222
Francis, Alban, 422
Freind, John, 441
French Academy, 15

Gabbey, Alan, xii, 19, 329–57
Galileo, 1, 10, 457
  absolute time/space and, 40, 48
  condemnation of, 387
  constant gravitation and, 110
  credit to, 15
  geometry and, 323
  gravity and, 5
  infinitesimals and, 76
  laws of motion and, 70
  mass and, 59
  mathematics and, 142
  metaphysics and, 258
  motion and, 154
  Newton's methodology and, 142–52

Gamma Draconis, 212
garden paths, 163–5
Garth, Samuel, 22
Gassendi, Pierre, 16, 375
Gauss, Carl Friedrich, 17
generalization
  by induction, 185–90
  weight/mass proportion and, 187–90
General Relativity, 5, 193–4, 223
General Scholium, 8, 13, 58, 85, 139
  induction and, 186
  methodology and, 140–1
Genesis, 387
geocentrism, 49–51, 178
Géométrie (Descartes), 10, 310, 313–14
geometry, 21, 57
  algebra and, 431–2, 439–40
  analysis vs. synthesis and, 324–5
  conic motion and, 93–5
  early computational methods and, 95–106
  experimentation and, 389
  Kepler's area law and, 152; see also Kepler's area law
  Leibniz and, 431–2
  lunar motion and, 120–4
  nature and, 323
  Newton's calculus and, 433–5
  parabola, 110–11, 219
  parallax, 212–13
  polygons, 91
  resistance forces and, 118–20
  see also curvature; mathematics
Geometry (Newton), 433–4
George II, 448
globuli, 229
Glymour, Clark, 174
Goclenius, Rudolph, 60
God, 243, 245, 249, 421, 423
  absolute time/space and, 47
  alchemy studies and, 24
  Apocalypse and, 391–400
  causal interactions and, 38
  composition theory and, 373
  dynamic analysis and, 316
  Joshua and, 457
  mathematics and, 371
  mechanical philosophy and, 330, 332, 346–50

God (*cont.*)
  metaphysics and, 259, 261, 266–75,
    279, 281–2, 288–90, 331–4
  Newton vs. Leibniz and, 431, 448–9,
    461–2
  Opticks and, 332
  prophecy and, 391–405
  space and, 390
Golinski, Jan, 27
Goodman, Nelson, 162
Grand Apostasy, 394
Grand Duchess Christina, 457
Grand Duke Cosimo II, 457
Grantham, 9
gravity, 5, 7–9, 12–14, 58, 195–201
  acceleration and, 183–5
  aether and, 207–8
  ancient sages and, 23
  aphelia at rest and, 180–1
  approximation and, 162–3
  causal interaction and, 152
  centripetal force and, 176–7, 183–5
  curvature method and, 100–6
  deduction and, 174–5
  Earth and, 182–5, 187–9
  entrenchment of law and, 162
  Euler on, 214
  falling apple myth and, 6
  general relativity and, 193–4, 223
  harmonic rule and, 177–80
  Huygens on, 140, 145
  induction and, 165–6, 185–90
  inference and, 175–81
  inverse-square law and, 141, 213–14;
    see also inverse-square law
  Jupiter's moons and, 175–7
  Kepler's area law and, 176–8
  laws of motion and, 70, 190–3;
    see also motion
  limitations of theory, 221–3
  mass and, 60
  mathematics and, 155–60
  mean solar distance and, 209
  Moon and, 120–4, 181–2
  Newtonian style and, 150, 154–60,
    155–6
  parabolic measurement and, 110–11
  particles and, 192–3
  Phenomena and Rules for, 139
  primary planets and, 178–81, 189–92

  rejection of Cartesian, 85
  resistance forces and, 118–20
  unification and, 181–5
  universal, 158, 162–3, 166, 190–4
  weight/mass proportion and, 187–90
  world systems resolution and, 193
great inequality, 215–17
Great Plague, 10
Greek Fathers, 416
Greenwich Observatory, 211
Gregory, David, 25, 207, 322, 324, 372,
    438
Gregory, James, 311
Grey, Zachary, 414–16
Guicciardini, Niccolò, xii, 21, 308–28
Gur, 360

Hall, A. Rupert, xii, 5, 14, 21, 27, 223,
    431–54
Hall, Francis, 431
Halley, Edmond, 6, 12, 22
  analysis and, 324
  celestial mechanics and, 202, 204, 208
  comets and, 218–19
  great inequality and, 215–16
  prophecy and, 390
Halley's Comet, 208, 222
Hansen, Peter Andreas, 218
harmonic rule, 177–80
  mean solar distance and, 208–9
  Newton and, 206–10
  unification of Moon and, 184
Harper, William, xii, 7, 174–201
Harriot, Thomas, 311
Harris, John, 25–6, 29, 364
Hartley, David, 344
Haynes, Hopton, 422–3
heliocentrism, 49–51, 178, 203
Herivel, John, 86–8, 95
hermeneutic method, 395–7, 403, 421
Hill, G. W., 121, 218
Hipparchus, 86
Historia et Origo Calculi Differentialis
    (Leibniz), 450
"Historical account of two Notable
    Corruptions of Scripture, An"
    (Newton), 410, 419
History of Fluxions (Raphson), 443
Hobbes, Thomas, 1, 315, 317, 334
Hoffman, J. E., 431

Hooke, Robert, 11, 15, 85, 431
   color and, 238
   controversy with, 12
   curvature and, 87
   experimentation and, 16
   Gamma Draconis and, 212
   harmonic rule and, 208
   Newton's methods and, 95–9, 102–3,
      106
   objections of, 400
   theory of light and, 231–2
Horologium Oscillatorium (Huygens),
      10, 15, 69, 142
   geometry and, 433
   methodology of, 143, 145
   Newtonian style and, 155
horoscopes, 23
Horrocks, Jeremiah, 15, 153, 206, 210,
      212
Horsley, Samuel, 418
Hudde, Johann, 311
Hume, David, 1, 3
   mechanical philosophy and, 349
   metaphysics and, 331, 335
Hutchinson, John, 418–19
Hutton, Charles, 29
Huygens, Christiaan, 10, 15, 126
   absolute space/time and, 33
   centrifugal force and, 206
   centripetal force and, 62
   gravity issues and, 13
   hypothetico-deductive method and,
      139–40
   inertia and, 148
   laws of motion and, 69–70
   Leibniz and, 432
   mathematics and, 142
   measurement and, 145–6
   microstructural forces and, 151
   Moon-test and, 182–3
   motion and, 154
   Newtonian style and, 142–52, 155
   uniform circular motion and, 89–90
hypotheses
   atomism and, 250–1
   deduction and, 139, 155–7, 174–5
   if-then propositions, 141–3, 150, 152,
      160–7
   induction and, 161, 164–6, 185–90
   Newtonian style and, 227–9

"Hypotheses non fingo," 13, 228
Hypothesis Explaining ye Properties of
   Light (Newton), 207

idolatry, 420
if-and-only-if condition, 146
if-then propositions, 142–3, 152
   secure arguing and, 141, 150, 160–7
imaginary numbers, 316
impact, 15, 57
impressed force, 62
impulsive forces
   continuous forces and, 70–5
   Kepler's area law and, 107–10
   Newton's methodology and, 148
   Second Law of Motion and, 65–8
   uniform circular motion and, 91
In Artem Analyticem Isagoge (Viète),
   309
indiscernibility, 40, 45–6
induction, 161, 185–6
   Newtonian style and, 165–6
   taxonomic hypotheses and, 164–5
   weight/mass proportion and, 187–90
inertia, 5, 10, 57
   composition theory and, 373
   contrapositive of, 148–9
   First Law of Motion and, 64–5
   Huygens and, 148
   Jupiter's moons and, 175–7
   Kepler's area law and, 205–6
   metaphysics and, 262
   Newton's concept of, 60–2
   orbital motion and, 11–12
   resistance forces and, 164
   separate laws for, 68–70
   tides and, 221
infant baptism, 420
inference, 161
   aphelia at rest and, 180–1
   centripetal force and, 176–7, 183–4
   empirical success and, 185
   gravity and, 174–5; see also gravity
   harmonic rule and, 177–80
   induction and, 185–90
   inverse-square law and, 177, 183–4
   Jupiter's moons and, 175–7
   Kepler's area law and, 176–8
   Moon-test and, 182–3
   primary planets and, 178–81

inference (*cont.*)
  tickets, 143
  unification and, 181–5
  universal interactive force and, 190–4
infinite series, 312
infinitesimals, 75–8
  analysis vs. synthesis and, 311–13
  curvature and, 91
  fluxions and, 313–16, 319–22
  imaginary numbers, 316
  spiral motion and, 96
  see also calculus
interpretive rules, 396–400
inverse fourth power term, 214
inverse problems, 93
inverse-square law, 6
  elliptical motion and, 12
  Euler on, 214
  force characterization and, 151
  gravity and, 85, 141, 214; *see also*
    gravity
  harmonic rule and, 180, 207–8
  Jupiter's moons and, 177
  lunar apse and, 213–15
  Mercury and, 223
  orbital motion and, 12
  particle gravitation and, 192–3
  unification of Moon and, 183–4
Isaac Newton: Adventurer in Thought
  (Hall), 27
Israelites, 413

James II, 422
I John 5:7, 409–10, 419, 421–3
Jones, William, 442, 444
Jonson, Ben, 25
Joshua, 457–8
Jupiter, 153, 167, 206, 376
  comets and, 219
  Euler on, 213–14
  Flamsteed and, 209
  great inequality and, 215–17
  mean solar distance and, 209
  moons of, 175–7

Kant, Immanuel, xiv, 1, 3, 5, 331
Kearsey, John, 311
Keill, John, 13, 440–2, 445–6
Kepler, Johannes, 7, 10
  absolute time/space and, 37

credit to, 15
  elliptical motion and, 93
  geocentrism vs. heliocentrism, 49–51
  great inequality and, 215
  harmonic rule and, 177–80, 184,
    206–10
  motion and, 12–13
  uniform circular motion and, 86
Kepler's area law, 6, 85, 97
  curvature method of computation
    and, 100–6
  derivation of, 87
  force measurement and, 107–10
  inertia and, 205–6
  Jupiter's moons and, 176–7
  justification of, 94
  limit and, 91
  mathematical to physical
    characterization and, 152–4
  Newtonian style and, 158–9, 204–6
  primary planets and, 178
  theory-mediated measurement and,
    144
"Key," 24–5
King, Peter, 409–10
Klopp, Onno, 455
Koyré, Alexandre, 13, 459
Kuhn, T. S., 194

Lacaille, Nicolas-Louis de, 213
Lagrange, Joseph Louis, 167, 216
Lakatos, Imre, 174
Lalande, J.-J. L., 219
La méthode des fluxions (de Buffon), 439
Laplace, Pierre-Simon, 7, 167
  Earth's figure and, 220
  great inequality and, 216–17
  limitations of gravitational theory,
    221
  lunar motion and, 122, 218
Law, Edmund, 419
law of inertia, *see* inertia
"Laws of Force, The" (Keill), 440
Laws of Motion, 205
Le Clerc, Jean, 422
Lectiones Opticae (Newton), 389
Lectures on Algebra, 11
Legendre, Adrien-Marie, 220
Leibniz, Gottfried Wilhelm, 1, 3, 21,
  450–1

absolute time/space and, 33, 37,
   39–41, 47–8
analysis vs. synthesis and, 323–5
calculus and, 433–5; *see also* calculus
Charta Volans and, 445–6
Cheyne and, 438
Clarke correspondence and, 14,
   455–63
Commercium Epistolicum and, 442–4
Duillier and, 436–8
geocentrism vs. heliocentrism, 51
geometry/algebra contrast and, 439–40
God and, 333–4
gravity and, 13–14, 183
Keill and, 440–2
mechanical philosophy and, 345
metaphysics and, 331, 335, 447–9
numerical series and, 431–2
plagiarism charges and, 436–7, 440–1,
   445
Principia error and, 444–5
publishing date controversies and,
   439–41
"Quadrature" and, 438–9
relativity and, 5
Scottish Newtonians and, 436–7
Tentamen controversy and, 436
Lepaute, N.-R. E., 219
Le Verrier, U. J. J., 222–3
Lexicon Philosophicum (Goclenius), 60
Lexicon Technicum (Harris), 25–6,
   29–30, 364
L'Hospital, Marquis de, 322, 439
libration, 203
light, 11, 389
   aether and, 238–45
   dispersion and, 232–8
   reflection/refraction and, 230, 232–8
   theory of, 229–32
   wave theory and, 232
   white, 230–1
   see also optics
limit, 91
Linus, Francis, 431
Lloyd, William, 412
Locke, John, xiv, 1, 3, 458
   curvature and, 95
   King and, 410
   metaphysics and, 272–3, 276–80,
      335

religion and, 418, 422
on science, 330
Logicae Artis Compendium (Sanderson),
   388
London, 9
Lucasian Professorship of Mathematics,
   10–11, 389
Lucretius, 23
lunar theory, 210–12
   apse, 213–15
   motion, 120–4
   see also Moon

Mace, Daniel, 409
Mach, Ernst, 59, 68
Maclaurin, Colin, 329, 335, 348–9
Magirus, Johannes, 60, 331
magnetism, 141, 203, 205
Mahometism, 412
Maier, Michael, 24, 371, 374–81
Maizeaux, Pierre Des, 450
Malebranche, Nicholas, 1
Mamiani, Maurizio, xii, 24, 387–408
Mandelbrote, Scott, xii, 24, 409–30
Manuel, Frank, 396
Marrow of Alchemy (Philalethes), 364
Mars, 206, 376
Mason, Charles, 218
mass, 6
   definition of, 58–60
   impulsive to continuous forces and,
      72–5
   infinitesimals and, 75–8
   proportion to weight, 187–90
Mathematicae Collectiones (Pappus),
   308–10, 317–18
*Mathematical and Philosophical
   Dictionary* (Hutton), 29
*Mathematical Elements of Natural
   Philosophy confirm'd by
   experiments* ('sGravesande), 329
*Mathematical Principles of Natural
   Philosophy* (Newton), *see Principia*
   (Newton)
mathematics, 13, 19, 390
   algebra and, 323; *see also* algebra
   analytical vs. synthetic proof and,
      308–15
   autonomy of, 331
   Berkeley on, 22–3

mathematics (*cont.*)
  binomial theorem, 312
  color, 241
  conservatism and, 20–1
  contrapositive of inertia and, 148–9
  core difficulty identification and, 17, 21
  curvature method of computation, 100–6
  defined, 330
  direct problems, 93
  Earth's figure and, 220–1
  experience and, 8–9
  fluxions and, 313–16, 319–22, 324; *see also* fluxions
  force characterization and, 15, 151–2
  Géométrie and, 310–11; *see also* geometry
  gravity and, 155–60; *see also* gravity
  harmonic rule and, 178–80
  Horologium Oscillatorium and, 142
  if-then propositions, 142–3
  imaginary numbers, 316
  inference tickets, 143
  infinite series, 312
  infinitesimals and, 75–8, 91, 96, 311–16, 319–22
  interpretive rules and, 397
  inverse problems, 93
  inverse-square law, 6; *see also* inverse-square law
  Kepler's area law, 85; *see also* Kepler's area law
  Legendre polynomials, 220
  limit and, 91
  Lucasian Professorship, 10–11
  lunar apse and, 213–15
  nature and, 85
  Newtonian style and, 78–81, 142–60
  numerical series and, 431–2
  optics and, 238, 243; *see also* optics
  Ozanam and, 310
  physical characterization and, 152–60
  slope, 86
  symbol manipulation and, 21
  thin films and, 239
  Two New Sciences and, 142
  see also calculus; curvature
Maupertuis, P. L. M. 158
Maxwell, James Clerk, 1
Mayer, Tobias, 217–18

Mead, Richard, 411
mechanical philosophy, 2, 139, 141–2, 150
  aether and, 340–2, 344
  characterization and, 337–40
  corporeality and, 342–3
  Descartes and, 346–50
  Duillier and, 337
  God and, 330–4, 346–50
  meaning of, 329–34
  mechanism obsession and, 333–4
  Peripatetics and, 329–30, 335–6
  religion and, 329
  universal conservation and, 345–6
Mede, Joseph, 387, 395
Meditations (Descartes), 2
Meli, Domenico Bertoloni, xi, 14, 435, 455–64
Mercator, Nicholas, 15
Mercury, 194, 206, 222–3
meridian transits, 212
Mersenne, Marin, 15, 141, 155
metaphysics, 2, 4, 295–307, 330
  absolute time/space and, 33–6
  Aristotle and, 257
  atomism and, 260–1
  bodies and, 275–6, 279–80
  deduction and, 257
  Descartes and, 256–65
  experience and, 270
  forces and, 283–8, 292–4
  geometry and, 262
  God and, 259, 261, 266–75, 279, 281–2, 288–90, 331–4
  gravity and, 282–3, 291
  hydrostatics and, 263
  ideas of substance and, 277–8, 281
  inertia and, 262
  Locke and, 272–3, 276–80, 335
  Maclaurin and, 335
  Maier and, 374–81
  mind and, 280–2
  motion and, 257–8, 260, 264–5, 289
  Newton's refutation and, 261–6
  Newton vs. Leibniz and, 447–9
  place and, 258–9, 265
  space and, 263–5, 267, 269
  waves and, 292
Method of Fluxions and Infinite Series (Newton), 313–16, 321–2

Method of Series and Fluxions
   (Newton), 86
Methodus Differentialis (Newton), 442
Micrographia (Hooke), 238
microstructural forces, 151
Middleton, Conyers, 413
Mill, John, 419
Mint, 9, 13, 26, 410, 422, 437
Moivre, Abraham de, 438, 444
Molyneux, Samuel, 212
momentum, 60, 121
Montagu, Charles, 450
Moon, 6, 81
   aberration and, 212–13
   comets and, 219
   empiricism and, 185
   Flamsteed and, 210–11
   harmonic rule and, 207
   Hill-Brown lunar theory and, 223
   Horrocks and, 210, 212
   Jupiter's, 175–7
   limitations of gravitational theory
      and, 221–3
   lunar apse and, 213–15
   lunar prediction accuracy and, 217–18
   motion of, 120–4, 210–15
   solar perturbation and, 210–12
   test, 182–3
   tides and, 221
   unification and, 181–5
More, Henry, 269, 316
Morgan, Augustus De, 442
Moses, 410–11
motion, 5–6, 10
   absolute space/time and, 33–6
   causal interactions and, 37–8
   contrapositive of inertia and, 148–9
   controversies over, 33–6, 38–49, 174
   curves and, 21
   empiricism and, 51–3
   First Law of, 64–5, 68–70
   geocentrism vs. heliocentrism, 49–51
   God and, 243
   impulsive to continuous forces and,
      70–2
   infinitesimals and, 75–8
   Keplerian, 7
   mathematical to physical
      characterization and, 152–60

Newton's methodology and, 36–8,
   143–4, 435
orbital, 11–12; *see also* orbital motion
pendulums and, 155
Second Law of, 65–70, 72–5
separate laws for, 68–70
Third Law of, 68, 190–3
uniform circular, 10, 86–93, 143–4
see also curvature; gravity
motive quantity, 64
Mystagogus, Cleidophorus, 374

Naachlass (Newton), 360
natural philosophy, 2
   analysis vs. synthesis and, 308–15
   biblical studies and, 387–91; *see also*
      biblical studies
   comprehensive approach to, 29–31
   division of science and, 330–1
   experimentalists and, 16–19
   first rule for, 160
   fourth rule for, 159
   gravity and, 174–5; *see also* gravity
   hermeneutic method and, 395–6
   Phenomena and Rules for, 139
   second rule for, 160–1
   secure arguing and, 160–7
   third rule for, 161
   truth and, 395
   see also science
Nauenberg, Michael, xii, 6, 85–137
Nautical Almanac, 217
*New and most Accurate Theory of the
   Moon's Motion, A* (Newton), 211
Newcomb, Simon, 194, 223
New Essays on Human Understanding
   (Leibniz), 272–3
Newman, William, xiii, 24–5, 358–69,
   374
Newton, Isaac
   alchemy and, 11–12, 17, 23–9, 370–86,
      390
   analysis and synthesis, 308–28
   anti-Catholicism of, 415–16
   biblical studies of, 11; *see also* biblical
      studies
   celestial mechanics and, 202–26
   centripetal force and, 62–4
   chemistry background of, 358–69
   comets and, 218–20

Newton, Isaac (*cont.*)
  comprehensive philosophy of, 29–31
  conservatism of, 20–1
  continuous forces and, 70–5
  curvature and, 85–137
  depth of commitment, 16–19
  eighteenth-century Christianity and,
    409–30
  elected Fellow, 10
  experimentation and, 16–19
  falling apple myth and, 6
  on force, 57, 60–84
  Galileo and, 1
  God and, 243, 245, 249, 316, 375–6;
    see also God
  great inequality and, 215–17
  harmonic rule and, 206–10
  impulsive forces and, 70–5
  on inertia, 60–2
  Kepler and, 202–6
  Leibniz and, 431–54; *see also* Leibniz,
    Gottfried Wilhelm
  limitations of gravitational theory,
    221–3
  Locke and, 410
  on mass, 58–60
  as mathematician, 19–23
  mechanical philosophy and, 329–57
  metaphysics and, 256–307
  methodology of, 138–43
  modern philosophy and, 3–4
  on motion, 60, 64–70
  myths of, 4–9
  optics and, 227–35; *see also* optics
  philosophical context of, 36–8
  prophecy and, 387–408
  rejection of Cartesian gravity, 85
  rejection of Trinity, 10–11, 23–4,
    409–10, 412–15, 419–23
  scholastic stature of, 1–2, 5
  as scientist, 14–19
  space/time philosophy of, 33–56
  synopsis of, 9–14
  time and, 70–5
  universal gravitation argument of,
    174–201; *see also* gravity
  worldview and, 2
Newtonian style, 78–81, 154, 159
  approximations and, 157–8
  arguing more securely, 141, 150, 160–7

  deductions and, 155–7
  derivation, 159
  entrenchment of law and, 161–2
  garden paths and, 163–5
  greater certainty and, 227–9
  inductive leaps and, 165–6
  Kepler's area law and, 158–9
  Rules for Natural Philosophy, 159–61
  see also Principia methodology
Nicene Creed, 420
Nichomachean Ethics (Aristotle), 60
Noah, 378, 421
Novum Lumen Chymicum
  (Sendivogius), 375
nutation, 212–13

*Observations upon the Prophecies of
  Daniel, and the Apocalypse of
  St John* (Newton), 240–1, 400, 409,
  413–15, 417
Occasionalists, 334
"Of Earth" (Newton), 387
"Of Refractions" (Newton), 233
"Of the Creation" (Newton), 387
Oldenburg, Henry, 363, 396, 400
Omerique, Hugo de, 434
"On Analysis by Infinite Series"
  (Newton), 11, 437
On Circular Motion (Newton), 91, 110
"On Colours" (Newton), 239, 241
"On Nature's Obvious Law and
  Processes in Vegetation" (Newton),
  27
opacity, 246
Opera Omnia (Newton), 418
Optical Lectures (Newton), 11, 229–30,
  234, 237
Opticks (Newton), 8, 13–14, 18
  aether and, 245
  alchemy and, 26, 371
  atomism and, 250, 251
  biblical studies and, 421
  chemistry and, 365
  color and, 246–8
  composition theory and, 372–3
  God and, 332
  greater certainty and, 228
  Hooke's death and, 438–9
  metaphysics and, 261, 335
  Queries of, 25, 28–9

taxonomic hypotheses and, 164–5
theory of light and, 230
optics, 12, 252–5, 330
    aberration and, 212–13
    aether and, 238–45
    alchemy and, 26–7
    atomism and, 245–51
    certain science and, 227–9
    color and, 10–11, 229–32, 237–49, 389,
        400
    dispersion and, 232–8
    light, 11, 229–45, 389
    opacity and, 246
    reflection/refraction and, 232–8
Opuscula Varii Argumenti (Euler), 213
orbital motion, 6, 11–12, 58, 125–6
    aberration and, 212–13
    absolute time/space and, 38–49
    causal interactions and, 37–8
    comets and, 218–20
    curvature method of computation,
        100–6
    geocentrism vs. heliocentrism, 49–51
    Kepler's area law, 107–10; see also
        Kepler's area law
    libration and, 203
    limitations of gravitational theory
        and, 221–3
    Magirus and, 331
    mathematical to physical
        characterization and, 153
    Moon and, 210–12; see also Moon
    Newtonian style and, 14; see also
        Newtonian style
    Newton vs. Leibniz and, 435
    puffy-cheeked, 202–3
    resistance forces and, 118–20
    spiral, 96, 106
    uniform circular, 10, 86–93, 143–4
    see also gravity
Organon (Aristotle), 308
Origine of Forms and Qualities, The
    (Boyle), 359
Ortus Medicinae (van Helmont), 361
oscillation, 155, 203, 435
Osiris, 377
Oughtred, William, 311
outward endeavor, 88
Ozanam, J., 310

Palitzsch, Johann George, 219
Pappus, 308–10, 317–18, 337
parabola, 110–11, 219
Paracelsian principles, 362
parallax, 212–13
Paraphrase and Notes on the Epistles of
    St. Paul, A (Locke), 410
Pardies, Ignace Gaston, 231
Paris Academy, 214, 216
Parliament, 12
Pascal, Blaise, 311
Patrick, Symon, 415
Pearce, Zachary, 413
Peirce, Charles Saunders, 161
Pell, John, 311
Pellisson, Paul, 457
Pemberton, Henry, 207, 318, 329, 438
pendulums, 155, 163–4
percussion, 62–3
Percy, Henry, 336
perigee, 100–6
Peripatetics, 329–30, 335–6
periphelia, 178
perturbation theory, 194, 211
    comets and, 218–20
    limitations of gravitational theory
        and, 222
    Mercury and, 222–3
phenomena
    Earth and, 182–5
    hermeneutic method and, 395–6
    inferences from, 175–81; see also
        inference
    Jupiter's moons and, 175–7
    Moon and, 181–5
    primary planets and, 178–81
    scientific reform and, 228
    see also gravity
Philalethes, Eirenaeus, 363–7, 374
Philosophiae Naturalis Principia
    Mathematica (Newton), see
    Principia (Newton)
Philosophiae Principia (Descartes), 64
Philosophical Principles of Natural
    Religion (Cheyne), 441
Philosophical Transactions of the Royal
    Society, 11, 230, 390
philosophy, xiv, 13–14
    absolute space/time and, 33–49
    atomism and, 250–1

philosophy (*cont.*)
  branches of, 320–30
  causal interactions and, 38
  deduction and, 139, 155–7, 174–5
  empirical world and, 16
  experimental, 2, 139, 150
  geocentrism vs. heliocentrism, 49–51
  induction and, 161, 164–6, 185–90
  mathematics and, 19–23; *see also*
    mathematics
  mechanical, 2, 139; *see also*
    mechanical philosophy
  modern, 3–4
  natural, 2; *see also* natural philosophy
  Newton's context and, 36–8
  practical, 329–30
  private imagination and, 395
  speculative, 329–30
  truth and, 395
  vs. science, 3–4
physical bobs, 155
physics, 390
  absolute time/space and, 33–6
  contrapositive of inertia and, 148–9
  force characterization and, 151
  group effort of, 15
  inertia and, 60–2
  mass and, 58–60
  mathematical characterization and,
    152–60
  Newtonian forces and, 147–52
  Newton's place in, 7–8
  worldview and, 5
  see also natural philosophy
Physiologiae Peripateticae Libri Sex
  (Magirus), 60, 331
planetary motion
  aether and, 207–8
  aphelia at rest and, 180–1
  general relativity and, 193–4
  harmonic rule for, 178–80
  induction and, 189–90
  Kepler's area law and, 178; *see also*
    Kepler's area law
  limitations of gravitational theory
    and, 221–3
  Magirus and, 331
  mean solar distance and, 208–9
  Newton vs. Leibniz and, 435
  parts of, 191–2

  see also celestial mechanics; orbital
    motion
Plato, 3, 86, 334
polygons, 91
polytheism, 394
Popper, Karl, 174
Porisms (Euclid), 324
Power, Henry, 337
practial philosophy, 329–30
Praxis (Newton), 379–80
precession, 144, 212–13
pressure, 57, 62–3
Prideaux, Humphrey, 415
Priestley, Joseph, 418
Principia (Newton), 2, 3, 7, 261
  alchemy and, 28
  analysis vs. synthesis, 308–28
  atomism and, 250–1
  beginnings of, 12
  biblical studies and, 423
  Book 1, 12, 58
  Book 2, 8, 12, 18, 21, 58
  Book 3, 12, 58
  calculus and, 433
  chemistry and, 360
  color and, 246
  composition theory and, 372
  Conclusio and, 360
  curvature and, 86; *see also* curvature
  elliptical motion and, 93–5
  error in, 444
  falling apple myth and, 6
  fame from, 9
  force measurement in, 106–17
  General Scholium, 8, 13, 58, 85,
    139–41, 186
  geocentrism vs. heliocentrism, 49–51
  gravity and, 174–5; *see also* gravity
  impulsive to continuous forces and,
    70–5
  infinitesimal discourse level and,
    75–8
  interpretive rules and, 396
  Laws of Motion, 64–70, 205; *see also*
    motion
  loose ends of, 167
  mass and, 58–60
  metaphysics and, 335
  publication of, 12–14
  refraction and, 235

structure of, 57–8
varieties of force in, 57
worldview and, 2
see also calculus
Principia methodology, 138, 168–73
axiomatic approach and, 142–3
deduction and, 139, 155–7, 174–5
force/motion differences and, 146–7
Galileo/Huygens methods and,
142–52
hypothetico-deductive approach and,
139–40
if-then propositions, 141–3, 150, 152,
160–7
induction and, 161, 164–6, 185–90
mathematical theory in, 142–7,
152–60; see also calculus;
mathematics
measurement and, 144–6
from motion to laws of force, 152–60
Newtonian style and, 147–60
proposition types, 144
reductio ad absurdum, 22
secure arguing and, 141, 150, 160–7
Principia Philosophiae (Descartes), 2,
85, 256, 258, 264
Principle of the Identity of
Indiscernibles, 40
prisca sapienta, 370–1, 374
Rosicrucianism and, 375–81
private imagination, 395, 397
prophecy, 420
Apocalypse and, 391–400
Book of Daniel, 24, 387–8, 394, 412,
414–15, 419, 421–2
Book of Revelation, 24, 387, 390–400,
421
figurative language and, 401–5
hermeneutic method and, 395–6
history and, 388
private imagination and, 395, 397
purpose of, 393–4
seventeenth-century natural
philosophy and, 387–91
Seventy Weeks, 412, 419, 422
substance of, 392–3
propositions, 144, 146–7
Ptolemy, 37, 51, 86
puffy-cheeked orbit, 202–3
Pyrotechny (Starkey), 359

Pyrrhonic skepticism, 3
Pythagoreans, 377, 404

"Quadrature" (Newton), 438–9
quam proxime, 96–7, 152–3, 156
fourth Rule of Natural Philosophy
and, 159
law entrenchment and, 161–2
Newtonian style and, 161–2
quantity of matter, see mass
quantity of motion, 60, 121
Queen Caroline, 411, 448–9
Leibniz–Clarke correspondence and,
455–63
"Questiones quaedam philosophicae"
(Newton), 229, 387

radii vectores, 203, 221
Ray, John, 421
rays, see light
Receuil de diverses pièces sur la
philosophie, la religion naturelle,
l'histoire, les mathématiques, etc
(Des Maizeaux), 450
reductio ad absurdum, 22
reflecting telescope, 11
reflection
explanation of, 232–8
white light and, 230–1
Reformation, 416, 420
refraction, 10, 389
explanation of, 232–8
Snell's law of, 15, 230, 235–6
white light and, 230–1
refrangibility, 230
regula Kepleriana, 206–7
Reichenbach, Hans, 34, 194
Reid, Thomas, 1
Relativity, 5, 37
absolute time/space and, 38–49
gravity and, 193–4, 223
religion
Act of Uniformity and, 421
Berkeley on, 22–3
Catholic Church, 415–16, 420, 422
Cheyne on, 441
Church of England, 10, 411, 414, 417,
420, 422–3
eighteenth-century Christianity and,
409–30

religion (*cont.*)
  false, 394, 420
  idolatry, 420
  Leibniz–Clarke correspondence and,
    455–63
  persecution and, 422
  rejection of Trinity and, 10–11, 23–4,
    409–10, 412–15, 419–23
  Society for Promoting Christian
    Knowledge, 411
  Toleration Act and, 422
  Whore of Babylon, 394
  see also biblical studies; God
Renaissance, 308–9, 316
resistance forces, 8, 118–20
  inertia and, 164
  Newtonian style and, 144, 163–4
"Resolve Problems by Motion, To"
  (Newton), 21
retrograde, 219
Revelation, Book of, 24, 391, 421
  Apocalypse and, 387, 390, 391–400
Ripley, George, 365
Roberval, Gilles Personne de, 311
Roman Catholic Church, 415–16, 420,
  422
Rosicrucianism, 375–81
rotation, 43–5
Royal Society, 11–13, 15
  aberration and, 212–13
  color and, 240
  harmonic rule and, 207
  Newton vs. Leibniz and, 441–2
  refraction and, 235
Rudolphine Tables (Kepler), 204, 206,
  215
Rules for the Direction of the Mind
  (Descartes), 259

sabbath, 420
Sanderson, Robert, 388, 391
Saturn, 153, 167, 206
  Euler on, 213–14
  great inequality and, 215–17
  mean solar distance and, 209
Sceptical Chymist, The (Boyle), 359
Schlick, Moritz, 34
Scholium Generale, 8, 13, 58, 85, 139
  induction and, 186
  methodology and, 140–1

science, 14–19
  analysis vs. synthesis and, 308–15
  defined, 330
  divisions of, 329–30
  greater certainty and, 227–9
  reform of, 227–9
  theoretical, 16–19
  vs. philosophy, 3–4
  see also natural philosophy;
    Newtonian style
Scottish Newtonians, 412, 436–7
Scripture, *see* biblical studies
Scripture-Doctrine of the Trinity, The
  (Clarke), 414, 423
Scripture Vindicated (Waterland), 414
Sendivogius, Michael, 24, 362, 374–5
Seventy Weeks prophecy, 412, 419, 422
'sGravesande, Willem Jacob, 329, 444
Shapiro, Alan, xiii, 11, 227–35
Shuckford, Samuel, 416–17
Simson, Robert, 324
skepticism, 3, 16, 334–5
Sleidan, J., 388, 394
Sloane, Hans, 441
slope, 86
Sluse, René F., 311
Smith, Barnabas, 9
Smith, Benjamin, 400, 409–11
Smith, George E., xiii, 1–32, 138–73
Snell's law of refraction, 15, 230, 235–6
Society for Promoting Christian
  Knowledge, 411
Solomon's Temple, 411
Sophia, Duchess of Hanover, 457
space, 5, 54–5
  causal interactions and, 37–8
  controversies over, 33–49, 174
  empiricism and, 51–3
  God and, 390
  Newton's definitions for, 38–49
  philosophical context and, 36–8
  worldview and, 49–51
Special Relativity, 5
speculative philosophy, 329–30
Spence, Joseph, 413
Spinoza, Benedict de, 1, 331, 333, 335
spiral motion, 96, 106
Starkey, George, 25, 359–60, 362, 374
Stein, Howard, xiii, 37, 184, 256–307
Stewart, Matthew, 324

Streete, Edward, 15, 153
Streete, Thomas, 205–6
Stukeley, William, 410–11, 417
Sun
  aether and, 207–8
  comets and, 219–20
  great inequality and, 215–17
  harmonic rule and, 180, 207
  Kepler and, 178, 203
  libration and, 203
  limitations of gravitational theory
    and, 221–3
  magnetism and, 205
  mathematical to physical
    characterization and, 153
  mean solar distance and, 208–9
  Moon and, 120–4, 210–12
  tides and, 221
Supplementum de Aquis Spadanis (van
  Helmont), 361
Sykes, Arthur Ashley, 417
Symbola Aureae Mensae (Maier), 374–5
symbolic algebra, see algebra
symmetry, 97–9
Synopsis Astronomiae Cometicae
  (Halley), 219
synthesis
  Arithmetica Universalis and, 319
  Euclid and, 308–9
  fluxions and, 313–15, 319–22, 324
  geometry and, 317–20, 322–5
  Leibniz dispute and, 321
  symbolic algebra and, 309, 311, 317,
    323
  Viète and, 309–11
syzygy, 221

Tabulae Astronomicae (Halley), 219
Tabulae Rudolphinae (Kepler), 204, 206,
  215
tangential forces, 88–90, 97
  limitations of gravitational theory,
    221
  resistance forces and, 118–20
  see also uniform circular motion
Taylor, Brook, 450
telescopes, 11
Telluris Theoria Sacra (Burnet), 366
Tentamen de Motuum Coelestium
  Causis (Leibniz), 435, 445

Tesauro, Emanuele, 401–2
Theodicée (Leibniz), 458, 462
theology, 10, 23–9
  dynamic analysis and, 316–17
  gravity issues and, 14
  see also biblical studies; prophecy
Theoria Lunae juxta Systema
  Newtonianum (Mayer), 217
Théorie de le terre (Clairaut), 220
theory-mediated measurement, 144
thin films, 228
  color and, 238–48
Third Law of Motion, 68
  gravitation toward planets and, 190–2
  inverse-square law and, 192–3
three-body problem, 141, 146, 213–14
tides, 220–1
time, 5
  causal interactions and, 37–8
  conic motion and, 94
  controversies over, 33–49, 174
  definitions for, 38–49
  empiricism and, 51–3
  impulsive to continuous forces and,
    70–5
  Kepler's area law and, 107–10; see also
    Kepler's area law
  philosophical context and, 36–8
  uniform circular motion and, 89–90
  worldview and, 49–53
I Timothy 3:16, 409–10, 419, 421–2
Tindal, Matthew, 413–14
Toleration Act, 422
Torricelli, Evangelista, 311
"Tractatus de quadratura curvarum"
  (Newton), 324
Traité de mécanique céleste (Laplace),
  217
Trattato (Newton), 396, 400
Treatise on Light (Huygens), 139–40
Trinity
  blasphemy and, 394
  Mace and, 409
  rejection of, 10–11, 23–4, 409–10,
    412–15, 419–23
  Waterland and, 413
Trinity College, 9–10
Trinity Notebook, 387–8
Trismegistus, Hermes, 371
two-body problems, 141

Two New Sciences (Galileo), 89, 142
"Two Notable Corruptions of Scripture"
    (Newton), 410, 419
Typhon, 379

unification, 181–4
    by induction, 185–90
uniform areal motion, 107
uniform circular motion, 10, 86
    curvature and, 87–93
    Newton's methodology and,
        143–4
    universal gravity, 158, 162–3, 166;
        see also gravity
Ussher, James, 412

vacuum, 37
van Helmont, Joan Baptista,
        359–60
    alchemy and, 375
    matter-theory and, 361–3
van Schooten, Frans, 310–11
Varignon, Pierre, 444, 450
velocity, 97, 144
Venus in Sole Visa (Horrocks), 206
via buccosa (puffy-cheeked orbit),
        202–3
Viète, François, 309–10
View of Sir Isaac Newton's Philosophy,
    A (Pemberton), 329
virtus movens, 204
vis inertiae, 61–2
vis insita, 60–2
vitriol, 361
Voltaire, 449
volume, 58–9
von Guericke, Otto, 445
vortices, 43, 205–6
    aether and, 208

harmonic rule and, 207
scientific reform and, 228

Wake, William, 457, 459
Wallis, John, 15, 434
    dynamic analysis and, 309, 311, 317
    fluxions and, 389
    microstructural forces and, 151
Warburton, William, 416–17
Waste Book (Newton), 87–8, 90, 94, 106
Waterland, Daniel, 413–14
wave theory, 232, 292; *see also* light
Webster, John, 360
weight, 60
    mass and, 59, 187–90
Westfall, Gloria, xiv
Westfall, Richard S., xiv, 400, 409
Whiston, William, 207, 440
    religion and, 409, 412–13, 422–3
white light, 230–1
Whiteside, D. T., 20, 75–6, 95, 433, 439
Whore of Babylon, 394
Wilson, Curtis, xiii, 7, 202–26
Wing, Vincent, 15, 153, 205–6
Wodrow, Robert, 412
Wolff, Christian, 1, 331
Woolsthorpe, 9–10, 388
World, The (Descartes), 258
World System (Galileo), 258
worldview
    absolute time/space and, 33–6
    empiricism and, 16–19, 51–3
    geocentrism vs. heliocentrism, 49–51
    space and time, 49–51
    world systems resolution and, 193
Wren, Christopher, 15, 151

Young, Arthur, 415
Y-Worth, William, 374